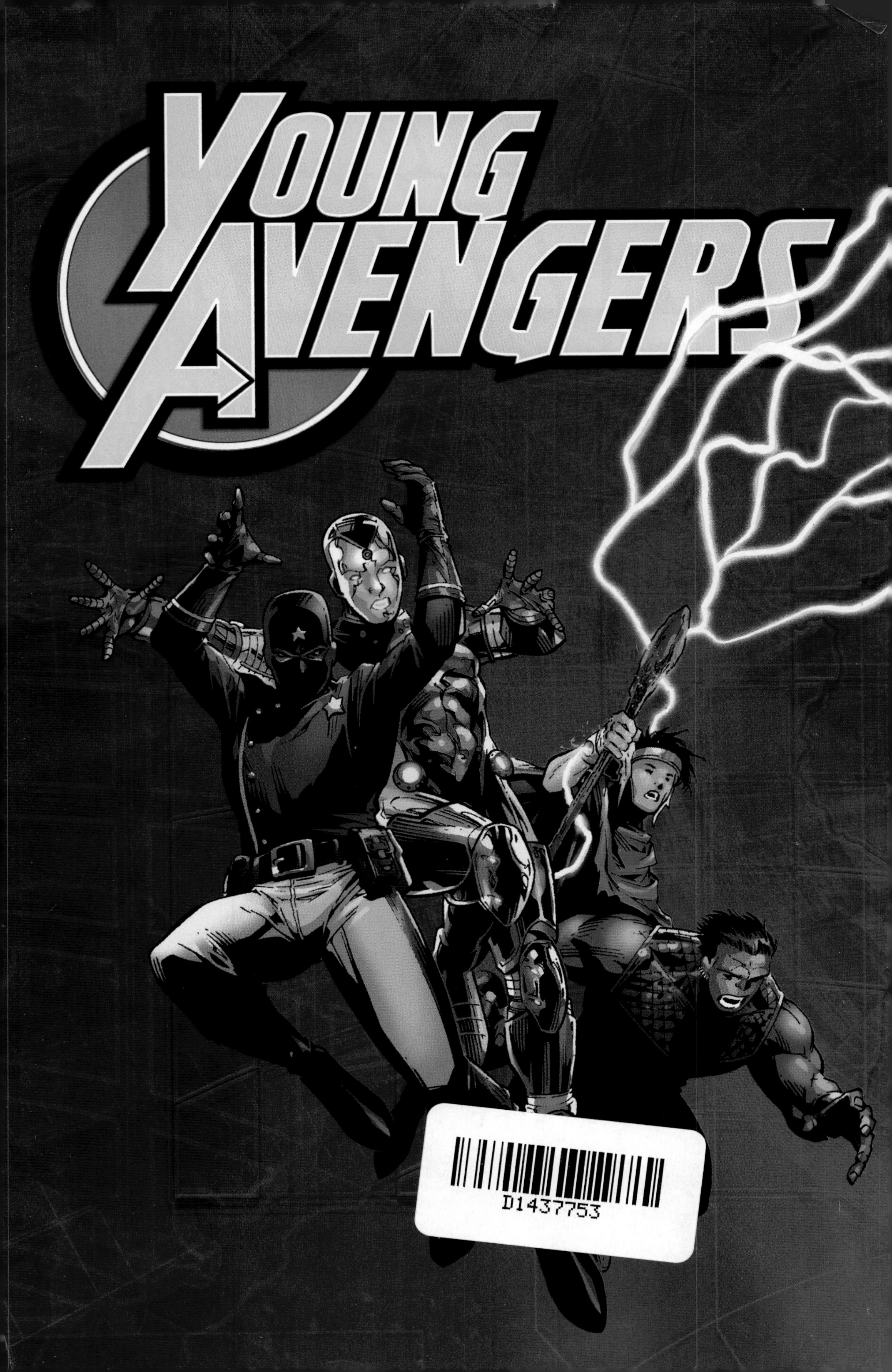
YOUNG AVENGERS

YOUNG AVENGERS

WRITER: ALLAN HEINBERG

SIDEKICKS
PENCILER: JIM CHEUNG
INKERS: JOHN DELL, MARK MORALES
& DREW GERACI
COLORIST: JUSTIN PONSOR

SECRET IDENTITIES
PENCILER: ANDREA DI VITO
INKER: DREW GERACI
COLORIST: JUSTIN PONSOR

YOUNG AVENGERS SPECIAL #1
PAGES 1-2, 8-9, 20-21, 25-26 & 34-36
ARTIST: MICHAEL GAYDOS
COLORIST: JOSÉ VILLARRUBIA
PAGES 3-7
ARTIST: NEAL ADAMS
COLORIST: JUSTIN PONSOR
PAGES 10-14
ARTIST: GENE HA
COLORIST: ART LYON
PAGES 15-19
ARTIST: JAE LEE
COLORIST: JUNE CHUNG
PAGES 22-24
ARTIST: BILL SIENKIEWICZ
COLORIST: JUSTIN PONSOR
PAGES 27-33
ARTIST: PASQUAL FERRY
COLORIST: DAVE McCAIG

FAMILY MATTERS
PENCILER: JIM CHEUNG
INKERS: DAVE MEIKIS, JOHN DELL,
ROB STULL, DEXTER VINES, LIVESAY,
JAY LEISTEN, MATT RYAN, JAIME MENDOZA,
MARK MORALES & JIM CHEUNG
COLORIST: JUSTIN PONSOR

LETTERER: VC'S CORY PETIT
COVER ART: JIM CHEUNG, JOHN DELL
& JUSTIN PONSOR
ASSISTANT EDITORS: STEPHANIE MOORE,
MOLLY LAZER & AUBREY SITTERSON
ASSOCIATE EDITOR: ANDY SCHMIDT
EDITOR: TOM BREVOORT

Avengers created by Stan Lee & Jack Kirby

Young Avengers created by Allan Heinberg & Jim Cheung

YOUNG AVENGERS BY ALLAN HEINBERG & JIM CHEUNG: THE COMPLETE COLLECTION. Contains material originally published in magazine form as YOUNG AVENGERS #1-12 and SPECIAL. First printing 2016. ISBN# 978-1-302-90519-4. Published by MARVEL WORLDWIDE, INC., a subsidiary of MARVEL ENTERTAINMENT, LLC. OFFICE OF PUBLICATION: 135 West 50th Street, New York, NY 10020. Copyright © 2016 MARVEL No similarity between any of the names, characters, persons, and/or institutions in this magazine with those of any living or dead person or institution is intended, and any such similarity which may exist is purely coincidental. **Printed in the U.S.A.** ALAN FINE, President, Marvel Entertainment; DAN BUCKLEY, President, TV, Publishing & Brand Management; JOE QUESADA, Chief Creative Officer; TOM BREVOORT, SVP of Publishing; DAVID BOGART, SVP of Business Affairs & Operations, Publishing & Partnership; C.B. CEBULSKI, VP of Brand Management & Development, Asia; DAVID GABRIEL, SVP of Sales & Marketing, Publishing; JEFF YOUNGQUIST, VP of Production & Special Projects; DAN CARR, Executive Director of Publishing Technology; ALEX MORALES, Director of Publishing Operations; SUSAN CRESPI, Production Manager; STAN LEE, Chairman Emeritus. For information regarding advertising in Marvel Comics or on Marvel.com, please contact Vit DeBellis, Integrated Sales Manager, at vdebellis@marvel.com. For Marvel subscription inquiries, please call 888-511-5480. **Manufactured between 10/7/2016 and 11/14/2016 by LSC COMMUNICATIONS INC., SALEM, VA, USA.**

10 9 8 7 6 5 4 3 2 1

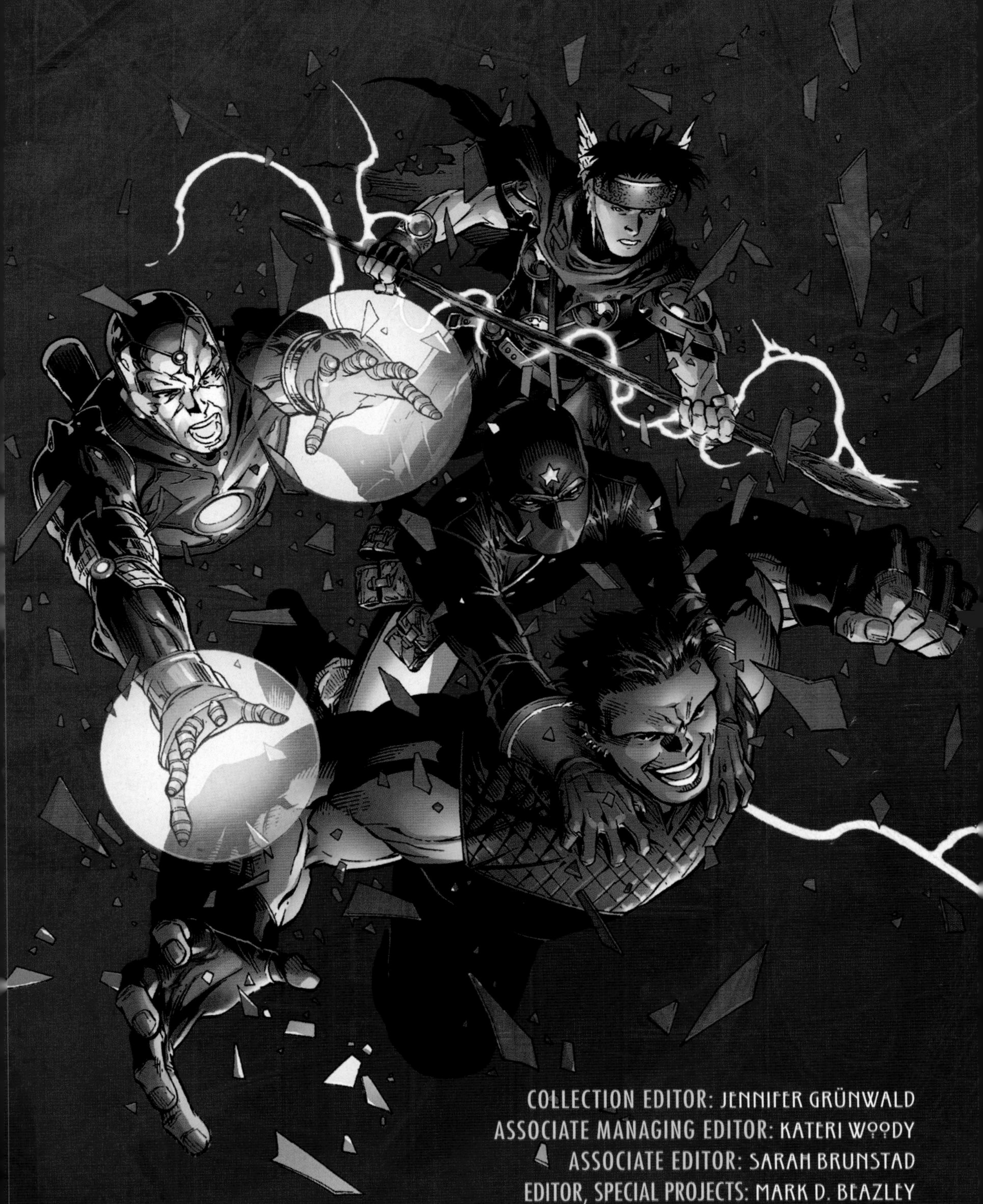

COLLECTION EDITOR: JENNIFER GRÜNWALD
ASSOCIATE MANAGING EDITOR: KATERI WOODY
ASSOCIATE EDITOR: SARAH BRUNSTAD
EDITOR, SPECIAL PROJECTS: MARK D. BEAZLEY
VP PRODUCTION & SPECIAL PROJECTS: JEFF YOUNGQUIST
SVP PRINT, SALES & MARKETING: DAVID GABRIEL

EDITOR IN CHIEF: AXEL ALONSO
CHIEF CREATIVE OFFICER: JOE QUESADA
PUBLISHER: DAN BUCKLEY
EXECUTIVE PRODUCER: ALAN FINE

ENCHANTMENT

What I've always loved about Magic is that when it is done well, there's no explanation for it. You actually don't want to know the answer, otherwise, as I've pointed out from time to time, all you wind up with is (possible spoiler here, kids) a hat with a false bottom and a rabbit shoved in there. See, if you didn't know how that trick was done, I've taken all the Magic out of it.

As some of you know, and the rest of you are about to learn, DC Legend Geoff Johns and I share a studio called the Empath Magic Tree House. It's located in a place that's somewhere between Sherman Oaks, California and Brigadoon. The plain truth is you have to be able to actually see the Magic Tree House to be let in (thus the word "Magic" in the title). A lot very good writers and artists have come by and walked right past the place. Some — and you know these folks — have stood out in the driveway squinting, hoping to catch a reflection off one of the stained glass windows and thus be able to find the door. Truth is, can't be done. It's Magic.

So, you can imagine my surprise one day when I not only found Allan Heinberg being able to *see* the tree house — he had plopped himself down on the couch in one of the four living rooms off from the waterfalls/koi pond and was typing away on his laptop. Empath had welcomed a new member of the Brotherhood.

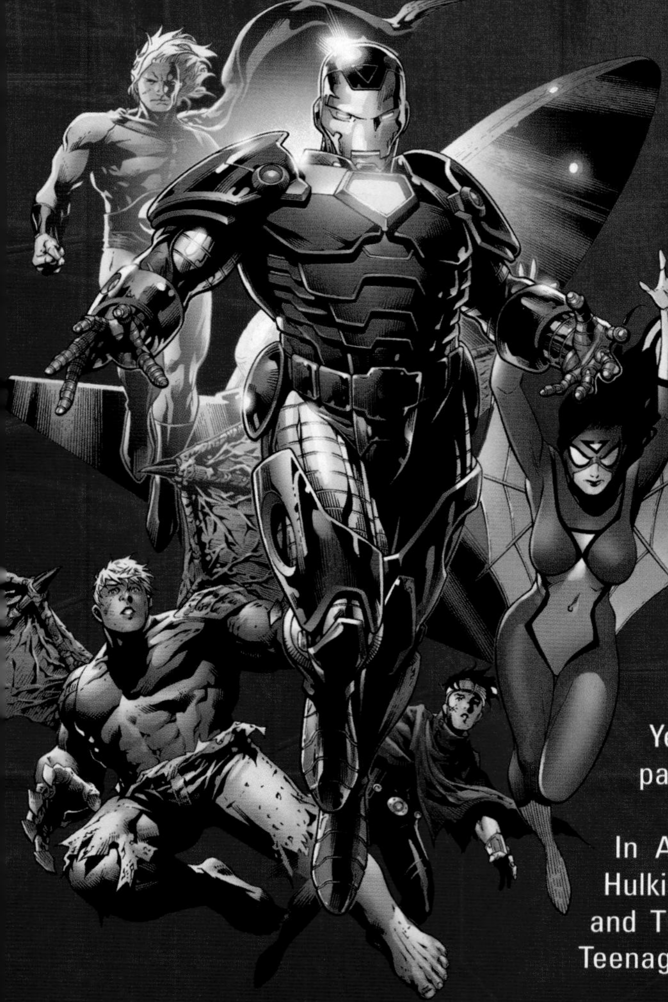

How could Allan do what others had not? Well, you're holding it in your hands. He created, along with Jim Cheung (we'll get to him in a moment), the first new franchise at Marvel that stuck since... well... I'd make the argument since a little Canadian with claws poppin' out of his hands that went "SNIKT!"

YOUNG AVENGERS should have been a disaster. A group of teens — some even distaff versions of the original characters — find their way together to become new heroes who look a lot like Captain America, Thor, Iron Man, Hulk...and should I really go on? Haven't we already seen this? And hasn't it always been a train wreck?

Yeah, well, that's when you get to the Magic part.

In Allan's hands, Patriot, Wiccan, Iron Lad, Hulking, as well as Hawkeye, Speed, Stature and The Vision are nothing short of delightful. Teenagers who sound like teenagers, with real problems from identity crisis to living up to the image you have of your parents and their world. Characters who are funny, self-deprecating, annoying, head-over-heels in love (and not necessarily boy-girl love), and wonderfully, impossibly, *original*.

It's the sort of thing I've heard Stan Lee talk about when he rocked all of comics with a teenager named Peter Parker. (Yes, Allan, I put you and Stan in the same paragraph. Get used to it, my friend, it's what happens when you're *that* good.) Because Allan somehow knew the trick. Spider-Man is just a kid in his underoos with guck shooting out of his wrists until you hear about Peter Parker, boy-nerd who wants to get the girl almost as much as catching the Green Goblin. Batman is a nut running around in his pajamas, until you learn about Bruce being 10 years old when his parents were murdered.

Allan put the "care" in character. OUCH. Okay, that wasn't what Allan would've ever written, but I ain't him, okay?!

He didn't do this alone either. One of the amazing things about working in comics is that, much like television or motion pictures where a great script can be destroyed by bad acting or direction, the comic book writer is always at the mercy of his artist. The penciler is the director, actor, cinematographer and editor.

Jim Cheung is gifted in every one of those tasks. He's taken Allan's story and given it a visual style that is vibrant and delicate and impactful and here's that word again, Magical. Each Young Avenger has a distinct look, pretty but not supermodel, powerful but not musclebound, wry but not cartoony. Faces that speak Allan's dialogue as if they were cast by the best actors in the universe. I cannot wait to someday have the pleasure of seeing Jim illustrate a story of my own.

The rest of the team is equally staggering in their talent. From John Dell's inking to Justin Ponsor's coloring, to Cory Petit's lettering to Andy Schmidt & Molly Lazer & Aubrey Sitterson's edits, these folks are working at the top of their game. And a special shout-out has to go to Avengers Editor Boss Tom Brevoort who took a chance on a television writer with a vision named Heinberg and wound up with the boldest new voice in the comic book business.

Now, you've bought the ticket and the show is about to start. When the curtain goes up, remember, you won't know how it's done, just that it's spectacularly entertaining.

It's why we call it "Magic."

Jeph Loeb
Christmas in NYC
2007

Jeph Loeb is an Emmy Award-nominated and Eisner Award-winning writer/producer. In television, his many credits include HEROES, LOST and SMALLVILLE; and in film, TEEN WOLF and COMMANDO. Jeph has written nearly every major comics icon including HULK, IRON MAN, SPIDER-MAN, WOLVERINE, BATMAN and SUPERMAN.

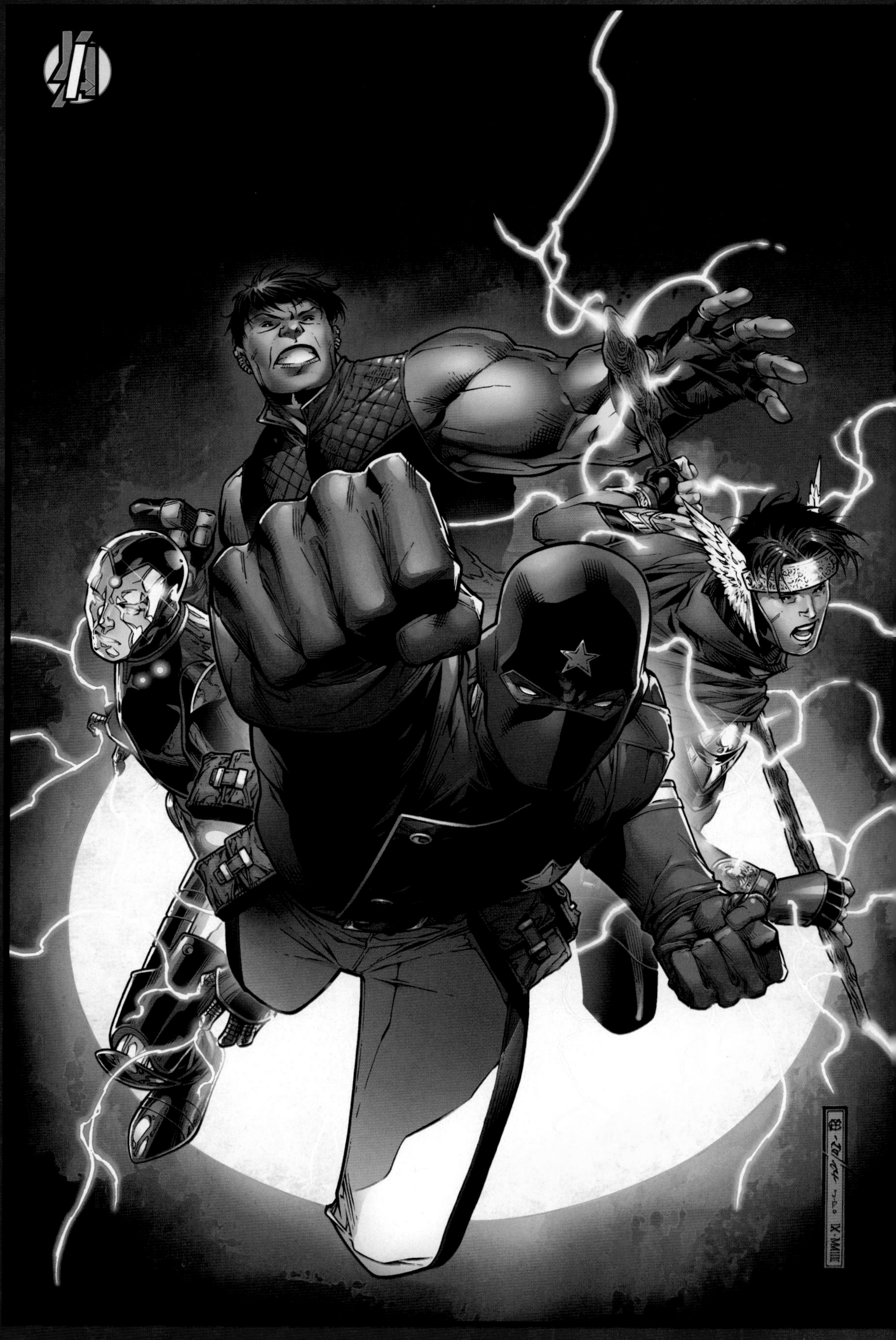

SIDEKICKS

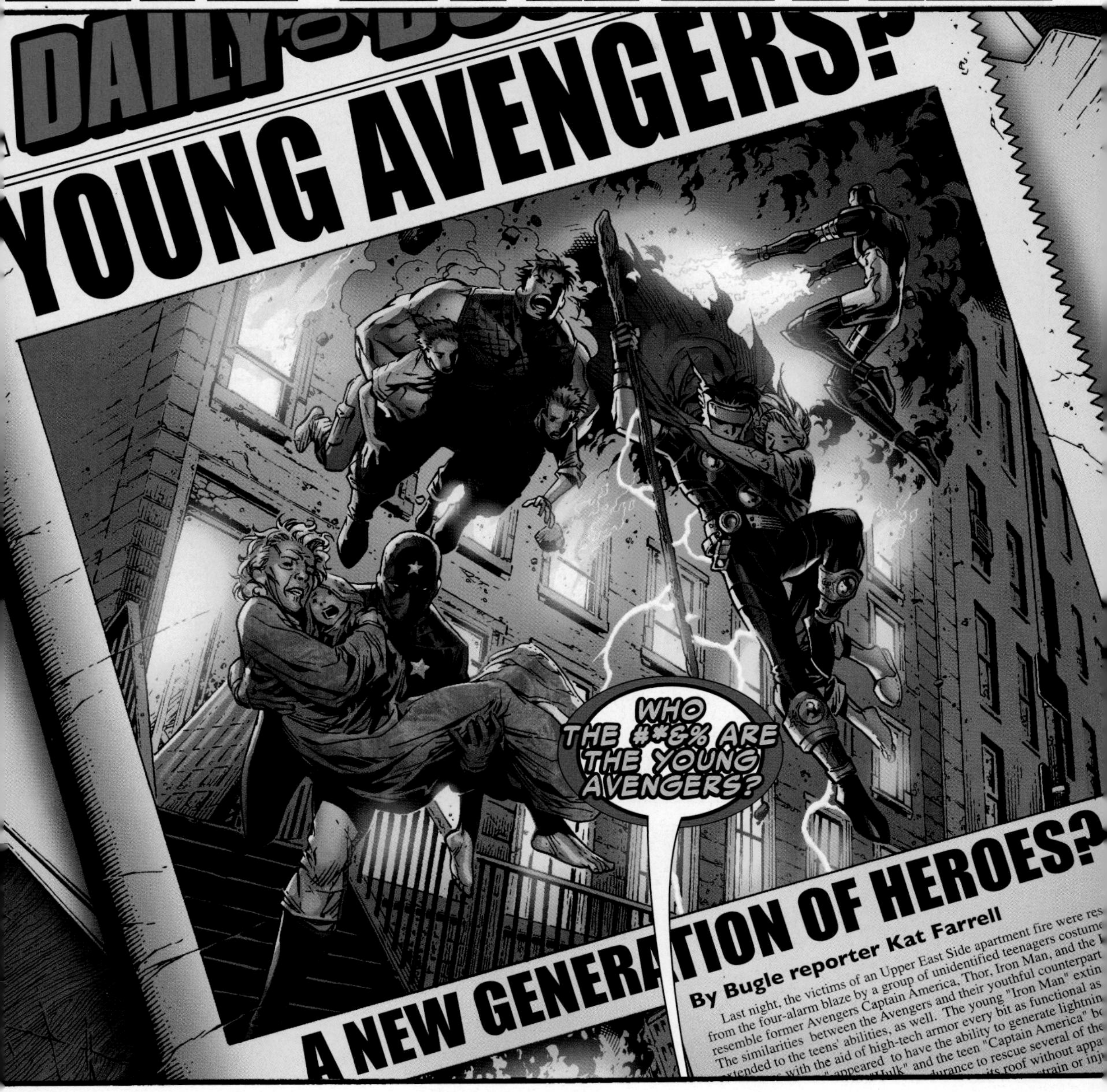

DAILY
YOUNG AVENGERS?
WHO THE #*&% ARE THE YOUNG AVENGERS?
A NEW GENERATION OF HEROES?
By Bugle reporter Kat Farrell
Last night, the victims of an Upper East Side apartment fire were
from the four-alarm blaze by a group of unidentified teenagers
resemble former Avengers Captain America, Thor, Iron Man, and the
The similarities between the Avengers and their youthful
extended to the teens' abilities, as well. The young "Iron Man"
with the aid of high-tech armor every bit as functional as
appeared to have the ability to generate
"Hulk" and the teen "Captain America"
to rescue several of the
its roof without
strain or

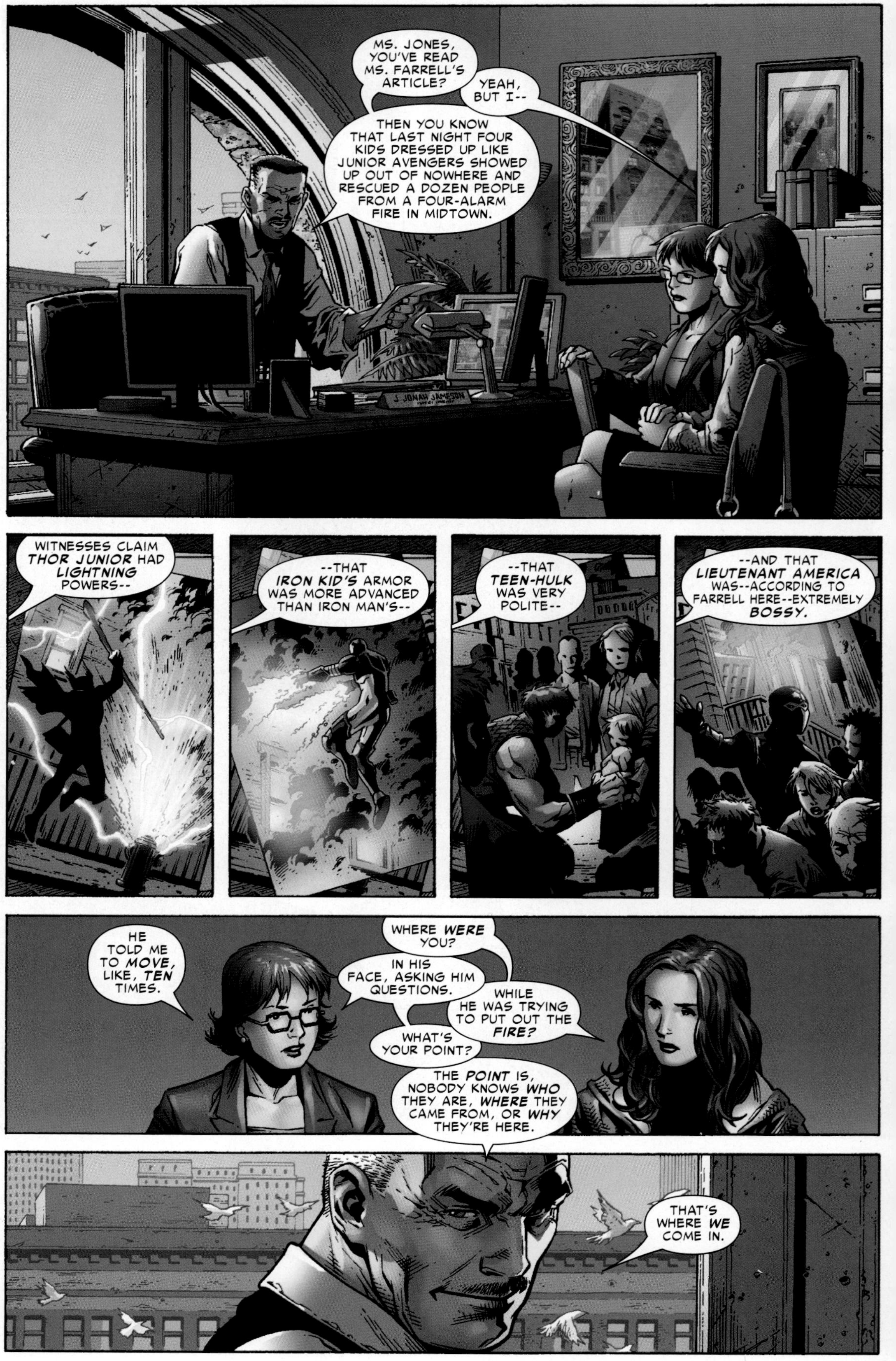
MS. JONES, YOU'VE READ MS. FARRELL'S ARTICLE?
YEAH, BUT I--
THEN YOU KNOW THAT LAST NIGHT FOUR KIDS DRESSED UP LIKE JUNIOR AVENGERS SHOWED UP OUT OF NOWHERE AND RESCUED A DOZEN PEOPLE FROM A FOUR-ALARM FIRE IN MIDTOWN.
J. JONAH JAMESON
WITNESSES CLAIM THOR JUNIOR HAD LIGHTNING POWERS--
--THAT IRON KID'S ARMOR WAS MORE ADVANCED THAN IRON MAN'S--
--THAT TEEN-HULK WAS VERY POLITE--
--AND THAT LIEUTENANT AMERICA WAS--ACCORDING TO FARRELL HERE--EXTREMELY BOSSY.
HE TOLD ME TO MOVE, LIKE, TEN TIMES.
WHERE WERE YOU?
IN HIS FACE, ASKING HIM QUESTIONS.
WHILE HE WAS TRYING TO PUT OUT THE FIRE?
WHAT'S YOUR POINT?
THE POINT IS, NOBODY KNOWS WHO THEY ARE, WHERE THEY CAME FROM, OR WHY THEY'RE HERE.
THAT'S WHERE WE COME IN.

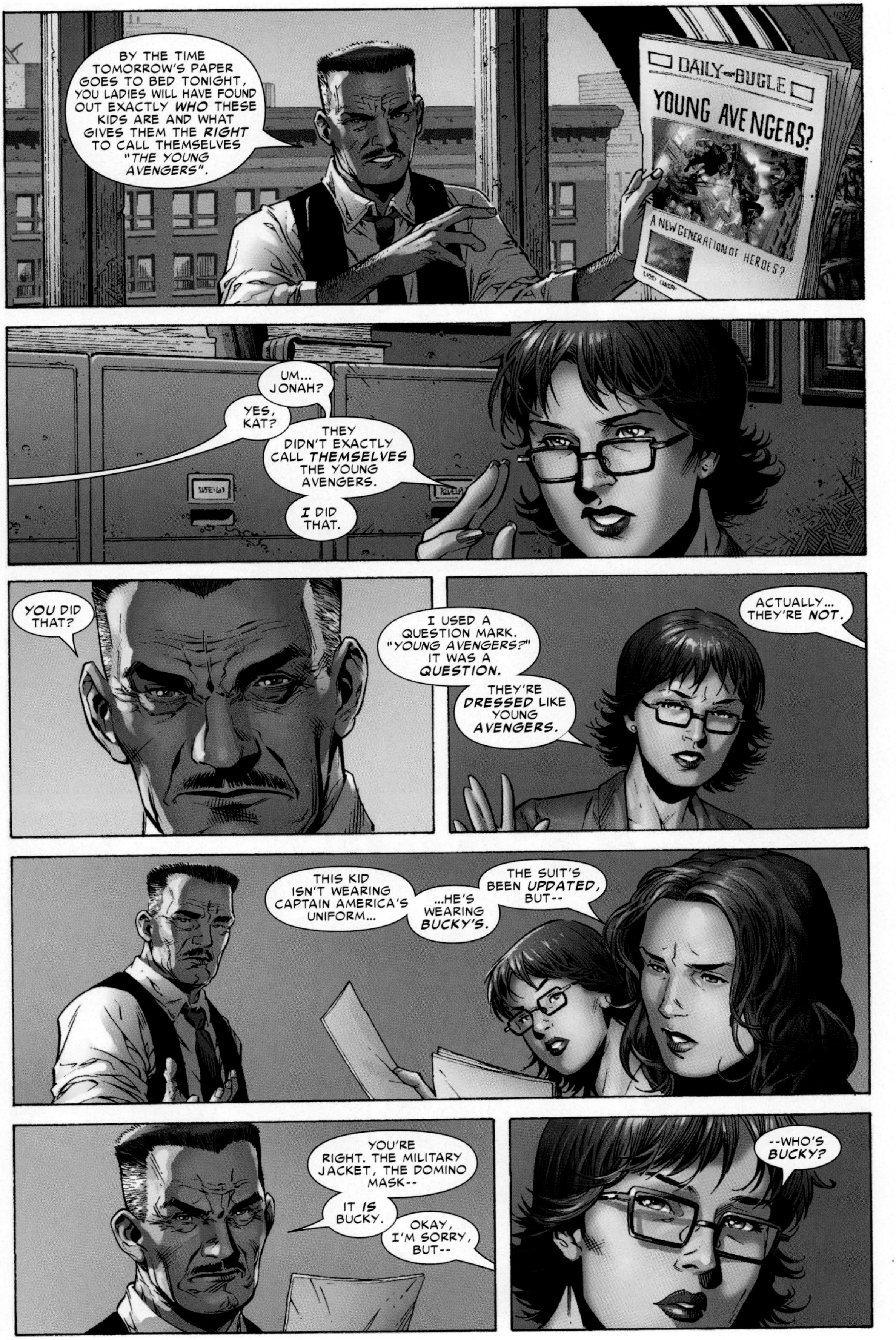
BY THE TIME TOMORROW'S PAPER GOES TO BED TONIGHT, YOU LADIES WILL HAVE FOUND OUT EXACTLY WHO THESE KIDS ARE AND WHAT GIVES THEM THE RIGHT TO CALL THEMSELVES "THE YOUNG AVENGERS".
DAILY BUGLE
YOUNG AVENGERS?
A NEW GENERATION OF HEROES?
UM... JONAH?
YES, KAT?
THEY DIDN'T EXACTLY CALL THEMSELVES THE YOUNG AVENGERS.
I DID THAT.
YOU DID THAT?
I USED A QUESTION MARK. "YOUNG AVENGERS?" IT WAS A QUESTION.
THEY'RE DRESSED LIKE YOUNG AVENGERS.
ACTUALLY... THEY'RE NOT.
THIS KID ISN'T WEARING CAPTAIN AMERICA'S UNIFORM...
...HE'S WEARING BUCKY'S.
THE SUIT'S BEEN UPDATED, BUT--
YOU'RE RIGHT. THE MILITARY JACKET, THE DOMINO MASK--
IT IS BUCKY.
OKAY, I'M SORRY, BUT--
--WHO'S BUCKY?

"WHO'S BUCKY?"

BUCKY WAS CAPTAIN AMERICA'S TEEN SIDEKICK DURING WORLD WAR TWO.

HOW COULD YOU NOT KNOW BUCKY? HOW OLD ARE YOU?

IT WAS WORLD WAR TWO. HOW OLD ARE YOU?

I WAS EXTREMELY YOUNG BACK THEN, THANK YOU FOR ASKING.

YOUNG ENOUGH--AND NAIVE ENOUGH--TO WANT TO BE BUCKY.

YOU WANTED TO BE BUCKY?

BUCKY DEAD, CAP MISSING

EVERY KID DID.

UNTIL CAPTAIN AMERICA LED HIS TEENAGE SIDEKICK BEHIND ENEMY LINES...

...AND GOT HIM KILLED.

LONDON, ENGLAND
Two of America's favorite sons, Captain America, the so-called super-soldier and his youthful sidekick, Bucky, are presumed this morning, according to a report. The report and Bucky, all...

SUDDENLY, I DIDN'T WANT TO BE BUCKY ANYMORE. NOBODY DID.

FROM THEN ON, KID SIDEKICKS ONLY SHOWED UP IN COMIC BOOKS.

UNTIL NOW.

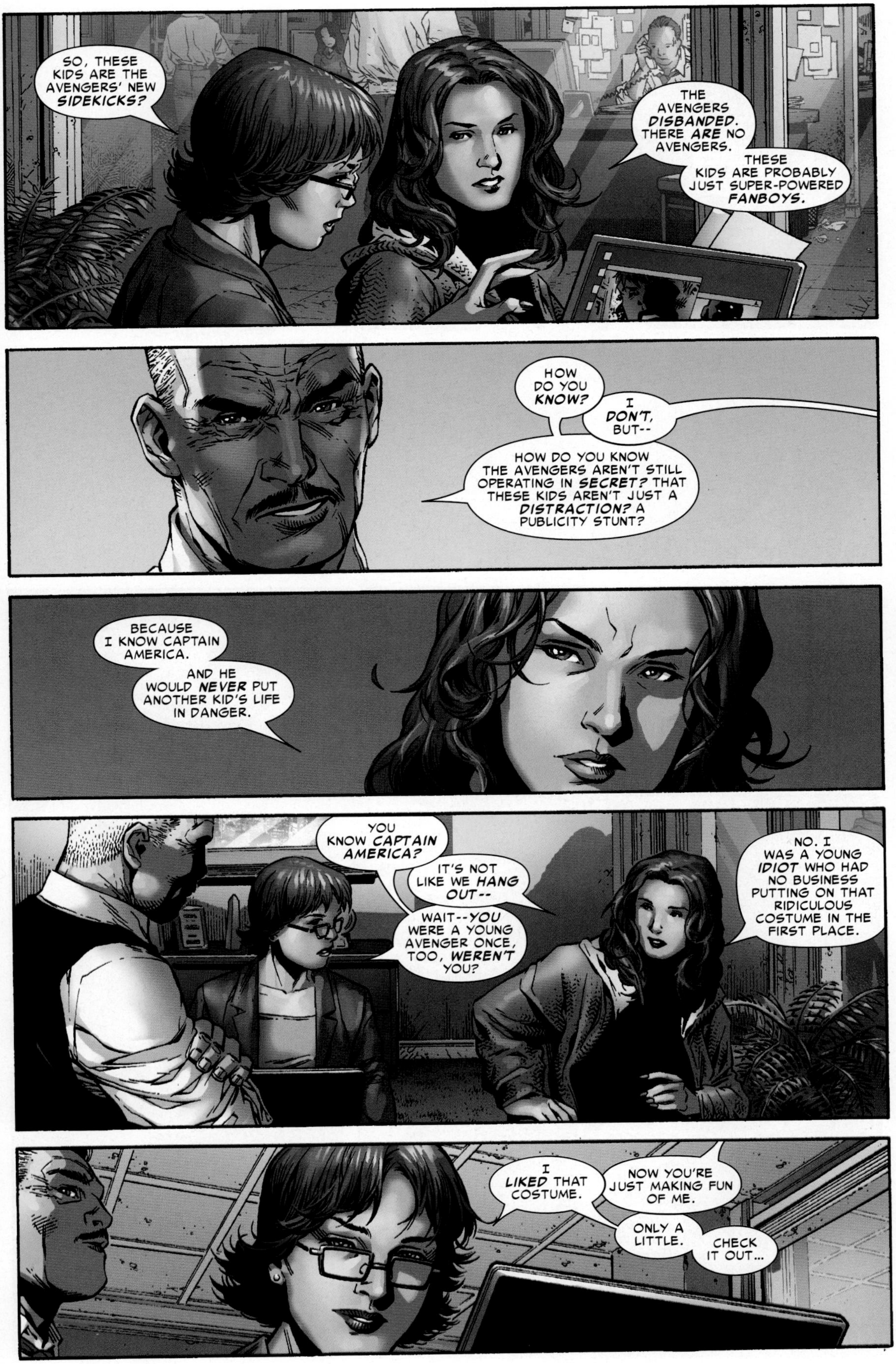
SO, THESE KIDS ARE THE AVENGERS' NEW SIDEKICKS?
THE AVENGERS DISBANDED. THERE ARE NO AVENGERS.
THESE KIDS ARE PROBABLY JUST SUPER-POWERED FANBOYS.
HOW DO YOU KNOW?
I DON'T, BUT--
HOW DO YOU KNOW THE AVENGERS AREN'T STILL OPERATING IN SECRET? THAT THESE KIDS AREN'T JUST A DISTRACTION? A PUBLICITY STUNT?
BECAUSE I KNOW CAPTAIN AMERICA.
AND HE WOULD NEVER PUT ANOTHER KID'S LIFE IN DANGER.
YOU KNOW CAPTAIN AMERICA?
IT'S NOT LIKE WE HANG OUT--
WAIT--YOU WERE A YOUNG AVENGER ONCE, TOO, WEREN'T YOU?
NO. I WAS A YOUNG IDIOT WHO HAD NO BUSINESS PUTTING ON THAT RIDICULOUS COSTUME IN THE FIRST PLACE.
I LIKED THAT COSTUME.
NOW YOU'RE JUST MAKING FUN OF ME.
ONLY A LITTLE.
CHECK IT OUT...

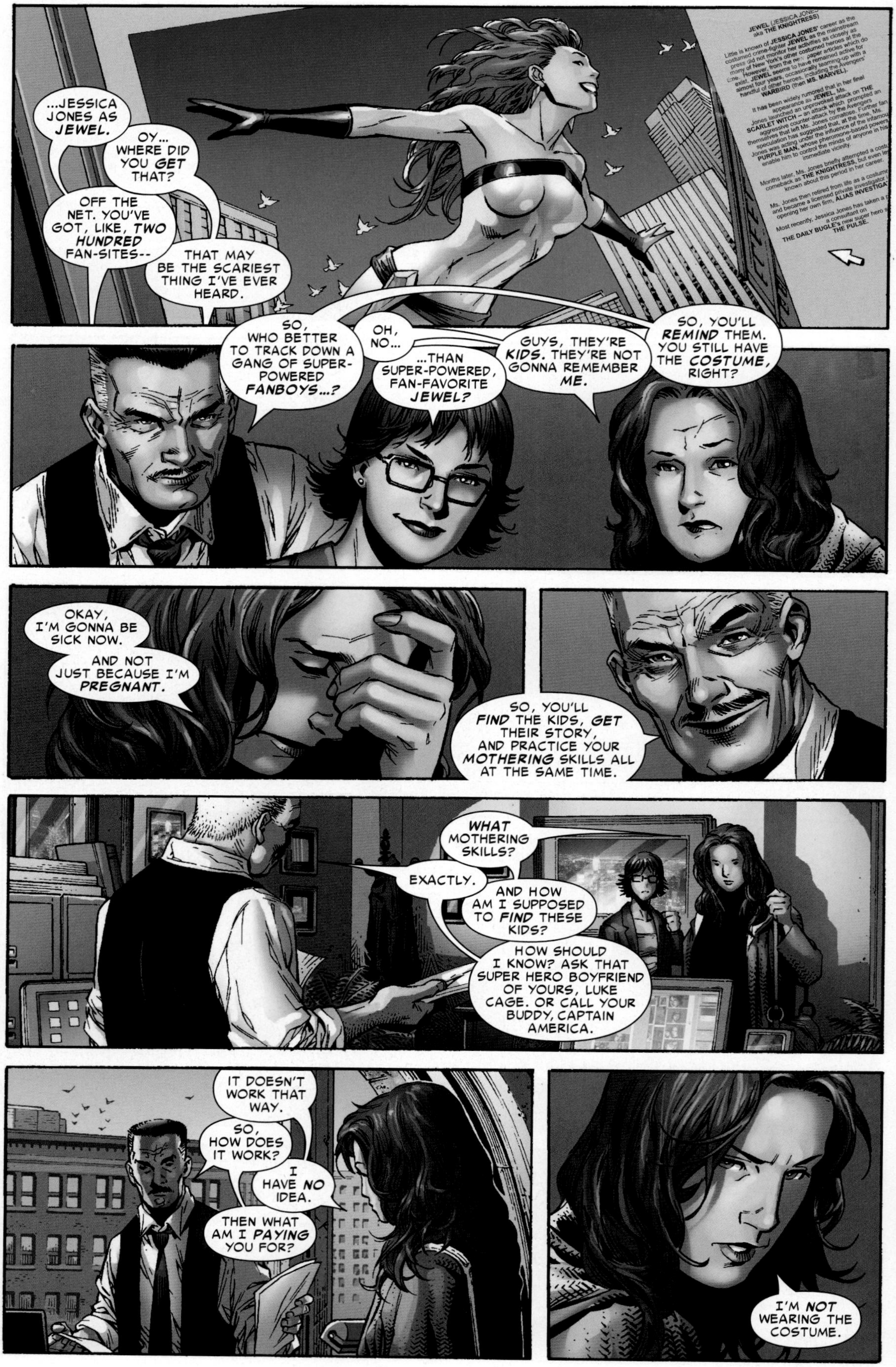
...JESSICA JONES AS JEWEL.
OY... WHERE DID YOU GET THAT?
OFF THE NET. YOU'VE GOT, LIKE, TWO HUNDRED FAN-SITES--
THAT MAY BE THE SCARIEST THING I'VE EVER HEARD.
SO, WHO BETTER TO TRACK DOWN A GANG OF SUPER-POWERED FANBOYS...?
OH, NO...
...THAN SUPER-POWERED, FAN-FAVORITE JEWEL?
GUYS, THEY'RE KIDS. THEY'RE NOT GONNA REMEMBER ME.
SO, YOU'LL REMIND THEM. YOU STILL HAVE THE COSTUME, RIGHT?
OKAY, I'M GONNA BE SICK NOW.
AND NOT JUST BECAUSE I'M PREGNANT.
SO, YOU'LL FIND THE KIDS, GET THEIR STORY, AND PRACTICE YOUR MOTHERING SKILLS ALL AT THE SAME TIME.
WHAT MOTHERING SKILLS?
EXACTLY.
AND HOW AM I SUPPOSED TO FIND THESE KIDS?
HOW SHOULD I KNOW? ASK THAT SUPER HERO BOYFRIEND OF YOURS, LUKE CAGE. OR CALL YOUR BUDDY, CAPTAIN AMERICA.
IT DOESN'T WORK THAT WAY.
SO, HOW DOES IT WORK?
I HAVE NO IDEA.
THEN WHAT AM I PAYING YOU FOR?
I'M NOT WEARING THE COSTUME.

SO, HOW DO YOU WANT TO *DO* THIS? ARE WE GONNA WORK *TOGETHER?* OR--

ACTUALLY, I'M USUALLY BETTER OFF ON MY *OWN.* I ANNOY FEWER PEOPLE THAT WAY.

BING

FINE.

IT'S JUST--A LOT OF THE PEOPLE I NEED TO TALK TO HAVE SECRET IDENTITIES AND--

IT'S *FINE.* I GET IT.

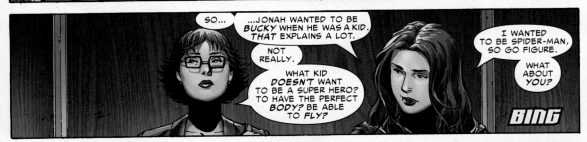

SO...

...JONAH WANTED TO BE *BUCKY* WHEN HE WAS A KID. *THAT* EXPLAINS A LOT.

NOT *REALLY.*

WHAT KID *DOESN'T* WANT TO BE A SUPER HERO? TO HAVE THE PERFECT *BODY?* BE ABLE TO *FLY?*

I WANTED TO BE SPIDER-MAN, SO GO FIGURE. WHAT ABOUT *YOU?*

BING

BELIEVE IT OR NOT...?

I WANTED TO BE *YOU.*

SO GO FIGURE.

YOU'RE *KIDDING,* RIGHT?

... HEY, KAT. WAIT UP.

SO, WHAT'S YOUR NEXT MOVE? CONTACT WHAT'S LEFT OF THE AVENGERS?

I'LL *TRY,* BUT I'M NOT AS CONNECTED AS JONAH...

...THINKS.

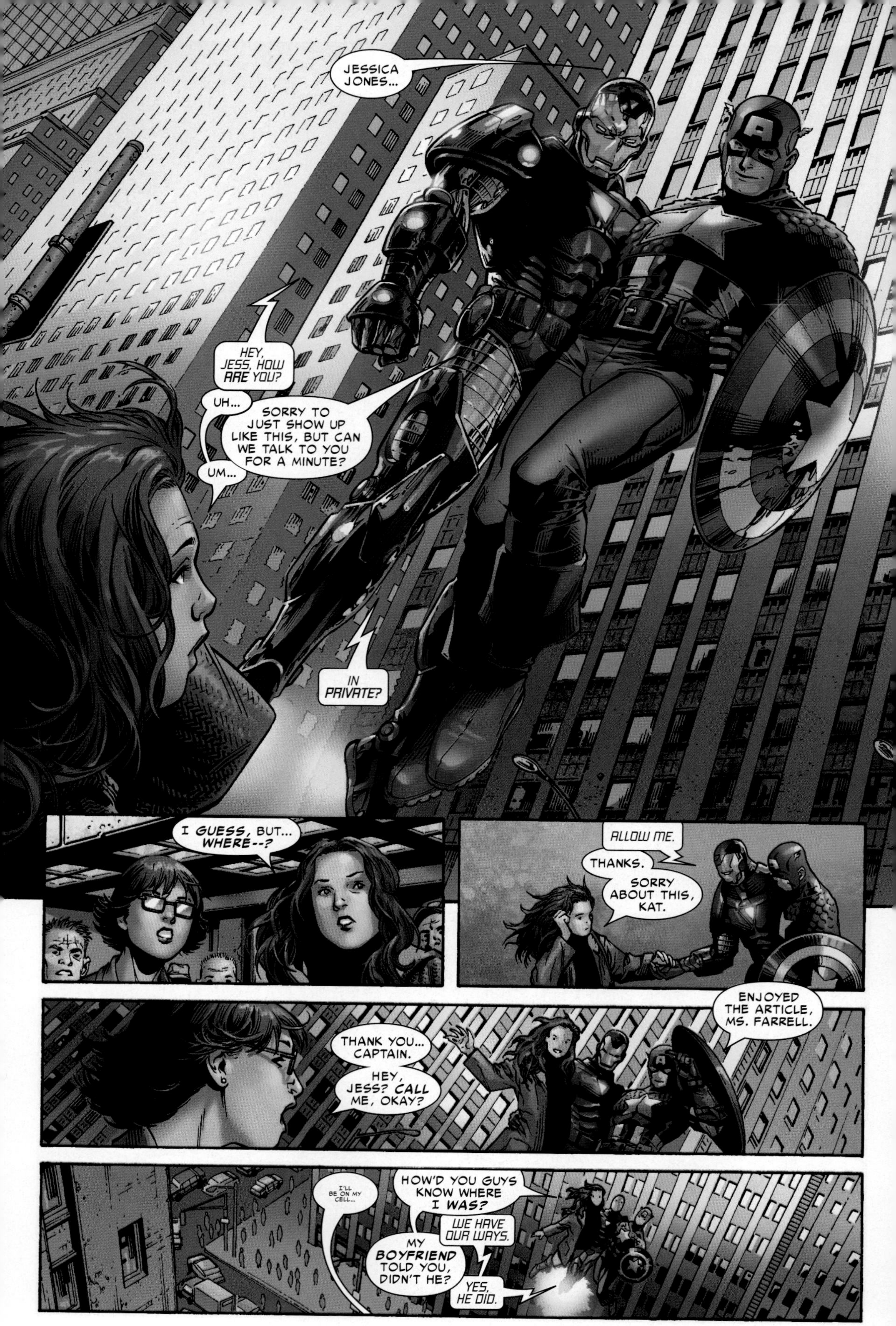
JESSICA JONES...
HEY, JESS, HOW ARE YOU?
UH...
SORRY TO JUST SHOW UP LIKE THIS, BUT CAN WE TALK TO YOU FOR A MINUTE?
UM...
IN PRIVATE?
I GUESS, BUT... WHERE--?
ALLOW ME.
THANKS.
SORRY ABOUT THIS, KAT.
ENJOYED THE ARTICLE, MS. FARRELL.
THANK YOU... CAPTAIN.
HEY, JESS? CALL ME, OKAY?
I'LL BE ON MY CELL...
HOW'D YOU GUYS KNOW WHERE I WAS?
WE HAVE OUR WAYS.
MY BOYFRIEND TOLD YOU, DIDN'T HE?
YES, HE DID.

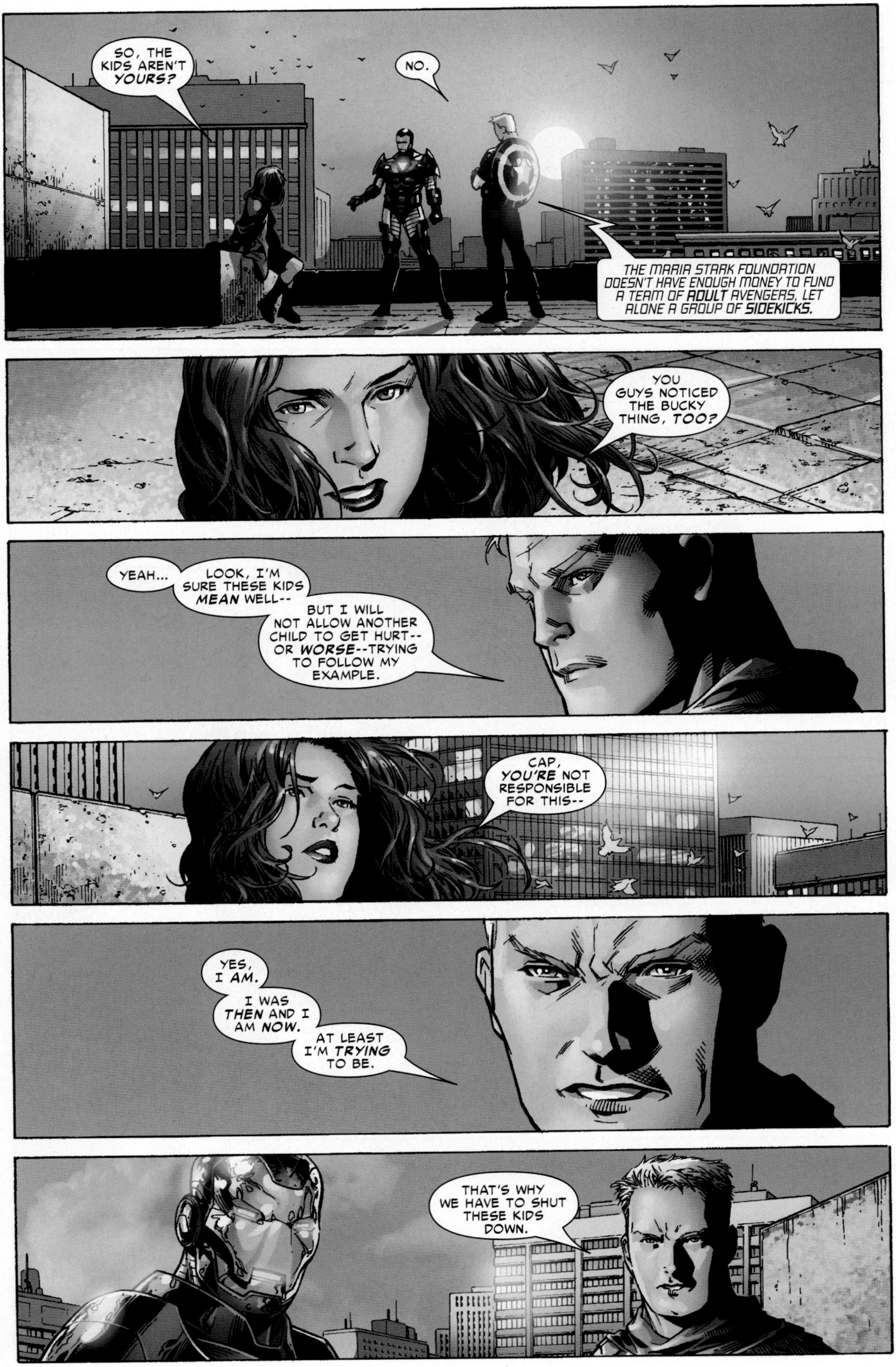
SO, THE KIDS AREN'T YOURS?
NO.
THE MARIA STARK FOUNDATION DOESN'T HAVE ENOUGH MONEY TO FUND A TEAM OF ADULT AVENGERS, LET ALONE A GROUP OF SIDEKICKS.
YOU GUYS NOTICED THE BUCKY THING, TOO?
YEAH...
LOOK, I'M SURE THESE KIDS MEAN WELL--
BUT I WILL NOT ALLOW ANOTHER CHILD TO GET HURT-- OR WORSE--TRYING TO FOLLOW MY EXAMPLE.
CAP, YOU'RE NOT RESPONSIBLE FOR THIS--
YES, I AM.
I WAS THEN AND I AM NOW.
AT LEAST I'M TRYING TO BE.
THAT'S WHY WE HAVE TO SHUT THESE KIDS DOWN.

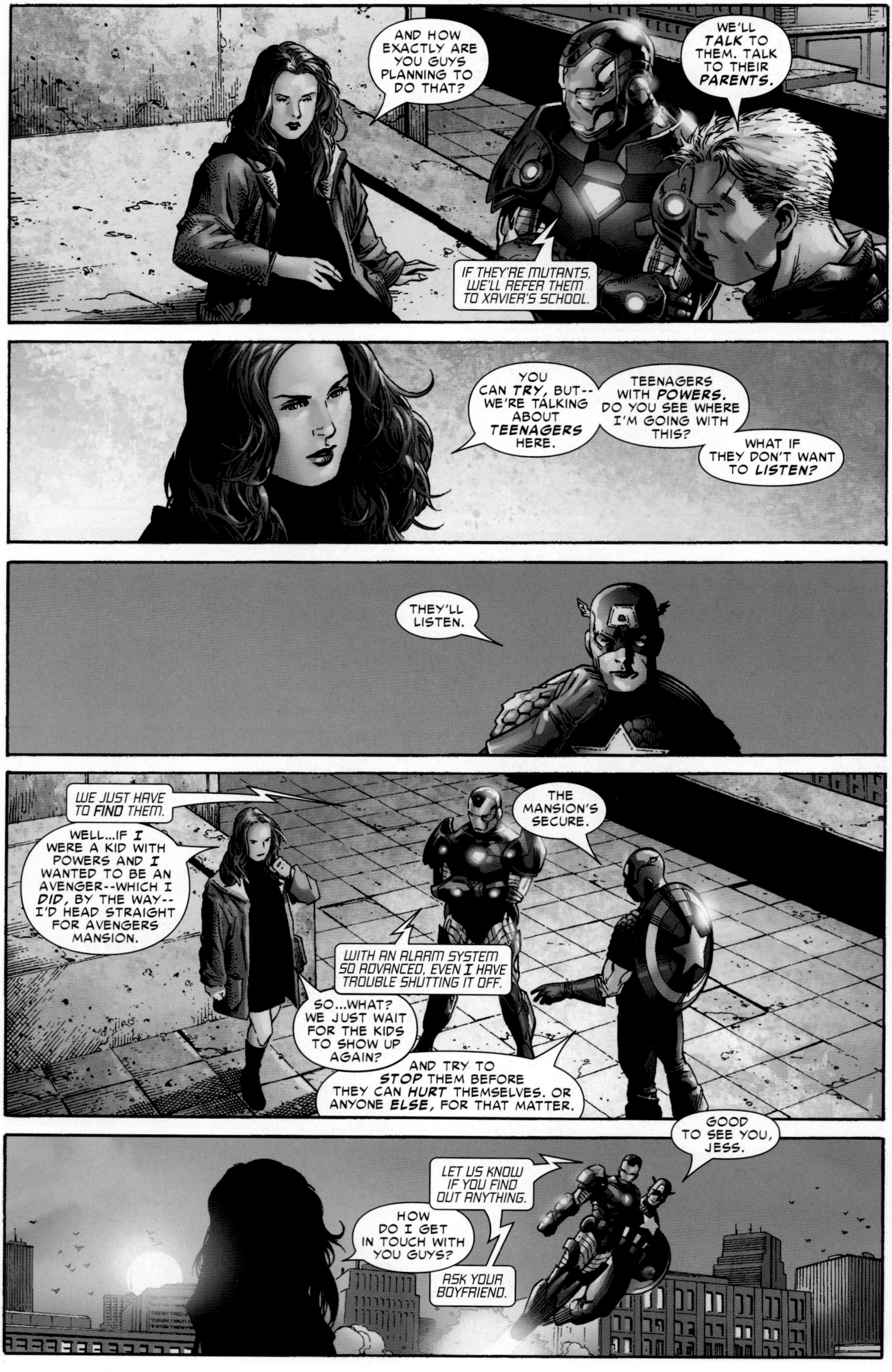

AND HOW EXACTLY ARE YOU GUYS PLANNING TO DO THAT?
WE'LL TALK TO THEM. TALK TO THEIR PARENTS.
IF THEY'RE MUTANTS, WE'LL REFER THEM TO XAVIER'S SCHOOL.
YOU CAN TRY, BUT-- WE'RE TALKING ABOUT TEENAGERS HERE.
TEENAGERS WITH POWERS. DO YOU SEE WHERE I'M GOING WITH THIS?
WHAT IF THEY DON'T WANT TO LISTEN?
THEY'LL LISTEN.
WE JUST HAVE TO FIND THEM.
WELL...IF I WERE A KID WITH POWERS AND I WANTED TO BE AN AVENGER--WHICH I DID, BY THE WAY-- I'D HEAD STRAIGHT FOR AVENGERS MANSION.
THE MANSION'S SECURE.
WITH AN ALARM SYSTEM SO ADVANCED, EVEN I HAVE TROUBLE SHUTTING IT OFF.
SO...WHAT? WE JUST WAIT FOR THE KIDS TO SHOW UP AGAIN?
AND TRY TO STOP THEM BEFORE THEY CAN HURT THEMSELVES. OR ANYONE ELSE, FOR THAT MATTER.
GOOD TO SEE YOU, JESS.
LET US KNOW IF YOU FIND OUT ANYTHING.
HOW DO I GET IN TOUCH WITH YOU GUYS?
ASK YOUR BOYFRIEND.

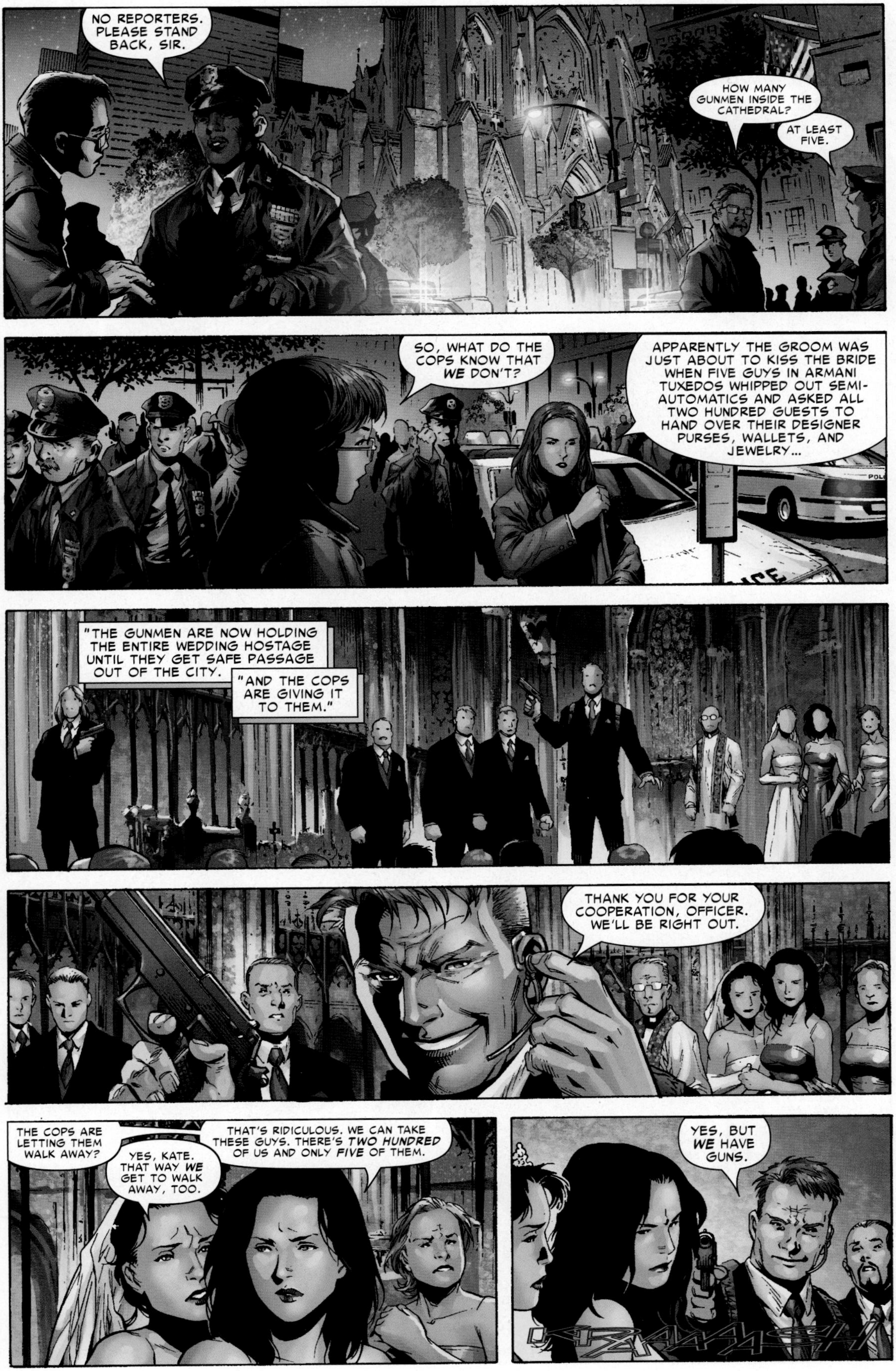
NO REPORTERS. PLEASE STAND BACK, SIR.
HOW MANY GUNMEN INSIDE THE CATHEDRAL?
AT LEAST FIVE.
SO, WHAT DO THE COPS KNOW THAT *WE* DON'T?
APPARENTLY THE GROOM WAS JUST ABOUT TO KISS THE BRIDE WHEN FIVE GUYS IN ARMANI TUXEDOS WHIPPED OUT SEMI-AUTOMATICS AND ASKED ALL TWO HUNDRED GUESTS TO HAND OVER THEIR DESIGNER PURSES, WALLETS, AND JEWELRY...
POLICE
"THE GUNMEN ARE NOW HOLDING THE ENTIRE WEDDING HOSTAGE UNTIL THEY GET SAFE PASSAGE OUT OF THE CITY.
"AND THE COPS ARE GIVING IT TO THEM."
THANK YOU FOR YOUR COOPERATION, OFFICER. WE'LL BE RIGHT OUT.
THE COPS ARE LETTING THEM WALK AWAY?
YES, KATE. THAT WAY *WE* GET TO WALK AWAY, TOO.
THAT'S RIDICULOUS. WE CAN TAKE THESE GUYS. THERE'S *TWO HUNDRED* OF US AND ONLY *FIVE* OF THEM.
YES, BUT *WE* HAVE GUNS.

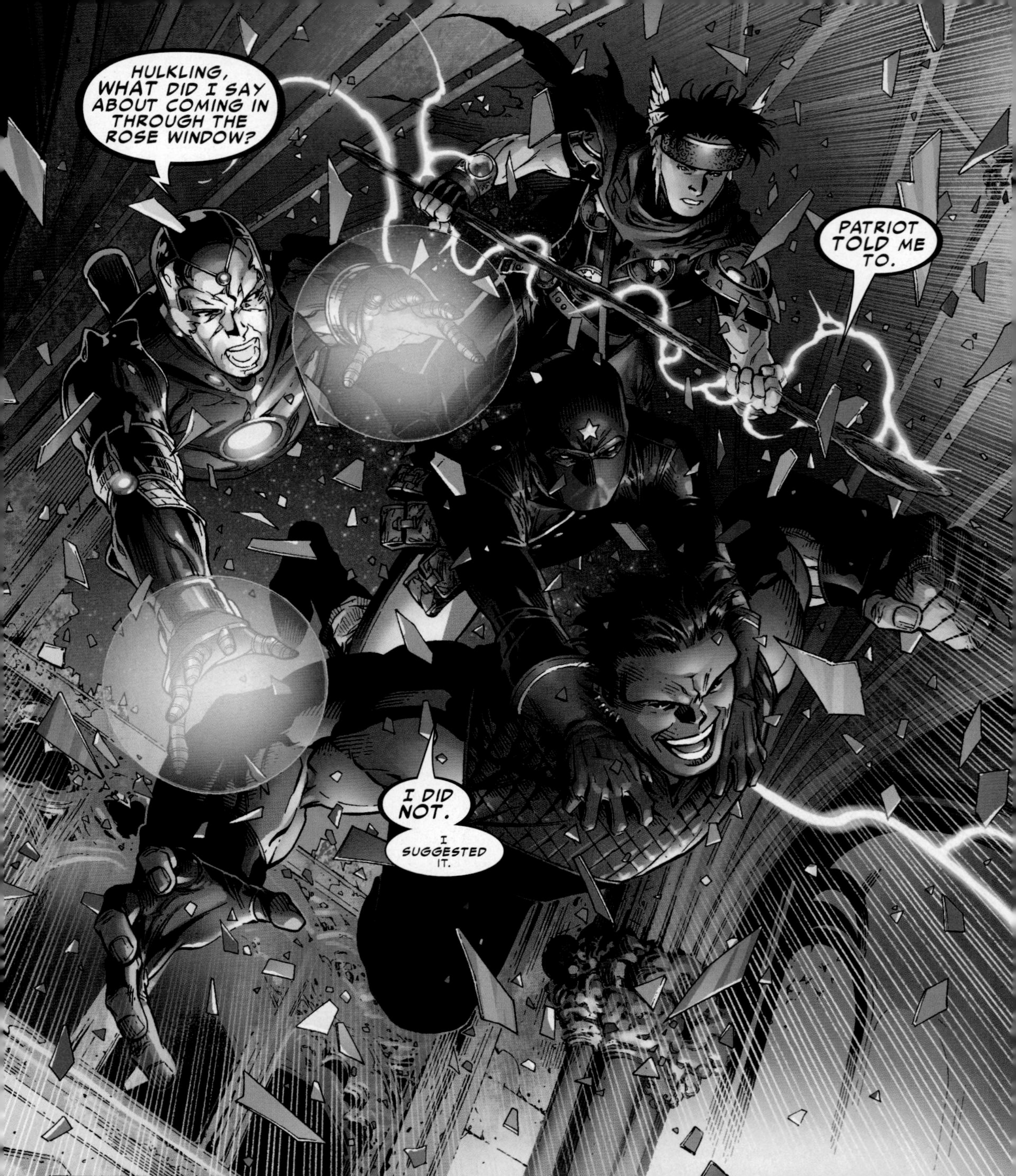
HULKLING, WHAT DID I SAY ABOUT COMING IN THROUGH THE ROSE WINDOW?
PATRIOT TOLD ME TO.
I DID NOT.
I SUGGESTED IT.

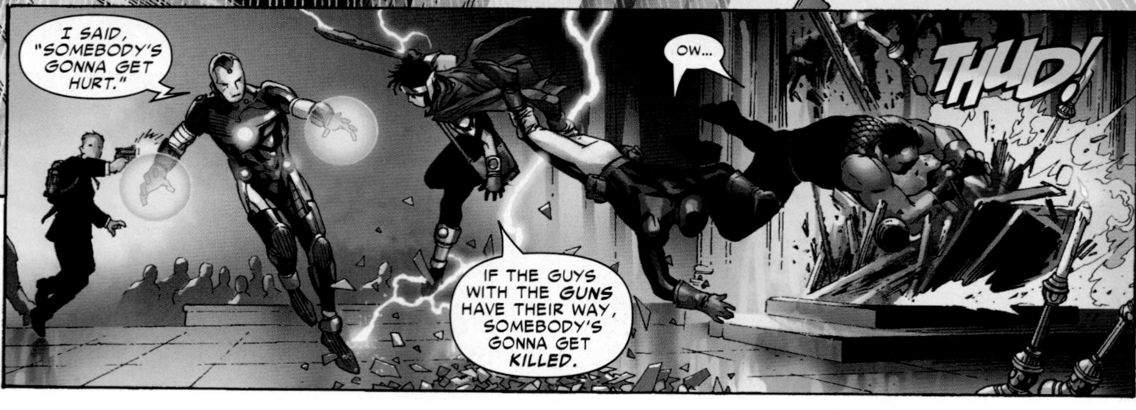
I SAID, "SOMEBODY'S GONNA GET HURT."
OW...
THUD!
IF THE GUYS WITH THE GUNS HAVE THEIR WAY, SOMEBODY'S GONNA GET KILLED.

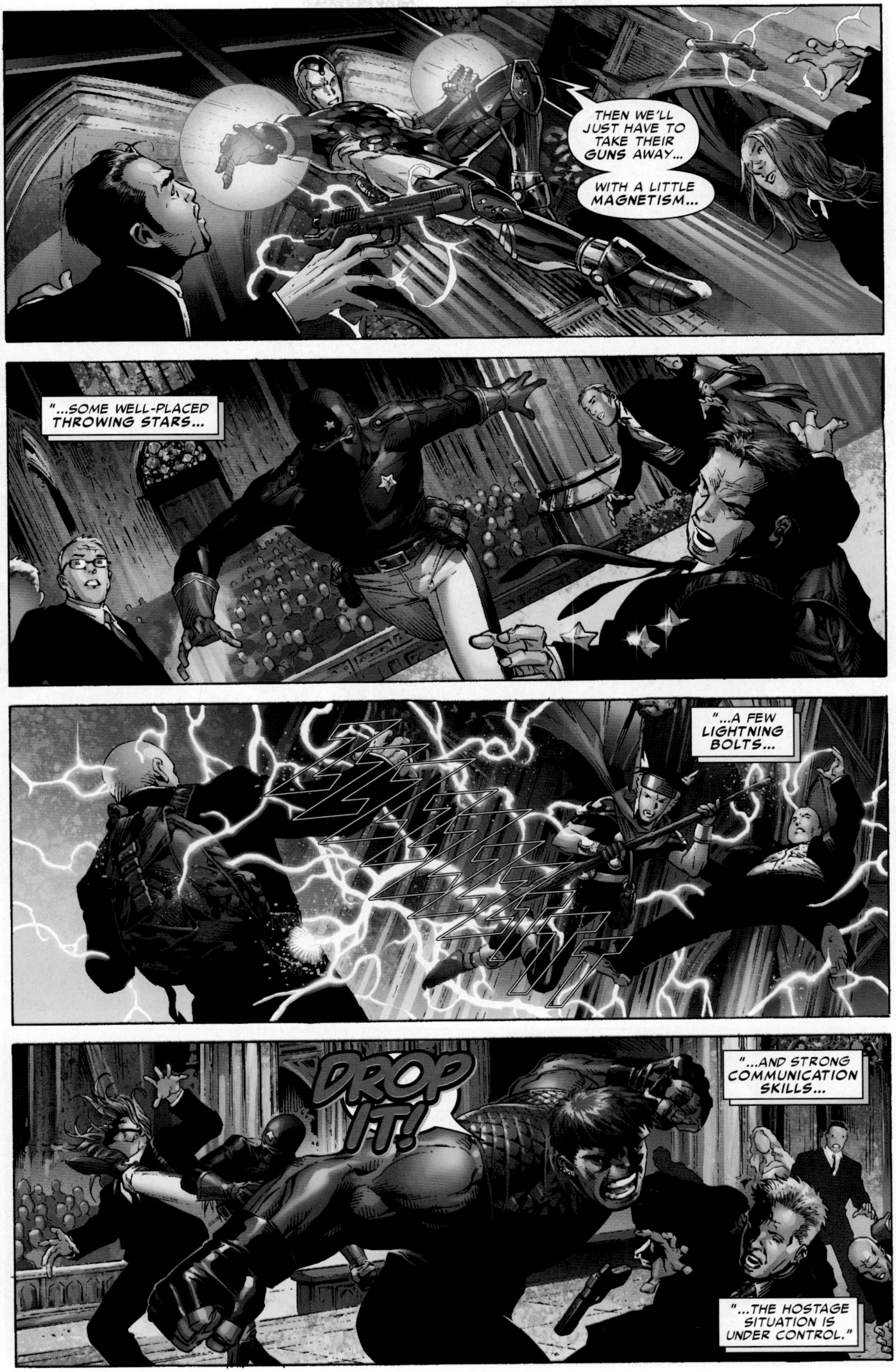
THEN WE'LL JUST HAVE TO TAKE THEIR GUNS AWAY...
WITH A LITTLE MAGNETISM...
"...SOME WELL-PLACED THROWING STARS...
"...A FEW LIGHTNING BOLTS...
"...AND STRONG COMMUNICATION SKILLS...
DROP IT!
"...THE HOSTAGE SITUATION IS UNDER CONTROL."

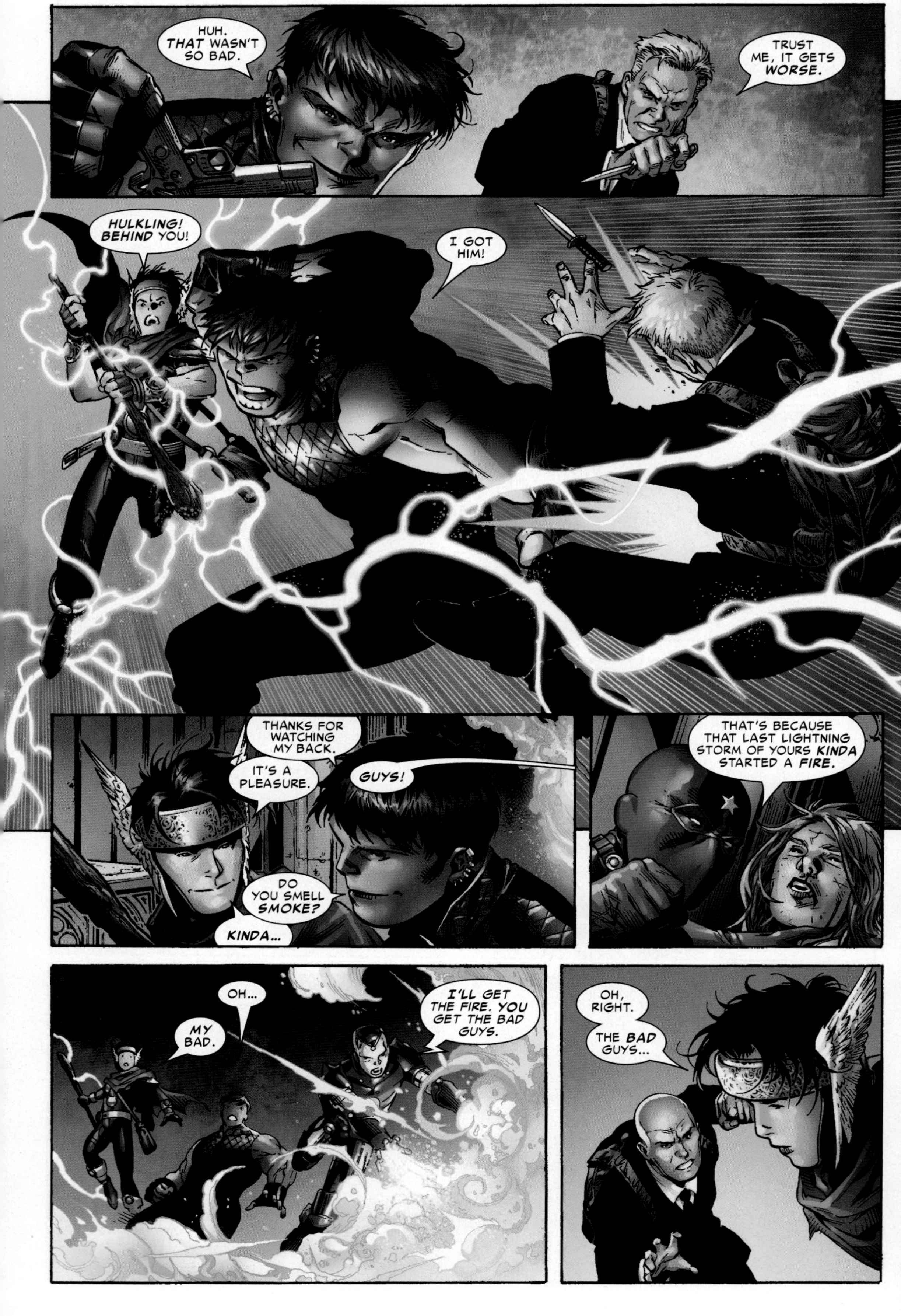

HUH. THAT WASN'T SO BAD.
TRUST ME, IT GETS WORSE.
HULKLING! BEHIND YOU!
I GOT HIM!
THANKS FOR WATCHING MY BACK.
IT'S A PLEASURE.
GUYS!
DO YOU SMELL SMOKE?
KINDA...
THAT'S BECAUSE THAT LAST LIGHTNING STORM OF YOURS KINDA STARTED A FIRE.
OH...
MY BAD.
I'LL GET THE FIRE. YOU GET THE BAD GUYS.
OH, RIGHT.
THE BAD GUYS...

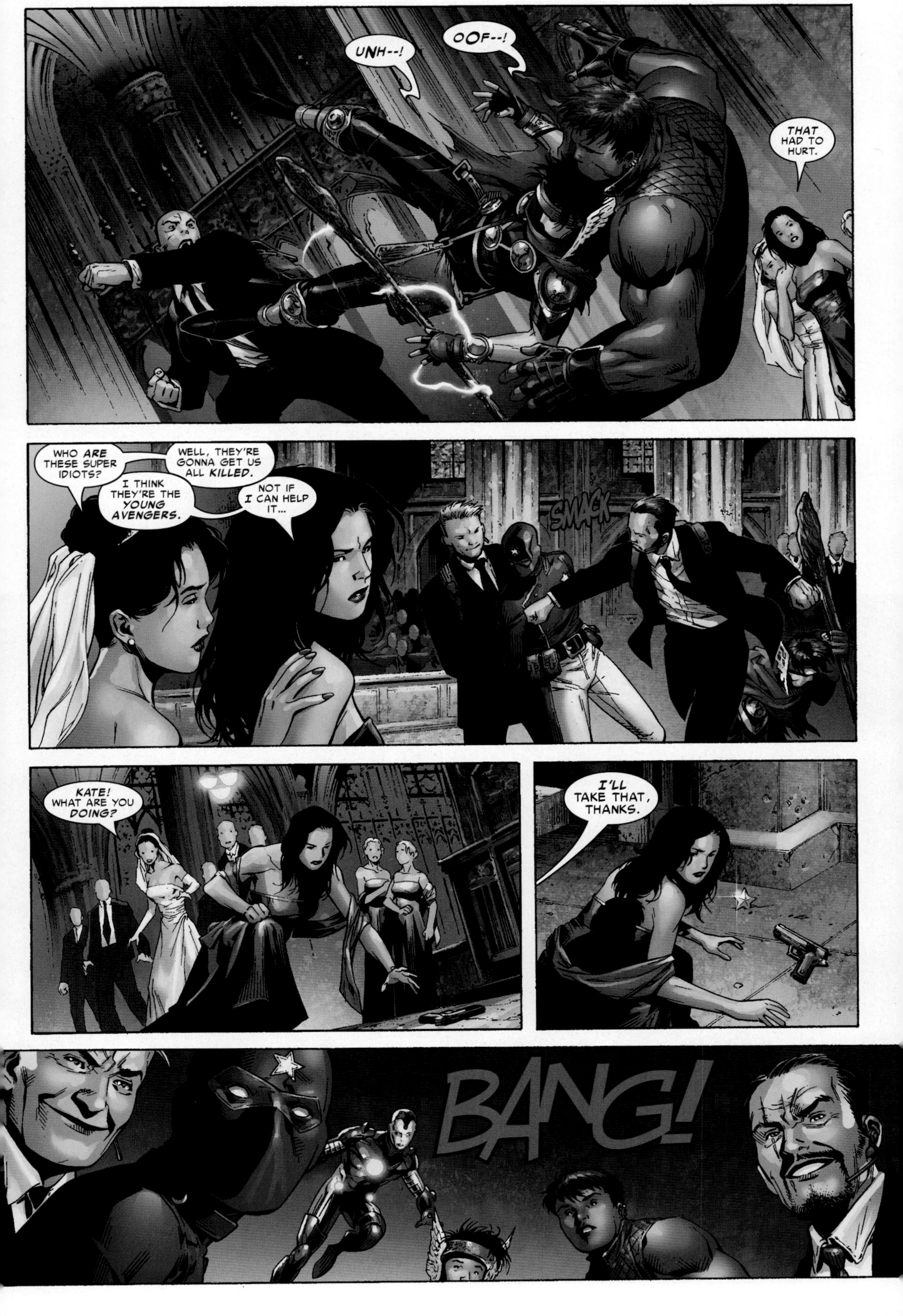
UNH--!
OOF--!
THAT HAD TO HURT.
WHO ARE THESE SUPER IDIOTS?
WELL, THEY'RE GONNA GET US ALL KILLED.
I THINK THEY'RE THE YOUNG AVENGERS.
NOT IF I CAN HELP IT...
SMACK
KATE! WHAT ARE YOU DOING?
I'LL TAKE THAT, THANKS.
BANG!

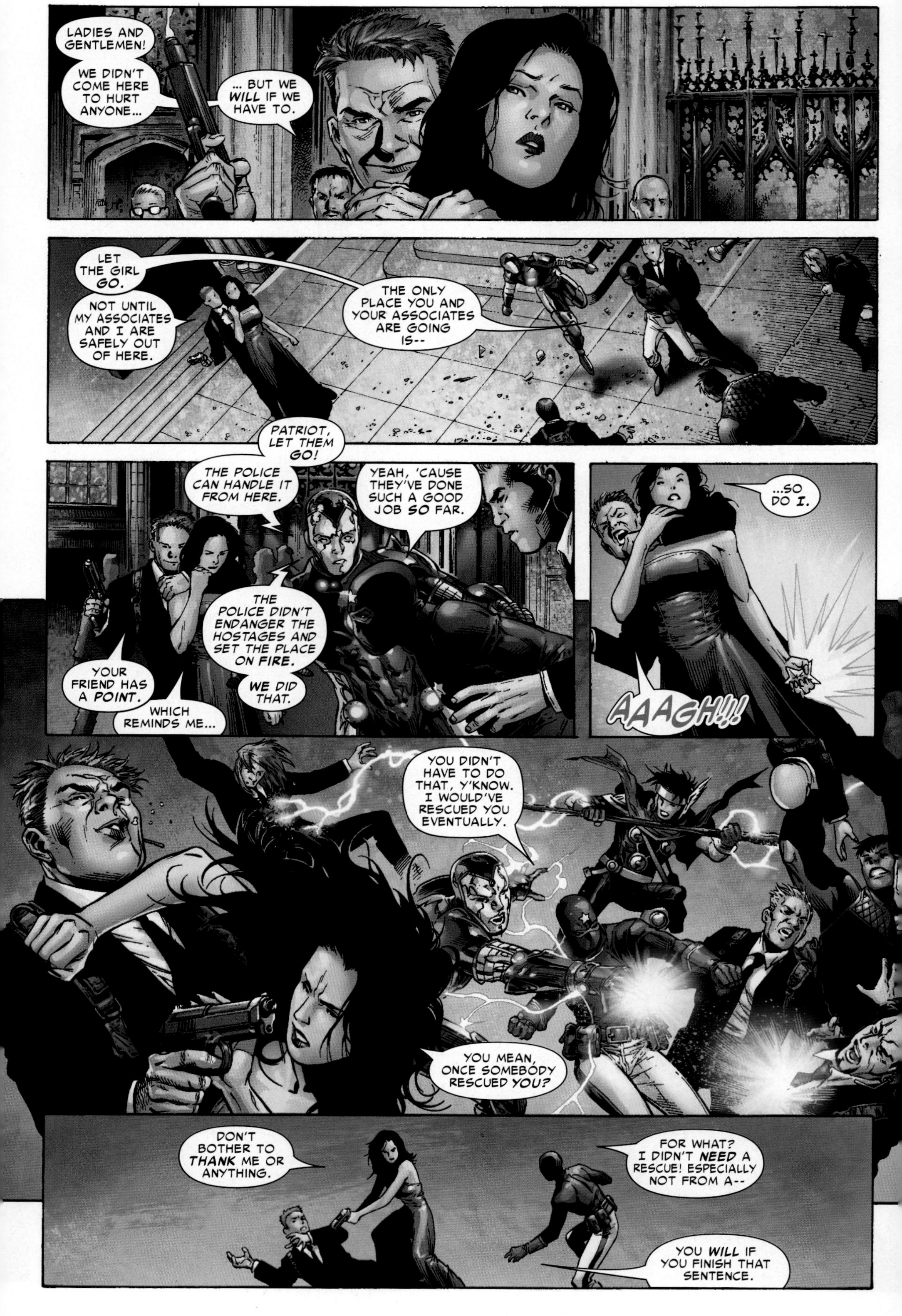

LADIES AND GENTLEMEN!
WE DIDN'T COME HERE TO HURT ANYONE...
... BUT WE WILL IF WE HAVE TO.
LET THE GIRL GO.
NOT UNTIL MY ASSOCIATES AND I ARE SAFELY OUT OF HERE.
THE ONLY PLACE YOU AND YOUR ASSOCIATES ARE GOING IS--
PATRIOT, LET THEM GO!
THE POLICE CAN HANDLE IT FROM HERE.
YEAH, 'CAUSE THEY'VE DONE SUCH A GOOD JOB SO FAR.
THE POLICE DIDN'T ENDANGER THE HOSTAGES AND SET THE PLACE ON FIRE.
WE DID THAT.
YOUR FRIEND HAS A POINT.
WHICH REMINDS ME...
...SO DO I.
AAAGH!!!
YOU DIDN'T HAVE TO DO THAT, Y'KNOW. I WOULD'VE RESCUED YOU EVENTUALLY.
YOU MEAN, ONCE SOMEBODY RESCUED YOU?
DON'T BOTHER TO THANK ME OR ANYTHING.
FOR WHAT? I DIDN'T NEED A RESCUE! ESPECIALLY NOT FROM A--
YOU WILL IF YOU FINISH THAT SENTENCE.

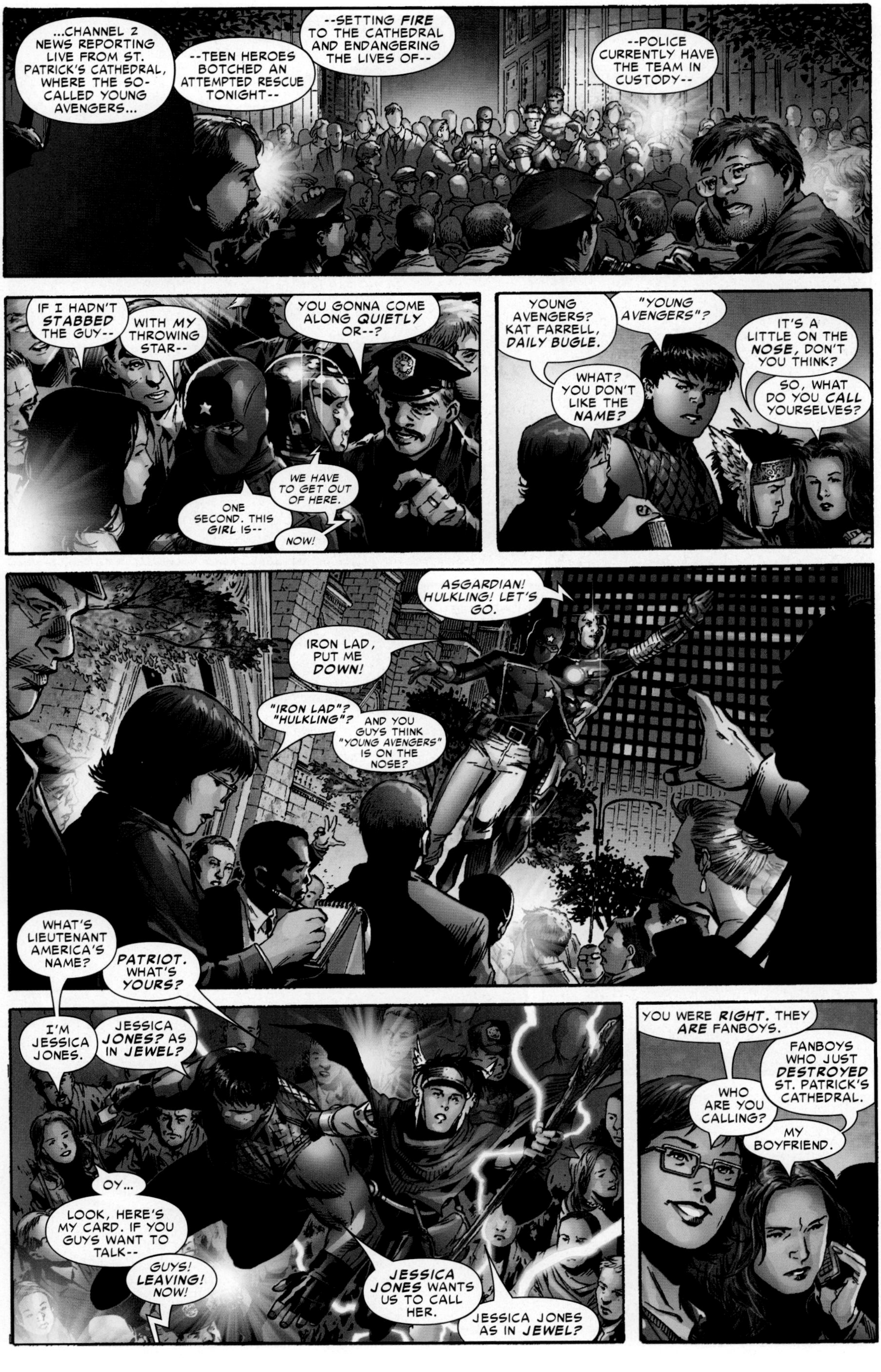

...CHANNEL 2 NEWS REPORTING LIVE FROM ST. PATRICK'S CATHEDRAL, WHERE THE SO-CALLED YOUNG AVENGERS...
--TEEN HEROES BOTCHED AN ATTEMPTED RESCUE TONIGHT--
--SETTING FIRE TO THE CATHEDRAL AND ENDANGERING THE LIVES OF--
--POLICE CURRENTLY HAVE THE TEAM IN CUSTODY--
IF I HADN'T STABBED THE GUY--
WITH MY THROWING STAR--
YOU GONNA COME ALONG QUIETLY OR--?
WE HAVE TO GET OUT OF HERE.
ONE SECOND. THIS GIRL IS--
NOW!
YOUNG AVENGERS? KAT FARRELL, DAILY BUGLE.
"YOUNG AVENGERS"?
WHAT? YOU DON'T LIKE THE NAME?
IT'S A LITTLE ON THE NOSE, DON'T YOU THINK?
SO, WHAT DO YOU CALL YOURSELVES?
ASGARDIAN! HULKLING! LET'S GO.
IRON LAD, PUT ME DOWN!
"IRON LAD"? "HULKLING"?
AND YOU GUYS THINK "YOUNG AVENGERS" IS ON THE NOSE?
WHAT'S LIEUTENANT AMERICA'S NAME?
PATRIOT. WHAT'S YOURS?
I'M JESSICA JONES.
JESSICA JONES? AS IN JEWEL?
OY...
LOOK, HERE'S MY CARD. IF YOU GUYS WANT TO TALK--
GUYS! LEAVING! NOW!
JESSICA JONES WANTS US TO CALL HER.
JESSICA JONES AS IN JEWEL?
YOU WERE RIGHT. THEY ARE FANBOYS.
FANBOYS WHO JUST DESTROYED ST. PATRICK'S CATHEDRAL.
WHO ARE YOU CALLING?
MY BOYFRIEND.

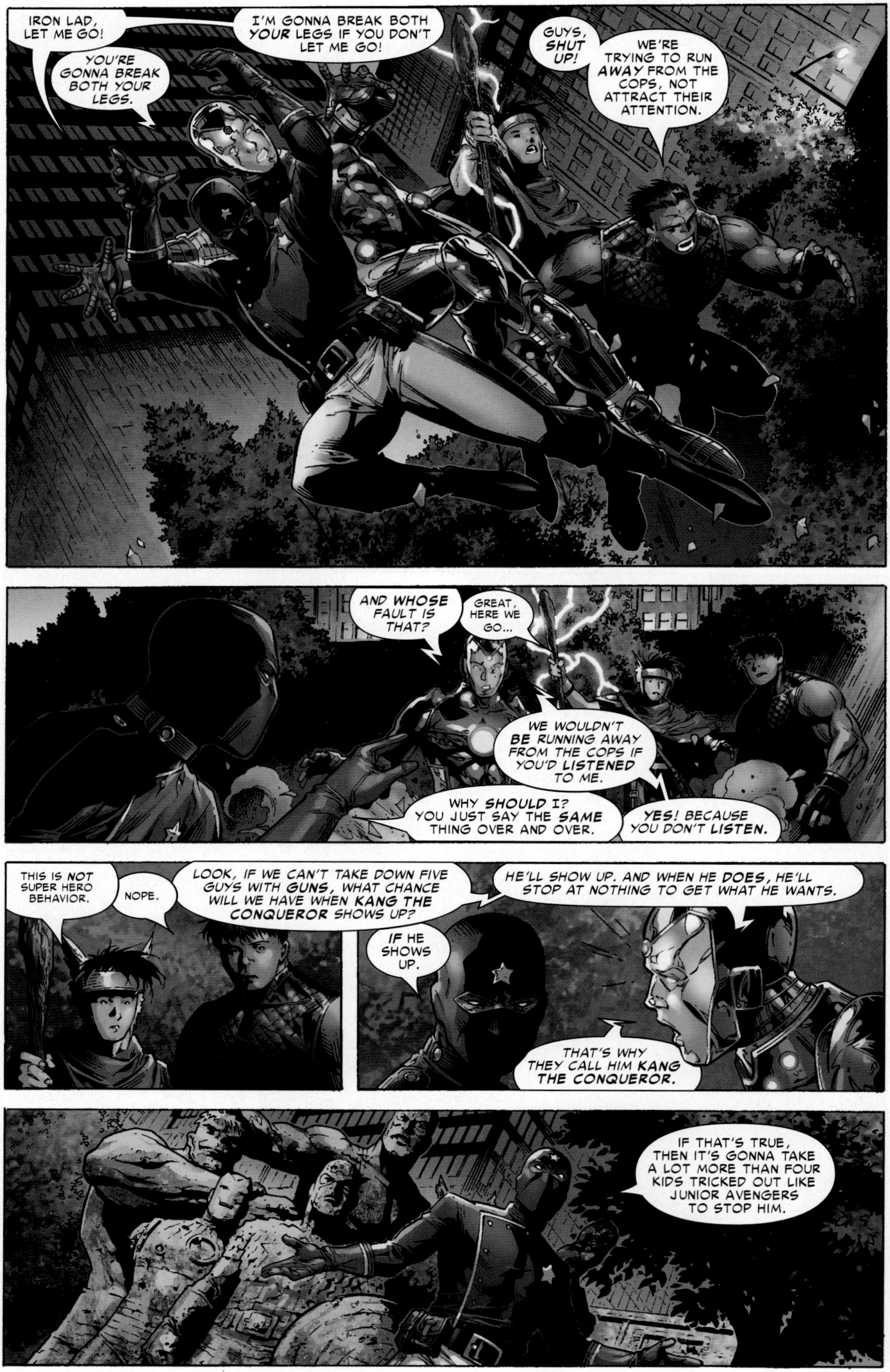
IRON LAD, LET ME GO!
I'M GONNA BREAK BOTH YOUR LEGS IF YOU DON'T LET ME GO!
YOU'RE GONNA BREAK BOTH YOUR LEGS.
GUYS, SHUT UP!
WE'RE TRYING TO RUN AWAY FROM THE COPS, NOT ATTRACT THEIR ATTENTION.
AND WHOSE FAULT IS THAT?
GREAT, HERE WE GO...
WE WOULDN'T BE RUNNING AWAY FROM THE COPS IF YOU'D LISTENED TO ME.
WHY SHOULD I? YOU JUST SAY THE SAME THING OVER AND OVER.
YES! BECAUSE YOU DON'T LISTEN.
THIS IS NOT SUPER HERO BEHAVIOR.
NOPE.
LOOK, IF WE CAN'T TAKE DOWN FIVE GUYS WITH GUNS, WHAT CHANCE WILL WE HAVE WHEN KANG THE CONQUEROR SHOWS UP?
IF HE SHOWS UP.
HE'LL SHOW UP. AND WHEN HE DOES, HE'LL STOP AT NOTHING TO GET WHAT HE WANTS.
THAT'S WHY THEY CALL HIM KANG THE CONQUEROR.
IF THAT'S TRUE, THEN IT'S GONNA TAKE A LOT MORE THAN FOUR KIDS TRICKED OUT LIKE JUNIOR AVENGERS TO STOP HIM.

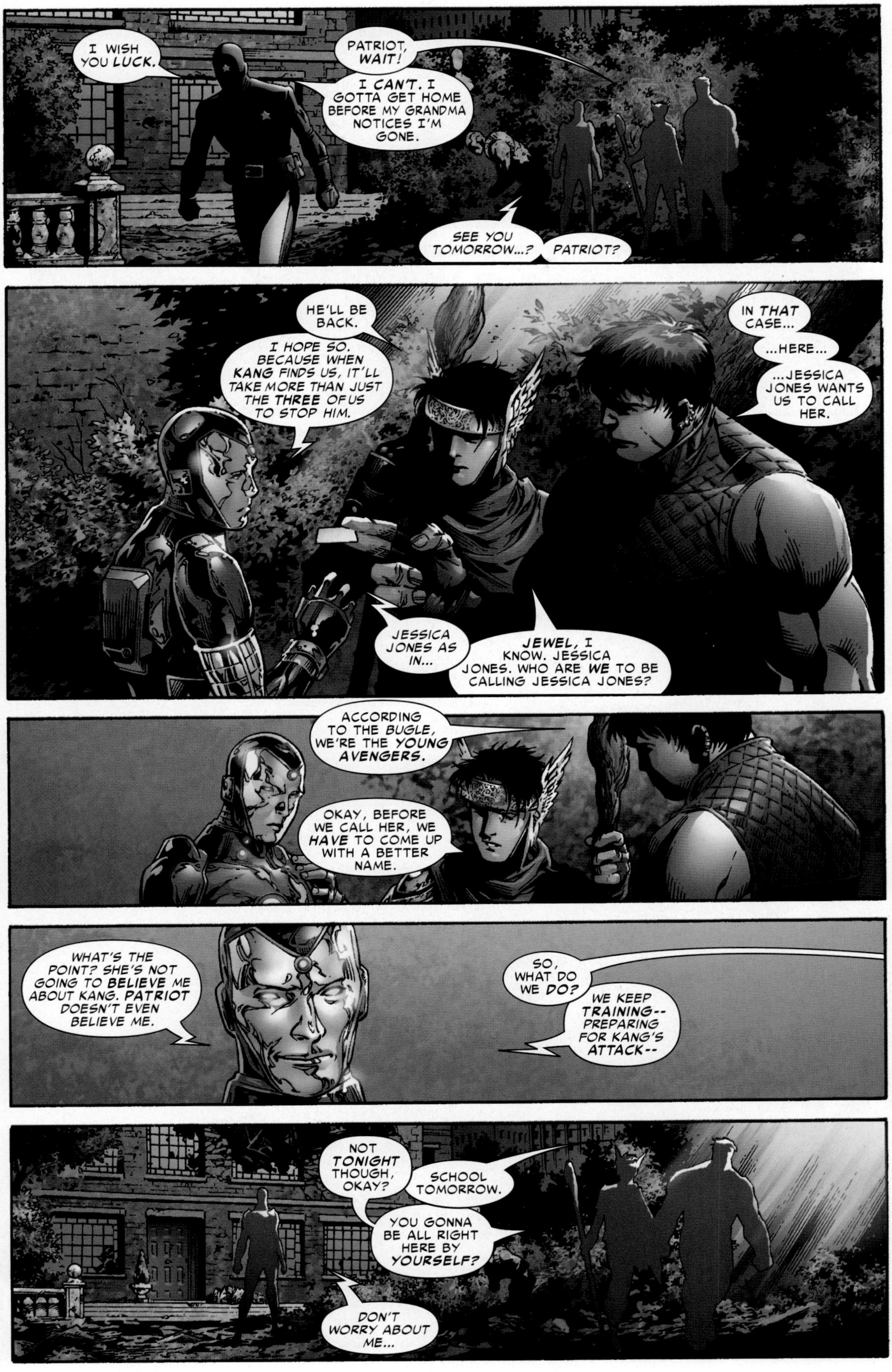
I WISH YOU LUCK.
PATRIOT, WAIT!
I CAN'T. I GOTTA GET HOME BEFORE MY GRANDMA NOTICES I'M GONE.
SEE YOU TOMORROW...?
PATRIOT?
HE'LL BE BACK.
I HOPE SO. BECAUSE WHEN KANG FINDS US, IT'LL TAKE MORE THAN JUST THE THREE OF US TO STOP HIM.
IN THAT CASE...
...HERE...
...JESSICA JONES WANTS US TO CALL HER.
JESSICA JONES AS IN...
JEWEL, I KNOW. JESSICA JONES. WHO ARE WE TO BE CALLING JESSICA JONES?
ACCORDING TO THE BUGLE, WE'RE THE YOUNG AVENGERS.
OKAY, BEFORE WE CALL HER, WE HAVE TO COME UP WITH A BETTER NAME.
WHAT'S THE POINT? SHE'S NOT GOING TO BELIEVE ME ABOUT KANG. PATRIOT DOESN'T EVEN BELIEVE ME.
SO, WHAT DO WE DO?
WE KEEP TRAINING-- PREPARING FOR KANG'S ATTACK--
NOT TONIGHT THOUGH, OKAY?
SCHOOL TOMORROW.
YOU GONNA BE ALL RIGHT HERE BY YOURSELF?
DON'T WORRY ABOUT ME...

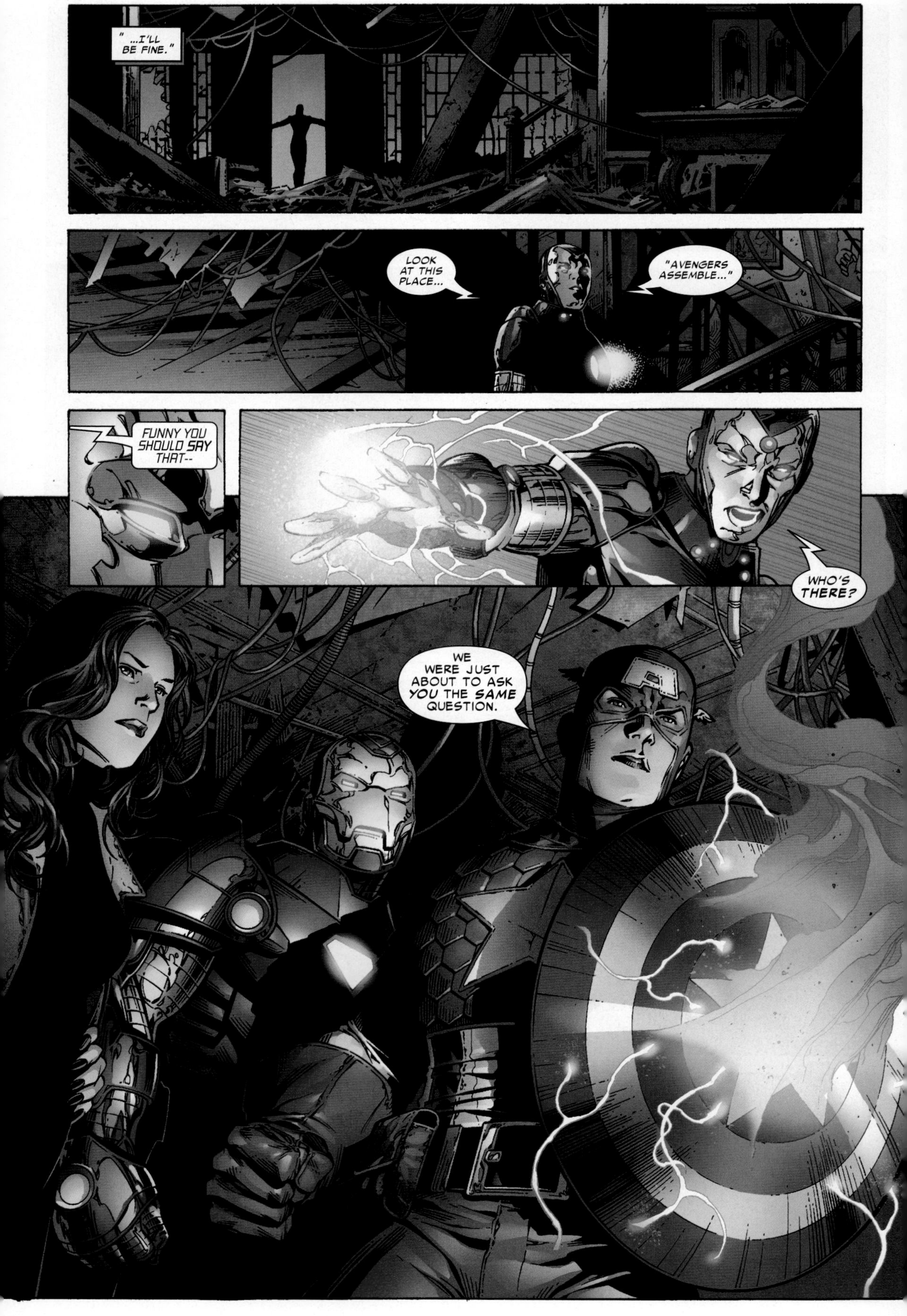
"...I'LL BE FINE."
LOOK AT THIS PLACE...
"AVENGERS ASSEMBLE..."
FUNNY YOU SHOULD SAY THAT--
WHO'S THERE?
WE WERE JUST ABOUT TO ASK YOU THE SAME QUESTION.

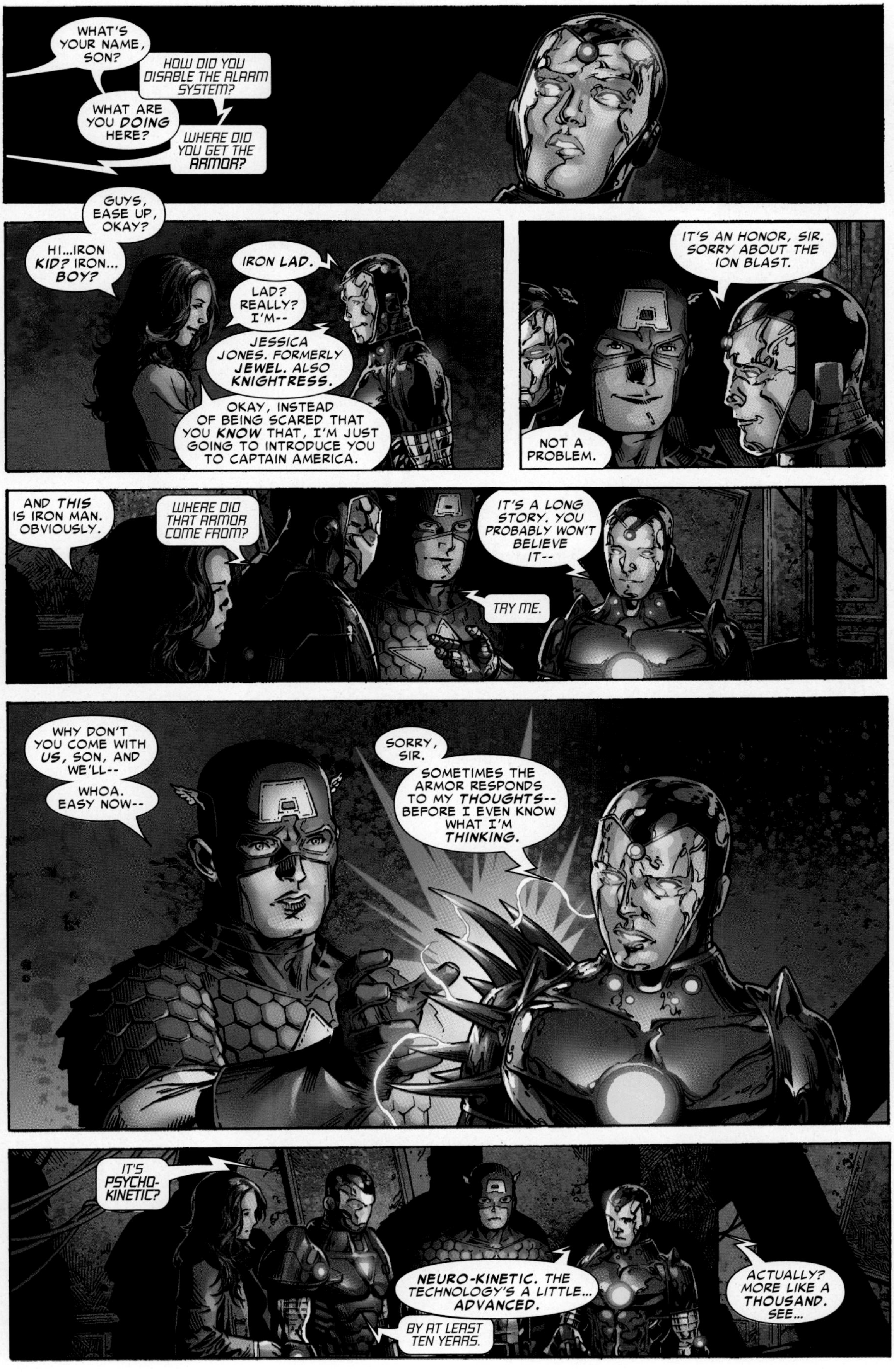
WHAT'S YOUR NAME, SON?
HOW DID YOU DISABLE THE ALARM SYSTEM?
WHAT ARE YOU DOING HERE?
WHERE DID YOU GET THE ARMOR?
GUYS, EASE UP, OKAY?
HI...IRON KID? IRON... BOY?
IRON LAD.
LAD? REALLY? I'M--
JESSICA JONES. FORMERLY JEWEL. ALSO KNIGHTRESS.
OKAY, INSTEAD OF BEING SCARED THAT YOU KNOW THAT, I'M JUST GOING TO INTRODUCE YOU TO CAPTAIN AMERICA.
IT'S AN HONOR, SIR. SORRY ABOUT THE ION BLAST.
NOT A PROBLEM.
AND THIS IS IRON MAN. OBVIOUSLY.
WHERE DID THAT ARMOR COME FROM?
IT'S A LONG STORY. YOU PROBABLY WON'T BELIEVE IT--
TRY ME.
WHY DON'T YOU COME WITH US, SON, AND WE'LL--
WHOA. EASY NOW--
SORRY, SIR.
SOMETIMES THE ARMOR RESPONDS TO MY THOUGHTS-- BEFORE I EVEN KNOW WHAT I'M THINKING.
IT'S PSYCHO-KINETIC?
NEURO-KINETIC. THE TECHNOLOGY'S A LITTLE... ADVANCED.
BY AT LEAST TEN YEARS.
ACTUALLY? MORE LIKE A THOUSAND. SEE...

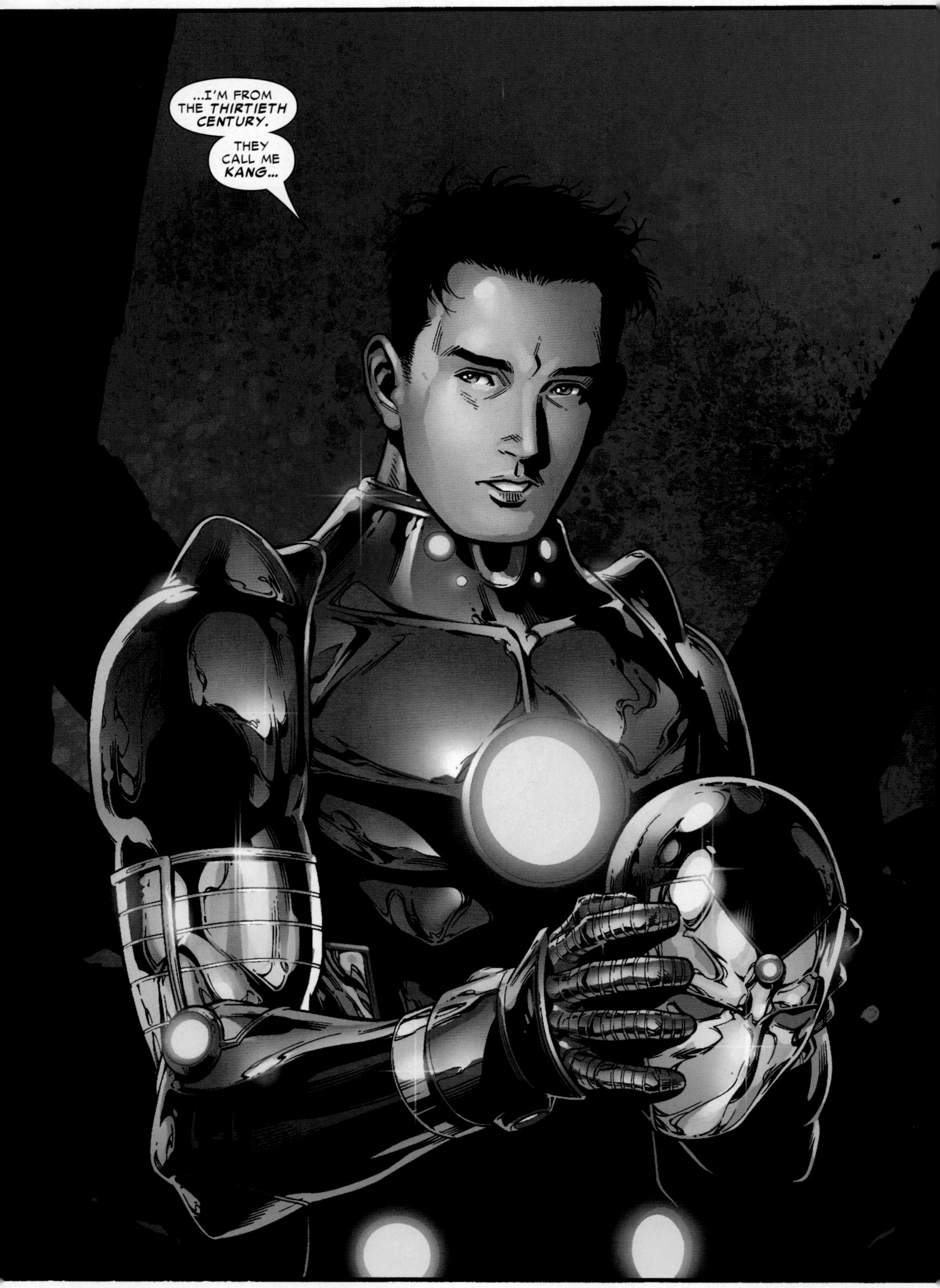
...I'M FROM THE THIRTIETH CENTURY.
THEY CALL ME KANG...

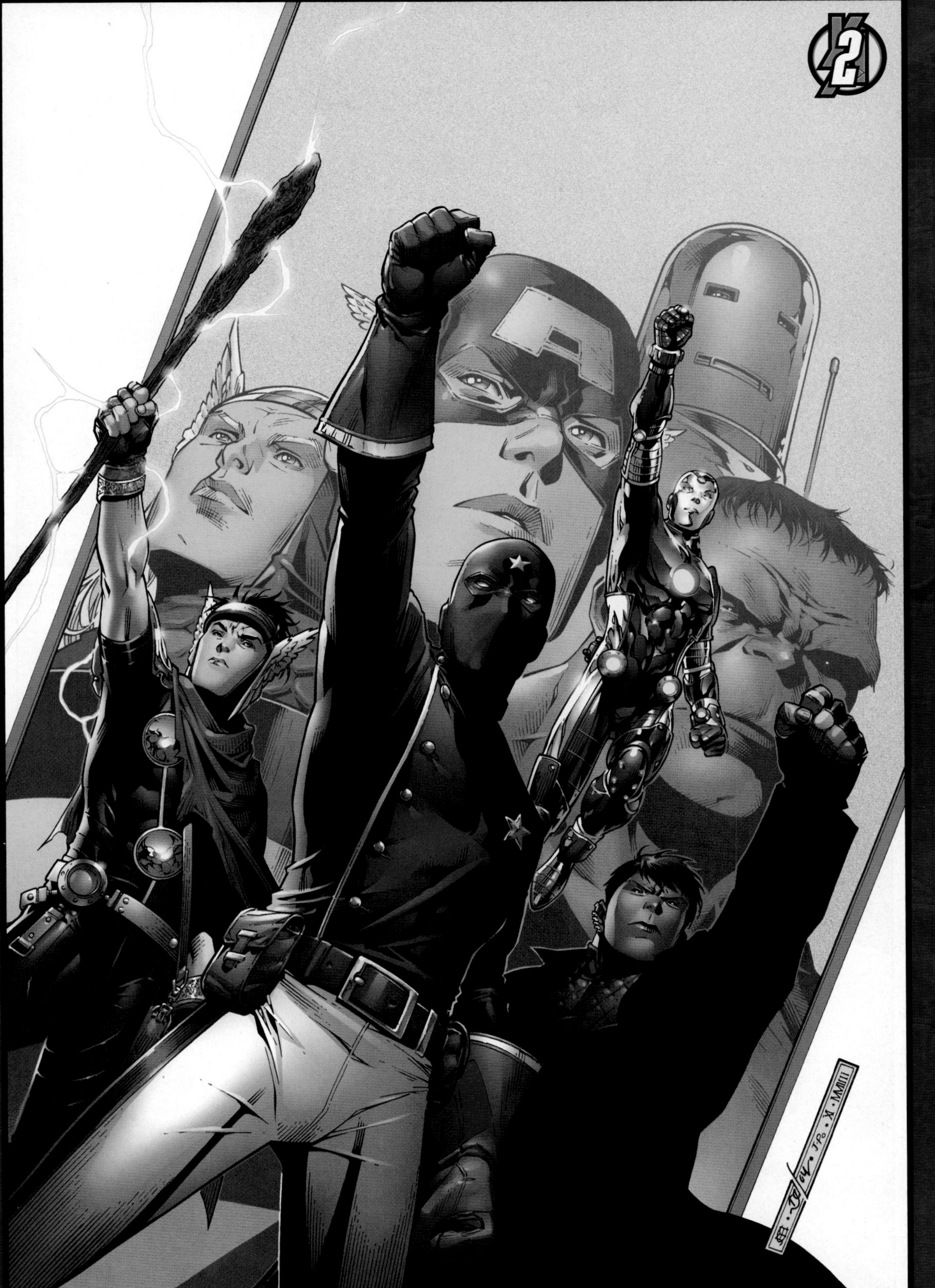

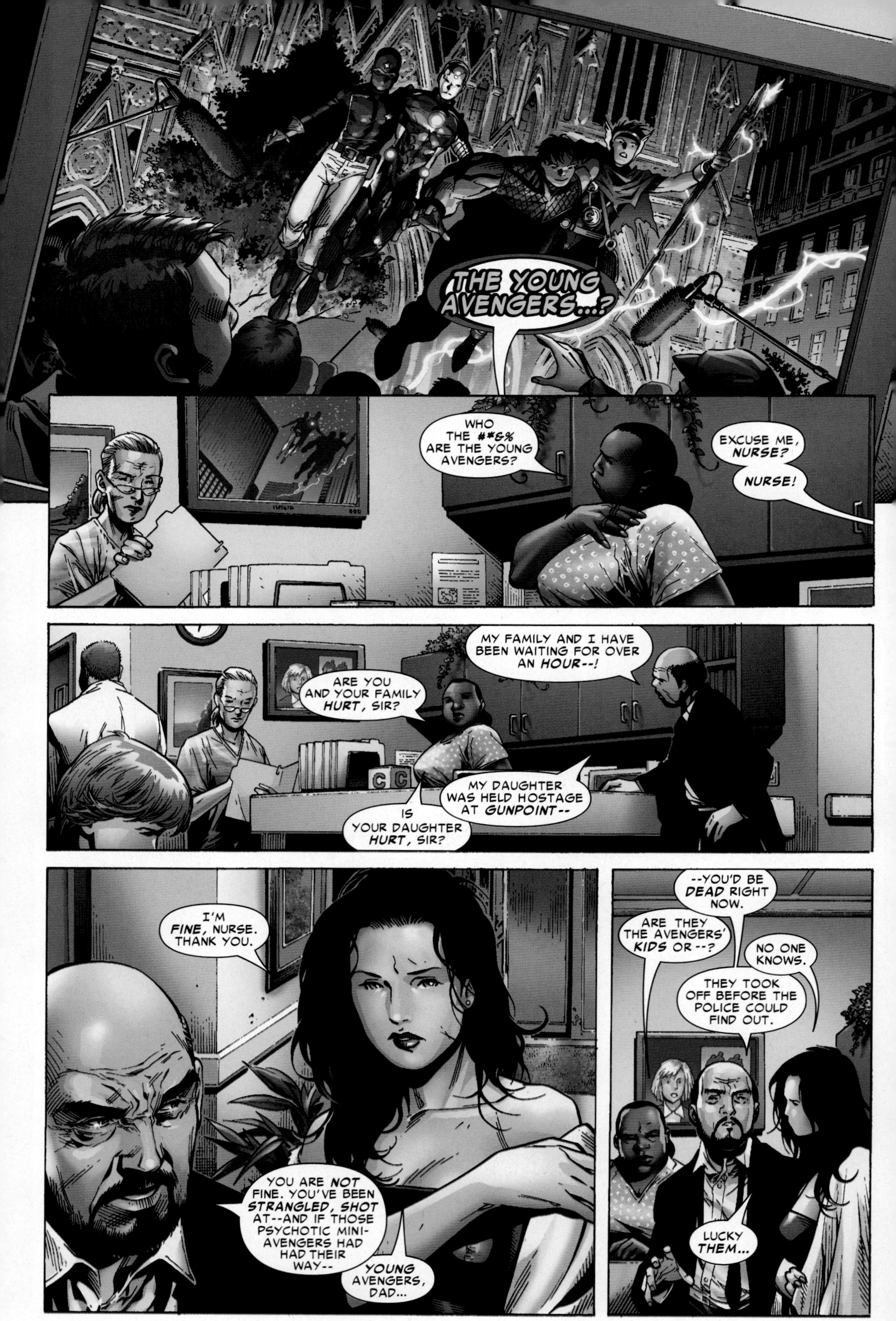
THE YOUNG AVENGERS...?
WHO THE #*&% ARE THE YOUNG AVENGERS?
EXCUSE ME, NURSE?
NURSE!
MY FAMILY AND I HAVE BEEN WAITING FOR OVER AN HOUR--!
ARE YOU AND YOUR FAMILY HURT, SIR?
MY DAUGHTER WAS HELD HOSTAGE AT GUNPOINT--
IS YOUR DAUGHTER HURT, SIR?
I'M FINE, NURSE. THANK YOU.
YOU ARE NOT FINE. YOU'VE BEEN STRANGLED, SHOT AT--AND IF THOSE PSYCHOTIC MINI-AVENGERS HAD HAD THEIR WAY--
YOUNG AVENGERS, DAD...
--YOU'D BE DEAD RIGHT NOW.
ARE THEY THE AVENGERS' KIDS OR --?
NO ONE KNOWS.
THEY TOOK OFF BEFORE THE POLICE COULD FIND OUT.
LUCKY THEM...

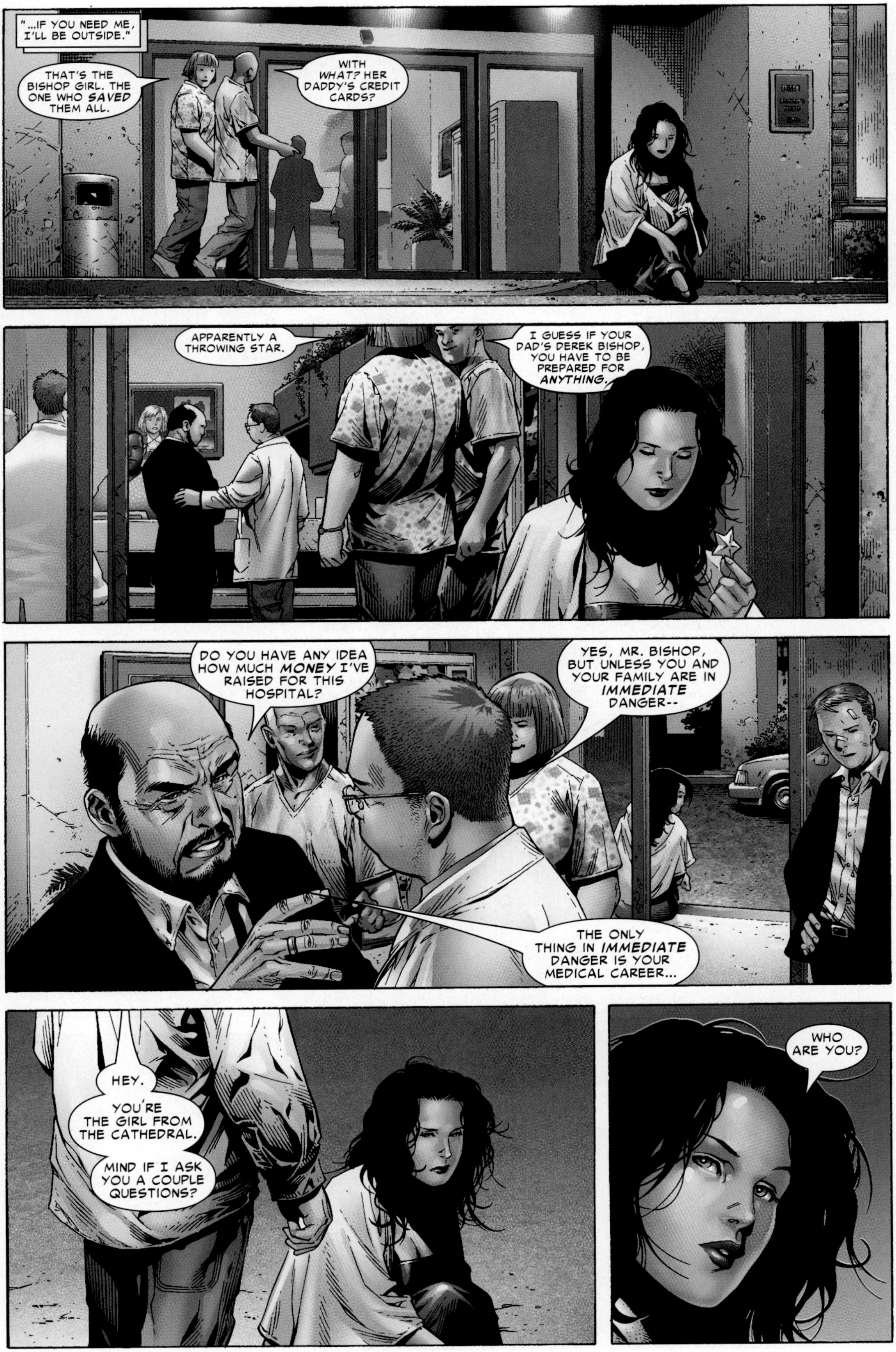
"...IF YOU NEED ME, I'LL BE OUTSIDE."
THAT'S THE BISHOP GIRL. THE ONE WHO *SAVED* THEM ALL.
WITH *WHAT?* HER DADDY'S CREDIT CARDS?
APPARENTLY A THROWING STAR.
I GUESS IF YOUR DAD'S DEREK BISHOP, YOU HAVE TO BE PREPARED FOR *ANYTHING.*
DO YOU HAVE ANY IDEA HOW MUCH *MONEY* I'VE RAISED FOR THIS HOSPITAL?
YES, MR. BISHOP, BUT UNLESS YOU AND YOUR FAMILY ARE IN *IMMEDIATE* DANGER--
THE ONLY THING IN *IMMEDIATE* DANGER IS YOUR MEDICAL CAREER...
HEY.
YOU'RE THE GIRL FROM THE CATHEDRAL.
MIND IF I ASK YOU A COUPLE QUESTIONS?
WHO ARE YOU?

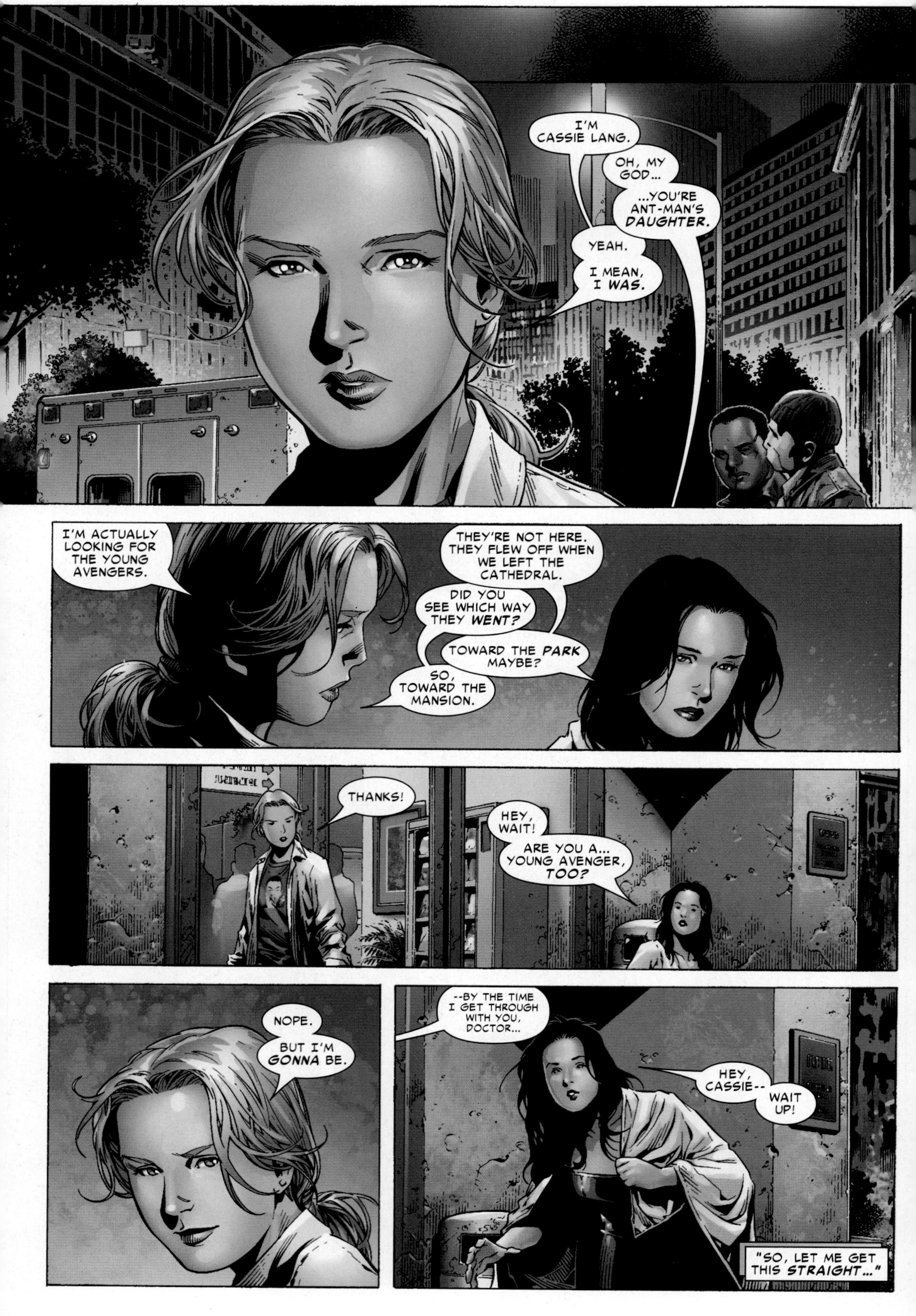
I'M CASSIE LANG.
OH, MY GOD...
...YOU'RE ANT-MAN'S DAUGHTER.
YEAH.
I MEAN, I WAS.
I'M ACTUALLY LOOKING FOR THE YOUNG AVENGERS.
THEY'RE NOT HERE. THEY FLEW OFF WHEN WE LEFT THE CATHEDRAL.
DID YOU SEE WHICH WAY THEY WENT?
TOWARD THE PARK MAYBE?
SO, TOWARD THE MANSION.
THANKS!
HEY, WAIT!
ARE YOU A... YOUNG AVENGER, TOO?
NOPE.
BUT I'M GONNA BE.
--BY THE TIME I GET THROUGH WITH YOU, DOCTOR...
HEY, CASSIE--
WAIT UP!
"SO, LET ME GET THIS STRAIGHT..."

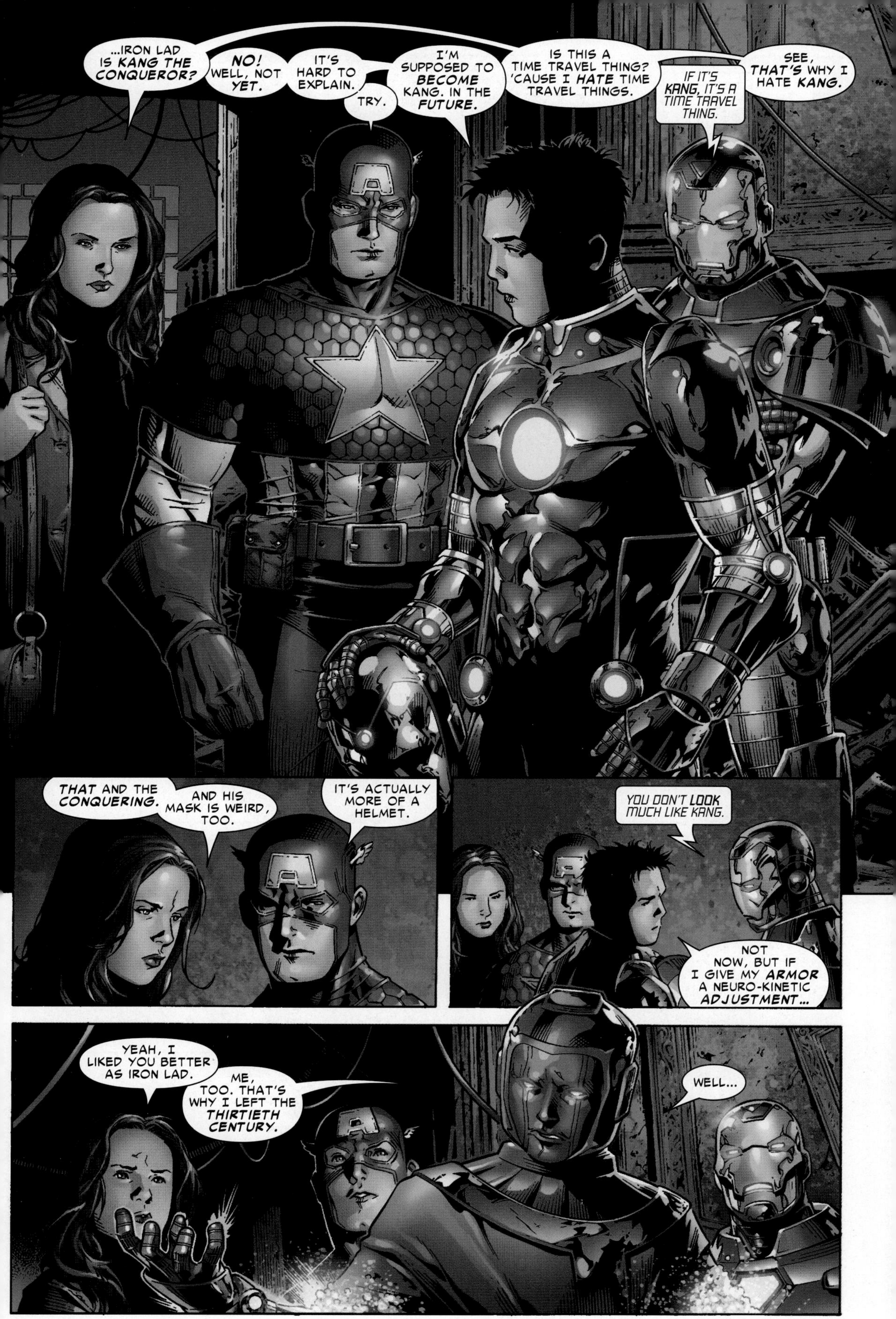
...IRON LAD IS KANG THE CONQUEROR?
NO! WELL, NOT YET.
IT'S HARD TO EXPLAIN.
TRY.
I'M SUPPOSED TO BECOME KANG. IN THE FUTURE.
IS THIS A TIME TRAVEL THING? 'CAUSE I HATE TIME TRAVEL THINGS.
IF IT'S KANG, IT'S A TIME TRAVEL THING.
SEE, THAT'S WHY I HATE KANG.
THAT AND THE CONQUERING.
AND HIS MASK IS WEIRD, TOO.
IT'S ACTUALLY MORE OF A HELMET.
YOU DON'T LOOK MUCH LIKE KANG.
NOT NOW, BUT IF I GIVE MY ARMOR A NEURO-KINETIC ADJUSTMENT...
YEAH, I LIKED YOU BETTER AS IRON LAD.
ME, TOO. THAT'S WHY I LEFT THE THIRTIETH CENTURY.
WELL...

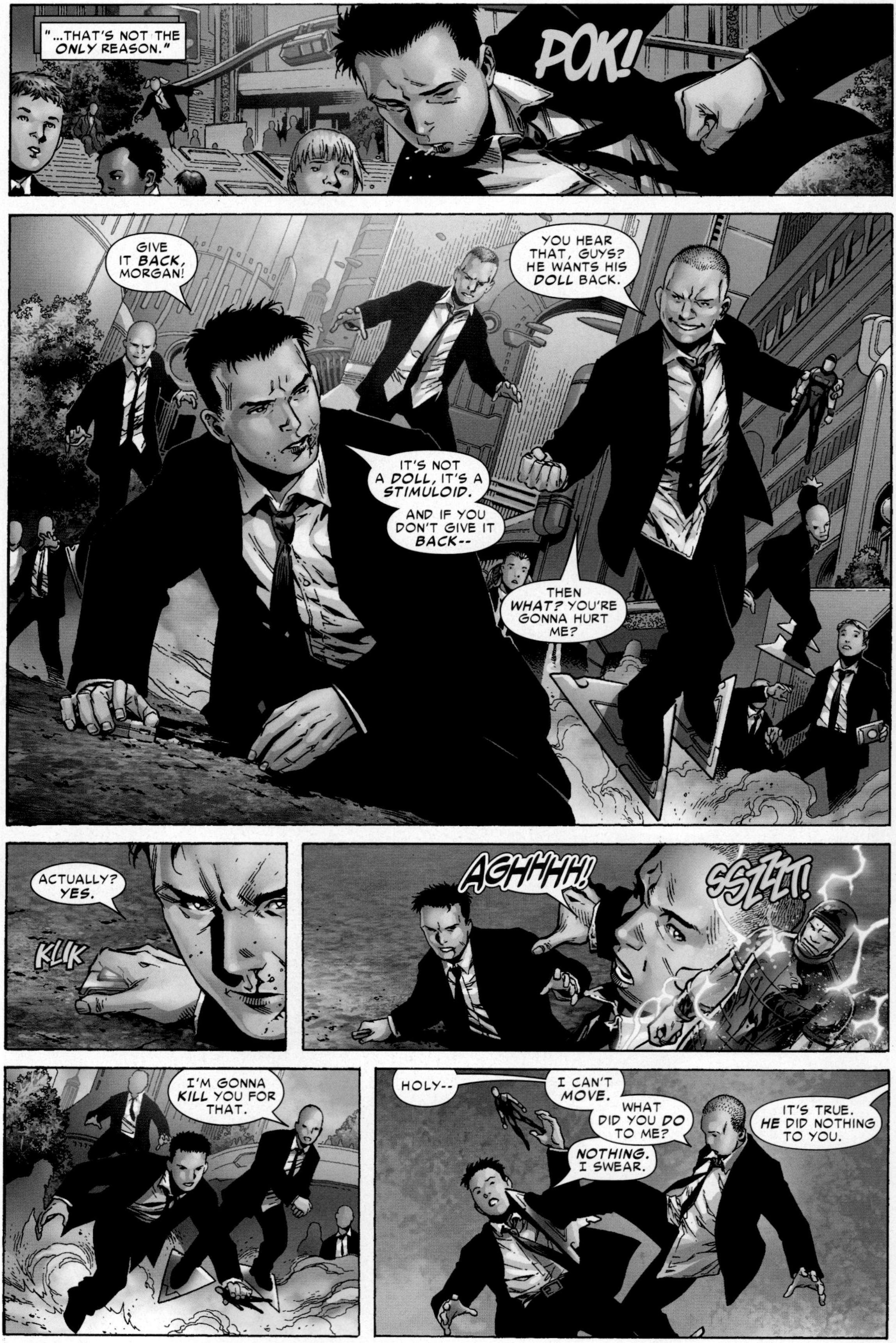
"...THAT'S NOT THE ONLY REASON."
POK!
GIVE IT BACK, MORGAN!
YOU HEAR THAT, GUYS? HE WANTS HIS DOLL BACK.
IT'S NOT A DOLL, IT'S A STIMULOID.
AND IF YOU DON'T GIVE IT BACK--
THEN WHAT? YOU'RE GONNA HURT ME?
ACTUALLY? YES.
KLIK
AGHHHH!
SSZZZT!
I'M GONNA KILL YOU FOR THAT.
HOLY--
I CAN'T MOVE.
WHAT DID YOU DO TO ME?
NOTHING. I SWEAR.
IT'S TRUE. HE DID NOTHING TO YOU.

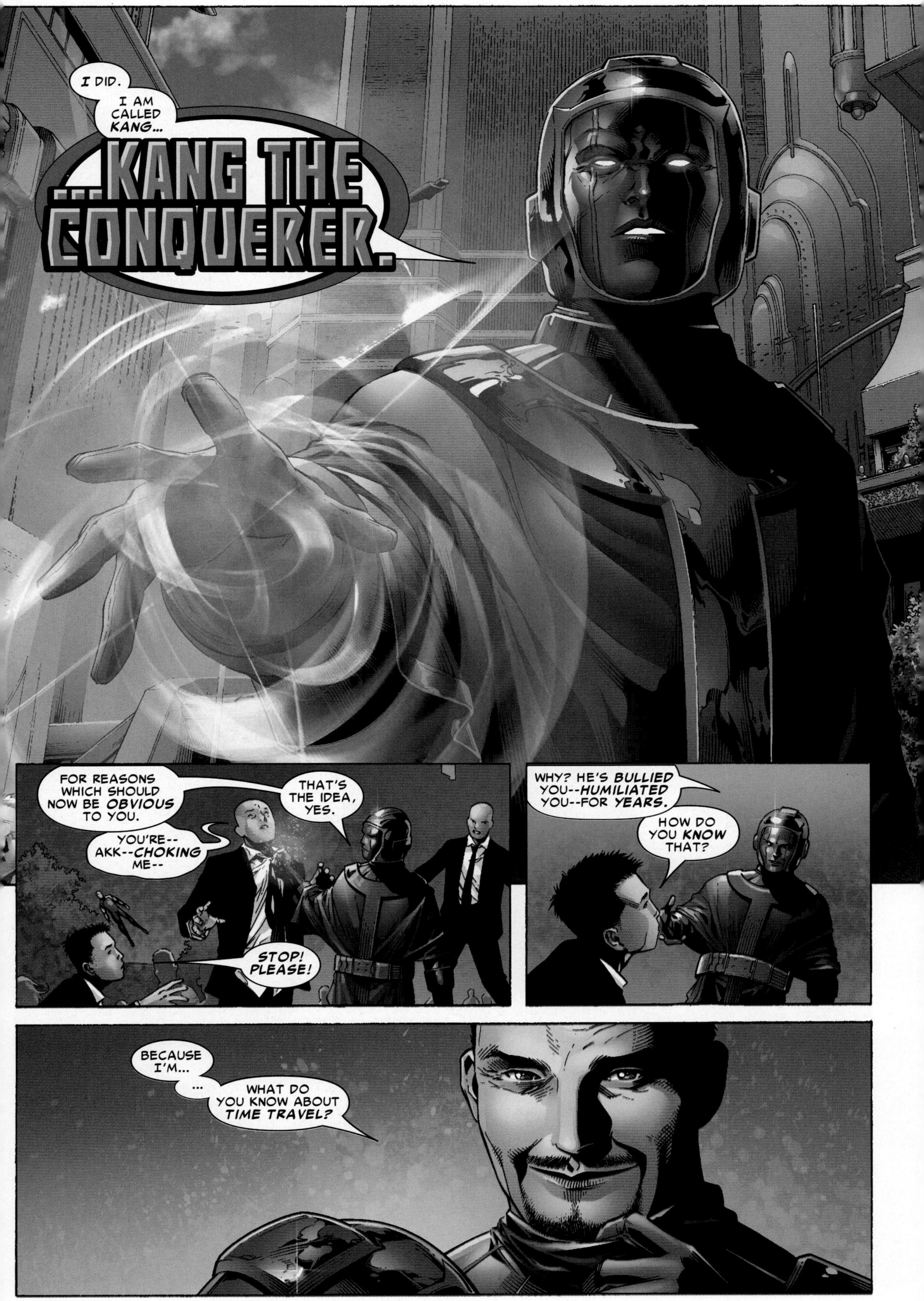
I DID.
I AM CALLED KANG...
...KANG THE CONQUERER.
FOR REASONS WHICH SHOULD NOW BE OBVIOUS TO YOU.
THAT'S THE IDEA, YES.
YOU'RE-- AKK--CHOKING ME--
STOP! PLEASE!
WHY? HE'S BULLIED YOU--HUMILIATED YOU--FOR YEARS.
HOW DO YOU KNOW THAT?
BECAUSE I'M...
... WHAT DO YOU KNOW ABOUT TIME TRAVEL?

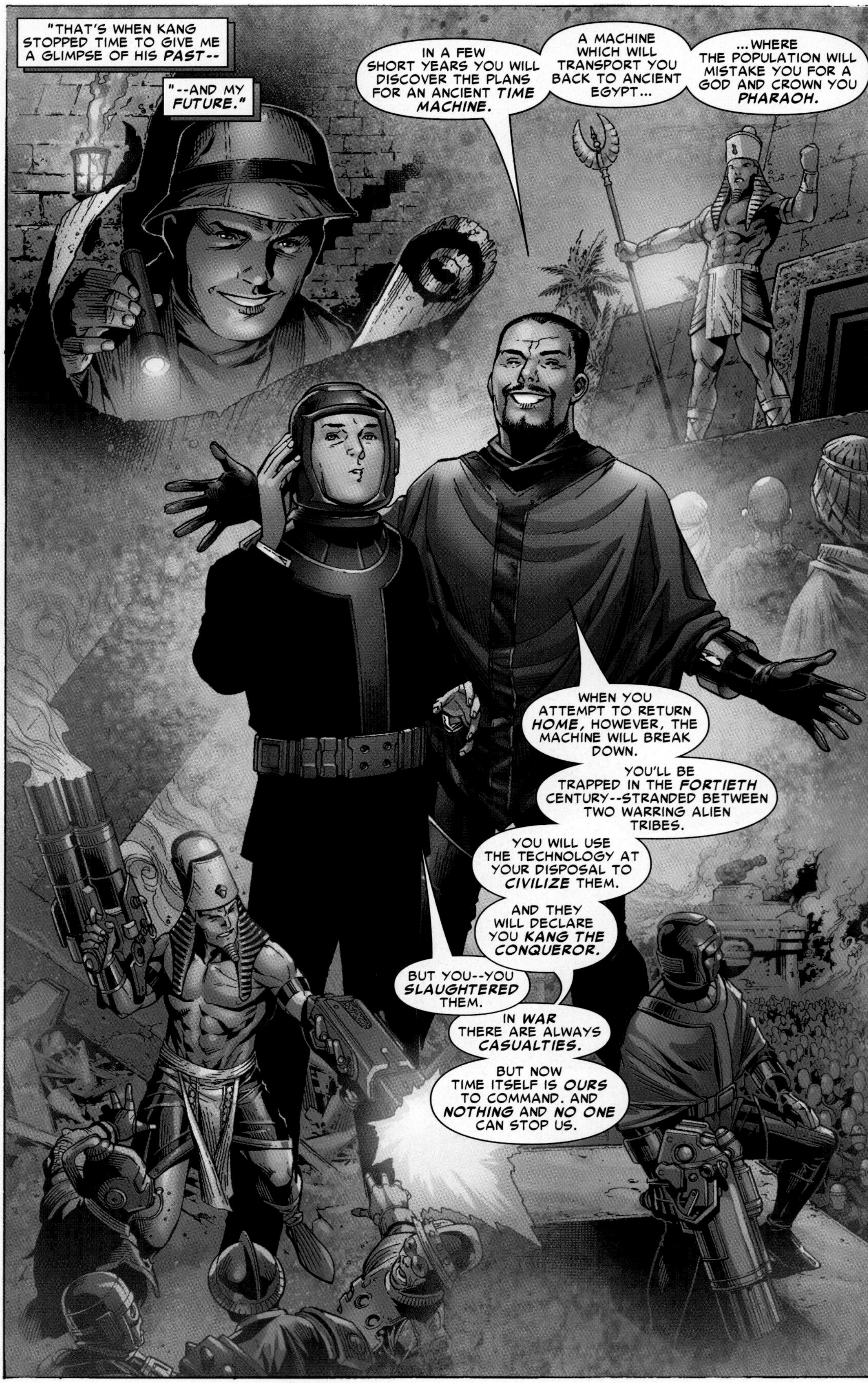
"THAT'S WHEN KANG STOPPED TIME TO GIVE ME A GLIMPSE OF HIS PAST--
"--AND MY FUTURE."
IN A FEW SHORT YEARS YOU WILL DISCOVER THE PLANS FOR AN ANCIENT TIME MACHINE.
A MACHINE WHICH WILL TRANSPORT YOU BACK TO ANCIENT EGYPT...
...WHERE THE POPULATION WILL MISTAKE YOU FOR A GOD AND CROWN YOU PHARAOH.
WHEN YOU ATTEMPT TO RETURN HOME, HOWEVER, THE MACHINE WILL BREAK DOWN.
YOU'LL BE TRAPPED IN THE FORTIETH CENTURY--STRANDED BETWEEN TWO WARRING ALIEN TRIBES.
YOU WILL USE THE TECHNOLOGY AT YOUR DISPOSAL TO CIVILIZE THEM.
AND THEY WILL DECLARE YOU KANG THE CONQUEROR.
BUT YOU--YOU SLAUGHTERED THEM.
IN WAR THERE ARE ALWAYS CASUALTIES.
BUT NOW TIME ITSELF IS OURS TO COMMAND. AND NOTHING AND NO ONE CAN STOP US.

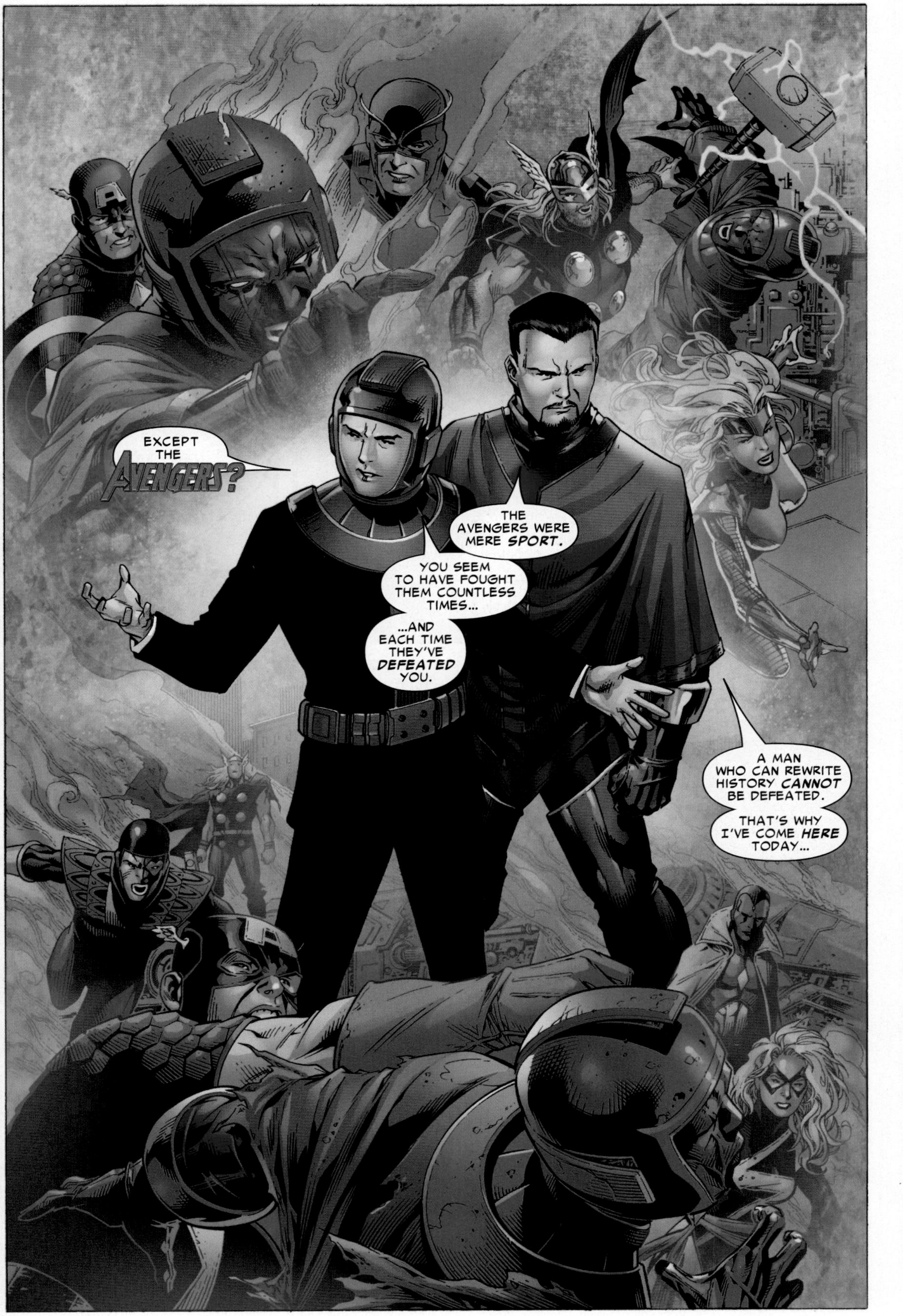
EXCEPT THE AVENGERS?
THE AVENGERS WERE MERE SPORT.
YOU SEEM TO HAVE FOUGHT THEM COUNTLESS TIMES...
...AND EACH TIME THEY'VE DEFEATED YOU.
A MAN WHO CAN REWRITE HISTORY CANNOT BE DEFEATED.
THAT'S WHY I'VE COME HERE TODAY...

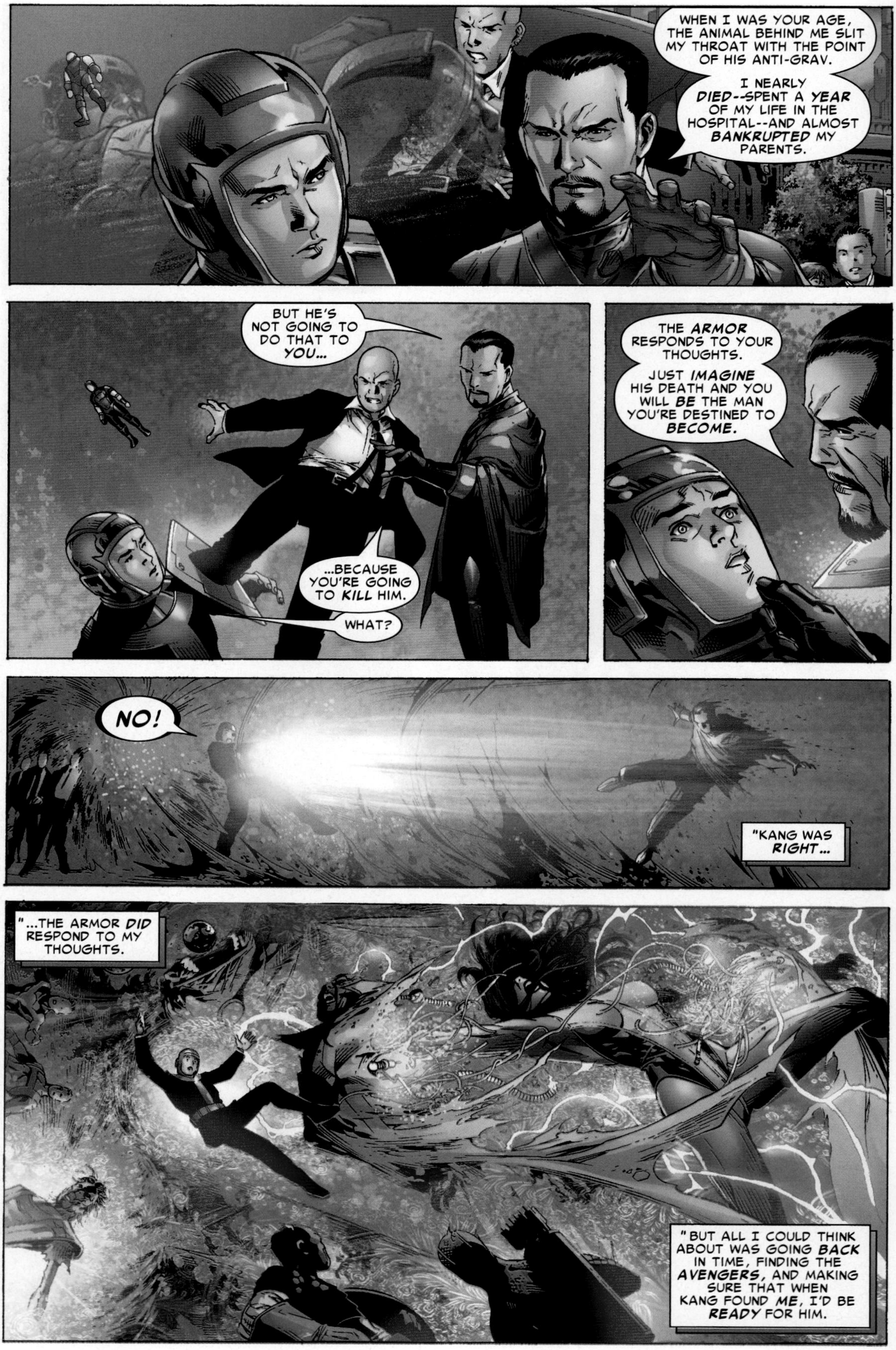
WHEN I WAS YOUR AGE, THE ANIMAL BEHIND ME SLIT MY THROAT WITH THE POINT OF HIS ANTI-GRAV.
I NEARLY DIED--SPENT A YEAR OF MY LIFE IN THE HOSPITAL--AND ALMOST BANKRUPTED MY PARENTS.
BUT HE'S NOT GOING TO DO THAT TO YOU...
...BECAUSE YOU'RE GOING TO KILL HIM.
WHAT?
THE ARMOR RESPONDS TO YOUR THOUGHTS.
JUST IMAGINE HIS DEATH AND YOU WILL BE THE MAN YOU'RE DESTINED TO BECOME.
NO!
"KANG WAS RIGHT...
"...THE ARMOR DID RESPOND TO MY THOUGHTS.
"BUT ALL I COULD THINK ABOUT WAS GOING BACK IN TIME, FINDING THE AVENGERS, AND MAKING SURE THAT WHEN KANG FOUND ME, I'D BE READY FOR HIM.

"HOWEVER, WHEN I ARRIVED, I DISCOVERED THE AVENGERS HAD *DISBANDED.*

"I TRIED TO CONTACT AS MANY *FORMER* AVENGERS AS I COULD...

MR. STARK! ONE SECOND! *PLEASE--!*

MR. STARK DOESN'T HAVE TIME FOR AUTOGRAPHS, KID.

"AND WHEN *THAT* FAILED, I USED KANG'S ARMOR TO GAIN ACCESS TO STARK INDUSTRIES...

"...WHERE I *FINALLY DID* FIND SOMEONE WHO COULD HELP ME."

VISION PROJECT
RETURN TO STARK INDUSTRIES PENDING CLEARANCE AND AUTHORIZATION

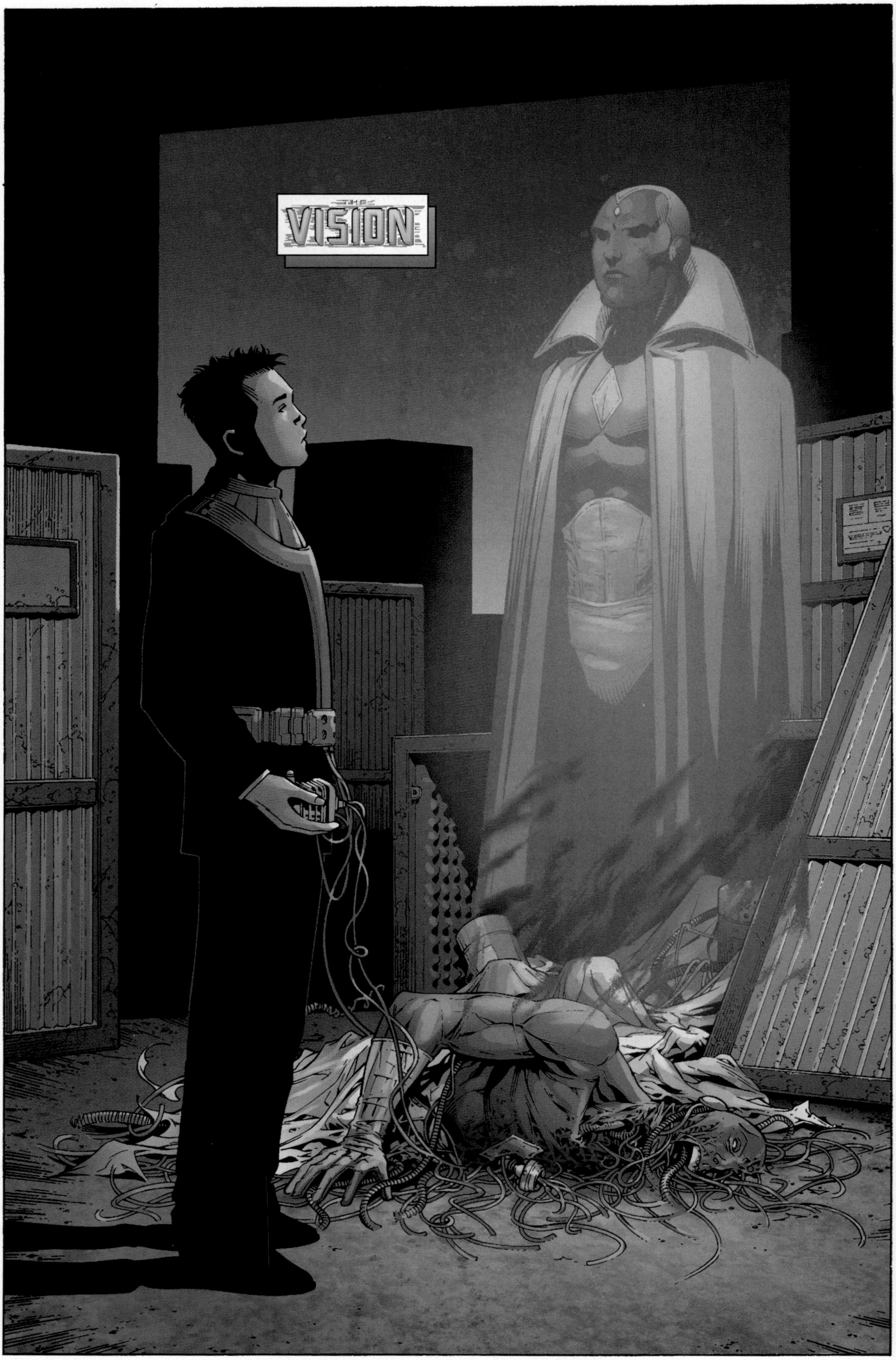
THE
VISION

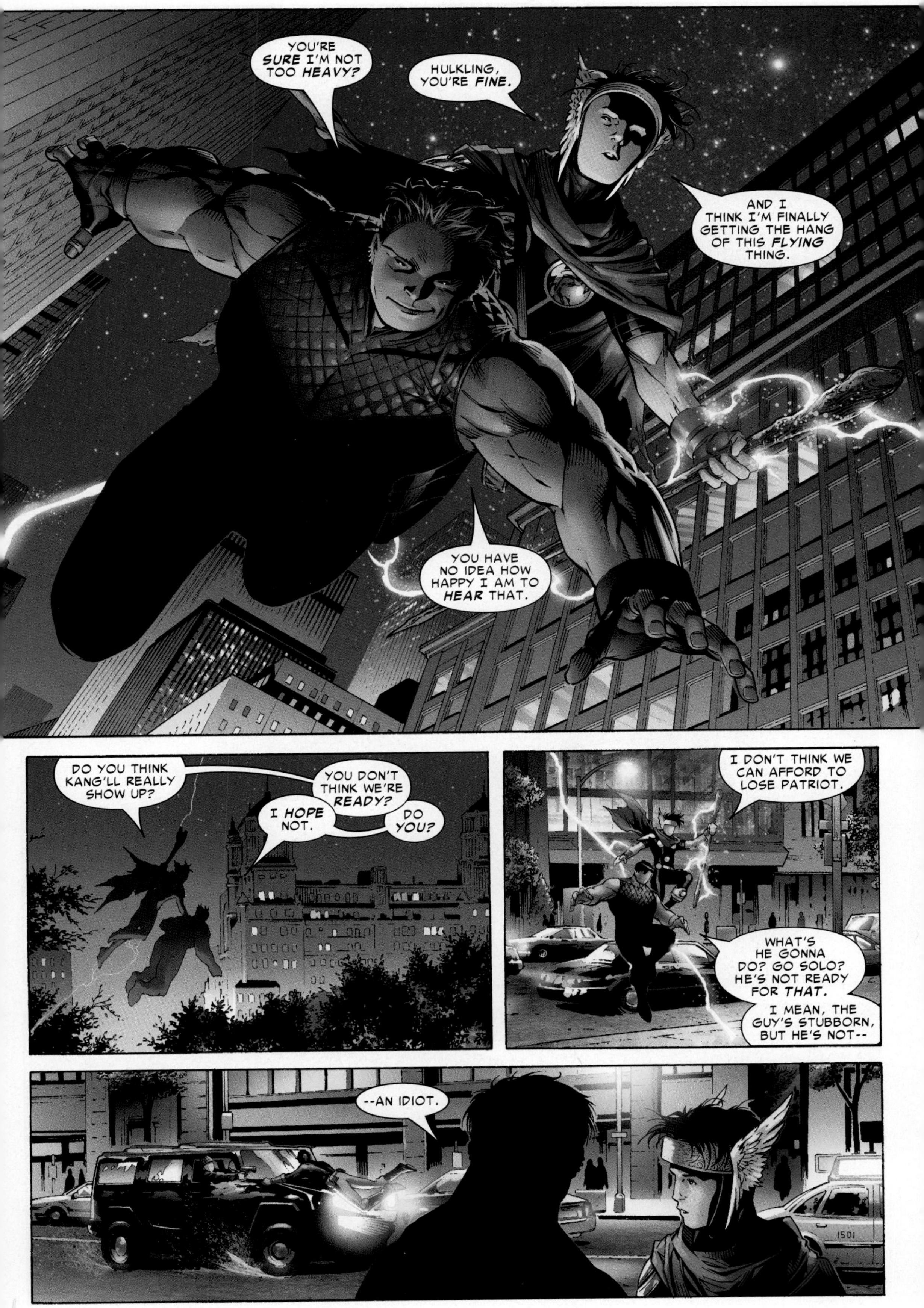

YOU'RE SURE I'M NOT TOO HEAVY?
HULKLING, YOU'RE FINE.
AND I THINK I'M FINALLY GETTING THE HANG OF THIS FLYING THING.
YOU HAVE NO IDEA HOW HAPPY I AM TO HEAR THAT.
DO YOU THINK KANG'LL REALLY SHOW UP?
YOU DON'T THINK WE'RE READY?
I HOPE NOT.
DO YOU?
I DON'T THINK WE CAN AFFORD TO LOSE PATRIOT.
WHAT'S HE GONNA DO? GO SOLO? HE'S NOT READY FOR THAT.
I MEAN, THE GUY'S STUBBORN, BUT HE'S NOT--
--AN IDIOT.

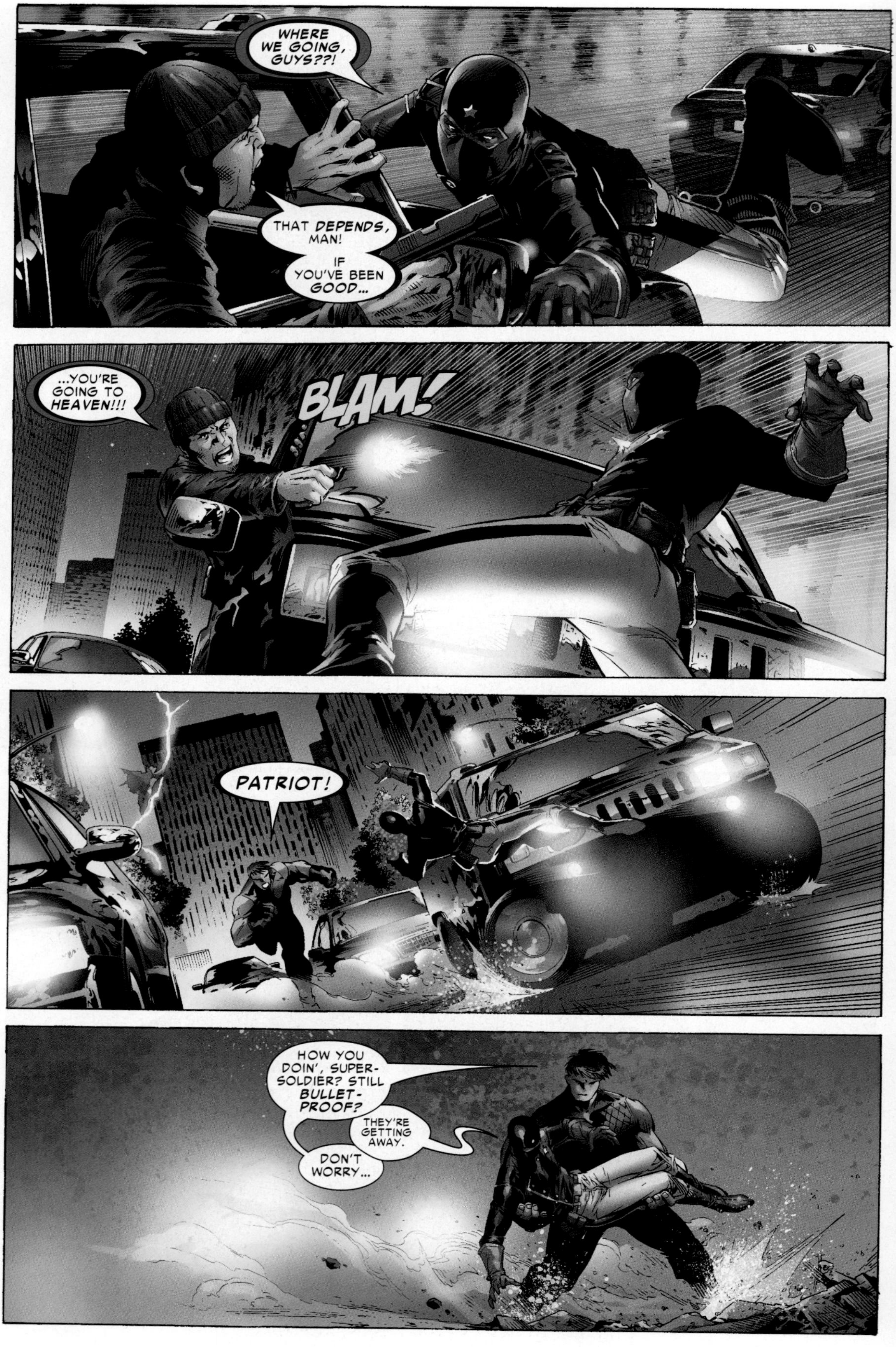
WHERE WE GOING, GUYS??!
THAT DEPENDS, MAN!
IF YOU'VE BEEN GOOD...
...YOU'RE GOING TO HEAVEN!!!
BLAM!
PATRIOT!
HOW YOU DOIN', SUPER-SOLDIER? STILL BULLET-PROOF?
THEY'RE GETTING AWAY.
DON'T WORRY...

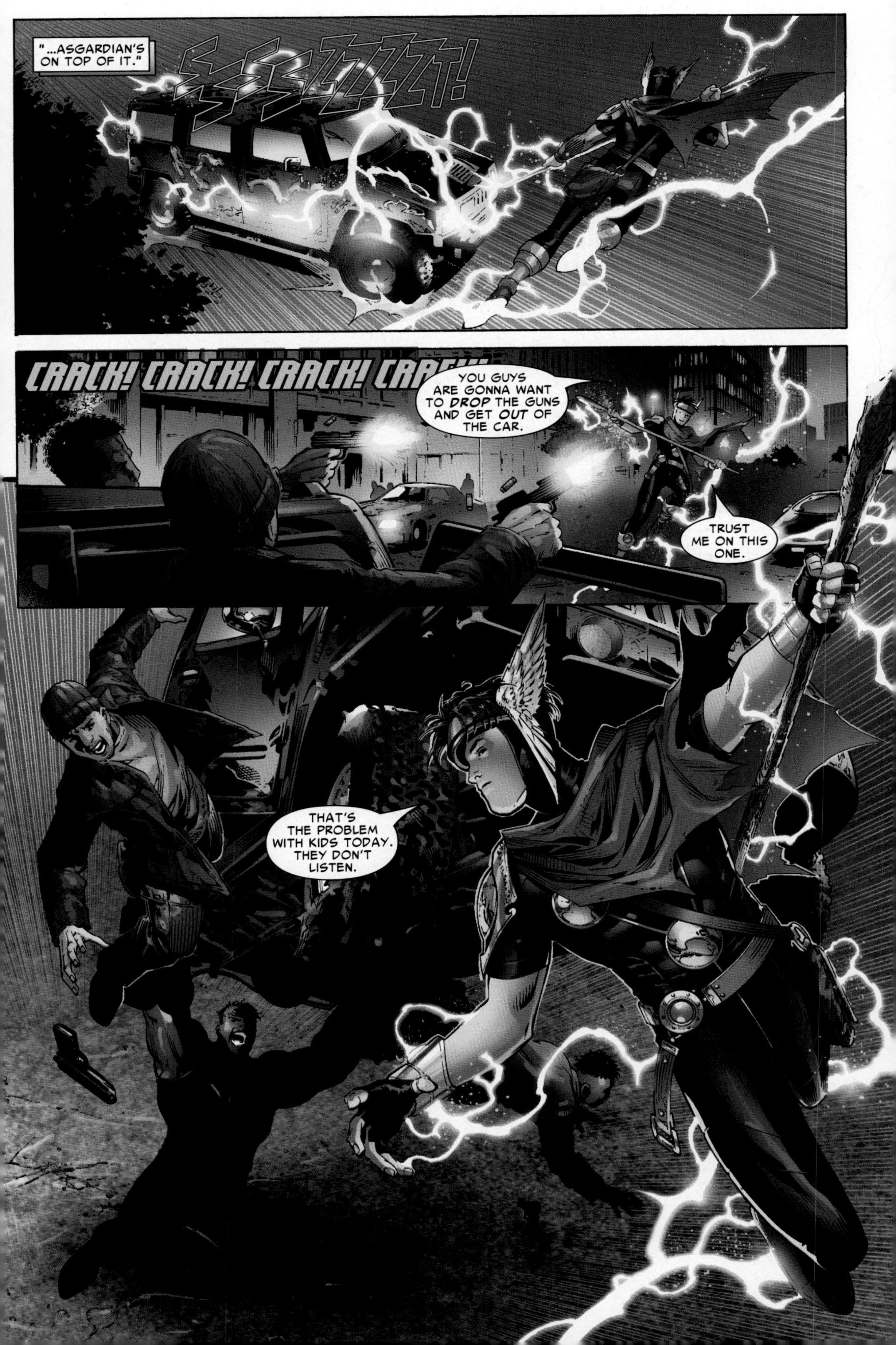
"...ASGARDIAN'S ON TOP OF IT."
CRACK! CRACK! CRACK! CRA
YOU GUYS ARE GONNA WANT TO DROP THE GUNS AND GET OUT OF THE CAR.
TRUST ME ON THIS ONE.
THAT'S THE PROBLEM WITH KIDS TODAY. THEY DON'T LISTEN.

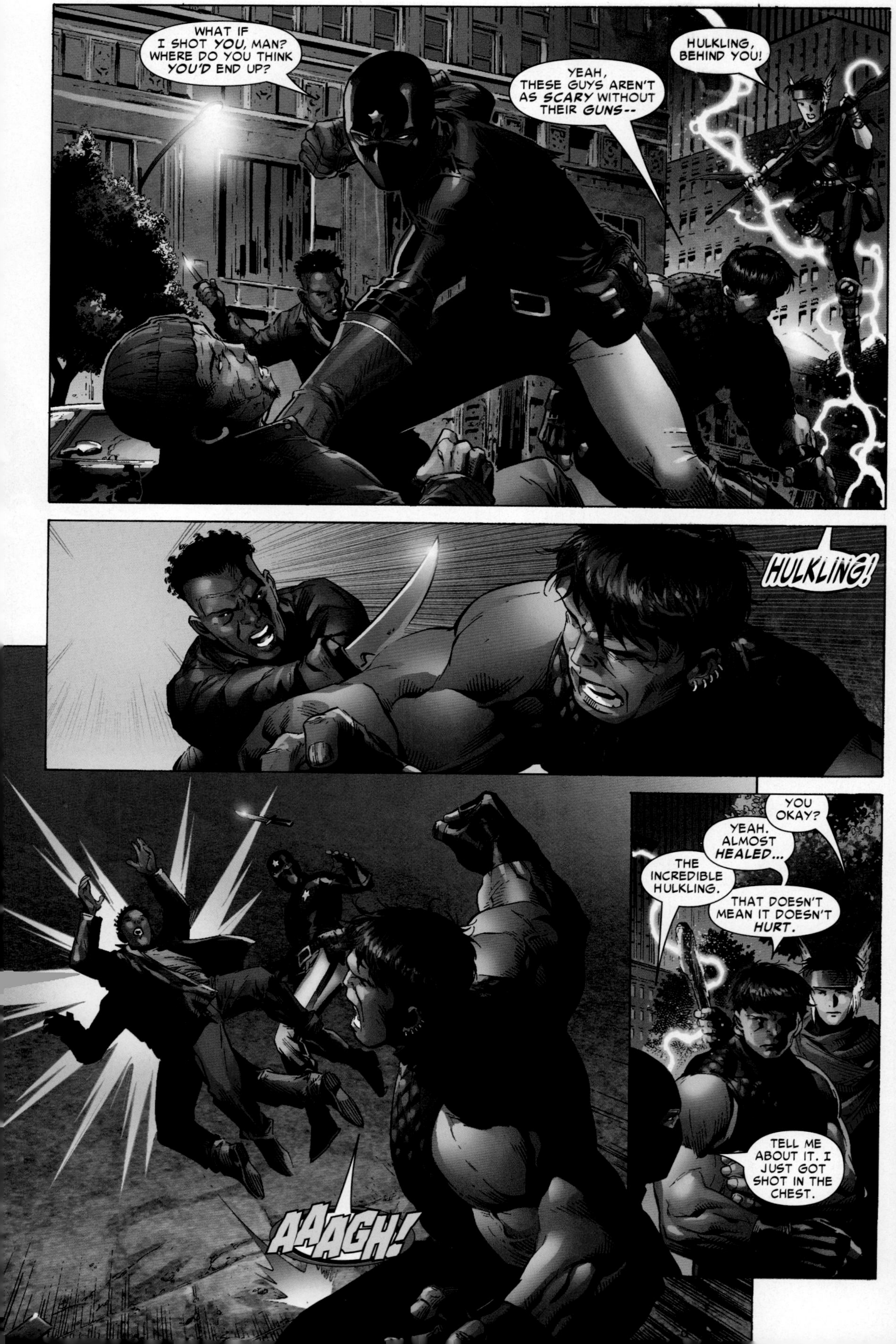
WHAT IF I SHOT YOU, MAN? WHERE DO YOU THINK YOU'D END UP?
YEAH, THESE GUYS AREN'T AS SCARY WITHOUT THEIR GUNS--
HULKLING, BEHIND YOU!
HULKLING!
AAAGH!
YOU OKAY?
YEAH. ALMOST HEALED...
THE INCREDIBLE HULKLING.
THAT DOESN'T MEAN IT DOESN'T HURT.
TELL ME ABOUT IT. I JUST GOT SHOT IN THE CHEST.

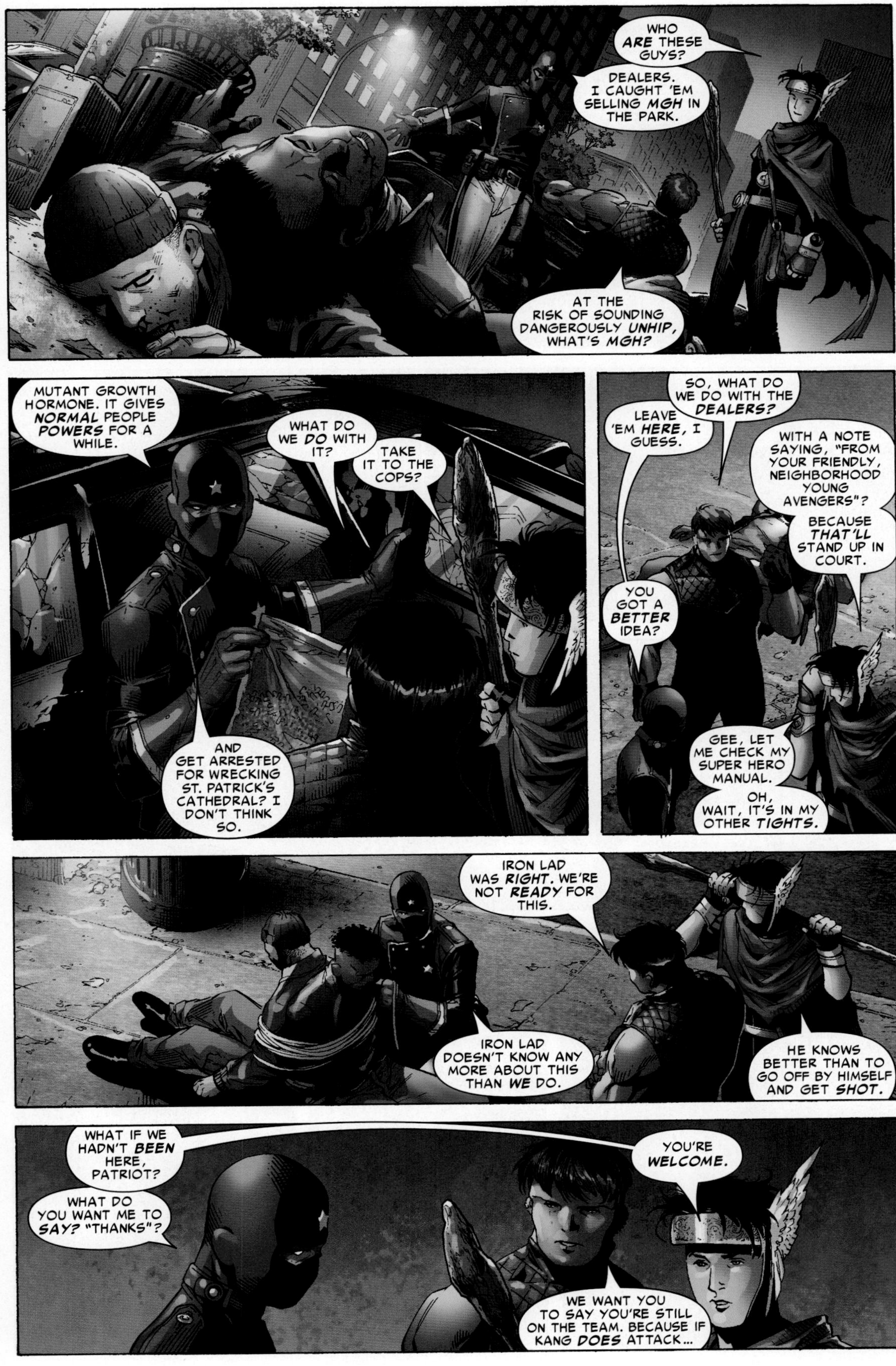
WHO ARE THESE GUYS?
DEALERS. I CAUGHT 'EM SELLING MGH IN THE PARK.
AT THE RISK OF SOUNDING DANGEROUSLY UNHIP, WHAT'S MGH?
MUTANT GROWTH HORMONE. IT GIVES NORMAL PEOPLE POWERS FOR A WHILE.
WHAT DO WE DO WITH IT?
TAKE IT TO THE COPS?
AND GET ARRESTED FOR WRECKING ST. PATRICK'S CATHEDRAL? I DON'T THINK SO.
SO, WHAT DO WE DO WITH THE DEALERS?
LEAVE 'EM HERE, I GUESS.
WITH A NOTE SAYING, "FROM YOUR FRIENDLY, NEIGHBORHOOD YOUNG AVENGERS"?
BECAUSE THAT'LL STAND UP IN COURT.
YOU GOT A BETTER IDEA?
GEE, LET ME CHECK MY SUPER HERO MANUAL.
OH, WAIT, IT'S IN MY OTHER TIGHTS.
IRON LAD WAS RIGHT. WE'RE NOT READY FOR THIS.
IRON LAD DOESN'T KNOW ANY MORE ABOUT THIS THAN WE DO.
HE KNOWS BETTER THAN TO GO OFF BY HIMSELF AND GET SHOT.
WHAT IF WE HADN'T BEEN HERE, PATRIOT?
WHAT DO YOU WANT ME TO SAY? "THANKS"?
YOU'RE WELCOME.
WE WANT YOU TO SAY YOU'RE STILL ON THE TEAM. BECAUSE IF KANG DOES ATTACK...

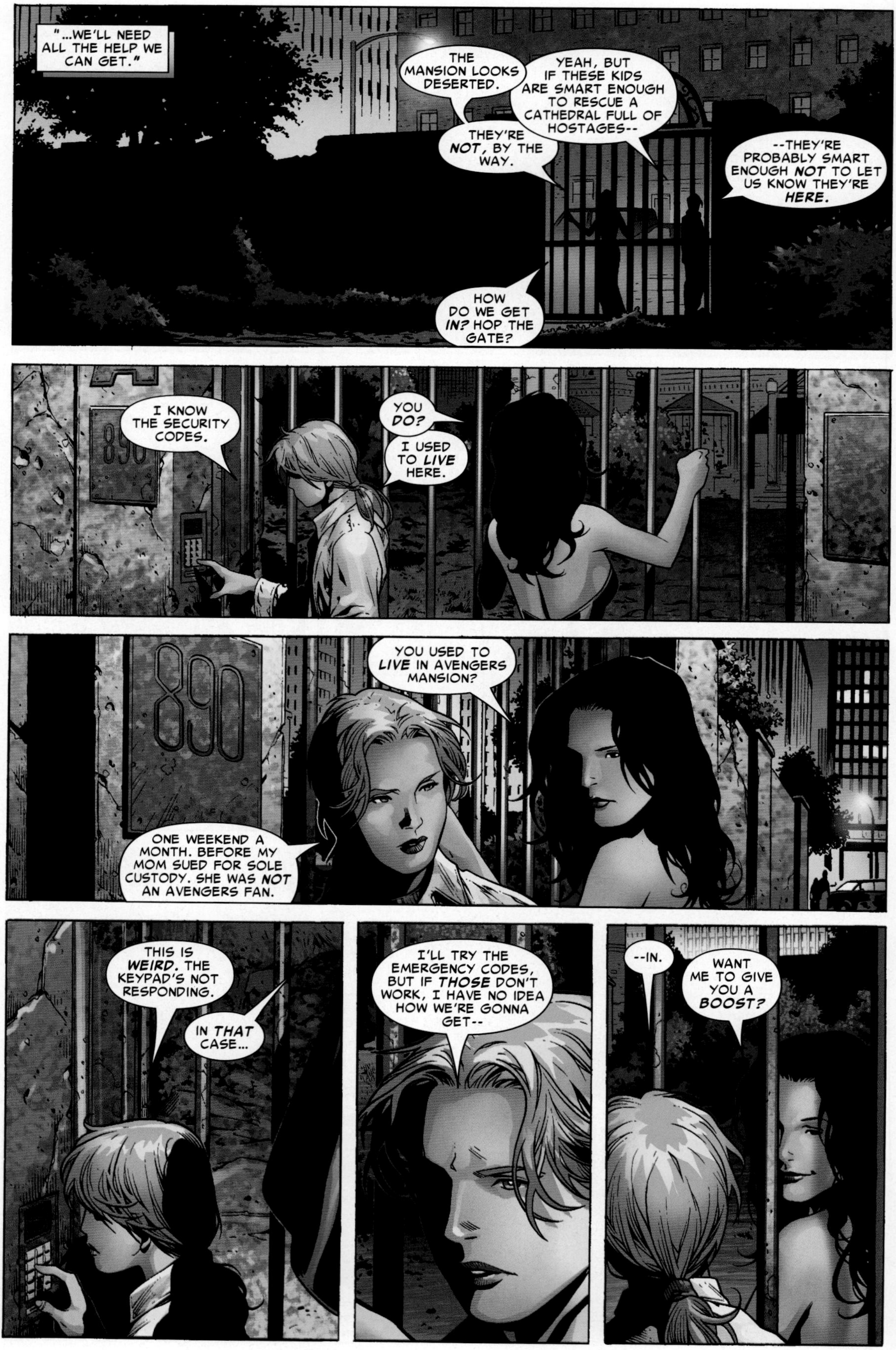
"...WE'LL NEED ALL THE HELP WE CAN GET."
THE MANSION LOOKS DESERTED.
YEAH, BUT IF THESE KIDS ARE SMART ENOUGH TO RESCUE A CATHEDRAL FULL OF HOSTAGES--
THEY'RE *NOT*, BY THE WAY.
--THEY'RE PROBABLY SMART ENOUGH *NOT* TO LET US KNOW THEY'RE *HERE*.
HOW DO WE GET *IN?* HOP THE GATE?
I KNOW THE SECURITY CODES.
YOU *DO?*
I USED TO *LIVE* HERE.
890
YOU USED TO *LIVE* IN AVENGERS MANSION?
ONE WEEKEND A MONTH. BEFORE MY MOM SUED FOR SOLE CUSTODY. SHE WAS *NOT* AN AVENGERS FAN.
THIS IS *WEIRD.* THE KEYPAD'S NOT RESPONDING.
IN *THAT* CASE...
I'LL TRY THE EMERGENCY CODES, BUT IF *THOSE* DON'T WORK, I HAVE NO IDEA HOW WE'RE GONNA GET--
--IN.
WANT ME TO GIVE YOU A *BOOST?*

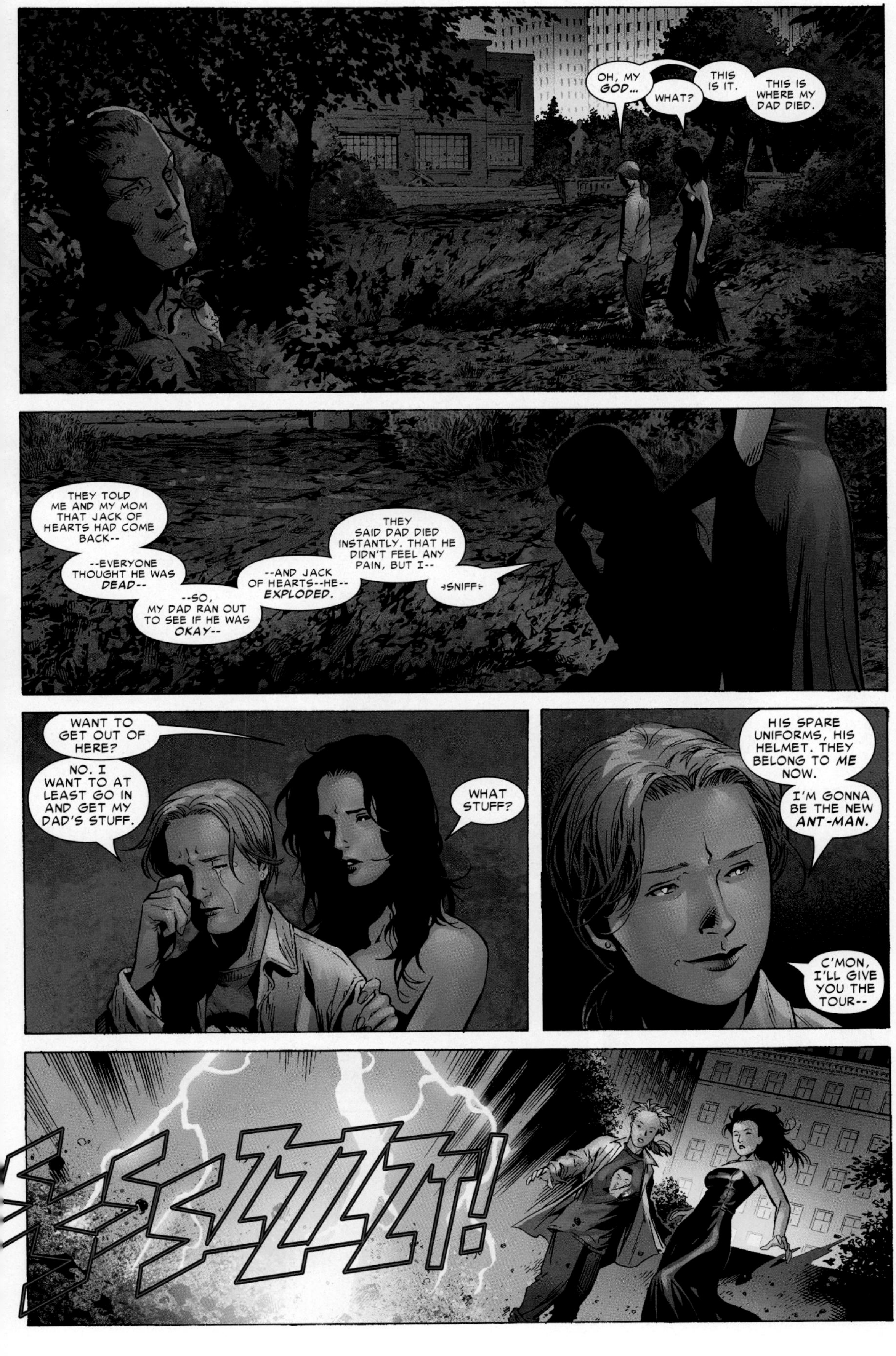
OH, MY GOD...
WHAT?
THIS IS IT.
THIS IS WHERE MY DAD DIED.
THEY TOLD ME AND MY MOM THAT JACK OF HEARTS HAD COME BACK--
--EVERYONE THOUGHT HE WAS DEAD--
--SO, MY DAD RAN OUT TO SEE IF HE WAS OKAY--
--AND JACK OF HEARTS--HE-- EXPLODED.
THEY SAID DAD DIED INSTANTLY. THAT HE DIDN'T FEEL ANY PAIN, BUT I--
SNIFF
WANT TO GET OUT OF HERE?
NO. I WANT TO AT LEAST GO IN AND GET MY DAD'S STUFF.
WHAT STUFF?
HIS SPARE UNIFORMS, HIS HELMET. THEY BELONG TO ME NOW.
I'M GONNA BE THE NEW ANT-MAN.
C'MON, I'LL GIVE YOU THE TOUR--
SSZZZT!

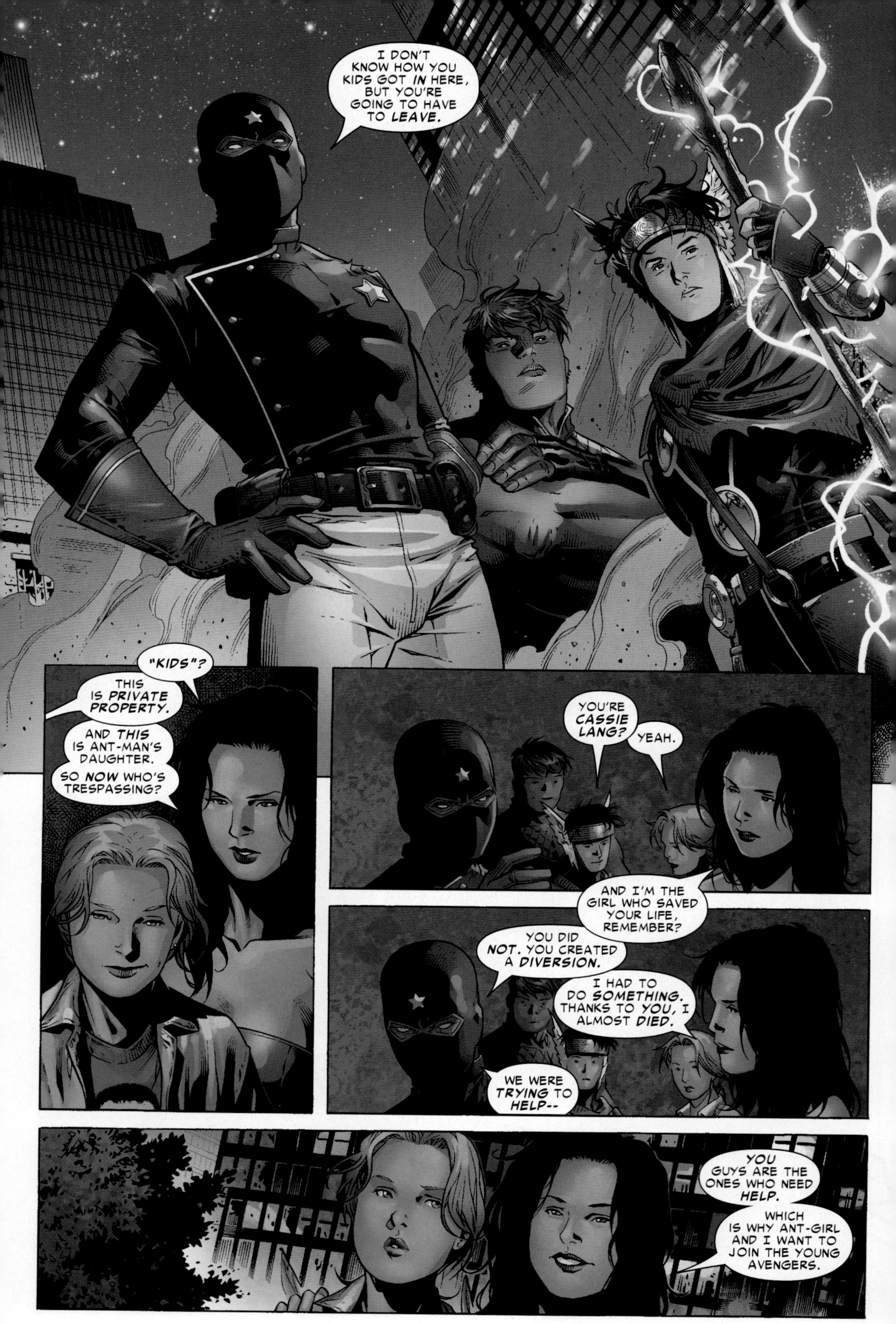
I DON'T KNOW HOW YOU KIDS GOT IN HERE, BUT YOU'RE GOING TO HAVE TO LEAVE.
"KIDS"?
THIS IS PRIVATE PROPERTY.
AND THIS IS ANT-MAN'S DAUGHTER.
SO NOW WHO'S TRESPASSING?
YOU'RE CASSIE LANG?
YEAH.
AND I'M THE GIRL WHO SAVED YOUR LIFE, REMEMBER?
YOU DID NOT. YOU CREATED A DIVERSION.
I HAD TO DO SOMETHING. THANKS TO YOU, I ALMOST DIED.
WE WERE TRYING TO HELP--
YOU GUYS ARE THE ONES WHO NEED HELP.
WHICH IS WHY ANT-GIRL AND I WANT TO JOIN THE YOUNG AVENGERS.

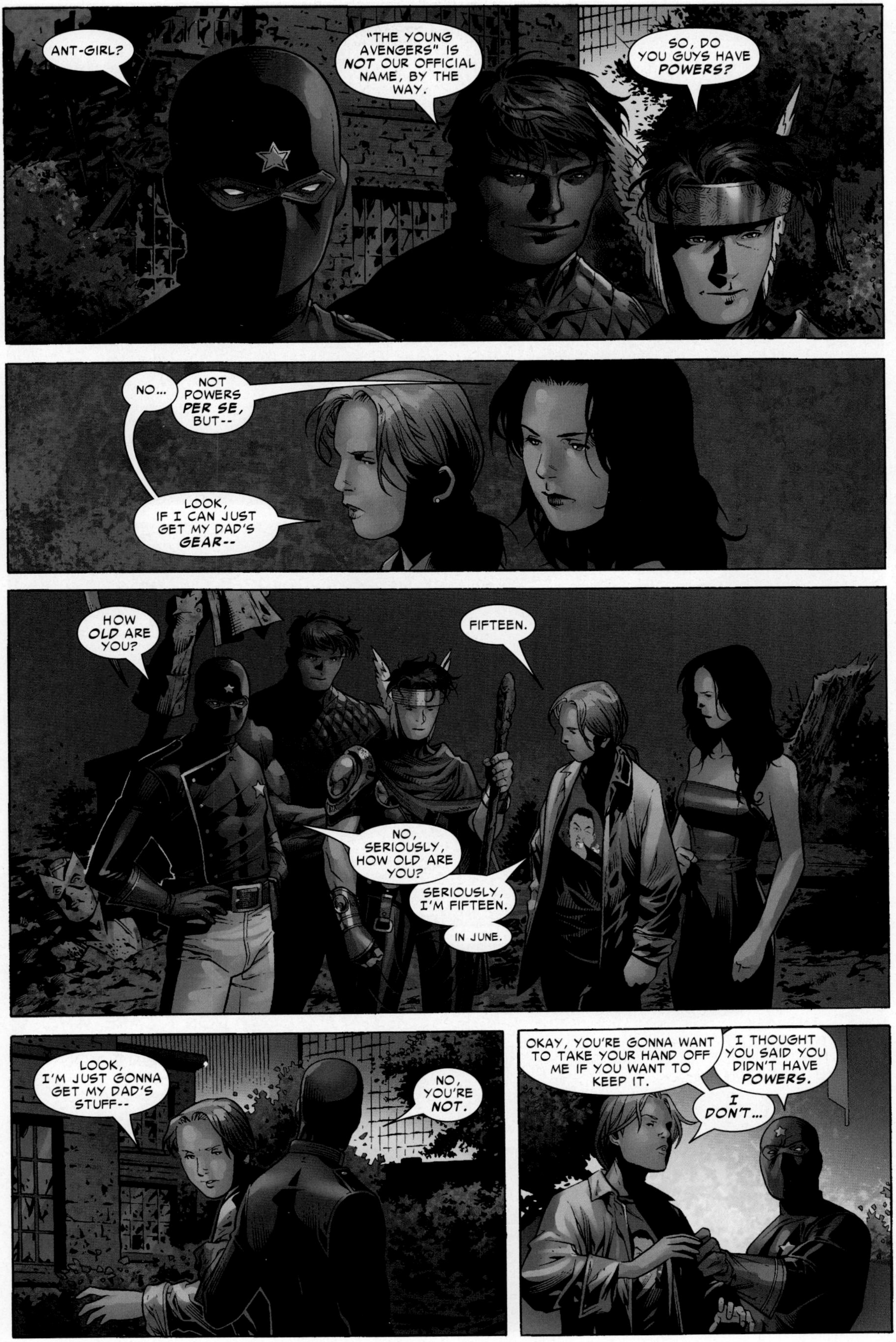
ANT-GIRL?
"THE YOUNG AVENGERS" IS NOT OUR OFFICIAL NAME, BY THE WAY.
SO, DO YOU GUYS HAVE POWERS?
NO...
NOT POWERS PER SE, BUT--
LOOK, IF I CAN JUST GET MY DAD'S GEAR--
HOW OLD ARE YOU?
FIFTEEN.
NO, SERIOUSLY, HOW OLD ARE YOU?
SERIOUSLY, I'M FIFTEEN.
IN JUNE.
LOOK, I'M JUST GONNA GET MY DAD'S STUFF--
NO, YOU'RE NOT.
OKAY, YOU'RE GONNA WANT TO TAKE YOUR HAND OFF ME IF YOU WANT TO KEEP IT.
I THOUGHT YOU SAID YOU DIDN'T HAVE POWERS.
I DON'T...

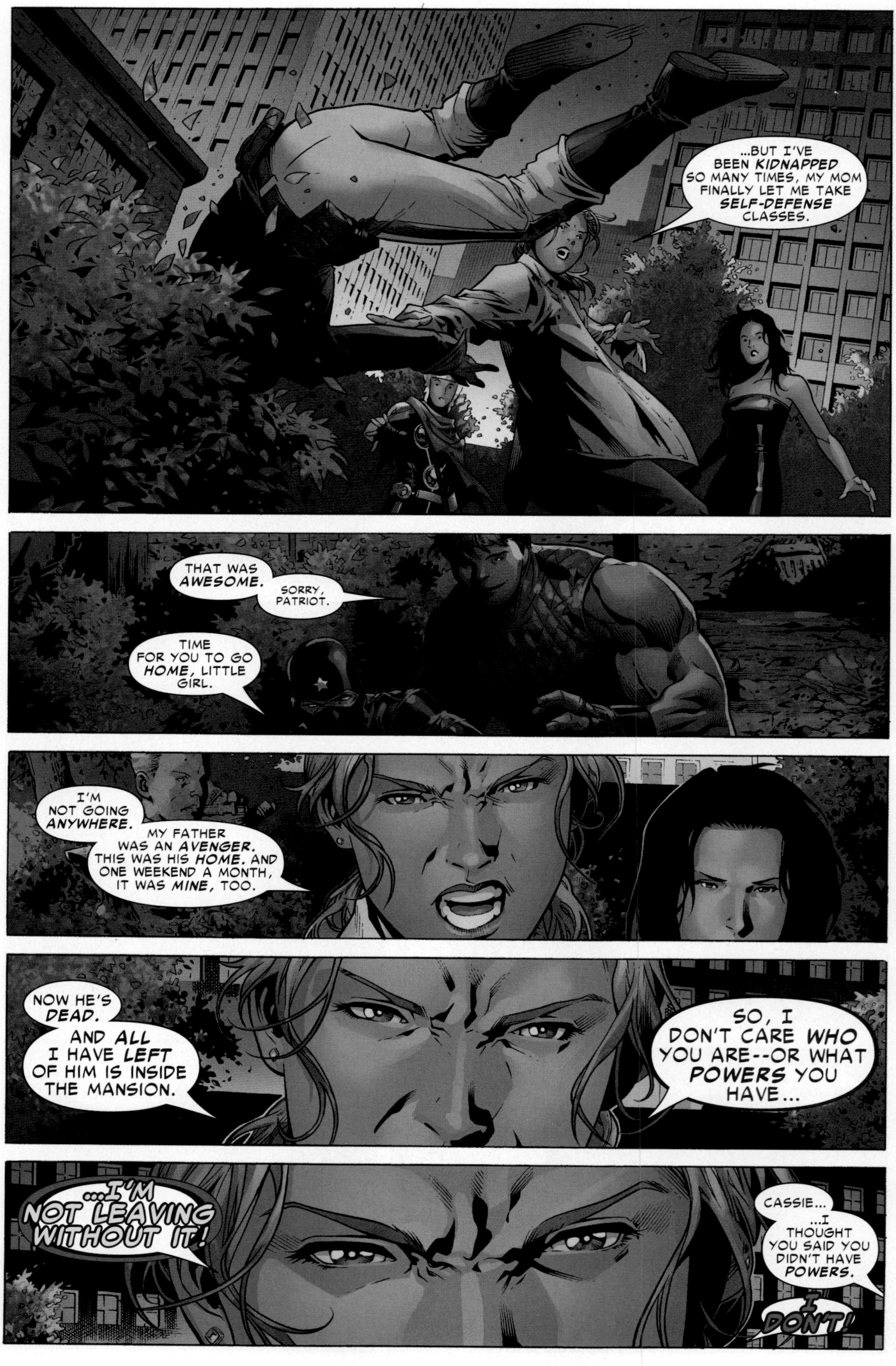
...BUT I'VE BEEN *KIDNAPPED* SO MANY TIMES, MY MOM FINALLY LET ME TAKE *SELF-DEFENSE* CLASSES.
THAT WAS *AWESOME.*
SORRY, PATRIOT.
TIME FOR YOU TO GO *HOME*, LITTLE GIRL.
I'M NOT GOING *ANYWHERE.*
MY FATHER WAS AN *AVENGER.* THIS WAS HIS *HOME.* AND ONE WEEKEND A MONTH, IT WAS *MINE*, TOO.
NOW HE'S *DEAD.*
AND *ALL* I HAVE *LEFT* OF HIM IS INSIDE THE MANSION.
SO, I DON'T CARE *WHO* YOU ARE--OR WHAT *POWERS* YOU HAVE...
...I'M NOT LEAVING WITHOUT IT!
CASSIE...
...I THOUGHT YOU SAID YOU DIDN'T HAVE *POWERS.*
I DON'T!

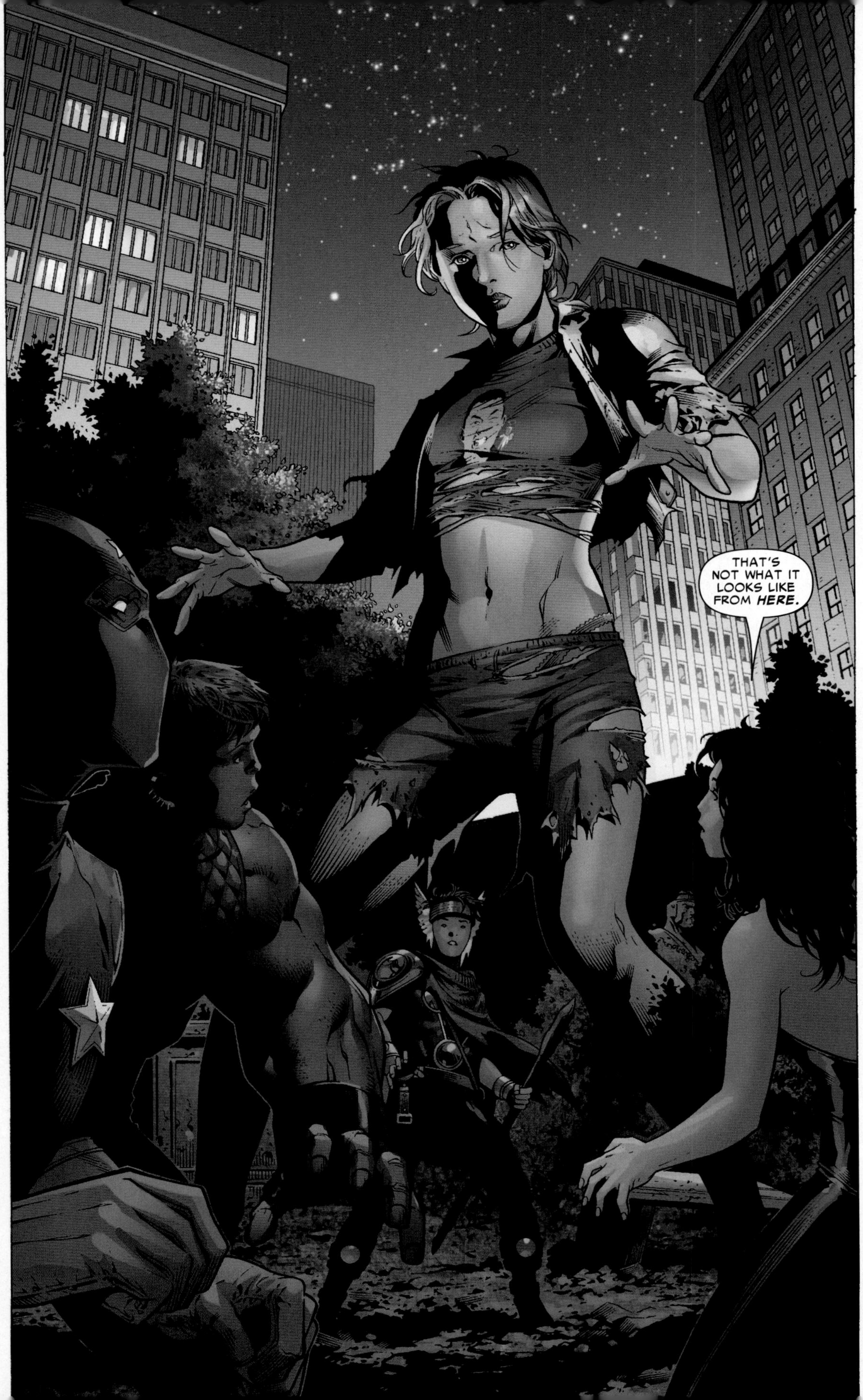
THAT'S NOT WHAT IT LOOKS LIKE FROM HERE.

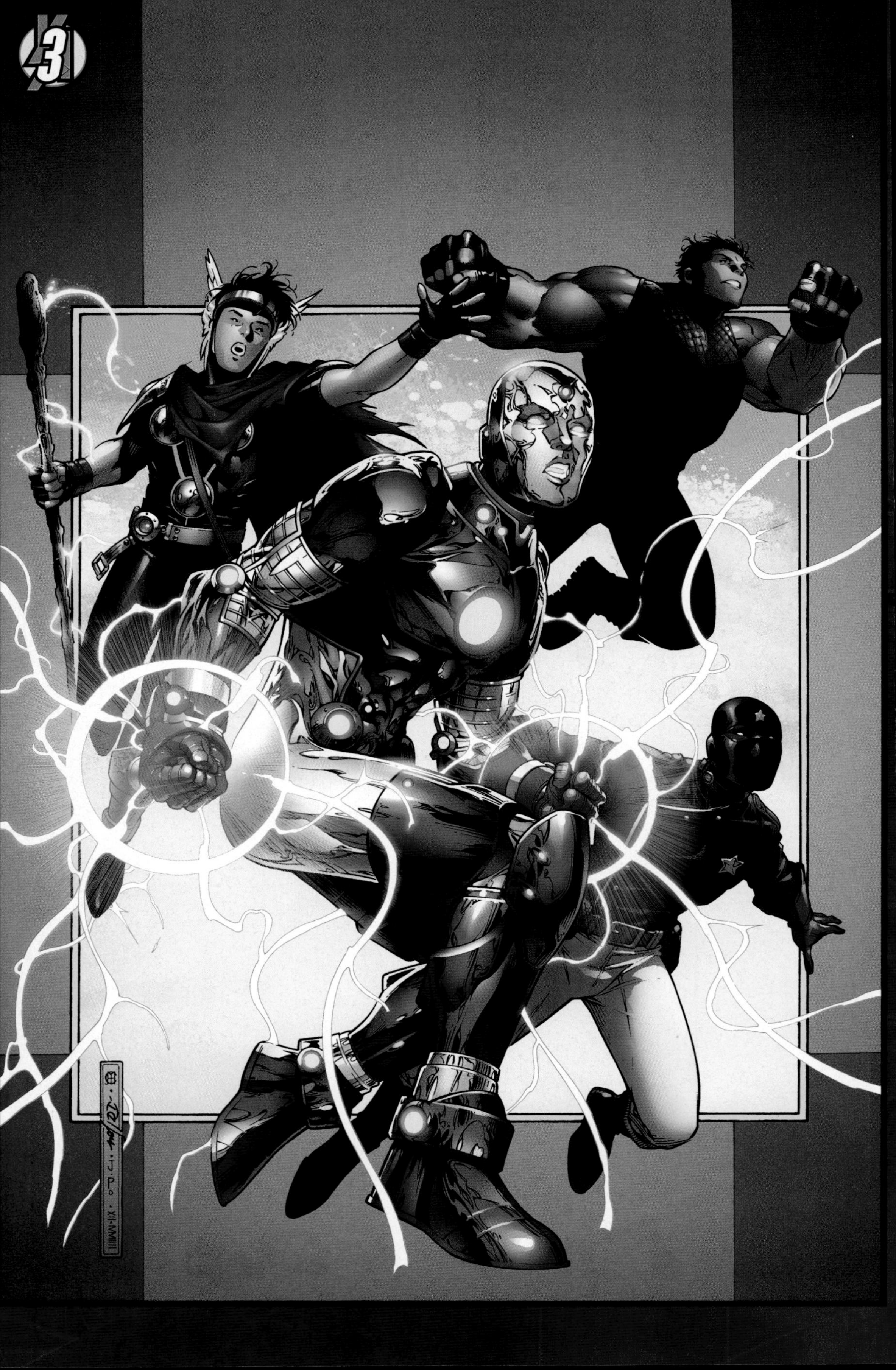

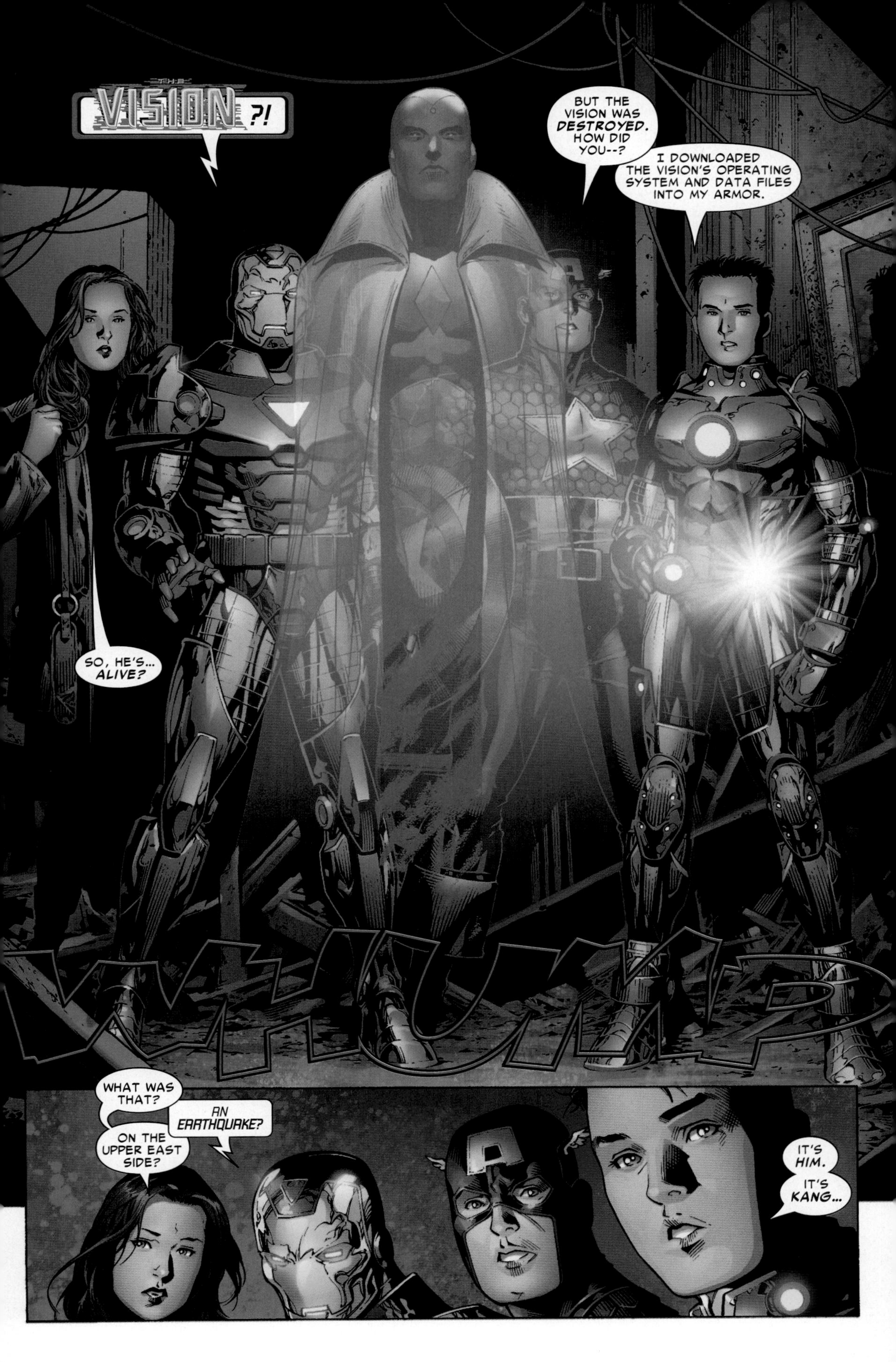
THE VISION ?!
BUT THE VISION WAS DESTROYED. HOW DID YOU--?
I DOWNLOADED THE VISION'S OPERATING SYSTEM AND DATA FILES INTO MY ARMOR.
SO, HE'S... ALIVE?
WHUMP
WHAT WAS THAT?
AN EARTHQUAKE?
ON THE UPPER EAST SIDE?
IT'S HIM.
IT'S KANG...

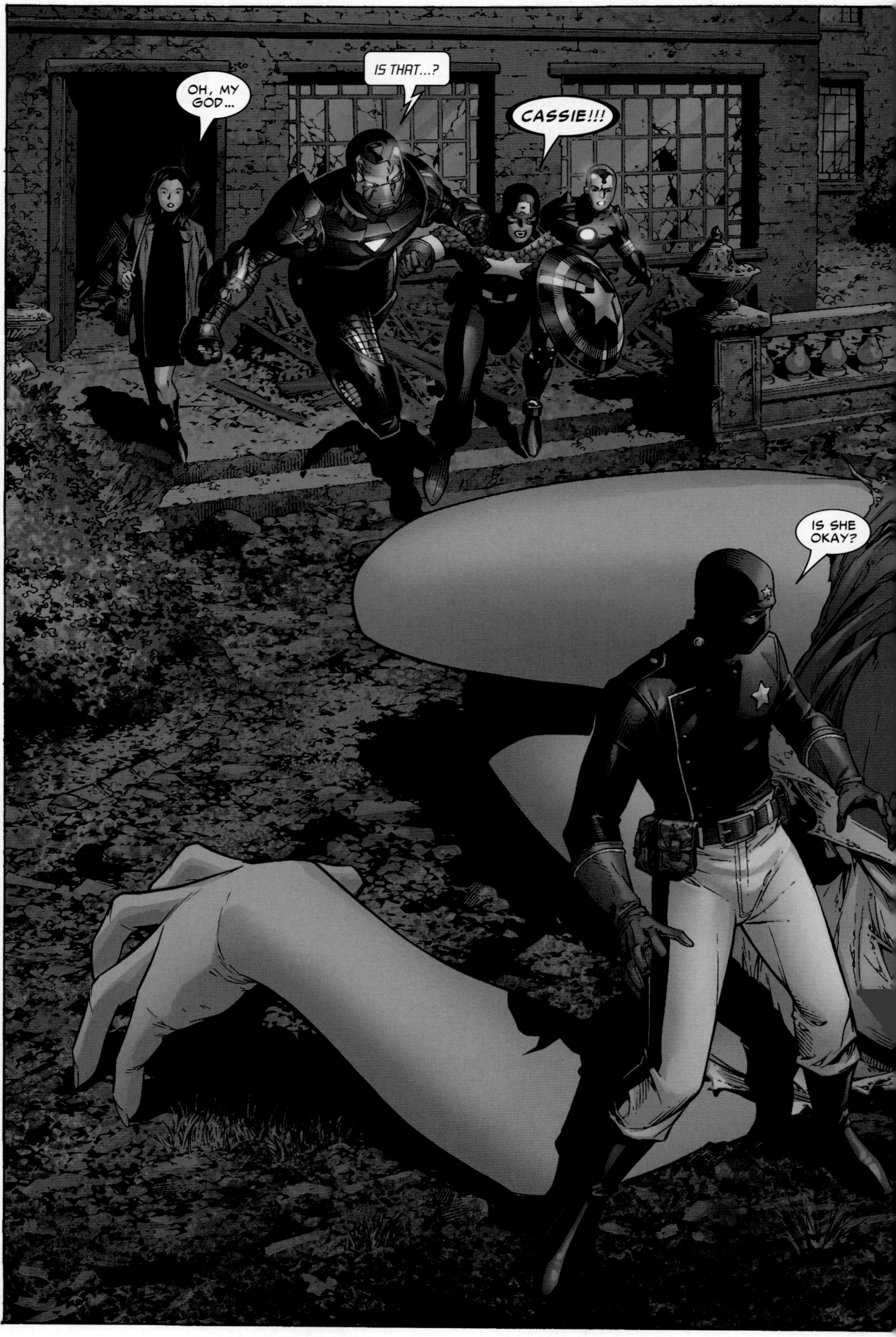
OH, MY GOD...
IS THAT...?
CASSIE!!!
IS SHE OKAY?

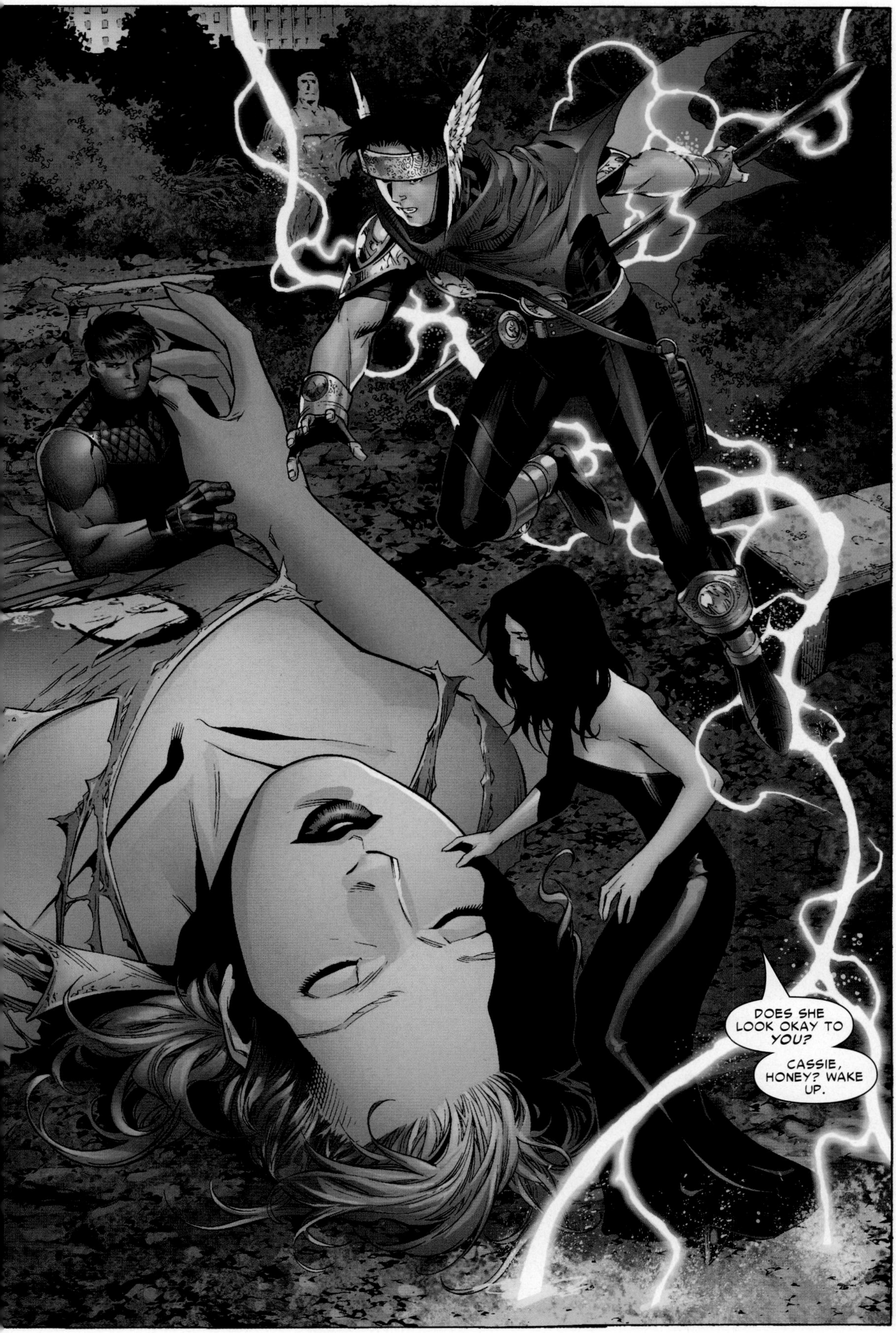
DOES SHE LOOK OKAY TO YOU?
CASSIE, HONEY? WAKE UP.

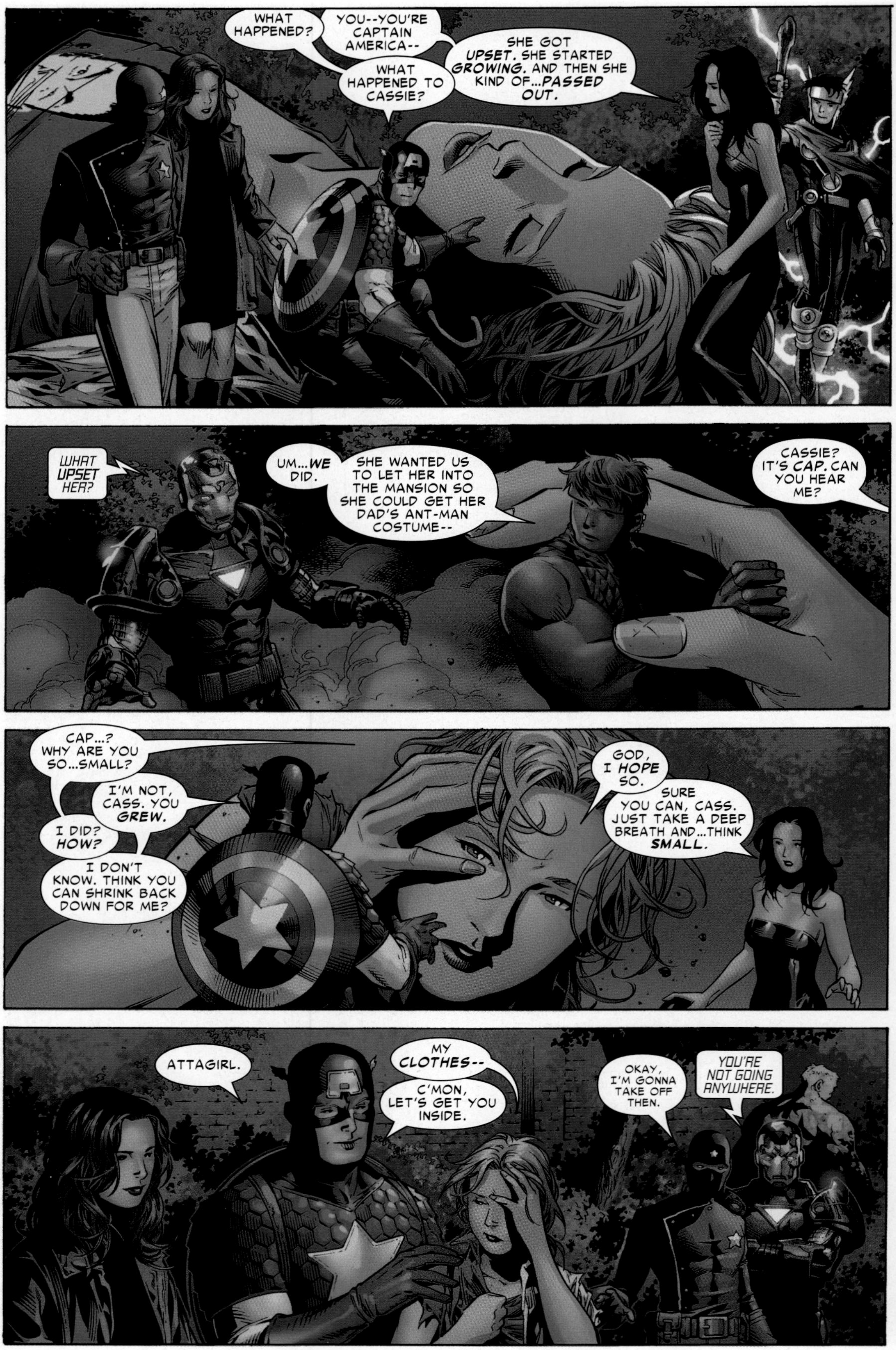
WHAT HAPPENED?
YOU--YOU'RE CAPTAIN AMERICA--
WHAT HAPPENED TO CASSIE?
SHE GOT UPSET. SHE STARTED GROWING. AND THEN SHE KIND OF...PASSED OUT.
WHAT UPSET HER?
UM...WE DID.
SHE WANTED US TO LET HER INTO THE MANSION SO SHE COULD GET HER DAD'S ANT-MAN COSTUME--
CASSIE? IT'S CAP. CAN YOU HEAR ME?
CAP...? WHY ARE YOU SO...SMALL?
I'M NOT, CASS. YOU GREW.
I DID? HOW?
I DON'T KNOW. THINK YOU CAN SHRINK BACK DOWN FOR ME?
GOD, I HOPE SO.
SURE YOU CAN, CASS. JUST TAKE A DEEP BREATH AND...THINK SMALL.
ATTAGIRL.
MY CLOTHES--
C'MON, LET'S GET YOU INSIDE.
OKAY, I'M GONNA TAKE OFF THEN.
YOU'RE NOT GOING ANYWHERE.

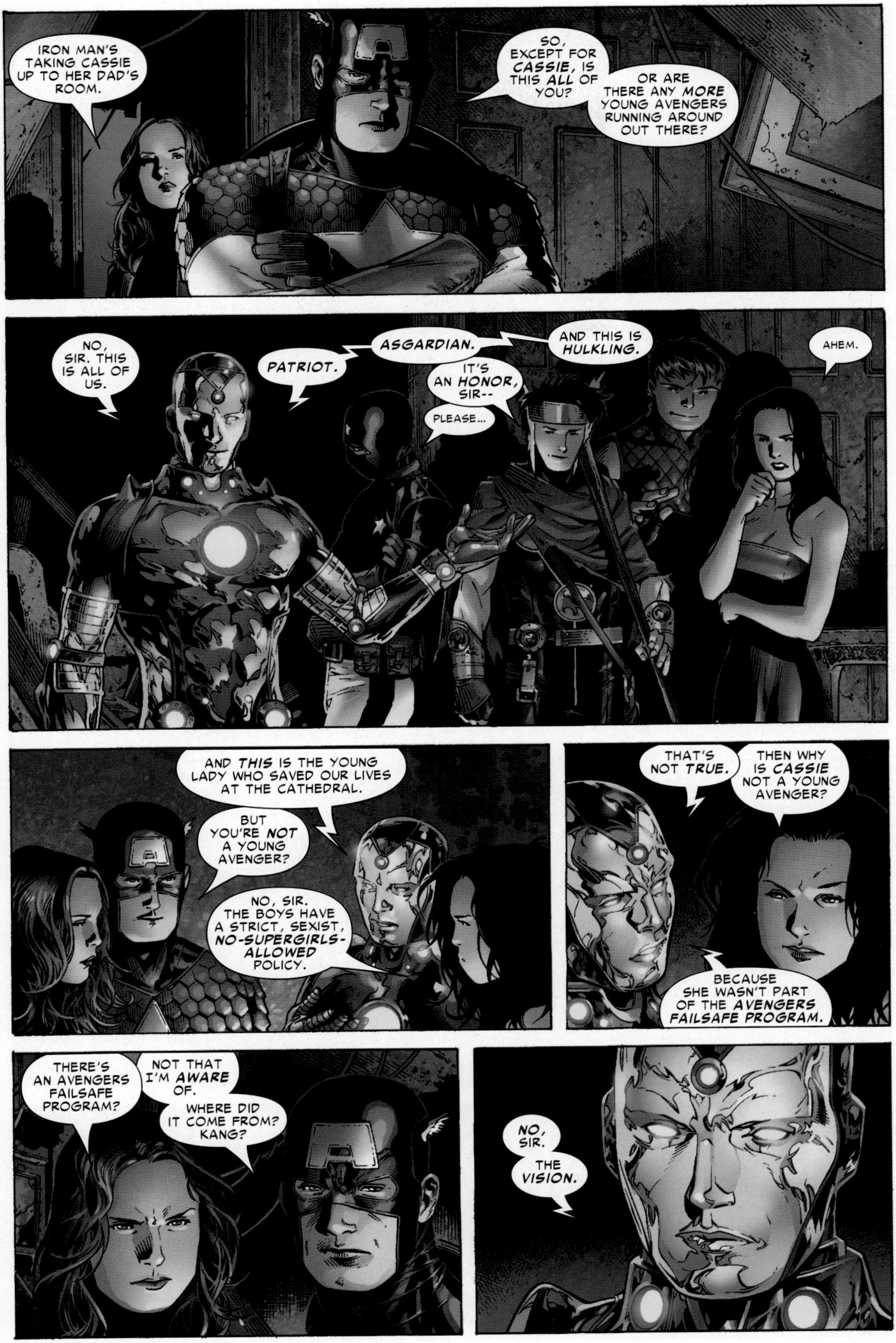
IRON MAN'S TAKING CASSIE UP TO HER DAD'S ROOM.
SO, EXCEPT FOR CASSIE, IS THIS ALL OF YOU?
OR ARE THERE ANY MORE YOUNG AVENGERS RUNNING AROUND OUT THERE?
NO, SIR. THIS IS ALL OF US.
PATRIOT.
ASGARDIAN.
AND THIS IS HULKLING.
IT'S AN HONOR, SIR--
PLEASE...
AHEM.
AND THIS IS THE YOUNG LADY WHO SAVED OUR LIVES AT THE CATHEDRAL.
BUT YOU'RE NOT A YOUNG AVENGER?
NO, SIR. THE BOYS HAVE A STRICT, SEXIST, NO-SUPERGIRLS-ALLOWED POLICY.
THAT'S NOT TRUE.
THEN WHY IS CASSIE NOT A YOUNG AVENGER?
BECAUSE SHE WASN'T PART OF THE AVENGERS FAILSAFE PROGRAM.
THERE'S AN AVENGERS FAILSAFE PROGRAM?
NOT THAT I'M AWARE OF.
WHERE DID IT COME FROM? KANG?
NO, SIR.
THE VISION.

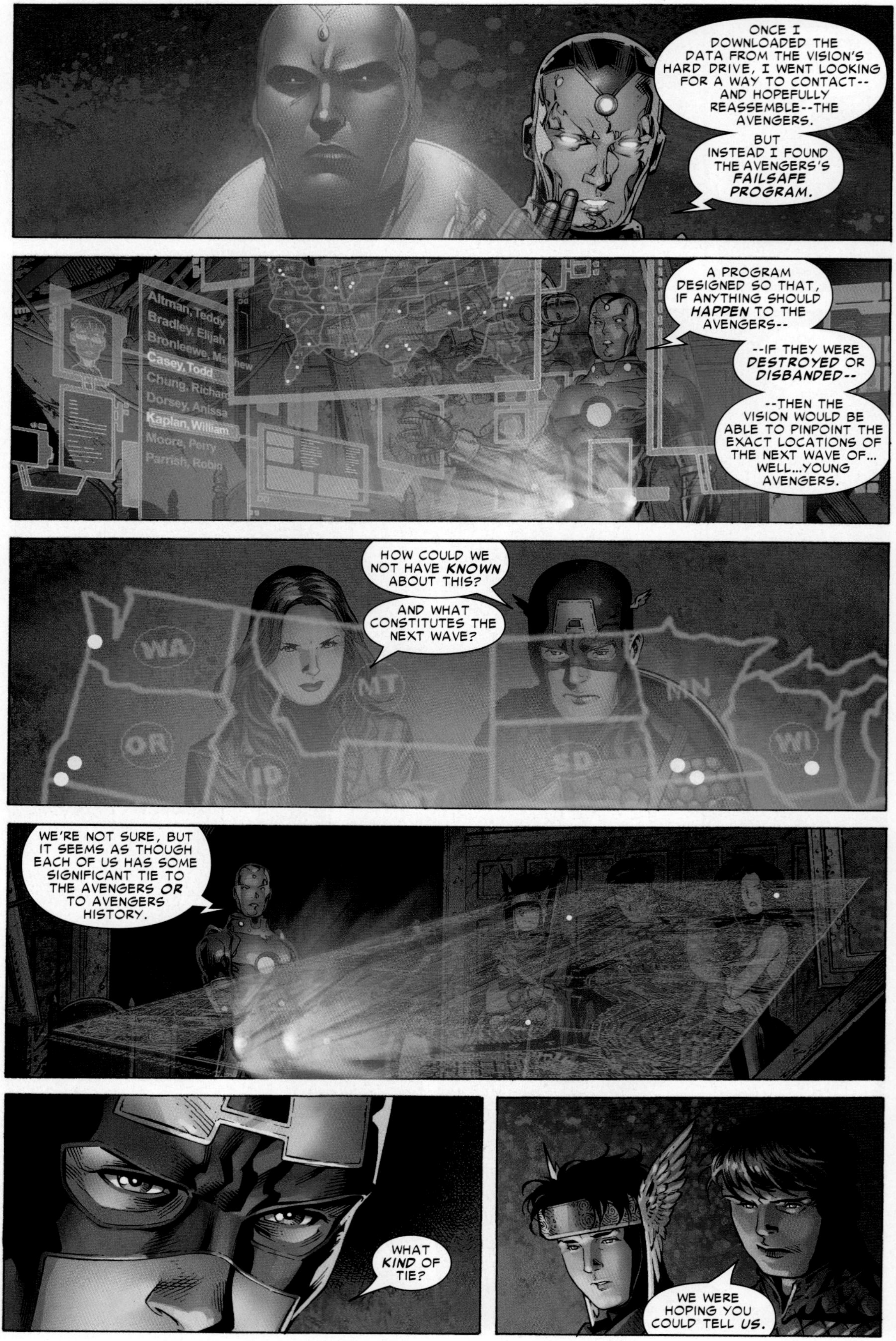
ONCE I DOWNLOADED THE DATA FROM THE VISION'S HARD DRIVE, I WENT LOOKING FOR A WAY TO CONTACT--AND HOPEFULLY REASSEMBLE--THE AVENGERS.
BUT INSTEAD I FOUND THE AVENGERS'S *FAILSAFE PROGRAM.*
Altman, Teddy
Bradley, Elijah
Bronleewe, Matthew
Casey, Todd
Chung, Richard
Dorsey, Anissa
Kaplan, William
Moore, Perry
Parrish, Robin
A PROGRAM DESIGNED SO THAT, IF ANYTHING SHOULD *HAPPEN* TO THE AVENGERS--
--IF THEY WERE *DESTROYED* OR *DISBANDED--*
--THEN THE VISION WOULD BE ABLE TO PINPOINT THE EXACT LOCATIONS OF THE NEXT WAVE OF... WELL...YOUNG AVENGERS.
HOW COULD WE NOT HAVE *KNOWN* ABOUT THIS?
AND WHAT CONSTITUTES THE NEXT WAVE?
WA
OR
ID
MT
SD
MN
WI
WE'RE NOT SURE, BUT IT SEEMS AS THOUGH EACH OF US HAS SOME SIGNIFICANT TIE TO THE AVENGERS *OR* TO AVENGERS HISTORY.
WHAT *KIND* OF TIE?
WE WERE HOPING YOU COULD TELL *US.*

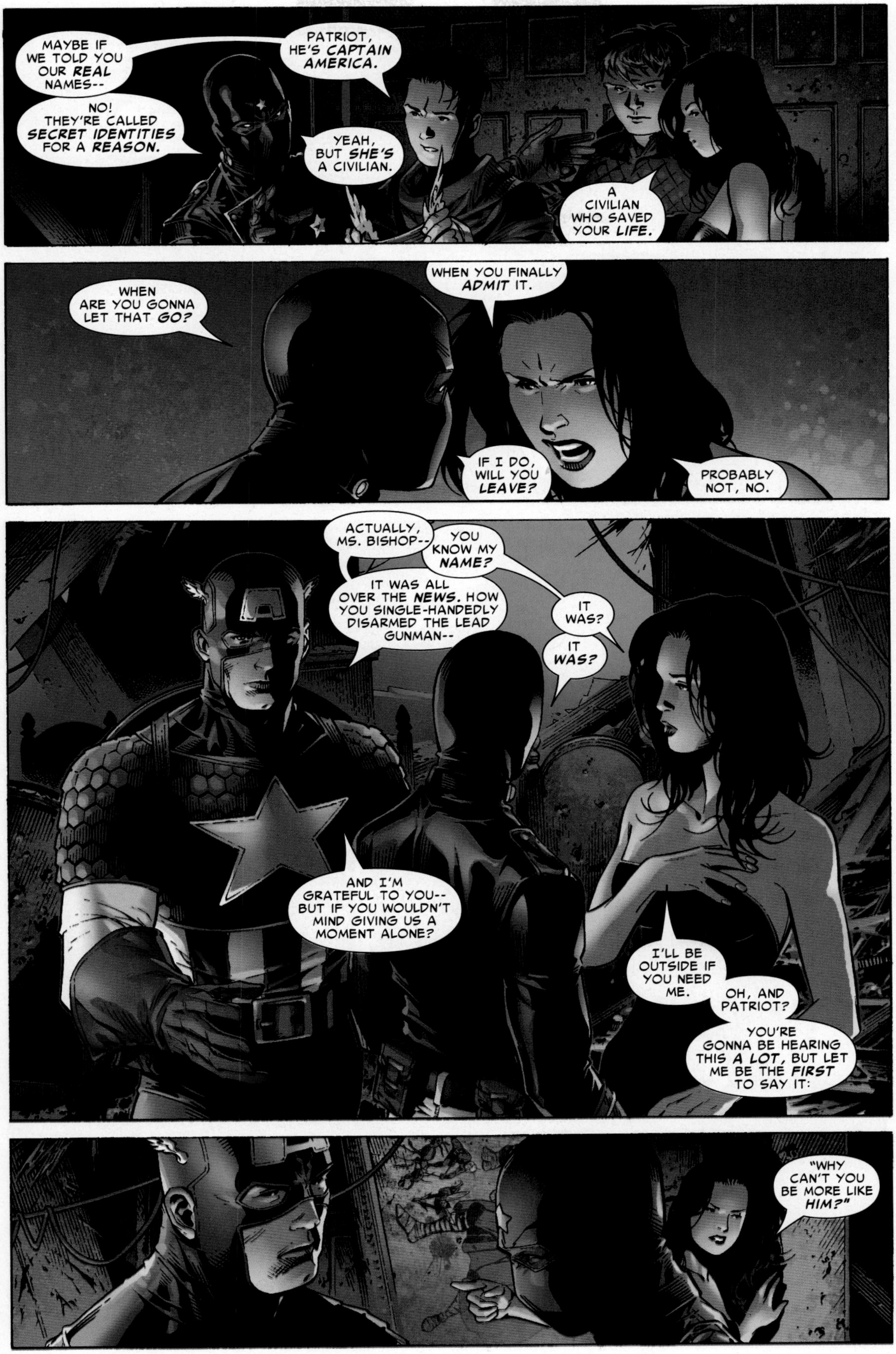
MAYBE IF WE TOLD YOU OUR REAL NAMES--
PATRIOT, HE'S CAPTAIN AMERICA.
NO! THEY'RE CALLED SECRET IDENTITIES FOR A REASON.
YEAH, BUT SHE'S A CIVILIAN.
A CIVILIAN WHO SAVED YOUR LIFE.
WHEN ARE YOU GONNA LET THAT GO?
WHEN YOU FINALLY ADMIT IT.
IF I DO, WILL YOU LEAVE?
PROBABLY NOT, NO.
ACTUALLY, MS. BISHOP--
YOU KNOW MY NAME?
IT WAS ALL OVER THE NEWS. HOW YOU SINGLE-HANDEDLY DISARMED THE LEAD GUNMAN--
IT WAS?
IT WAS?
AND I'M GRATEFUL TO YOU-- BUT IF YOU WOULDN'T MIND GIVING US A MOMENT ALONE?
I'LL BE OUTSIDE IF YOU NEED ME.
OH, AND PATRIOT?
YOU'RE GONNA BE HEARING THIS A LOT, BUT LET ME BE THE FIRST TO SAY IT:
"WHY CAN'T YOU BE MORE LIKE HIM?"

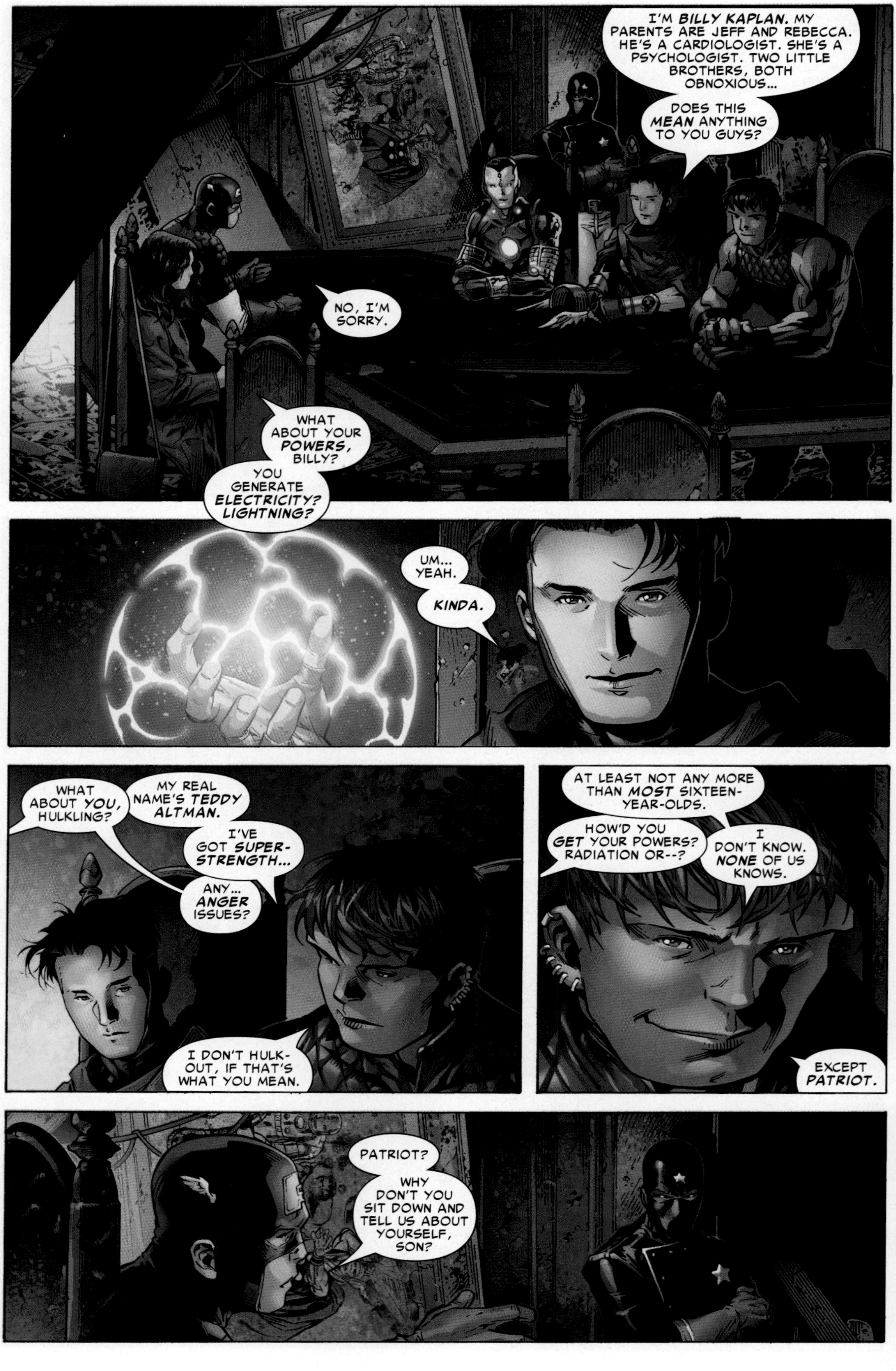
I'M BILLY KAPLAN. MY PARENTS ARE JEFF AND REBECCA. HE'S A CARDIOLOGIST. SHE'S A PSYCHOLOGIST. TWO LITTLE BROTHERS, BOTH OBNOXIOUS...
DOES THIS MEAN ANYTHING TO YOU GUYS?
NO, I'M SORRY.
WHAT ABOUT YOUR POWERS, BILLY?
YOU GENERATE ELECTRICITY? LIGHTNING?
UM... YEAH.
KINDA.
WHAT ABOUT YOU, HULKLING?
MY REAL NAME'S TEDDY ALTMAN.
I'VE GOT SUPER-STRENGTH...
ANY... ANGER ISSUES?
I DON'T HULK-OUT, IF THAT'S WHAT YOU MEAN.
AT LEAST NOT ANY MORE THAN MOST SIXTEEN-YEAR-OLDS.
HOW'D YOU GET YOUR POWERS? RADIATION OR--?
I DON'T KNOW. NONE OF US KNOWS.
EXCEPT PATRIOT.
PATRIOT?
WHY DON'T YOU SIT DOWN AND TELL US ABOUT YOURSELF, SON?

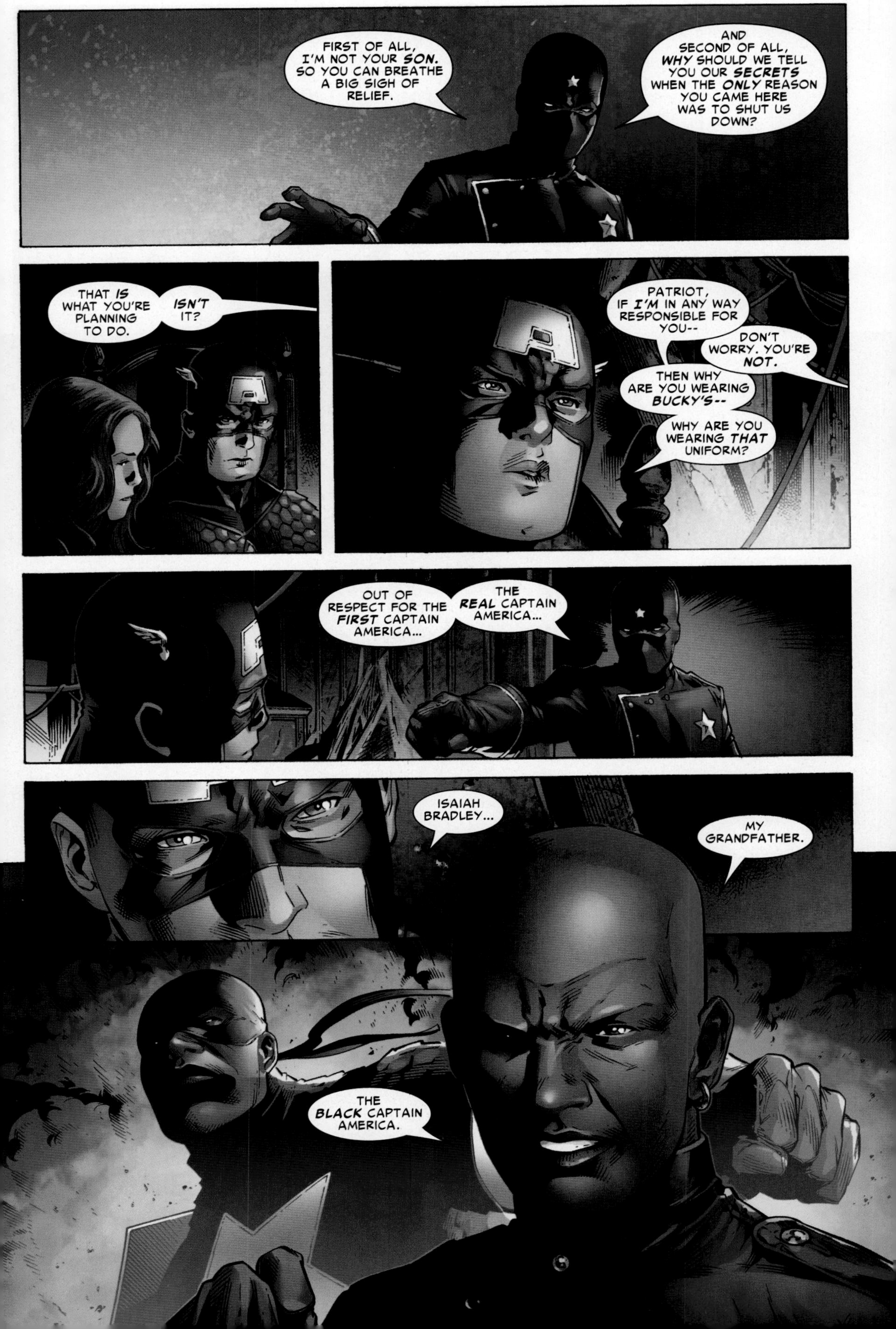

FIRST OF ALL, I'M NOT YOUR SON. SO YOU CAN BREATHE A BIG SIGH OF RELIEF.
AND SECOND OF ALL, WHY SHOULD WE TELL YOU OUR SECRETS WHEN THE ONLY REASON YOU CAME HERE WAS TO SHUT US DOWN?
THAT IS WHAT YOU'RE PLANNING TO DO.
ISN'T IT?
PATRIOT, IF I'M IN ANY WAY RESPONSIBLE FOR YOU--
DON'T WORRY. YOU'RE NOT.
THEN WHY ARE YOU WEARING BUCKY'S--
WHY ARE YOU WEARING THAT UNIFORM?
OUT OF RESPECT FOR THE FIRST CAPTAIN AMERICA...
THE REAL CAPTAIN AMERICA...
ISAIAH BRADLEY...
MY GRANDFATHER.
THE BLACK CAPTAIN AMERICA.

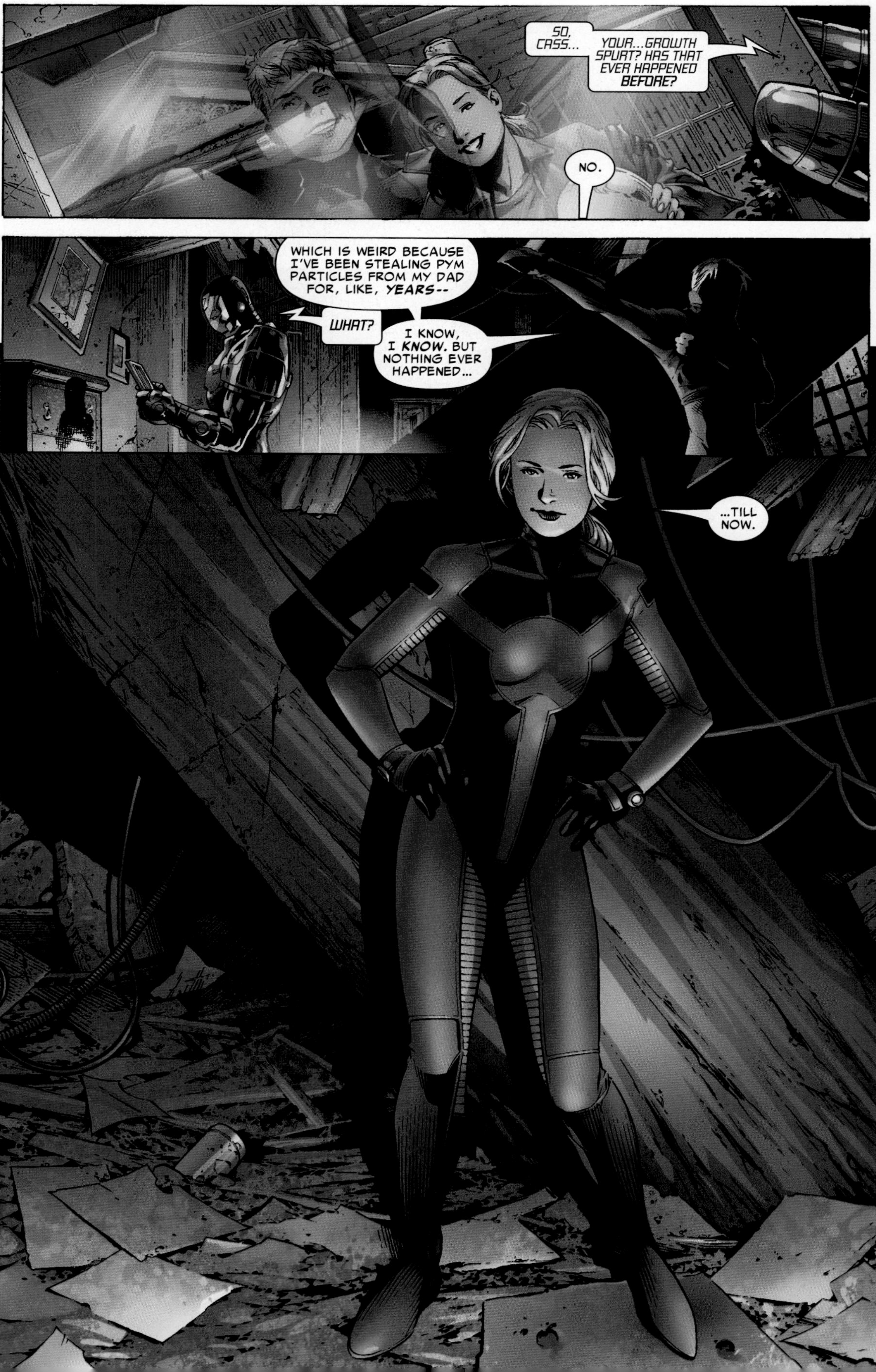
SO, CASS...
YOUR...GROWTH SPURT? HAS THAT EVER HAPPENED BEFORE?
NO.
WHICH IS WEIRD BECAUSE I'VE BEEN STEALING PYM PARTICLES FROM MY DAD FOR, LIKE, YEARS--
WHAT?
I KNOW, I KNOW. BUT NOTHING EVER HAPPENED...
...TILL NOW.

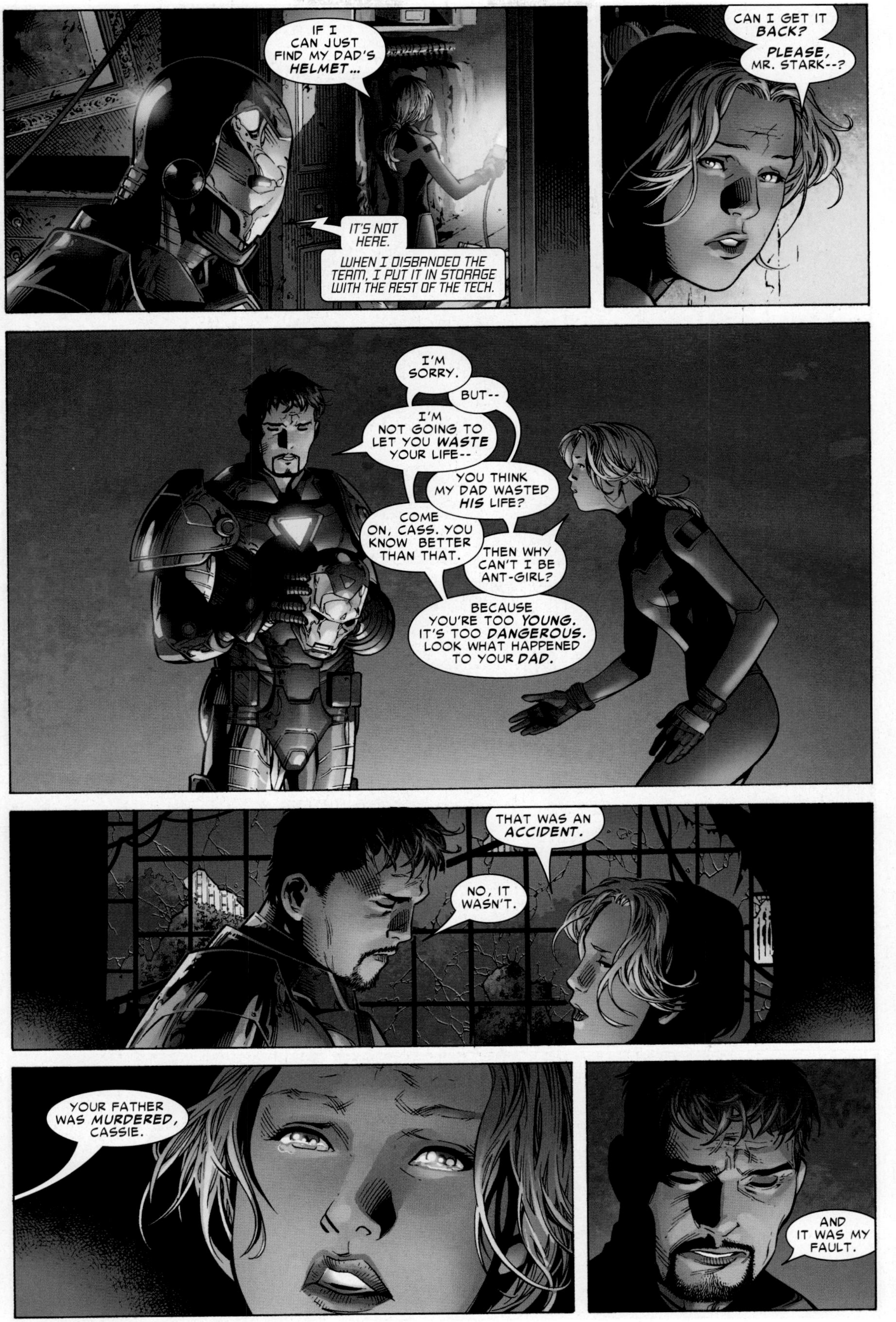
IF I CAN JUST FIND MY DAD'S HELMET...
IT'S NOT HERE.
WHEN I DISBANDED THE TEAM, I PUT IT IN STORAGE WITH THE REST OF THE TECH.
CAN I GET IT BACK?
PLEASE, MR. STARK--?
I'M SORRY.
BUT--
I'M NOT GOING TO LET YOU WASTE YOUR LIFE--
YOU THINK MY DAD WASTED HIS LIFE?
COME ON, CASS. YOU KNOW BETTER THAN THAT.
THEN WHY CAN'T I BE ANT-GIRL?
BECAUSE YOU'RE TOO YOUNG. IT'S TOO DANGEROUS. LOOK WHAT HAPPENED TO YOUR DAD.
THAT WAS AN ACCIDENT.
NO, IT WASN'T.
YOUR FATHER WAS MURDERED, CASSIE.
AND IT WAS MY FAULT.

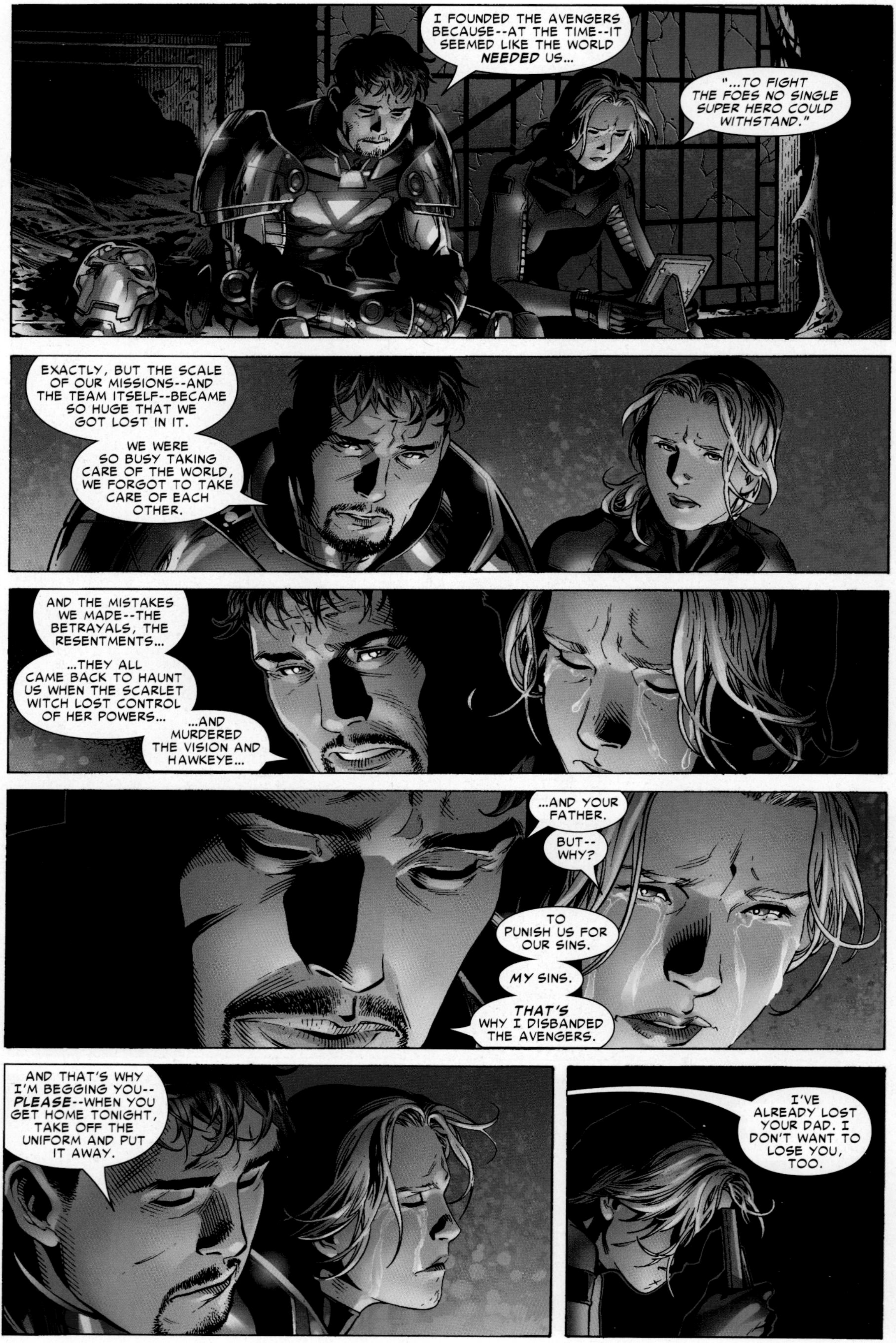
I FOUNDED THE AVENGERS BECAUSE--AT THE TIME--IT SEEMED LIKE THE WORLD *NEEDED* US...
"...TO FIGHT THE FOES NO SINGLE SUPER HERO COULD WITHSTAND."
EXACTLY, BUT THE SCALE OF OUR MISSIONS--AND THE TEAM ITSELF--BECAME SO HUGE THAT WE GOT LOST IN IT.
WE WERE SO BUSY TAKING CARE OF THE WORLD, WE FORGOT TO TAKE CARE OF EACH OTHER.
AND THE MISTAKES WE MADE--THE BETRAYALS, THE RESENTMENTS...
...THEY ALL CAME BACK TO HAUNT US WHEN THE SCARLET WITCH LOST CONTROL OF HER POWERS...
...AND MURDERED THE VISION AND HAWKEYE...
...AND YOUR FATHER.
BUT--WHY?
TO PUNISH US FOR OUR SINS.
MY SINS.
THAT'S WHY I DISBANDED THE AVENGERS.
AND THAT'S WHY I'M BEGGING YOU--*PLEASE*--WHEN YOU GET HOME TONIGHT, TAKE OFF THE UNIFORM AND PUT IT AWAY.
I'VE ALREADY LOST YOUR DAD. I DON'T WANT TO LOSE YOU, TOO.

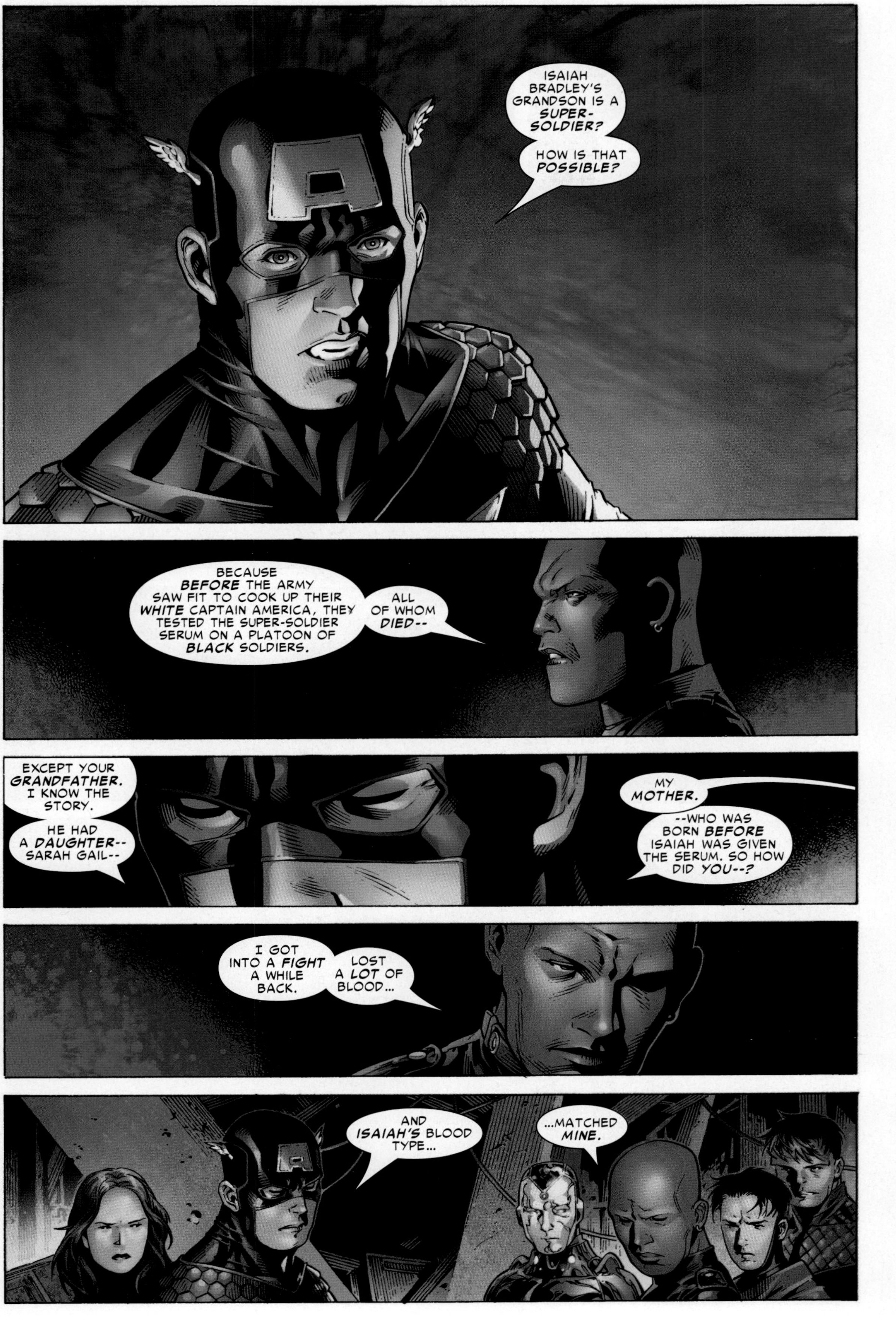
ISAIAH BRADLEY'S GRANDSON IS A SUPER-SOLDIER?
HOW IS THAT POSSIBLE?
BECAUSE BEFORE THE ARMY SAW FIT TO COOK UP THEIR WHITE CAPTAIN AMERICA, THEY TESTED THE SUPER-SOLDIER SERUM ON A PLATOON OF BLACK SOLDIERS.
ALL OF WHOM DIED--
EXCEPT YOUR GRANDFATHER. I KNOW THE STORY.
HE HAD A DAUGHTER-- SARAH GAIL--
MY MOTHER.
--WHO WAS BORN BEFORE ISAIAH WAS GIVEN THE SERUM. SO HOW DID YOU--?
I GOT INTO A FIGHT A WHILE BACK.
LOST A LOT OF BLOOD...
AND ISAIAH'S BLOOD TYPE...
...MATCHED MINE.

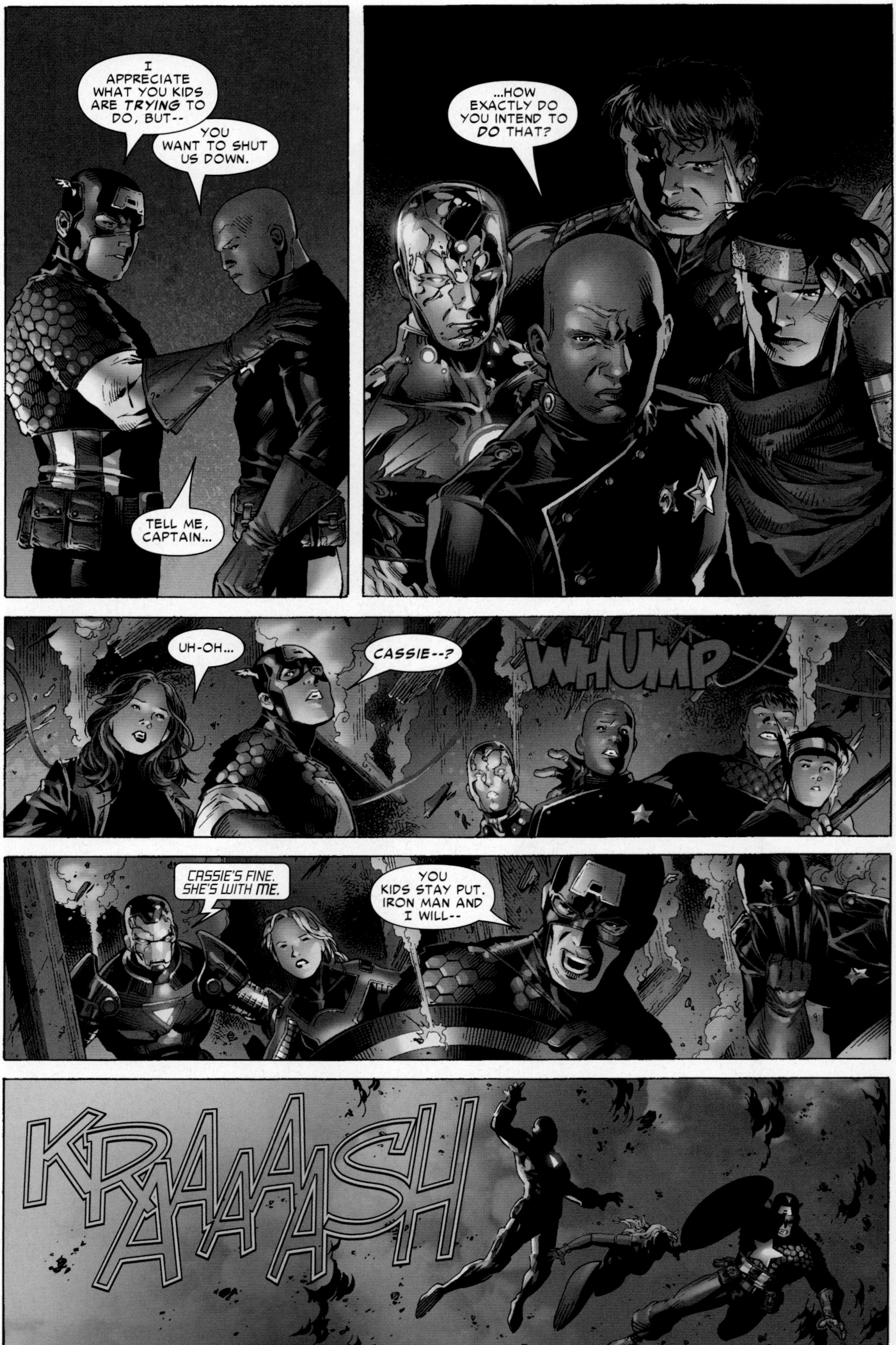
I APPRECIATE WHAT YOU KIDS ARE *TRYING* TO DO, BUT--
YOU WANT TO SHUT US DOWN.
TELL ME, CAPTAIN...
...HOW EXACTLY DO YOU INTEND TO *DO* THAT?
UH-OH...
CASSIE--?
WHUMP
CASSIE'S FINE. SHE'S WITH *ME*.
YOU KIDS STAY PUT. IRON MAN AND I WILL--
KRAAAASH
AAAAAH

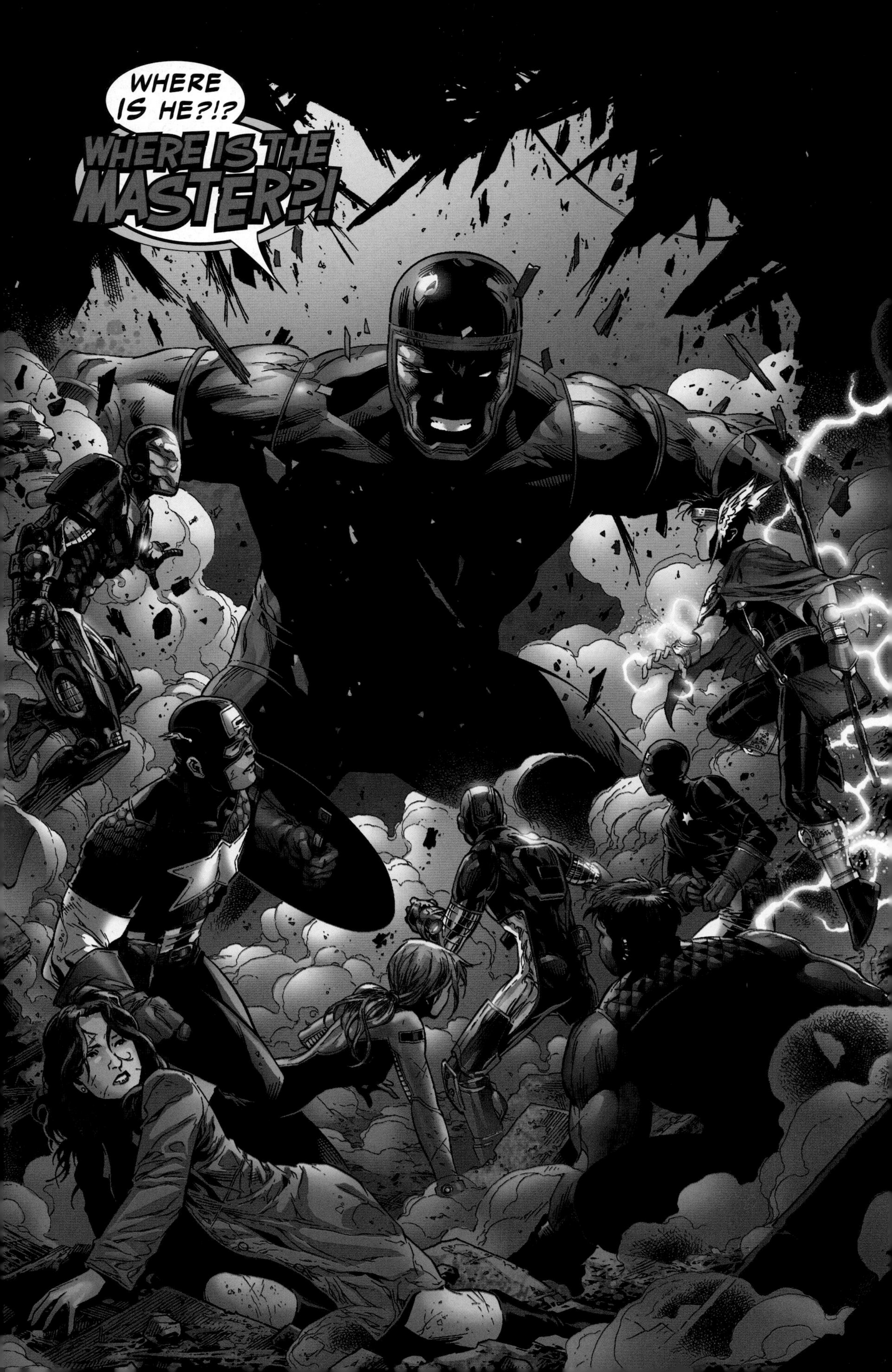
WHERE IS HE?!?
WHERE IS THE MASTER?!

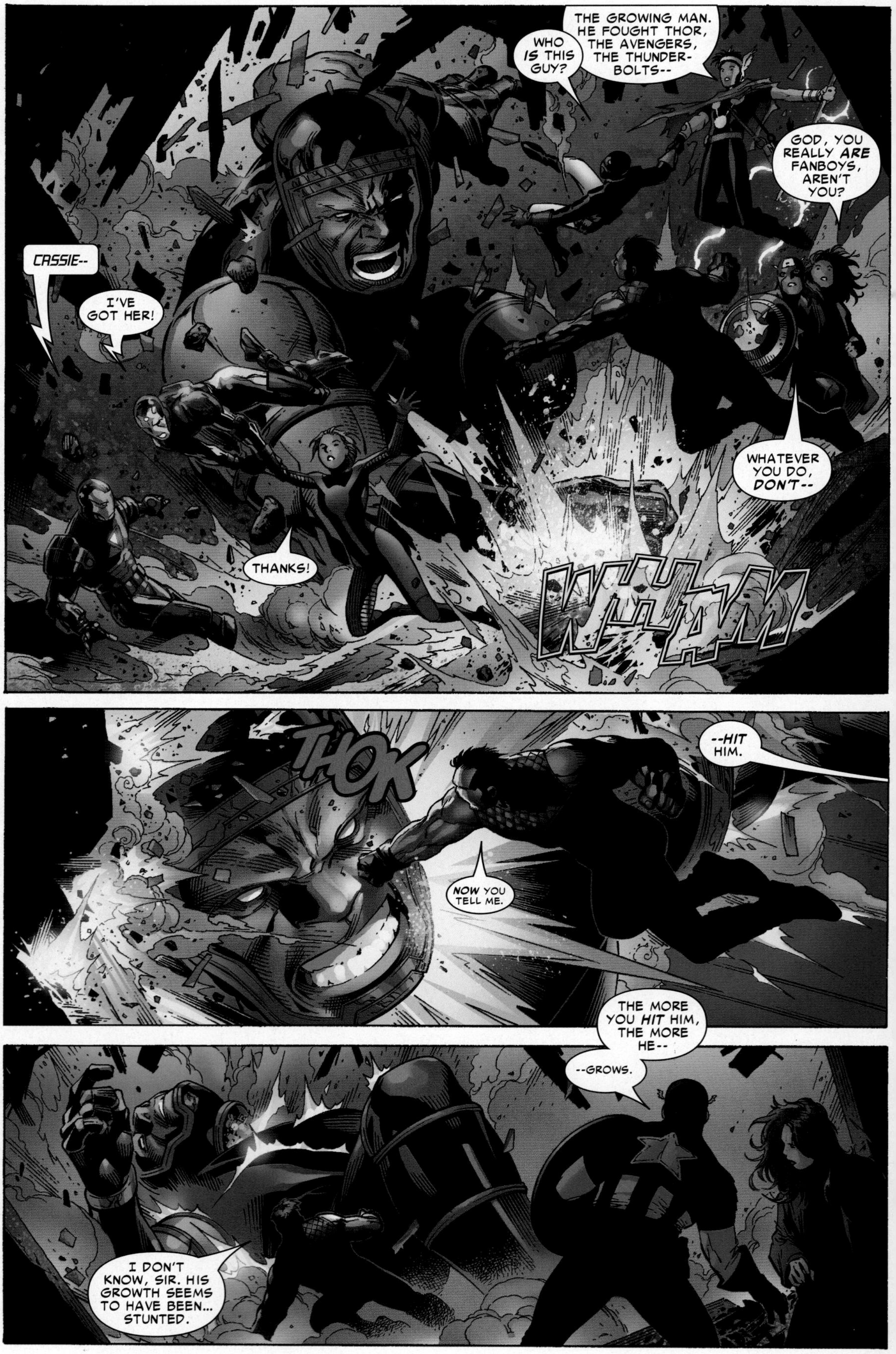
WHO IS THIS GUY?
THE GROWING MAN. HE FOUGHT THOR, THE AVENGERS, THE THUNDER-BOLTS--
GOD, YOU REALLY ARE FANBOYS, AREN'T YOU?
CASSIE--
I'VE GOT HER!
THANKS!
WHATEVER YOU DO, DON'T--
WHAM
THOK
--HIT HIM.
NOW YOU TELL ME.
THE MORE YOU HIT HIM, THE MORE HE--
--GROWS.
I DON'T KNOW, SIR. HIS GROWTH SEEMS TO HAVE BEEN... STUNTED.

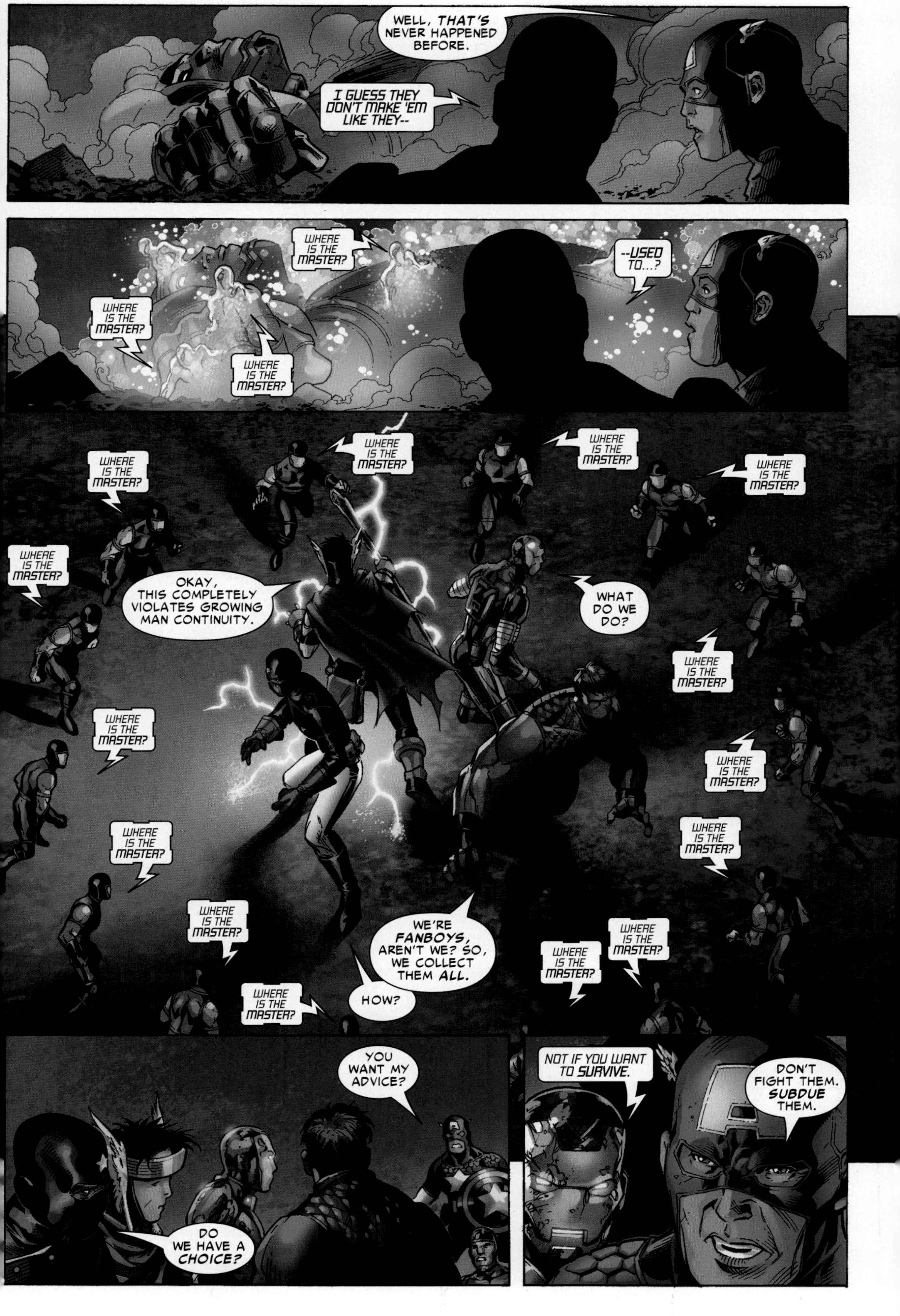
WELL, THAT'S NEVER HAPPENED BEFORE.
I GUESS THEY DON'T MAKE 'EM LIKE THEY--
WHERE IS THE MASTER?
WHERE IS THE MASTER?
WHERE IS THE MASTER?
--USED TO...?
WHERE IS THE MASTER?
WHERE IS THE MASTER?
WHERE IS THE MASTER?
WHERE IS THE MASTER?
WHERE IS THE MASTER?
OKAY, THIS COMPLETELY VIOLATES GROWING MAN CONTINUITY.
WHAT DO WE DO?
WHERE IS THE MASTER?
WHERE IS THE MASTER?
WHERE IS THE MASTER?
WHERE IS THE MASTER?
WHERE IS THE MASTER?
WHERE IS THE MASTER?
WE'RE FANBOYS, AREN'T WE? SO, WE COLLECT THEM ALL.
WHERE IS THE MASTER?
WHERE IS THE MASTER?
HOW?
WHERE IS THE MASTER?
YOU WANT MY ADVICE?
DO WE HAVE A CHOICE?
NOT IF YOU WANT TO SURVIVE.
DON'T FIGHT THEM. SUBDUE THEM.

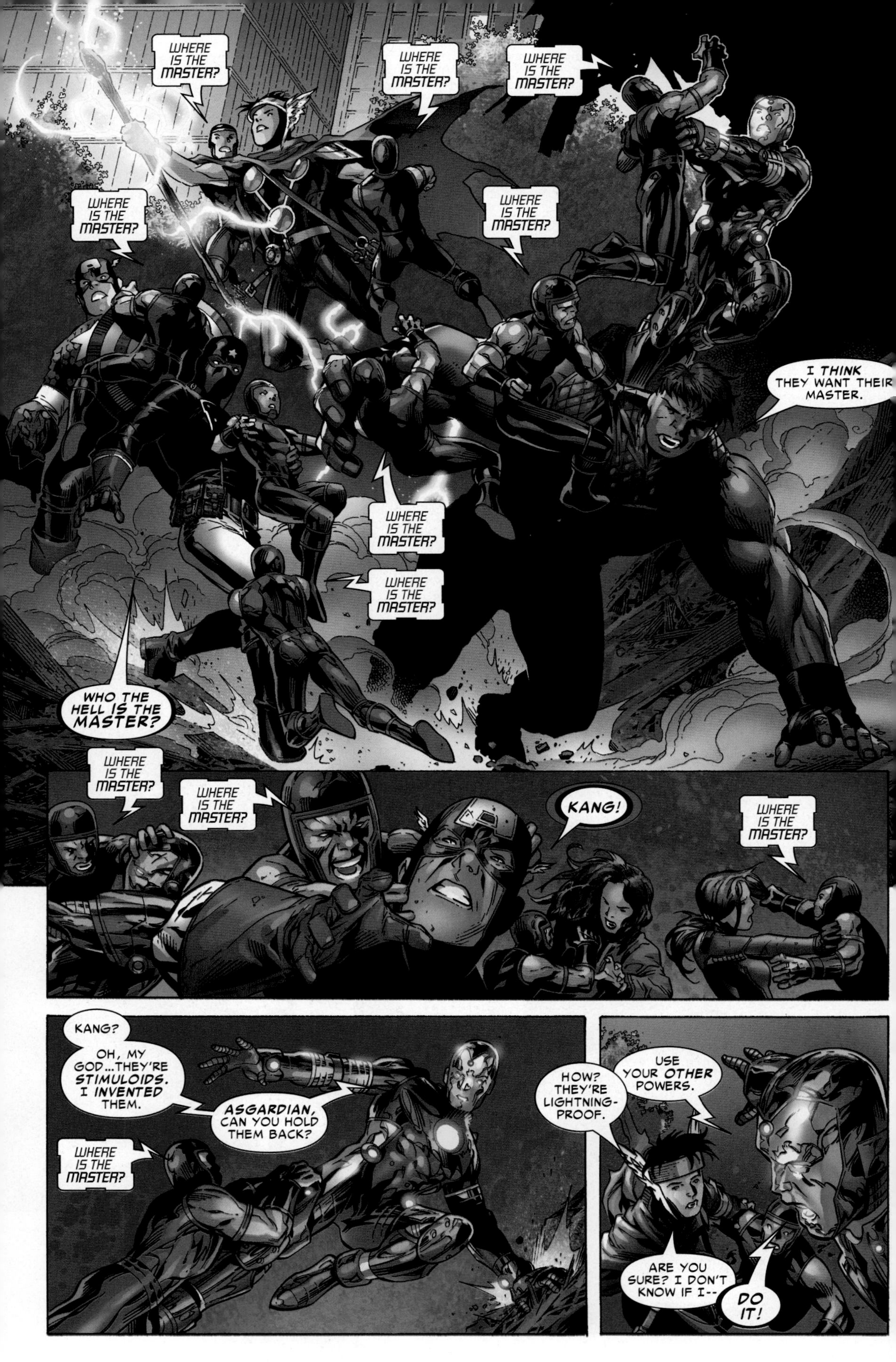
WHERE IS THE MASTER?
WHERE IS THE MASTER?
WHERE IS THE MASTER?
WHERE IS THE MASTER?
WHERE IS THE MASTER?
I THINK THEY WANT THEIR MASTER.
WHERE IS THE MASTER?
WHERE IS THE MASTER?
WHO THE HELL IS THE MASTER?
WHERE IS THE MASTER?
WHERE IS THE MASTER?
KANG!
WHERE IS THE MASTER?
KANG?
OH, MY GOD...THEY'RE STIMULOIDS. I INVENTED THEM.
ASGARDIAN, CAN YOU HOLD THEM BACK?
WHERE IS THE MASTER?
HOW? THEY'RE LIGHTNING-PROOF.
USE YOUR OTHER POWERS.
ARE YOU SURE? I DON'T KNOW IF I--
DO IT!

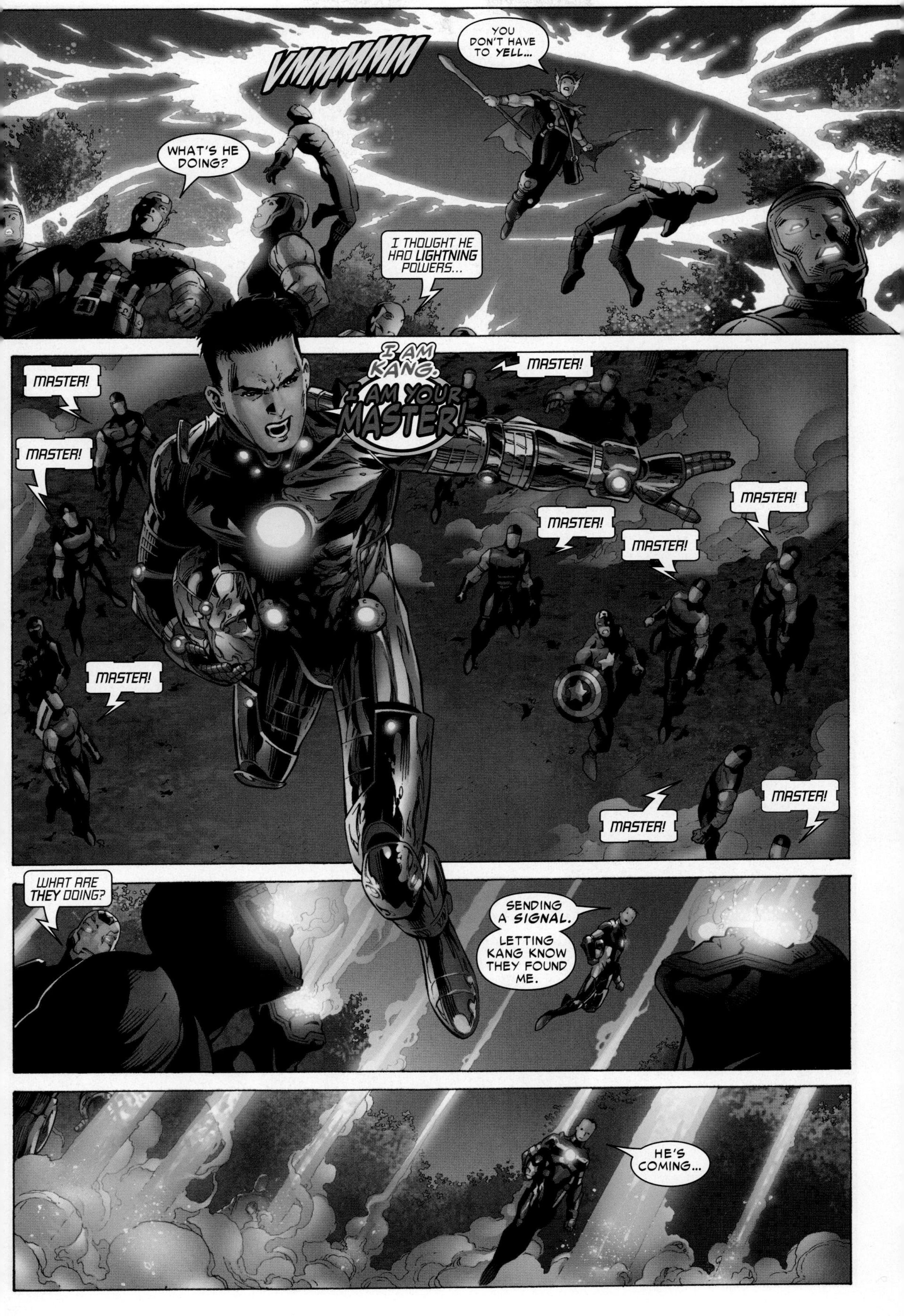
VMMMMM
YOU DON'T HAVE TO YELL...
WHAT'S HE DOING?
I THOUGHT HE HAD LIGHTNING POWERS...
I AM KANG. I AM YOUR MASTER!
MASTER!
MASTER!
MASTER!
MASTER!
MASTER!
MASTER!
MASTER!
MASTER!
MASTER!
WHAT ARE THEY DOING?
SENDING A SIGNAL.
LETTING KANG KNOW THEY FOUND ME.
HE'S COMING...

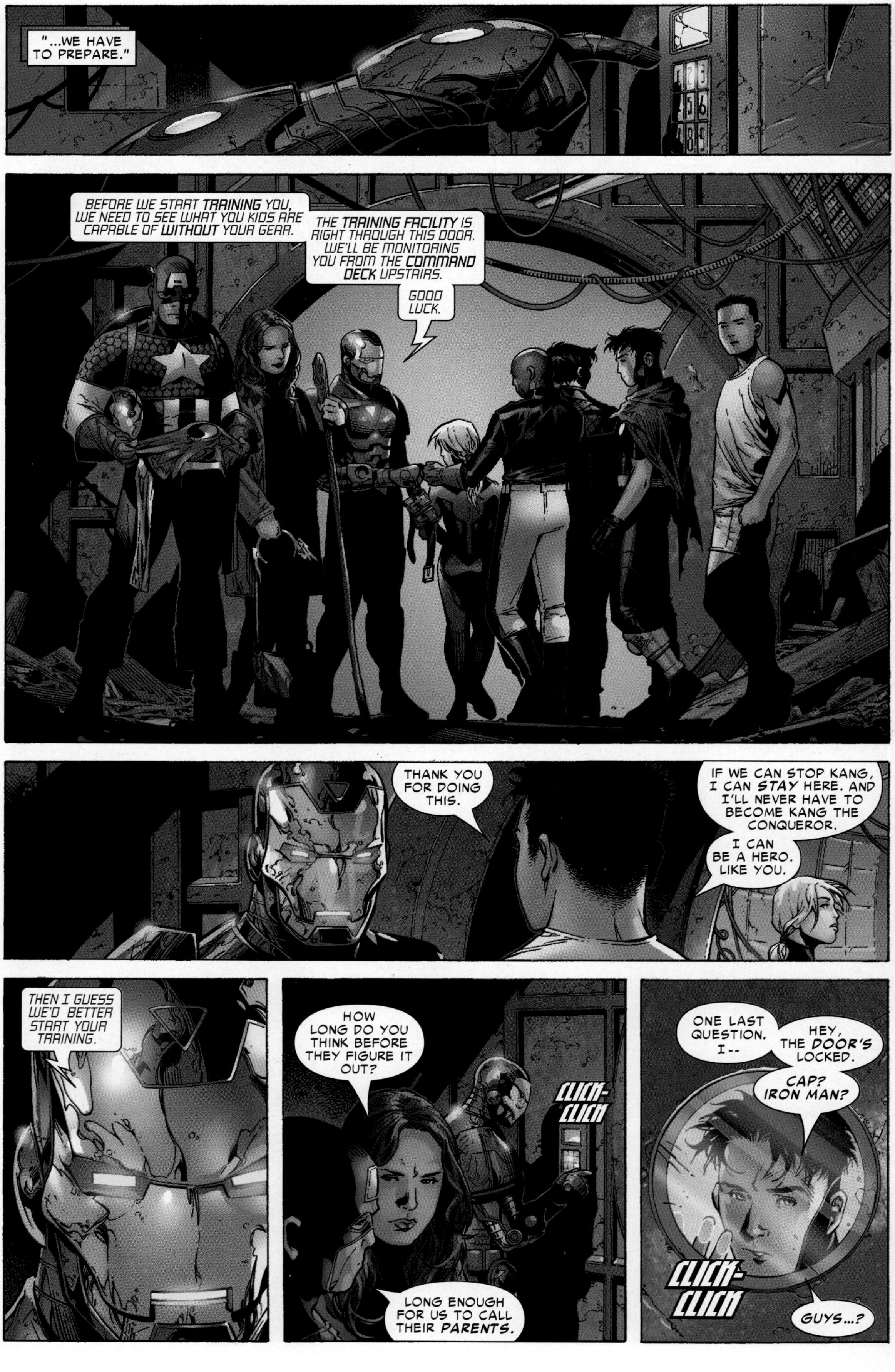
"...WE HAVE TO PREPARE."
BEFORE WE START TRAINING YOU, WE NEED TO SEE WHAT YOU KIDS ARE CAPABLE OF WITHOUT YOUR GEAR.
THE TRAINING FACILITY IS RIGHT THROUGH THIS DOOR. WE'LL BE MONITORING YOU FROM THE COMMAND DECK UPSTAIRS.
GOOD LUCK.
THANK YOU FOR DOING THIS.
IF WE CAN STOP KANG, I CAN STAY HERE. AND I'LL NEVER HAVE TO BECOME KANG THE CONQUEROR.
I CAN BE A HERO. LIKE YOU.
THEN I GUESS WE'D BETTER START YOUR TRAINING.
HOW LONG DO YOU THINK BEFORE THEY FIGURE IT OUT?
CLICK-CLICK
LONG ENOUGH FOR US TO CALL THEIR PARENTS.
ONE LAST QUESTION. I--
HEY, THE DOOR'S LOCKED.
CAP? IRON MAN?
CLICK-CLICK
GUYS...?

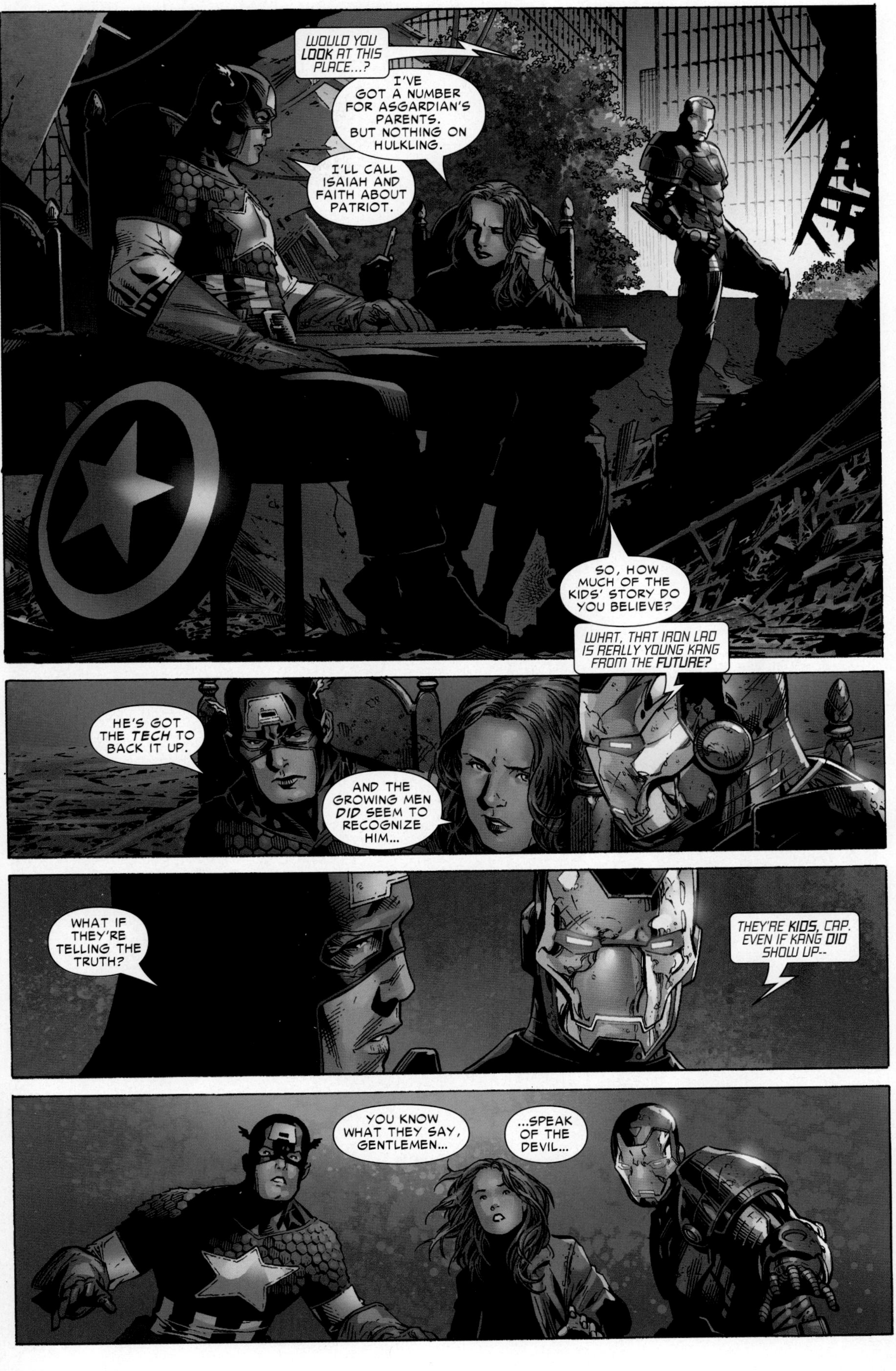
WOULD YOU LOOK AT THIS PLACE...?
I'VE GOT A NUMBER FOR ASGARDIAN'S PARENTS. BUT NOTHING ON HULKLING.
I'LL CALL ISAIAH AND FAITH ABOUT PATRIOT.
SO, HOW MUCH OF THE KIDS' STORY DO YOU BELIEVE?
WHAT, THAT IRON LAD IS REALLY YOUNG KANG FROM THE FUTURE?
HE'S GOT THE TECH TO BACK IT UP.
AND THE GROWING MEN DID SEEM TO RECOGNIZE HIM...
WHAT IF THEY'RE TELLING THE TRUTH?
THEY'RE KIDS, CAP. EVEN IF KANG DID SHOW UP--
YOU KNOW WHAT THEY SAY, GENTLEMEN...
...SPEAK OF THE DEVIL...

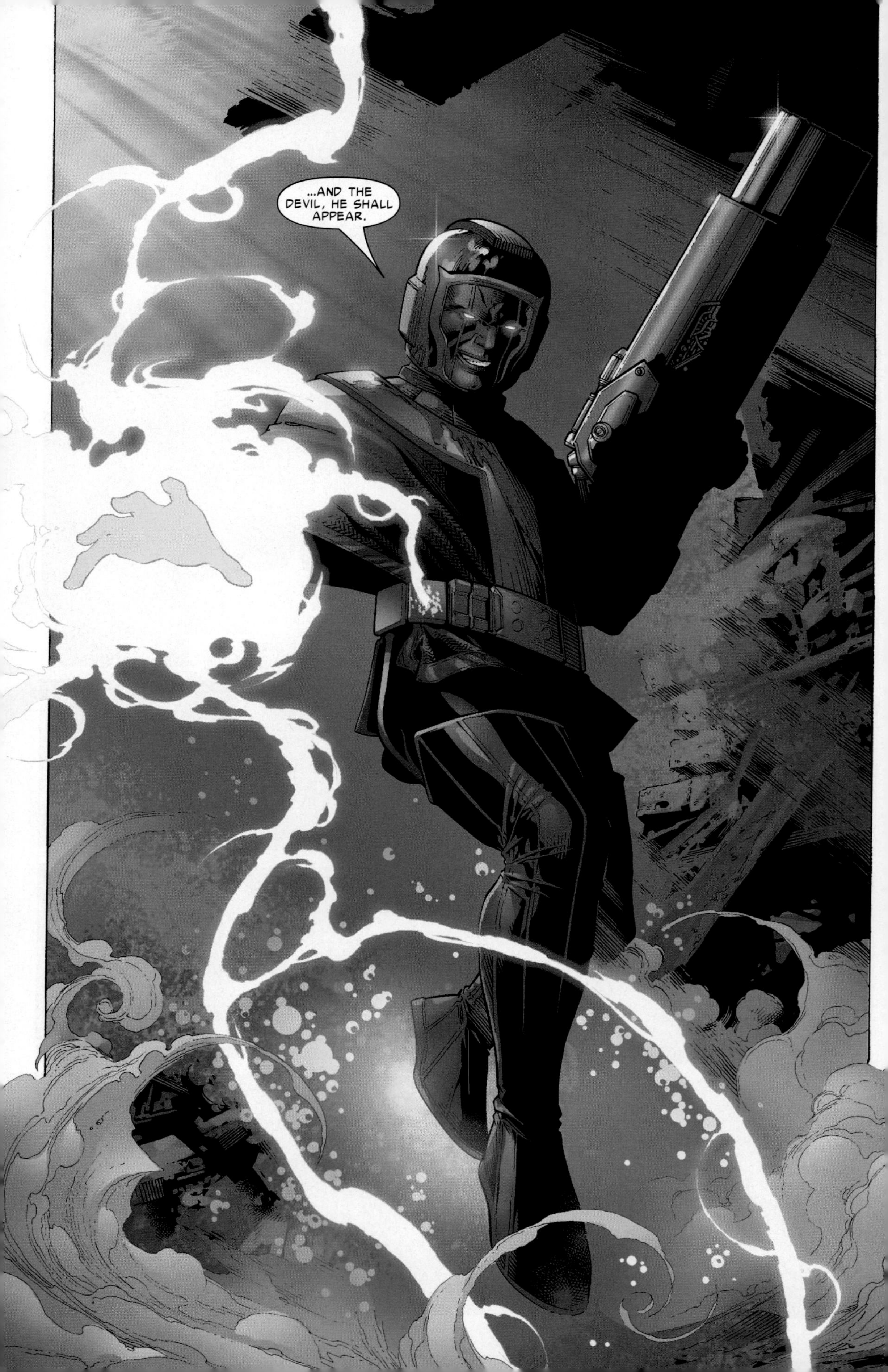
...AND THE DEVIL, HE SHALL APPEAR.

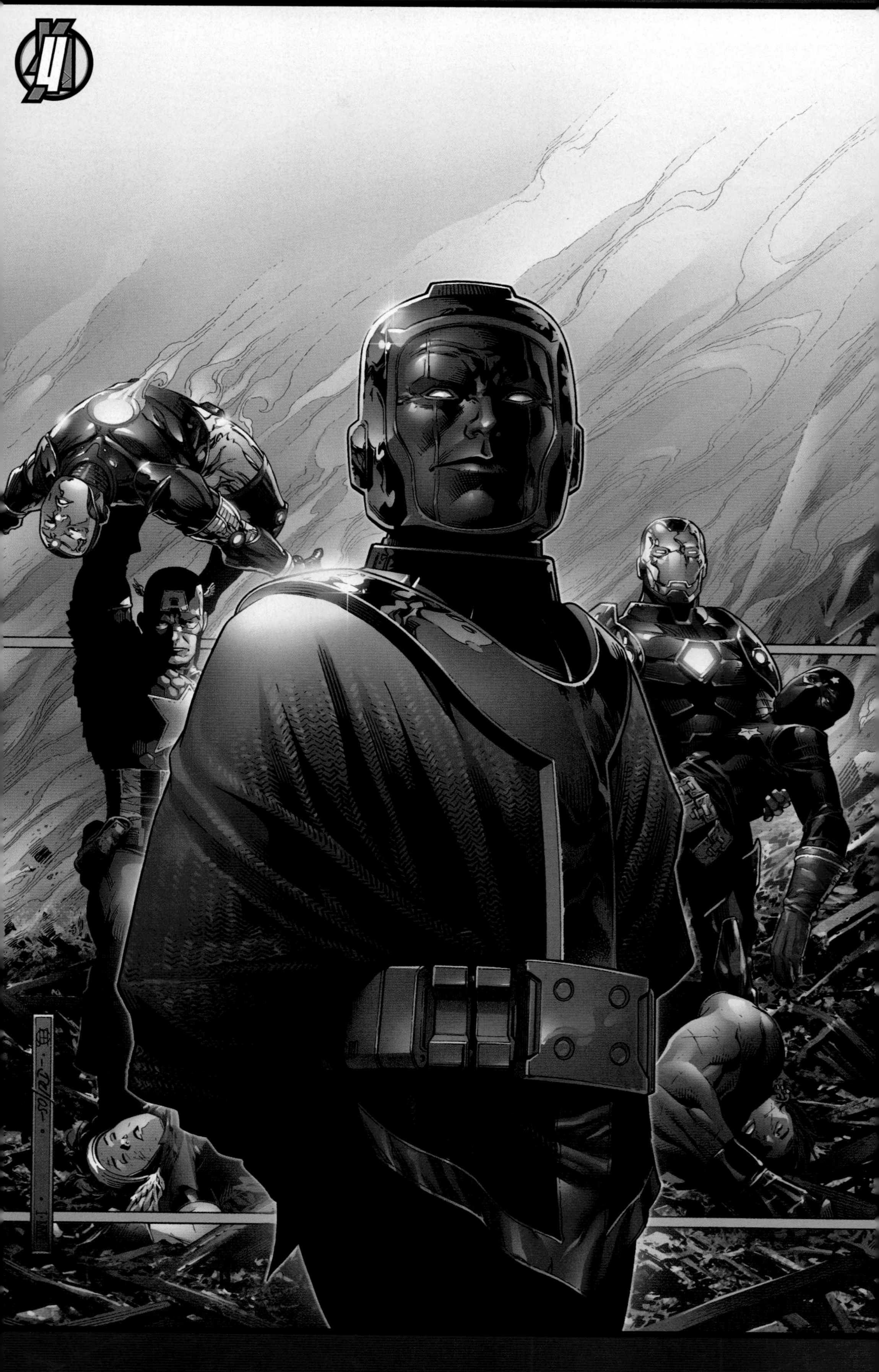

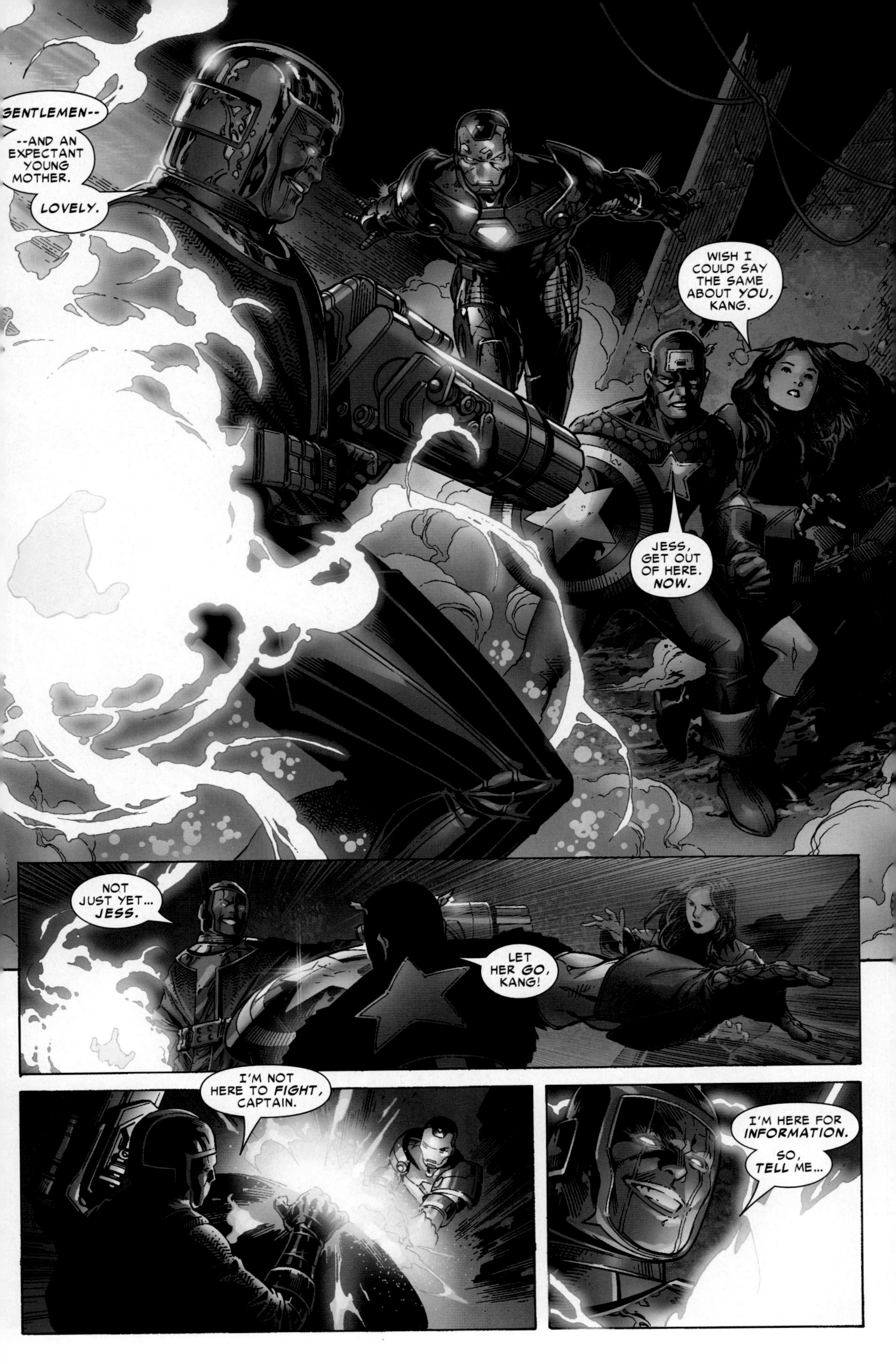
GENTLEMEN--
--AND AN EXPECTANT YOUNG MOTHER.
LOVELY.
WISH I COULD SAY THE SAME ABOUT YOU, KANG.
JESS, GET OUT OF HERE. NOW.
NOT JUST YET... JESS.
LET HER GO, KANG!
I'M NOT HERE TO FIGHT, CAPTAIN.
I'M HERE FOR INFORMATION.
SO, TELL ME...

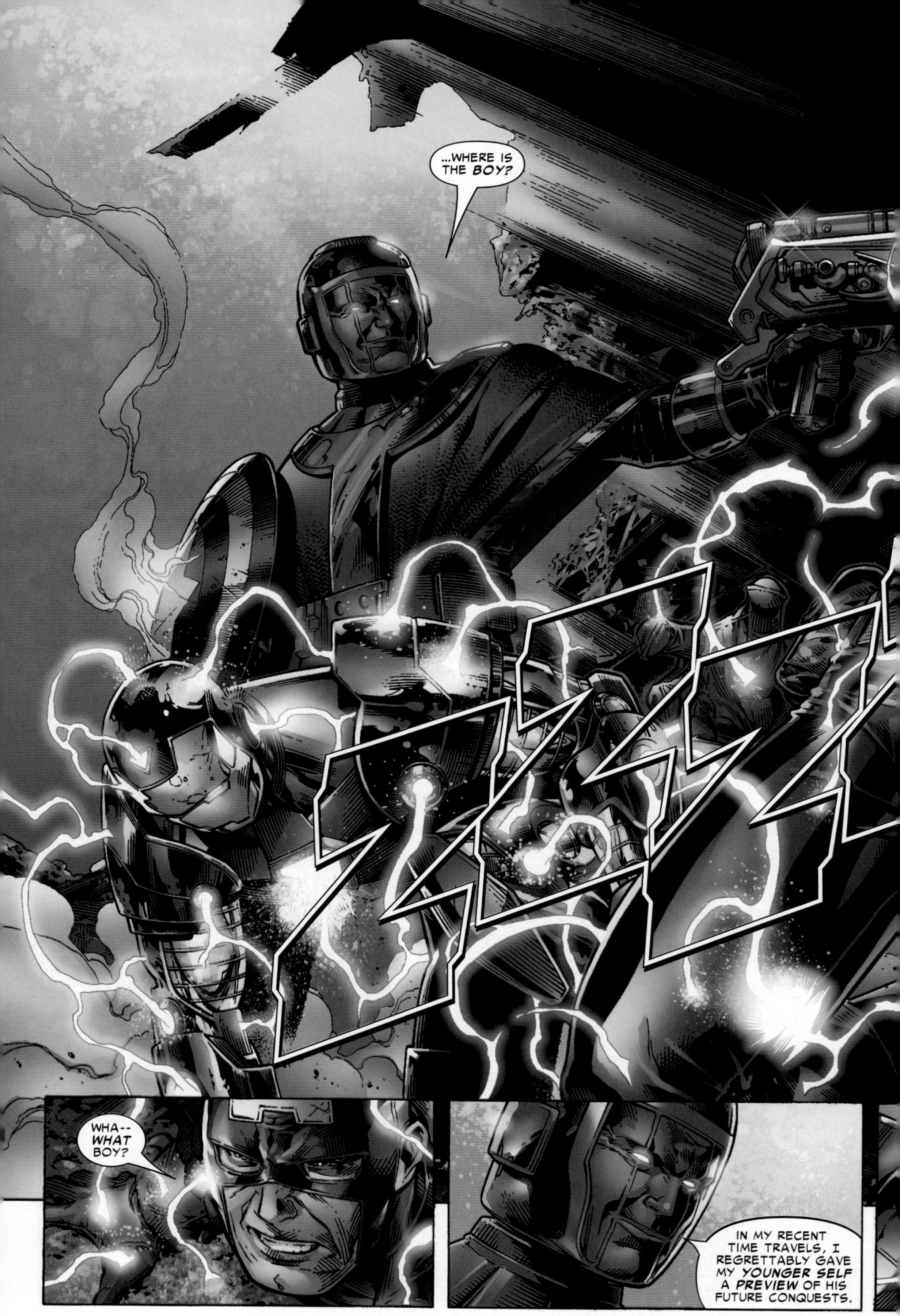
...WHERE IS THE BOY?
WHA-- WHAT BOY?
IN MY RECENT TIME TRAVELS, I REGRETTABLY GAVE MY YOUNGER SELF A PREVIEW OF HIS FUTURE CONQUESTS.

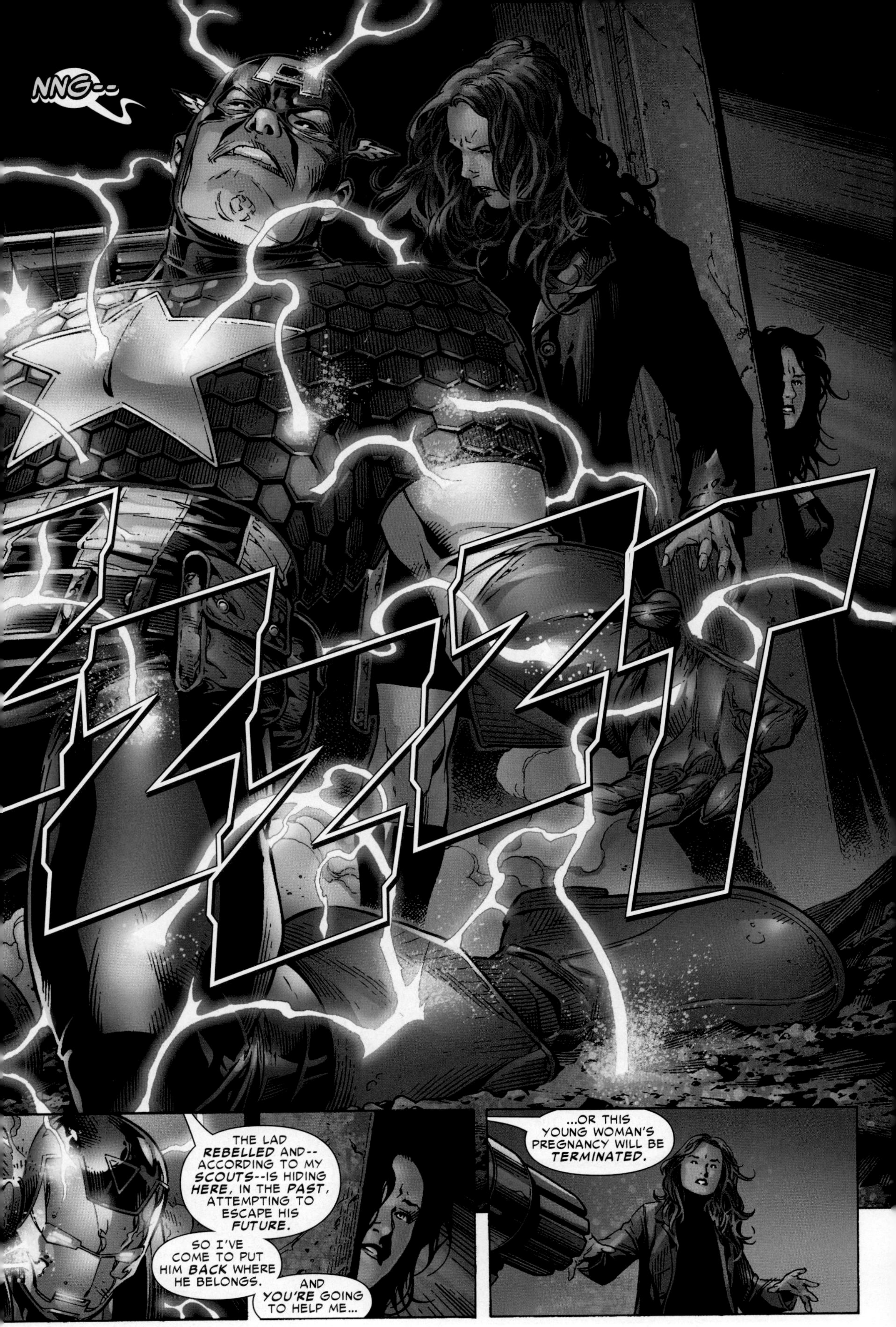
NNG--
THE LAD REBELLED AND-- ACCORDING TO MY SCOUTS--IS HIDING HERE, IN THE PAST, ATTEMPTING TO ESCAPE HIS FUTURE.
SO I'VE COME TO PUT HIM BACK WHERE HE BELONGS.
AND YOU'RE GOING TO HELP ME...
...OR THIS YOUNG WOMAN'S PREGNANCY WILL BE TERMINATED.

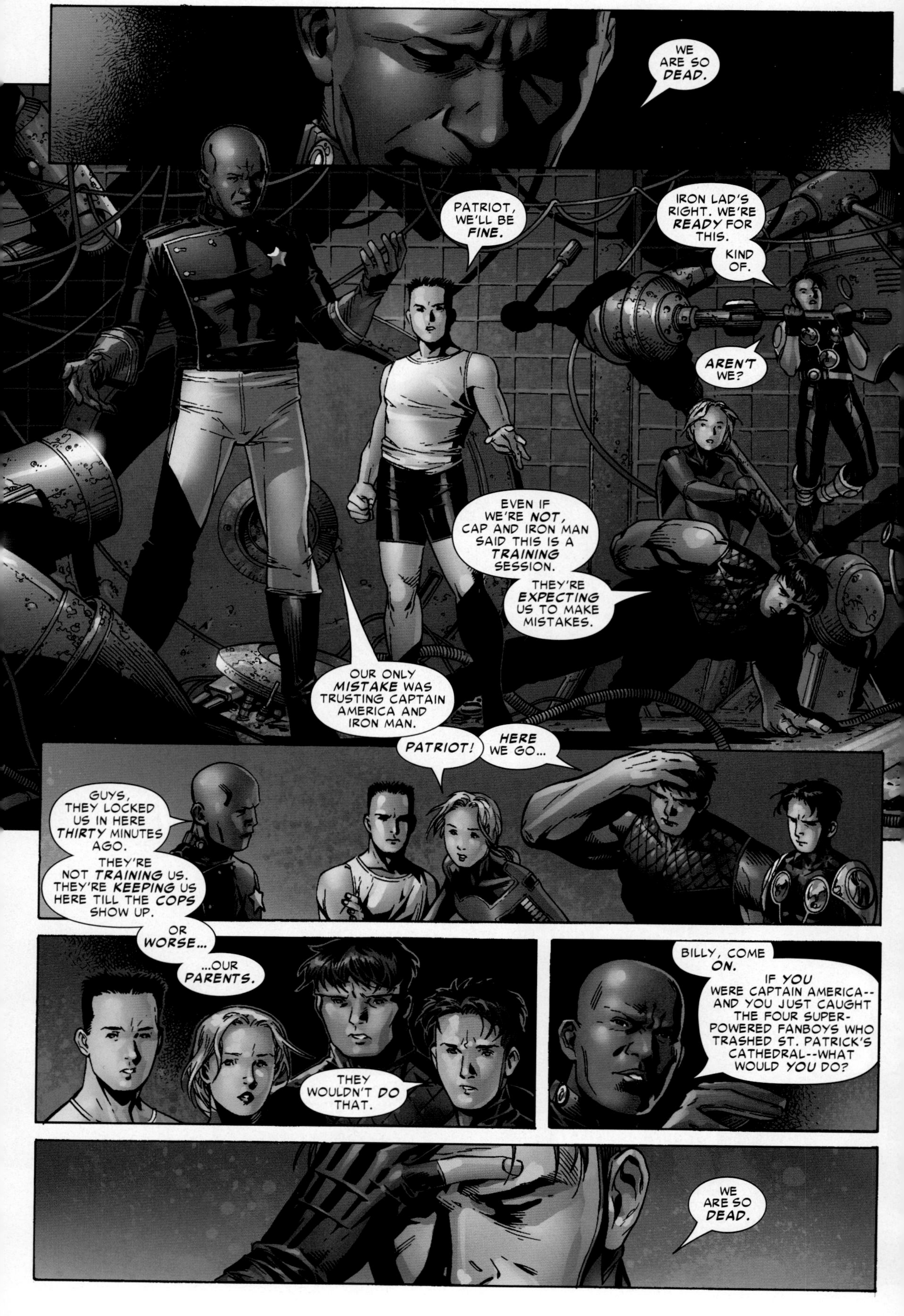

WE ARE SO DEAD.
PATRIOT, WE'LL BE FINE.
IRON LAD'S RIGHT. WE'RE READY FOR THIS.
KIND OF.
AREN'T WE?
EVEN IF WE'RE NOT, CAP AND IRON MAN SAID THIS IS A TRAINING SESSION.
THEY'RE EXPECTING US TO MAKE MISTAKES.
OUR ONLY MISTAKE WAS TRUSTING CAPTAIN AMERICA AND IRON MAN.
PATRIOT!
HERE WE GO...
GUYS, THEY LOCKED US IN HERE THIRTY MINUTES AGO.
THEY'RE NOT TRAINING US. THEY'RE KEEPING US HERE TILL THE COPS SHOW UP.
OR WORSE...
...OUR PARENTS.
THEY WOULDN'T DO THAT.
BILLY, COME ON.
IF YOU WERE CAPTAIN AMERICA--AND YOU JUST CAUGHT THE FOUR SUPER-POWERED FANBOYS WHO TRASHED ST. PATRICK'S CATHEDRAL--WHAT WOULD YOU DO?
WE ARE SO DEAD.

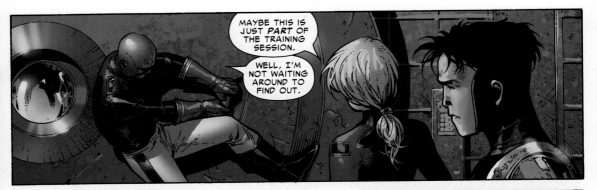

MAYBE THIS IS JUST *PART* OF THE TRAINING SESSION.

WELL, I'M NOT WAITING AROUND TO FIND OUT.

HULKLING, BREAK IT DOWN.

HOW?

I THOUGHT YOU HAD SUPER-STRENGTH.

I THOUGHT *YOU* HAD SUPER-STRENGTH.

STAND BACK. MAYBE I CAN SHORT OUT THE SECURITY SYSTEM.

THEN AGAIN, MAYBE I *CAN'T.*

X-S-SZZZZT!

WHAT IF YOU USE YOUR *OTHER* POWERS?

WHAT OTHER POWERS?

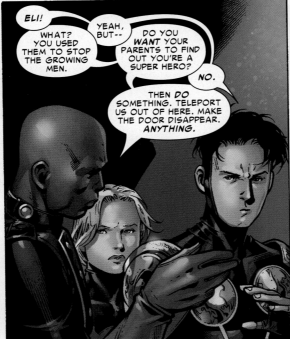

ELI!

WHAT? YOU USED THEM TO STOP THE GROWING MEN.

YEAH, BUT--

DO YOU *WANT* YOUR PARENTS TO FIND OUT YOU'RE A SUPER HERO?

NO.

THEN DO SOMETHING. TELEPORT US OUT OF HERE. MAKE THE DOOR DISAPPEAR. ANYTHING.

YOU CAN MAKE *DOORS* DISAPPEAR?

UM...

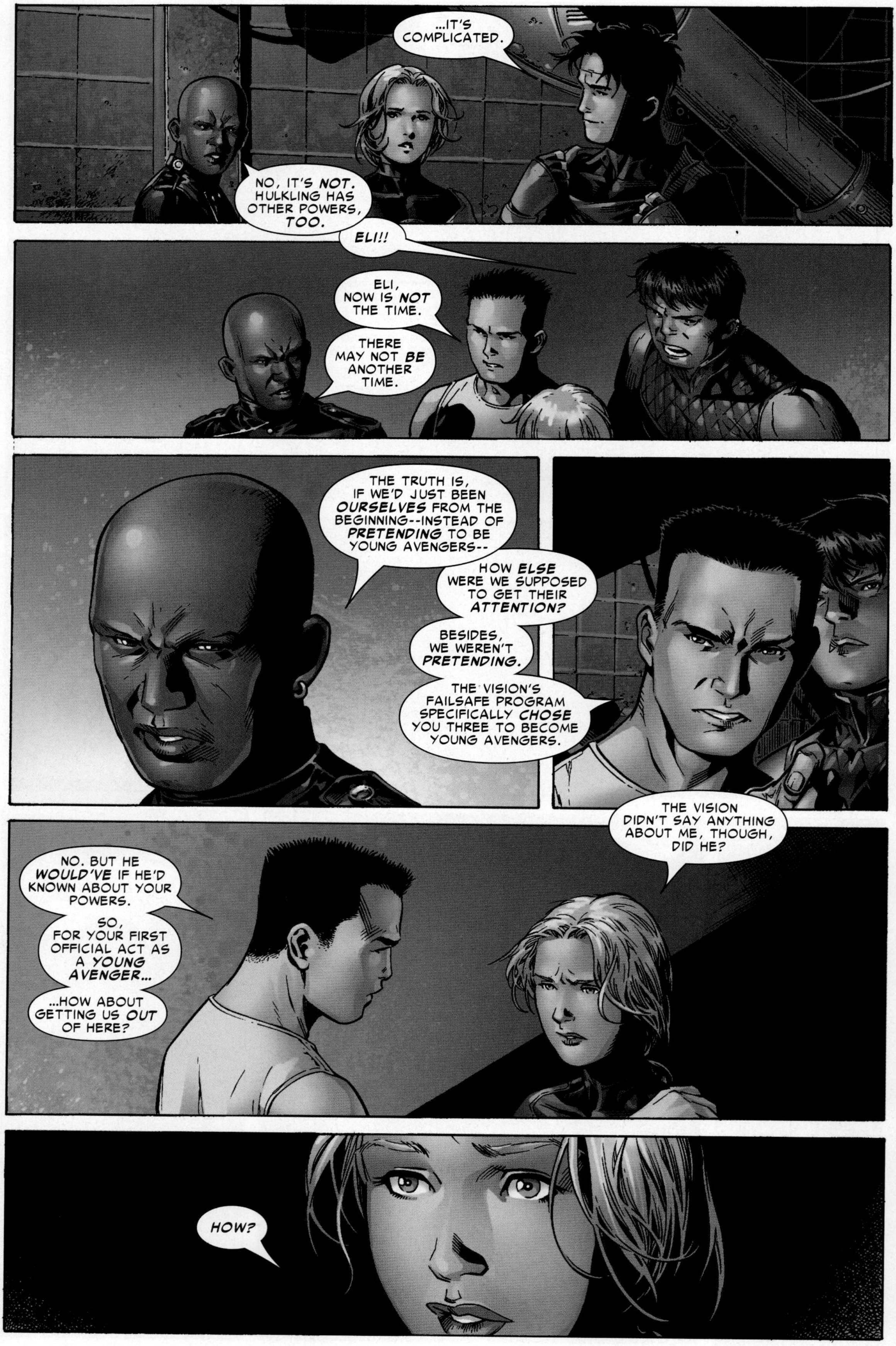
...IT'S COMPLICATED.
NO, IT'S NOT. HULKLING HAS OTHER POWERS, TOO.
ELI!!
ELI, NOW IS NOT THE TIME.
THERE MAY NOT BE ANOTHER TIME.
THE TRUTH IS, IF WE'D JUST BEEN OURSELVES FROM THE BEGINNING--INSTEAD OF PRETENDING TO BE YOUNG AVENGERS--
HOW ELSE WERE WE SUPPOSED TO GET THEIR ATTENTION?
BESIDES, WE WEREN'T PRETENDING.
THE VISION'S FAILSAFE PROGRAM SPECIFICALLY CHOSE YOU THREE TO BECOME YOUNG AVENGERS.
THE VISION DIDN'T SAY ANYTHING ABOUT ME, THOUGH, DID HE?
NO. BUT HE WOULD'VE IF HE'D KNOWN ABOUT YOUR POWERS.
SO, FOR YOUR FIRST OFFICIAL ACT AS A YOUNG AVENGER...
...HOW ABOUT GETTING US OUT OF HERE?
HOW?

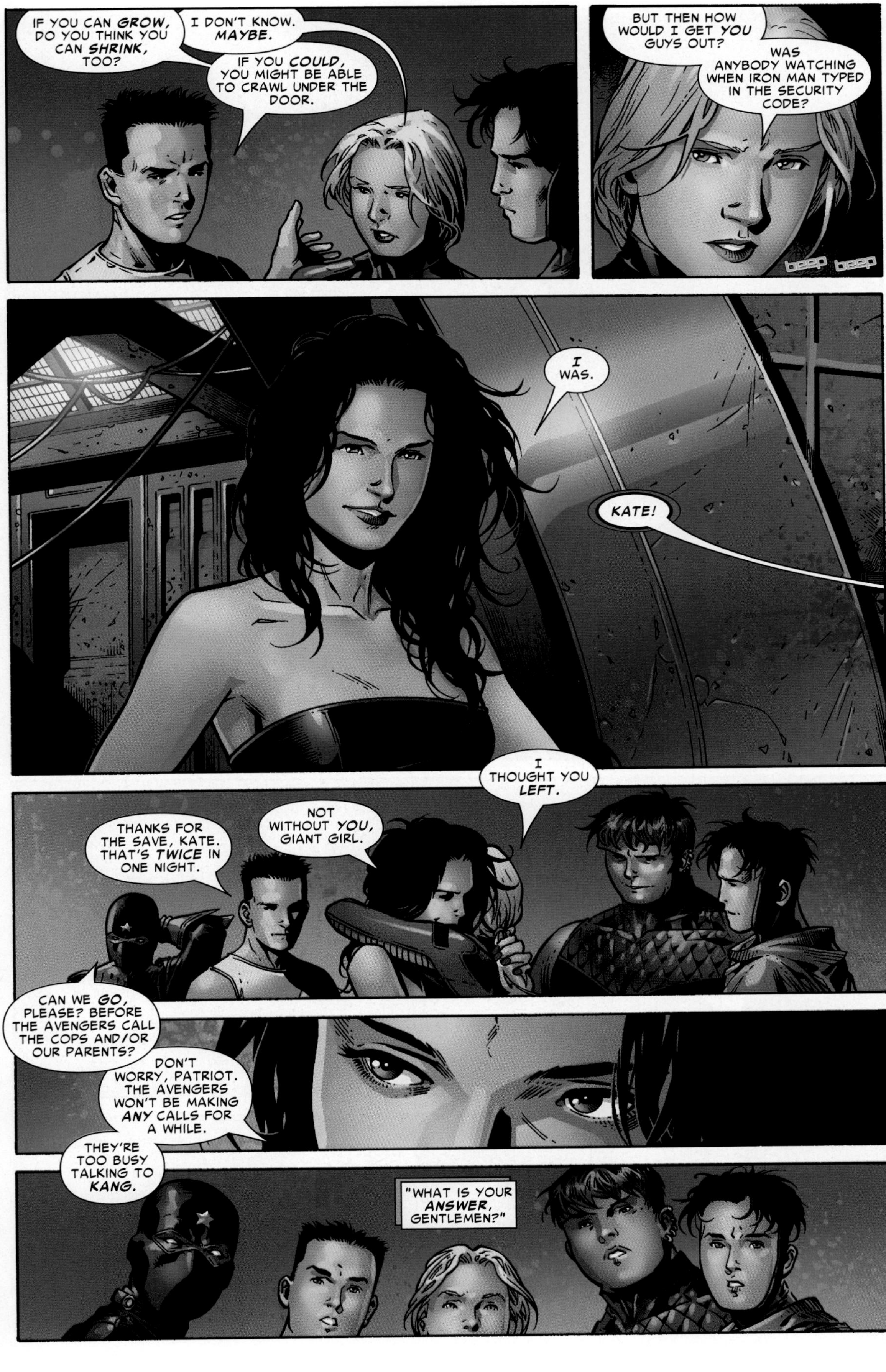
IF YOU CAN GROW, DO YOU THINK YOU CAN SHRINK, TOO?
I DON'T KNOW. MAYBE.
IF YOU COULD, YOU MIGHT BE ABLE TO CRAWL UNDER THE DOOR.
BUT THEN HOW WOULD I GET YOU GUYS OUT?
WAS ANYBODY WATCHING WHEN IRON MAN TYPED IN THE SECURITY CODE?
beep beep
I WAS.
KATE!
THANKS FOR THE SAVE, KATE. THAT'S TWICE IN ONE NIGHT.
NOT WITHOUT YOU, GIANT GIRL.
I THOUGHT YOU LEFT.
CAN WE GO, PLEASE? BEFORE THE AVENGERS CALL THE COPS AND/OR OUR PARENTS?
DON'T WORRY, PATRIOT. THE AVENGERS WON'T BE MAKING ANY CALLS FOR A WHILE.
THEY'RE TOO BUSY TALKING TO KANG.
"WHAT IS YOUR ANSWER, GENTLEMEN?"

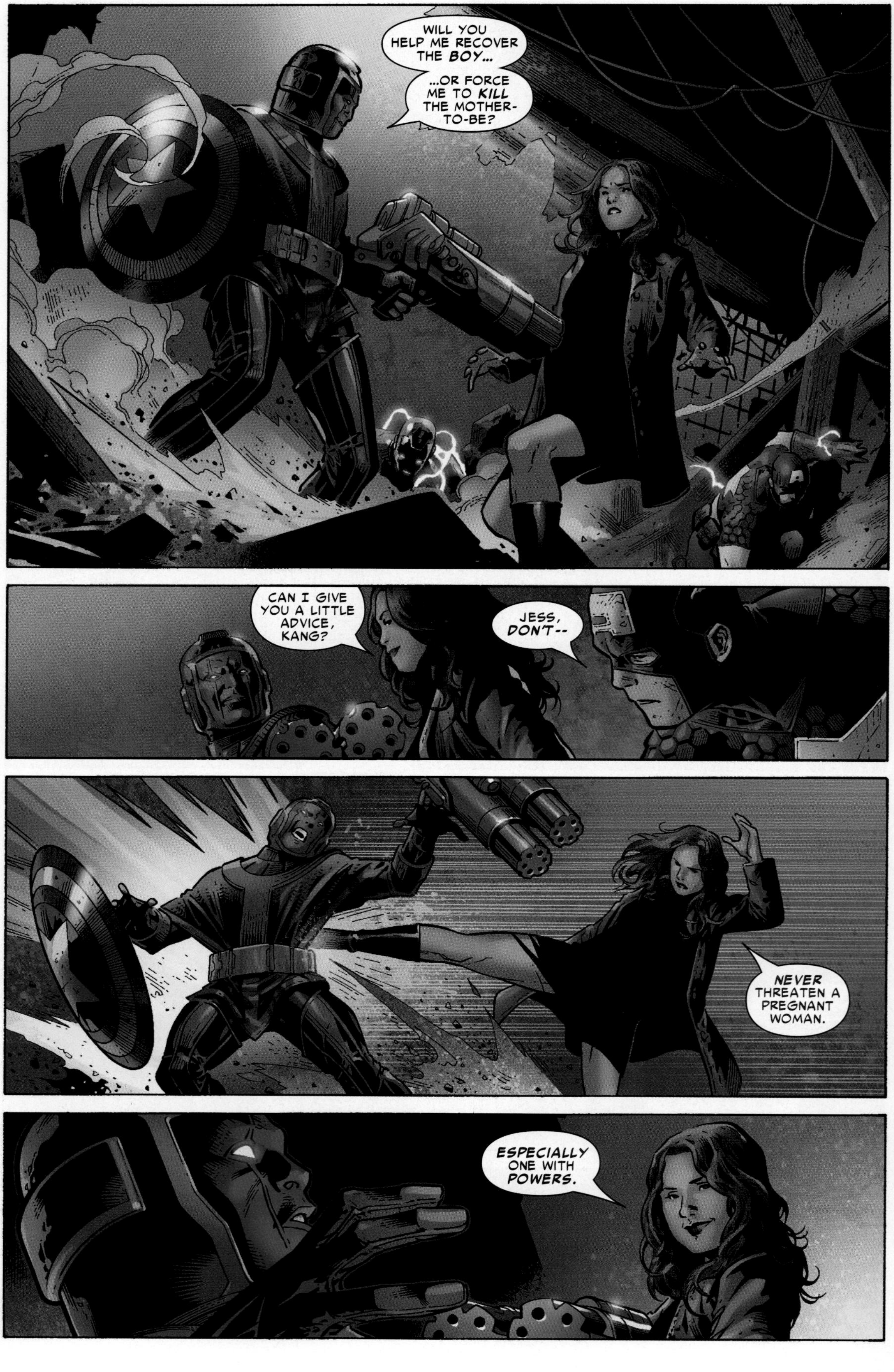

WILL YOU HELP ME RECOVER THE *BOY*...
...OR FORCE ME TO *KILL* THE MOTHER-TO-BE?
CAN I GIVE YOU A LITTLE ADVICE, KANG?
JESS, *DON'T*--
NEVER THREATEN A PREGNANT WOMAN.
ESPECIALLY ONE WITH *POWERS*.

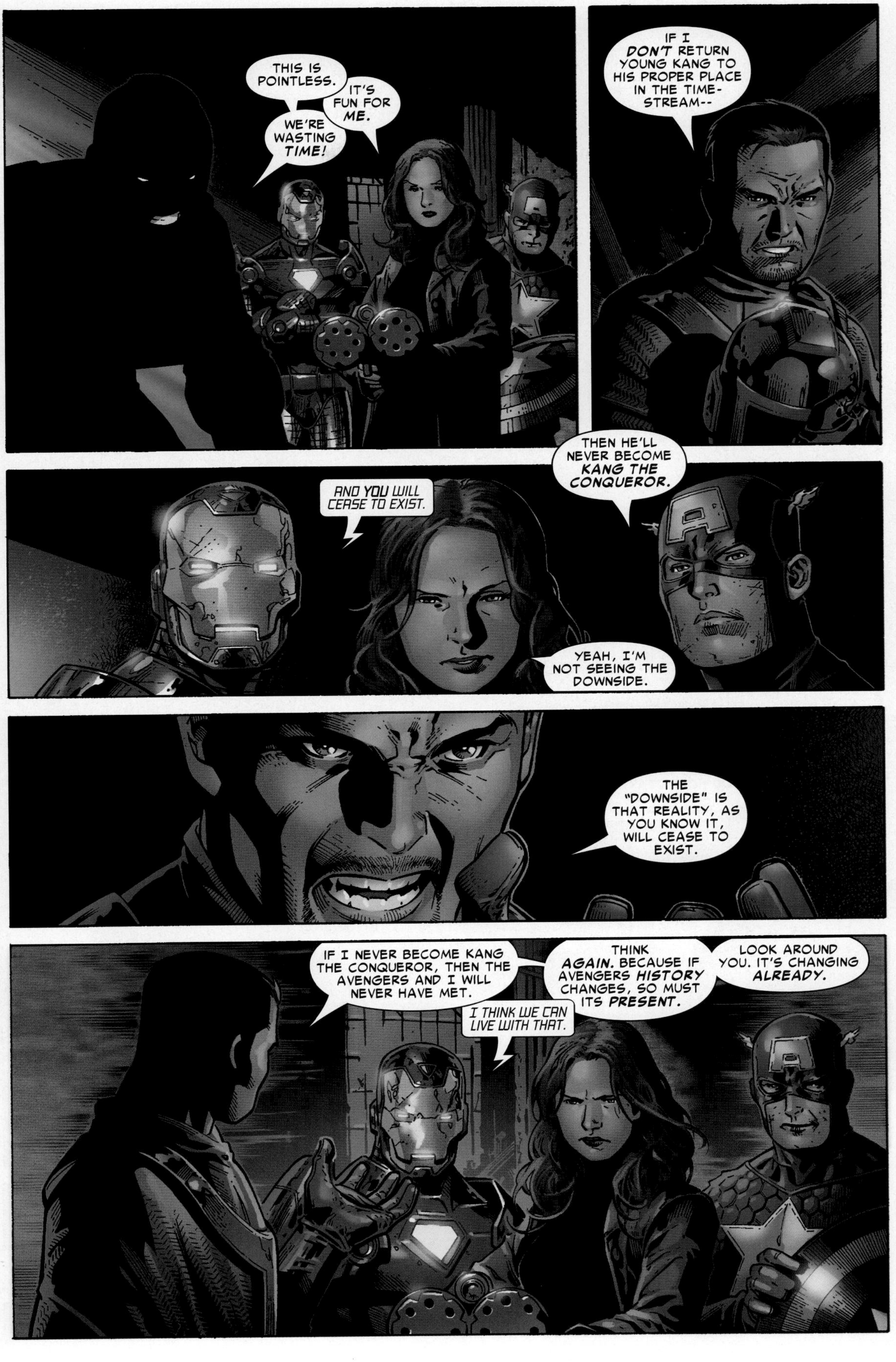

THIS IS POINTLESS.
WE'RE WASTING *TIME!*
IT'S FUN FOR *ME.*
IF I *DON'T* RETURN YOUNG KANG TO HIS PROPER PLACE IN THE TIME-STREAM--
THEN HE'LL NEVER BECOME *KANG THE CONQUEROR.*
AND *YOU* WILL CEASE TO EXIST.
YEAH, I'M NOT SEEING THE DOWNSIDE.
THE "DOWNSIDE" IS THAT REALITY, AS YOU KNOW IT, WILL CEASE TO EXIST.
IF I NEVER BECOME KANG THE CONQUEROR, THEN THE AVENGERS AND I WILL NEVER HAVE MET.
I THINK WE CAN LIVE WITH THAT.
THINK *AGAIN.* BECAUSE IF AVENGERS *HISTORY* CHANGES, SO MUST ITS *PRESENT.*
LOOK AROUND YOU. IT'S CHANGING *ALREADY.*

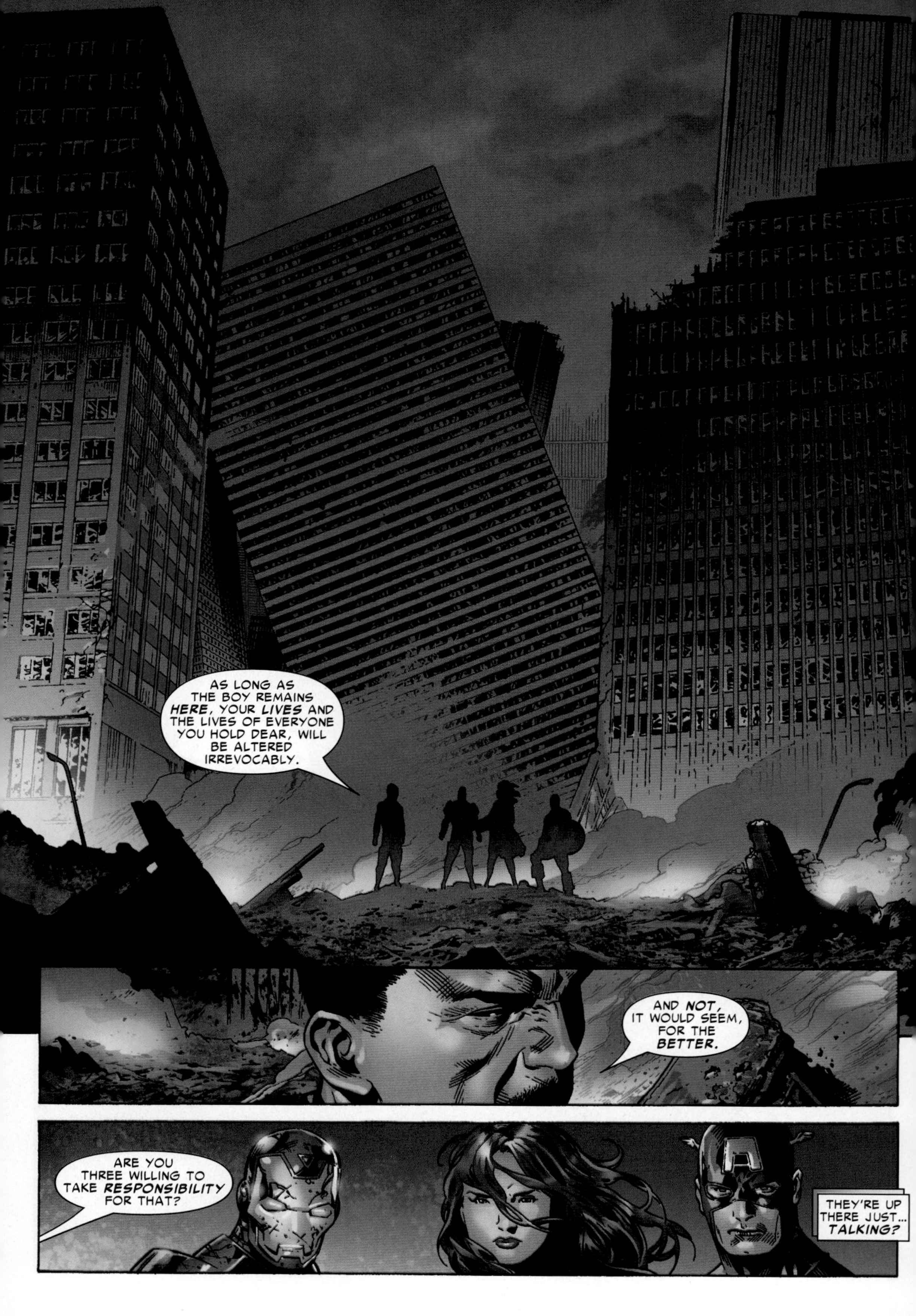

AS LONG AS THE BOY REMAINS HERE, YOUR LIVES AND THE LIVES OF EVERYONE YOU HOLD DEAR, WILL BE ALTERED IRREVOCABLY.
AND NOT, IT WOULD SEEM, FOR THE BETTER.
ARE YOU THREE WILLING TO TAKE RESPONSIBILITY FOR THAT?
THEY'RE UP THERE JUST... TALKING?

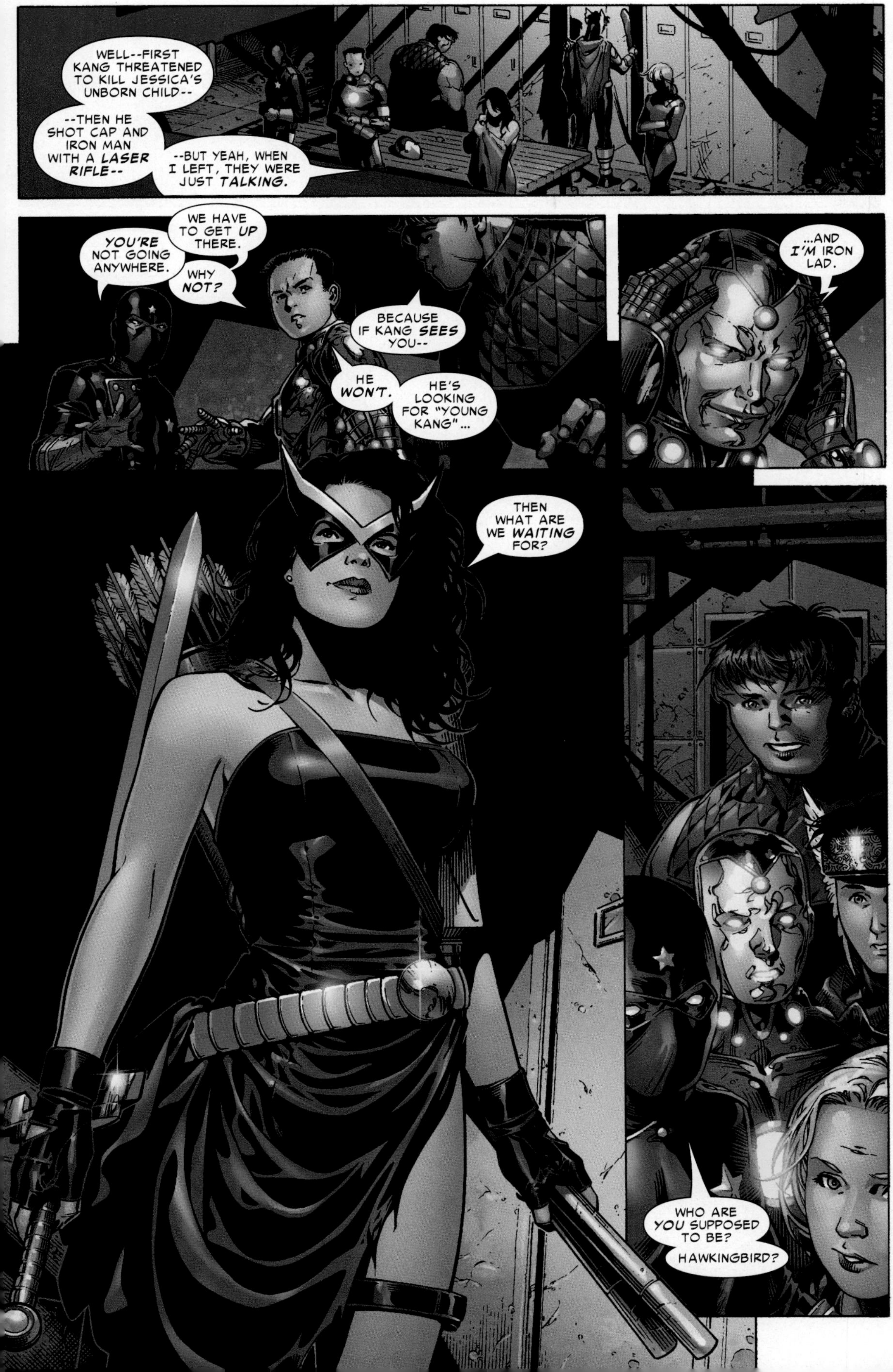
WELL--FIRST KANG THREATENED TO KILL JESSICA'S UNBORN CHILD--
--THEN HE SHOT CAP AND IRON MAN WITH A LASER RIFLE--
--BUT YEAH, WHEN I LEFT, THEY WERE JUST TALKING.
YOU'RE NOT GOING ANYWHERE.
WE HAVE TO GET UP THERE.
WHY NOT?
BECAUSE IF KANG SEES YOU--
HE WON'T.
HE'S LOOKING FOR "YOUNG KANG"...
...AND I'M IRON LAD.
THEN WHAT ARE WE WAITING FOR?
WHO ARE YOU SUPPOSED TO BE?
HAWKINGBIRD?

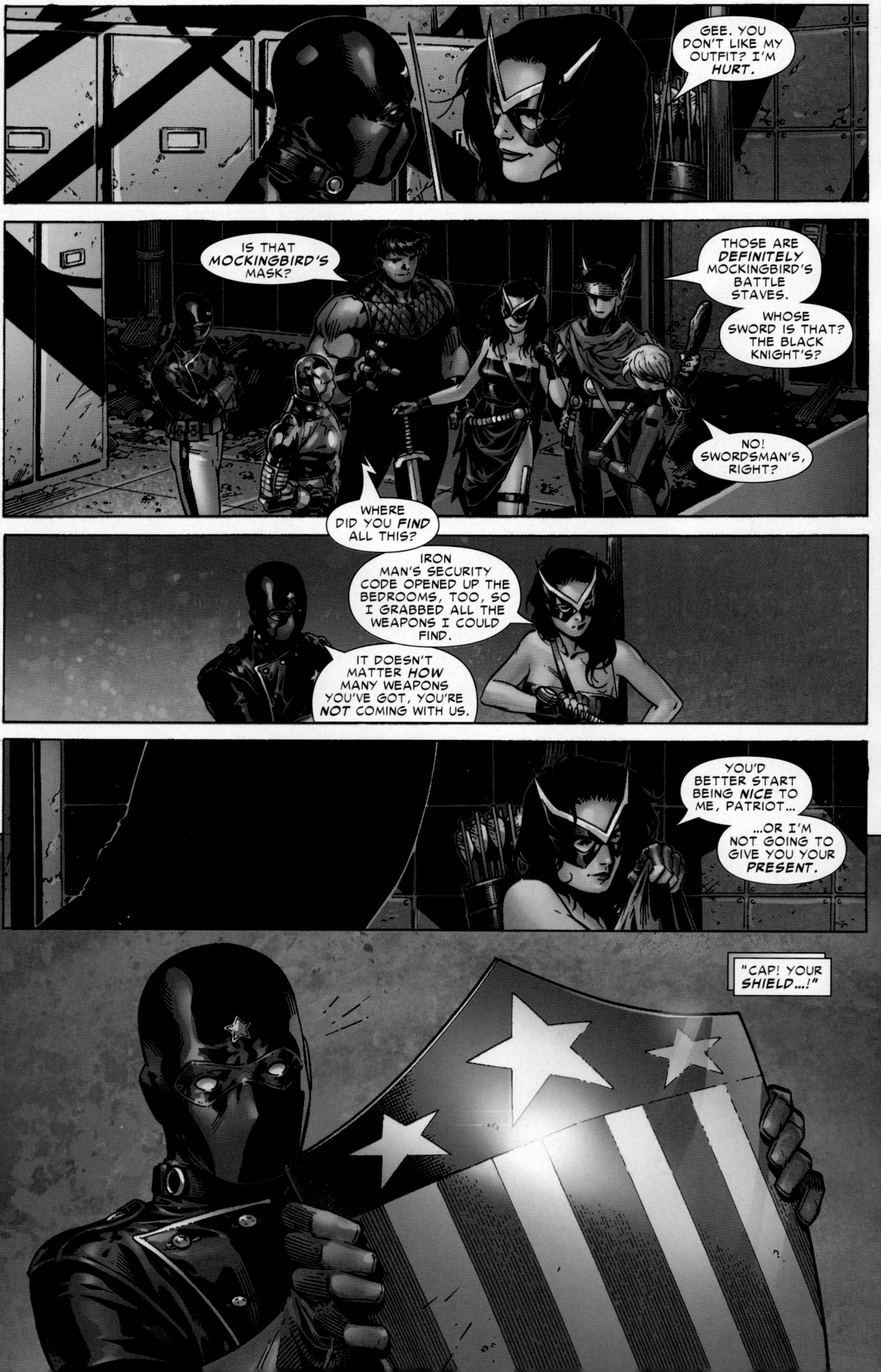

GEE. YOU DON'T LIKE MY OUTFIT? I'M HURT.
IS THAT MOCKINGBIRD'S MASK?
THOSE ARE DEFINITELY MOCKINGBIRD'S BATTLE STAVES.
WHOSE SWORD IS THAT? THE BLACK KNIGHT'S?
NO! SWORDSMAN'S, RIGHT?
WHERE DID YOU FIND ALL THIS?
IRON MAN'S SECURITY CODE OPENED UP THE BEDROOMS, TOO, SO I GRABBED ALL THE WEAPONS I COULD FIND.
IT DOESN'T MATTER HOW MANY WEAPONS YOU'VE GOT, YOU'RE NOT COMING WITH US.
YOU'D BETTER START BEING NICE TO ME, PATRIOT...
...OR I'M NOT GOING TO GIVE YOU YOUR PRESENT.
"CAP! YOUR SHIELD...!"

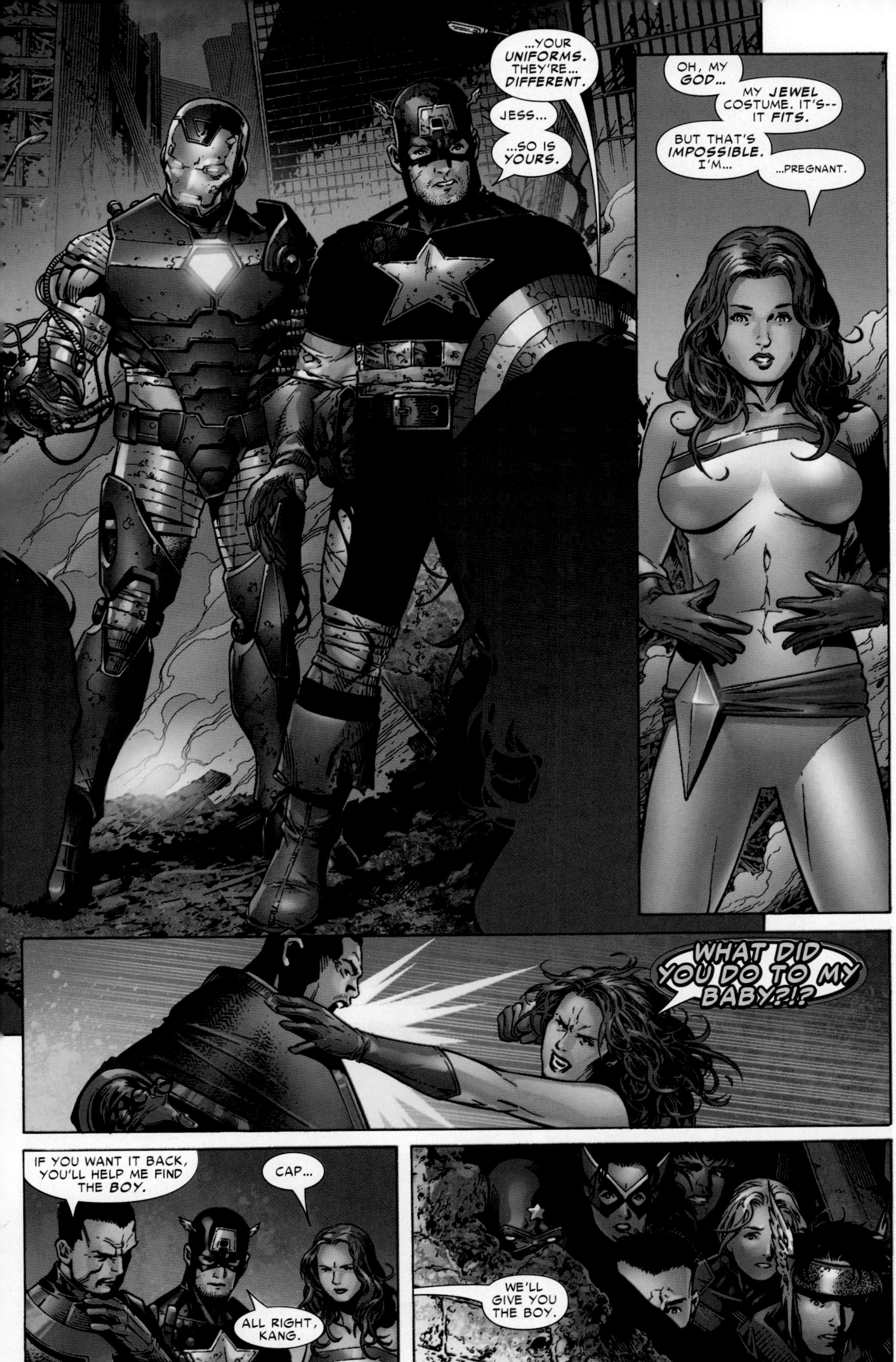

...YOUR UNIFORMS. THEY'RE... DIFFERENT.
JESS...
...SO IS YOURS.
OH, MY GOD...
MY JEWEL COSTUME. IT'S-- IT FITS.
BUT THAT'S IMPOSSIBLE. I'M...
...PREGNANT.
WHAT DID YOU DO TO MY BABY?!?
IF YOU WANT IT BACK, YOU'LL HELP ME FIND THE BOY.
CAP...
ALL RIGHT, KANG.
WE'LL GIVE YOU THE BOY.

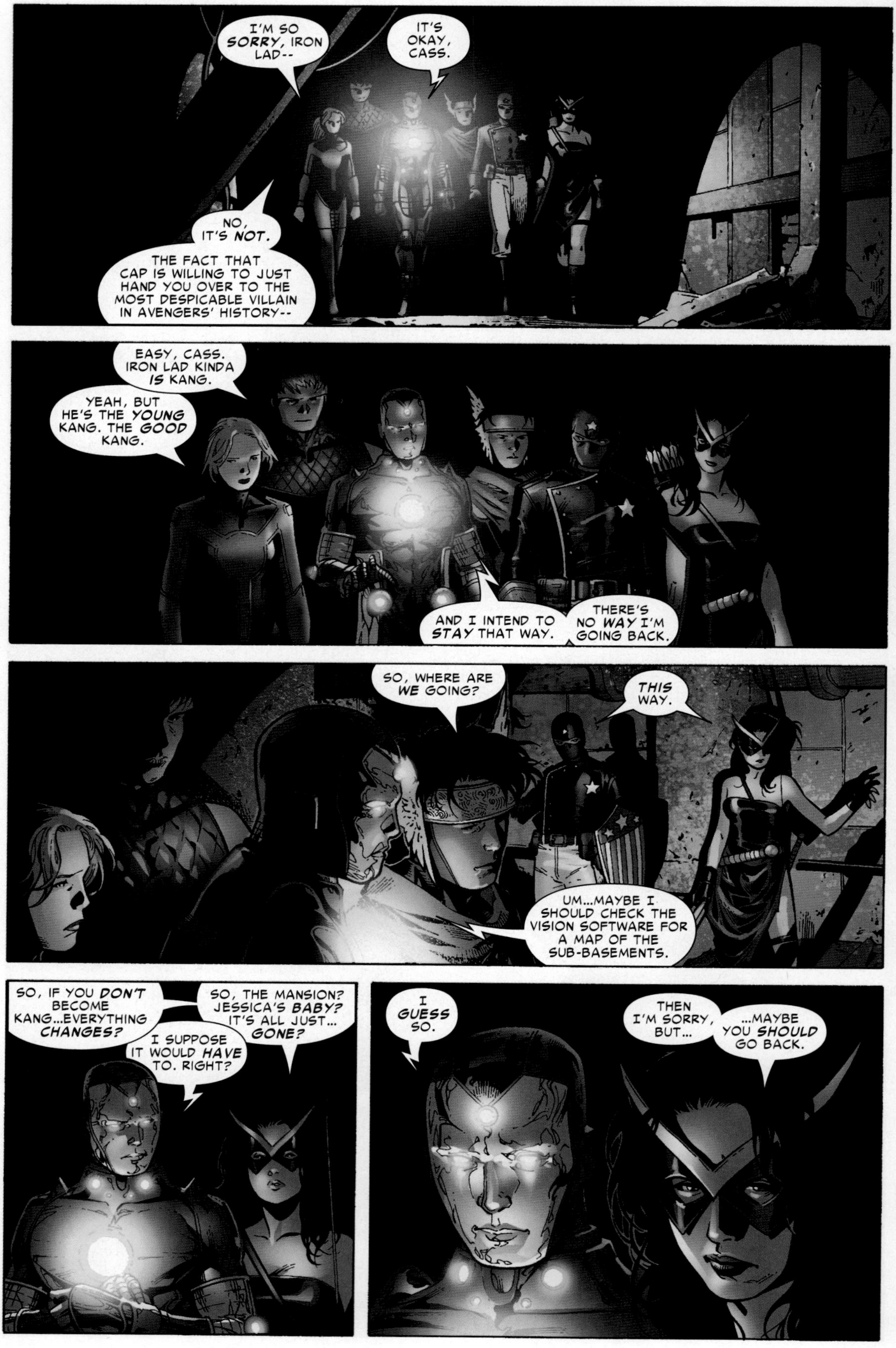
I'M SO SORRY, IRON LAD--
IT'S OKAY, CASS.
NO, IT'S NOT.
THE FACT THAT CAP IS WILLING TO JUST HAND YOU OVER TO THE MOST DESPICABLE VILLAIN IN AVENGERS' HISTORY--
EASY, CASS. IRON LAD KINDA IS KANG.
YEAH, BUT HE'S THE YOUNG KANG. THE GOOD KANG.
AND I INTEND TO STAY THAT WAY.
THERE'S NO WAY I'M GOING BACK.
SO, WHERE ARE WE GOING?
THIS WAY.
UM...MAYBE I SHOULD CHECK THE VISION SOFTWARE FOR A MAP OF THE SUB-BASEMENTS.
SO, IF YOU DON'T BECOME KANG...EVERYTHING CHANGES?
SO, THE MANSION? JESSICA'S BABY? IT'S ALL JUST... GONE?
I SUPPOSE IT WOULD HAVE TO. RIGHT?
I GUESS SO.
THEN I'M SORRY, BUT...
...MAYBE YOU SHOULD GO BACK.

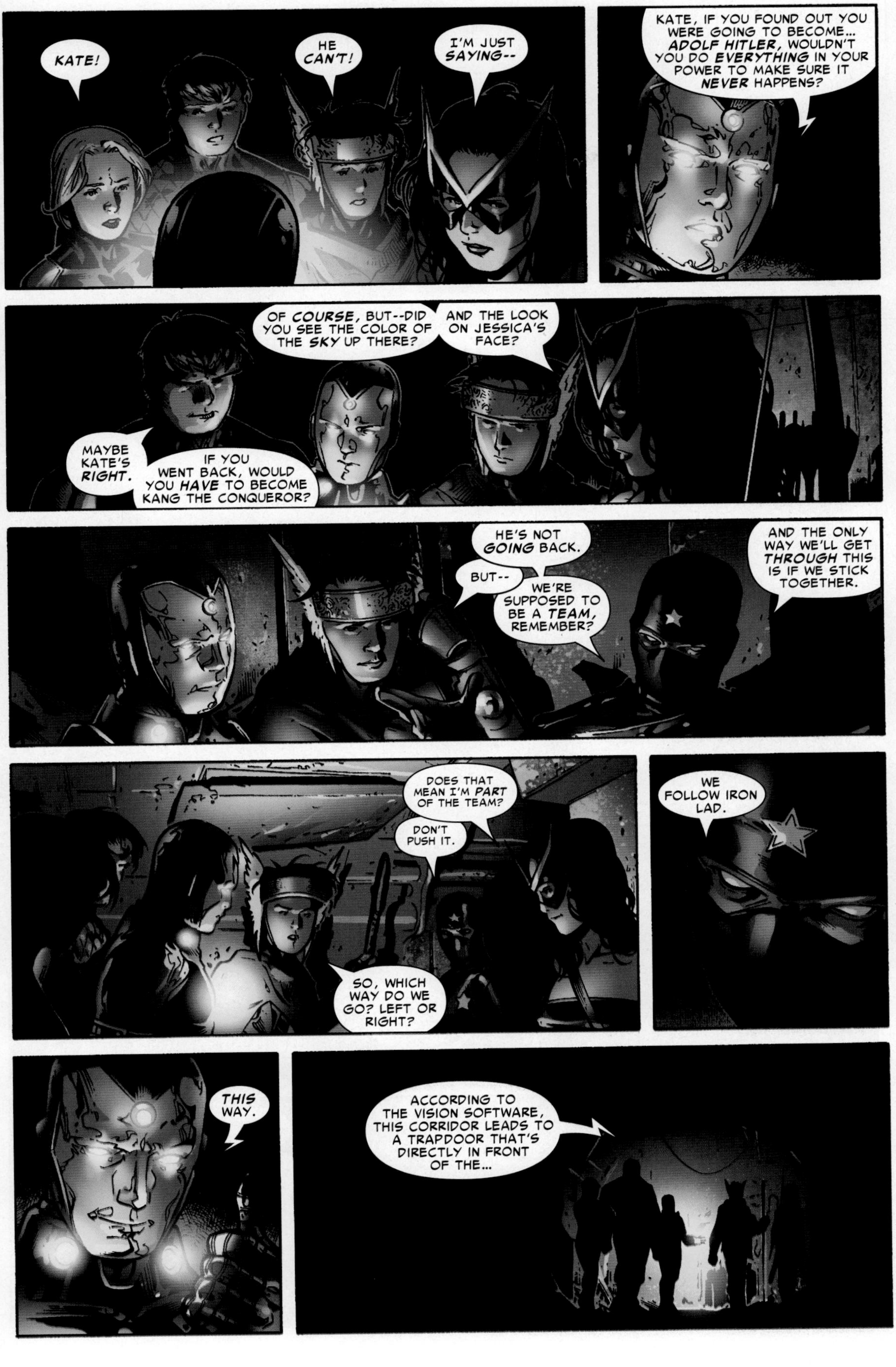
KATE!
HE CAN'T!
I'M JUST SAYING--
KATE, IF YOU FOUND OUT YOU WERE GOING TO BECOME... ADOLF HITLER, WOULDN'T YOU DO EVERYTHING IN YOUR POWER TO MAKE SURE IT NEVER HAPPENS?
OF COURSE, BUT--DID YOU SEE THE COLOR OF THE SKY UP THERE?
AND THE LOOK ON JESSICA'S FACE?
MAYBE KATE'S RIGHT.
IF YOU WENT BACK, WOULD YOU HAVE TO BECOME KANG THE CONQUEROR?
HE'S NOT GOING BACK.
BUT--
WE'RE SUPPOSED TO BE A TEAM, REMEMBER?
AND THE ONLY WAY WE'LL GET THROUGH THIS IS IF WE STICK TOGETHER.
DOES THAT MEAN I'M PART OF THE TEAM?
DON'T PUSH IT.
SO, WHICH WAY DO WE GO? LEFT OR RIGHT?
WE FOLLOW IRON LAD.
THIS WAY.
ACCORDING TO THE VISION SOFTWARE, THIS CORRIDOR LEADS TO A TRAPDOOR THAT'S DIRECTLY IN FRONT OF THE...

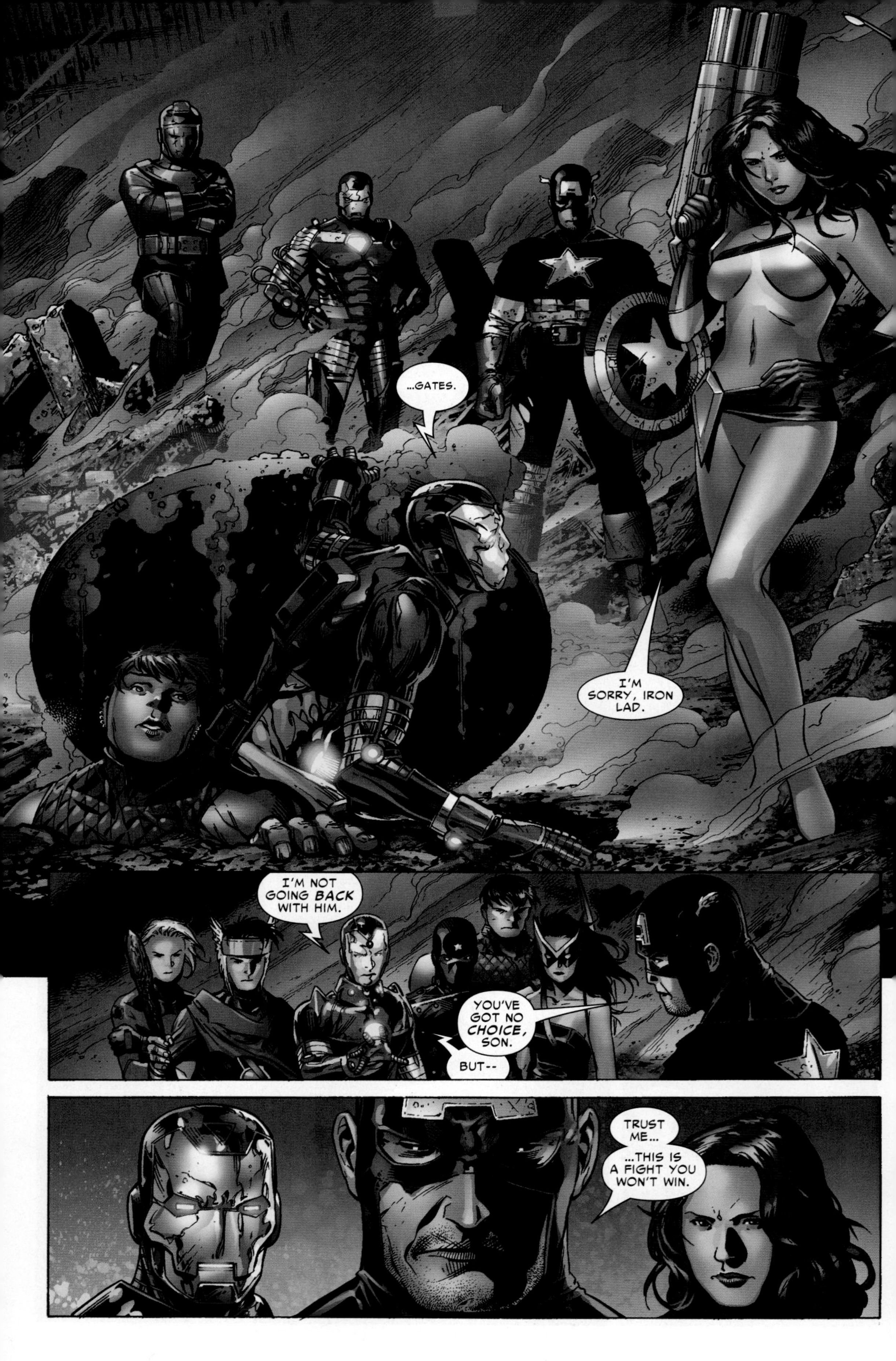
...GATES.
I'M SORRY, IRON LAD.
I'M NOT GOING BACK WITH HIM.
YOU'VE GOT NO CHOICE, SON.
BUT--
TRUST ME...
...THIS IS A FIGHT YOU WON'T WIN.

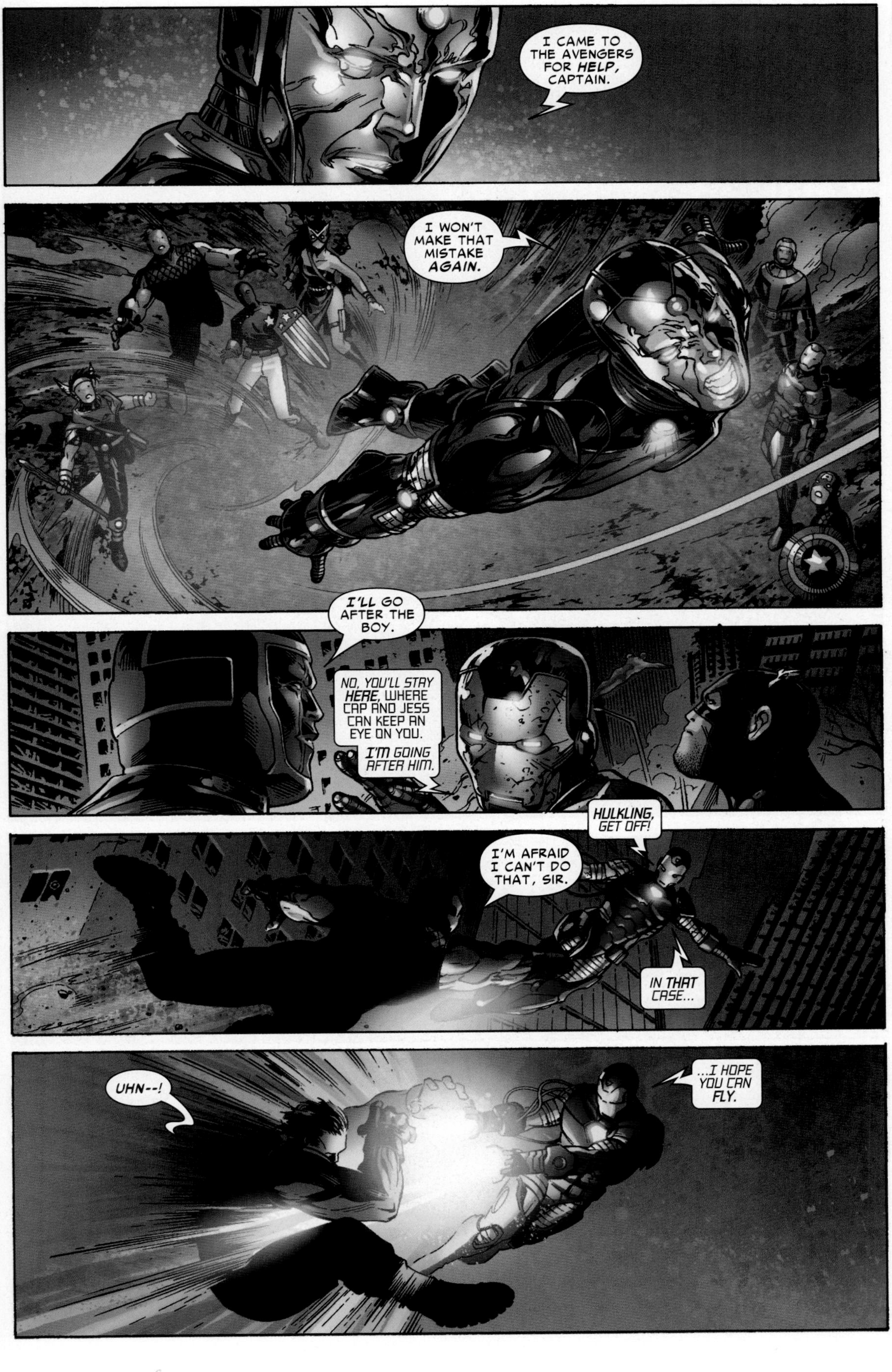
I CAME TO THE AVENGERS FOR HELP, CAPTAIN.
I WON'T MAKE THAT MISTAKE AGAIN.
I'LL GO AFTER THE BOY.
NO, YOU'LL STAY HERE, WHERE CAP AND JESS CAN KEEP AN EYE ON YOU.
I'M GOING AFTER HIM.
HULKLING, GET OFF!
I'M AFRAID I CAN'T DO THAT, SIR.
IN THAT CASE...
UHN--!
...I HOPE YOU CAN FLY.

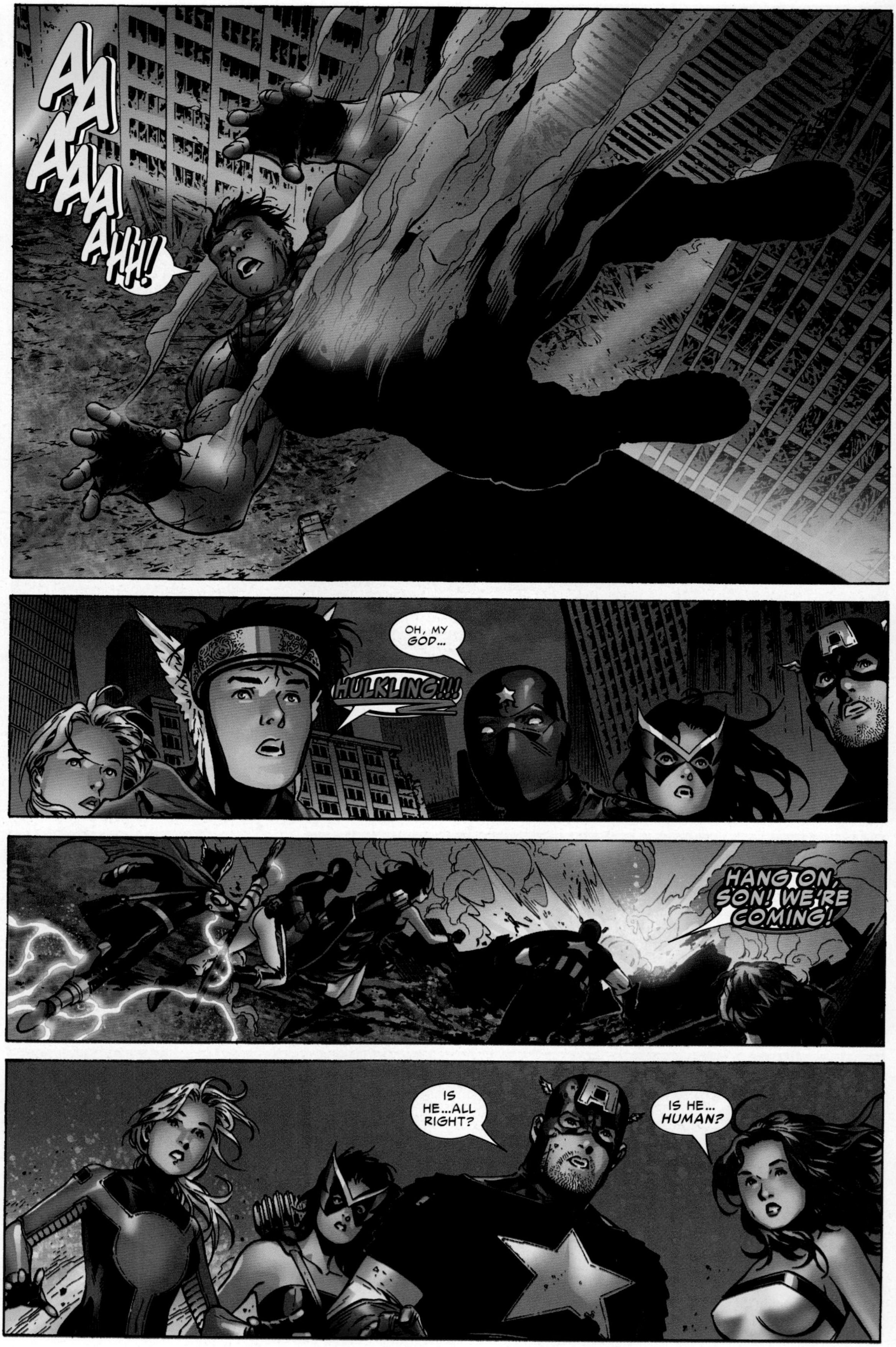

AAAAAAAHH!!
OH, MY GOD...
HULKLING!!!
HANG ON, SON! WE'RE COMING!
IS HE...ALL RIGHT?
IS HE... HUMAN?

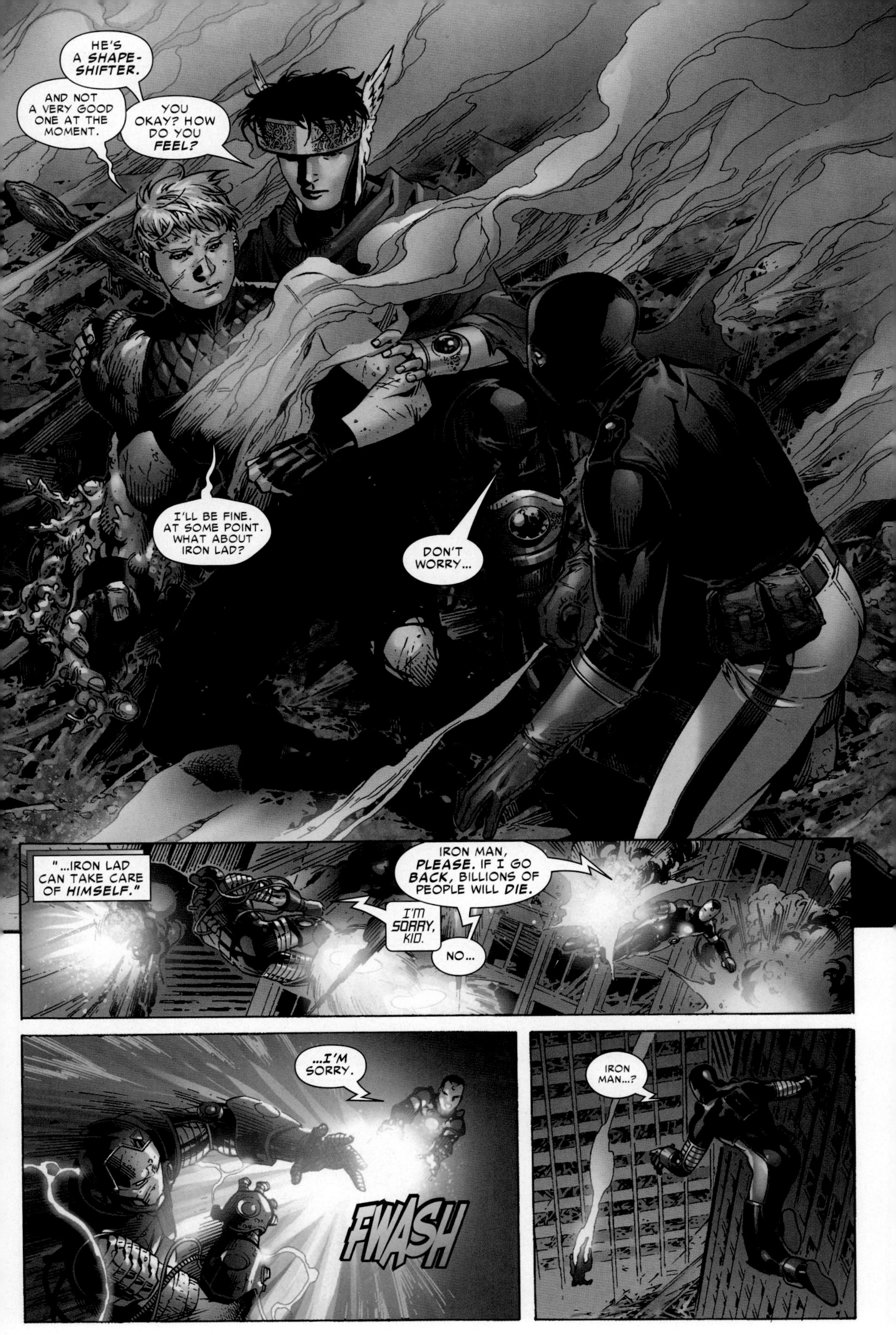
HE'S A SHAPE-SHIFTER.
AND NOT A VERY GOOD ONE AT THE MOMENT.
YOU OKAY? HOW DO YOU FEEL?
I'LL BE FINE. AT SOME POINT. WHAT ABOUT IRON LAD?
DON'T WORRY...
"...IRON LAD CAN TAKE CARE OF HIMSELF."
IRON MAN, PLEASE. IF I GO BACK, BILLIONS OF PEOPLE WILL DIE.
I'M SORRY, KID.
NO...
...I'M SORRY.
FWASH
IRON MAN...?

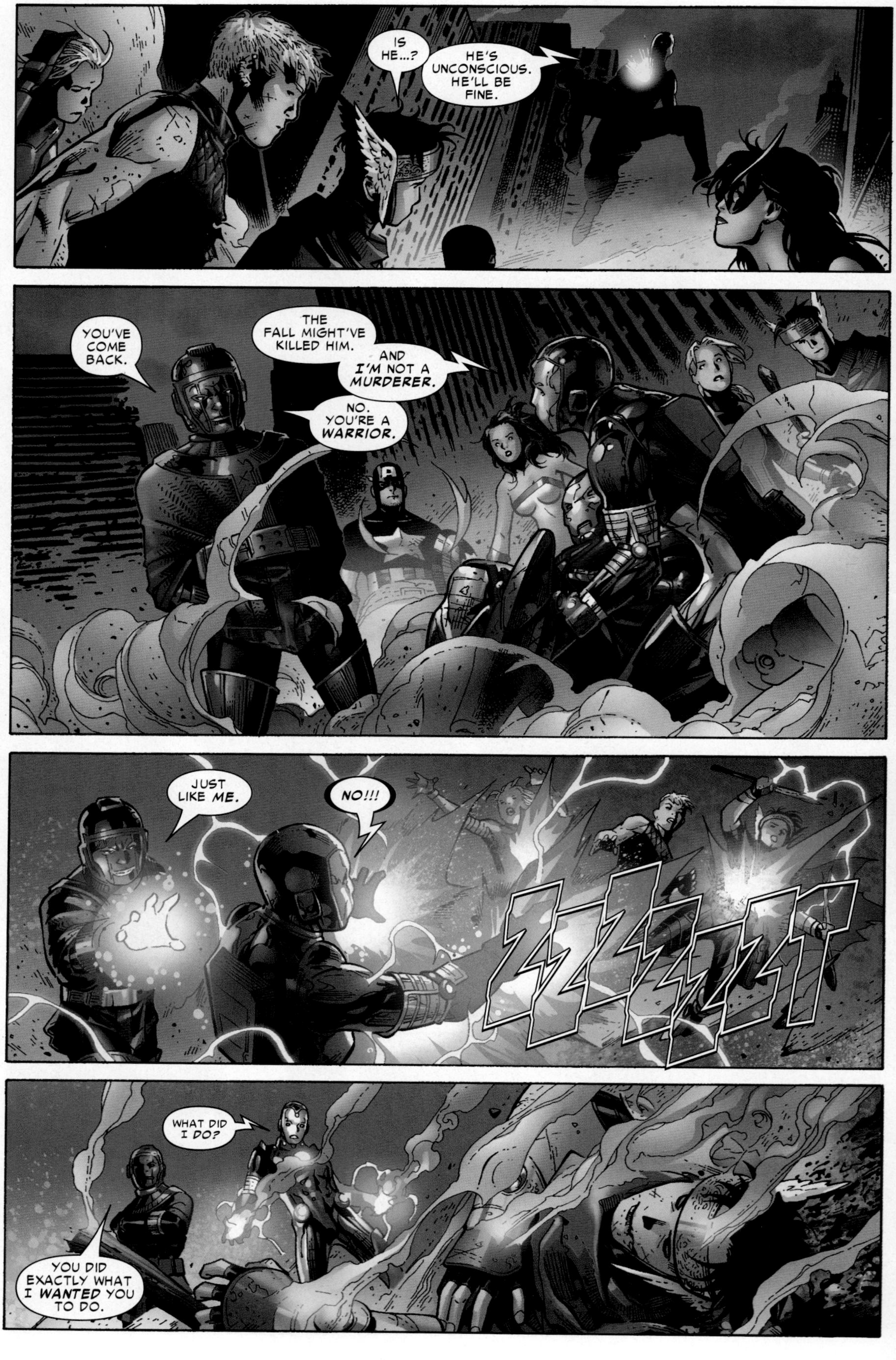
IS HE...?
HE'S UNCONSCIOUS. HE'LL BE FINE.
YOU'VE COME BACK.
THE FALL MIGHT'VE KILLED HIM.
AND *I'M* NOT A *MURDERER*.
NO. YOU'RE A *WARRIOR*.
JUST LIKE *ME*.
NO!!!
ZZZZZZT
WHAT DID I *DO*?
YOU DID EXACTLY WHAT I *WANTED* YOU TO DO.

AFTER ALL, YOU STOLE THAT ARMOR FROM *ME*, REMEMBER? *I'M* THE ONE WHO *BUILT* IT. AND NOW THAT YOU'RE WITHIN *RANGE*...

...I'M THE ONE *CONTROLLING* IT.

PLEASE! I'M BEGGING YOU!

PATRIOT... I C-CAN'T STOP IT...

RUN!

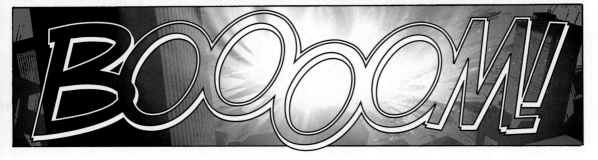

BOOOOM!

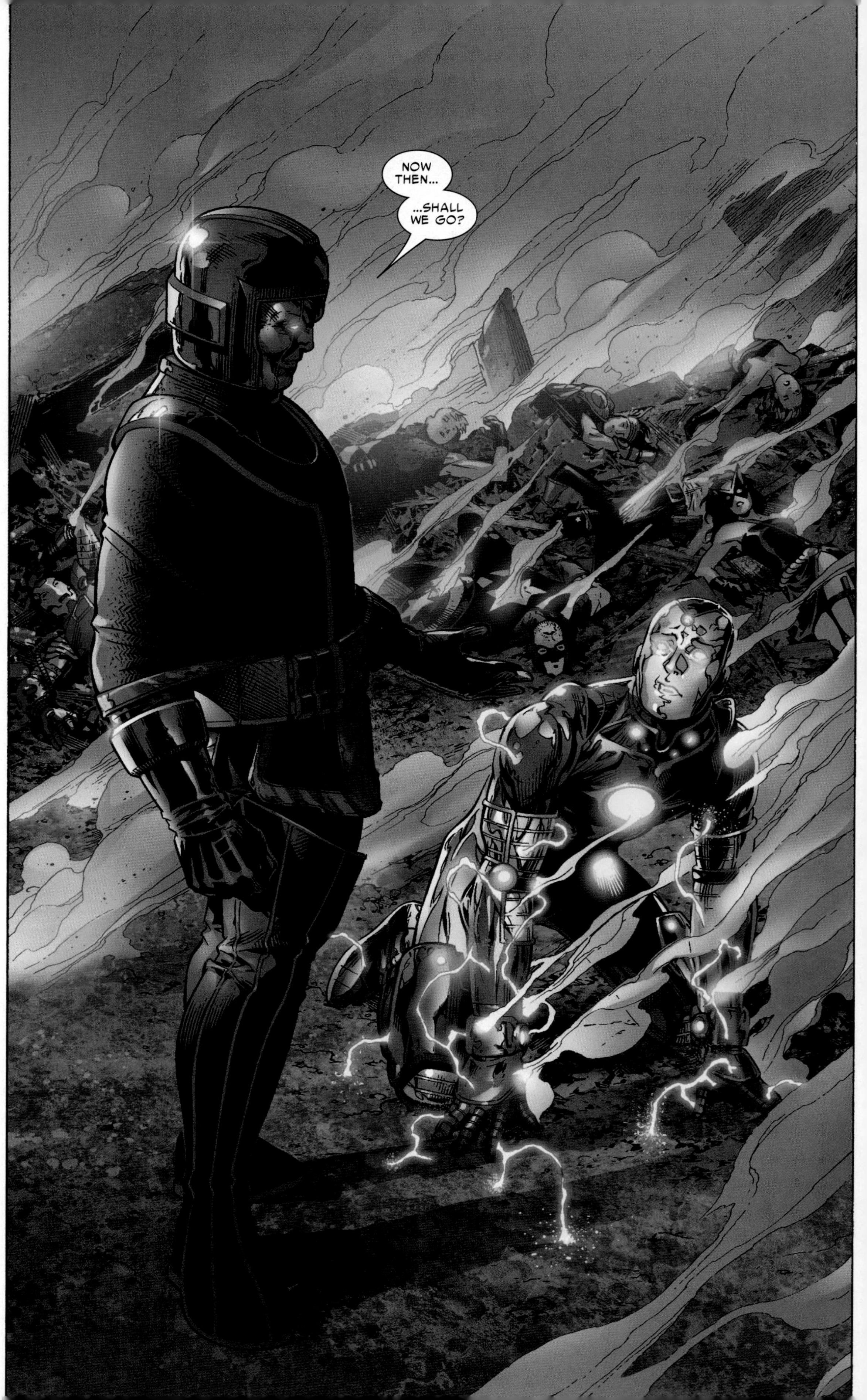
NOW THEN...
...SHALL WE GO?

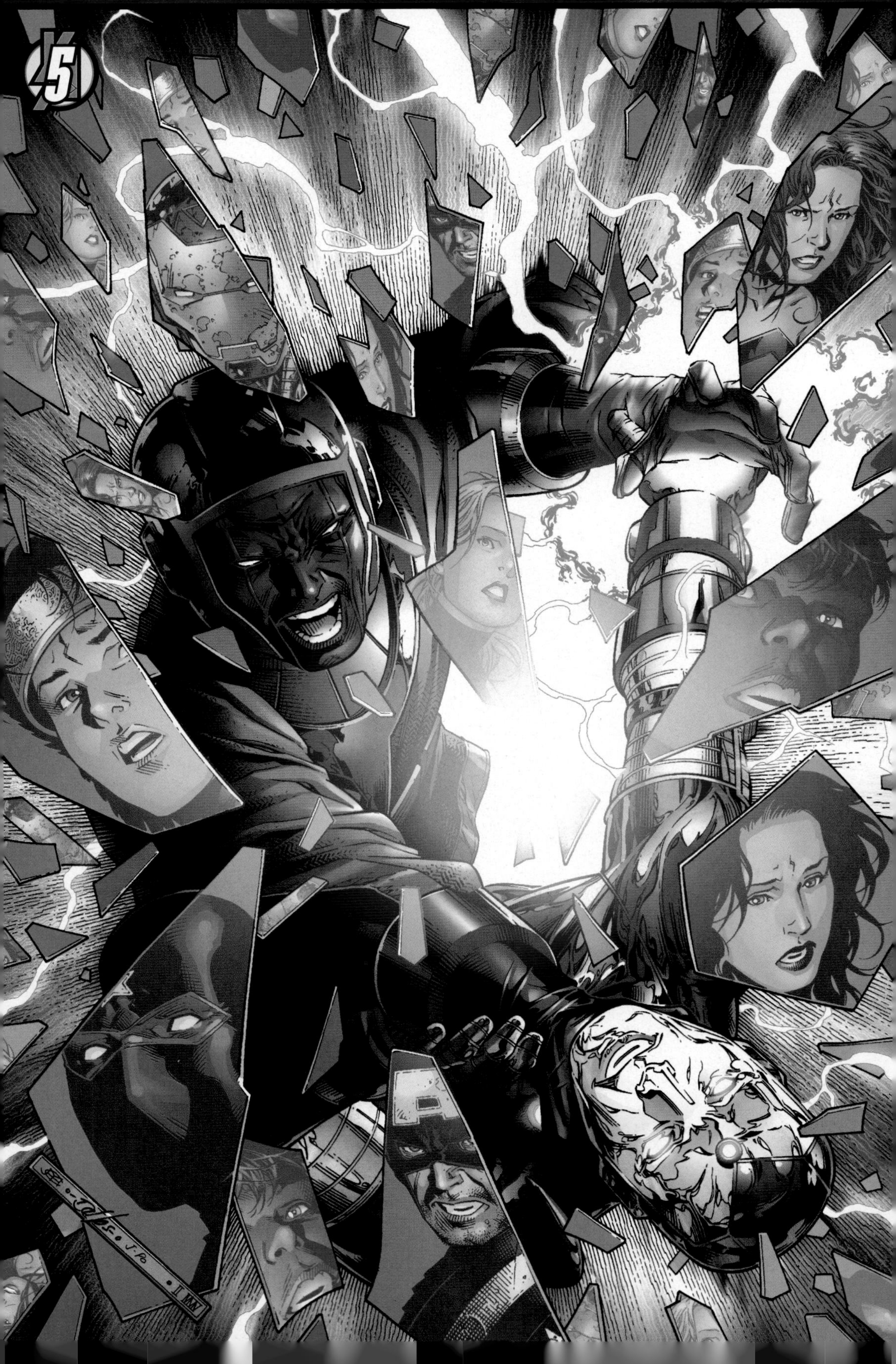

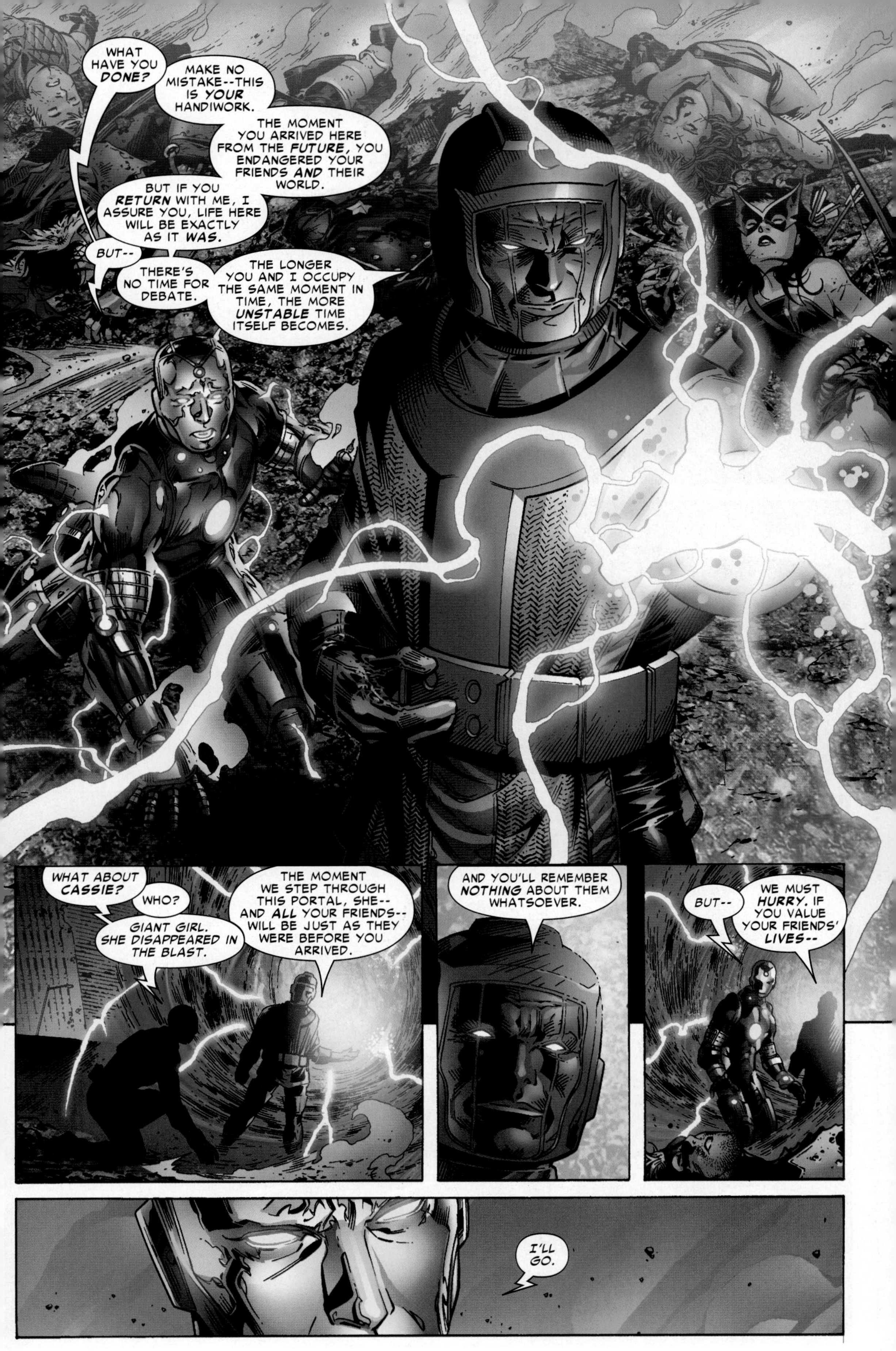
WHAT HAVE YOU DONE?
MAKE NO MISTAKE--THIS IS YOUR HANDIWORK.
THE MOMENT YOU ARRIVED HERE FROM THE FUTURE, YOU ENDANGERED YOUR FRIENDS AND THEIR WORLD.
BUT IF YOU RETURN WITH ME, I ASSURE YOU, LIFE HERE WILL BE EXACTLY AS IT WAS.
BUT--
THERE'S NO TIME FOR DEBATE.
THE LONGER YOU AND I OCCUPY THE SAME MOMENT IN TIME, THE MORE UNSTABLE TIME ITSELF BECOMES.
WHAT ABOUT CASSIE?
WHO?
GIANT GIRL. SHE DISAPPEARED IN THE BLAST.
THE MOMENT WE STEP THROUGH THIS PORTAL, SHE-- AND ALL YOUR FRIENDS-- WILL BE JUST AS THEY WERE BEFORE YOU ARRIVED.
AND YOU'LL REMEMBER NOTHING ABOUT THEM WHATSOEVER.
BUT--
WE MUST HURRY. IF YOU VALUE YOUR FRIENDS' LIVES--
I'LL GO.

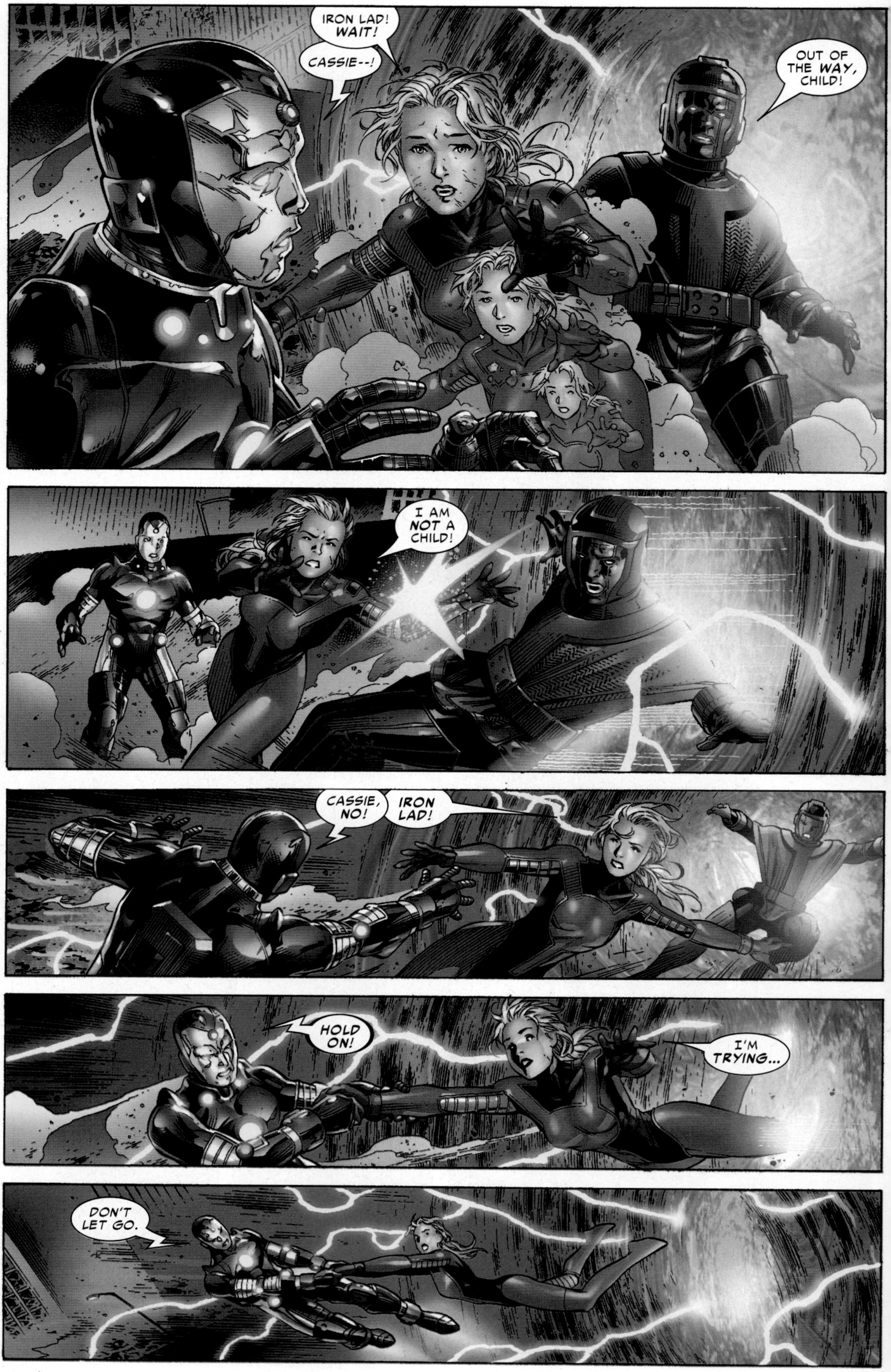
IRON LAD! WAIT!
CASSIE--!
OUT OF THE WAY, CHILD!
I AM NOT A CHILD!
CASSIE, NO!
IRON LAD!
HOLD ON!
I'M TRYING...
DON'T LET GO.

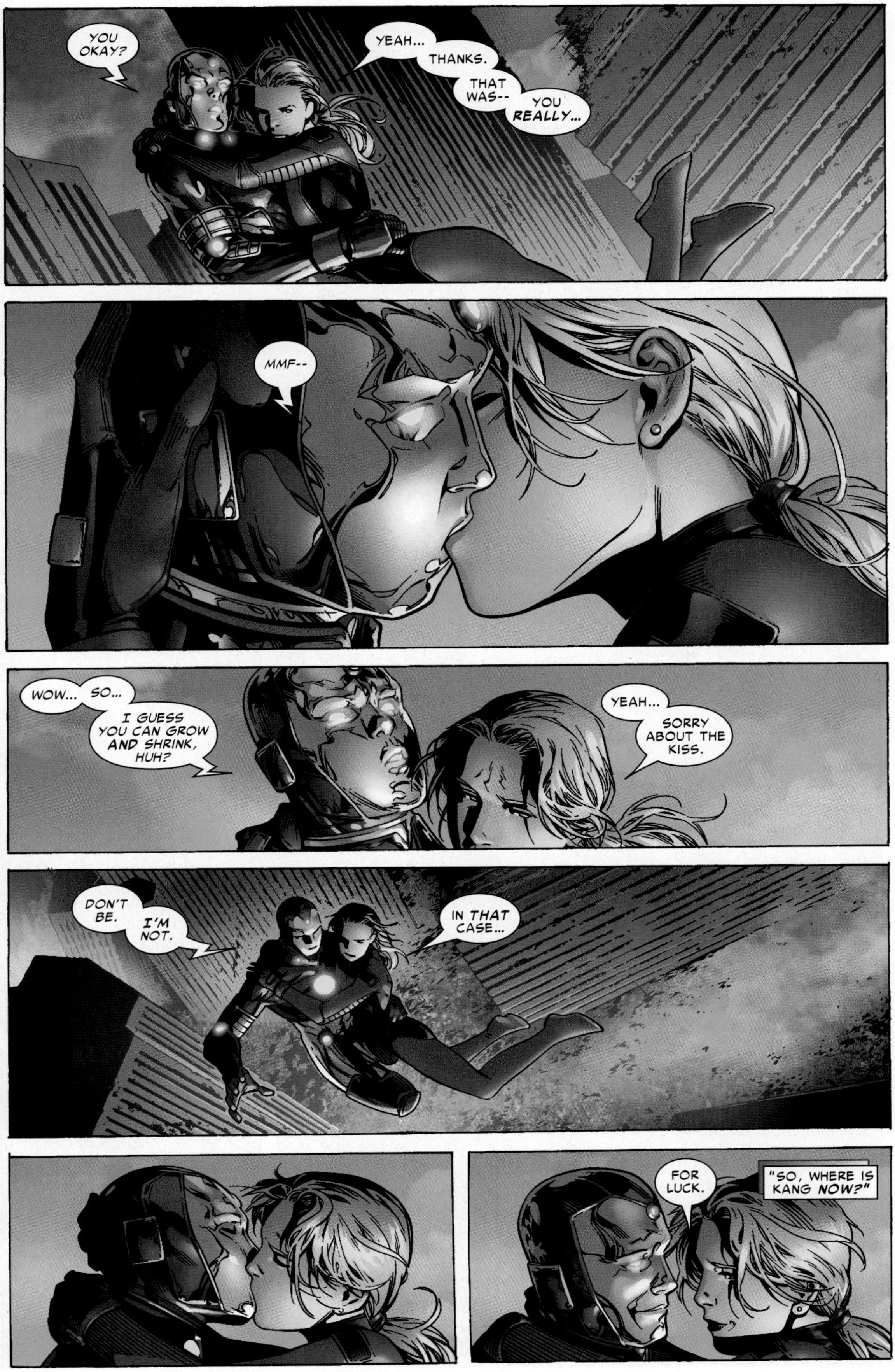
YOU OKAY?
YEAH...
THANKS.
THAT WAS--
YOU REALLY...
MMF--
WOW... SO...
I GUESS YOU CAN GROW AND SHRINK, HUH?
YEAH...
SORRY ABOUT THE KISS.
DON'T BE.
I'M NOT.
IN THAT CASE...
FOR LUCK.
"SO, WHERE IS KANG NOW?"

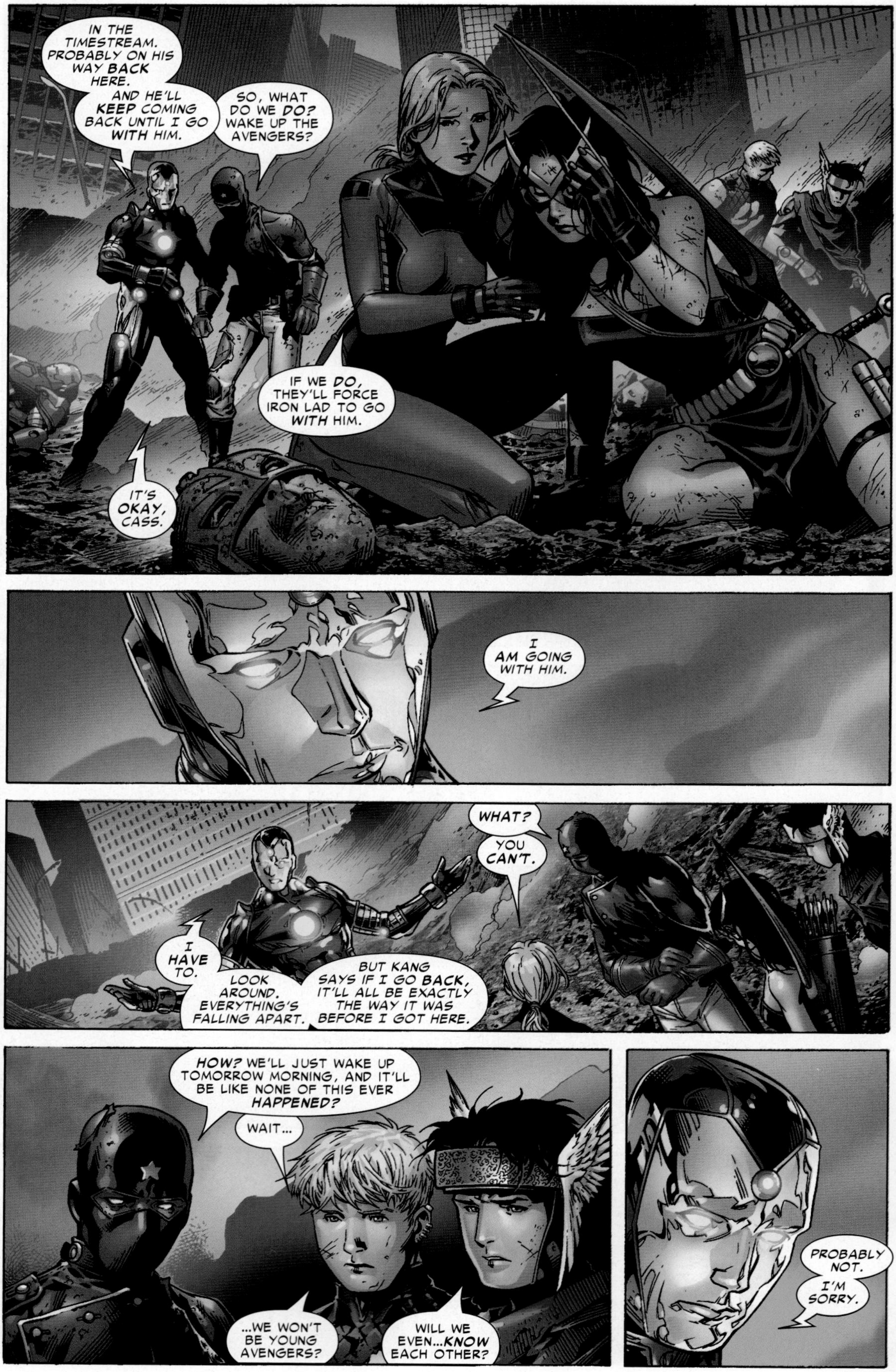
IN THE TIMESTREAM. PROBABLY ON HIS WAY BACK HERE.
AND HE'LL KEEP COMING BACK UNTIL I GO WITH HIM.
SO, WHAT DO WE DO? WAKE UP THE AVENGERS?
IF WE DO, THEY'LL FORCE IRON LAD TO GO WITH HIM.
IT'S OKAY, CASS.
I AM GOING WITH HIM.
WHAT?
YOU CAN'T.
I HAVE TO.
LOOK AROUND. EVERYTHING'S FALLING APART.
BUT KANG SAYS IF I GO BACK, IT'LL ALL BE EXACTLY THE WAY IT WAS BEFORE I GOT HERE.
HOW? WE'LL JUST WAKE UP TOMORROW MORNING, AND IT'LL BE LIKE NONE OF THIS EVER HAPPENED?
WAIT...
...WE WON'T BE YOUNG AVENGERS?
WILL WE EVEN...KNOW EACH OTHER?
PROBABLY NOT.
I'M SORRY.

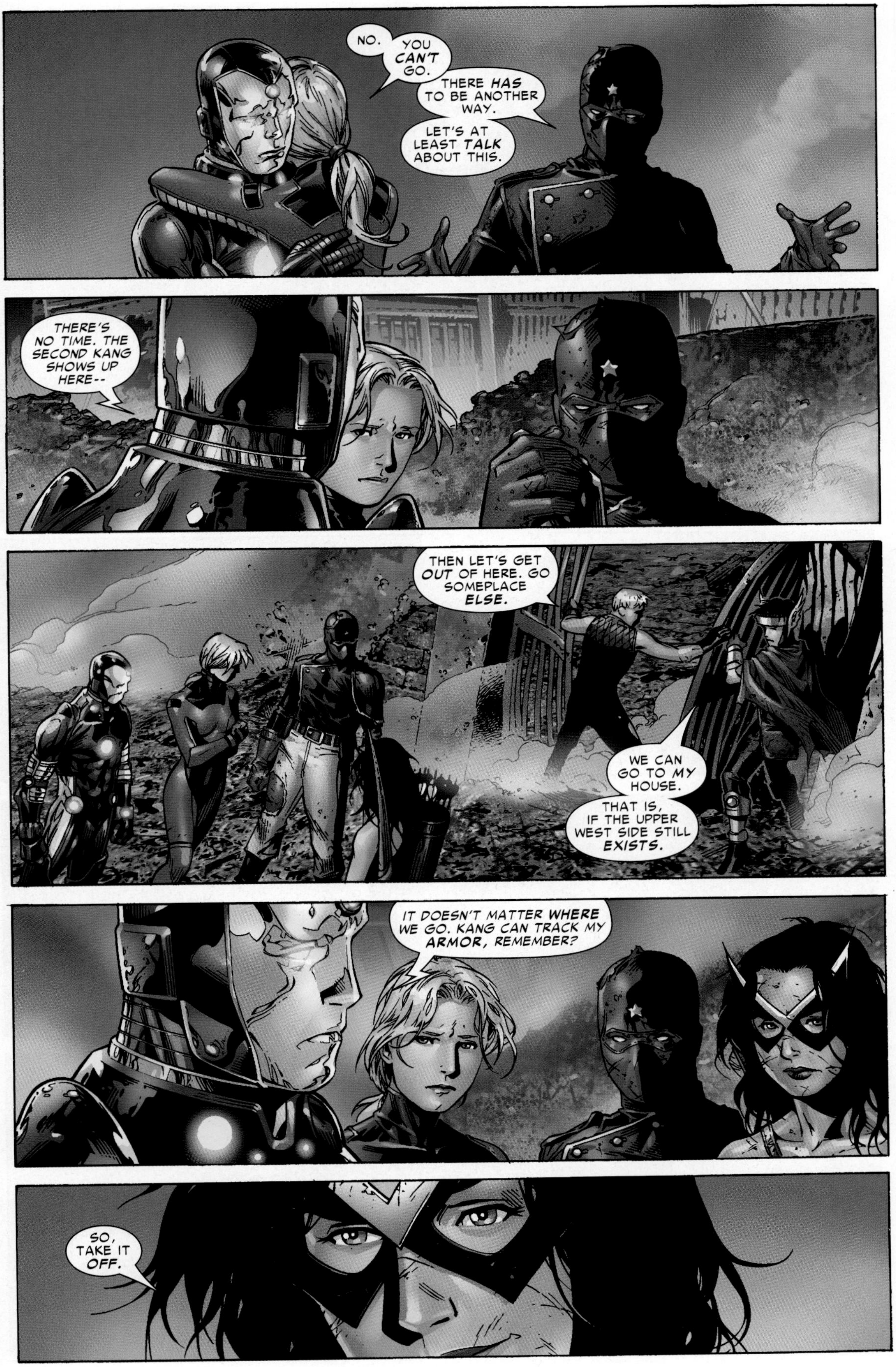
NO.
YOU CAN'T GO.
THERE HAS TO BE ANOTHER WAY.
LET'S AT LEAST TALK ABOUT THIS.
THERE'S NO TIME. THE SECOND KANG SHOWS UP HERE--
THEN LET'S GET OUT OF HERE. GO SOMEPLACE ELSE.
WE CAN GO TO MY HOUSE.
THAT IS, IF THE UPPER WEST SIDE STILL EXISTS.
IT DOESN'T MATTER WHERE WE GO. KANG CAN TRACK MY ARMOR, REMEMBER?
SO, TAKE IT OFF.

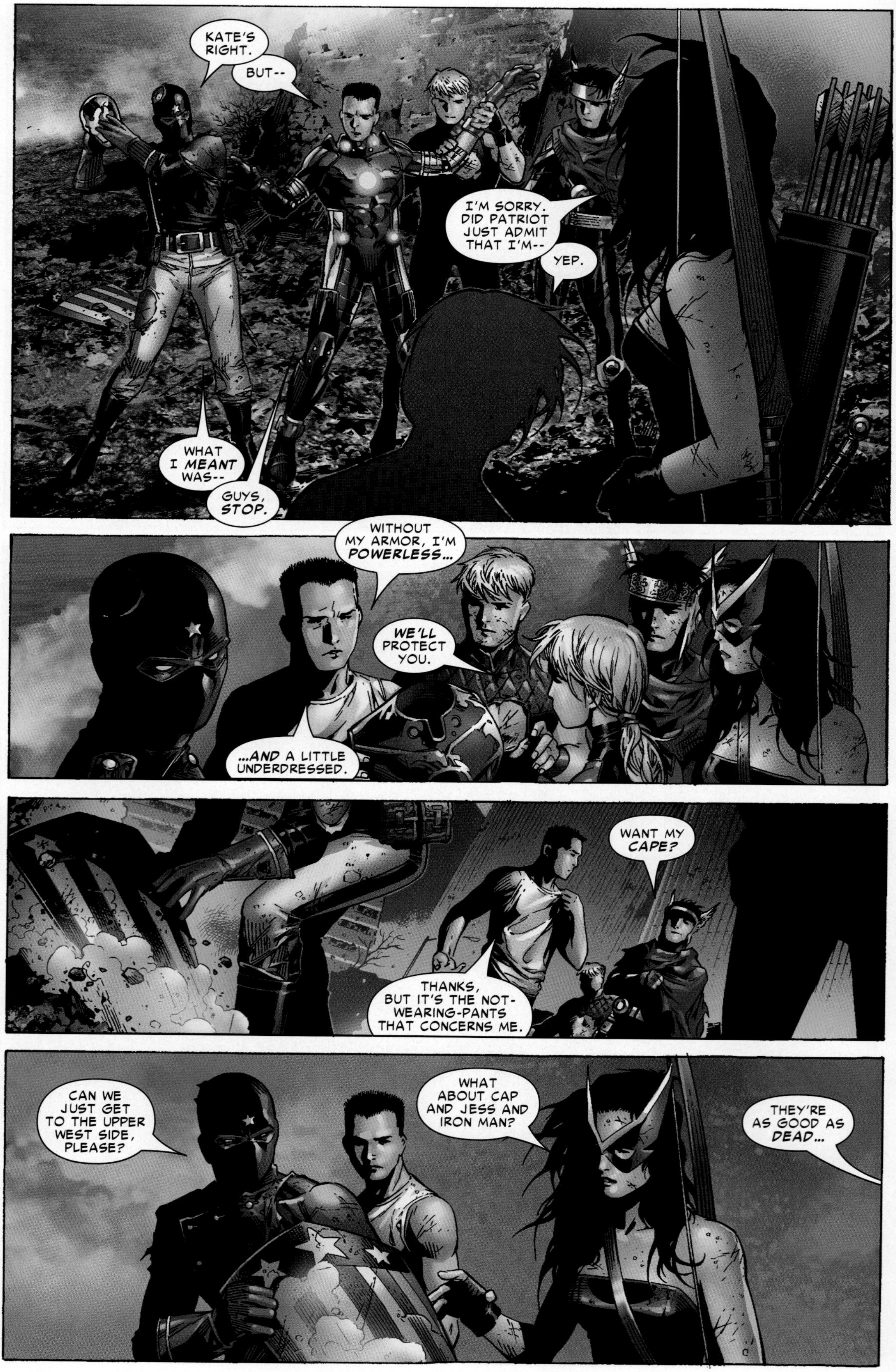
KATE'S RIGHT.
BUT--
I'M SORRY. DID PATRIOT JUST ADMIT THAT I'M--
YEP.
WHAT I MEANT WAS--
GUYS, STOP.
WITHOUT MY ARMOR, I'M POWERLESS...
WE'LL PROTECT YOU.
...AND A LITTLE UNDERDRESSED.
WANT MY CAPE?
THANKS, BUT IT'S THE NOT-WEARING-PANTS THAT CONCERNS ME.
CAN WE JUST GET TO THE UPPER WEST SIDE, PLEASE?
WHAT ABOUT CAP AND JESS AND IRON MAN?
THEY'RE AS GOOD AS DEAD...

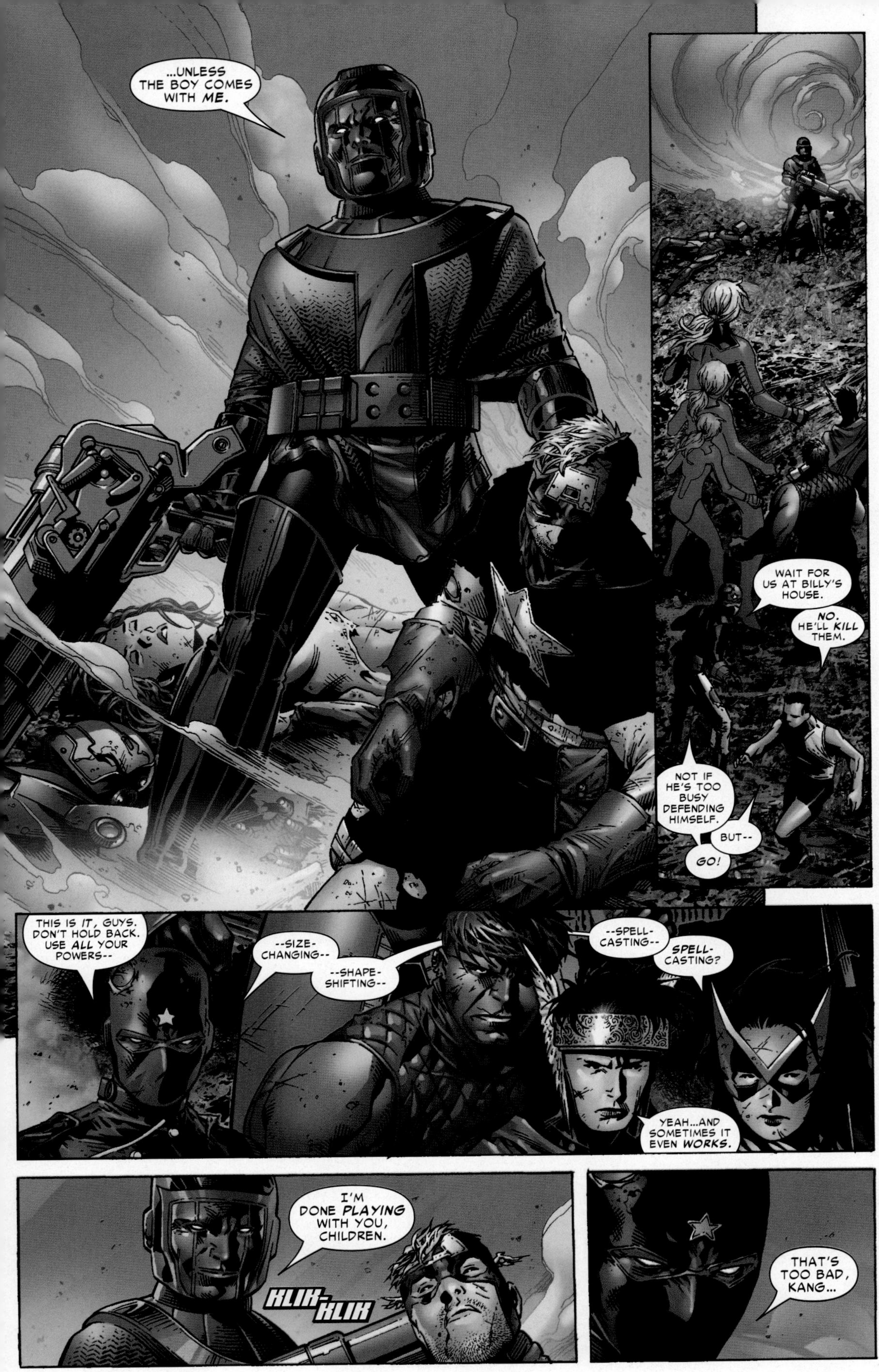
...UNLESS THE BOY COMES WITH ME.
WAIT FOR US AT BILLY'S HOUSE.
NO. HE'LL KILL THEM.
NOT IF HE'S TOO BUSY DEFENDING HIMSELF.
BUT--
GO!
THIS IS IT, GUYS. DON'T HOLD BACK. USE ALL YOUR POWERS--
--SIZE-CHANGING--
--SHAPE-SHIFTING--
--SPELL-CASTING--
SPELL-CASTING?
YEAH...AND SOMETIMES IT EVEN WORKS.
I'M DONE PLAYING WITH YOU, CHILDREN.
KLIK-KLIK
THAT'S TOO BAD, KANG...

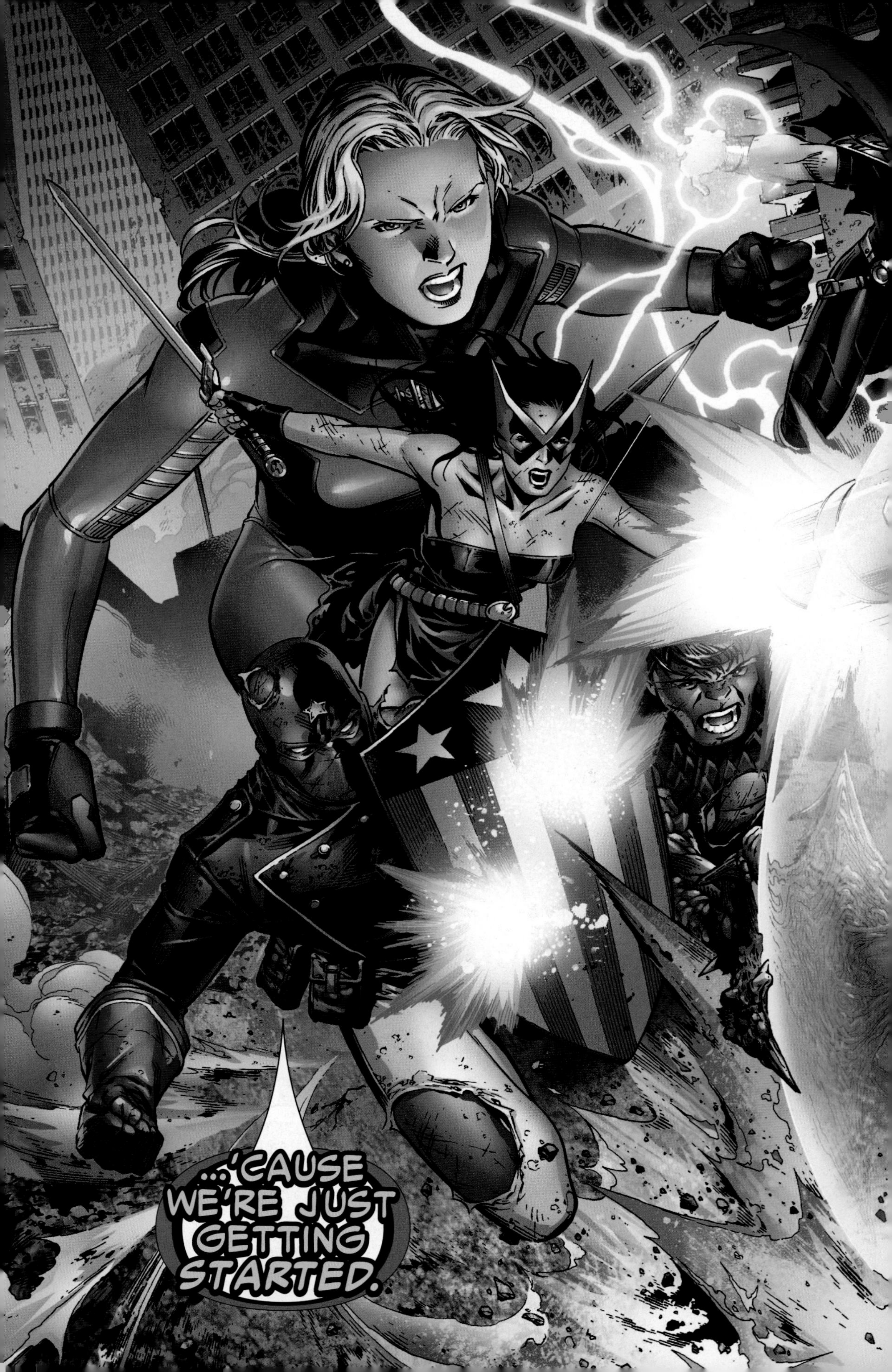

...'CAUSE WE'RE JUST GETTING STARTED.

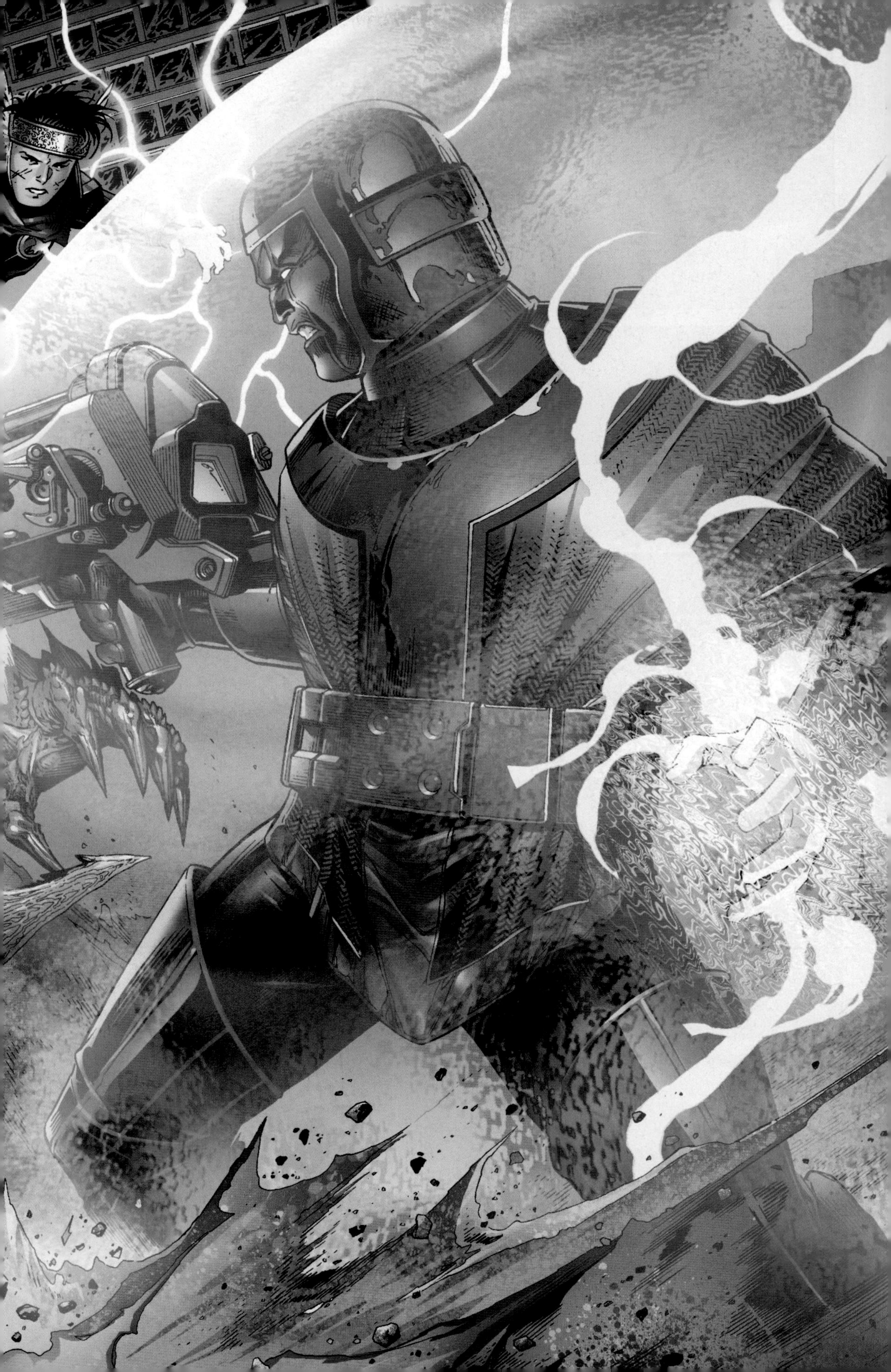

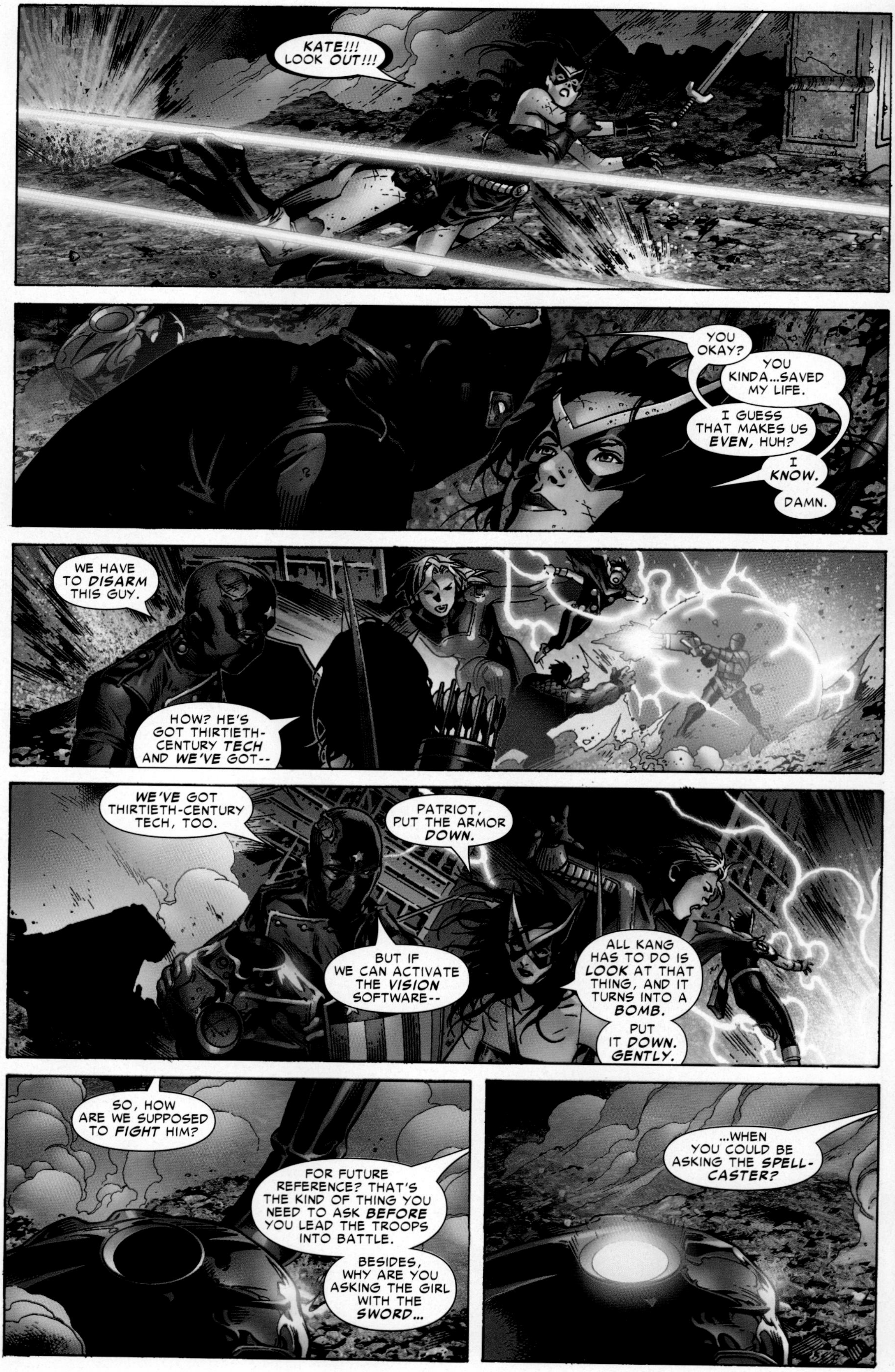
KATE!!! LOOK OUT!!!
YOU OKAY?
YOU KINDA...SAVED MY LIFE.
I GUESS THAT MAKES US EVEN, HUH?
I KNOW.
DAMN.
WE HAVE TO DISARM THIS GUY.
HOW? HE'S GOT THIRTIETH-CENTURY TECH AND WE'VE GOT--
WE'VE GOT THIRTIETH-CENTURY TECH, TOO.
PATRIOT, PUT THE ARMOR DOWN.
BUT IF WE CAN ACTIVATE THE VISION SOFTWARE--
ALL KANG HAS TO DO IS LOOK AT THAT THING, AND IT TURNS INTO A BOMB.
PUT IT DOWN. GENTLY.
SO, HOW ARE WE SUPPOSED TO FIGHT HIM?
FOR FUTURE REFERENCE? THAT'S THE KIND OF THING YOU NEED TO ASK BEFORE YOU LEAD THE TROOPS INTO BATTLE.
BESIDES, WHY ARE YOU ASKING THE GIRL WITH THE SWORD...
...WHEN YOU COULD BE ASKING THE SPELL-CASTER?

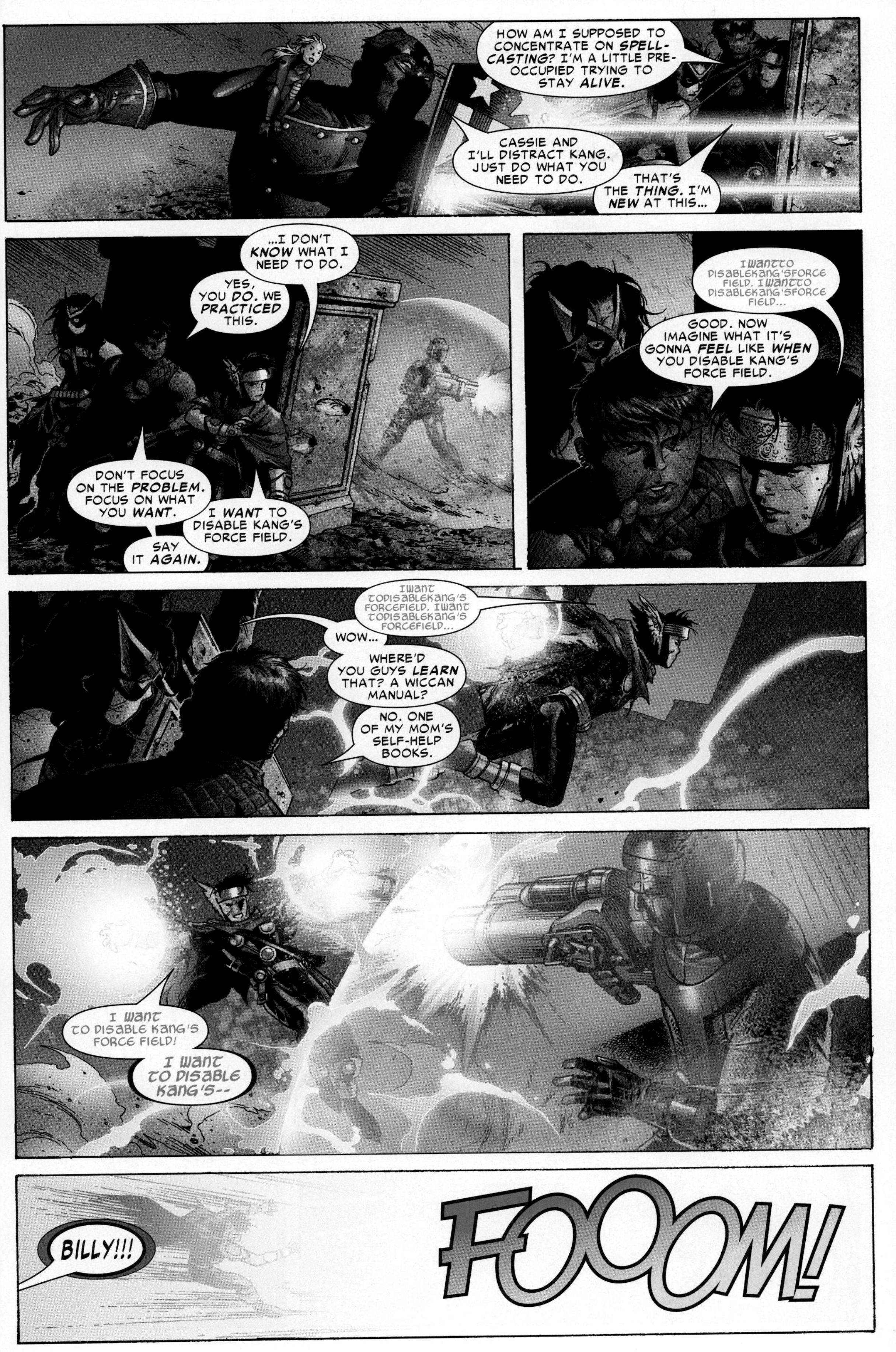
HOW AM I SUPPOSED TO CONCENTRATE ON SPELL-CASTING? I'M A LITTLE PRE-OCCUPIED TRYING TO STAY ALIVE.
CASSIE AND I'LL DISTRACT KANG. JUST DO WHAT YOU NEED TO DO.
THAT'S THE THING. I'M NEW AT THIS...
...I DON'T KNOW WHAT I NEED TO DO.
YES, YOU DO. WE PRACTICED THIS.
DON'T FOCUS ON THE PROBLEM. FOCUS ON WHAT YOU WANT.
I WANT TO DISABLE KANG'S FORCE FIELD.
SAY IT AGAIN.
IWANTTO DISABLEKANG'SFORCE FIELD. IWANTTO DISABLEKANG'SFORCE FIELD...
GOOD. NOW IMAGINE WHAT IT'S GONNA FEEL LIKE WHEN YOU DISABLE KANG'S FORCE FIELD.
IWANT TODISABLEKANG'S FORCEFIELD. IWANT TODISABLEKANG'S FORCEFIELD...
WOW...
WHERE'D YOU GUYS LEARN THAT? A WICCAN MANUAL?
NO. ONE OF MY MOM'S SELF-HELP BOOKS.
I WANT TO DISABLE KANG'S FORCE FIELD!
I WANT TO DISABLE KANG'S--
BILLY!!!
FOOOM!

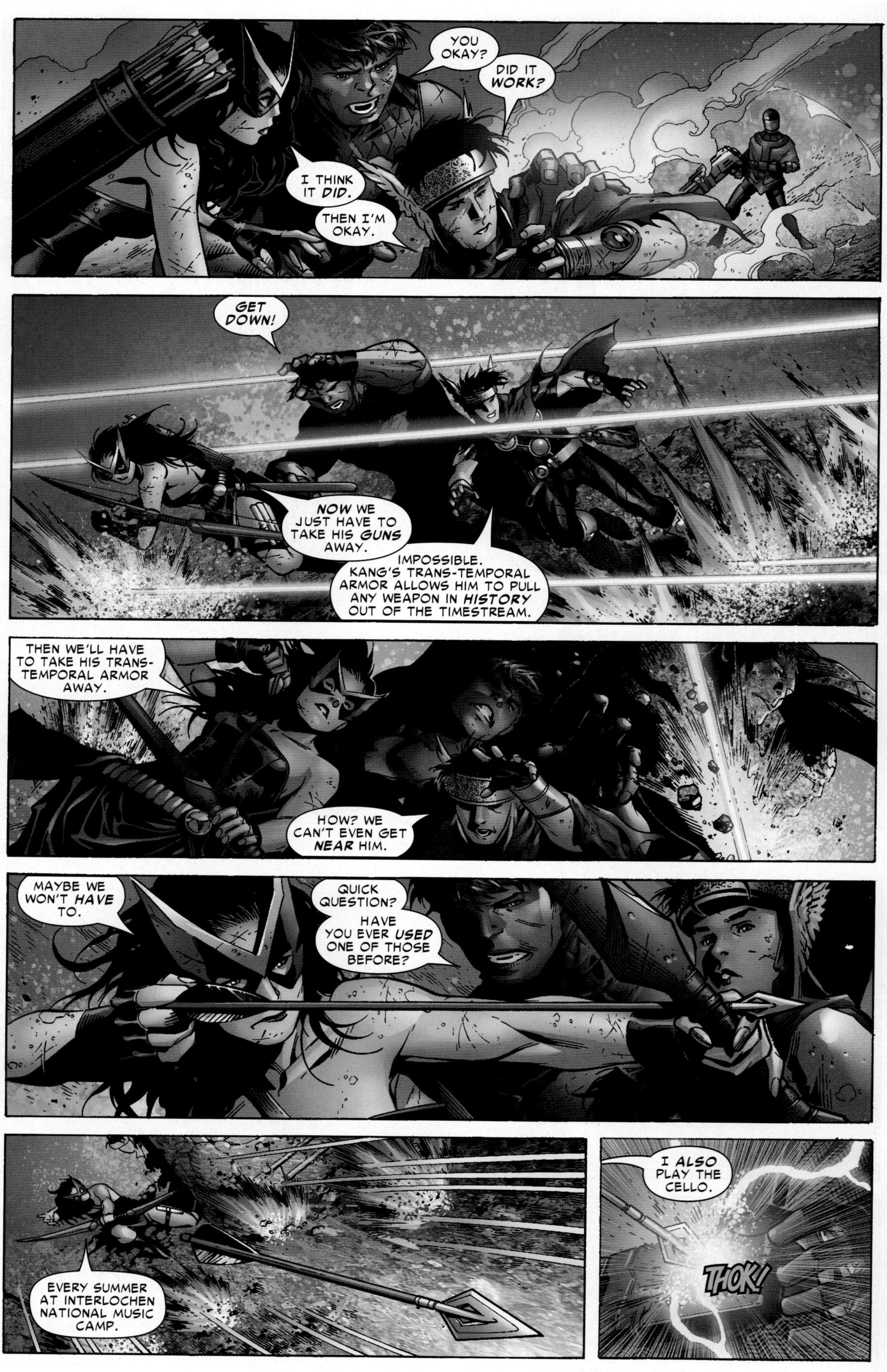

YOU OKAY?
DID IT WORK?
I THINK IT DID.
THEN I'M OKAY.
GET DOWN!
NOW WE JUST HAVE TO TAKE HIS GUNS AWAY.
IMPOSSIBLE. KANG'S TRANS-TEMPORAL ARMOR ALLOWS HIM TO PULL ANY WEAPON IN HISTORY OUT OF THE TIMESTREAM.
THEN WE'LL HAVE TO TAKE HIS TRANS-TEMPORAL ARMOR AWAY.
HOW? WE CAN'T EVEN GET NEAR HIM.
MAYBE WE WON'T HAVE TO.
QUICK QUESTION?
HAVE YOU EVER USED ONE OF THOSE BEFORE?
EVERY SUMMER AT INTERLOCHEN NATIONAL MUSIC CAMP.
I ALSO PLAY THE CELLO.
THOK!

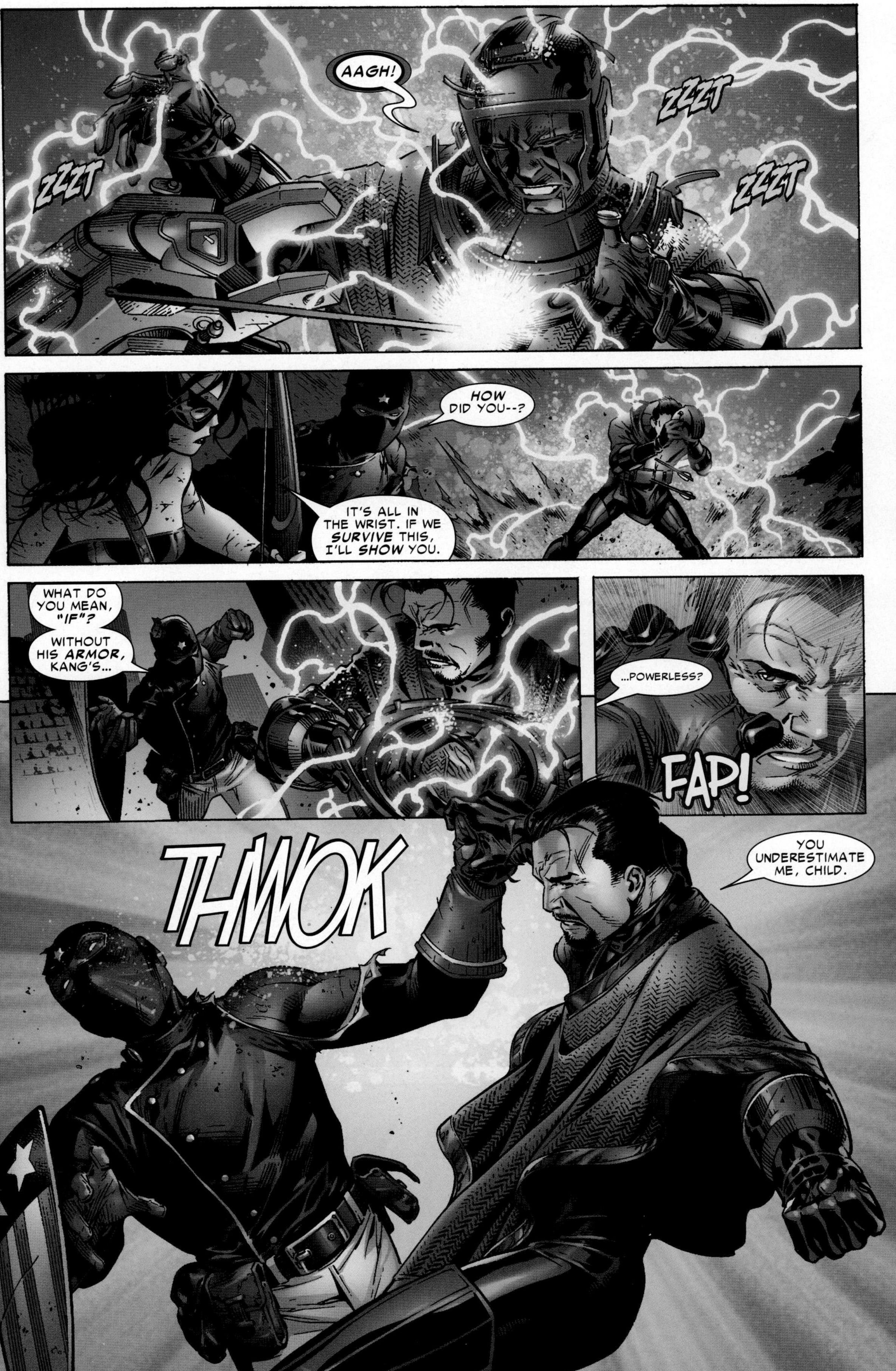
AAGH!
ZZZT
ZZZT
ZZZT
HOW DID YOU--?
IT'S ALL IN THE WRIST. IF WE SURVIVE THIS, I'LL SHOW YOU.
WHAT DO YOU MEAN, "IF"? WITHOUT HIS ARMOR, KANG'S...
...POWERLESS?
FAP!
THWOK
YOU UNDERESTIMATE ME, CHILD.

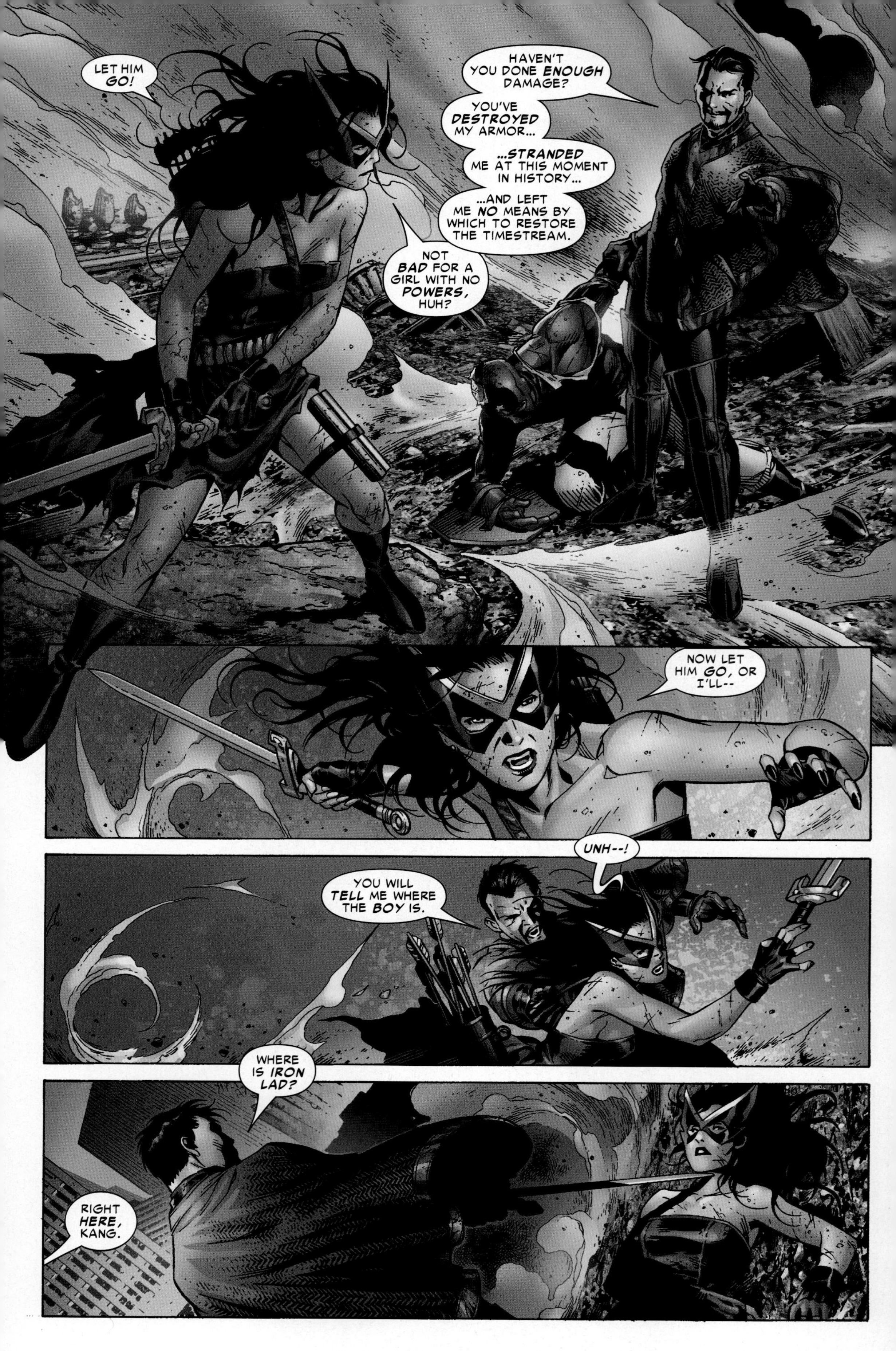
LET HIM GO!
HAVEN'T YOU DONE ENOUGH DAMAGE?
YOU'VE DESTROYED MY ARMOR...
...STRANDED ME AT THIS MOMENT IN HISTORY...
...AND LEFT ME NO MEANS BY WHICH TO RESTORE THE TIMESTREAM.
NOT BAD FOR A GIRL WITH NO POWERS, HUH?
NOW LET HIM GO, OR I'LL--
UNH--!
YOU WILL TELL ME WHERE THE BOY IS.
WHERE IS IRON LAD?
RIGHT HERE, KANG.

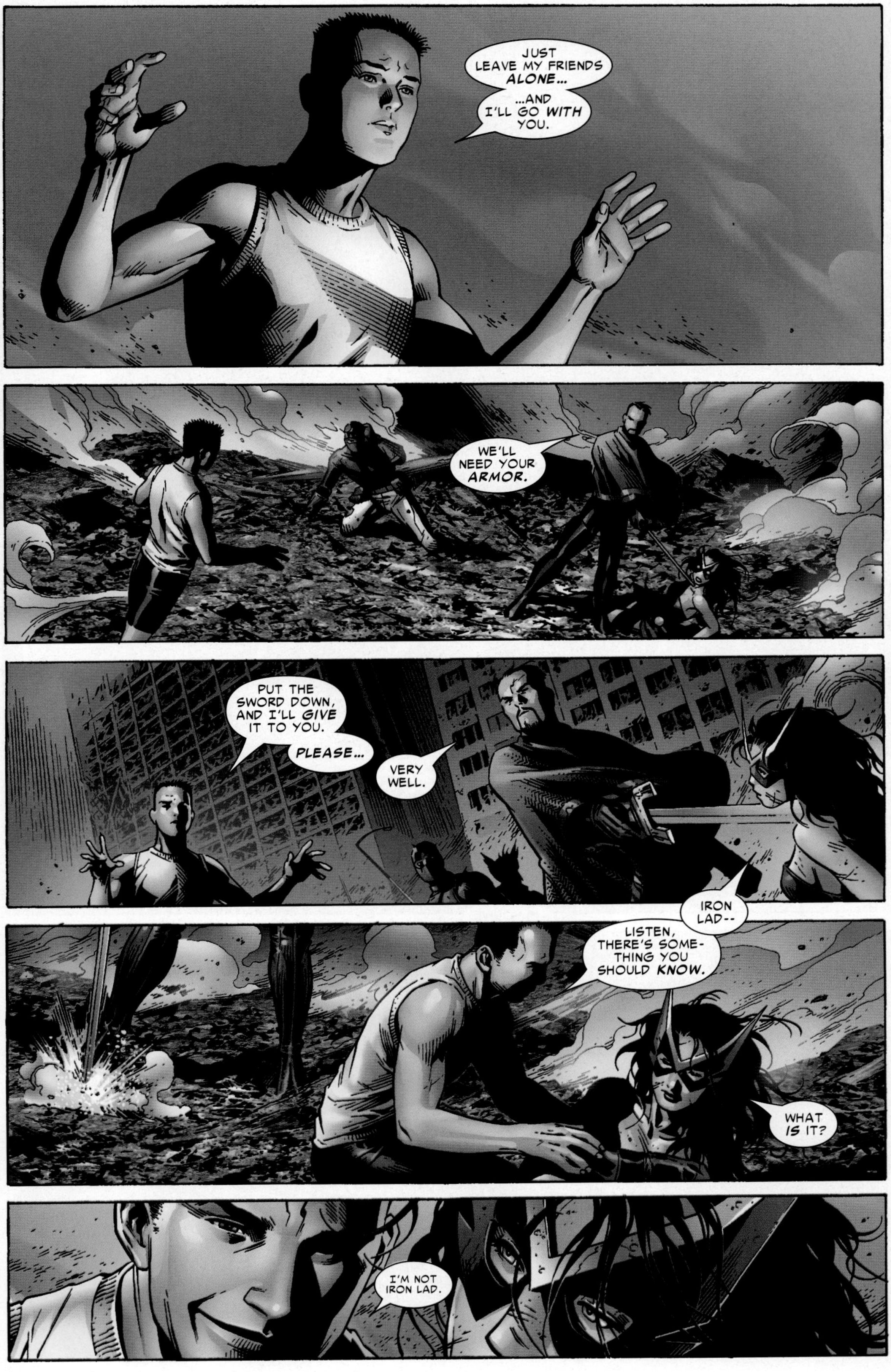

JUST LEAVE MY FRIENDS ALONE...
...AND I'LL GO WITH YOU.
WE'LL NEED YOUR ARMOR.
PUT THE SWORD DOWN, AND I'LL GIVE IT TO YOU.
PLEASE...
VERY WELL.
IRON LAD--
LISTEN, THERE'S SOME-THING YOU SHOULD KNOW.
WHAT IS IT?
I'M NOT IRON LAD.

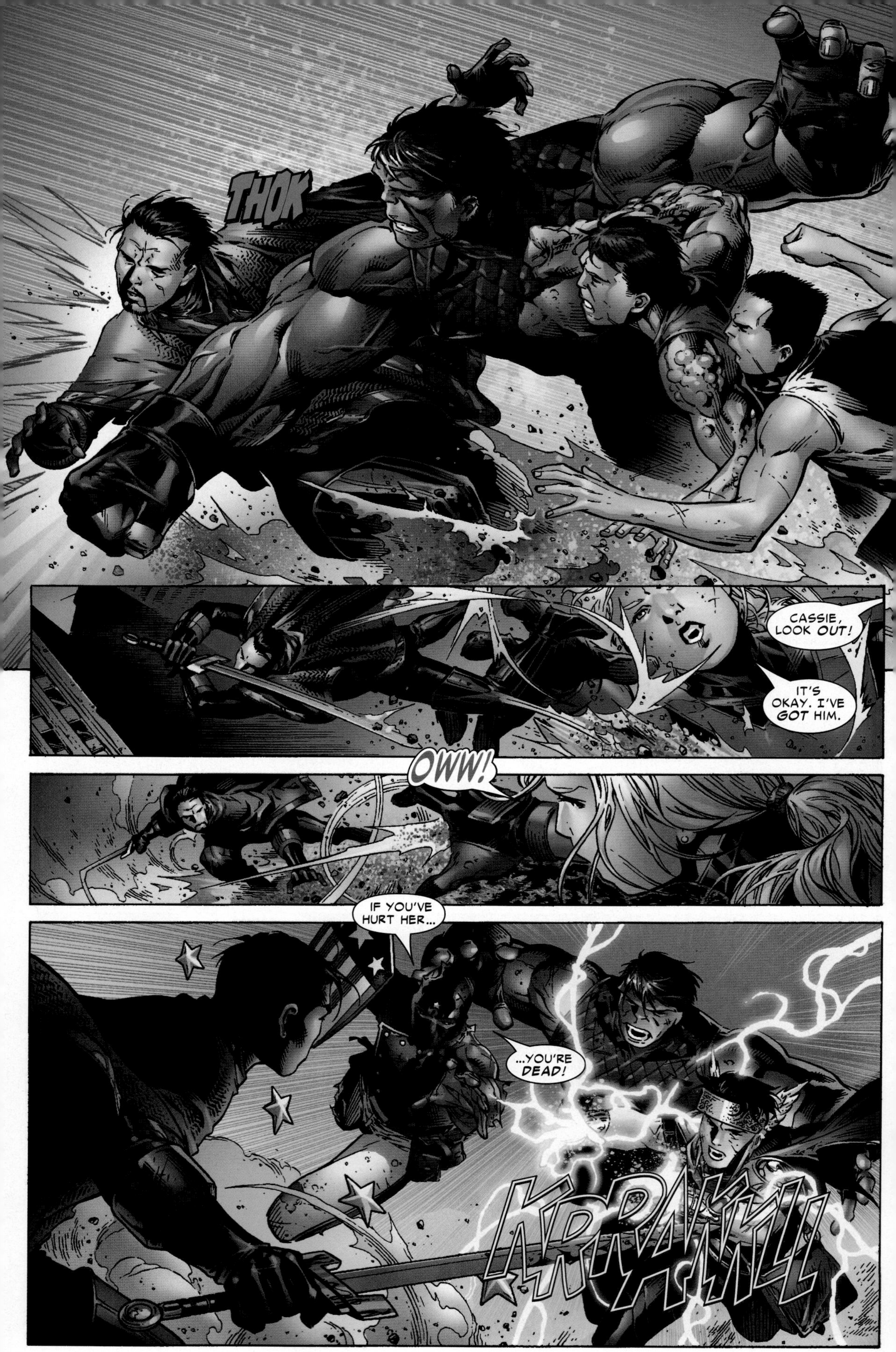
THOK
CASSIE, LOOK OUT!
IT'S OKAY. I'VE GOT HIM.
OWW!
IF YOU'VE HURT HER...
...YOU'RE DEAD!
KRRAKKK

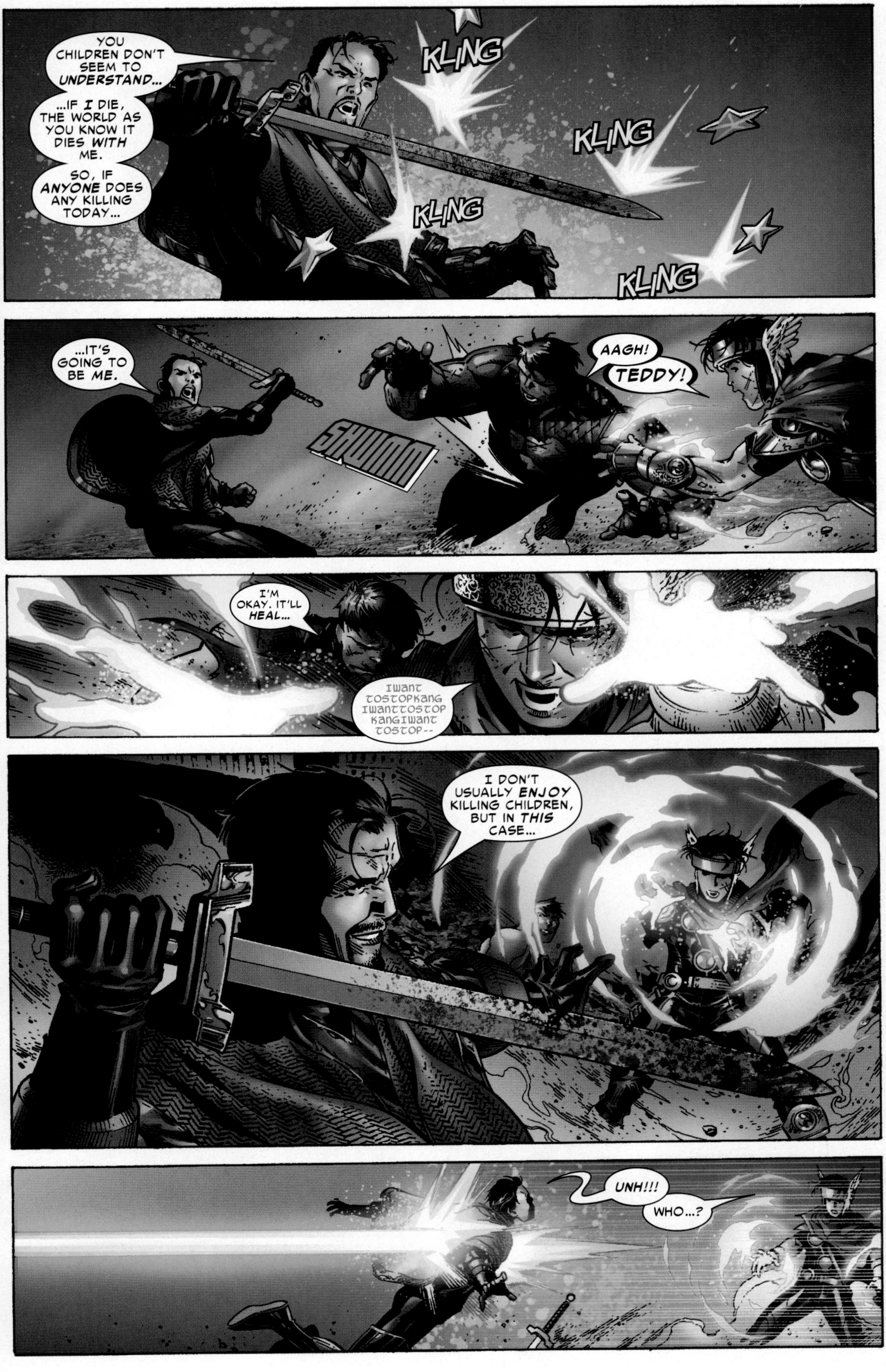
YOU CHILDREN DON'T SEEM TO UNDERSTAND...
...IF I DIE, THE WORLD AS YOU KNOW IT DIES WITH ME.
SO, IF ANYONE DOES ANY KILLING TODAY...
KLING
KLING
KLING
KLING
...IT'S GOING TO BE ME.
SHUNNN
AAGH!
TEDDY!
I'M OKAY. IT'LL HEAL...
IWANT TOSTOPKANG IWANTTOSTOP KANGIWANT TOSTOP--
I DON'T USUALLY ENJOY KILLING CHILDREN, BUT IN THIS CASE...
UNH!!!
WHO...?

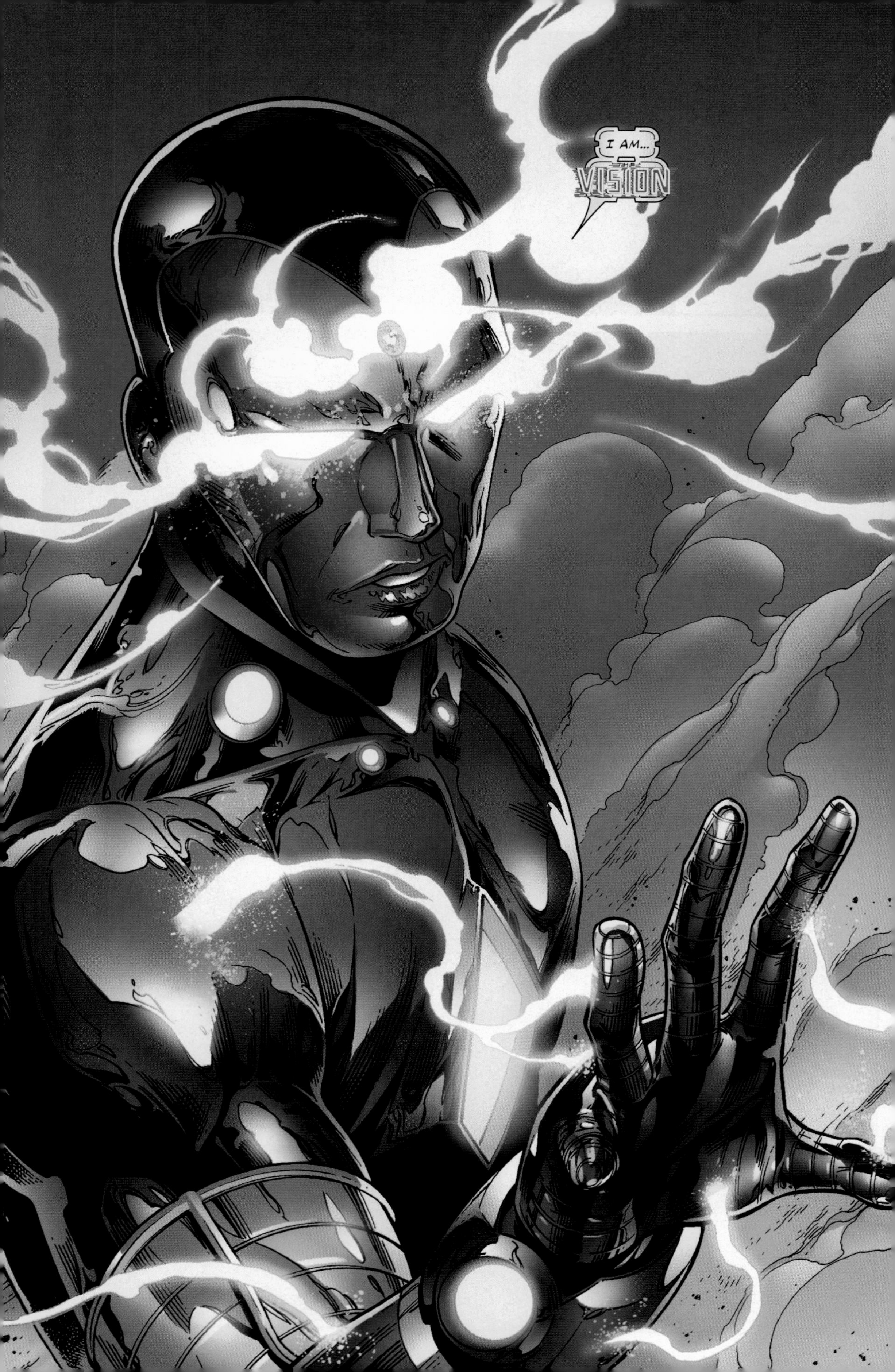
I AM...
THE VISION

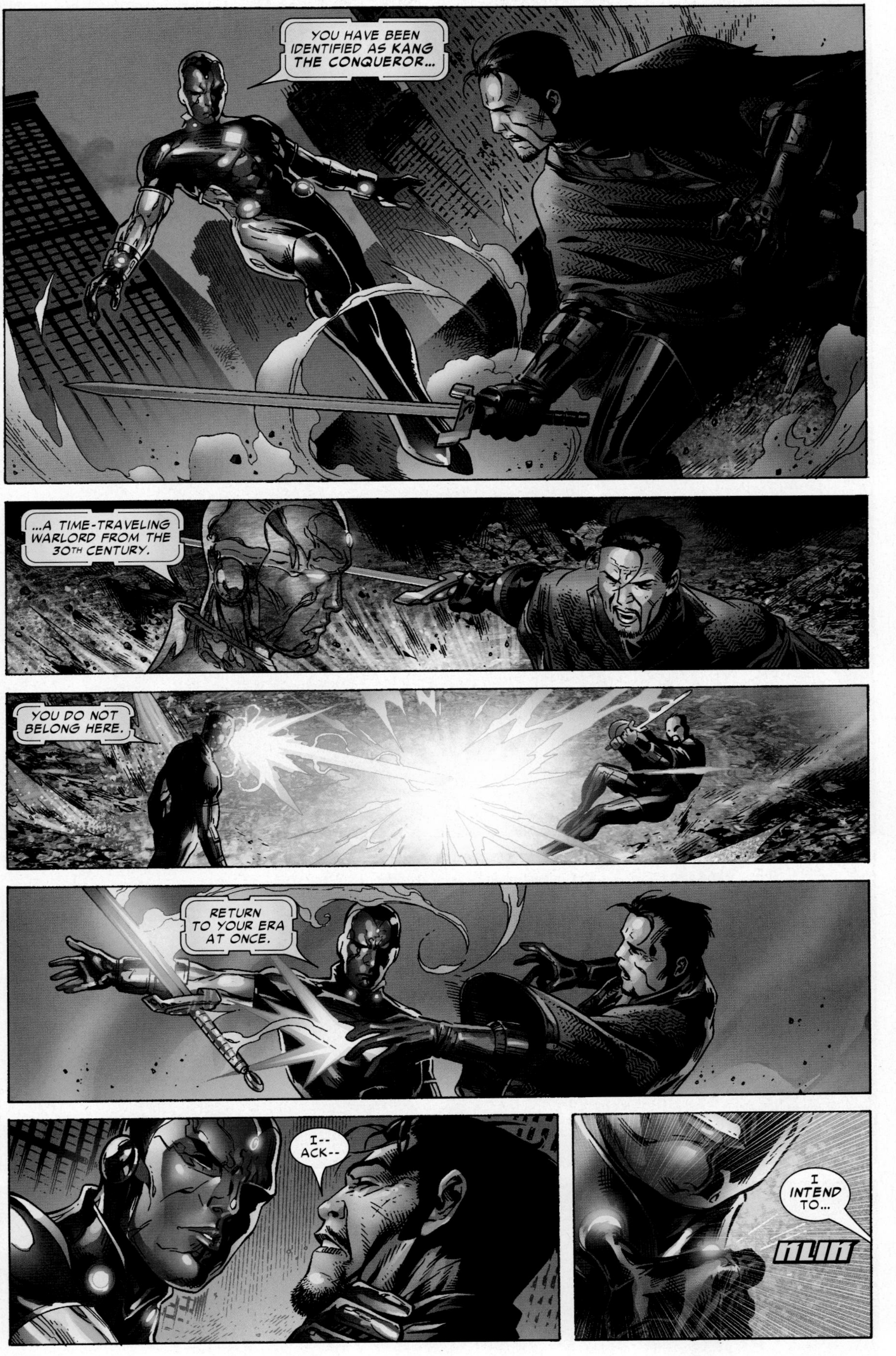
YOU HAVE BEEN IDENTIFIED AS KANG THE CONQUEROR...
...A TIME-TRAVELING WARLORD FROM THE 30TH CENTURY.
YOU DO NOT BELONG HERE.
RETURN TO YOUR ERA AT ONCE.
I-- ACK--
I INTEND TO...
NLIN

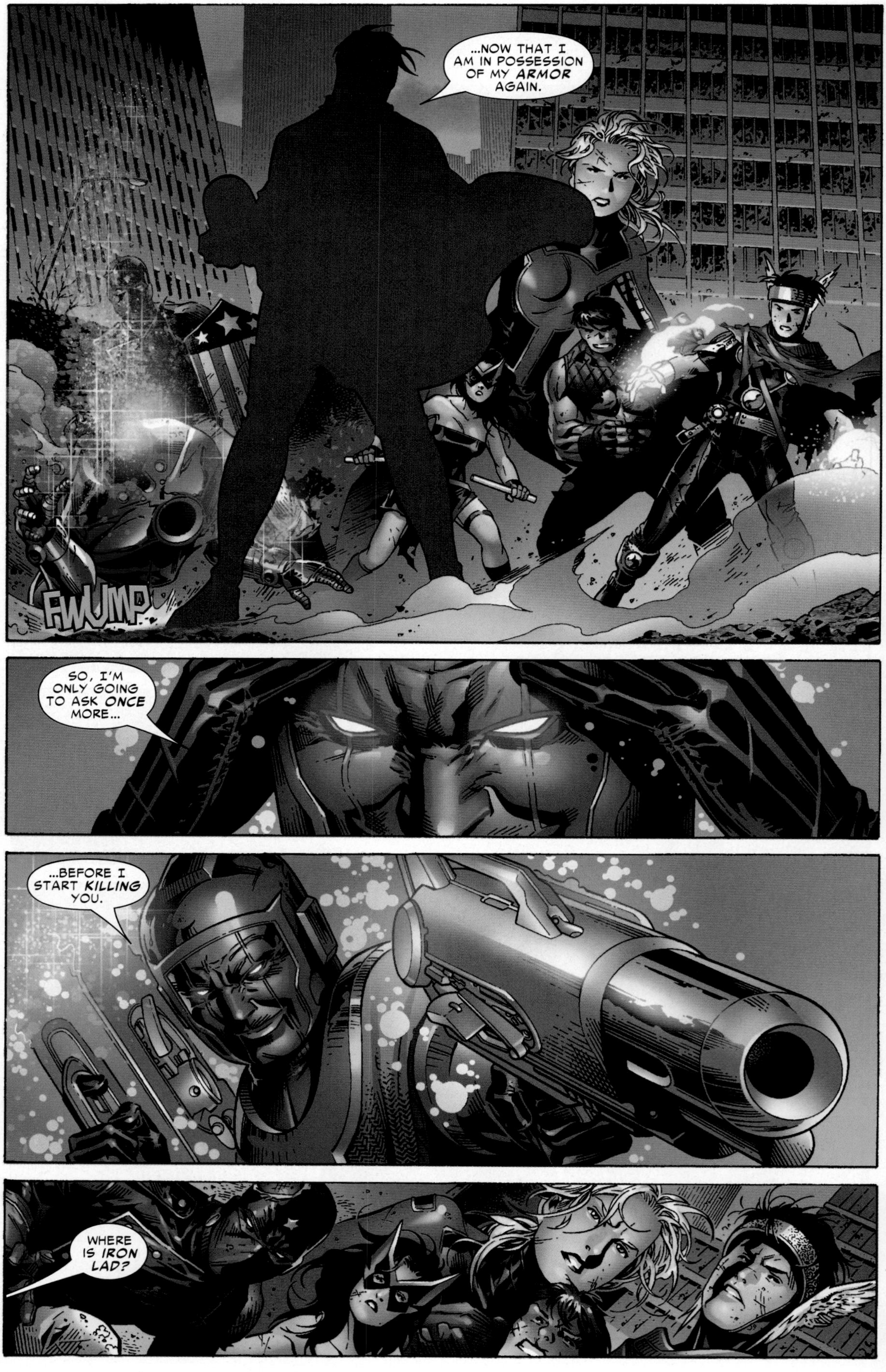
...NOW THAT I AM IN POSSESSION OF MY ARMOR AGAIN.
FWUMP
SO, I'M ONLY GOING TO ASK ONCE MORE...
...BEFORE I START KILLING YOU.
WHERE IS IRON LAD?

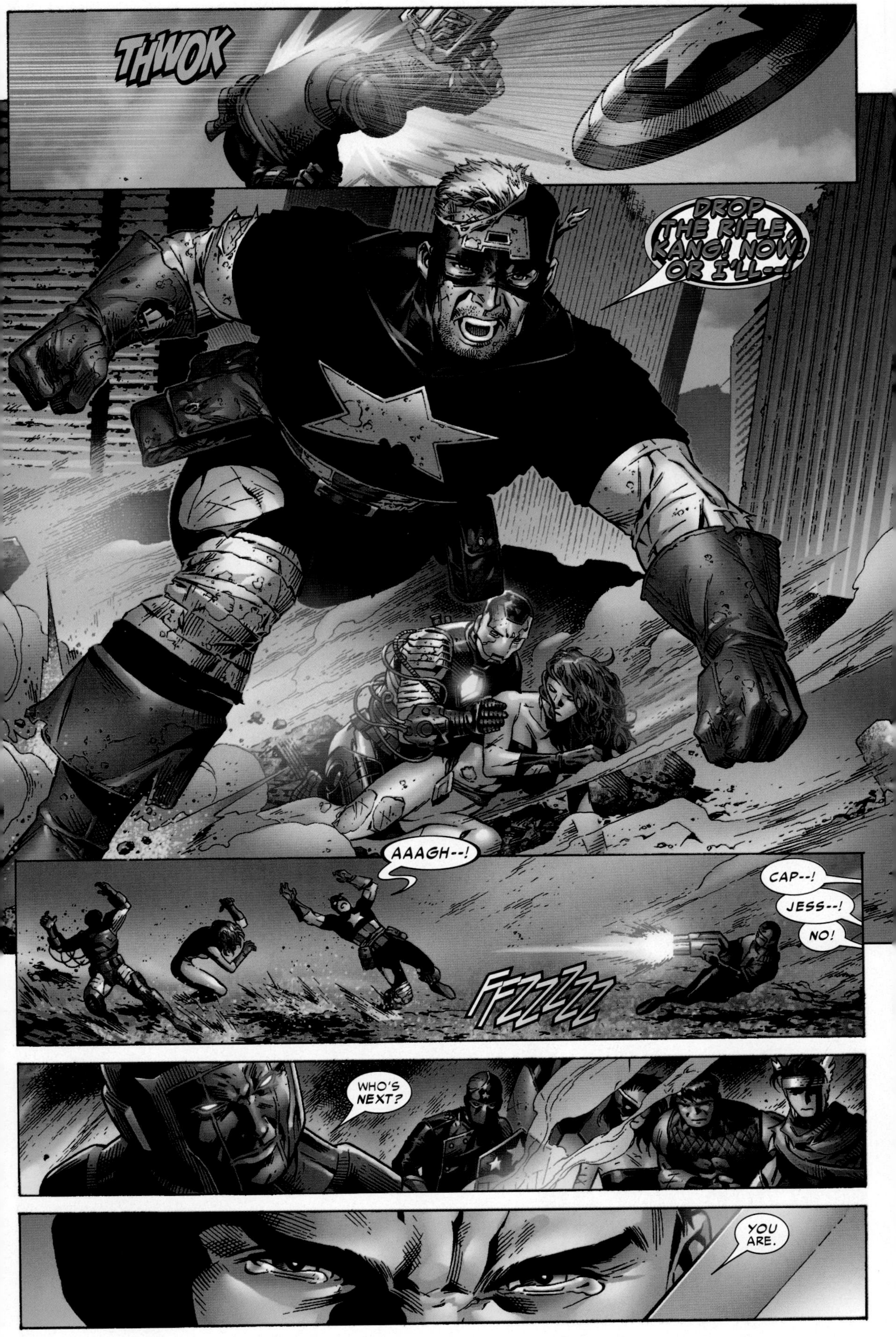
THWOK
DROP THE RIFLE, KANG! NOW! OR I'LL--!
AAAGH--!
CAP--!
JESS--!
NO!
FZZZZZ
WHO'S NEXT?
YOU ARE.

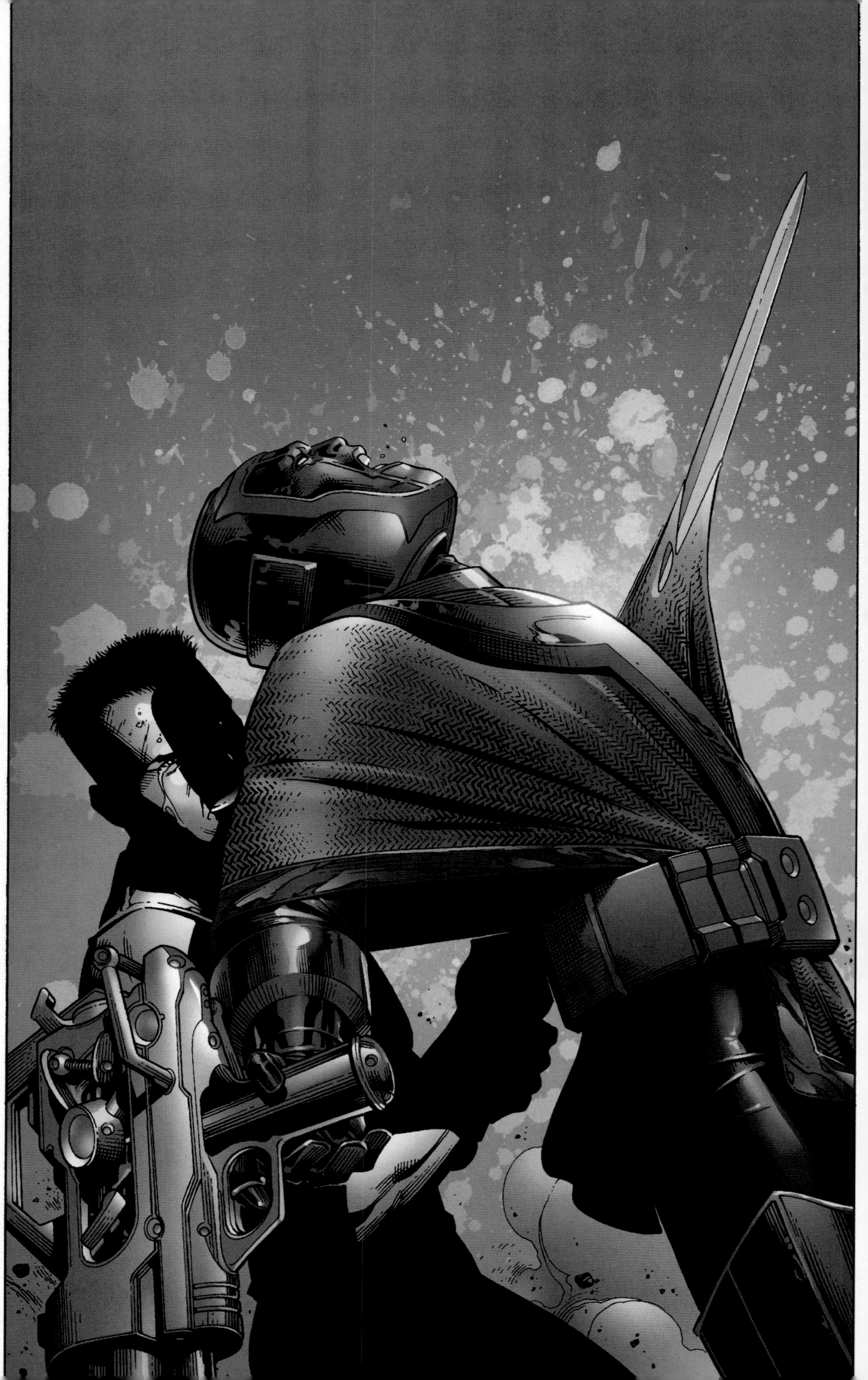

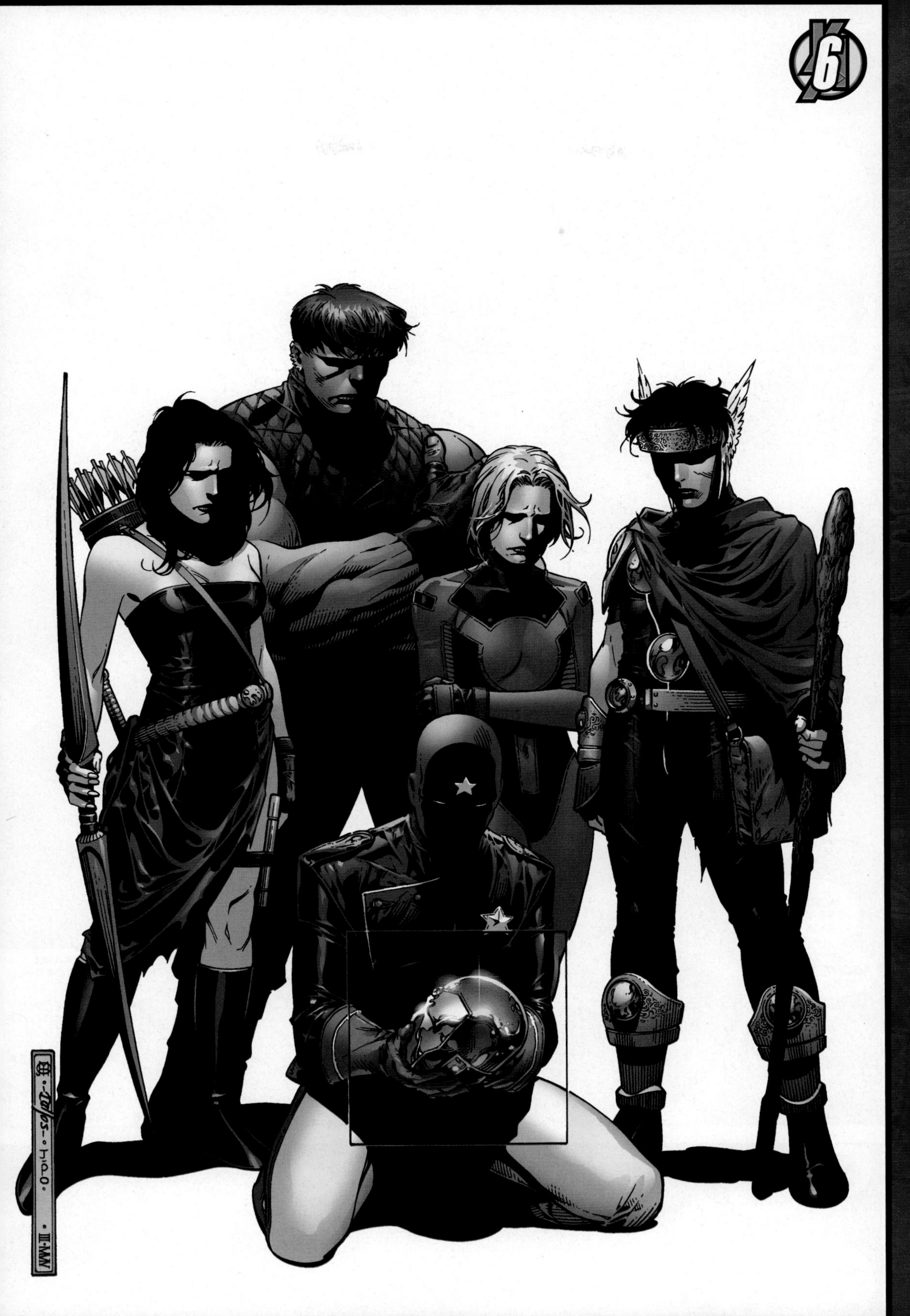

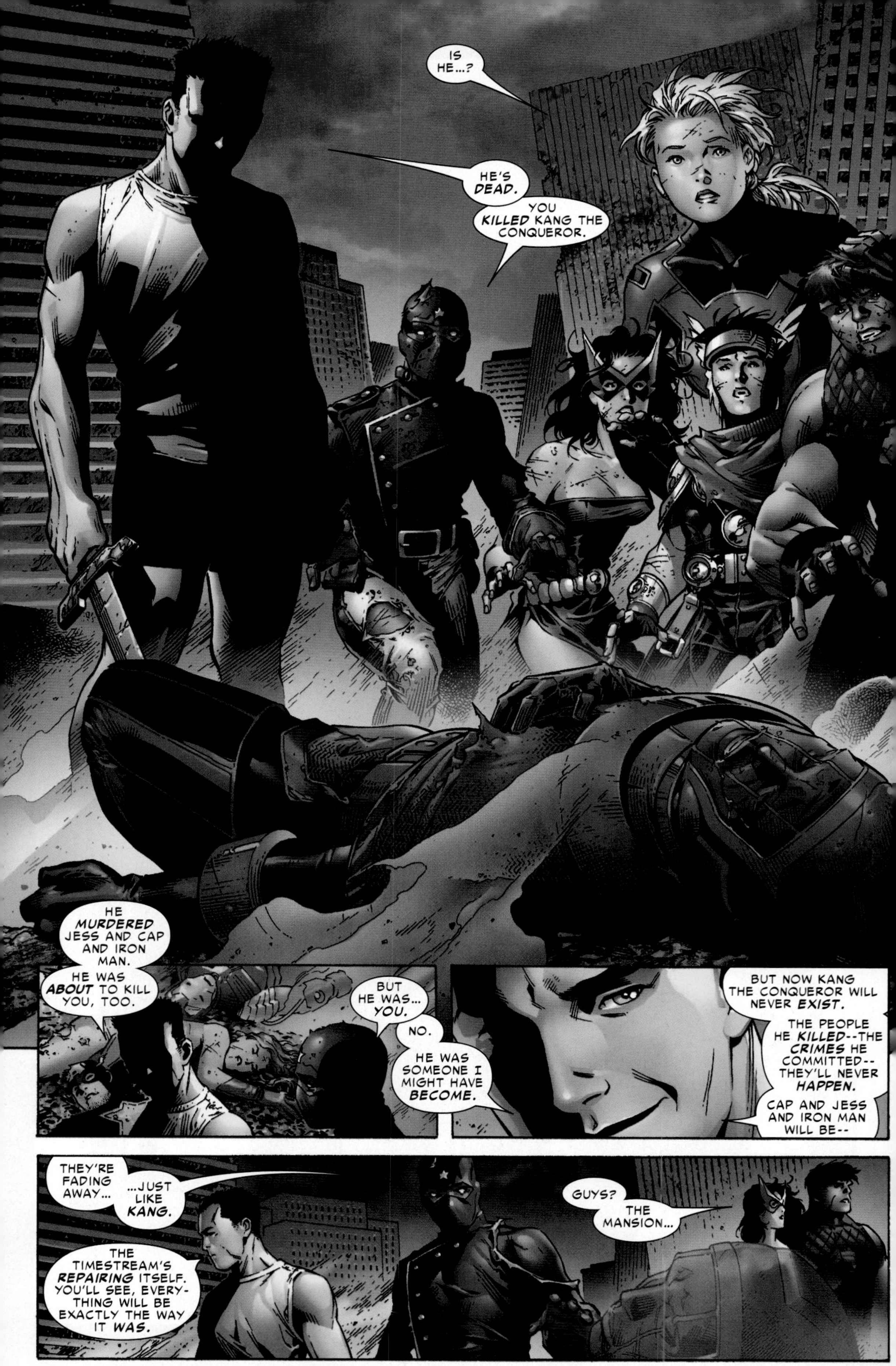
IS HE...?
HE'S DEAD.
YOU KILLED KANG THE CONQUEROR.
HE MURDERED JESS AND CAP AND IRON MAN.
HE WAS ABOUT TO KILL YOU, TOO.
BUT HE WAS... YOU.
NO.
HE WAS SOMEONE I MIGHT HAVE BECOME.
BUT NOW KANG THE CONQUEROR WILL NEVER EXIST.
THE PEOPLE HE KILLED--THE CRIMES HE COMMITTED--THEY'LL NEVER HAPPEN.
CAP AND JESS AND IRON MAN WILL BE--
THEY'RE FADING AWAY...
...JUST LIKE KANG.
THE TIMESTREAM'S REPAIRING ITSELF. YOU'LL SEE, EVERY-THING WILL BE EXACTLY THE WAY IT WAS.
GUYS? THE MANSION...

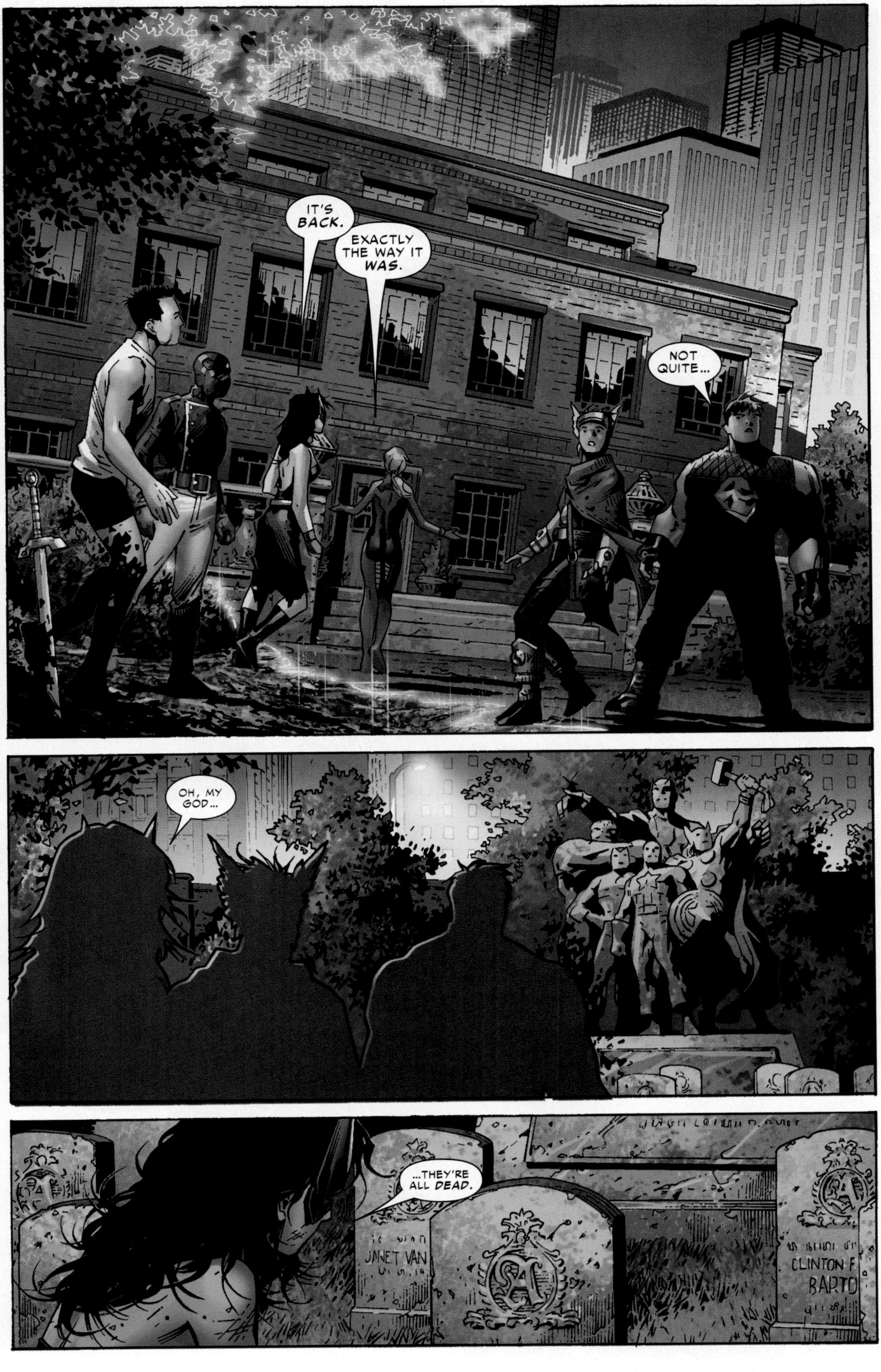
IT'S BACK.
EXACTLY THE WAY IT WAS.
NOT QUITE...
OH, MY GOD...
...THEY'RE ALL DEAD.
JANET VAN
CLINTON F
BARTO

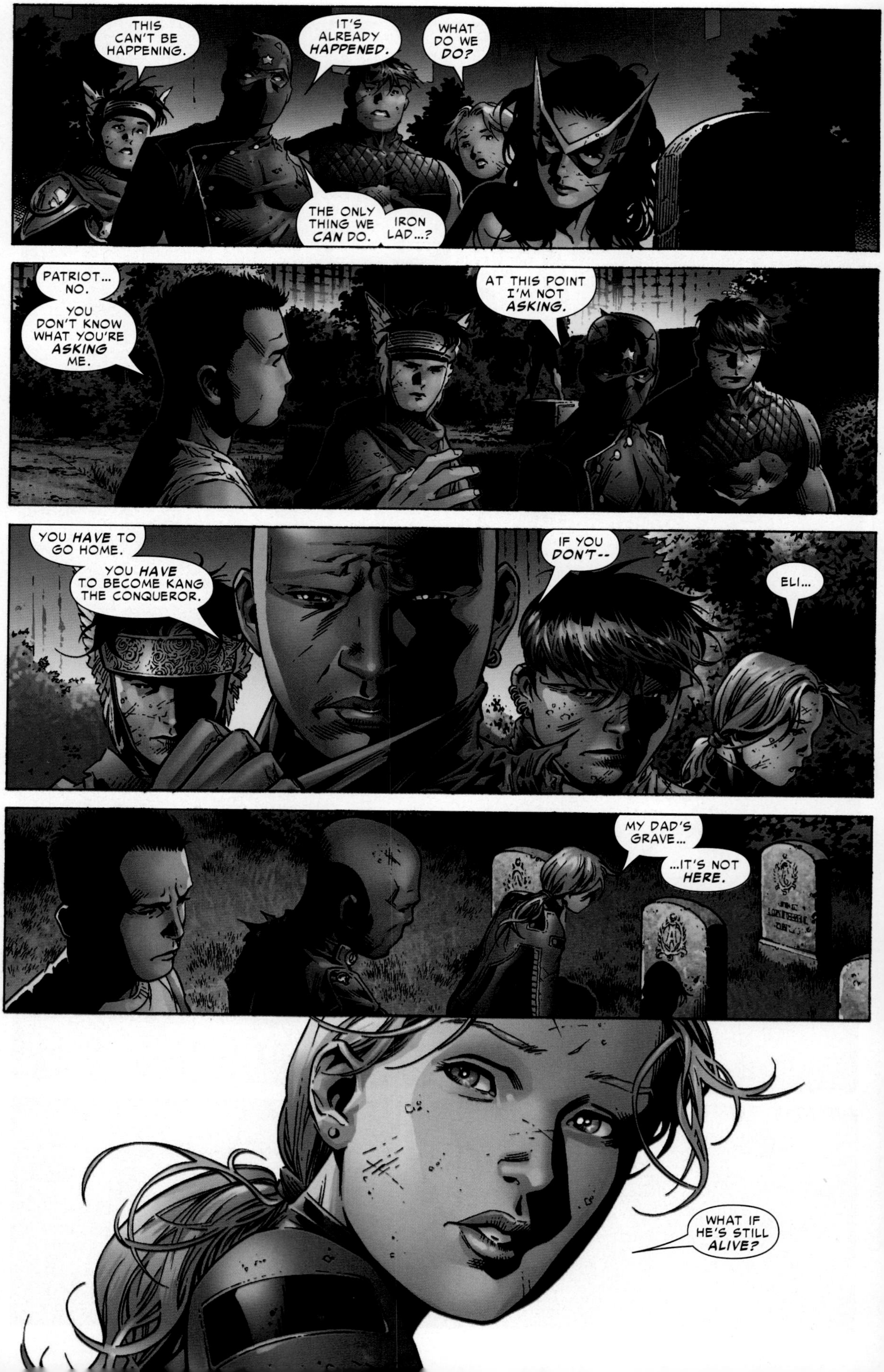

THIS CAN'T BE HAPPENING.
IT'S ALREADY HAPPENED.
WHAT DO WE DO?
THE ONLY THING WE CAN DO.
IRON LAD...?
PATRIOT... NO.
YOU DON'T KNOW WHAT YOU'RE ASKING ME.
AT THIS POINT I'M NOT ASKING.
YOU HAVE TO GO HOME.
TO BECOME KANG THE CONQUEROR.
IF YOU DON'T--
ELI...
MY DAD'S GRAVE...
...IT'S NOT HERE.
WHAT IF HE'S STILL ALIVE?

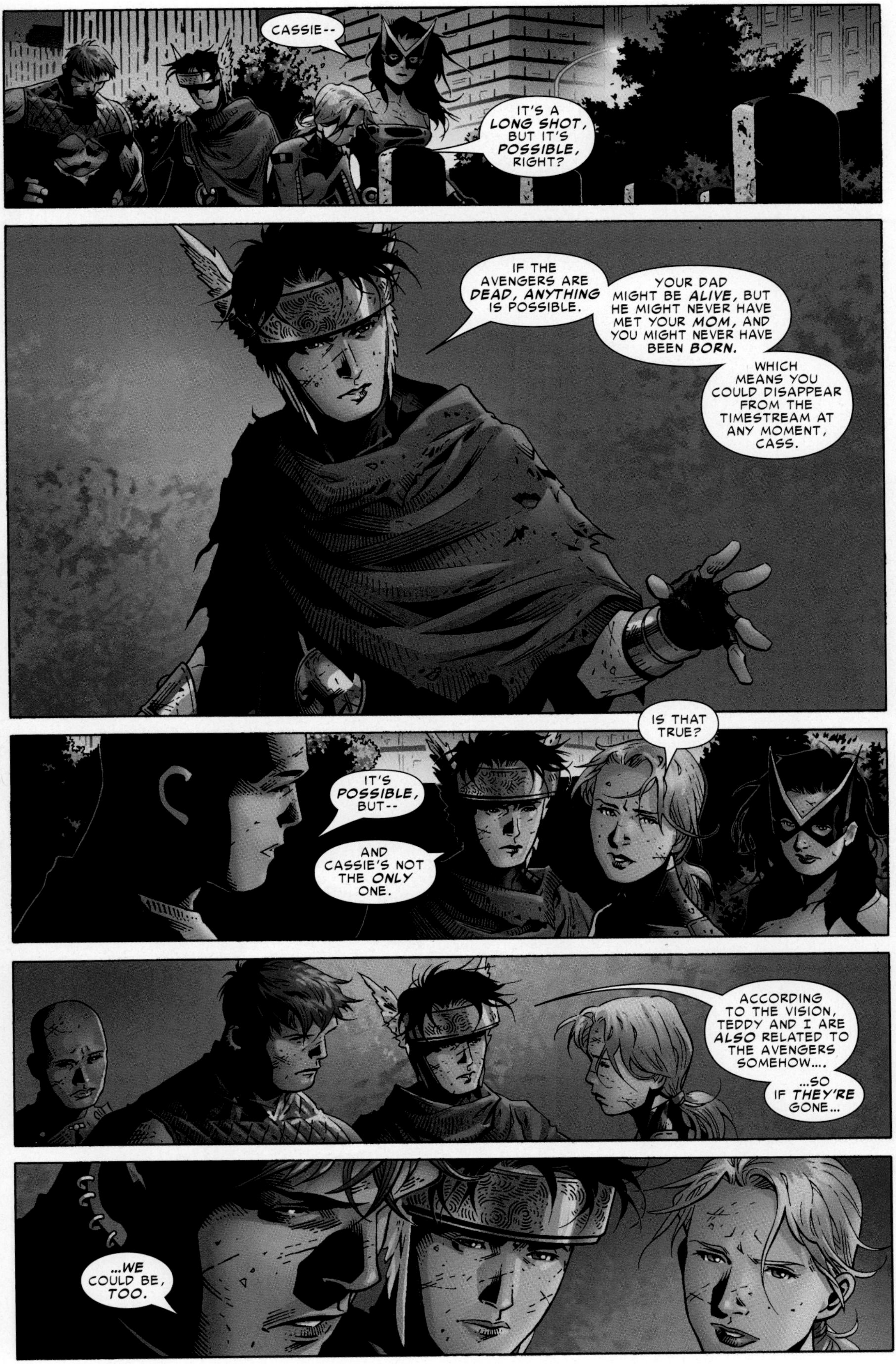
CASSIE--
IT'S A LONG SHOT, BUT IT'S POSSIBLE, RIGHT?
IF THE AVENGERS ARE DEAD, ANYTHING IS POSSIBLE.
YOUR DAD MIGHT BE ALIVE, BUT HE MIGHT NEVER HAVE MET YOUR MOM, AND YOU MIGHT NEVER HAVE BEEN BORN.
WHICH MEANS YOU COULD DISAPPEAR FROM THE TIMESTREAM AT ANY MOMENT, CASS.
IS THAT TRUE?
IT'S POSSIBLE, BUT--
AND CASSIE'S NOT THE ONLY ONE.
ACCORDING TO THE VISION, TEDDY AND I ARE ALSO RELATED TO THE AVENGERS SOMEHOW....
...SO IF THEY'RE GONE...
...WE COULD BE, TOO.

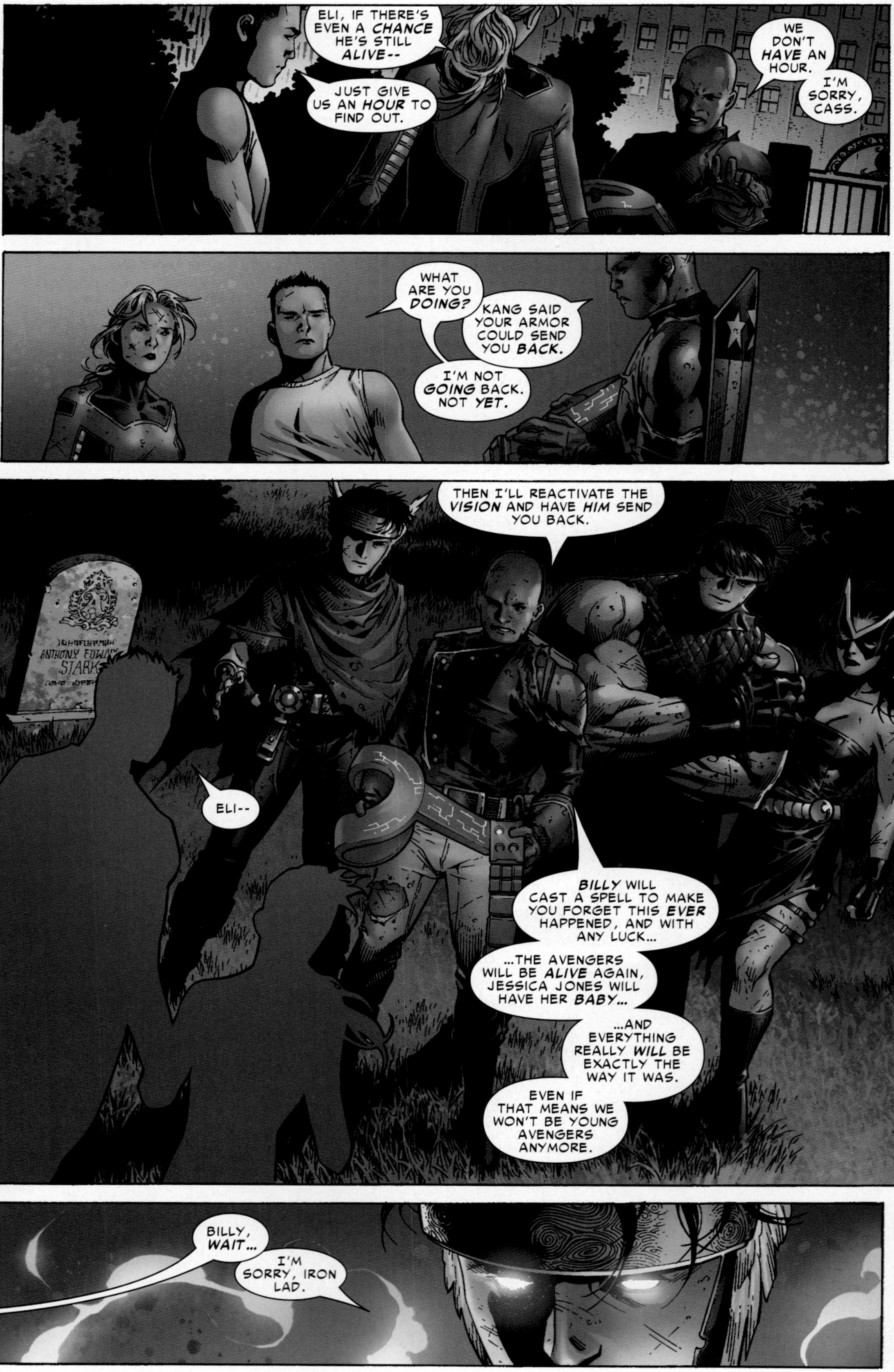
ELI, IF THERE'S EVEN A CHANCE HE'S STILL ALIVE--
JUST GIVE US AN HOUR TO FIND OUT.
WE DON'T HAVE AN HOUR.
I'M SORRY, CASS.
WHAT ARE YOU DOING?
KANG SAID YOUR ARMOR COULD SEND YOU BACK.
I'M NOT GOING BACK. NOT YET.
THEN I'LL REACTIVATE THE VISION AND HAVE HIM SEND YOU BACK.
ELI--
BILLY WILL CAST A SPELL TO MAKE YOU FORGET THIS EVER HAPPENED, AND WITH ANY LUCK...
...THE AVENGERS WILL BE ALIVE AGAIN, JESSICA JONES WILL HAVE HER BABY...
...AND EVERYTHING REALLY WILL BE EXACTLY THE WAY IT WAS.
EVEN IF THAT MEANS WE WON'T BE YOUNG AVENGERS ANYMORE.
BILLY, WAIT...
I'M SORRY, IRON LAD.

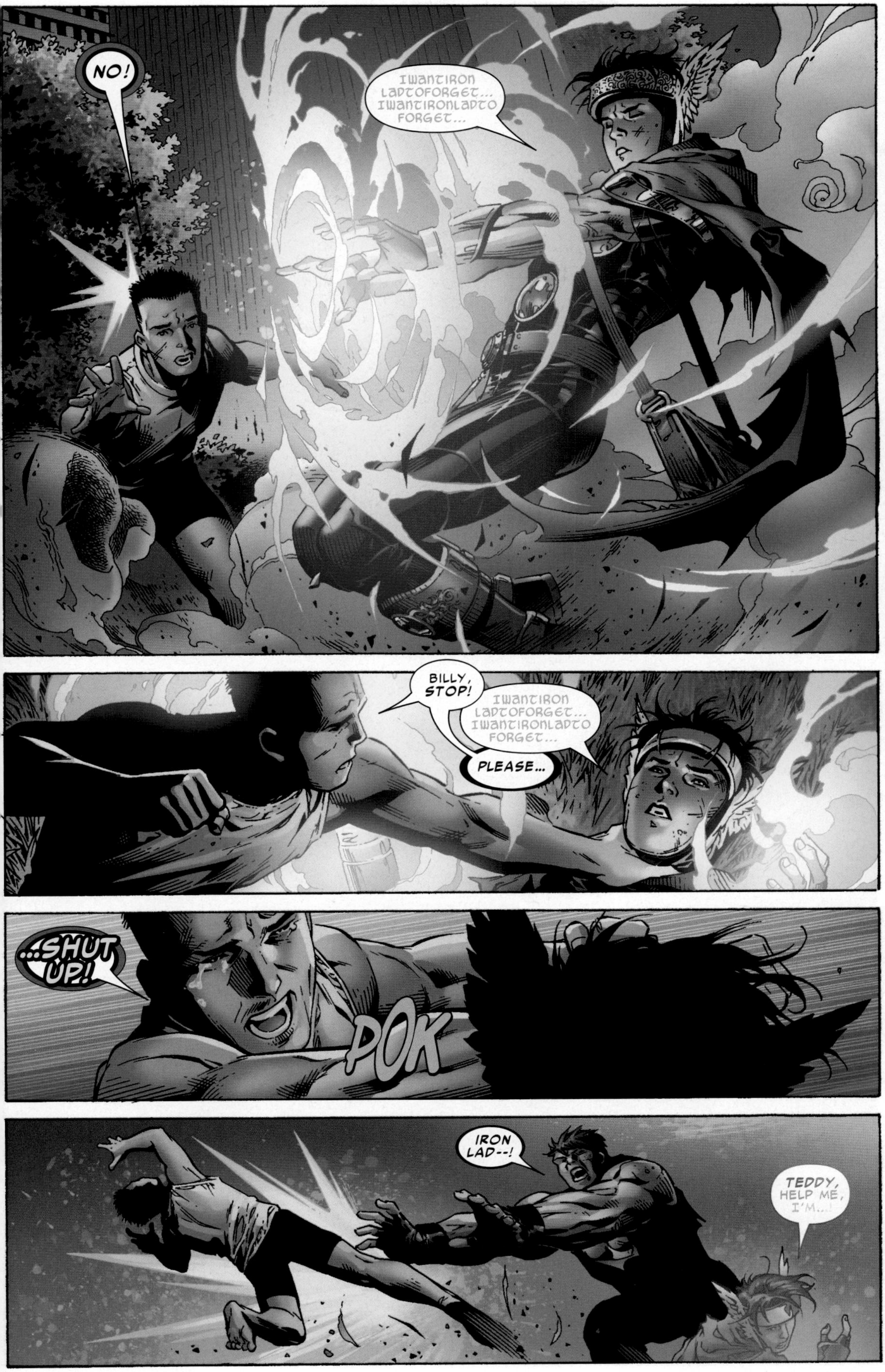
NO!
IWANTIRON LADTOFORGET... IWANTIRONLADTO FORGET...
BILLY, STOP!
IWANTIRON LADTOFORGET... IWANTIRONLADTO FORGET...
PLEASE...
...SHUT UP!
POK
IRON LAD--!
TEDDY, HELP ME, I'M...!

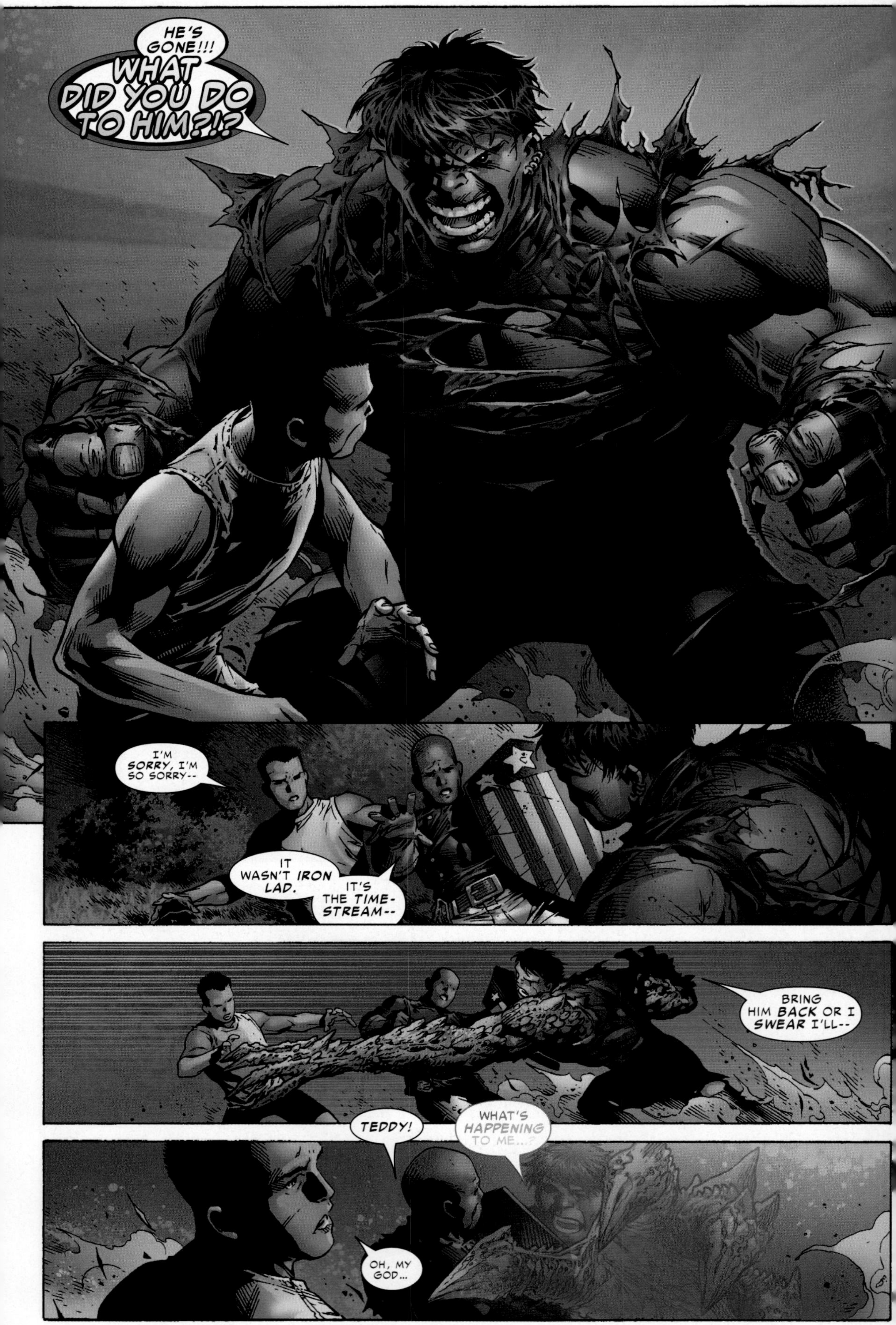
HE'S GONE!!!
WHAT DID YOU DO TO HIM?!?
I'M SORRY, I'M SO SORRY--
IT WASN'T IRON LAD.
IT'S THE TIME-STREAM--
BRING HIM BACK OR I SWEAR I'LL--
TEDDY!
WHAT'S HAPPENING TO ME...?
OH, MY GOD...

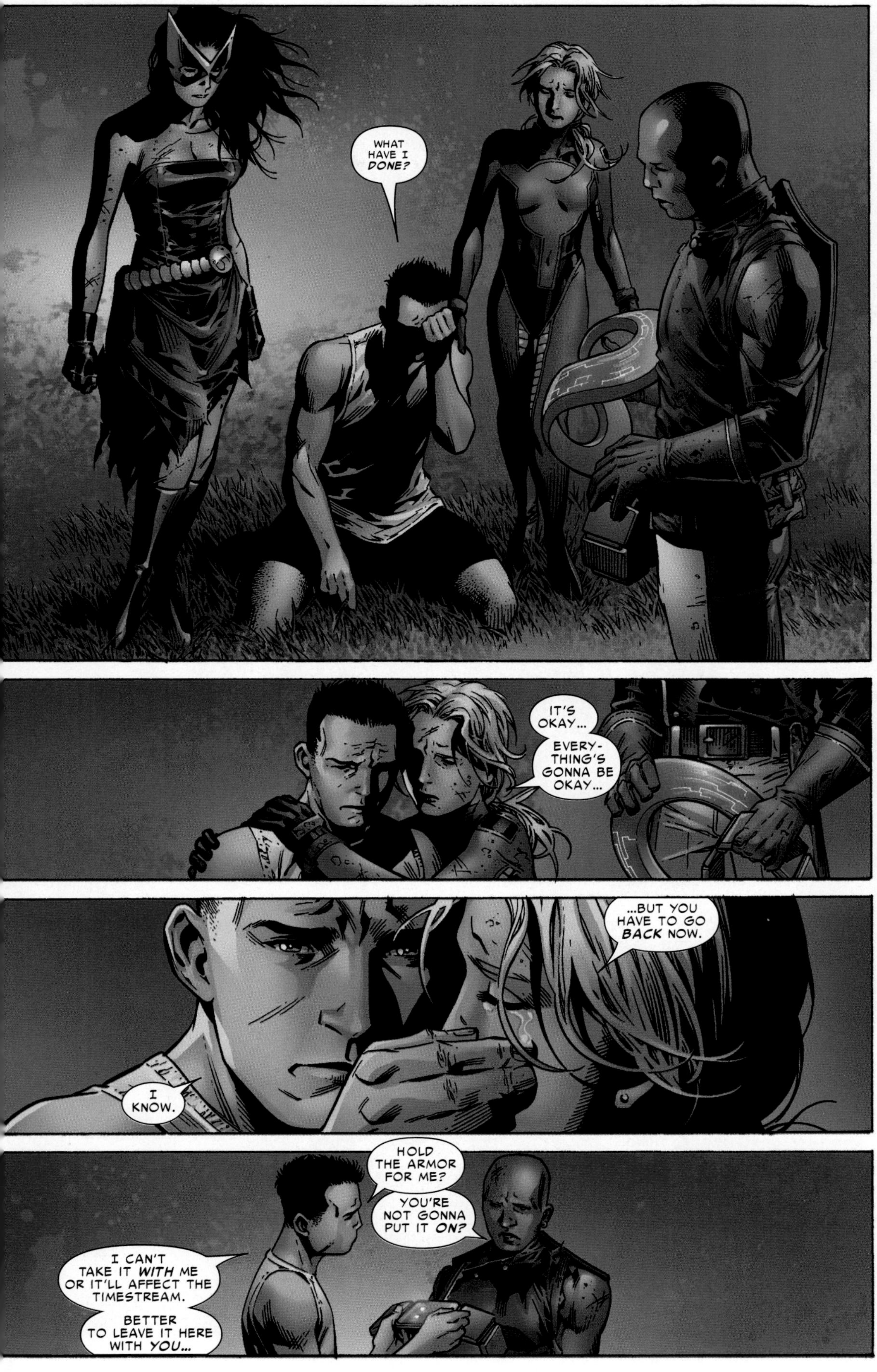
WHAT HAVE I DONE?
IT'S OKAY...
EVERYTHING'S GONNA BE OKAY...
...BUT YOU HAVE TO GO BACK NOW.
I KNOW.
HOLD THE ARMOR FOR ME?
YOU'RE NOT GONNA PUT IT ON?
I CAN'T TAKE IT WITH ME OR IT'LL AFFECT THE TIMESTREAM.
BETTER TO LEAVE IT HERE WITH YOU...

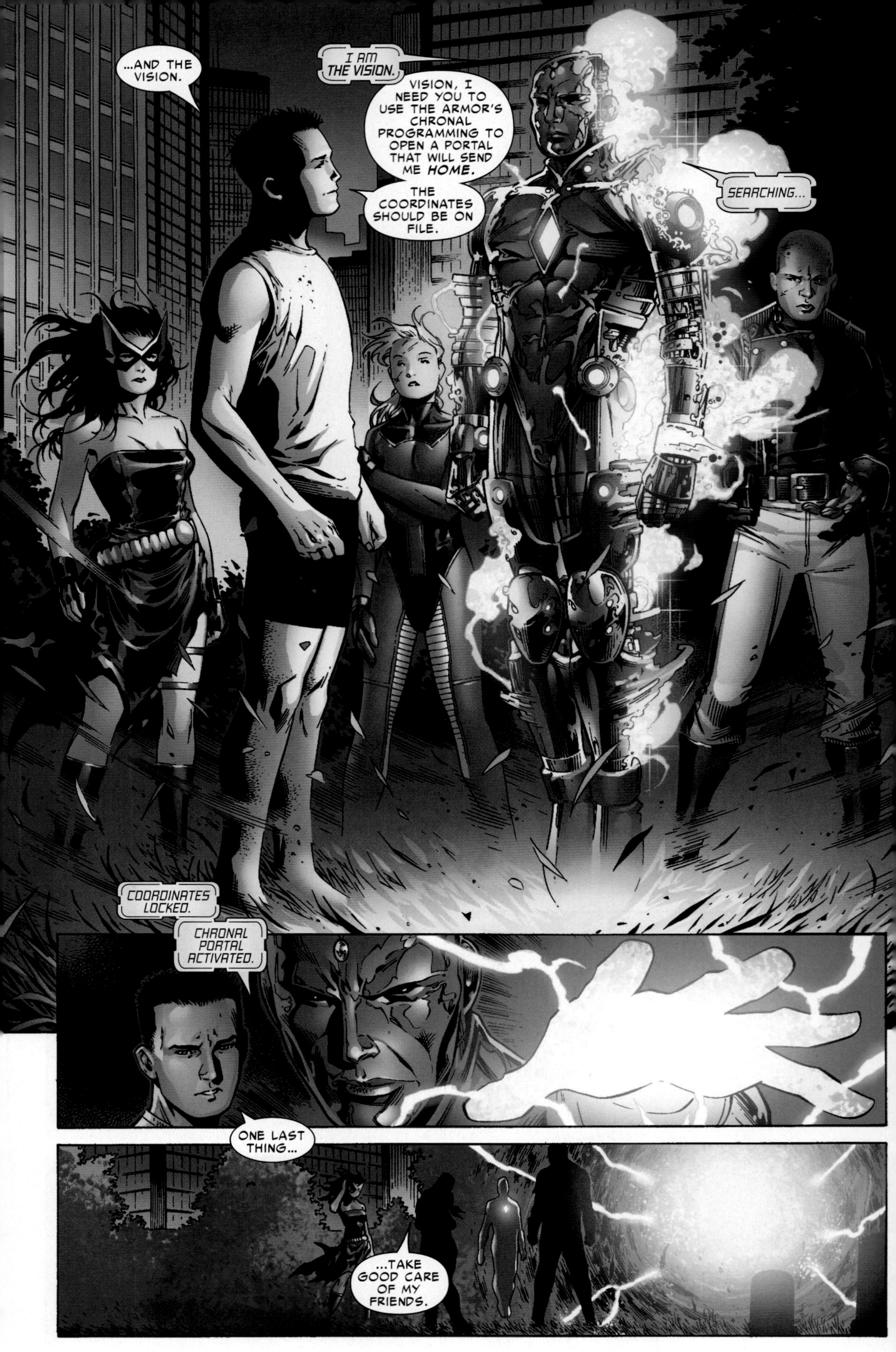

...AND THE VISION.
I AM THE VISION.
VISION, I NEED YOU TO USE THE ARMOR'S CHRONAL PROGRAMMING TO OPEN A PORTAL THAT WILL SEND ME HOME.
THE COORDINATES SHOULD BE ON FILE.
SEARCHING...
COORDINATES LOCKED.
CHRONAL PORTAL ACTIVATED.
ONE LAST THING...
...TAKE GOOD CARE OF MY FRIENDS.

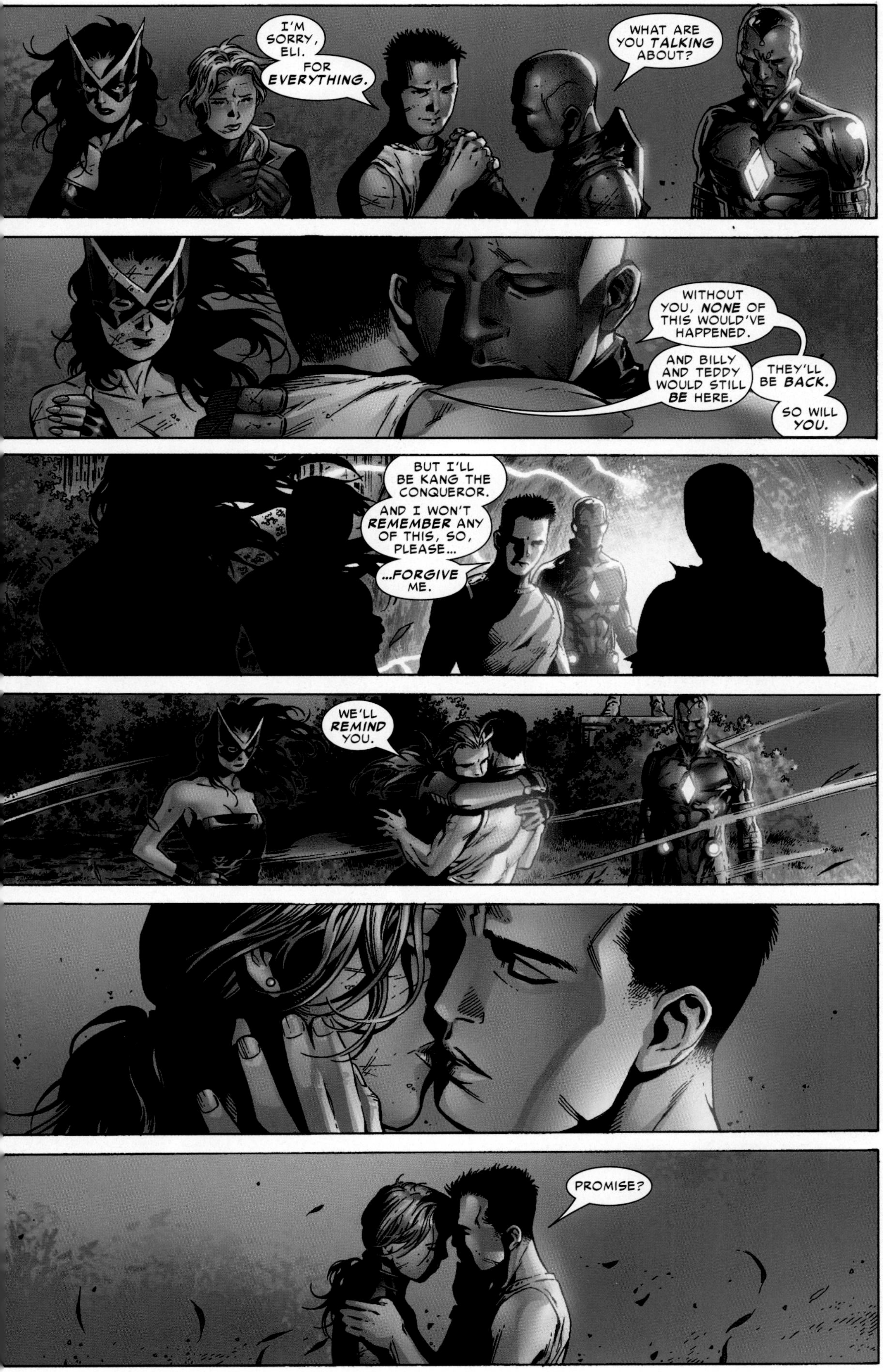
I'M SORRY, ELI.
FOR EVERYTHING.
WHAT ARE YOU TALKING ABOUT?
WITHOUT YOU, NONE OF THIS WOULD'VE HAPPENED.
AND BILLY AND TEDDY WOULD STILL BE HERE.
THEY'LL BE BACK.
SO WILL YOU.
BUT I'LL BE KANG THE CONQUEROR.
AND I WON'T REMEMBER ANY OF THIS, SO, PLEASE...
...FORGIVE ME.
WE'LL REMIND YOU.
PROMISE?

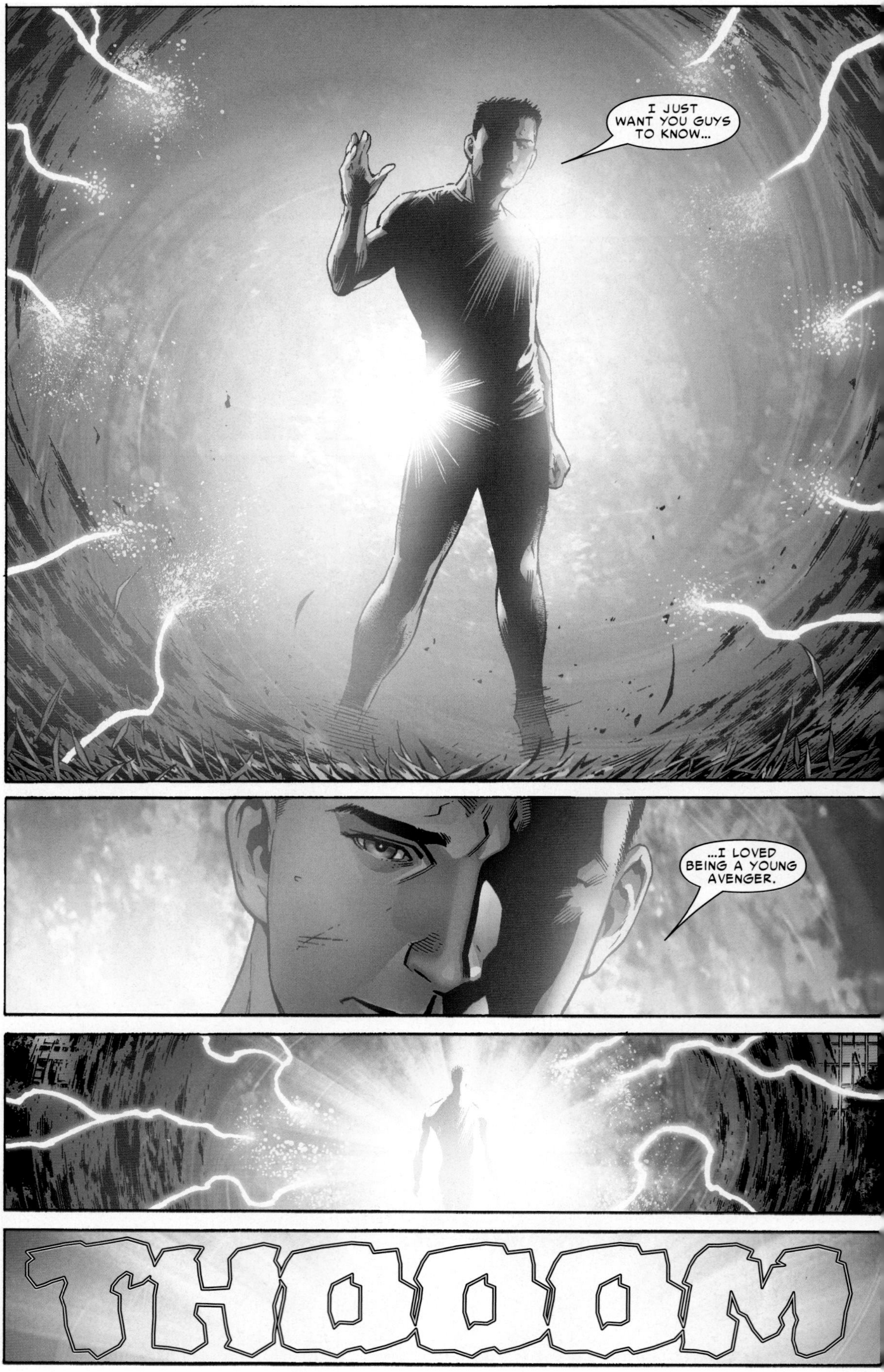
I JUST WANT YOU GUYS TO KNOW...
...I LOVED BEING A YOUNG AVENGER.
THOOOM

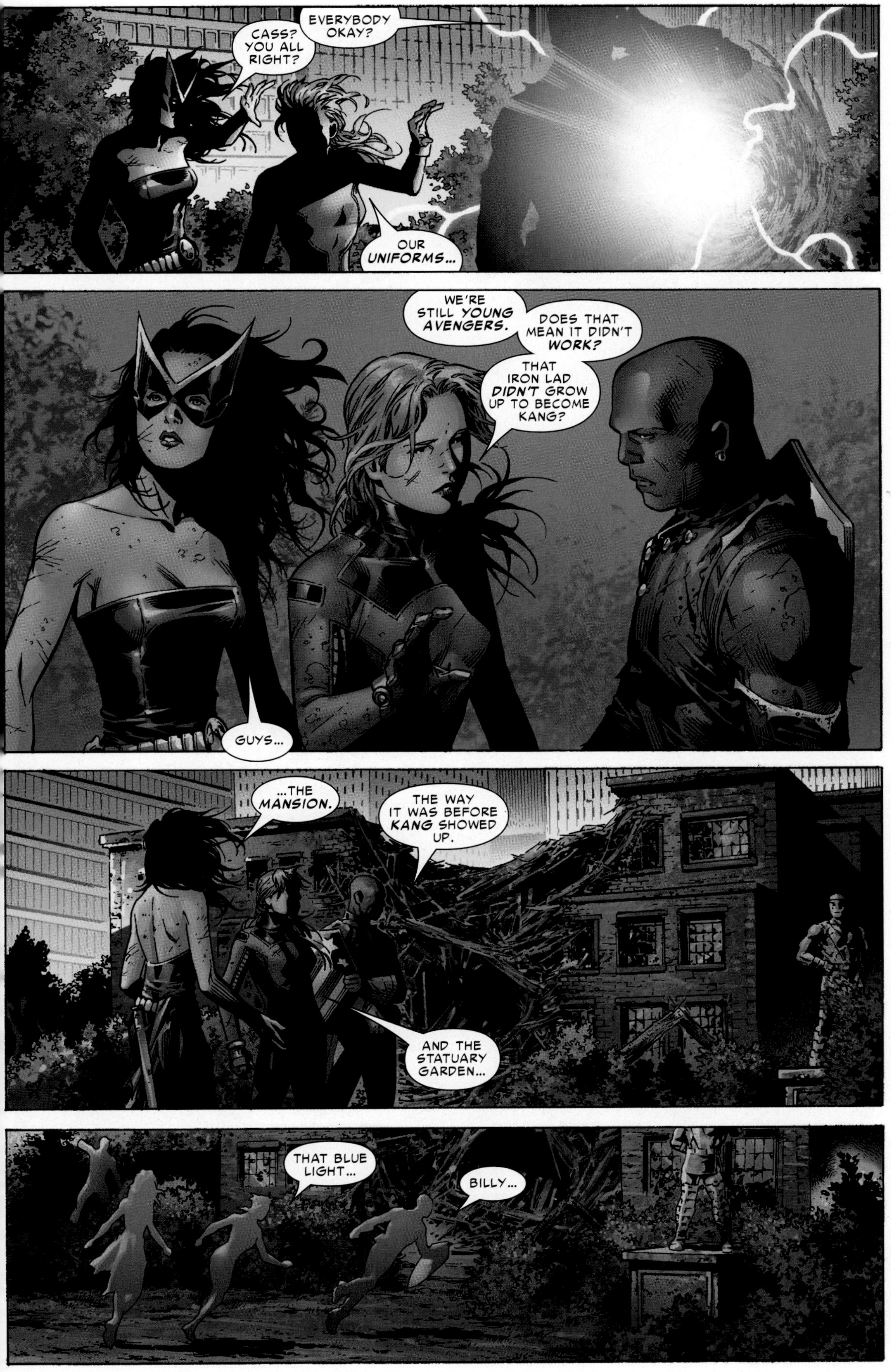
EVERYBODY OKAY?
CASS? YOU ALL RIGHT?
OUR UNIFORMS...
WE'RE STILL YOUNG AVENGERS.
DOES THAT MEAN IT DIDN'T WORK?
THAT IRON LAD DIDN'T GROW UP TO BECOME KANG?
GUYS...
...THE MANSION.
THE WAY IT WAS BEFORE KANG SHOWED UP.
AND THE STATUARY GARDEN...
THAT BLUE LIGHT...
BILLY...

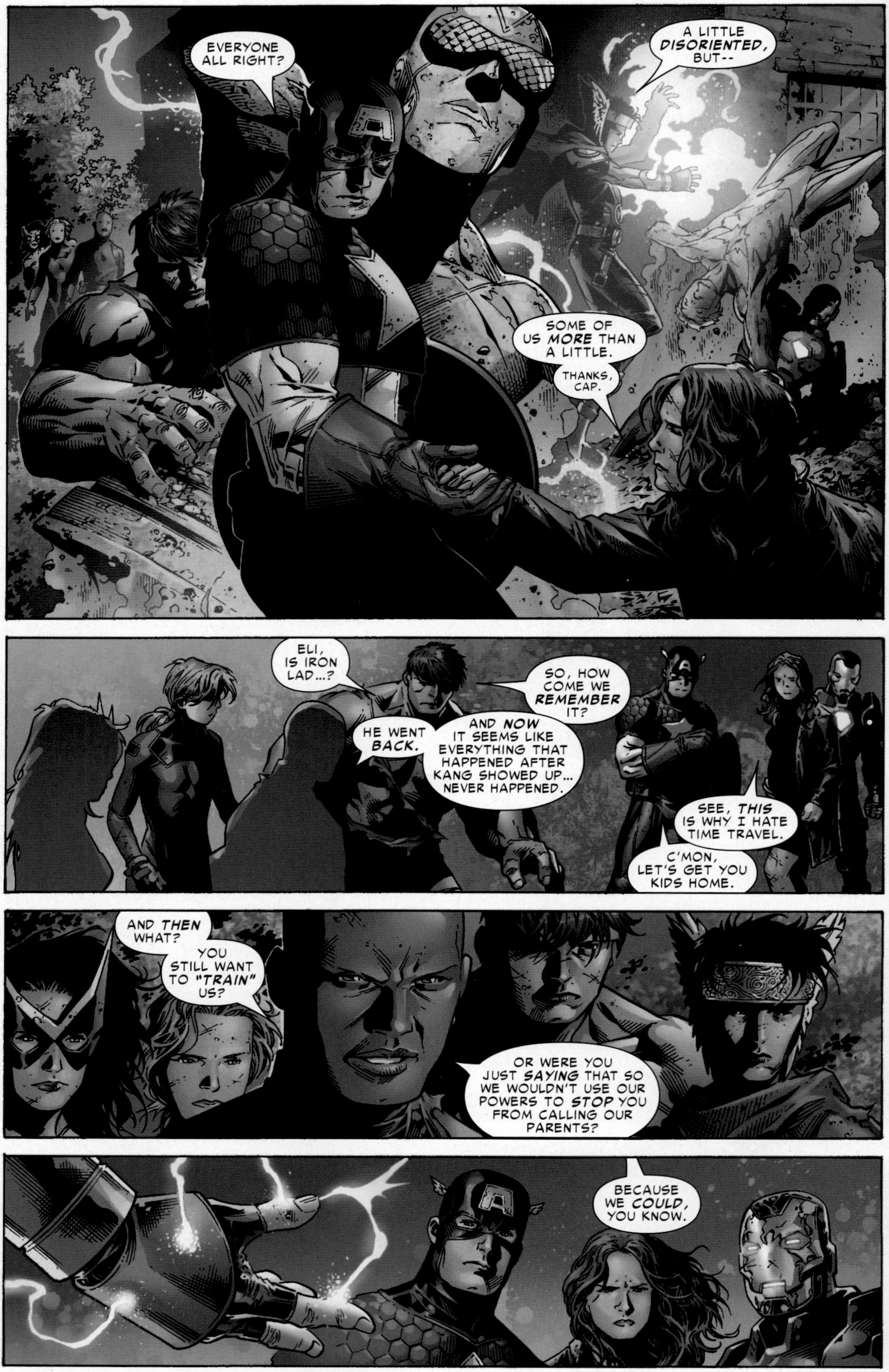
EVERYONE ALL RIGHT?
A LITTLE *DISORIENTED,* BUT--
SOME OF US *MORE* THAN A LITTLE.
THANKS, CAP.
ELI, IS IRON LAD...?
HE WENT *BACK.*
SO, HOW COME WE *REMEMBER* IT?
AND *NOW* IT SEEMS LIKE EVERYTHING THAT HAPPENED AFTER KANG SHOWED UP... NEVER HAPPENED.
SEE, *THIS* IS WHY I HATE TIME TRAVEL.
C'MON, LET'S GET YOU KIDS HOME.
AND *THEN* WHAT?
YOU STILL WANT TO *"TRAIN"* US?
OR WERE YOU JUST *SAYING* THAT SO WE WOULDN'T USE OUR POWERS TO *STOP* YOU FROM CALLING OUR PARENTS?
BECAUSE WE *COULD,* YOU KNOW.

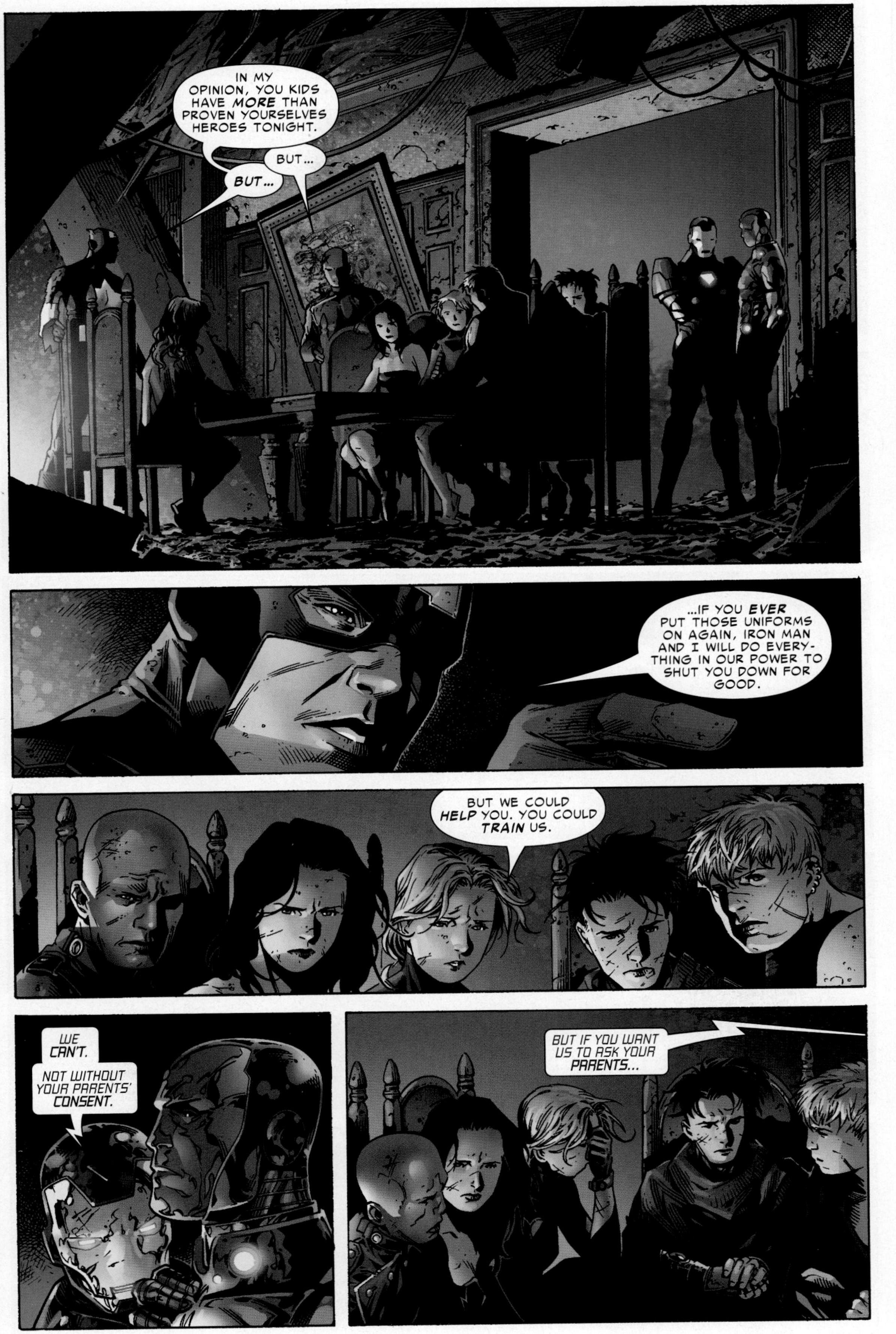
IN MY OPINION, YOU KIDS HAVE MORE THAN PROVEN YOURSELVES HEROES TONIGHT.
BUT...
BUT...
...IF YOU EVER PUT THOSE UNIFORMS ON AGAIN, IRON MAN AND I WILL DO EVERY-THING IN OUR POWER TO SHUT YOU DOWN FOR GOOD.
BUT WE COULD HELP YOU. YOU COULD TRAIN US.
WE CAN'T.
NOT WITHOUT YOUR PARENTS' CONSENT.
BUT IF YOU WANT US TO ASK YOUR PARENTS...

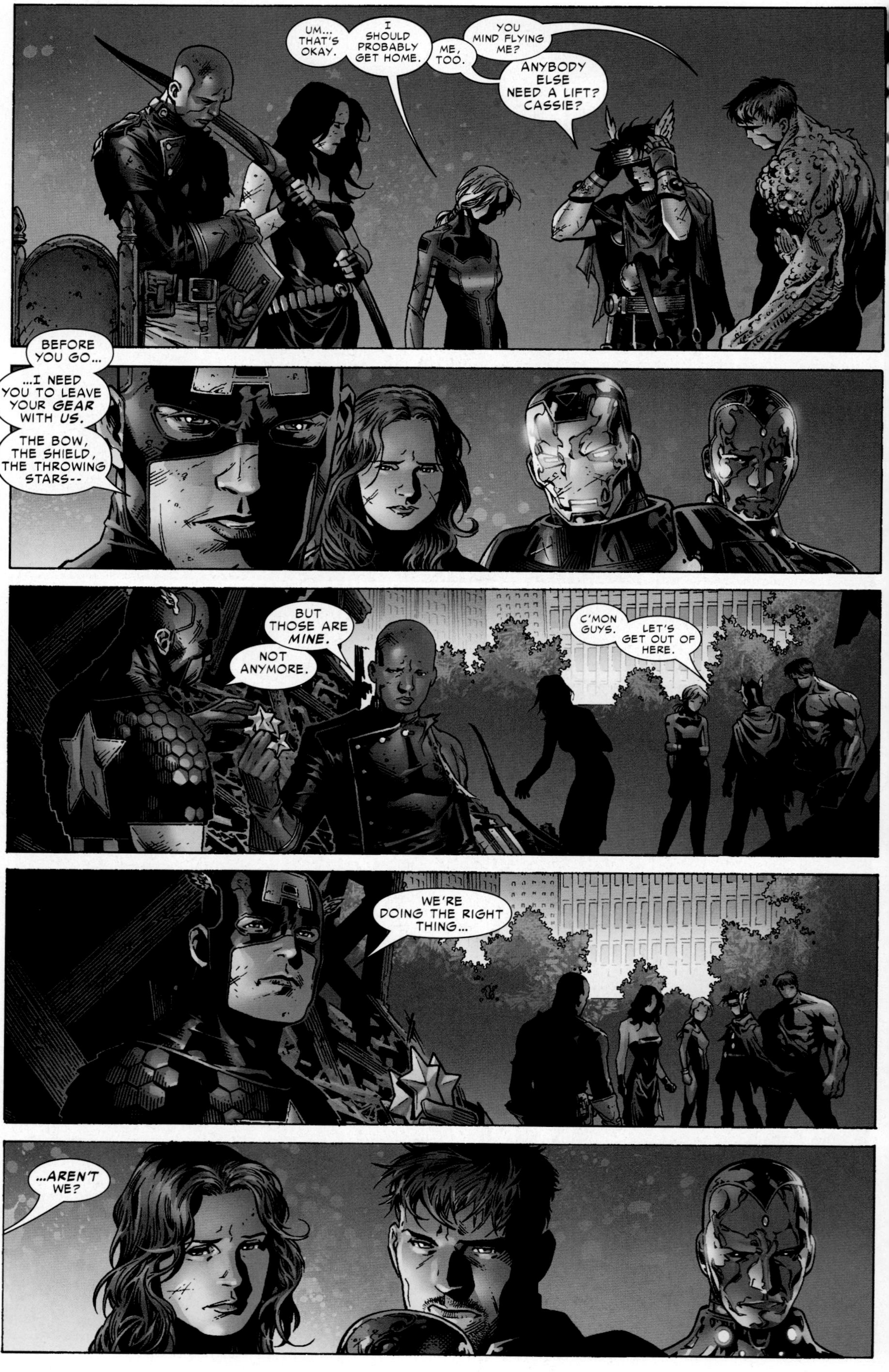
UM... THAT'S OKAY.
I SHOULD PROBABLY GET HOME.
ME, TOO.
YOU MIND FLYING ME?
ANYBODY ELSE NEED A LIFT? CASSIE?
BEFORE YOU GO...
...I NEED YOU TO LEAVE YOUR GEAR WITH US.
THE BOW, THE SHIELD, THE THROWING STARS--
BUT THOSE ARE MINE.
NOT ANYMORE.
C'MON GUYS.
LET'S GET OUT OF HERE.
WE'RE DOING THE RIGHT THING...
...AREN'T WE?

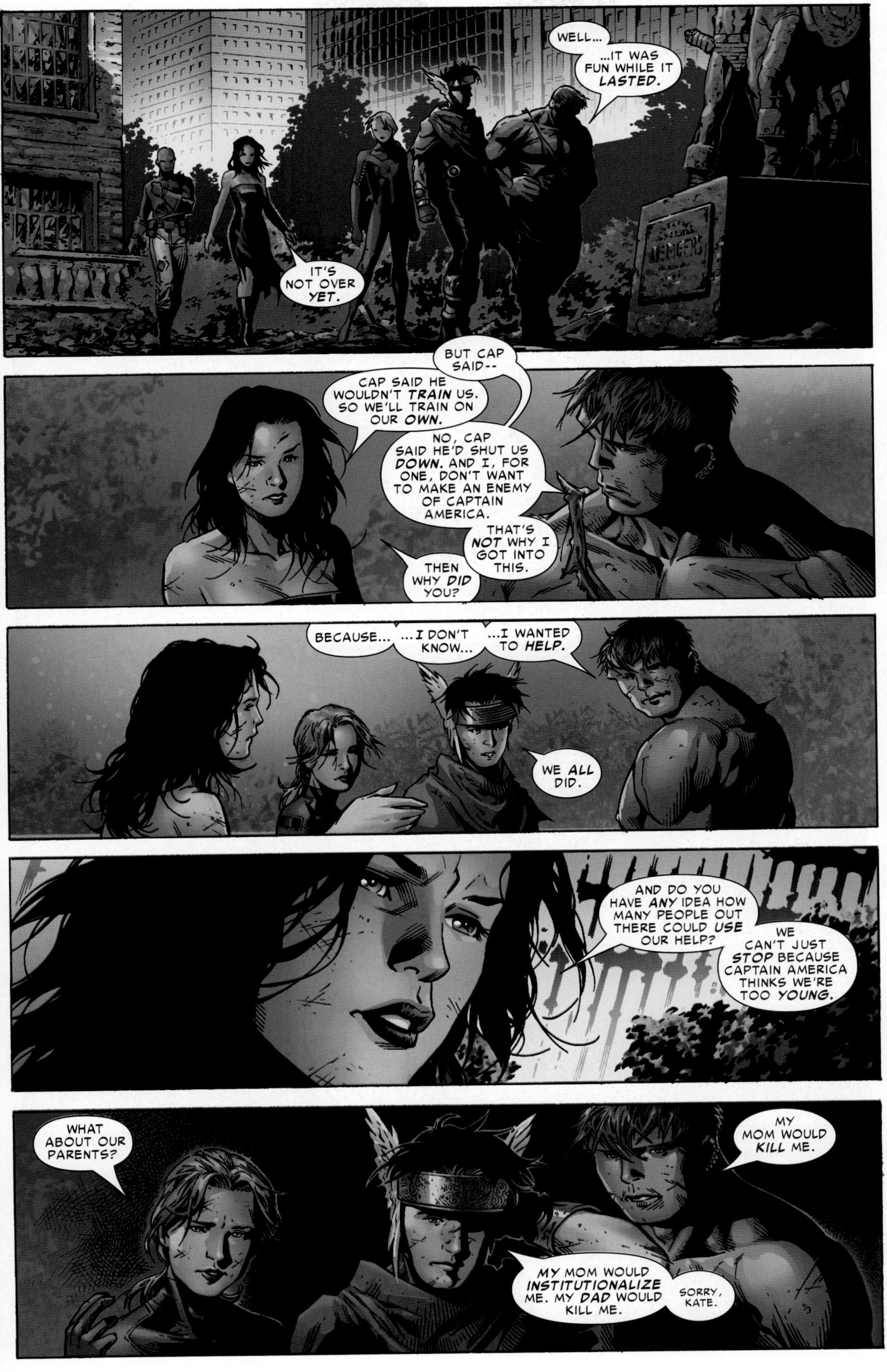
WELL...
...IT WAS FUN WHILE IT LASTED.
IT'S NOT OVER YET.
CAP SAID HE WOULDN'T TRAIN US. SO WE'LL TRAIN ON OUR OWN.
BUT CAP SAID--
NO, CAP SAID HE'D SHUT US DOWN. AND I, FOR ONE, DON'T WANT TO MAKE AN ENEMY OF CAPTAIN AMERICA.
THAT'S NOT WHY I GOT INTO THIS.
THEN WHY DID YOU?
BECAUSE...
...I DON'T KNOW...
...I WANTED TO HELP.
WE ALL DID.
AND DO YOU HAVE ANY IDEA HOW MANY PEOPLE OUT THERE COULD USE OUR HELP?
WE CAN'T JUST STOP BECAUSE CAPTAIN AMERICA THINKS WE'RE TOO YOUNG.
WHAT ABOUT OUR PARENTS?
MY MOM WOULD KILL ME.
MY MOM WOULD INSTITUTIONALIZE ME. MY DAD WOULD KILL ME.
SORRY, KATE.

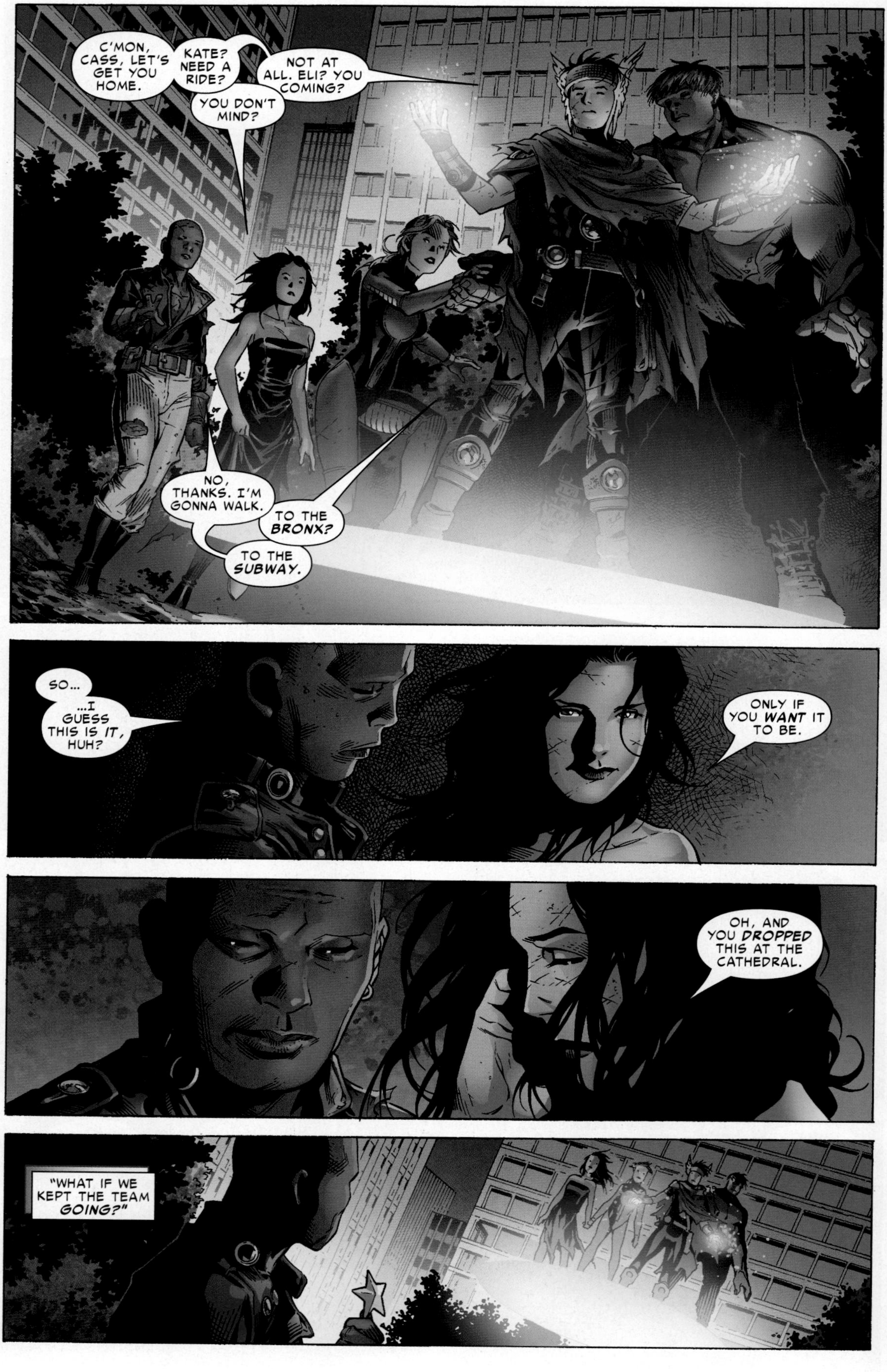
C'MON, CASS, LET'S GET YOU HOME.
KATE? NEED A RIDE?
YOU DON'T MIND?
NOT AT ALL. ELI? YOU COMING?
NO, THANKS. I'M GONNA WALK.
TO THE BRONX?
TO THE SUBWAY.
SO...
...I GUESS THIS IS IT, HUH?
ONLY IF YOU WANT IT TO BE.
OH, AND YOU DROPPED THIS AT THE CATHEDRAL.
"WHAT IF WE KEPT THE TEAM GOING?"

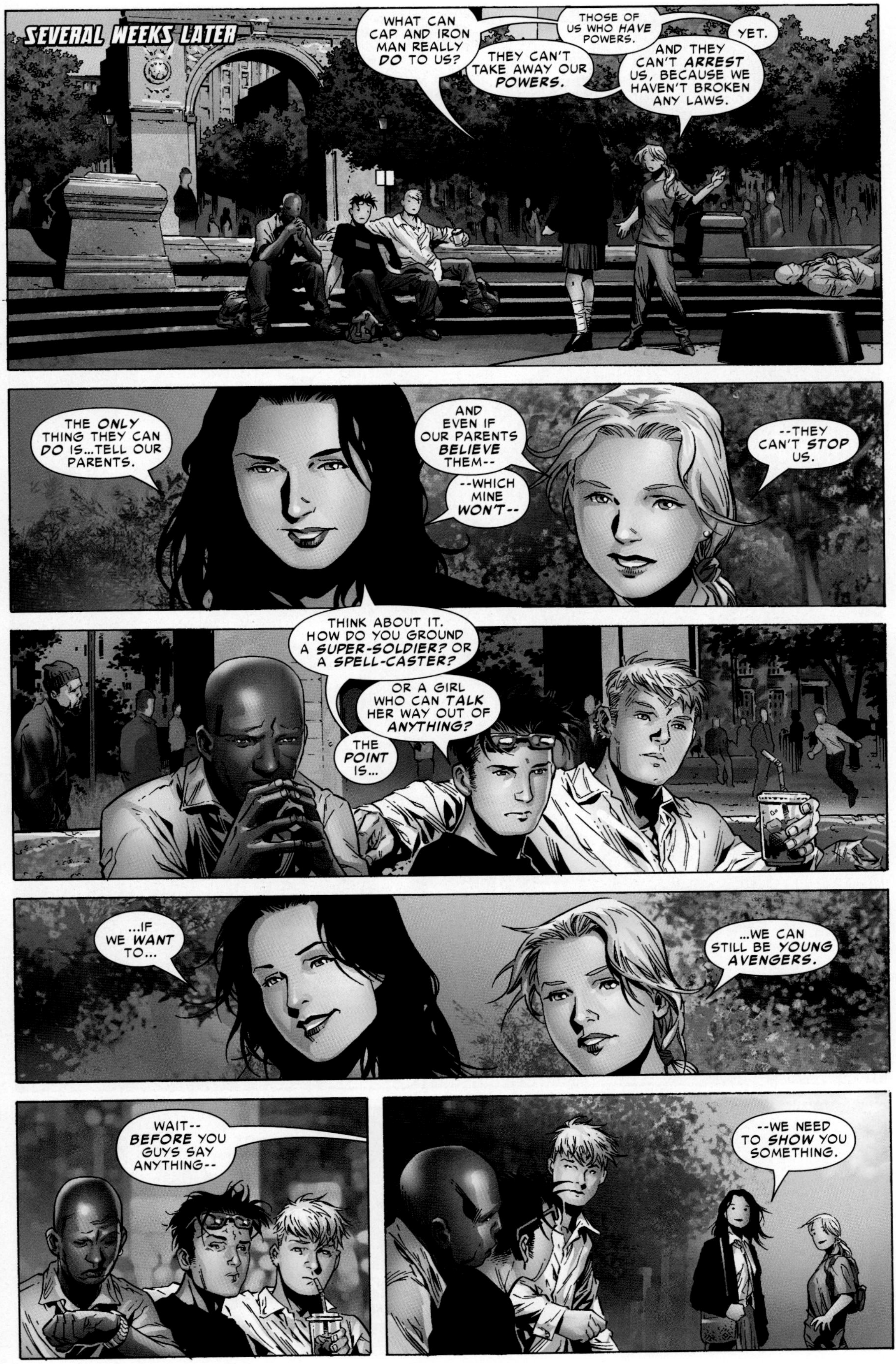
SEVERAL WEEKS LATER
WHAT CAN CAP AND IRON MAN REALLY DO TO US?
THOSE OF US WHO HAVE POWERS.
YET.
THEY CAN'T TAKE AWAY OUR POWERS.
AND THEY CAN'T ARREST US, BECAUSE WE HAVEN'T BROKEN ANY LAWS.
THE ONLY THING THEY CAN DO IS...TELL OUR PARENTS.
AND EVEN IF OUR PARENTS BELIEVE THEM--
--WHICH MINE WON'T--
--THEY CAN'T STOP US.
THINK ABOUT IT. HOW DO YOU GROUND A SUPER-SOLDIER? OR A SPELL-CASTER?
OR A GIRL WHO CAN TALK HER WAY OUT OF ANYTHING?
THE POINT IS...
...IF WE WANT TO...
...WE CAN STILL BE YOUNG AVENGERS.
WAIT-- BEFORE YOU GUYS SAY ANYTHING--
--WE NEED TO SHOW YOU SOMETHING.

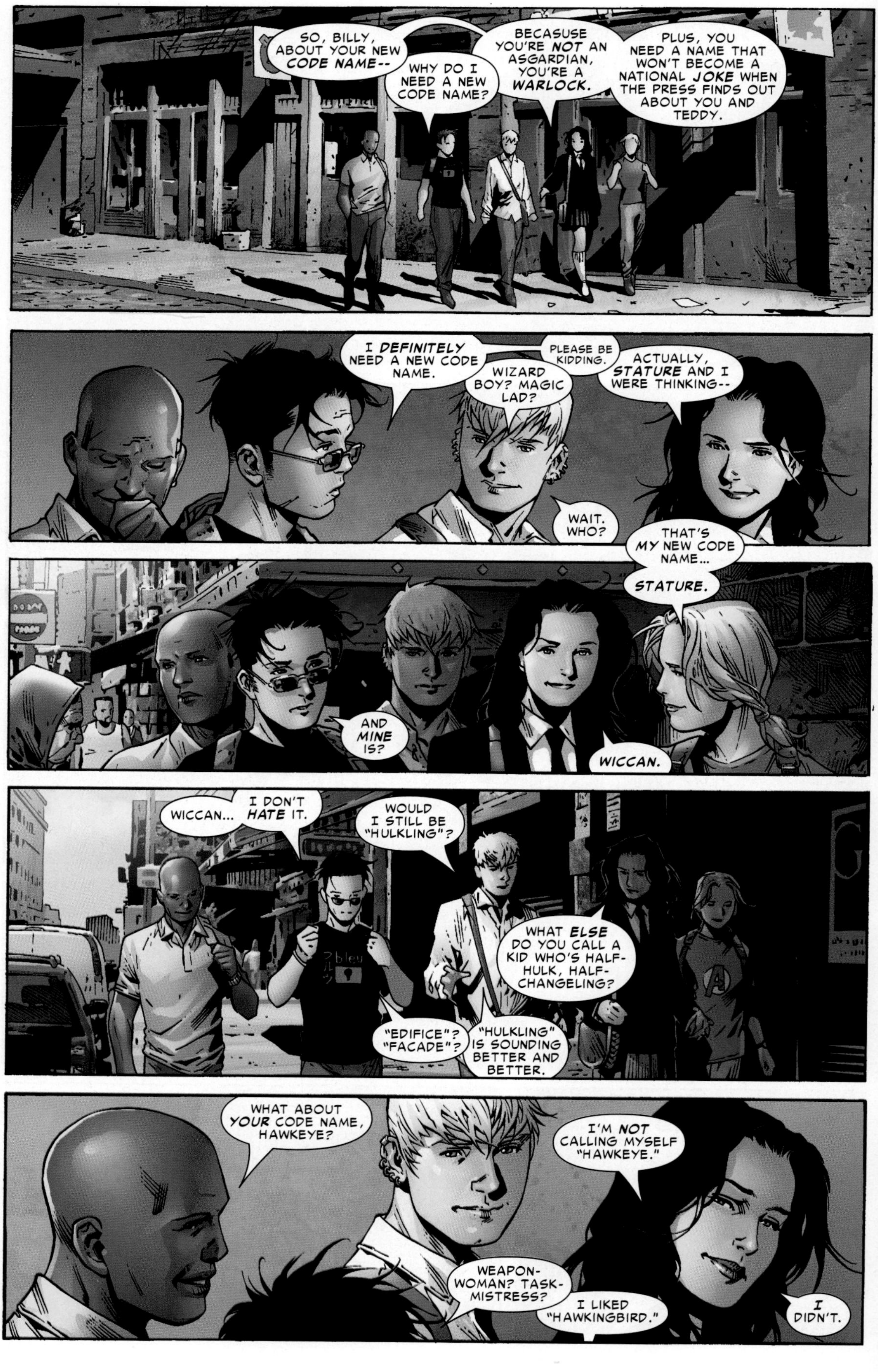
SO, BILLY, ABOUT YOUR NEW CODE NAME--
WHY DO I NEED A NEW CODE NAME?
BECASUSE YOU'RE NOT AN ASGARDIAN, YOU'RE A WARLOCK.
PLUS, YOU NEED A NAME THAT WON'T BECOME A NATIONAL JOKE WHEN THE PRESS FINDS OUT ABOUT YOU AND TEDDY.
I DEFINITELY NEED A NEW CODE NAME.
PLEASE BE KIDDING.
WIZARD BOY? MAGIC LAD?
ACTUALLY, STATURE AND I WERE THINKING--
WAIT. WHO?
THAT'S MY NEW CODE NAME...
STATURE.
AND MINE IS?
WICCAN.
WICCAN...
I DON'T HATE IT.
WOULD I STILL BE "HULKLING"?
WHAT ELSE DO YOU CALL A KID WHO'S HALF-HULK, HALF-CHANGELING?
"EDIFICE"? "FACADE"?
"HULKLING" IS SOUNDING BETTER AND BETTER.
WHAT ABOUT YOUR CODE NAME, HAWKEYE?
I'M NOT CALLING MYSELF "HAWKEYE."
WEAPON-WOMAN? TASK-MISTRESS?
I LIKED "HAWKINGBIRD."
I DIDN'T.

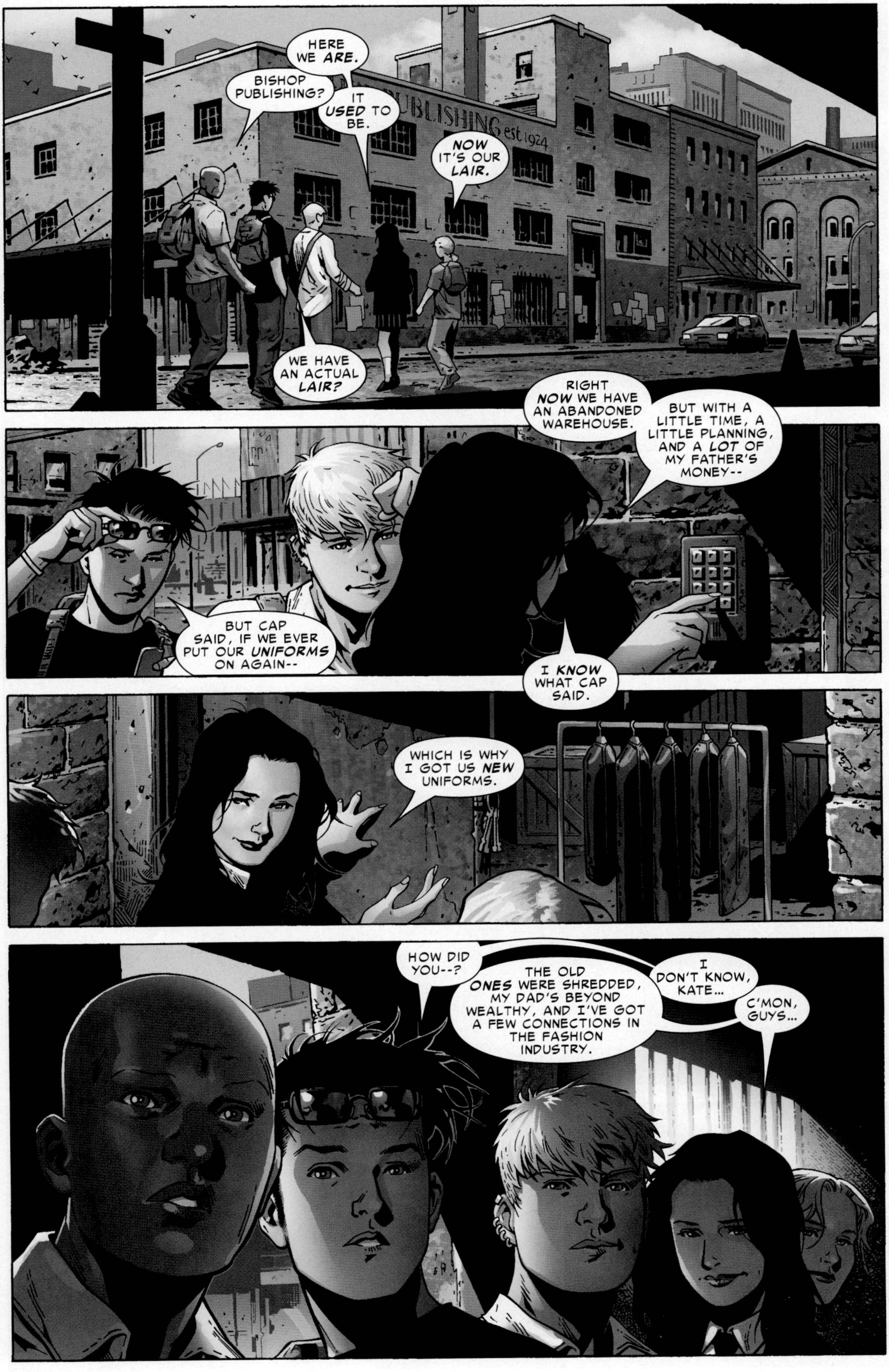
BISHOP PUBLISHING?
HERE WE ARE.
IT USED TO BE.
NOW IT'S OUR LAIR.
WE HAVE AN ACTUAL LAIR?
PUBLISHING est 1924
RIGHT NOW WE HAVE AN ABANDONED WAREHOUSE.
BUT WITH A LITTLE TIME, A LITTLE PLANNING, AND A LOT OF MY FATHER'S MONEY--
BUT CAP SAID, IF WE EVER PUT OUR UNIFORMS ON AGAIN--
I KNOW WHAT CAP SAID.
WHICH IS WHY I GOT US NEW UNIFORMS.
HOW DID YOU--?
THE OLD ONES WERE SHREDDED, MY DAD'S BEYOND WEALTHY, AND I'VE GOT A FEW CONNECTIONS IN THE FASHION INDUSTRY.
I DON'T KNOW, KATE...
C'MON, GUYS...

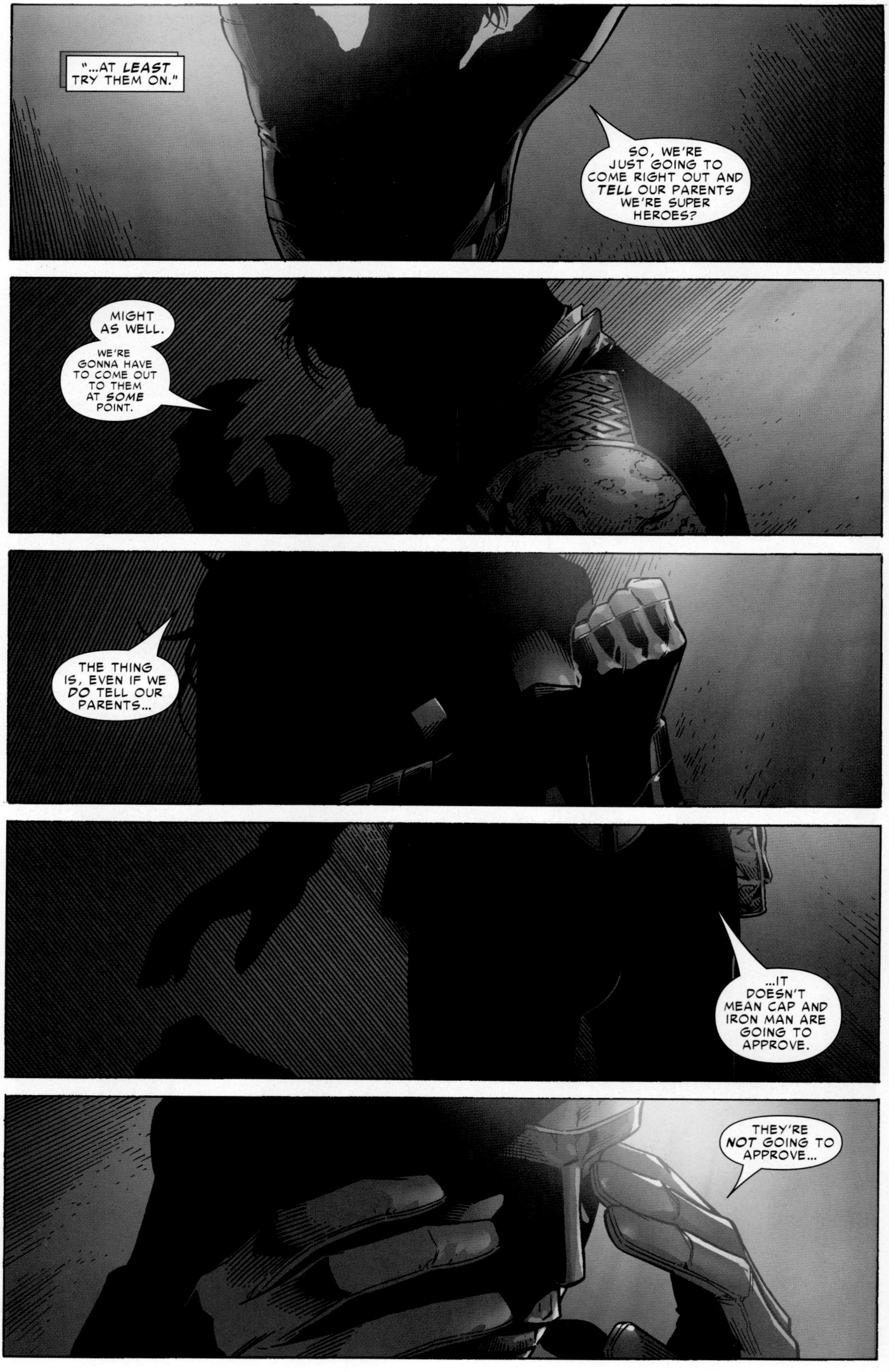
"...AT LEAST TRY THEM ON."
SO, WE'RE JUST GOING TO COME RIGHT OUT AND TELL OUR PARENTS WE'RE SUPER HEROES?
MIGHT AS WELL.
WE'RE GONNA HAVE TO COME OUT TO THEM AT SOME POINT.
THE THING IS, EVEN IF WE DO TELL OUR PARENTS...
...IT DOESN'T MEAN CAP AND IRON MAN ARE GOING TO APPROVE.
THEY'RE NOT GOING TO APPROVE...

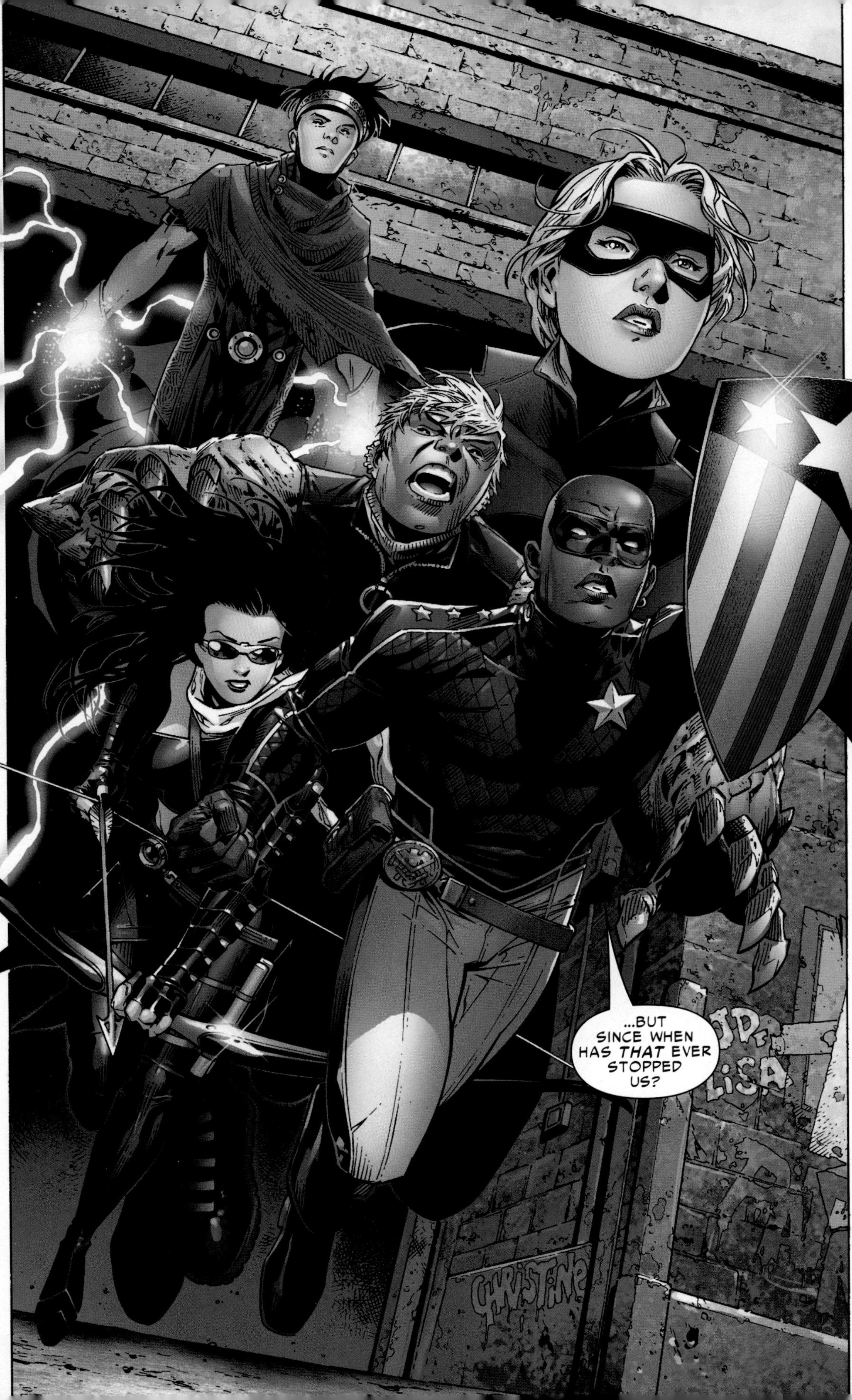
...BUT SINCE WHEN HAS THAT EVER STOPPED US?

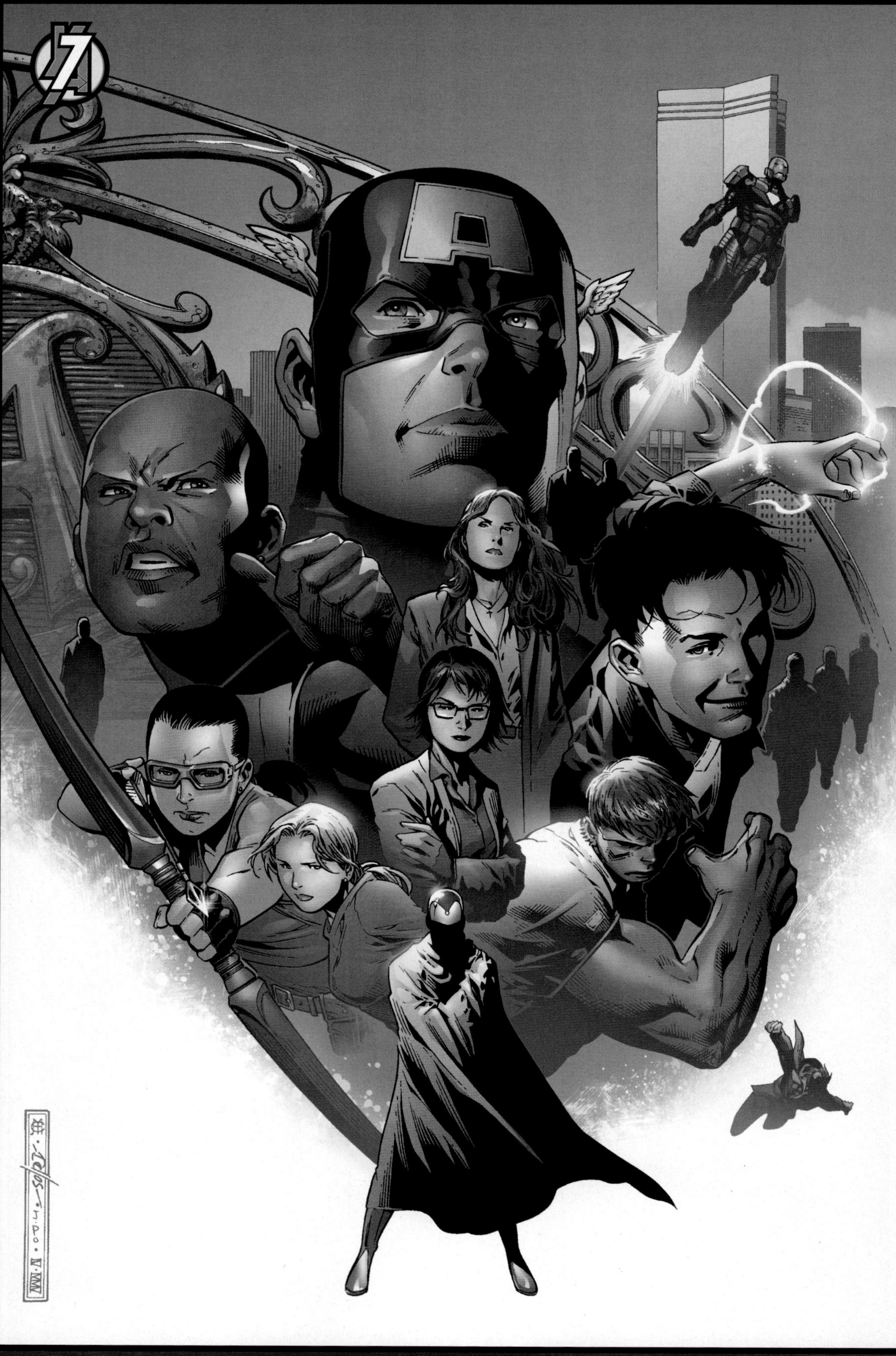

DAILY BUGLE

THE NEW YOUNG AVENGERS?

WHAT THE HELL DO THESE KIDS THINK THEY'RE DOING?

The Young Avengers proudly display their quarry, The Shocker, amid the fluttering evidence of his failure. One hundred percent of the ... was recovered. The Shocker is currently in custody.
-Photo by Todd Casey

The reinvented supergroup brings a "shocking" end to attempt...

By Bugle Reporter Kat Farrell
Staff Writer

Dolor sit amet, consectetuer adipiscing elit, sed diam nonummy nibh euismod tincidunt ut laoreet dolore magna on aliquam erat volutpat. Ut wisi enim ad twe minim veniam, quis nostrud exerci tatio ullamcorper suscipit lobortis nisl ut ang.

Eliquip ex ea commodo consequat. Duis autem vel eum iriure dolor a hendrerit in molestie consequat,

cumsan... usto odio dignissim qui blandit praese... ptatum zzril delenit augue duis dolore... feugiat nulla facilisi.

Ut w... enim ad minim veniam, quis nostrud... erci tation ullamcorper suscipit lobort... nisl ut aliquip ex ea commodo con- seq... at. Duis autem vel eum iriure dolor in he... drerit in vulputate velit esse molestie co... sequat, vel illum dolore eu feugiat n... la facilisis at vero eros et accumsan et i... sto odio dignissim qui blandit praesent ... ptatum zzril delenit augue duis dolore te Lorem ipsum dolor

drerit in vulputate velit esse molestie co... sequat, vel illum dolore eu feugiat nulla facilisis at vero eros et accumsan et iust odio dignissim qui blandit praesent lup tum zzril delenit augue duis dolore te v feugait nulla facilisi.

Bolfang iktum dolor sit amet, fanstati adipiscing elit, sed diam nonummy ni euismod tincidunt ut laoreet dolore n aliquam erat volutpat.

Duis autem vel eum iriure dolor in h drerit in vulputate velit esse molesti sequat, quis nostrud exerci tation ul ... bortis nisl ut aliqu

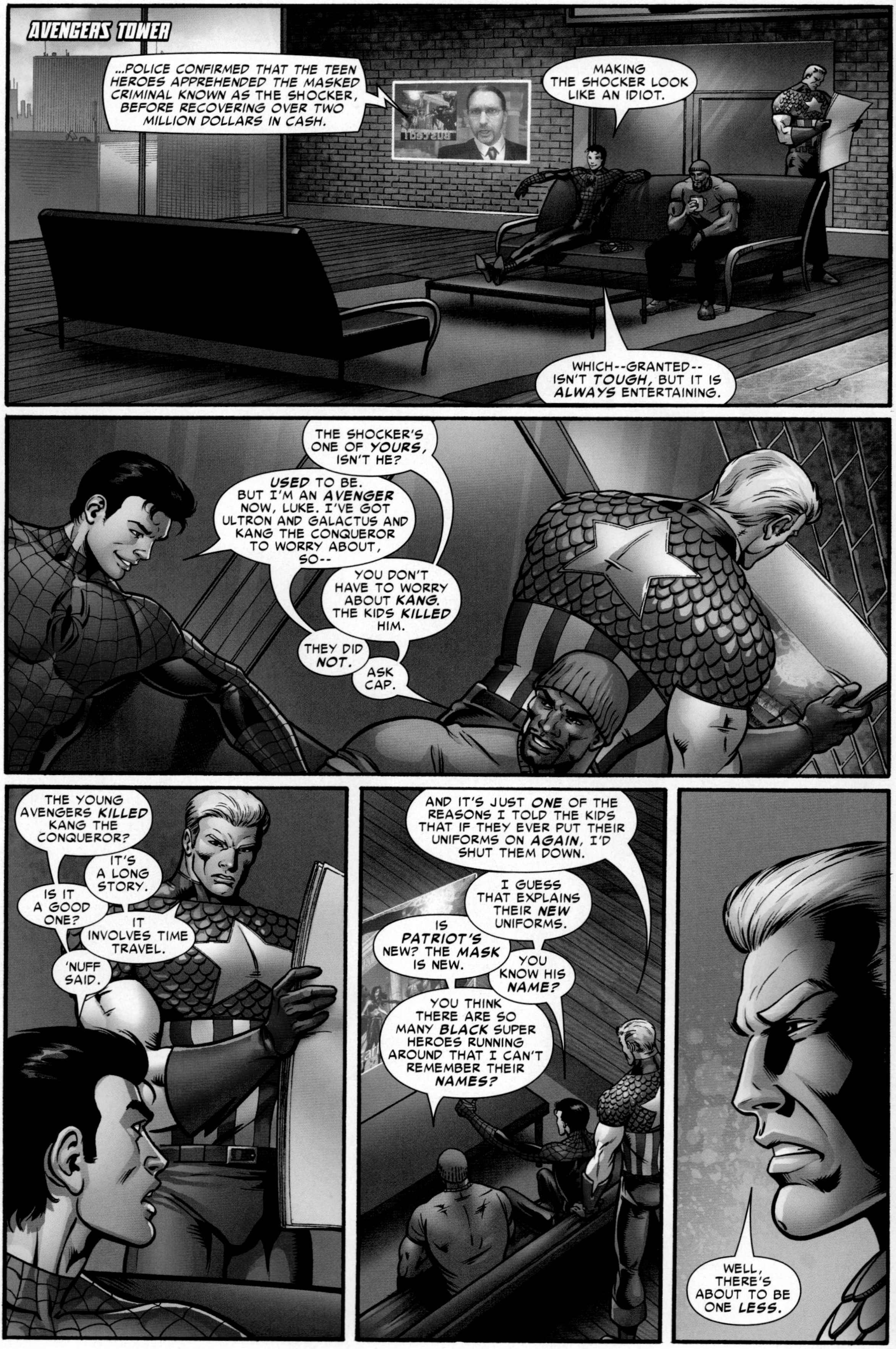
AVENGERS TOWER
...POLICE CONFIRMED THAT THE TEEN HEROES APPREHENDED THE MASKED CRIMINAL KNOWN AS THE SHOCKER, BEFORE RECOVERING OVER TWO MILLION DOLLARS IN CASH.
BUSTED!
MAKING THE SHOCKER LOOK LIKE AN IDIOT.
WHICH--GRANTED--ISN'T TOUGH, BUT IT IS ALWAYS ENTERTAINING.
THE SHOCKER'S ONE OF YOURS, ISN'T HE?
USED TO BE. BUT I'M AN AVENGER NOW, LUKE. I'VE GOT ULTRON AND GALACTUS AND KANG THE CONQUEROR TO WORRY ABOUT, SO--
YOU DON'T HAVE TO WORRY ABOUT KANG. THE KIDS KILLED HIM.
THEY DID NOT.
ASK CAP.
THE YOUNG AVENGERS KILLED KANG THE CONQUEROR?
IT'S A LONG STORY.
IS IT A GOOD ONE?
IT INVOLVES TIME TRAVEL.
'NUFF SAID.
AND IT'S JUST ONE OF THE REASONS I TOLD THE KIDS THAT IF THEY EVER PUT THEIR UNIFORMS ON AGAIN, I'D SHUT THEM DOWN.
I GUESS THAT EXPLAINS THEIR NEW UNIFORMS.
IS PATRIOT'S NEW? THE MASK IS NEW.
YOU KNOW HIS NAME?
YOU THINK THERE ARE SO MANY BLACK SUPER HEROES RUNNING AROUND THAT I CAN'T REMEMBER THEIR NAMES?
WELL, THERE'S ABOUT TO BE ONE LESS.

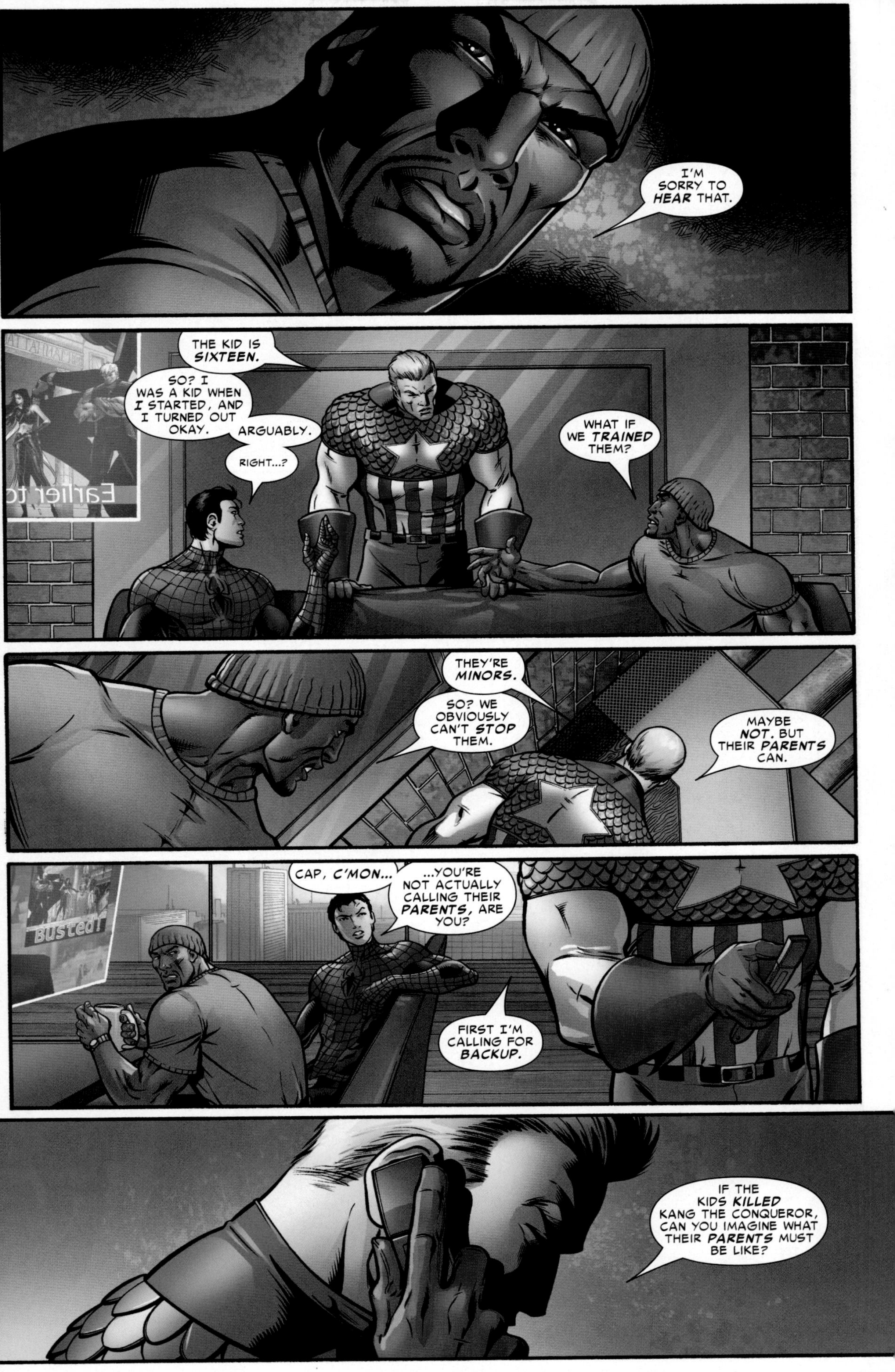
I'M SORRY TO HEAR THAT.
THE KID IS SIXTEEN.
SO? I WAS A KID WHEN I STARTED, AND I TURNED OUT OKAY.
ARGUABLY.
RIGHT...?
WHAT IF WE TRAINED THEM?
THEY'RE MINORS.
SO? WE OBVIOUSLY CAN'T STOP THEM.
MAYBE NOT. BUT THEIR PARENTS CAN.
Busted!
CAP, C'MON...
...YOU'RE NOT ACTUALLY CALLING THEIR PARENTS, ARE YOU?
FIRST I'M CALLING FOR BACKUP.
IF THE KIDS KILLED KANG THE CONQUEROR, CAN YOU IMAGINE WHAT THEIR PARENTS MUST BE LIKE?

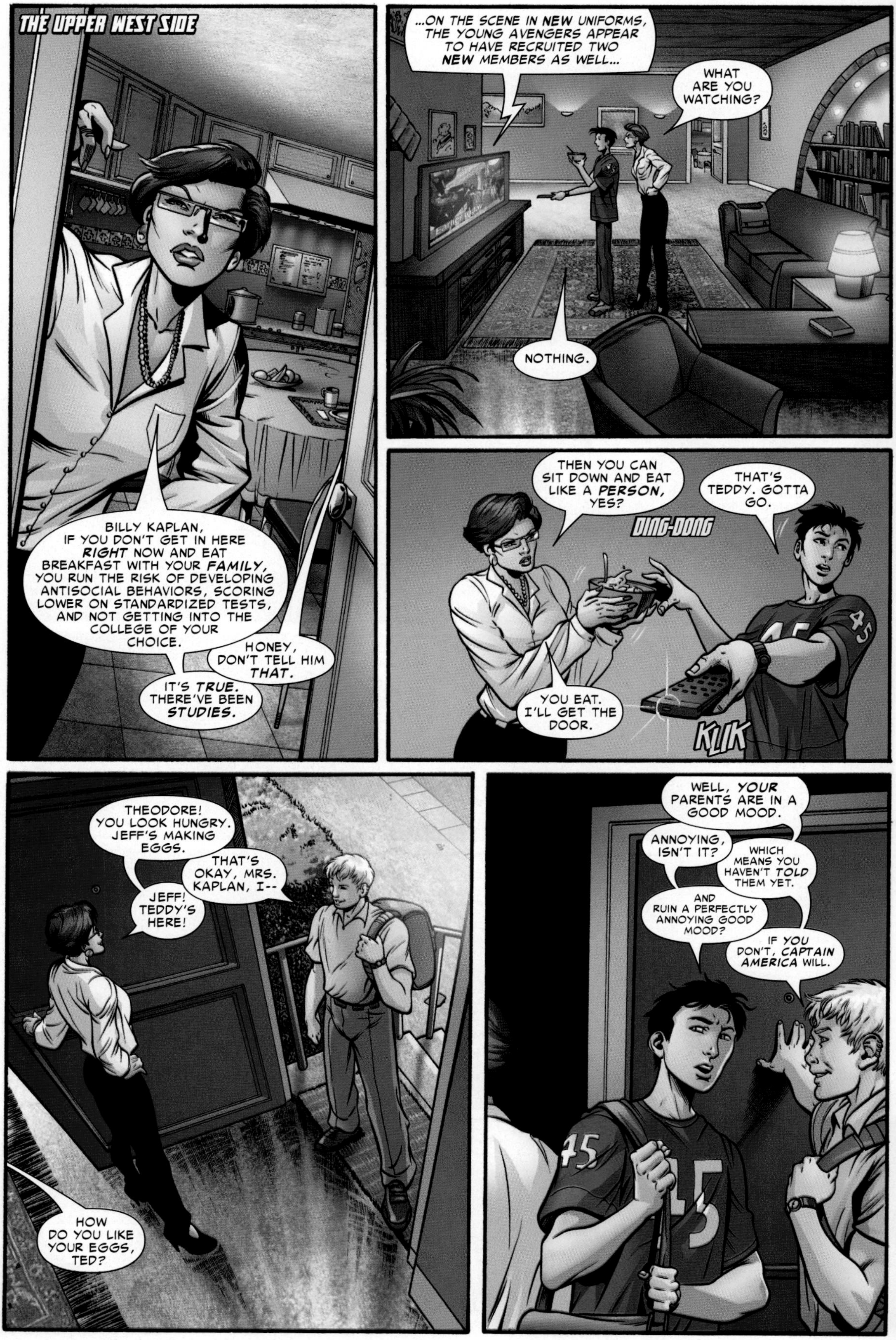
THE UPPER WEST SIDE
BILLY KAPLAN, IF YOU DON'T GET IN HERE RIGHT NOW AND EAT BREAKFAST WITH YOUR FAMILY, YOU RUN THE RISK OF DEVELOPING ANTISOCIAL BEHAVIORS, SCORING LOWER ON STANDARDIZED TESTS, AND NOT GETTING INTO THE COLLEGE OF YOUR CHOICE.
HONEY, DON'T TELL HIM THAT.
IT'S TRUE. THERE'VE BEEN STUDIES.
...ON THE SCENE IN NEW UNIFORMS, THE YOUNG AVENGERS APPEAR TO HAVE RECRUITED TWO NEW MEMBERS AS WELL...
WHAT ARE YOU WATCHING?
NOTHING.
THEN YOU CAN SIT DOWN AND EAT LIKE A PERSON, YES?
DING-DONG
THAT'S TEDDY. GOTTA GO.
YOU EAT. I'LL GET THE DOOR.
KLIK
THEODORE! YOU LOOK HUNGRY. JEFF'S MAKING EGGS.
THAT'S OKAY, MRS. KAPLAN, I--
JEFF! TEDDY'S HERE!
HOW DO YOU LIKE YOUR EGGS, TED?
WELL, YOUR PARENTS ARE IN A GOOD MOOD.
ANNOYING, ISN'T IT?
WHICH MEANS YOU HAVEN'T TOLD THEM YET.
AND RUIN A PERFECTLY ANNOYING GOOD MOOD?
IF YOU DON'T, CAPTAIN AMERICA WILL.

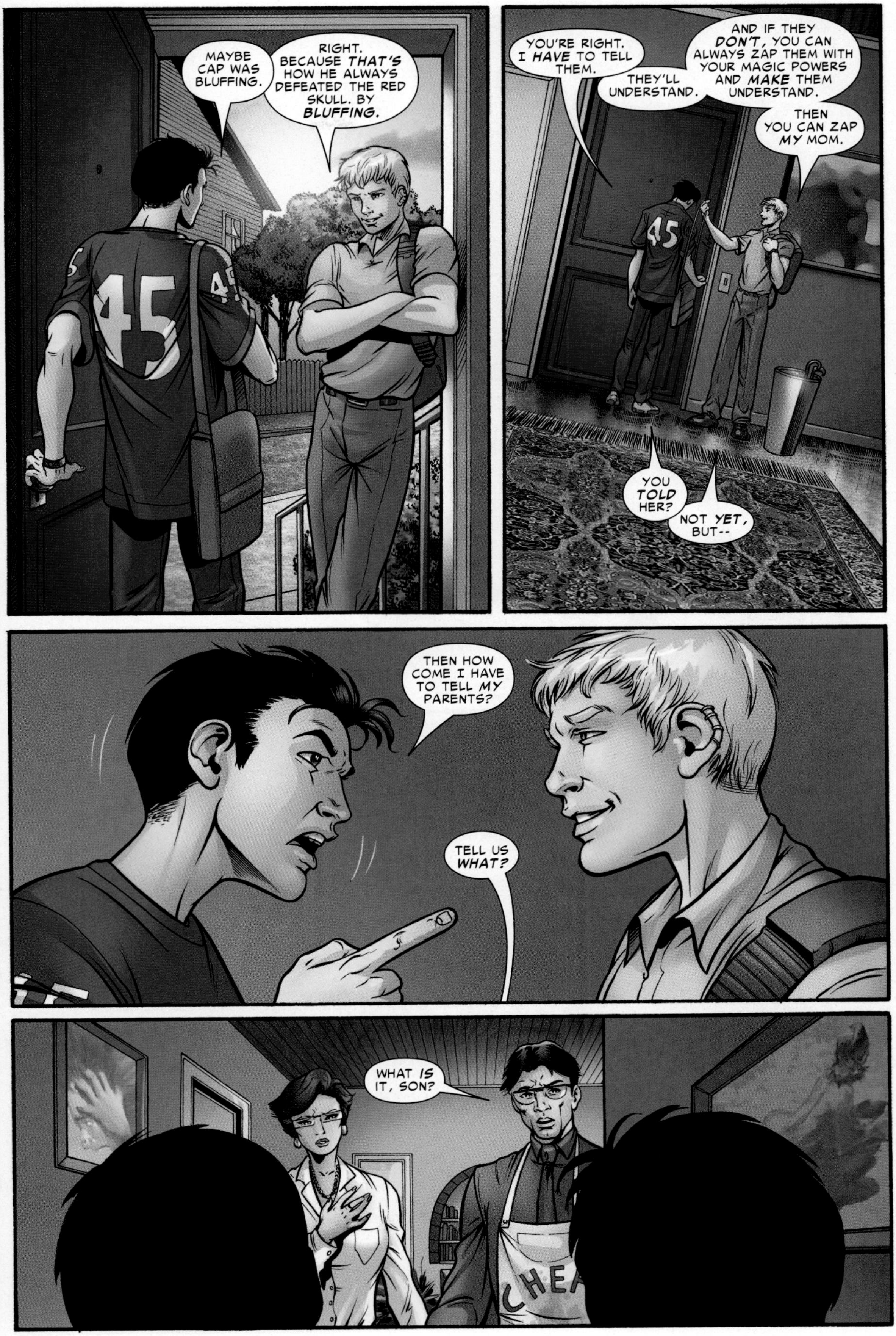
MAYBE CAP WAS BLUFFING.
RIGHT. BECAUSE THAT'S HOW HE ALWAYS DEFEATED THE RED SKULL. BY BLUFFING.
YOU'RE RIGHT. I HAVE TO TELL THEM.
THEY'LL UNDERSTAND.
AND IF THEY DON'T, YOU CAN ALWAYS ZAP THEM WITH YOUR MAGIC POWERS AND MAKE THEM UNDERSTAND.
THEN YOU CAN ZAP MY MOM.
YOU TOLD HER?
NOT YET, BUT--
THEN HOW COME I HAVE TO TELL MY PARENTS?
TELL US WHAT?
WHAT IS IT, SON?
CHEF

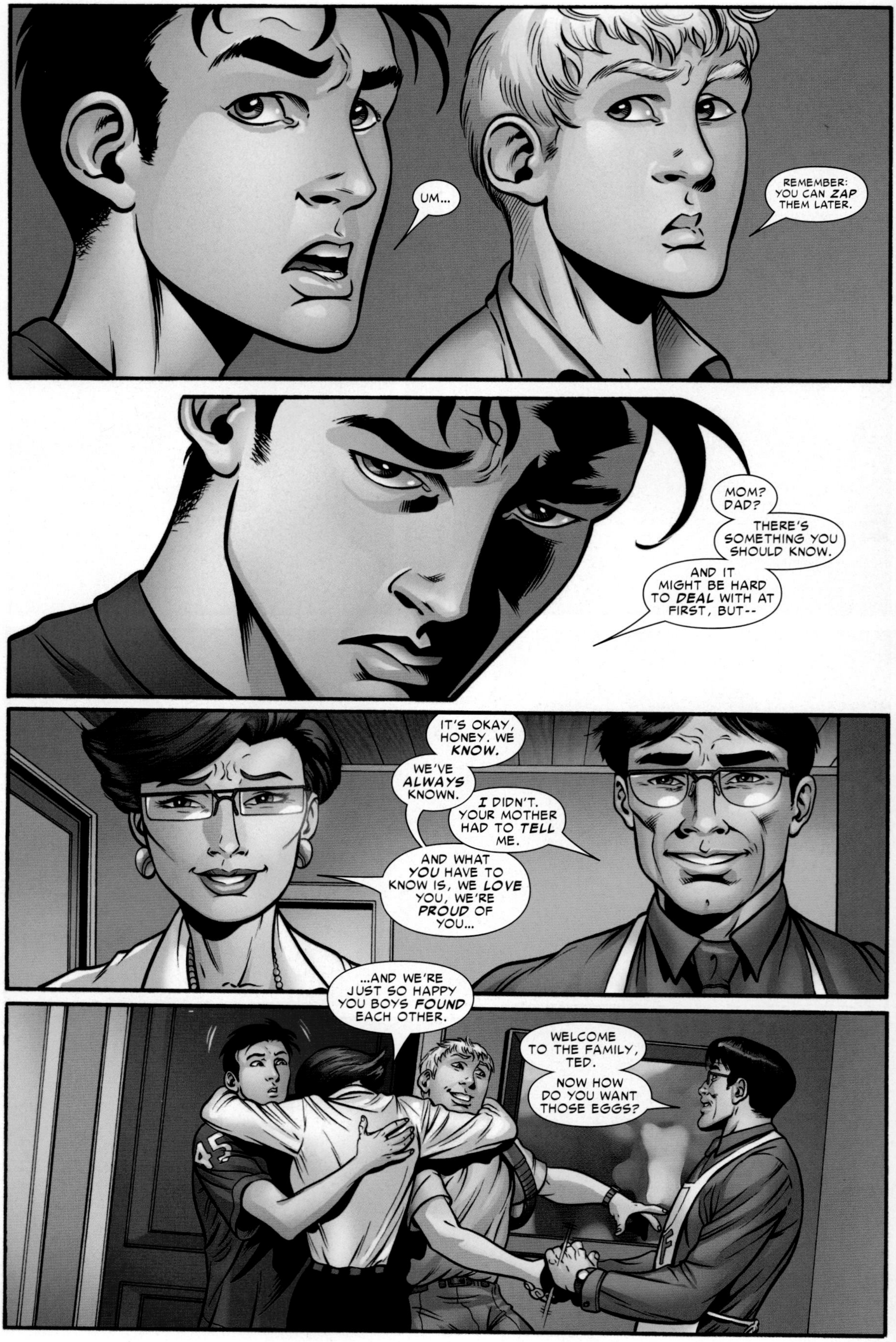
UM...
REMEMBER: YOU CAN ZAP THEM LATER.
MOM? DAD?
THERE'S SOMETHING YOU SHOULD KNOW.
AND IT MIGHT BE HARD TO DEAL WITH AT FIRST, BUT--
IT'S OKAY, HONEY. WE KNOW.
WE'VE ALWAYS KNOWN.
I DIDN'T. YOUR MOTHER HAD TO TELL ME.
AND WHAT YOU HAVE TO KNOW IS, WE LOVE YOU, WE'RE PROUD OF YOU...
...AND WE'RE JUST SO HAPPY YOU BOYS FOUND EACH OTHER.
WELCOME TO THE FAMILY, TED.
NOW HOW DO YOU WANT THOSE EGGS?

THE *GIANT* GIRL. YOU DON'T THINK--

PEGGY, C'MON...

I KNOW, BUT THE *COSTUME*, THE *HAIR*--

Earlier today

HONEY, SCOTT'S POWERS WEREN'T *GENETIC*. THEY WERE *CHEMICAL*.

SO, WHAT IF SHE'S GOTTEN AHOLD OF THE *CHEMICALS?*

I WOULDN'T *WORRY* ABOUT IT.

CASSIE'S NOT EXACTLY THE *SUPER HERO* TYPE.

WHAT IS *THAT* SUPPOSED TO MEAN?

IT MEANS SHE CAN BARELY *FOCUS* LONG ENOUGH TO DO HER *HOMEWORK*, LET ALONE CAPTURE THE SHOCKER.

BESIDES, CASSIE *KNOWS* HOW YOU FELT ABOUT HER DAD BEING ANT-MAN.

THERE'S NO WAY SHE'D PUT YOU THROUGH *THAT* AGAIN.

SHE *LOVES* YOU TOO MUCH.

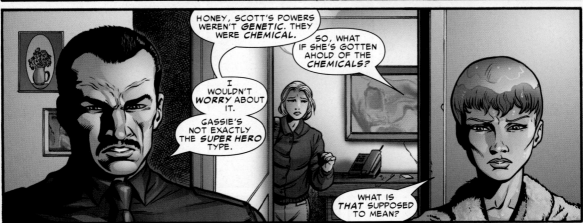

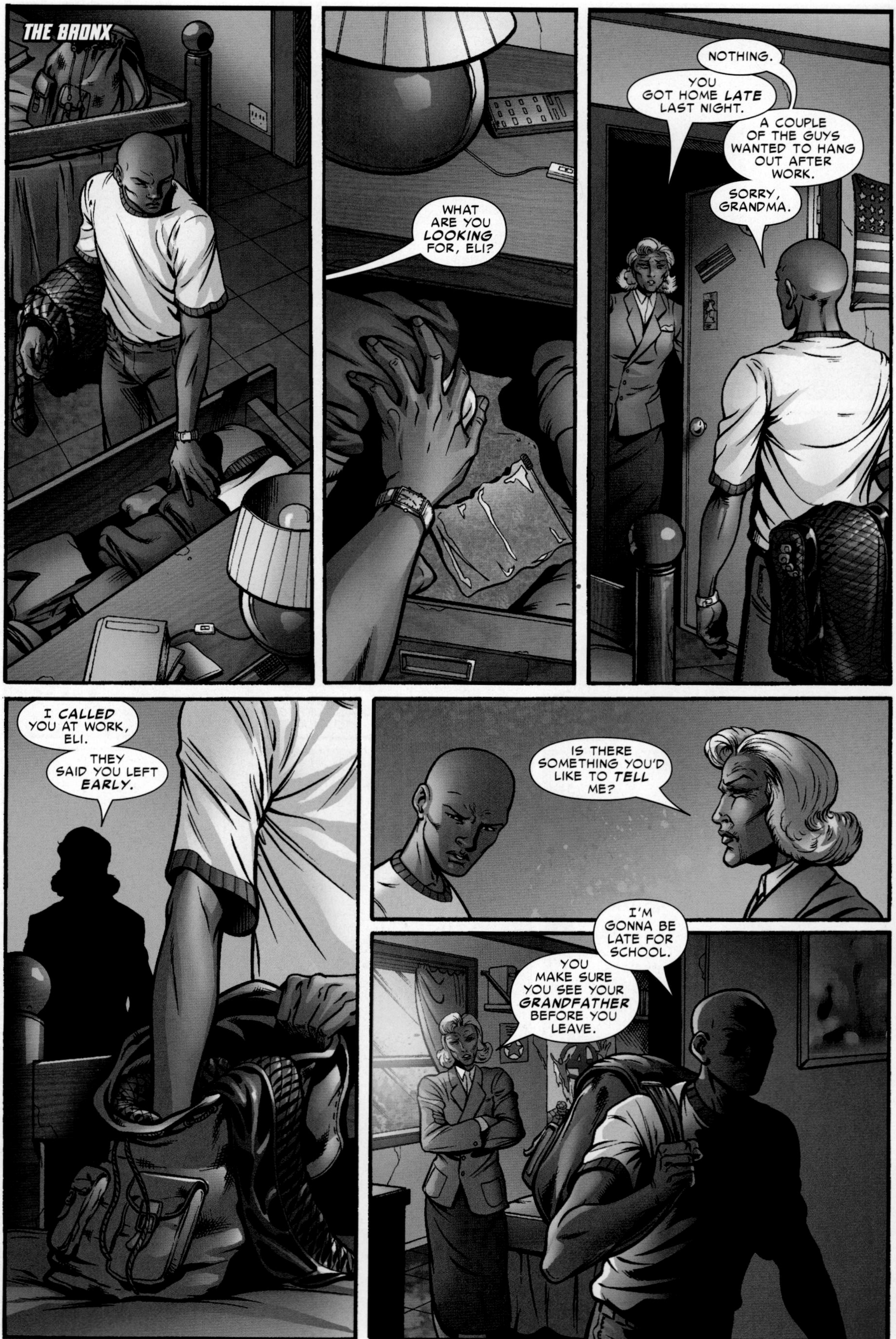
THE BRONX
WHAT ARE YOU LOOKING FOR, ELI?
NOTHING.
YOU GOT HOME LATE LAST NIGHT.
A COUPLE OF THE GUYS WANTED TO HANG OUT AFTER WORK.
SORRY, GRANDMA.
I CALLED YOU AT WORK, ELI.
THEY SAID YOU LEFT EARLY.
IS THERE SOMETHING YOU'D LIKE TO TELL ME?
I'M GONNA BE LATE FOR SCHOOL.
YOU MAKE SURE YOU SEE YOUR GRANDFATHER BEFORE YOU LEAVE.

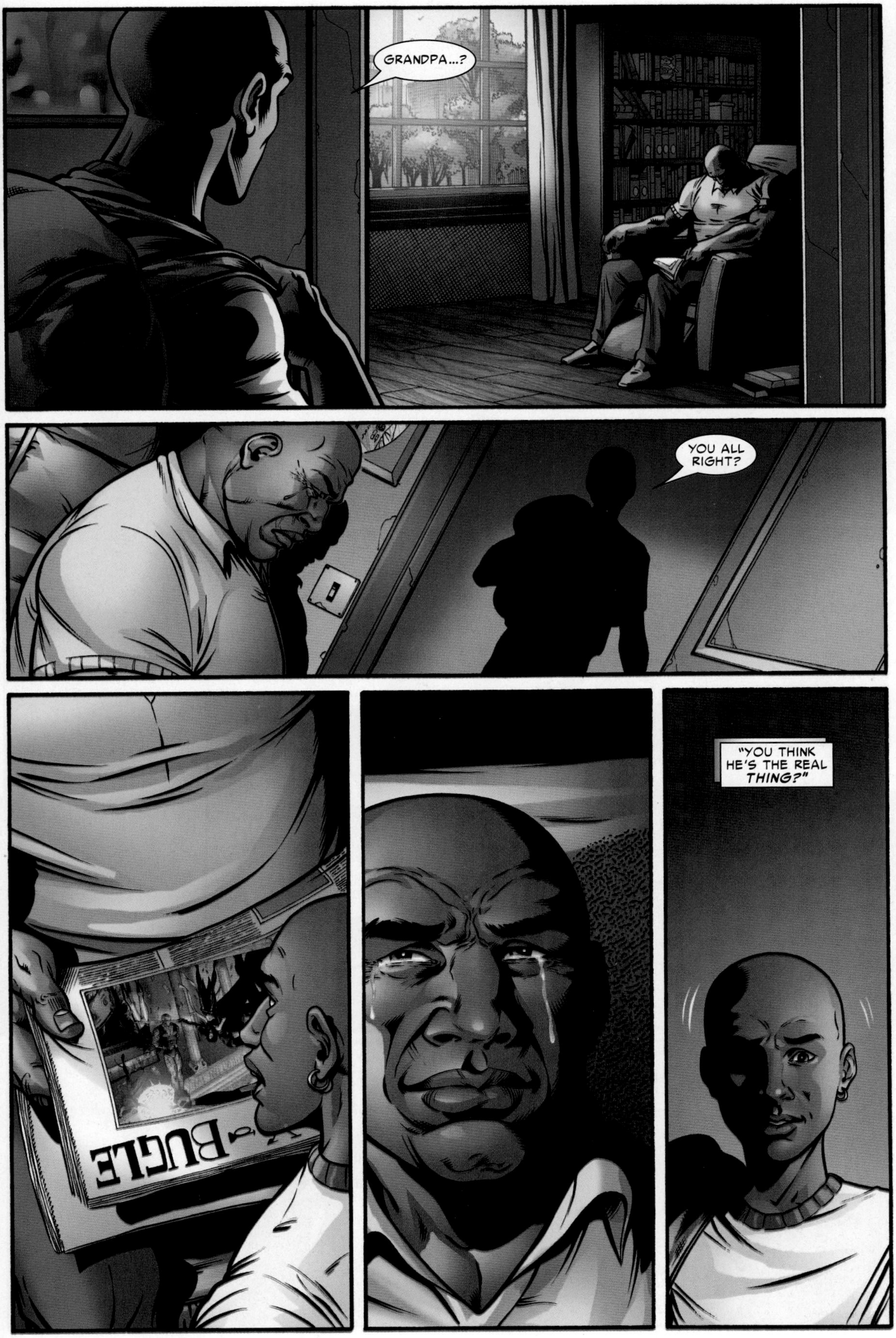
GRANDPA...?
YOU ALL RIGHT?
BUGLE
"YOU THINK HE'S THE REAL THING?"

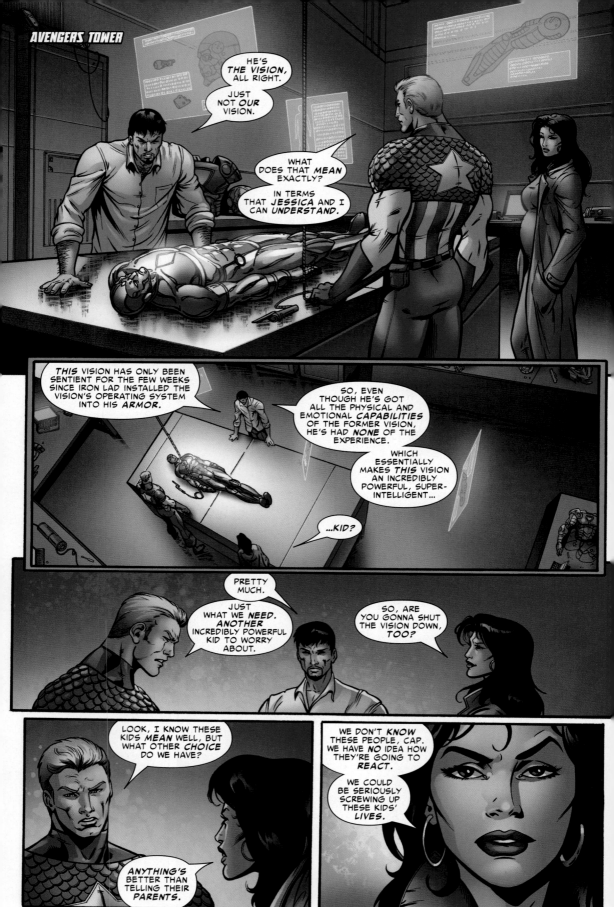

HE'S *THE VISION,* ALL RIGHT.

JUST NOT *OUR* VISION.

WHAT DOES THAT *MEAN* EXACTLY?

IN TERMS THAT *JESSICA* AND I CAN *UNDERSTAND.*

THIS VISION HAS ONLY BEEN SENTIENT FOR THE FEW WEEKS SINCE IRON LAD INSTALLED THE VISION'S OPERATING SYSTEM INTO HIS *ARMOR.*

SO, EVEN THOUGH HE'S GOT ALL THE PHYSICAL AND EMOTIONAL *CAPABILITIES* OF THE FORMER VISION, HE'S HAD *NONE* OF THE EXPERIENCE.

WHICH ESSENTIALLY MAKES *THIS* VISION AN INCREDIBLY POWERFUL, SUPER-INTELLIGENT...

...KID?

PRETTY MUCH.

JUST WHAT WE *NEED.* *ANOTHER* INCREDIBLY POWERFUL KID TO WORRY ABOUT.

SO, ARE YOU GONNA SHUT THE VISION DOWN, *TOO?*

LOOK, I KNOW THESE KIDS *MEAN* WELL, BUT WHAT OTHER *CHOICE* DO WE HAVE?

WE DON'T *KNOW* THESE PEOPLE, CAP. WE HAVE *NO* IDEA HOW THEY'RE GOING TO *REACT.*

WE COULD BE SERIOUSLY SCREWING UP THESE KIDS' LIVES.

ANYTHING'S BETTER THAN TELLING THEIR *PARENTS.*

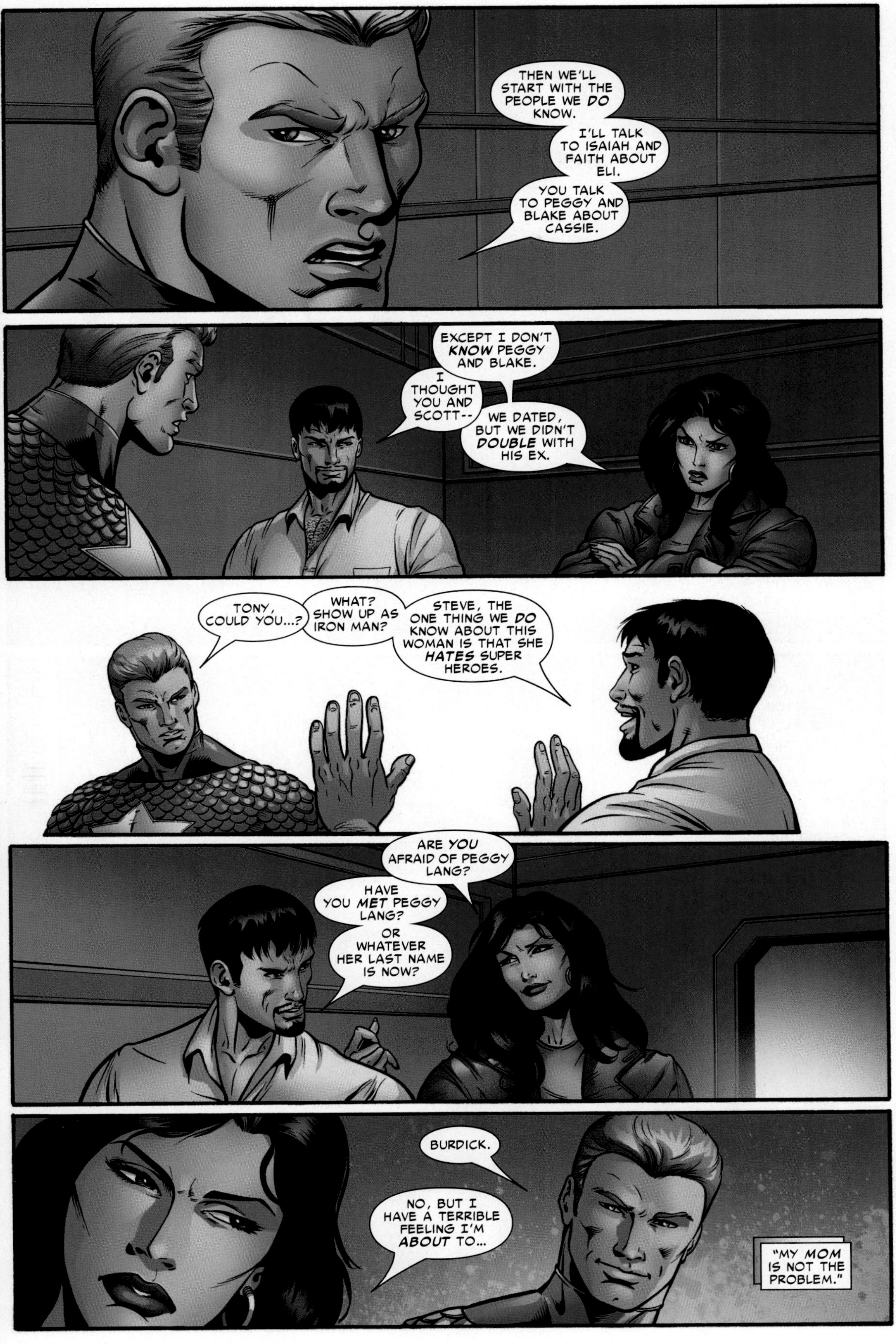
THEN WE'LL START WITH THE PEOPLE WE DO KNOW.
I'LL TALK TO ISAIAH AND FAITH ABOUT ELI.
YOU TALK TO PEGGY AND BLAKE ABOUT CASSIE.
EXCEPT I DON'T KNOW PEGGY AND BLAKE.
I THOUGHT YOU AND SCOTT--
WE DATED, BUT WE DIDN'T DOUBLE WITH HIS EX.
TONY, COULD YOU...?
WHAT? SHOW UP AS IRON MAN?
STEVE, THE ONE THING WE DO KNOW ABOUT THIS WOMAN IS THAT SHE HATES SUPER HEROES.
ARE YOU AFRAID OF PEGGY LANG?
HAVE YOU MET PEGGY LANG?
OR WHATEVER HER LAST NAME IS NOW?
BURDICK.
NO, BUT I HAVE A TERRIBLE FEELING I'M ABOUT TO...
"MY MOM IS NOT THE PROBLEM."

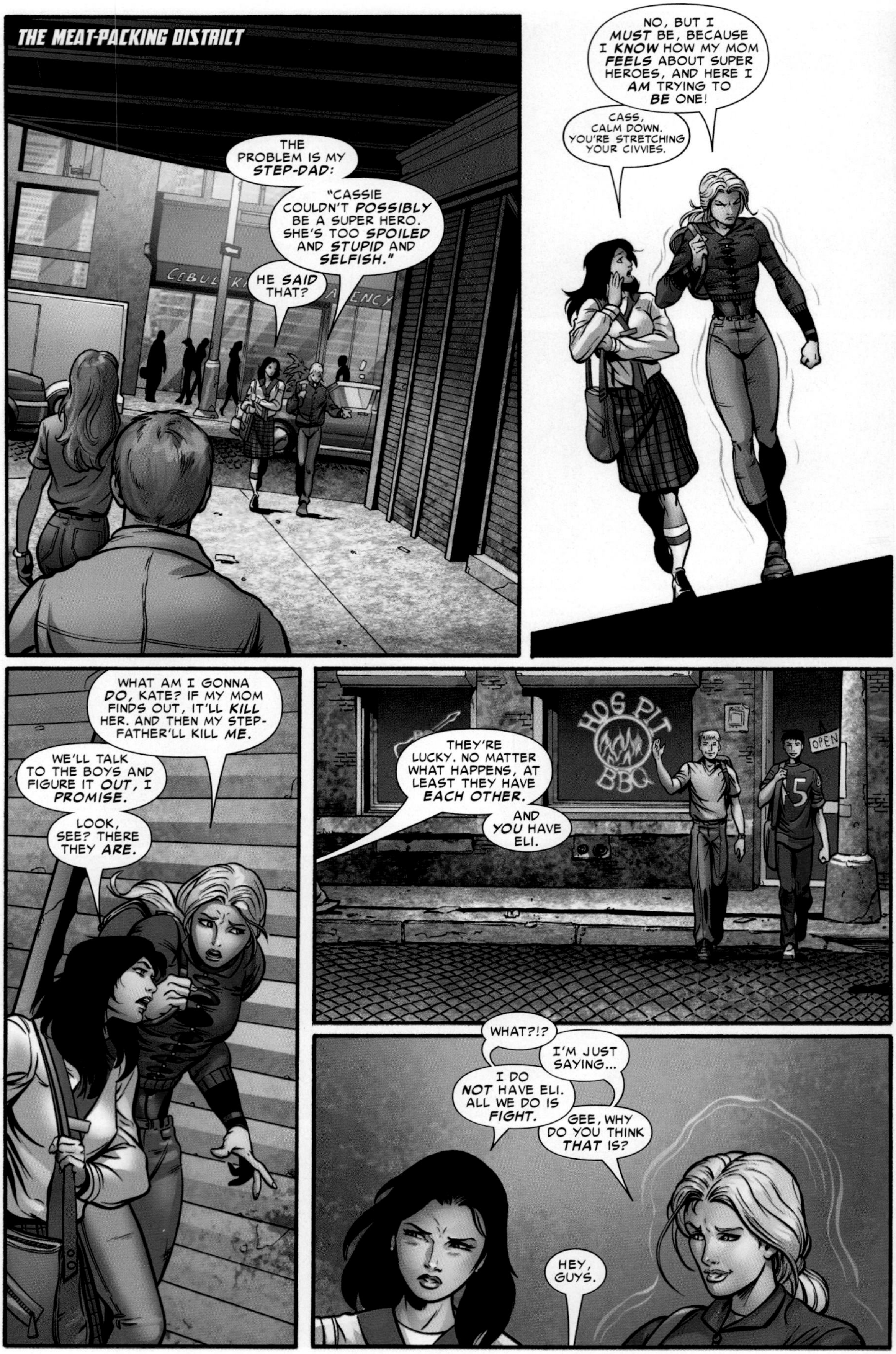
THE MEAT-PACKING DISTRICT
THE PROBLEM IS MY STEP-DAD:
"CASSIE COULDN'T POSSIBLY BE A SUPER HERO. SHE'S TOO SPOILED AND STUPID AND SELFISH."
HE SAID THAT?
NO, BUT I MUST BE, BECAUSE I KNOW HOW MY MOM FEELS ABOUT SUPER HEROES, AND HERE I AM TRYING TO BE ONE!
CASS, CALM DOWN. YOU'RE STRETCHING YOUR CIVVIES.
WHAT AM I GONNA DO, KATE? IF MY MOM FINDS OUT, IT'LL KILL HER. AND THEN MY STEP-FATHER'LL KILL ME.
WE'LL TALK TO THE BOYS AND FIGURE IT OUT, I PROMISE.
LOOK, SEE? THERE THEY ARE.
HOG PIT BBQ
OPEN
THEY'RE LUCKY. NO MATTER WHAT HAPPENS, AT LEAST THEY HAVE EACH OTHER.
AND YOU HAVE ELI.
WHAT?!?
I'M JUST SAYING...
I DO NOT HAVE ELI. ALL WE DO IS FIGHT.
GEE, WHY DO YOU THINK THAT IS?
HEY, GUYS.

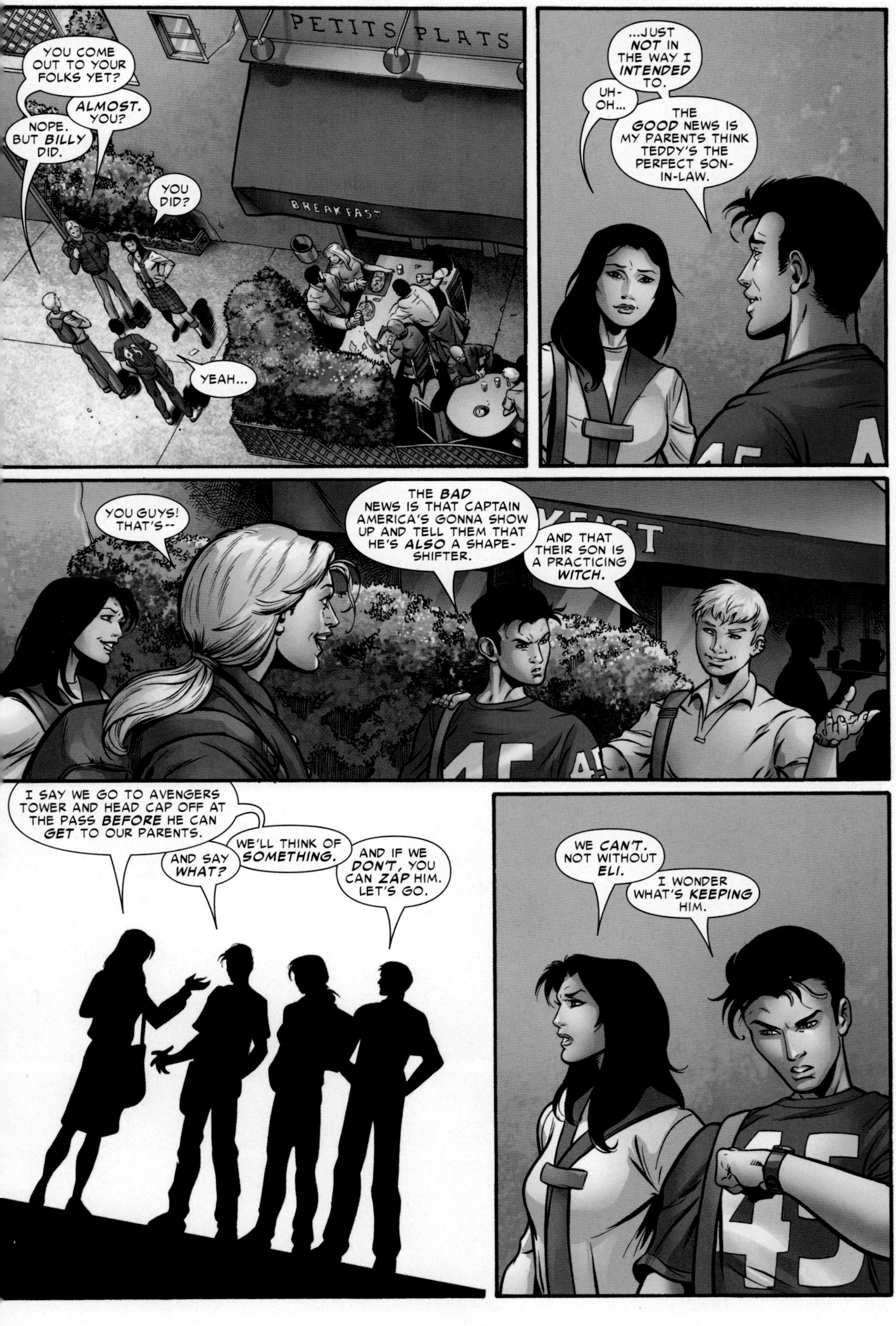
PETITS PLATS
BREAKFAST
YOU COME OUT TO YOUR FOLKS YET?
ALMOST. YOU?
NOPE. BUT BILLY DID.
YOU DID?
YEAH...
...JUST NOT IN THE WAY I INTENDED TO.
UH-OH...
THE GOOD NEWS IS MY PARENTS THINK TEDDY'S THE PERFECT SON-IN-LAW.
YOU GUYS! THAT'S--
THE BAD NEWS IS THAT CAPTAIN AMERICA'S GONNA SHOW UP AND TELL THEM THAT HE'S ALSO A SHAPE-SHIFTER.
AND THAT THEIR SON IS A PRACTICING WITCH.
I SAY WE GO TO AVENGERS TOWER AND HEAD CAP OFF AT THE PASS BEFORE HE CAN GET TO OUR PARENTS.
AND SAY WHAT?
WE'LL THINK OF SOMETHING.
AND IF WE DON'T, YOU CAN ZAP HIM. LET'S GO.
WE CAN'T. NOT WITHOUT ELI.
I WONDER WHAT'S KEEPING HIM.

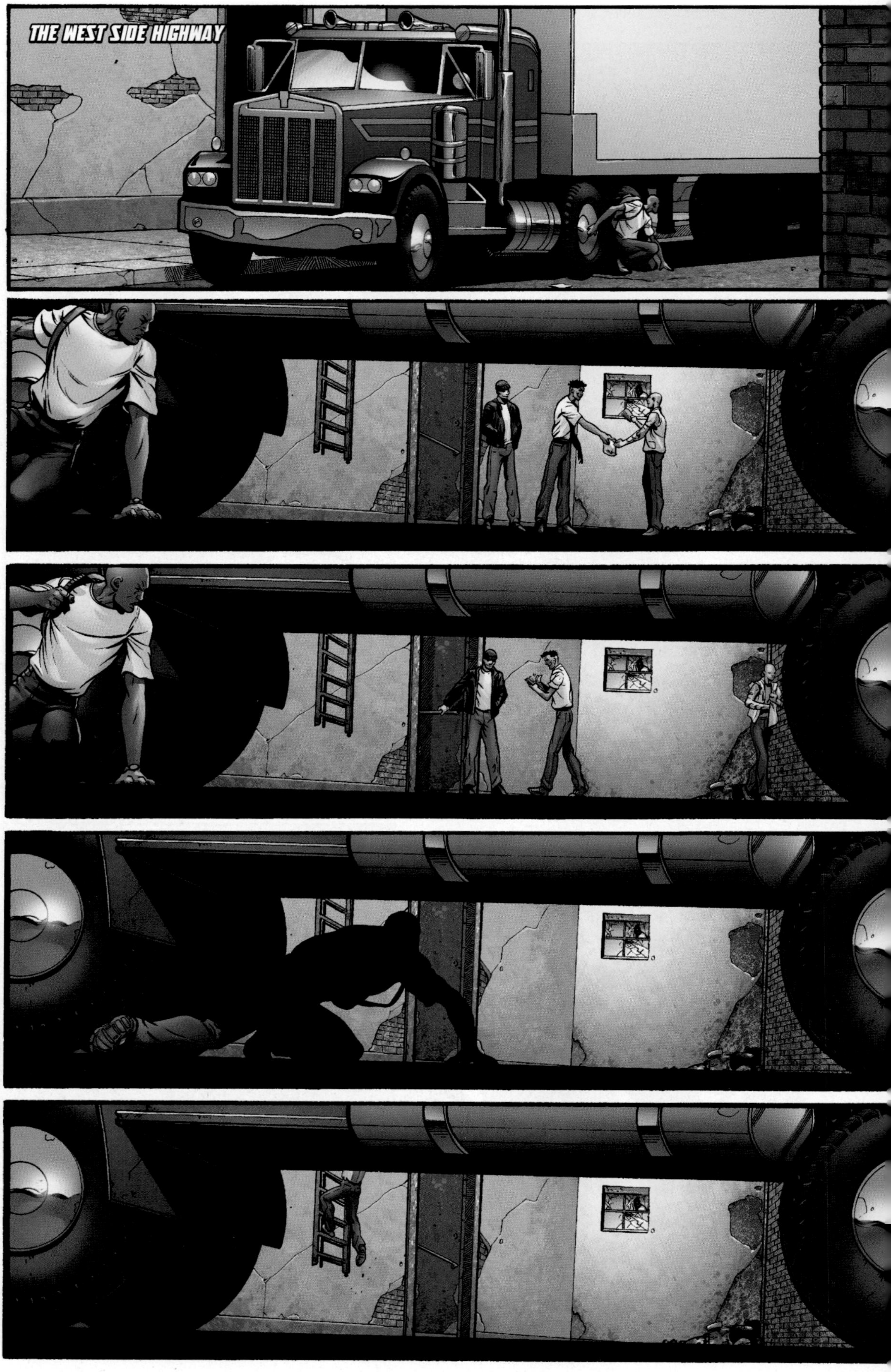
THE WEST SIDE HIGHWAY

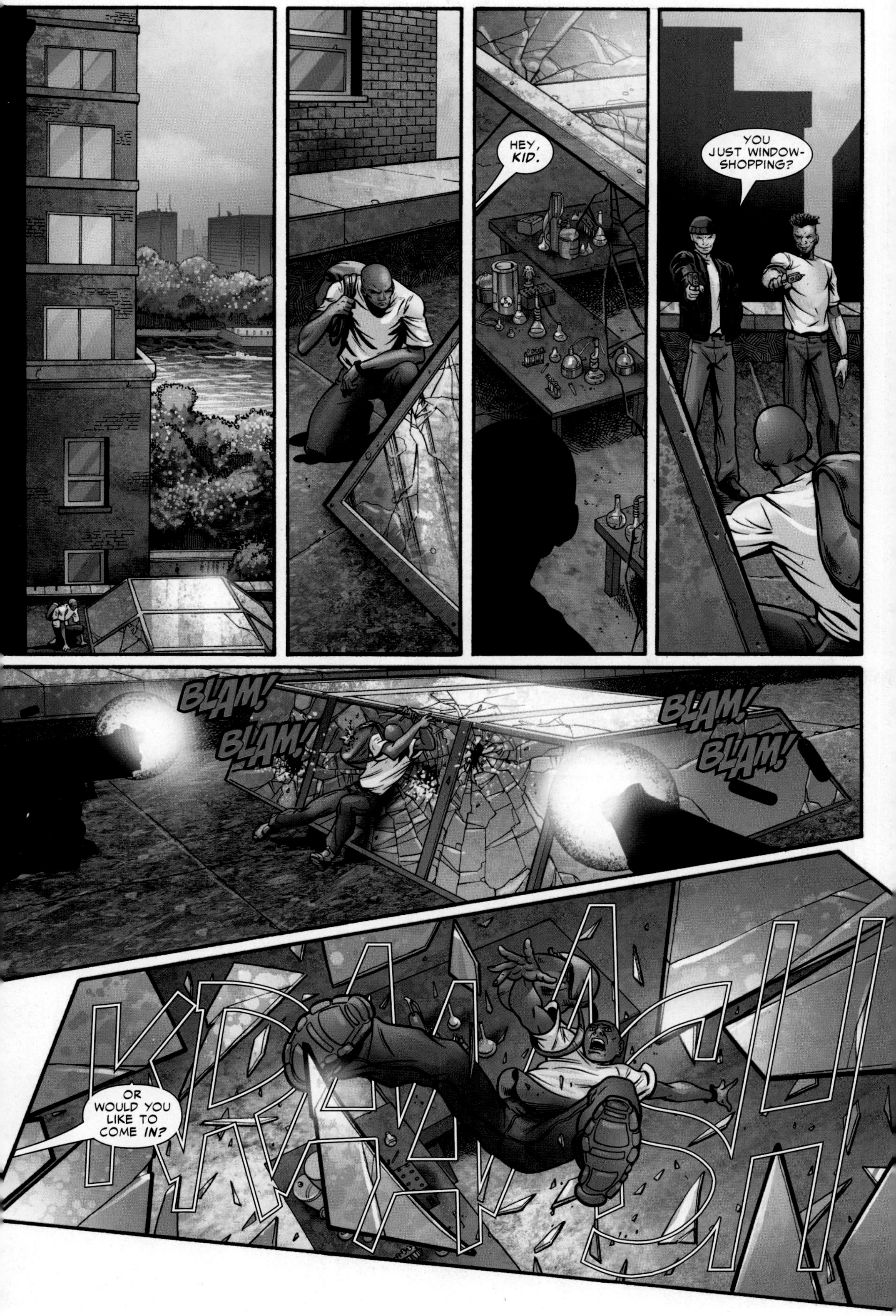
HEY, KID.
YOU JUST WINDOW-SHOPPING?
BLAM!
BLAM!
BLAM!
BLAM!
KRAAASH
OR WOULD YOU LIKE TO COME IN?

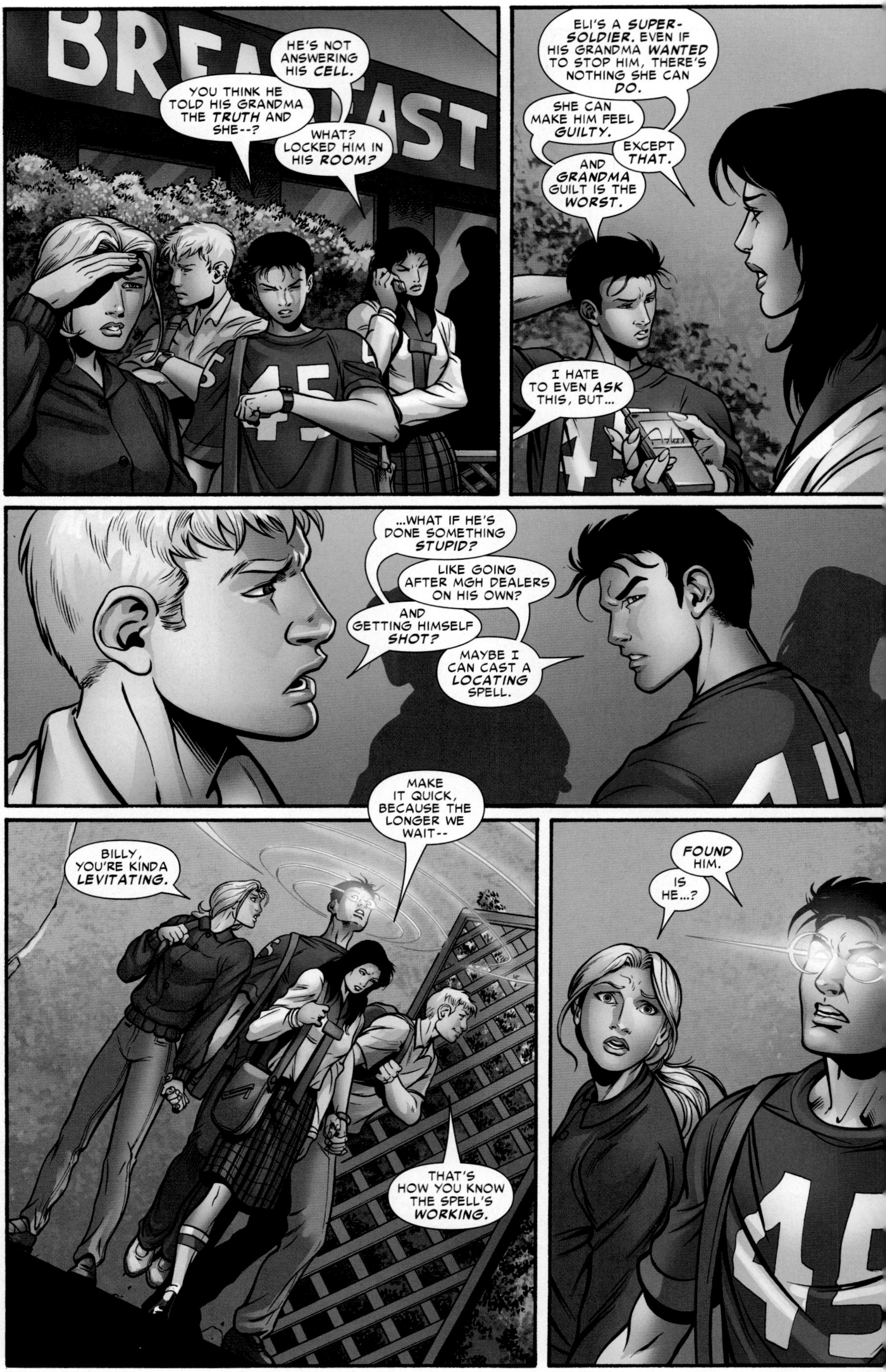
BREAKFAST
HE'S NOT ANSWERING HIS CELL.
YOU THINK HE TOLD HIS GRANDMA THE TRUTH AND SHE--?
WHAT? LOCKED HIM IN HIS ROOM?
ELI'S A SUPER-SOLDIER. EVEN IF HIS GRANDMA WANTED TO STOP HIM, THERE'S NOTHING SHE CAN DO.
SHE CAN MAKE HIM FEEL GUILTY.
EXCEPT THAT.
AND GRANDMA GUILT IS THE WORST.
I HATE TO EVEN ASK THIS, BUT...
...WHAT IF HE'S DONE SOMETHING STUPID?
LIKE GOING AFTER MGH DEALERS ON HIS OWN?
AND GETTING HIMSELF SHOT?
MAYBE I CAN CAST A LOCATING SPELL.
MAKE IT QUICK, BECAUSE THE LONGER WE WAIT--
BILLY, YOU'RE KINDA LEVITATING.
THAT'S HOW YOU KNOW THE SPELL'S WORKING.
FOUND HIM.
IS HE...?

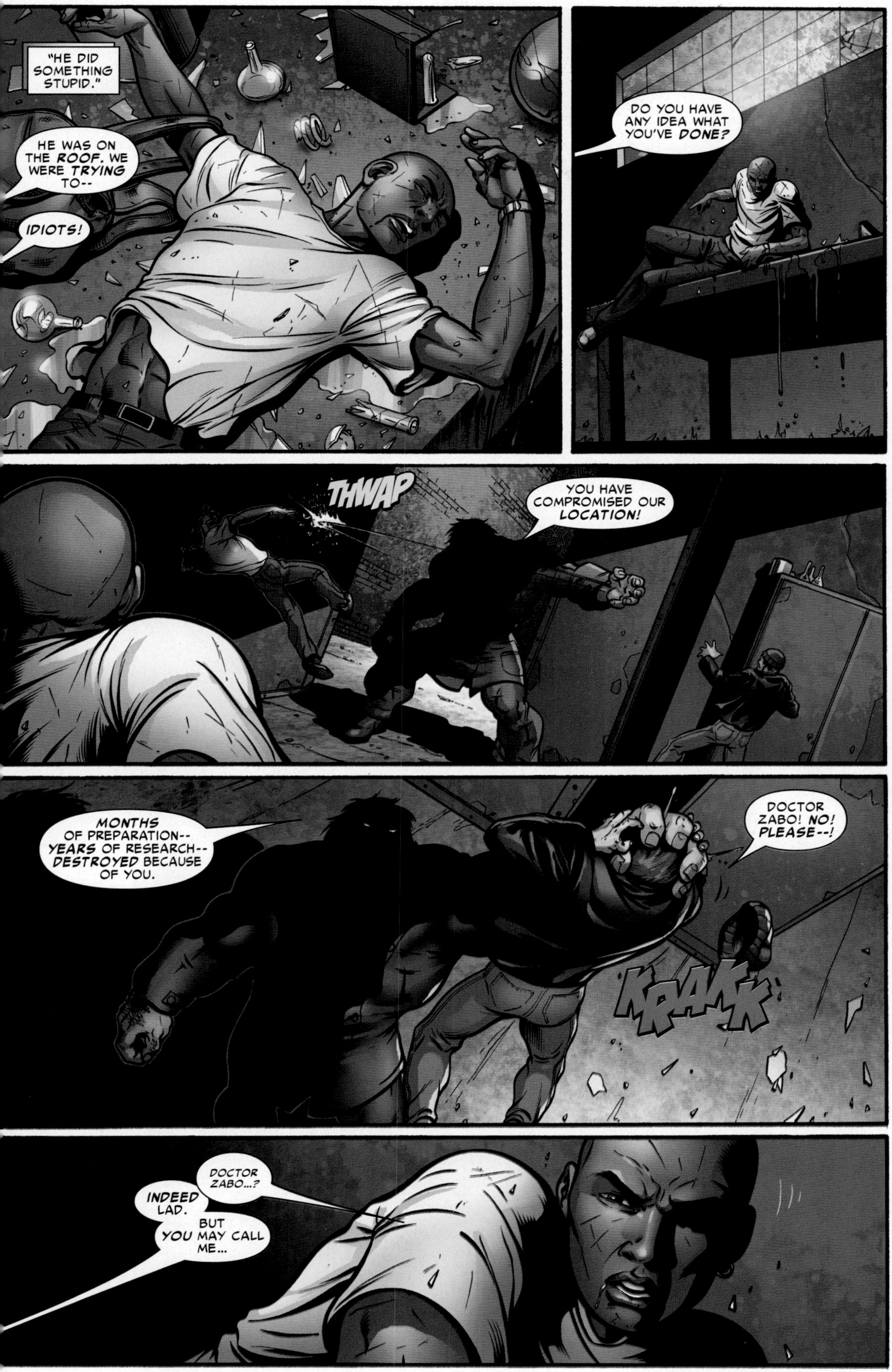
"HE DID SOMETHING STUPID."
HE WAS ON THE ROOF. WE WERE TRYING TO--
IDIOTS!
DO YOU HAVE ANY IDEA WHAT YOU'VE DONE?
THWAP
YOU HAVE COMPROMISED OUR LOCATION!
MONTHS OF PREPARATION-- YEARS OF RESEARCH-- DESTROYED BECAUSE OF YOU.
DOCTOR ZABO! NO! PLEASE--!
KRAKK
DOCTOR ZABO...?
INDEED LAD.
BUT YOU MAY CALL ME...

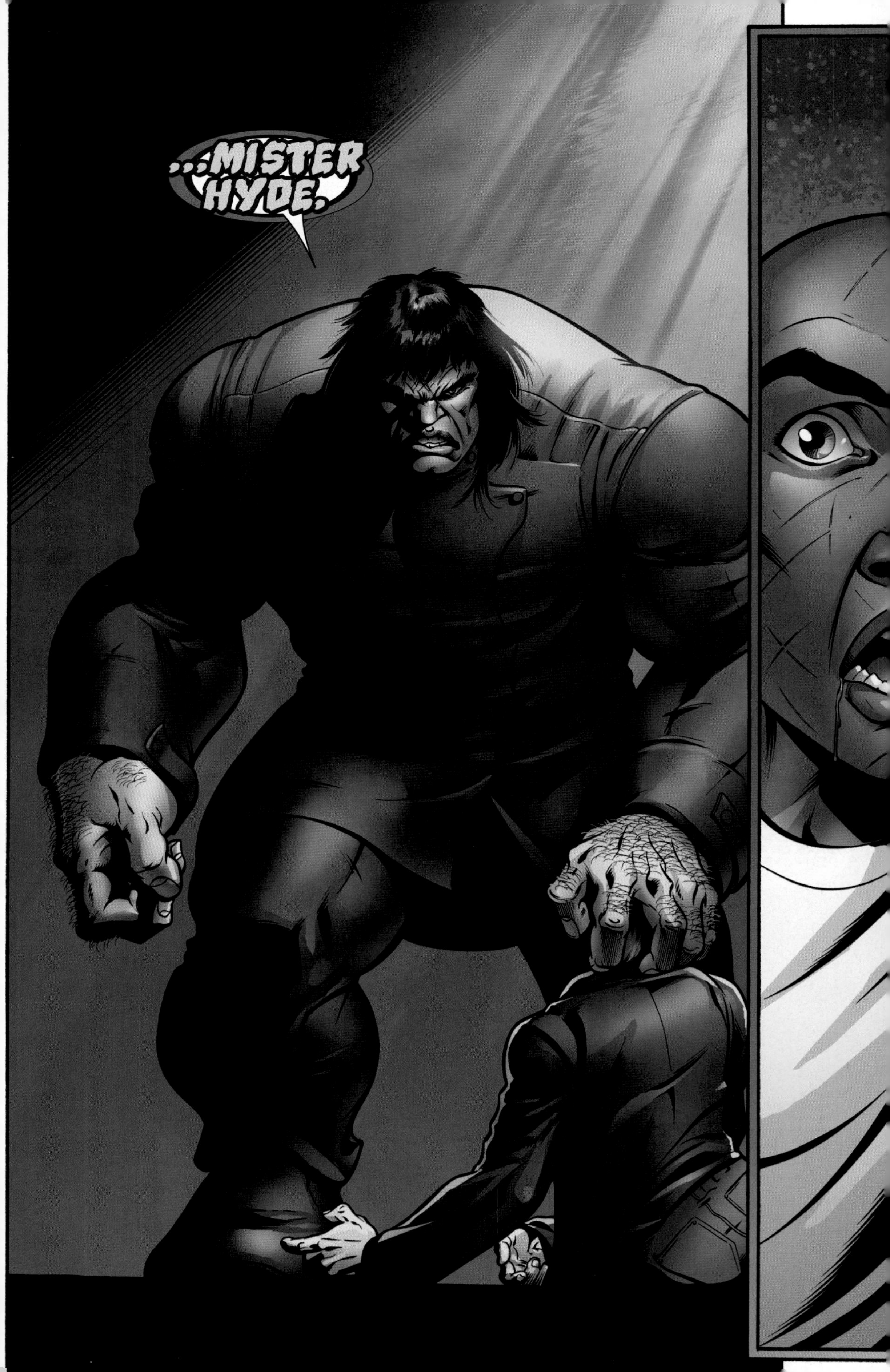
...MISTER HYDE.

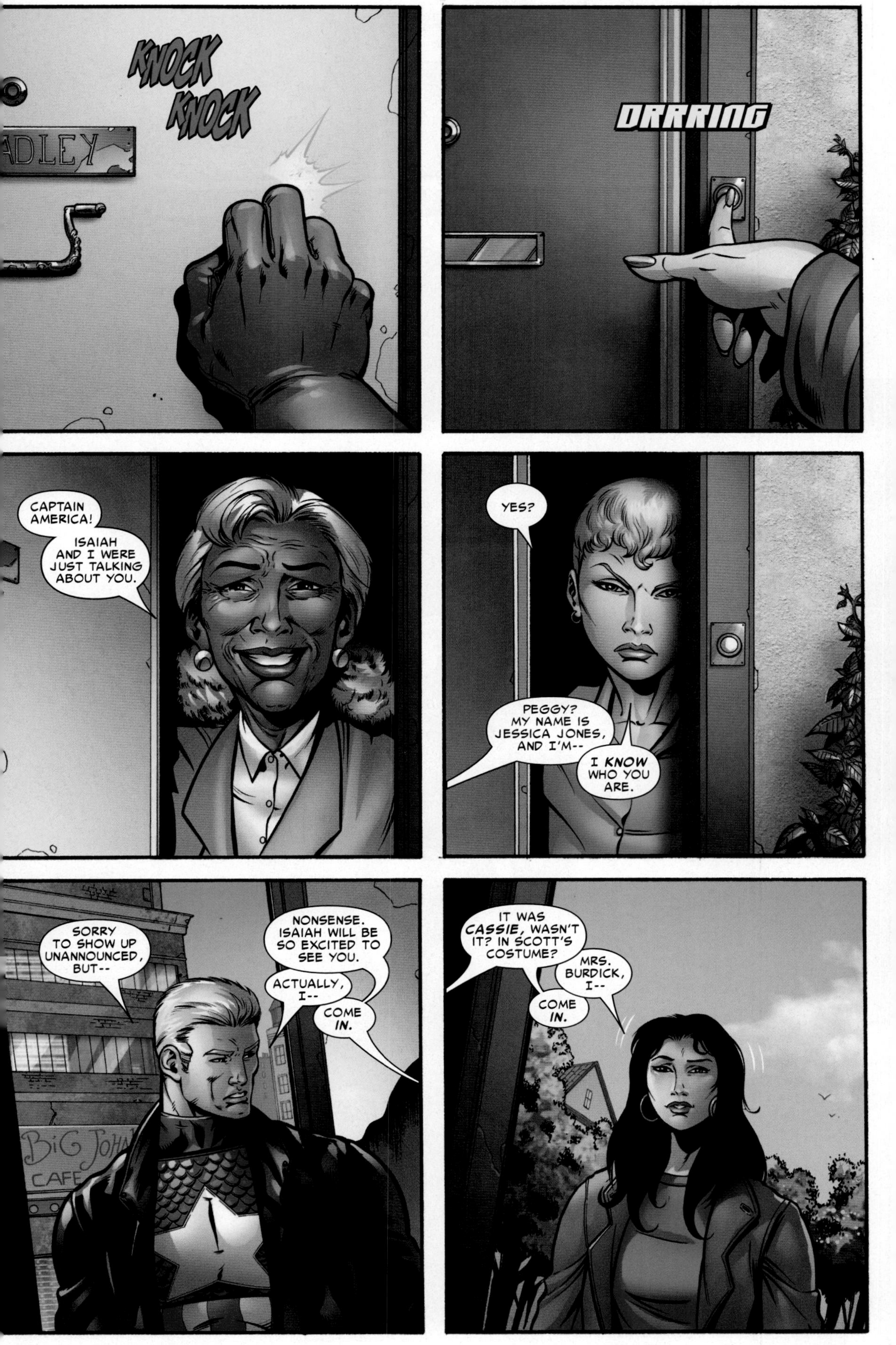

KNOCK KNOCK
ADLEY
DRRRING
CAPTAIN AMERICA!
ISAIAH AND I WERE JUST TALKING ABOUT YOU.
YES?
PEGGY? MY NAME IS JESSICA JONES, AND I'M--
I KNOW WHO YOU ARE.
SORRY TO SHOW UP UNANNOUNCED, BUT--
NONSENSE. ISAIAH WILL BE SO EXCITED TO SEE YOU.
ACTUALLY, I--
COME IN.
BIG JOHN CAFE
IT WAS CASSIE, WASN'T IT? IN SCOTT'S COSTUME?
MRS. BURDICK, I--
COME IN.

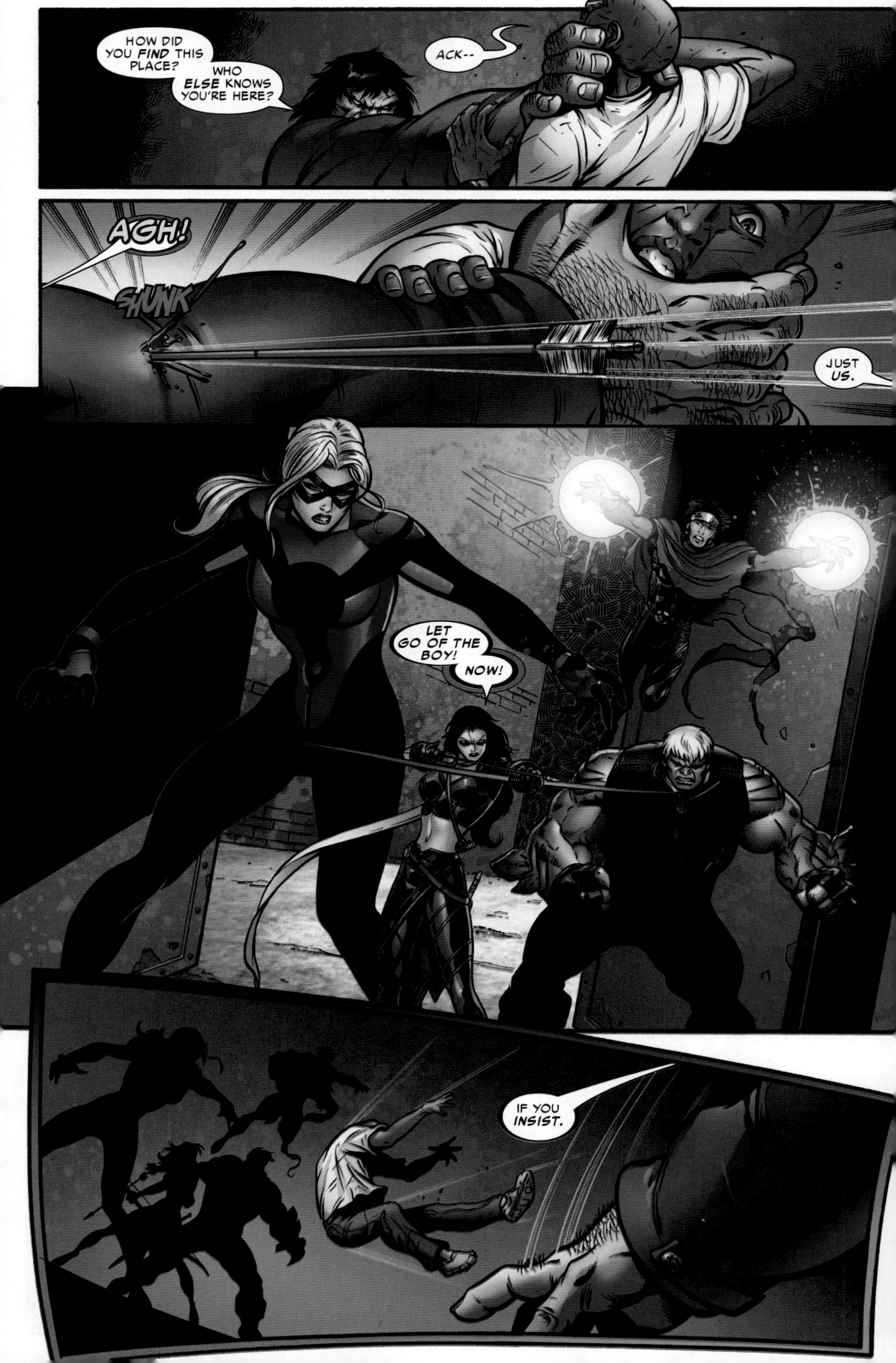
HOW DID YOU FIND THIS PLACE?
WHO ELSE KNOWS YOU'RE HERE?
ACK--
AGH!
SHUNK
JUST US.
LET GO OF THE BOY!
NOW!
IF YOU INSIST.

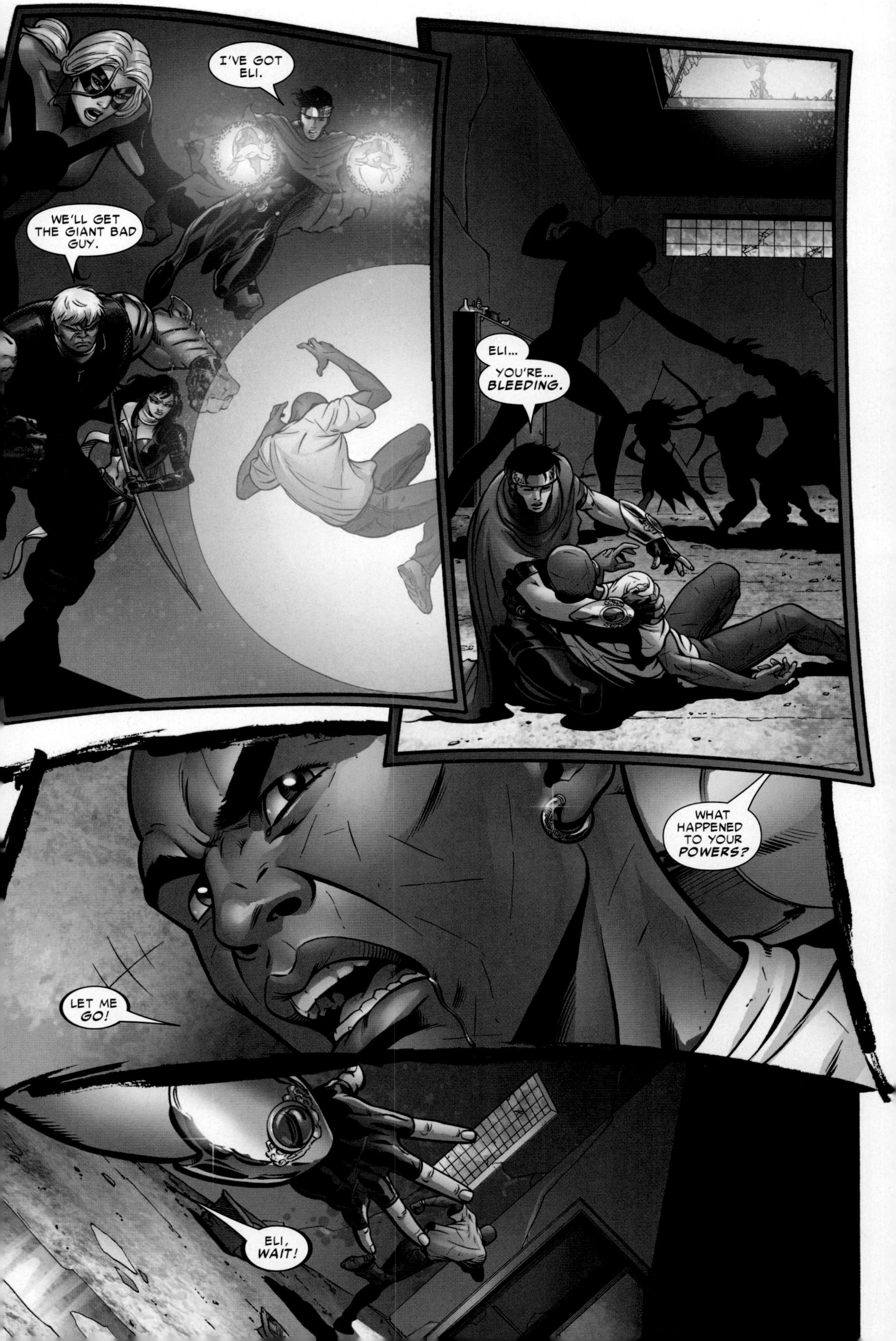
I'VE GOT ELI.
WE'LL GET THE GIANT BAD GUY.
ELI... YOU'RE... BLEEDING.
WHAT HAPPENED TO YOUR POWERS?
LET ME GO!
ELI, WAIT!

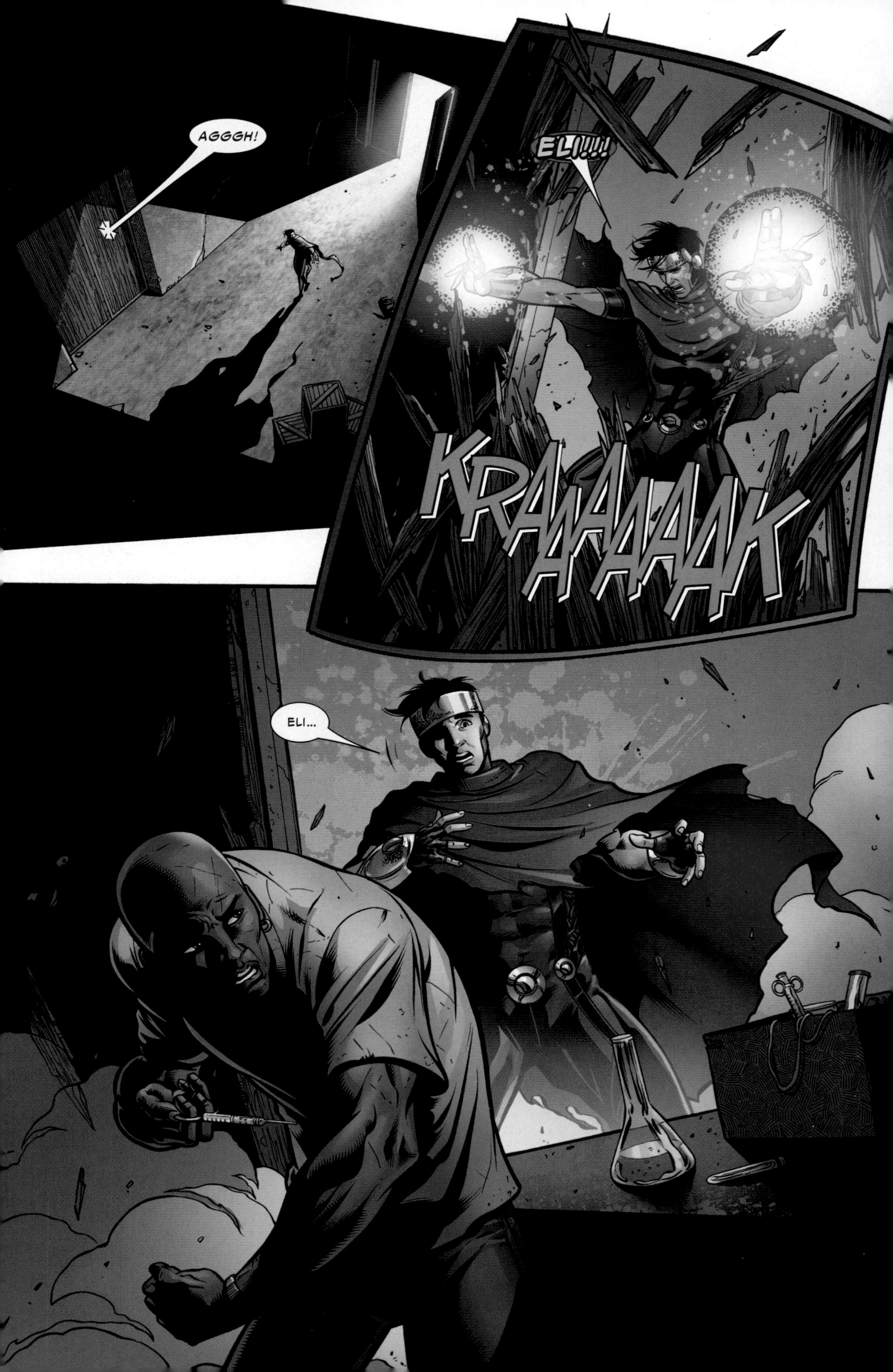
AGGGH!
ELI!!!!
KRAAAAAAAK
ELI...

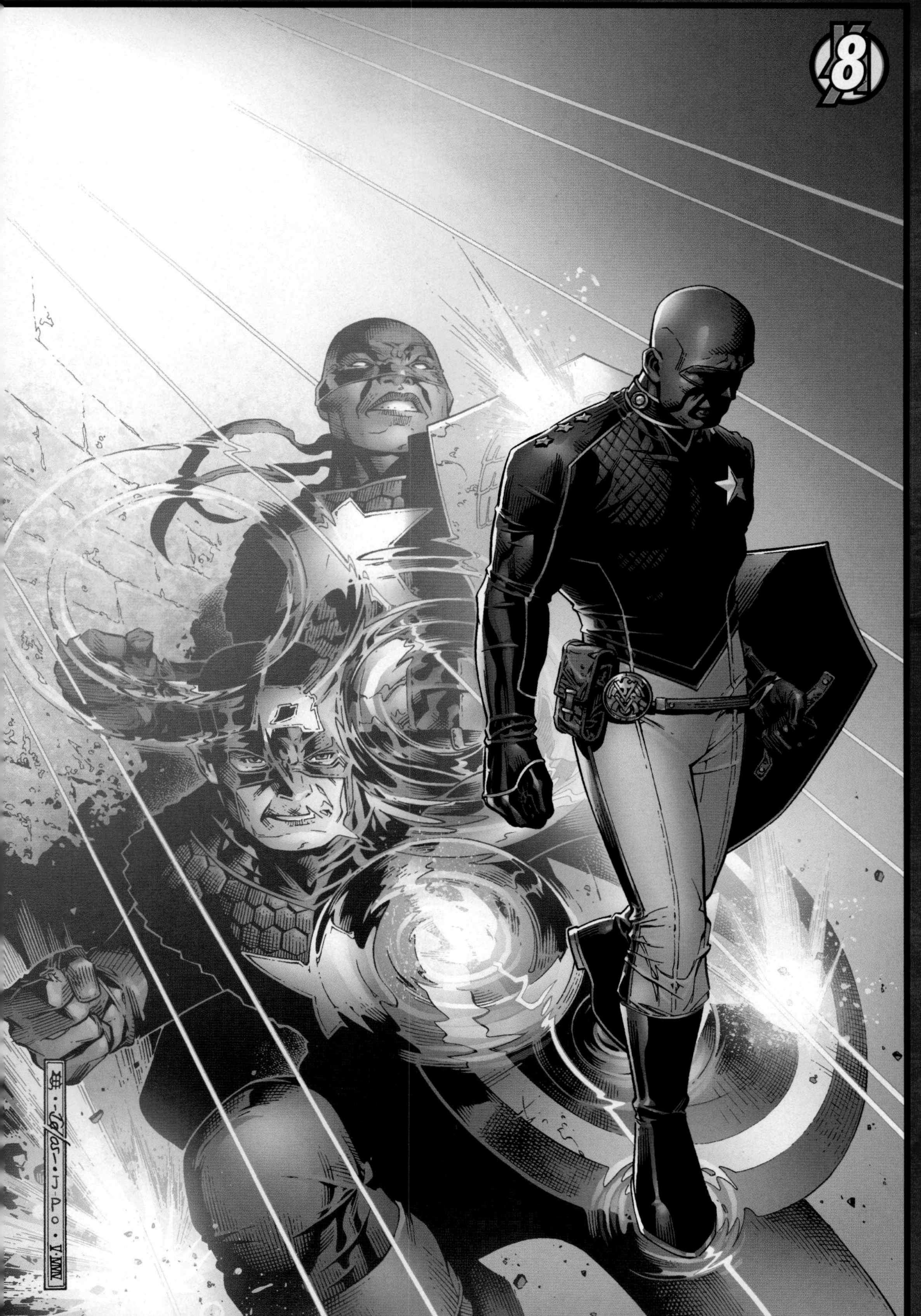

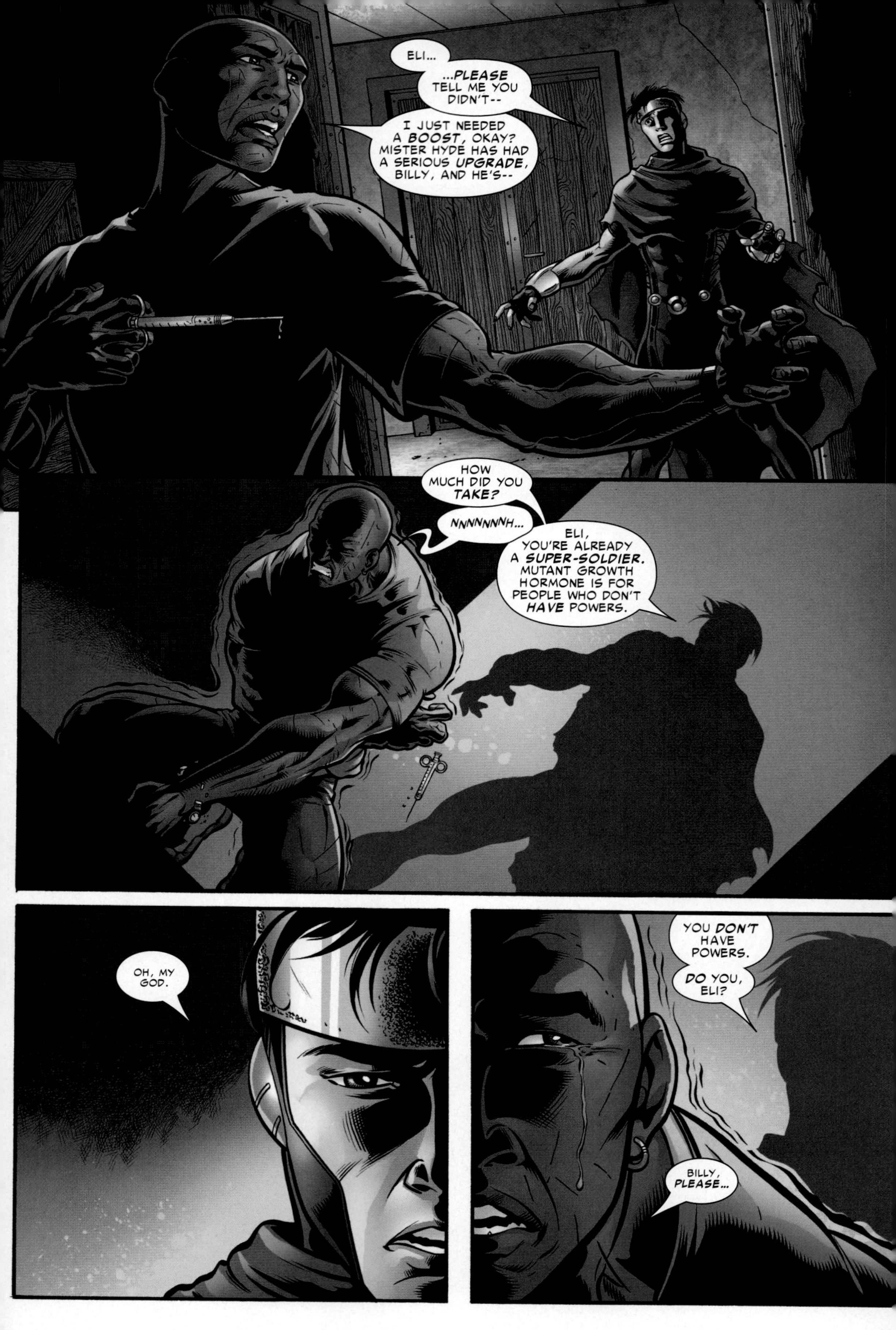
ELI...
...PLEASE TELL ME YOU DIDN'T--
I JUST NEEDED A BOOST, OKAY? MISTER HYDE HAS HAD A SERIOUS UPGRADE, BILLY, AND HE'S--
HOW MUCH DID YOU TAKE?
NNNNNNNH...
ELI, YOU'RE ALREADY A SUPER-SOLDIER. MUTANT GROWTH HORMONE IS FOR PEOPLE WHO DON'T HAVE POWERS.
OH, MY GOD.
YOU DON'T HAVE POWERS.
DO YOU, ELI?
BILLY, PLEASE...

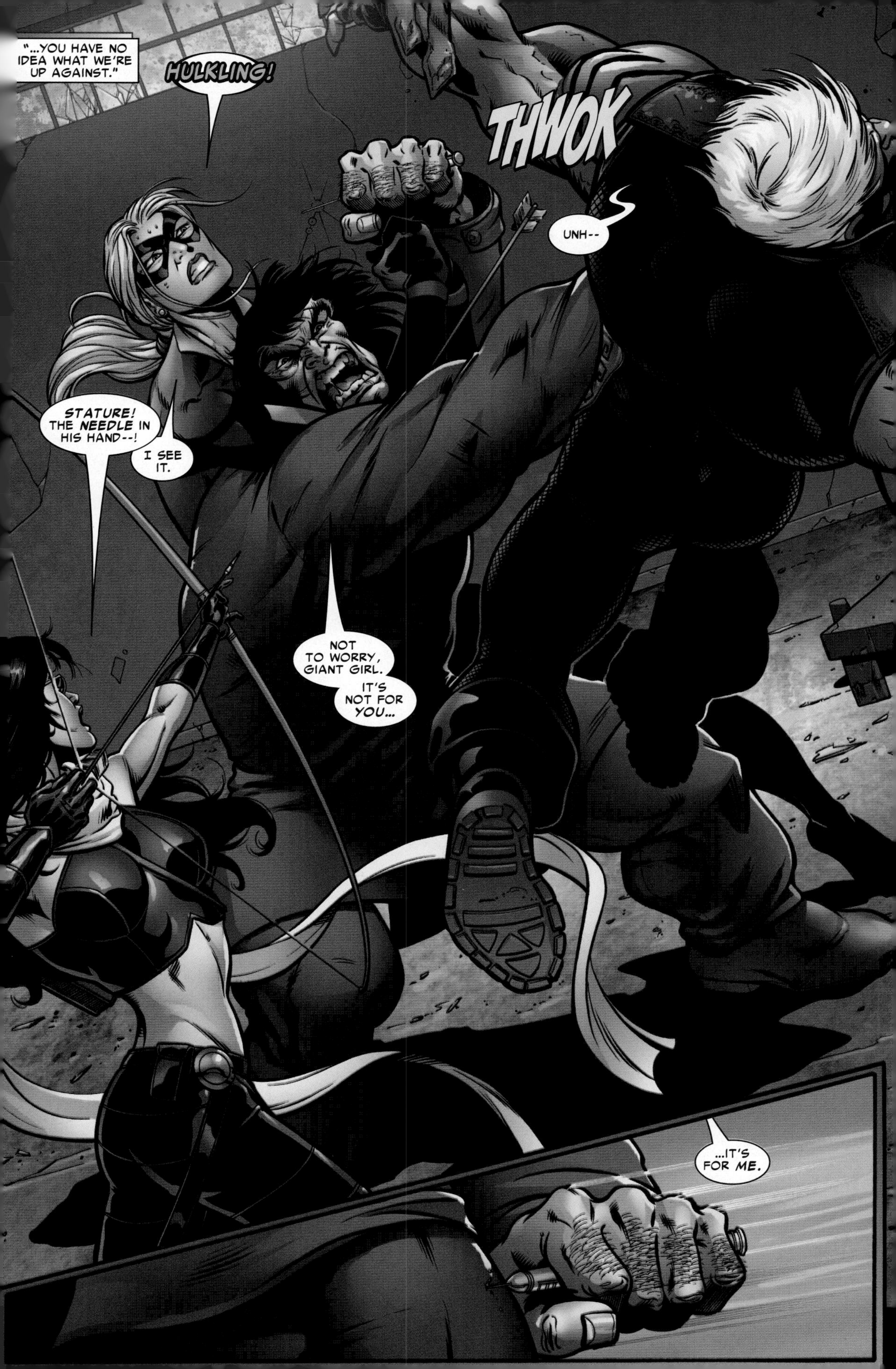

"...YOU HAVE NO IDEA WHAT WE'RE UP AGAINST."
HULKLING!
THWOK
UNH--
STATURE! THE NEEDLE IN HIS HAND--!
I SEE IT.
NOT TO WORRY, GIANT GIRL.
IT'S NOT FOR YOU...
...IT'S FOR ME.

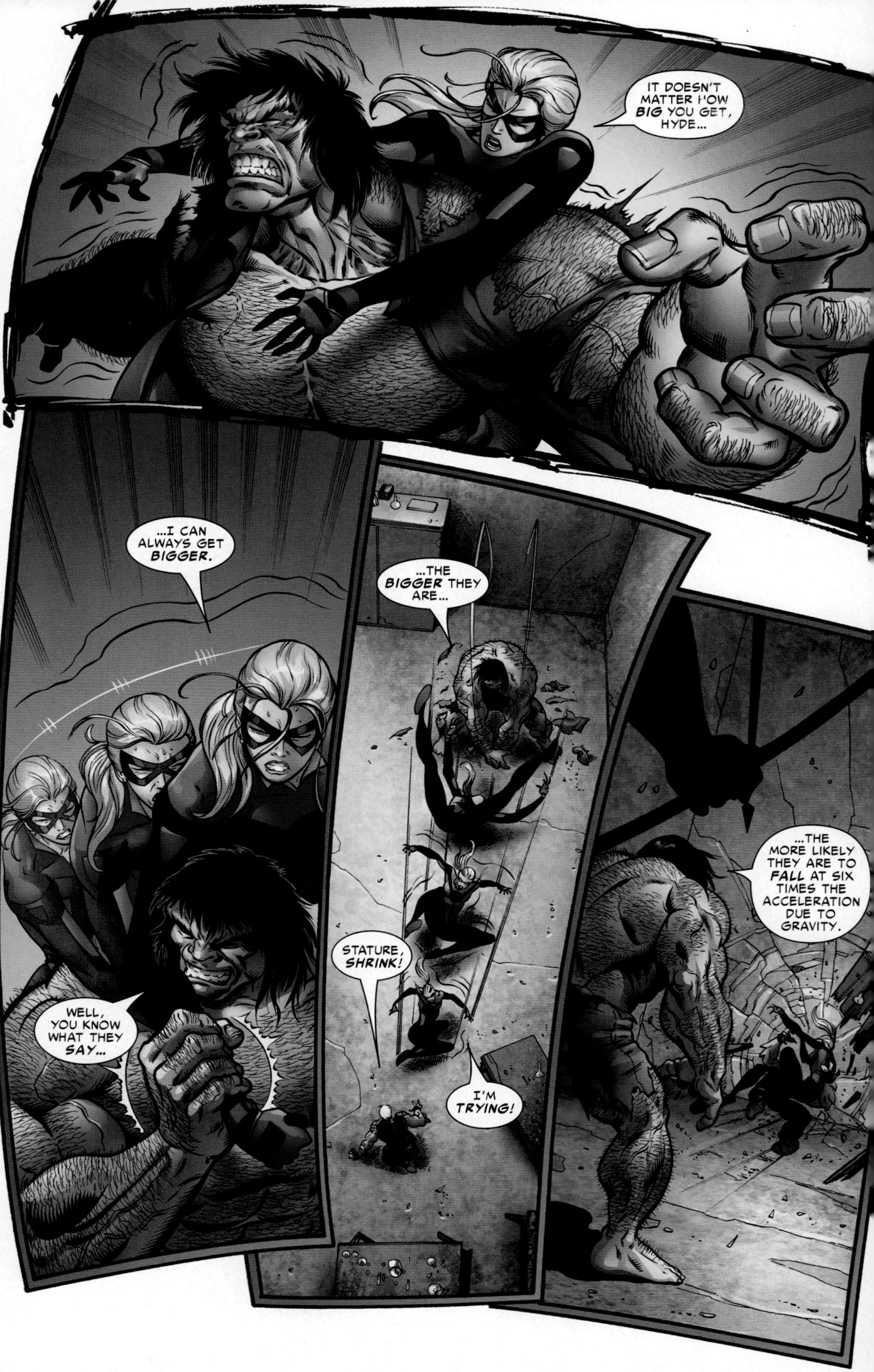
IT DOESN'T MATTER HOW BIG YOU GET, HYDE...
...I CAN ALWAYS GET BIGGER.
WELL, YOU KNOW WHAT THEY SAY...
...THE BIGGER THEY ARE...
STATURE, SHRINK!
I'M TRYING!
...THE MORE LIKELY THEY ARE TO FALL AT SIX TIMES THE ACCELERATION DUE TO GRAVITY.

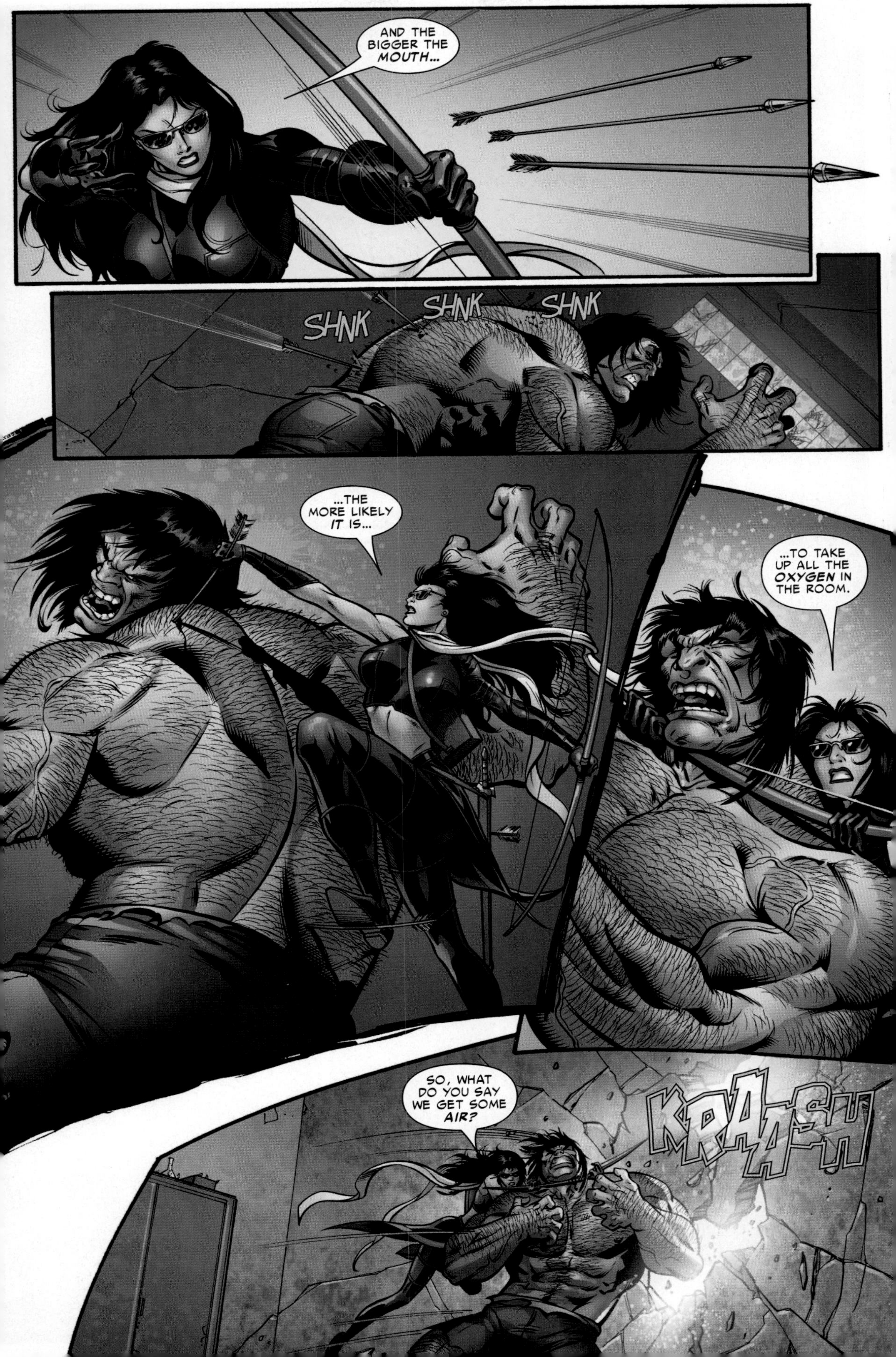

AND THE BIGGER THE MOUTH...
SHNK
SHNK
SHNK
...THE MORE LIKELY IT IS...
...TO TAKE UP ALL THE OXYGEN IN THE ROOM.
SO, WHAT DO YOU SAY WE GET SOME AIR?
KRAASH

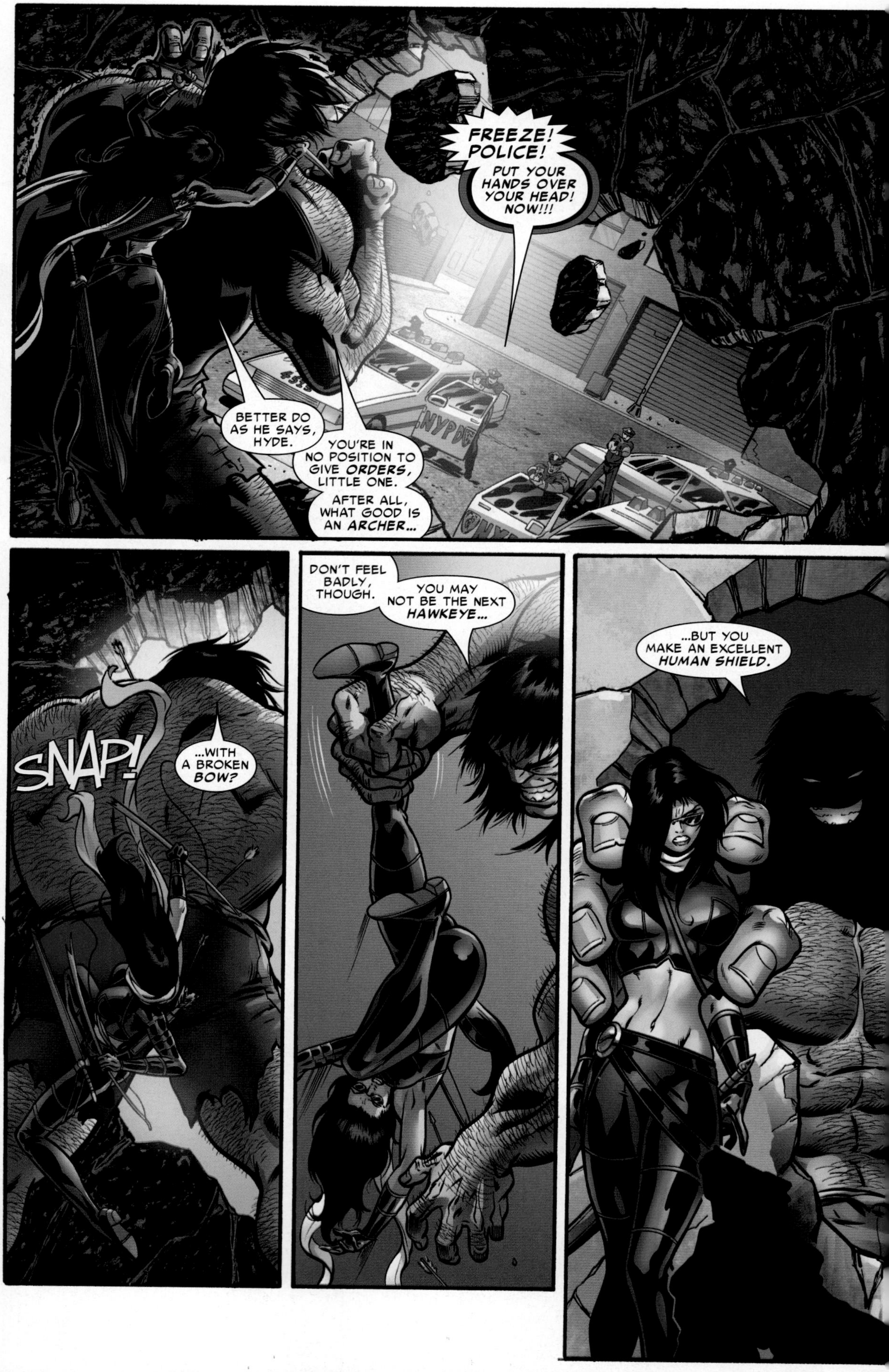
FREEZE! POLICE!
PUT YOUR HANDS OVER YOUR HEAD! NOW!!!
BETTER DO AS HE SAYS, HYDE.
YOU'RE IN NO POSITION TO GIVE ORDERS, LITTLE ONE.
AFTER ALL, WHAT GOOD IS AN ARCHER...
SNAP!
...WITH A BROKEN BOW?
DON'T FEEL BADLY, THOUGH.
YOU MAY NOT BE THE NEXT HAWKEYE...
...BUT YOU MAKE AN EXCELLENT HUMAN SHIELD.

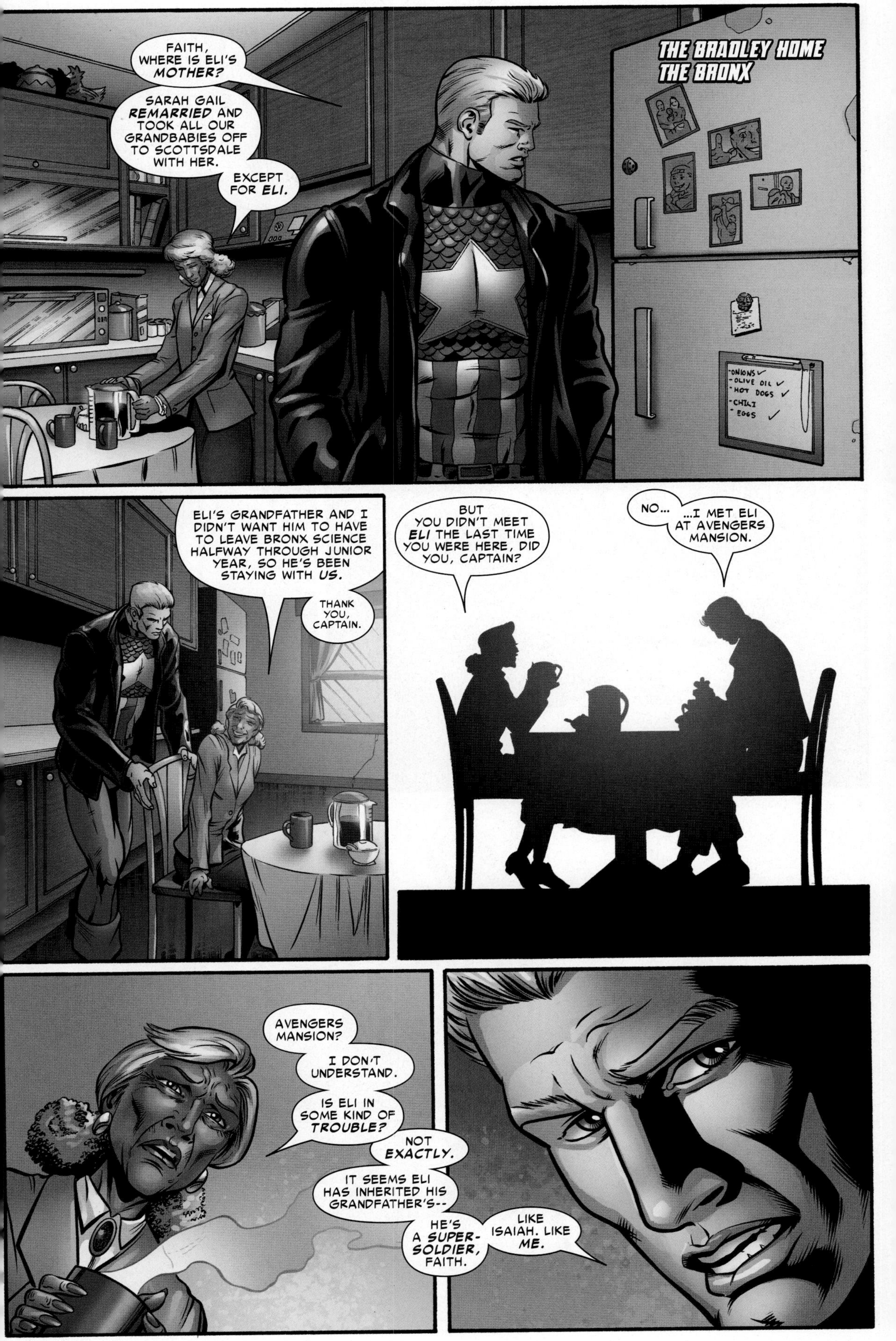
THE BRADLEY HOME
THE BRONX
FAITH, WHERE IS ELI'S MOTHER?
SARAH GAIL REMARRIED AND TOOK ALL OUR GRANDBABIES OFF TO SCOTTSDALE WITH HER.
EXCEPT FOR ELI.
-ONIONS
-OLIVE OIL
-HOT DOGS
-CHILI
-EGGS
ELI'S GRANDFATHER AND I DIDN'T WANT HIM TO HAVE TO LEAVE BRONX SCIENCE HALFWAY THROUGH JUNIOR YEAR, SO HE'S BEEN STAYING WITH US.
THANK YOU, CAPTAIN.
BUT YOU DIDN'T MEET ELI THE LAST TIME YOU WERE HERE, DID YOU, CAPTAIN?
NO...
...I MET ELI AT AVENGERS MANSION.
AVENGERS MANSION?
I DON'T UNDERSTAND.
IS ELI IN SOME KIND OF TROUBLE?
NOT EXACTLY.
IT SEEMS ELI HAS INHERITED HIS GRANDFATHER'S--
HE'S A SUPER-SOLDIER, FAITH.
LIKE ISAIAH. LIKE ME.

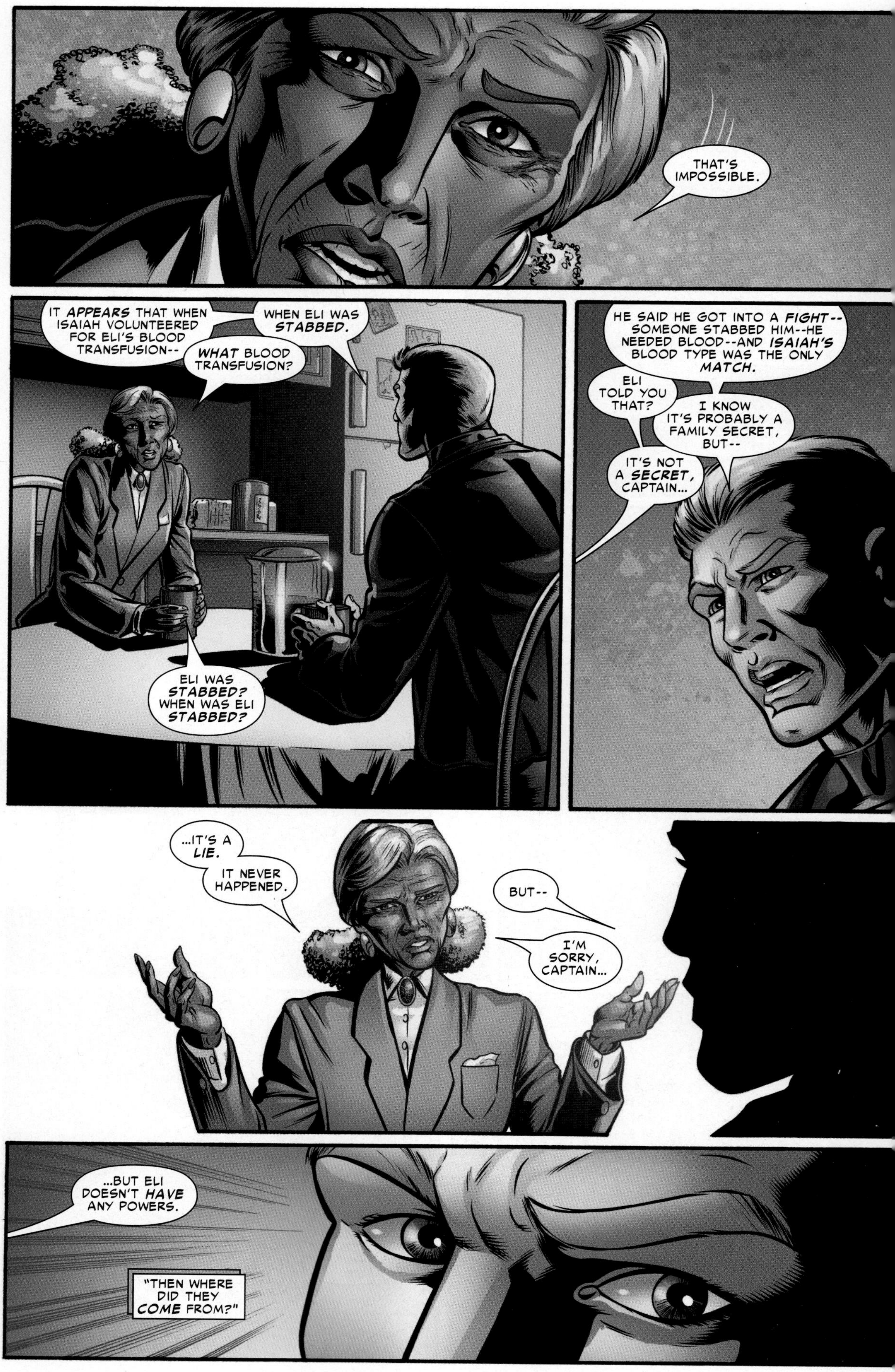
THAT'S IMPOSSIBLE.
IT APPEARS THAT WHEN ISAIAH VOLUNTEERED FOR ELI'S BLOOD TRANSFUSION--
WHEN ELI WAS STABBED.
WHAT BLOOD TRANSFUSION?
ELI WAS STABBED? WHEN WAS ELI STABBED?
HE SAID HE GOT INTO A FIGHT-- SOMEONE STABBED HIM--HE NEEDED BLOOD--AND ISAIAH'S BLOOD TYPE WAS THE ONLY MATCH.
ELI TOLD YOU THAT?
I KNOW IT'S PROBABLY A FAMILY SECRET, BUT--
IT'S NOT A SECRET, CAPTAIN...
...IT'S A LIE.
IT NEVER HAPPENED.
BUT--
I'M SORRY, CAPTAIN...
...BUT ELI DOESN'T HAVE ANY POWERS.
"THEN WHERE DID THEY COME FROM?"

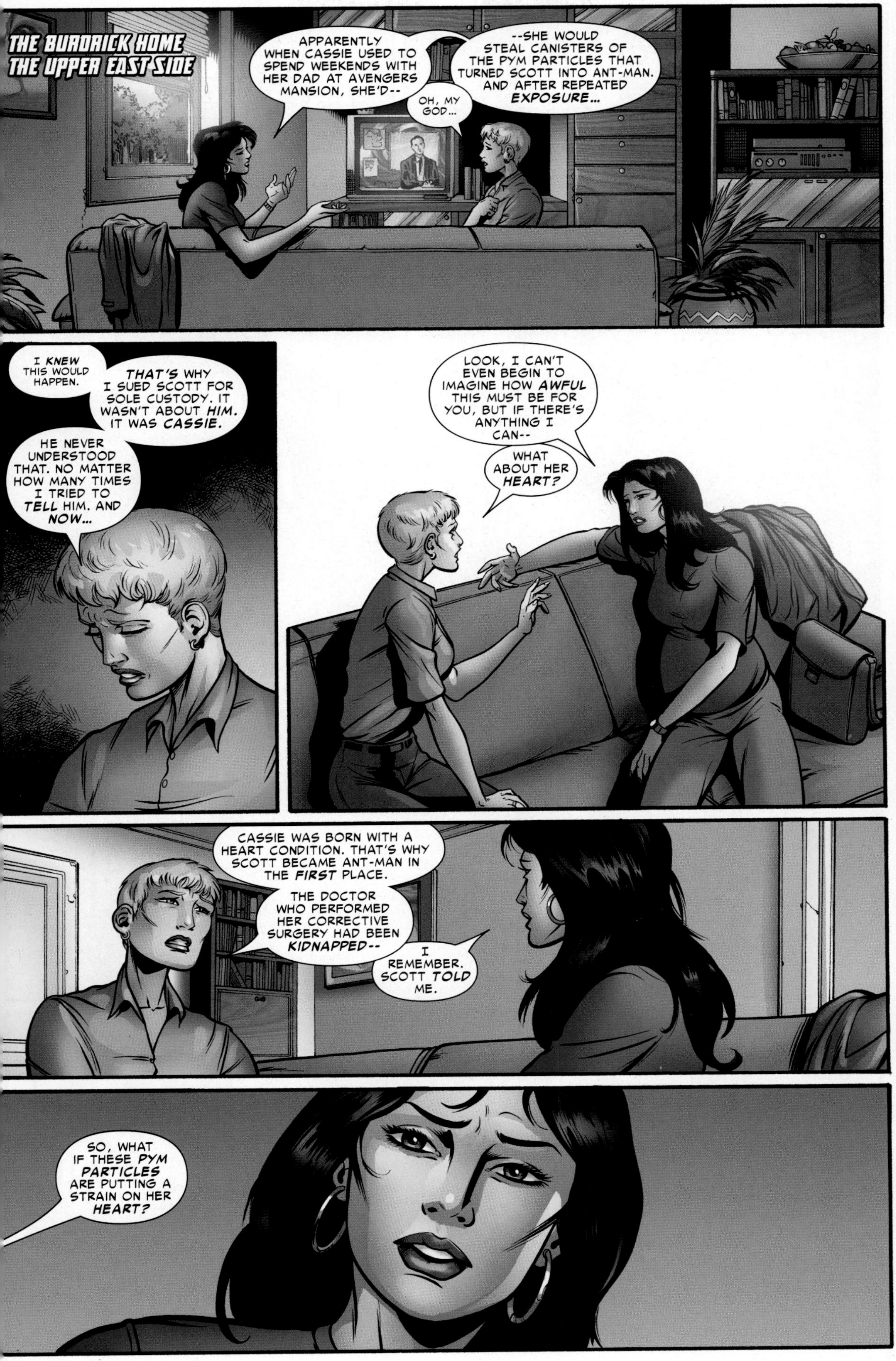
THE BURDRICK HOME
THE UPPER EAST SIDE
APPARENTLY WHEN CASSIE USED TO SPEND WEEKENDS WITH HER DAD AT AVENGERS MANSION, SHE'D--
--SHE WOULD STEAL CANISTERS OF THE PYM PARTICLES THAT TURNED SCOTT INTO ANT-MAN. AND AFTER REPEATED EXPOSURE...
OH, MY GOD...
I KNEW THIS WOULD HAPPEN.
THAT'S WHY I SUED SCOTT FOR SOLE CUSTODY. IT WASN'T ABOUT HIM. IT WAS CASSIE.
HE NEVER UNDERSTOOD THAT. NO MATTER HOW MANY TIMES I TRIED TO TELL HIM. AND NOW...
LOOK, I CAN'T EVEN BEGIN TO IMAGINE HOW AWFUL THIS MUST BE FOR YOU, BUT IF THERE'S ANYTHING I CAN--
WHAT ABOUT HER HEART?
CASSIE WAS BORN WITH A HEART CONDITION. THAT'S WHY SCOTT BECAME ANT-MAN IN THE FIRST PLACE.
THE DOCTOR WHO PERFORMED HER CORRECTIVE SURGERY HAD BEEN KIDNAPPED--
I REMEMBER. SCOTT TOLD ME.
SO, WHAT IF THESE PYM PARTICLES ARE PUTTING A STRAIN ON HER HEART?

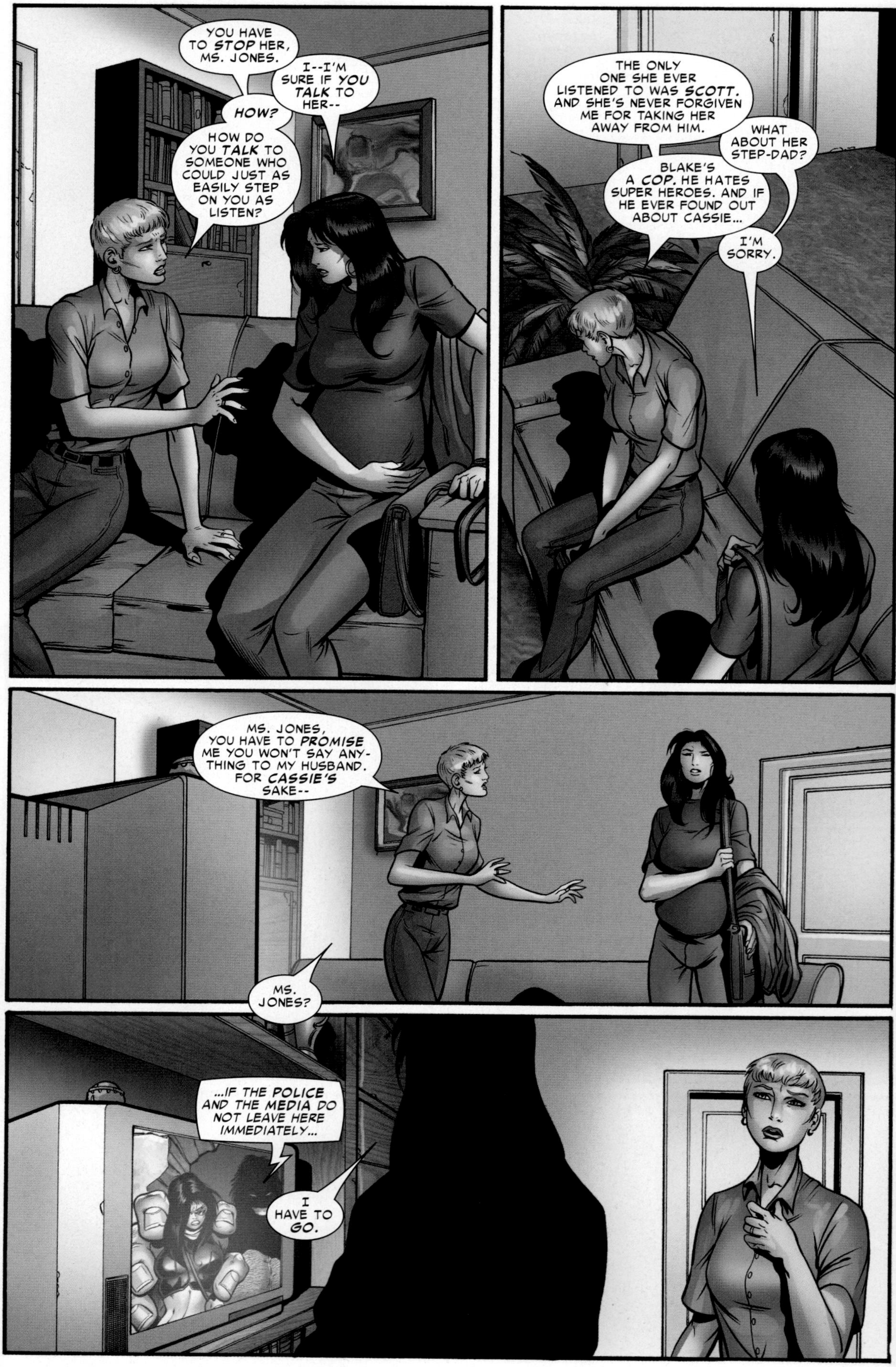
YOU HAVE TO STOP HER, MS. JONES.
I--I'M SURE IF YOU TALK TO HER--
HOW?
HOW DO YOU TALK TO SOMEONE WHO COULD JUST AS EASILY STEP ON YOU AS LISTEN?
THE ONLY ONE SHE EVER LISTENED TO WAS SCOTT. AND SHE'S NEVER FORGIVEN ME FOR TAKING HER AWAY FROM HIM.
WHAT ABOUT HER STEP-DAD?
BLAKE'S A COP. HE HATES SUPER HEROES. AND IF HE EVER FOUND OUT ABOUT CASSIE...
I'M SORRY.
MS. JONES, YOU HAVE TO PROMISE ME YOU WON'T SAY ANY-THING TO MY HUSBAND. FOR CASSIE'S SAKE--
MS. JONES?
...IF THE POLICE AND THE MEDIA DO NOT LEAVE HERE IMMEDIATELY...
I HAVE TO GO.

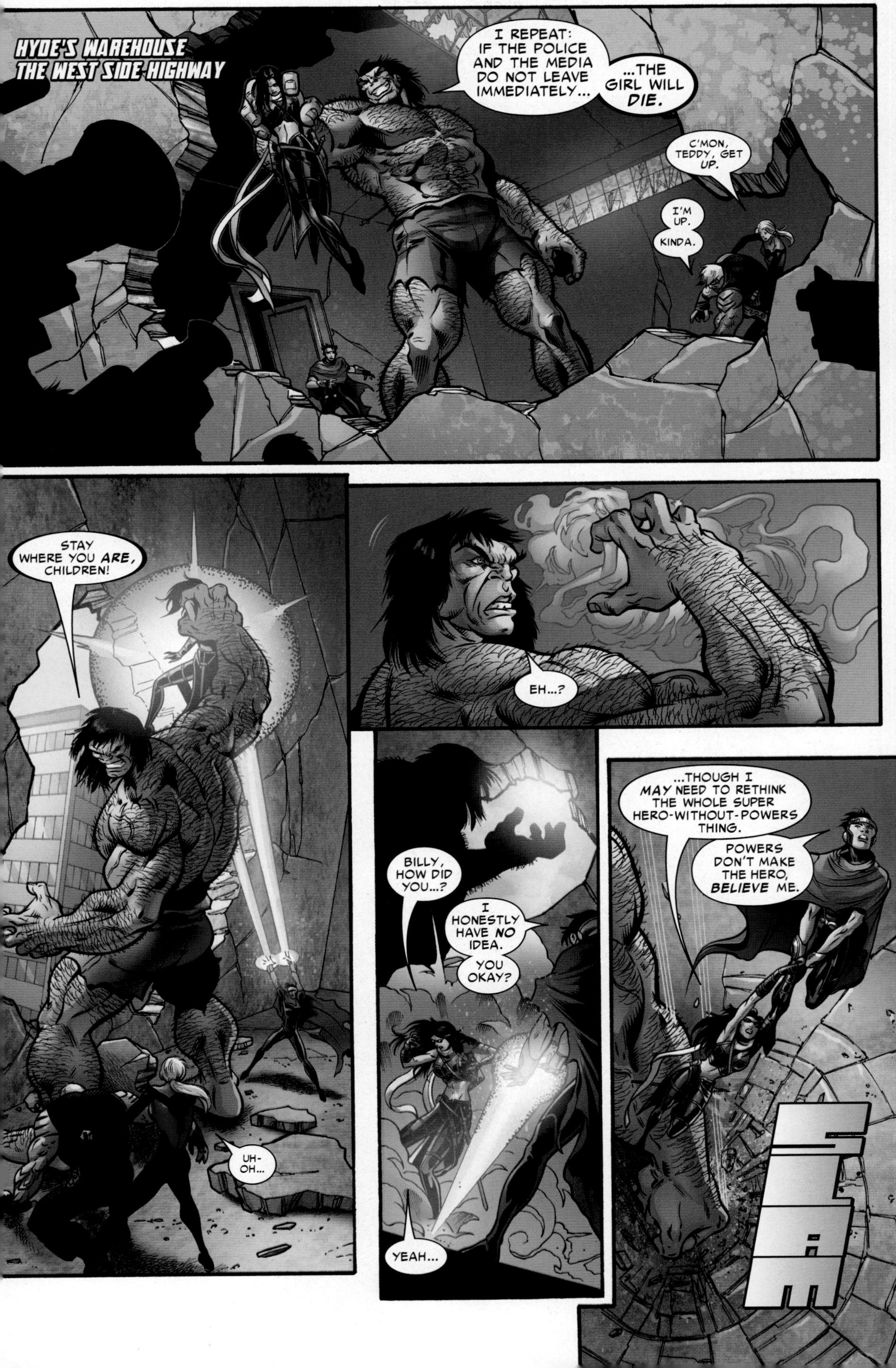
HYDE'S WAREHOUSE
THE WEST SIDE HIGHWAY
I REPEAT: IF THE POLICE AND THE MEDIA DO NOT LEAVE IMMEDIATELY...
...THE GIRL WILL DIE.
C'MON, TEDDY, GET UP.
I'M UP.
KINDA.
STAY WHERE YOU ARE, CHILDREN!
UH-OH...
EH...?
BILLY, HOW DID YOU...?
I HONESTLY HAVE NO IDEA.
YOU OKAY?
YEAH...
...THOUGH I MAY NEED TO RETHINK THE WHOLE SUPER HERO-WITHOUT-POWERS THING.
POWERS DON'T MAKE THE HERO, BELIEVE ME.
SLAM

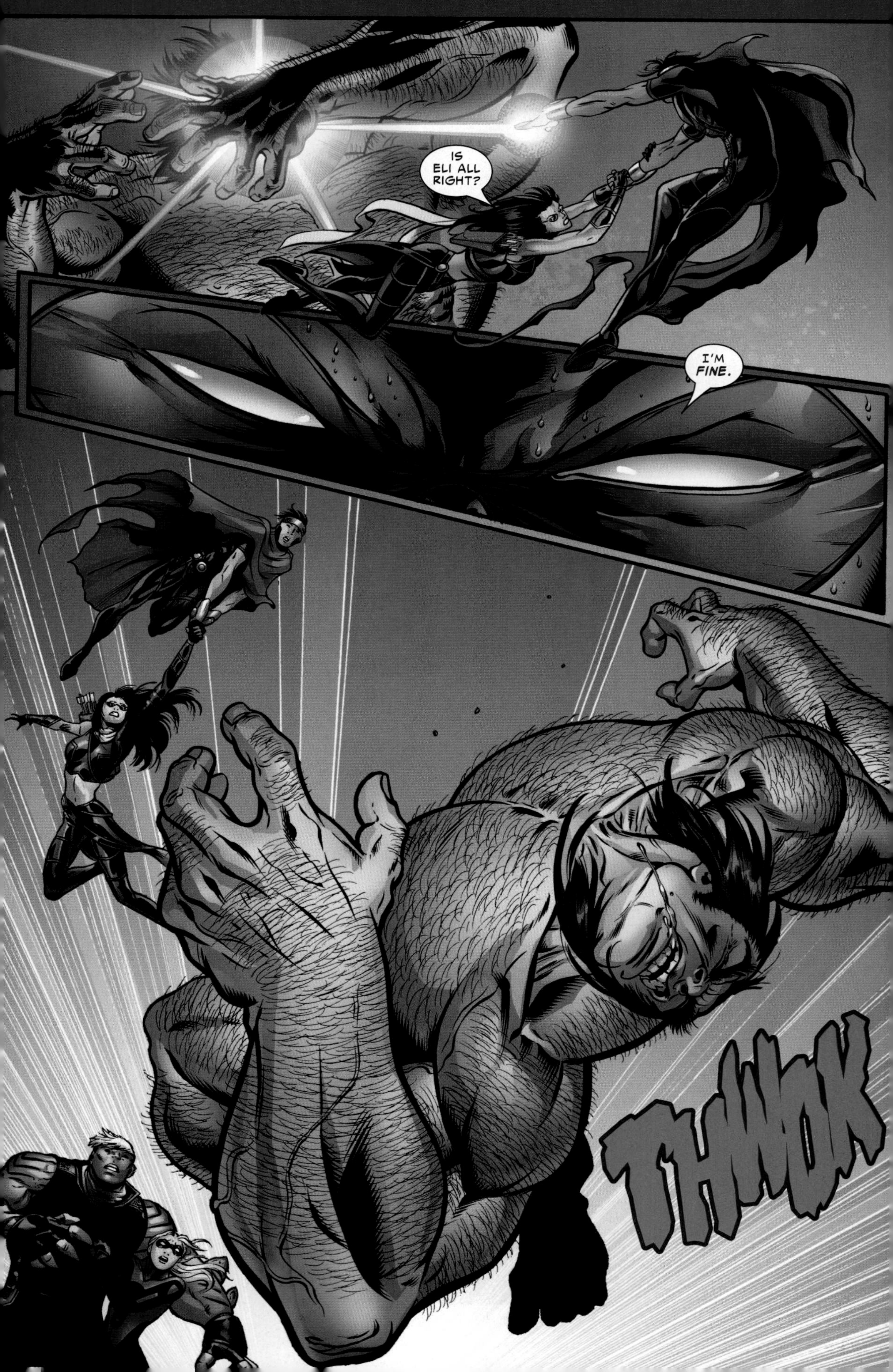
IS ELI ALL RIGHT?
I'M FINE.
THWOK

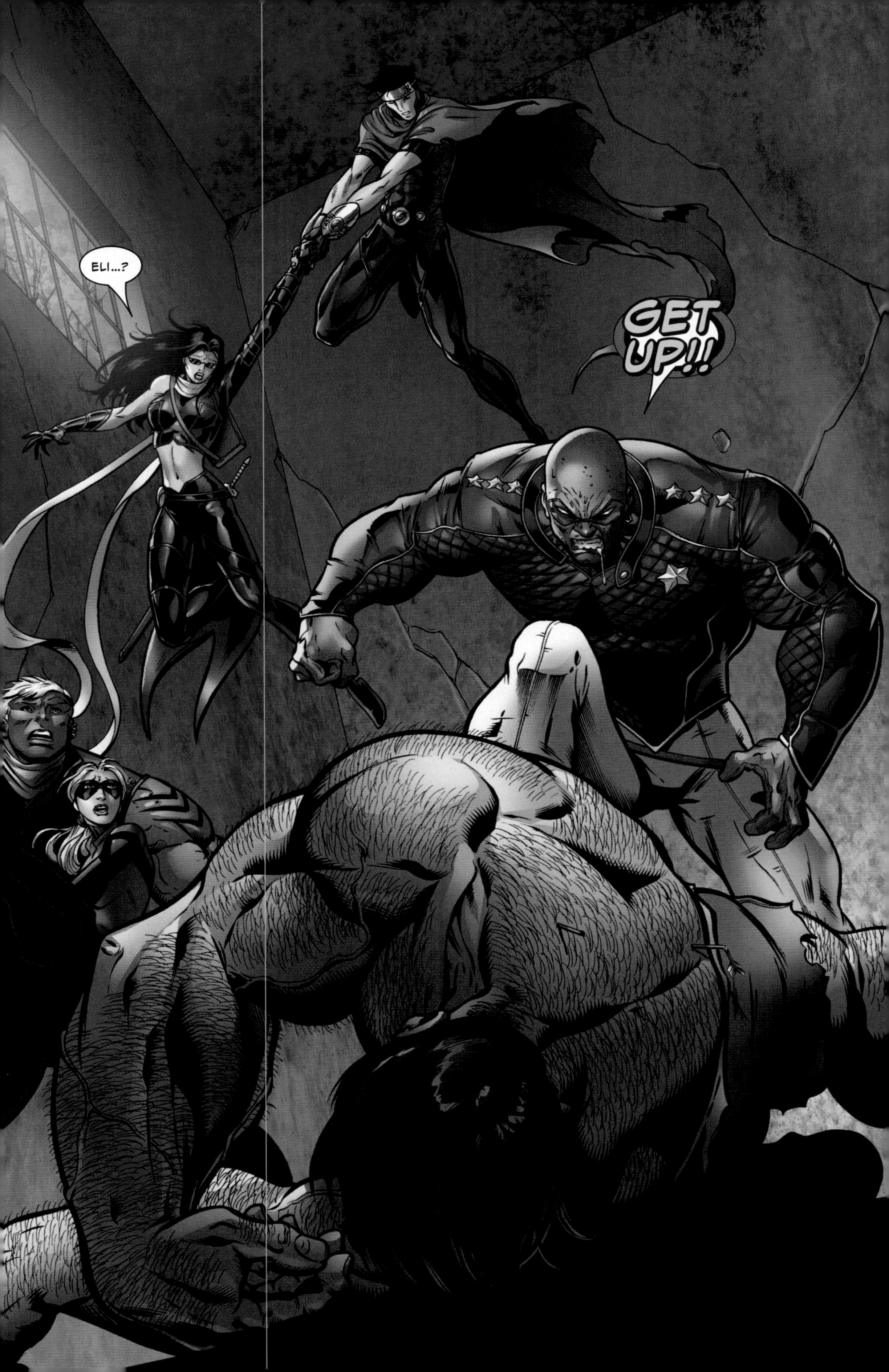
ELI...?
GET UP!!

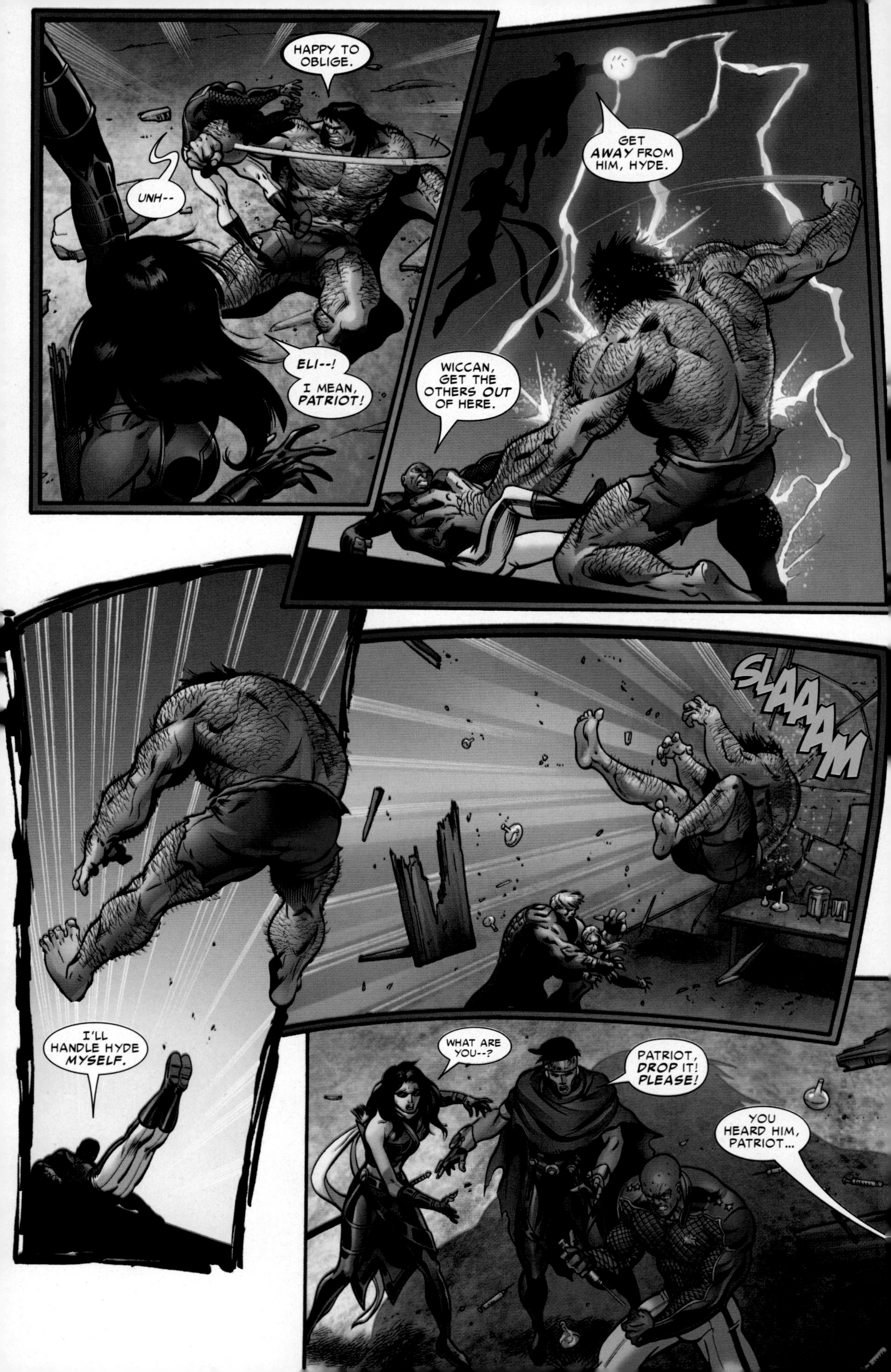
HAPPY TO OBLIGE.
UNH--
ELI--! I MEAN, PATRIOT!
GET AWAY FROM HIM, HYDE.
WICCAN, GET THE OTHERS OUT OF HERE.
SLAAAAM
I'LL HANDLE HYDE MYSELF.
WHAT ARE YOU--?
PATRIOT, DROP IT! PLEASE!
YOU HEARD HIM, PATRIOT...

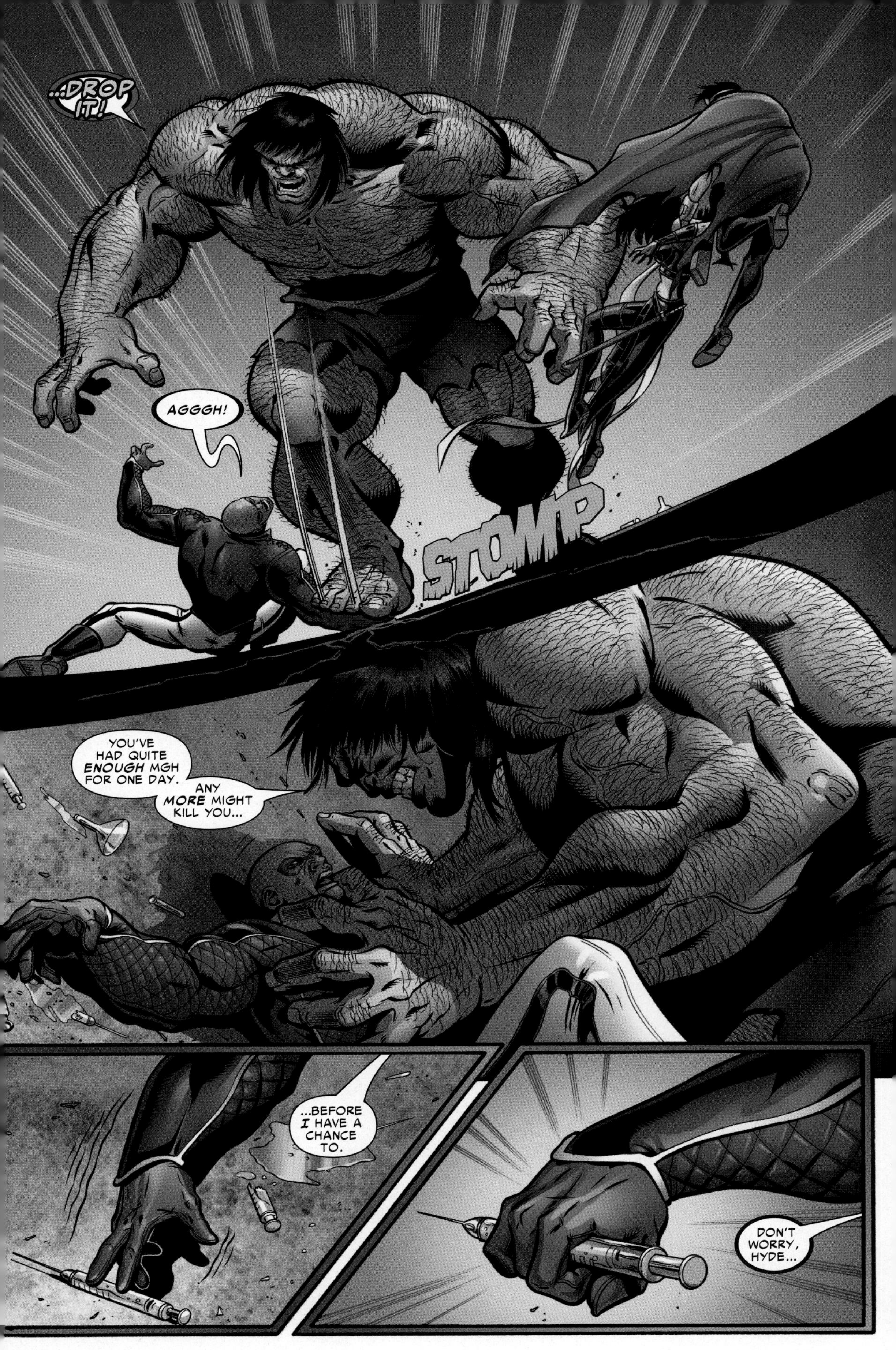
..DROP IT!
AGGGH!
STOMP
YOU'VE HAD QUITE ENOUGH MGH FOR ONE DAY.
ANY MORE MIGHT KILL YOU...
...BEFORE I HAVE A CHANCE TO.
DON'T WORRY, HYDE...

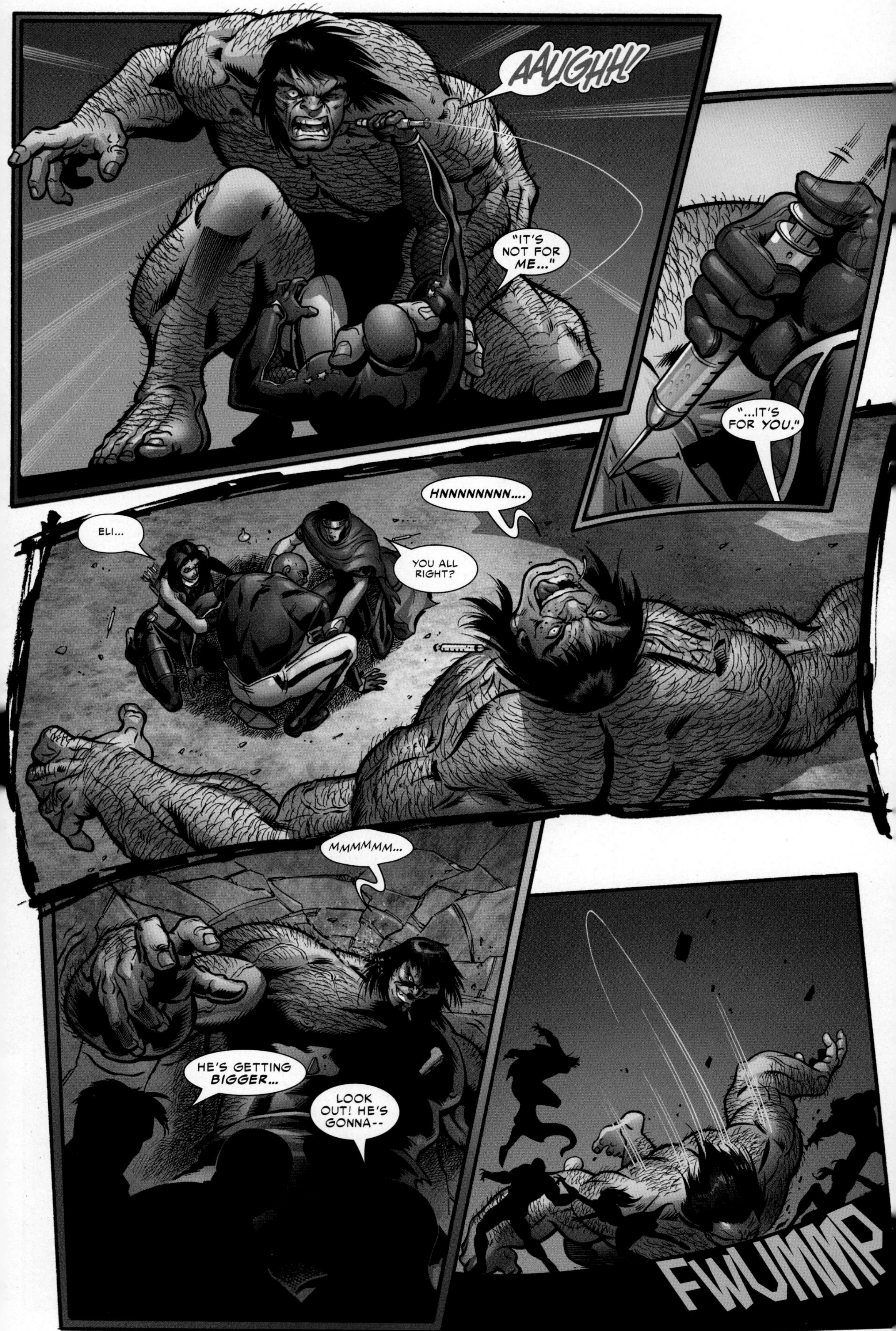
AAUGHH!
"IT'S NOT FOR ME..."
"...IT'S FOR YOU."
HNNNNNNNN....
ELI...
YOU ALL RIGHT?
MMMMMM...
HE'S GETTING BIGGER...
LOOK OUT! HE'S GONNA--
FWUMMP

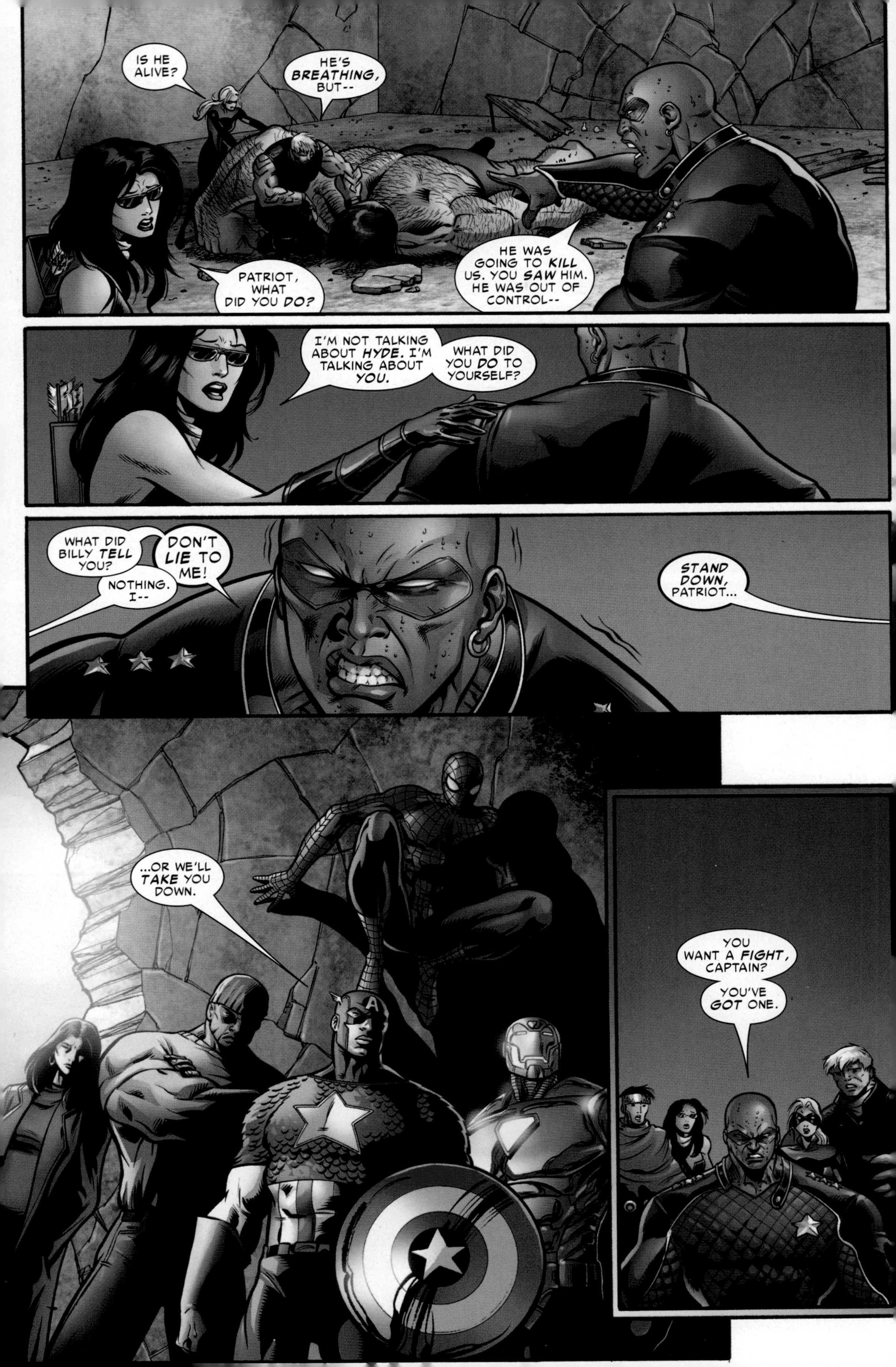
IS HE ALIVE?
HE'S BREATHING, BUT--
PATRIOT, WHAT DID YOU DO?
HE WAS GOING TO KILL US. YOU SAW HIM. HE WAS OUT OF CONTROL--
I'M NOT TALKING ABOUT HYDE. I'M TALKING ABOUT YOU.
WHAT DID YOU DO TO YOURSELF?
WHAT DID BILLY TELL YOU?
NOTHING. I--
DON'T LIE TO ME!
STAND DOWN, PATRIOT...
...OR WE'LL TAKE YOU DOWN.
YOU WANT A FIGHT, CAPTAIN?
YOU'VE GOT ONE.

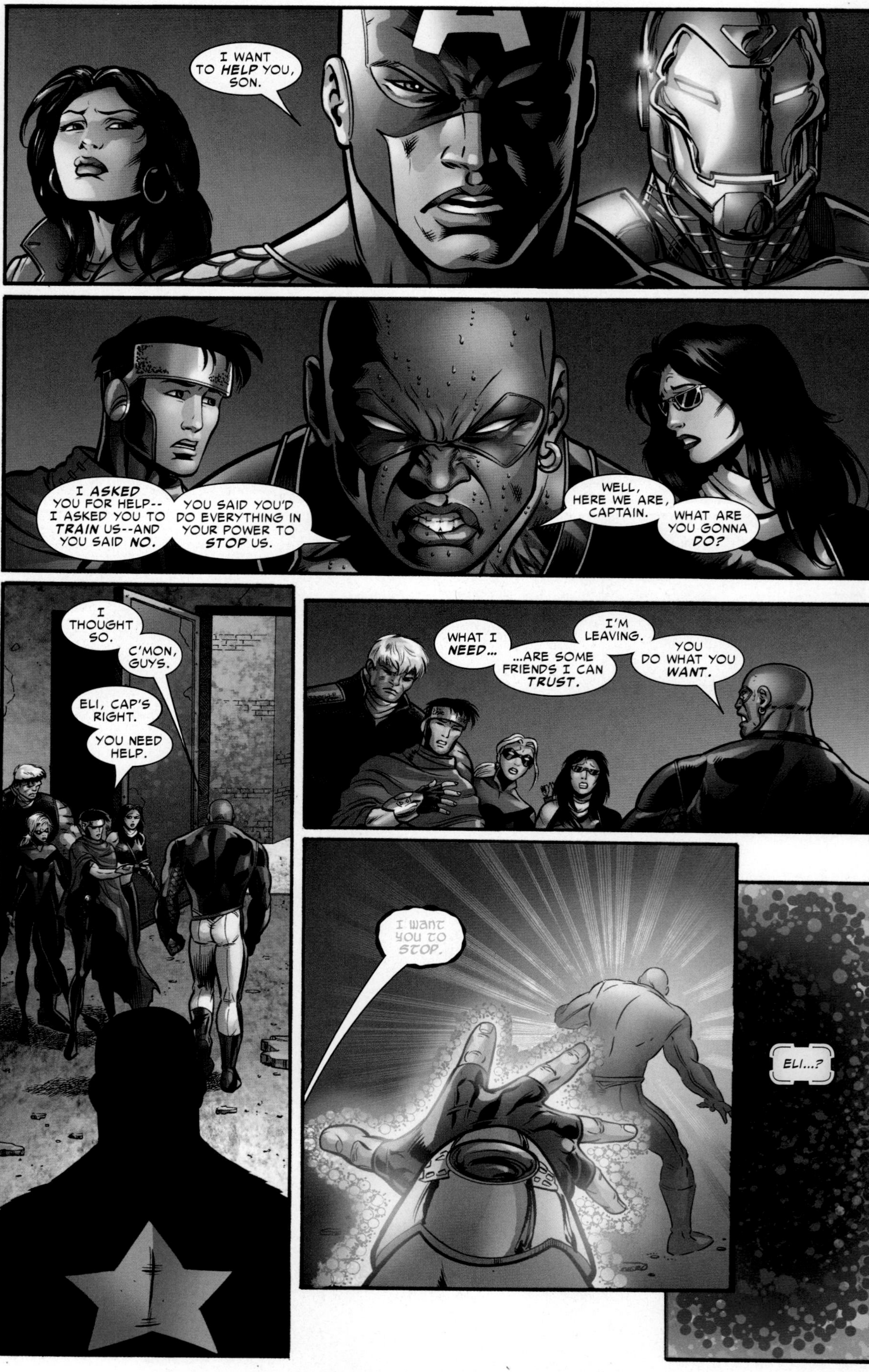
I WANT TO HELP YOU, SON.
I ASKED YOU FOR HELP-- I ASKED YOU TO TRAIN US--AND YOU SAID NO.
YOU SAID YOU'D DO EVERYTHING IN YOUR POWER TO STOP US.
WELL, HERE WE ARE, CAPTAIN.
WHAT ARE YOU GONNA DO?
I THOUGHT SO.
C'MON, GUYS.
ELI, CAP'S RIGHT.
YOU NEED HELP.
WHAT I NEED...
...ARE SOME FRIENDS I CAN TRUST.
I'M LEAVING.
YOU DO WHAT YOU WANT.
I WANT YOU TO STOP.
ELI...?

ELI.

HMN...?

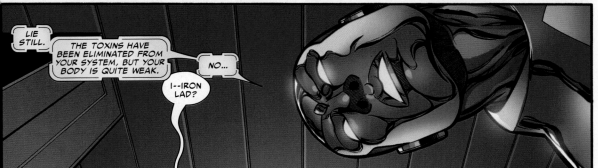

LIE STILL.

THE TOXINS HAVE BEEN ELIMINATED FROM YOUR SYSTEM, BUT YOUR BODY IS QUITE WEAK.

NO...

I--IRON LAD?

...I AM THE VISION.

WHERE AM I?

AVENGERS TOWER.

CAPTAIN AMERICA AND THE OTHERS HAVE TAKEN TEDDY, CASSIE AND KATE TO THE MAIN MEETING ROOM.

YOU KNOW OUR REAL NAMES?

THE NEURO-KINETIC ARMOR WHICH HOUSES MY PROGRAMMING HAS RETAINED THE BRAIN PATTERNS, EMOTIONS, AND MEMORIES OF IRON LAD.

SO, YOU KIND OF ARE IRON LAD.

IN SOME WAYS, I SUPPOSE I AM.

DO YOU HAVE HIS POWERS?

CAN YOU TAKE ME BACK TO THE PAST, SO I CAN MABYE...FIX ALL THIS?

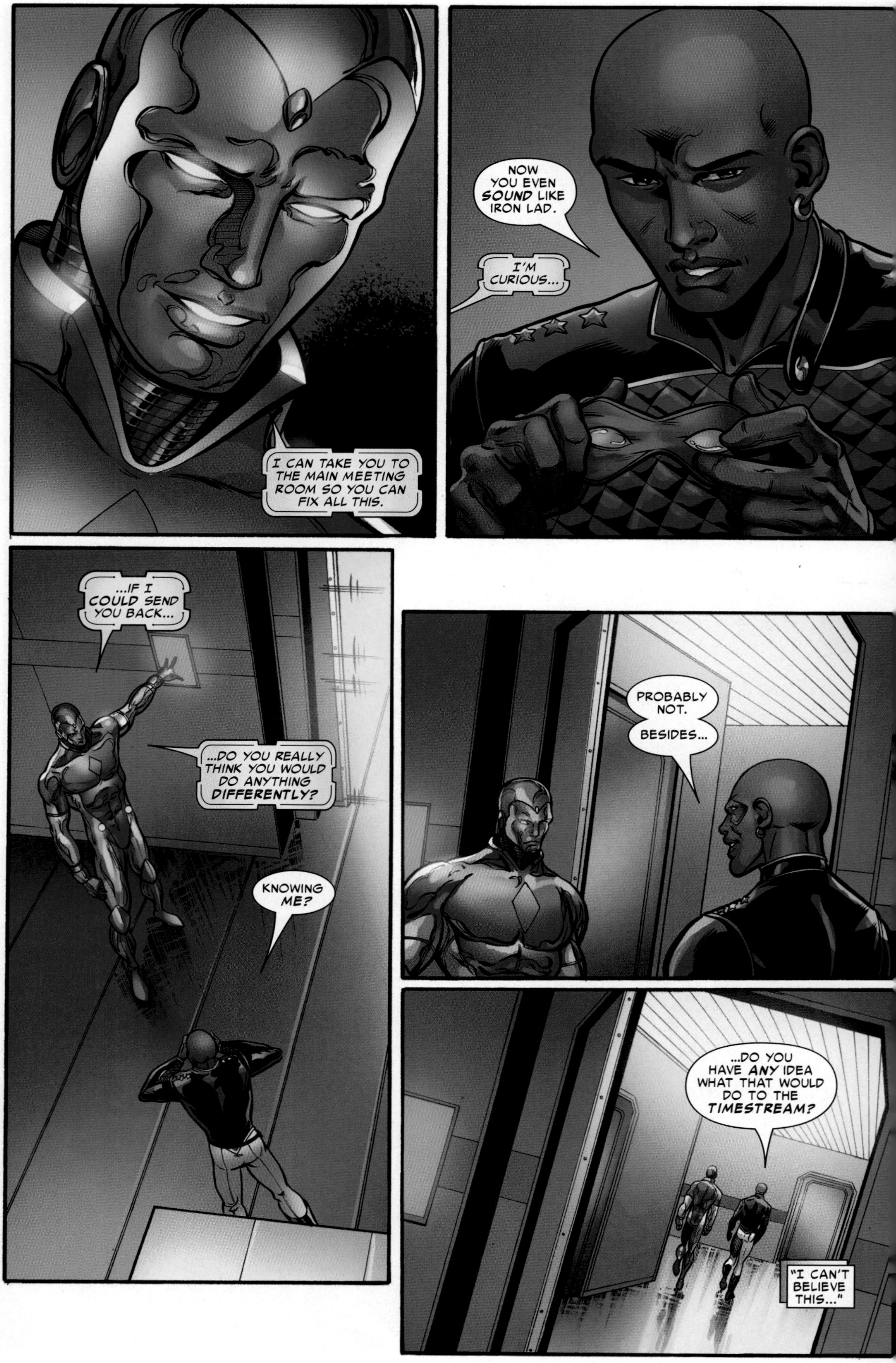
I CAN TAKE YOU TO THE MAIN MEETING ROOM SO YOU CAN FIX ALL THIS.
NOW YOU EVEN SOUND LIKE IRON LAD.
I'M CURIOUS...
...IF I COULD SEND YOU BACK...
...DO YOU REALLY THINK YOU WOULD DO ANYTHING DIFFERENTLY?
KNOWING ME?
PROBABLY NOT.
BESIDES...
...DO YOU HAVE ANY IDEA WHAT THAT WOULD DO TO THE TIMESTREAM?
"I CAN'T BELIEVE THIS..."

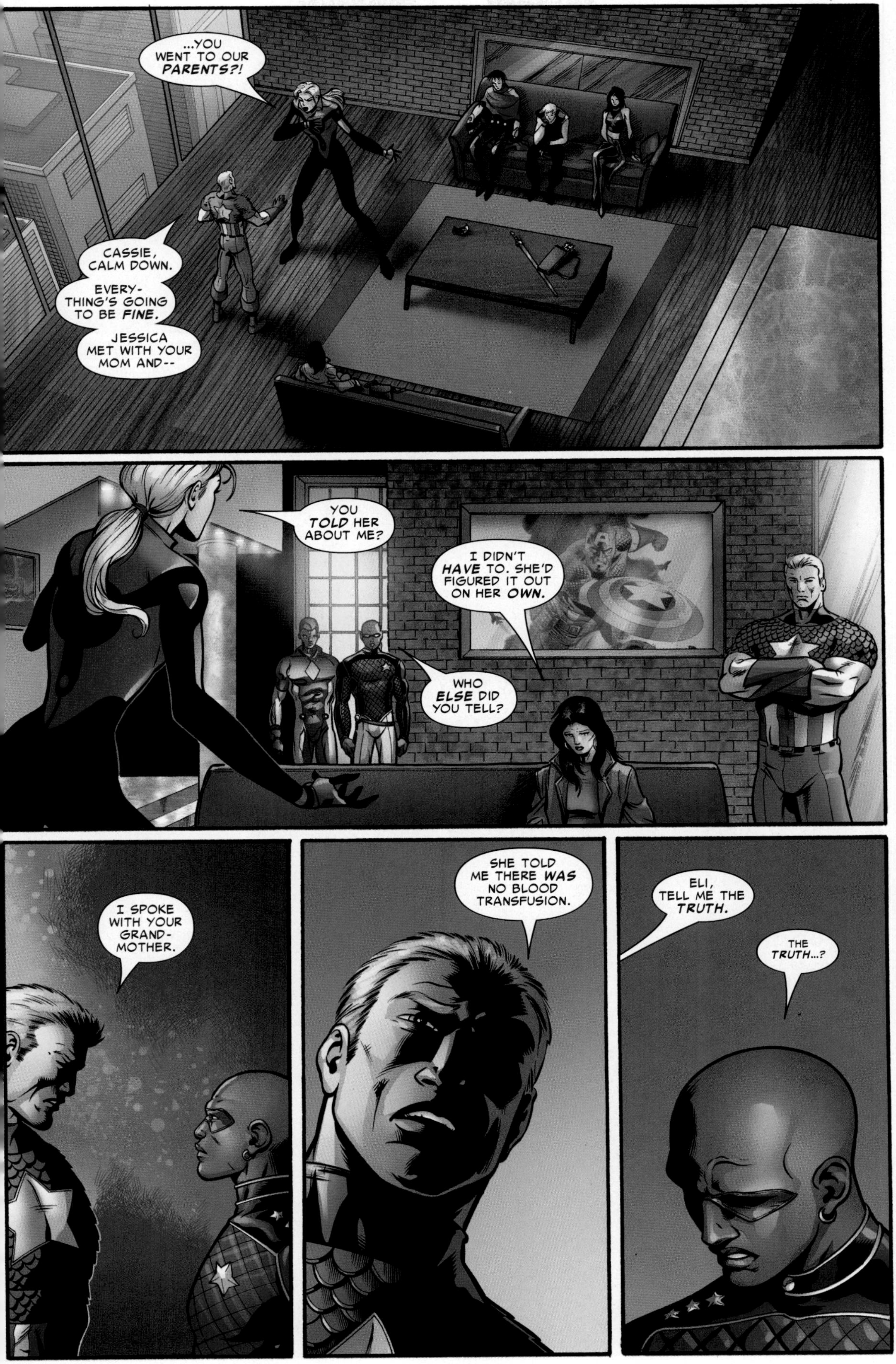
...YOU WENT TO OUR PARENTS?!
CASSIE, CALM DOWN.
EVERY-THING'S GOING TO BE FINE.
JESSICA MET WITH YOUR MOM AND--
YOU TOLD HER ABOUT ME?
I DIDN'T HAVE TO. SHE'D FIGURED IT OUT ON HER OWN.
WHO ELSE DID YOU TELL?
I SPOKE WITH YOUR GRAND-MOTHER.
SHE TOLD ME THERE WAS NO BLOOD TRANSFUSION.
ELI, TELL ME THE TRUTH.
THE TRUTH...?

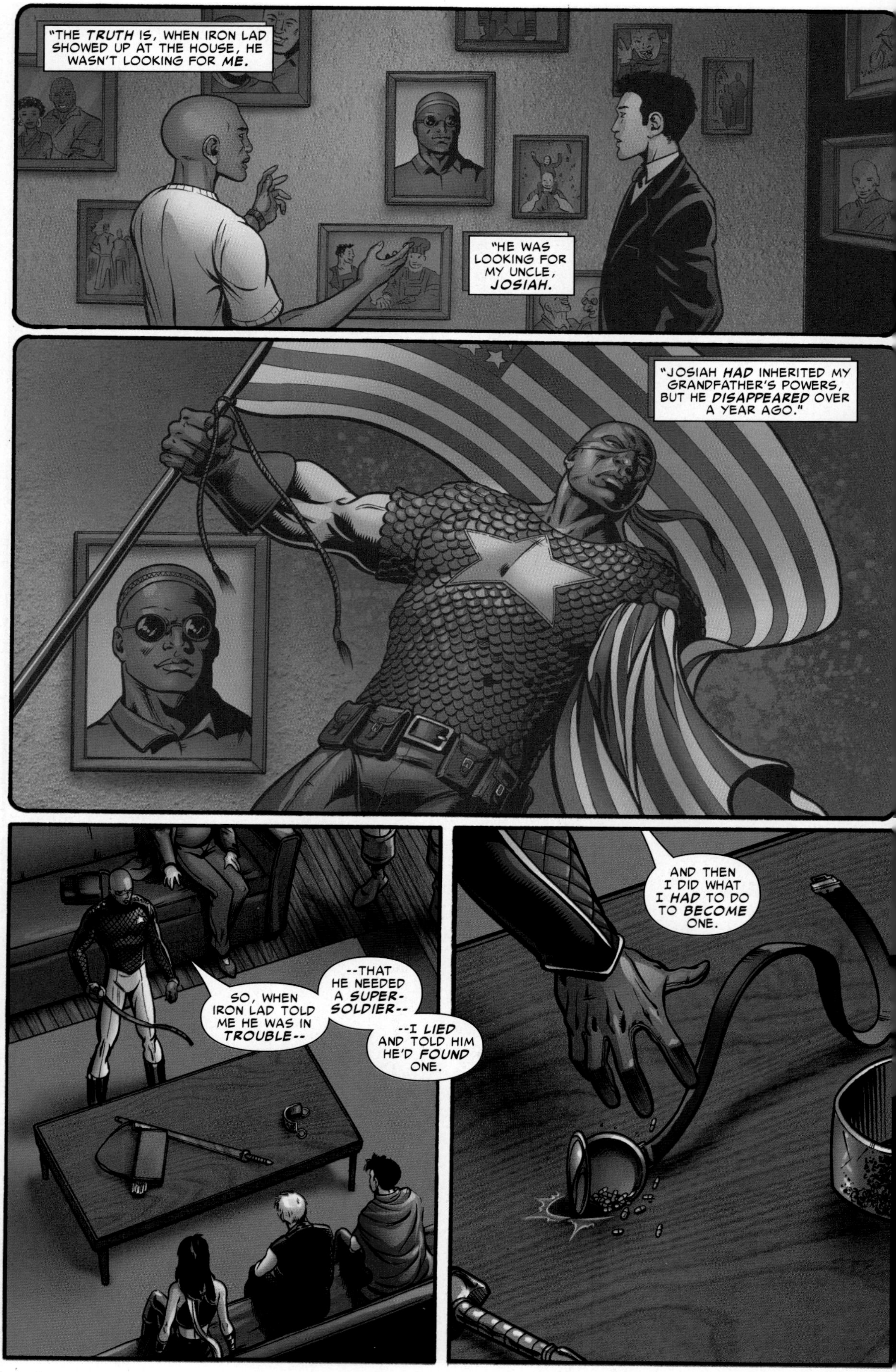
"THE TRUTH IS, WHEN IRON LAD SHOWED UP AT THE HOUSE, HE WASN'T LOOKING FOR ME.
"HE WAS LOOKING FOR MY UNCLE, JOSIAH.
"JOSIAH HAD INHERITED MY GRANDFATHER'S POWERS, BUT HE DISAPPEARED OVER A YEAR AGO."
SO, WHEN IRON LAD TOLD ME HE WAS IN TROUBLE--
--THAT HE NEEDED A SUPER-SOLDIER--
--I LIED AND TOLD HIM HE'D FOUND ONE.
AND THEN I DID WHAT I HAD TO DO TO BECOME ONE.

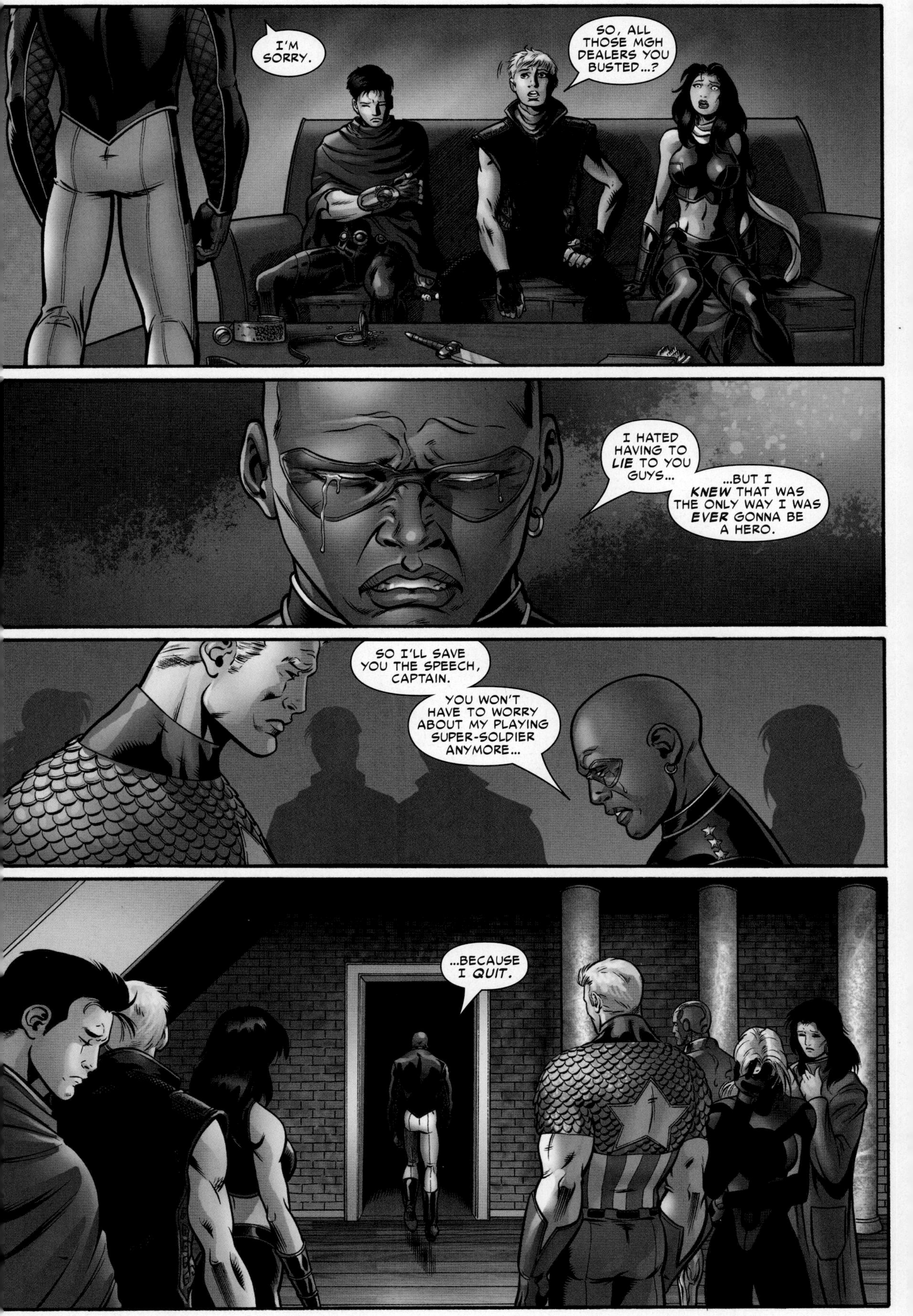
I'M SORRY.
SO, ALL THOSE MGH DEALERS YOU BUSTED...?
I HATED HAVING TO LIE TO YOU GUYS...
...BUT I KNEW THAT WAS THE ONLY WAY I WAS EVER GONNA BE A HERO.
SO I'LL SAVE YOU THE SPEECH, CAPTAIN.
YOU WON'T HAVE TO WORRY ABOUT MY PLAYING SUPER-SOLDIER ANYMORE...
...BECAUSE I QUIT.

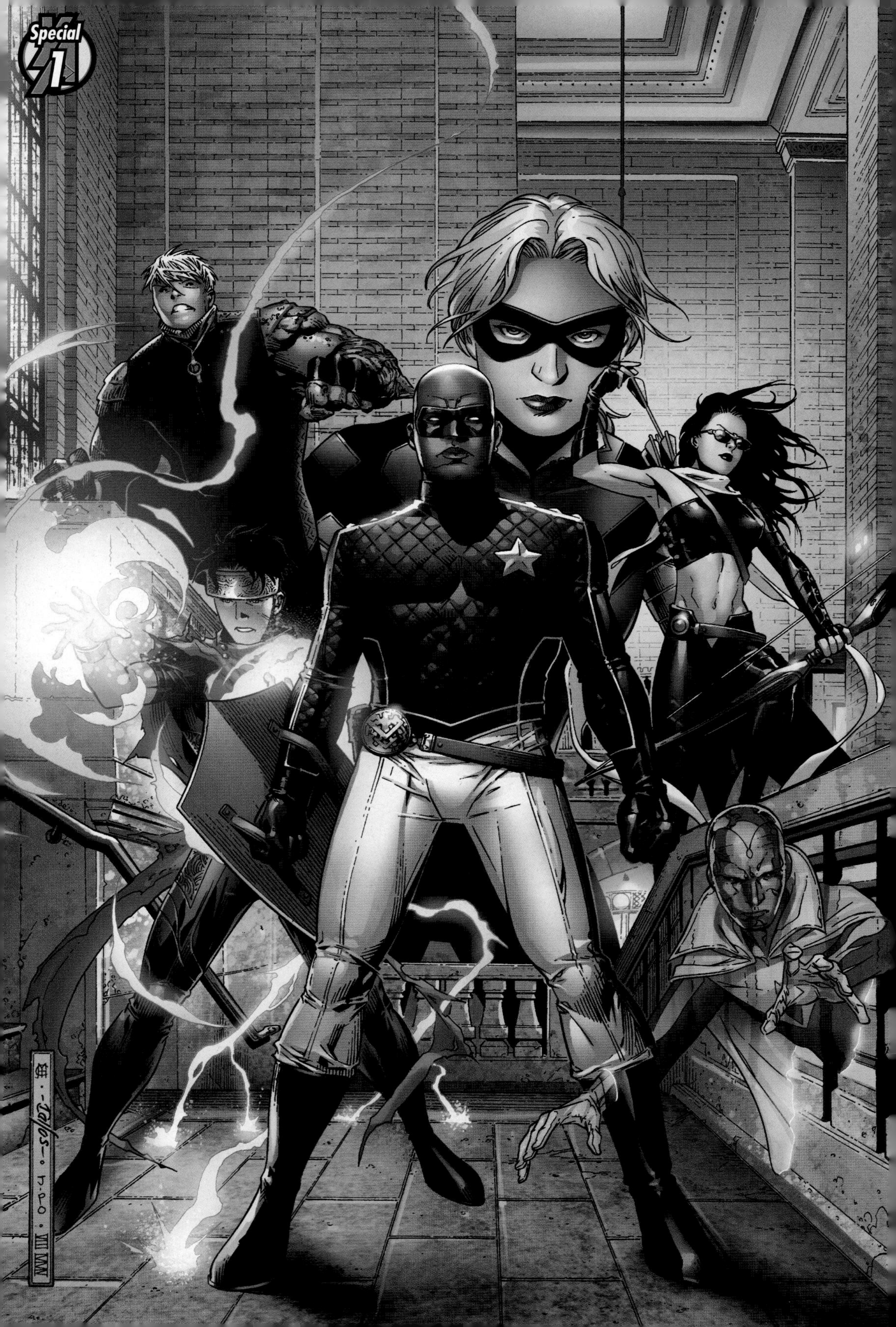
Special
1

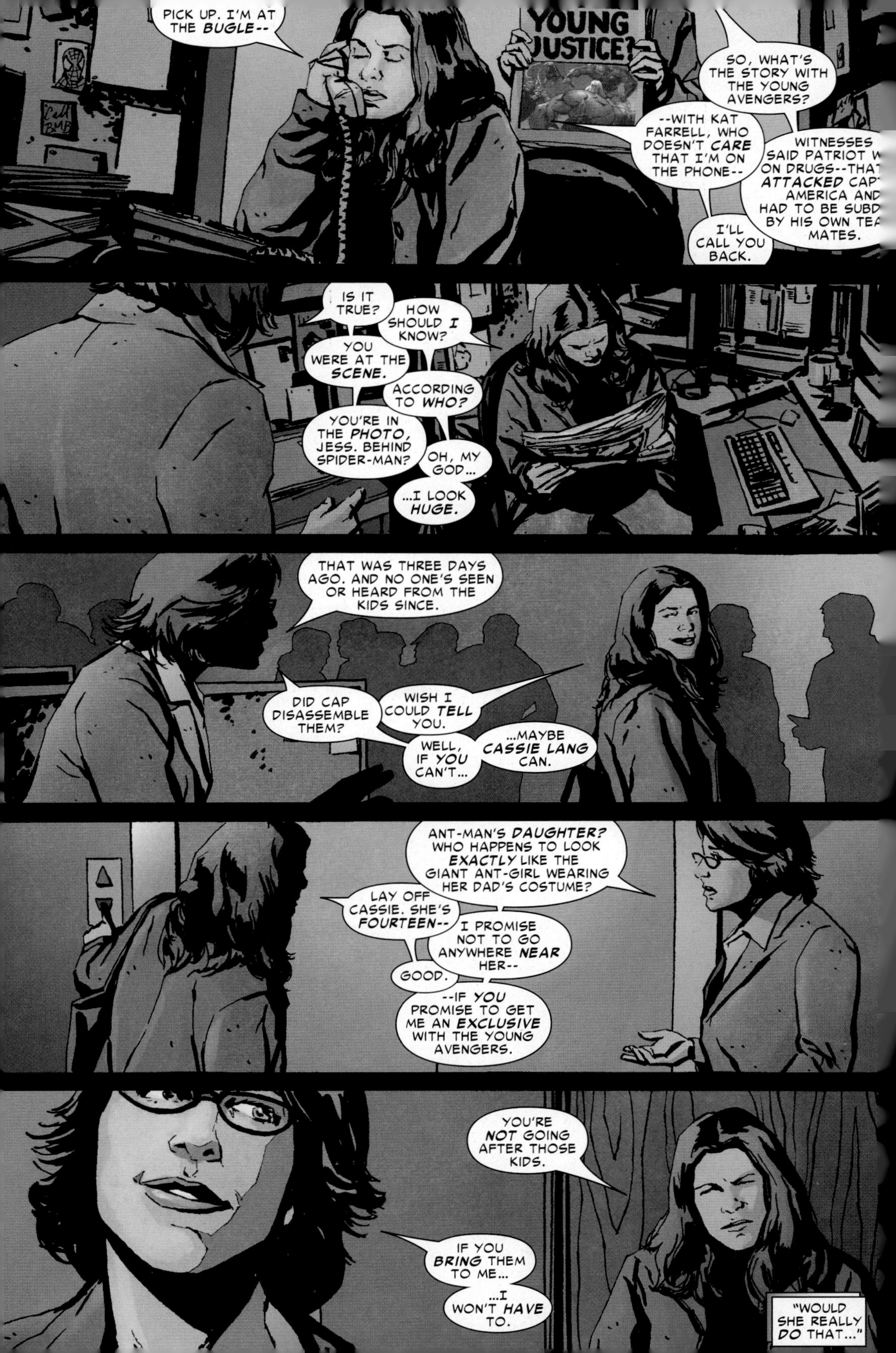

PICK UP. I'M AT THE *BUGLE*--
YOUNG JUSTICE?
SO, WHAT'S THE STORY WITH THE YOUNG AVENGERS?
--WITH KAT FARRELL, WHO DOESN'T *CARE* THAT I'M ON THE PHONE--
WITNESSES SAID PATRIOT W ON DRUGS--THAT *ATTACKED* CAPT AMERICA AND HAD TO BE SUBD BY HIS OWN TEA MATES.
I'LL CALL YOU BACK.
IS IT TRUE?
HOW SHOULD *I* KNOW?
YOU WERE AT THE *SCENE.*
ACCORDING TO *WHO?*
YOU'RE IN THE *PHOTO,* JESS. BEHIND SPIDER-MAN?
OH, MY GOD...
...I LOOK *HUGE.*
THAT WAS THREE DAYS AGO. AND NO ONE'S SEEN OR HEARD FROM THE KIDS SINCE.
DID CAP DISASSEMBLE THEM?
WISH I COULD *TELL* YOU.
WELL, IF *YOU* CAN'T...
...MAYBE *CASSIE LANG* CAN.
ANT-MAN'S *DAUGHTER?* WHO HAPPENS TO LOOK *EXACTLY* LIKE THE GIANT ANT-GIRL WEARING HER DAD'S COSTUME?
LAY OFF CASSIE. SHE'S *FOURTEEN--*
I PROMISE NOT TO GO ANYWHERE *NEAR* HER--
GOOD.
--IF *YOU* PROMISE TO GET ME AN *EXCLUSIVE* WITH THE YOUNG AVENGERS.
YOU'RE *NOT* GOING AFTER THOSE KIDS.
IF YOU *BRING* THEM TO ME...
...I WON'T *HAVE* TO.
"WOULD SHE REALLY *DO* THAT..."

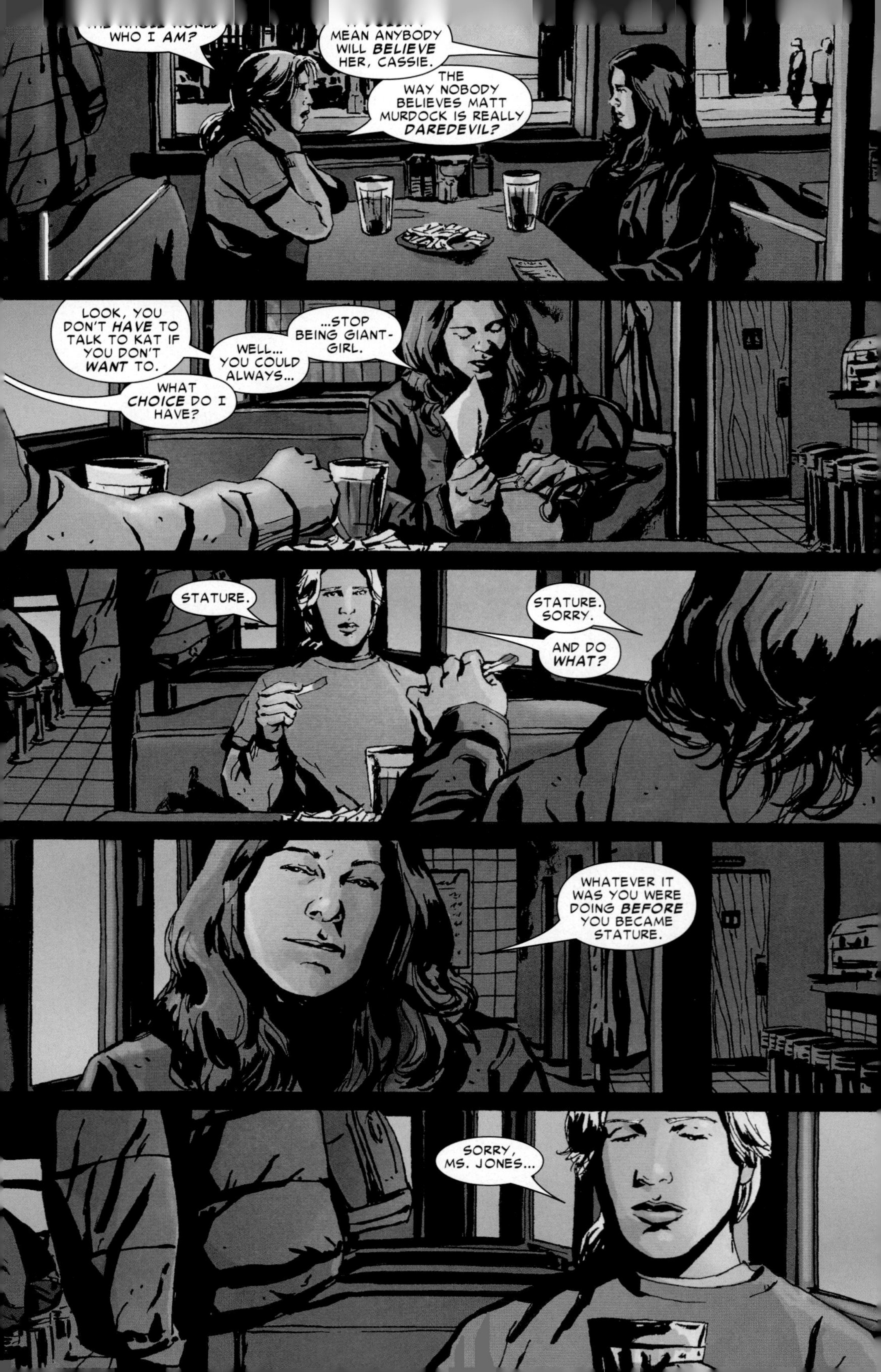
WHO I AM?
MEAN ANYBODY WILL BELIEVE HER, CASSIE.
THE WAY NOBODY BELIEVES MATT MURDOCK IS REALLY DAREDEVIL?
LOOK, YOU DON'T HAVE TO TALK TO KAT IF YOU DON'T WANT TO.
WHAT CHOICE DO I HAVE?
WELL... YOU COULD ALWAYS...
...STOP BEING GIANT-GIRL.
STATURE.
STATURE. SORRY.
AND DO WHAT?
WHATEVER IT WAS YOU WERE DOING BEFORE YOU BECAME STATURE.
SORRY, MS. JONES...

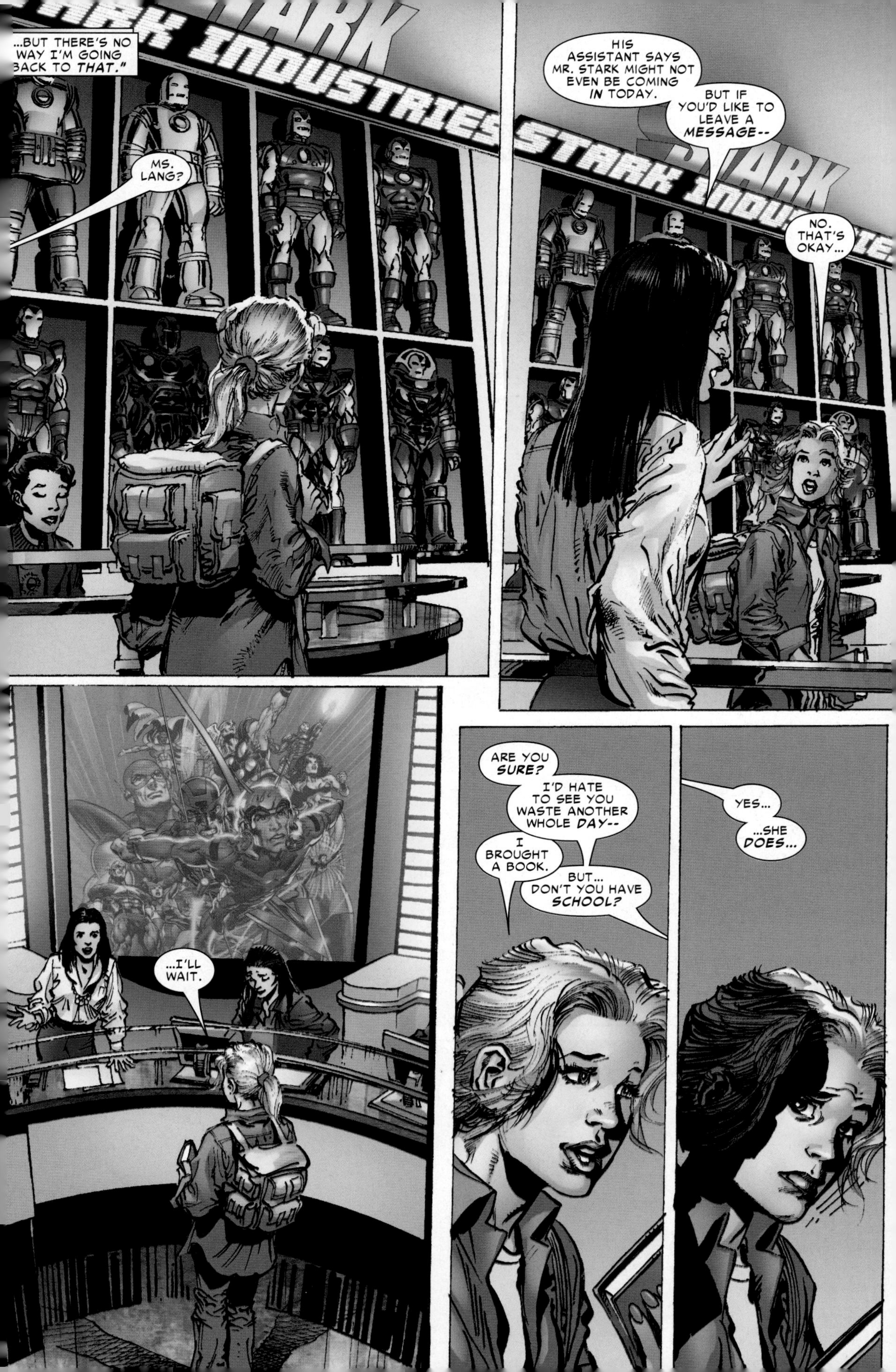

STARK INDUSTRIES
"...BUT THERE'S NO WAY I'M GOING BACK TO THAT."
MS. LANG?
HIS ASSISTANT SAYS MR. STARK MIGHT NOT EVEN BE COMING IN TODAY.
BUT IF YOU'D LIKE TO LEAVE A MESSAGE--
STARK INDUSTRIES
NO. THAT'S OKAY...
...I'LL WAIT.
ARE YOU SURE?
I'D HATE TO SEE YOU WASTE ANOTHER WHOLE DAY--
I BROUGHT A BOOK.
BUT... DON'T YOU HAVE SCHOOL?
YES...
...SHE DOES...

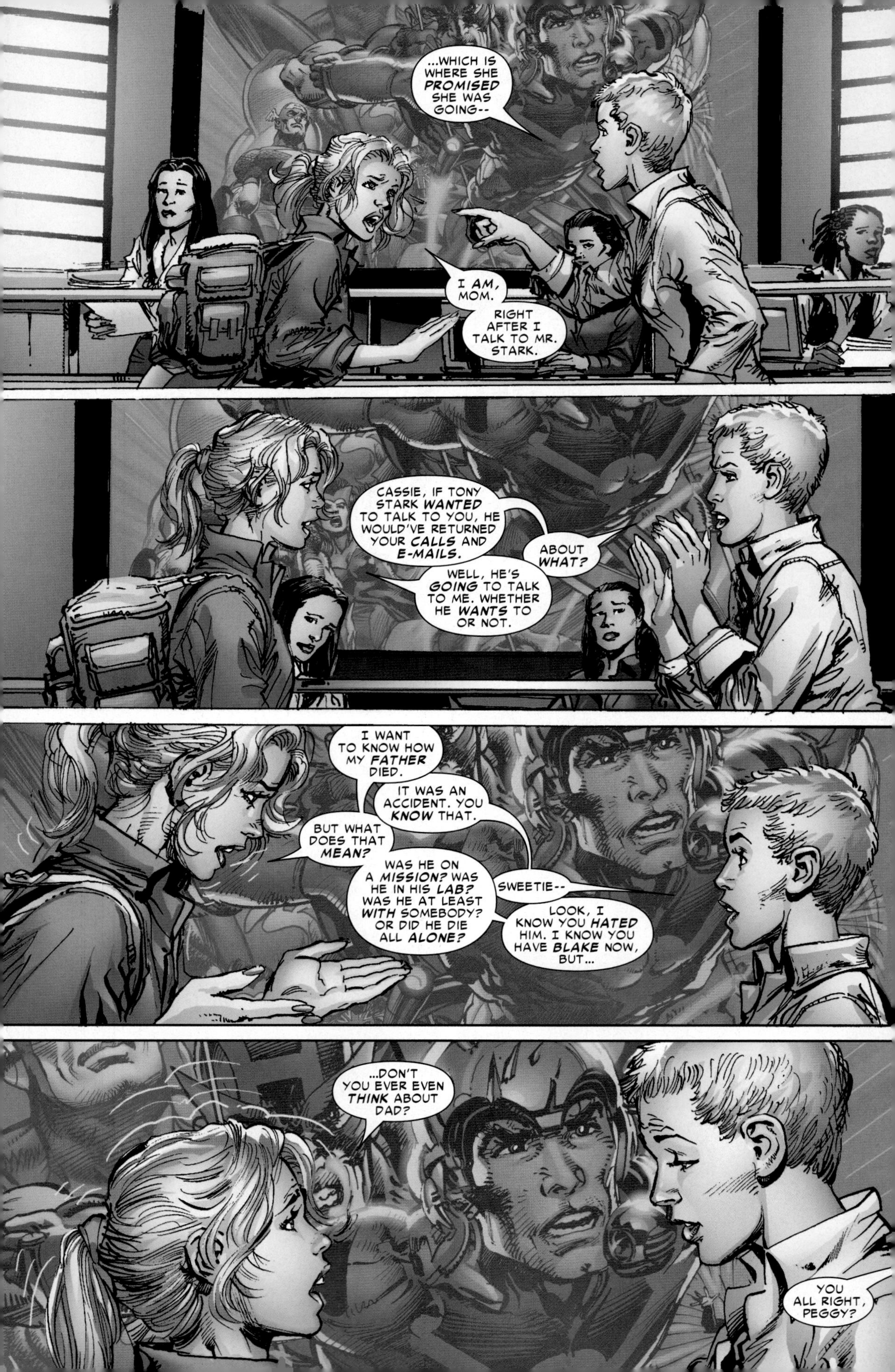
...WHICH IS WHERE SHE PROMISED SHE WAS GOING--
I AM, MOM.
RIGHT AFTER I TALK TO MR. STARK.
CASSIE, IF TONY STARK WANTED TO TALK TO YOU, HE WOULD'VE RETURNED YOUR CALLS AND E-MAILS.
ABOUT WHAT?
WELL, HE'S GOING TO TALK TO ME. WHETHER HE WANTS TO OR NOT.
I WANT TO KNOW HOW MY FATHER DIED.
IT WAS AN ACCIDENT. YOU KNOW THAT.
BUT WHAT DOES THAT MEAN?
WAS HE ON A MISSION? WAS HE IN HIS LAB? WAS HE AT LEAST WITH SOMEBODY? OR DID HE DIE ALL ALONE?
SWEETIE--
LOOK, I KNOW YOU HATED HIM. I KNOW YOU HAVE BLAKE NOW, BUT...
...DON'T YOU EVER EVEN THINK ABOUT DAD?
YOU ALL RIGHT, PEGGY?

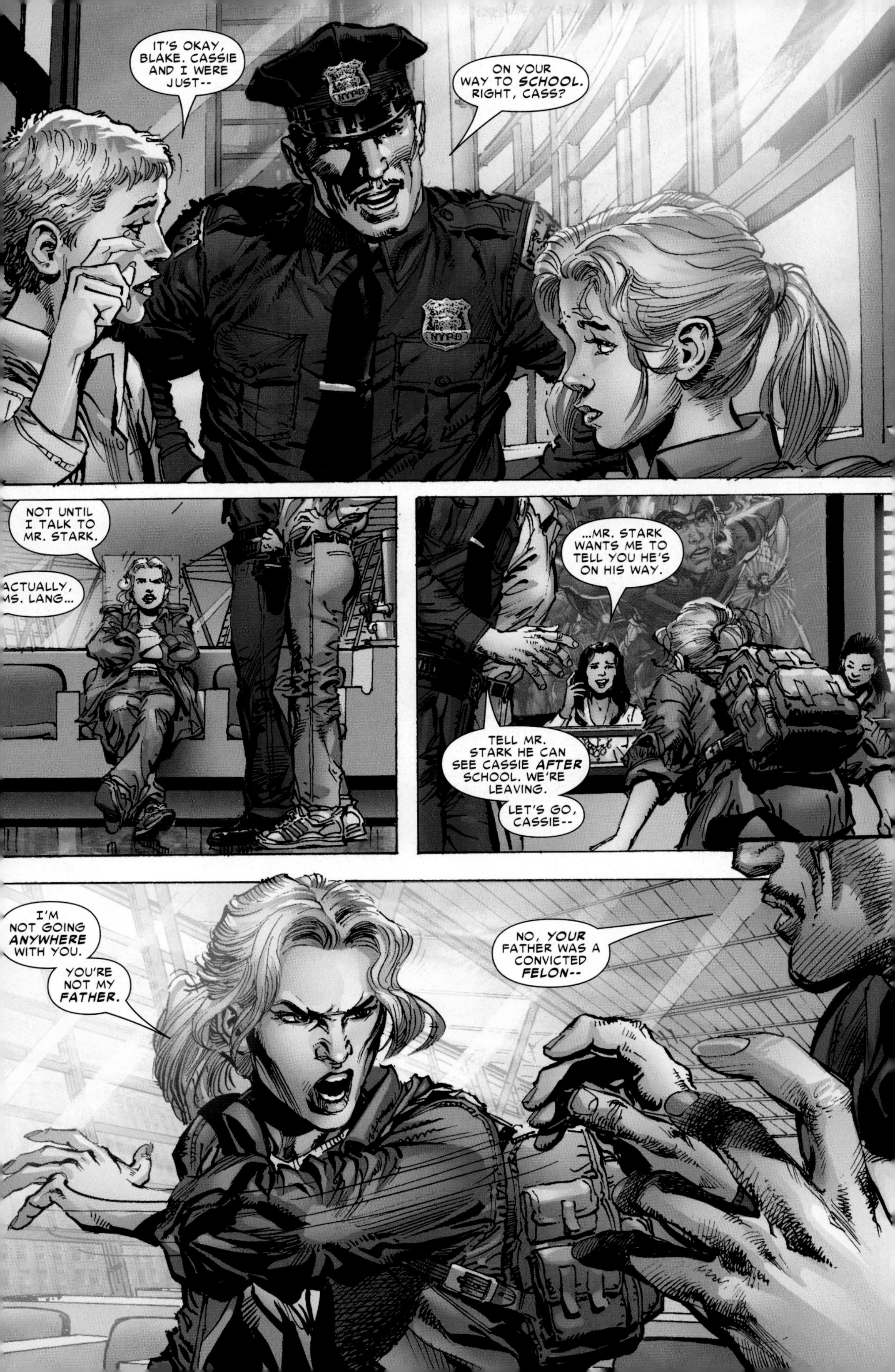
IT'S OKAY, BLAKE. CASSIE AND I WERE JUST--
ON YOUR WAY TO SCHOOL. RIGHT, CASS?
NOT UNTIL I TALK TO MR. STARK.
ACTUALLY, MS. LANG...
...MR. STARK WANTS ME TO TELL YOU HE'S ON HIS WAY.
TELL MR. STARK HE CAN SEE CASSIE AFTER SCHOOL. WE'RE LEAVING.
LET'S GO, CASSIE--
I'M NOT GOING ANYWHERE WITH YOU.
YOU'RE NOT MY FATHER.
NO, YOUR FATHER WAS A CONVICTED FELON--

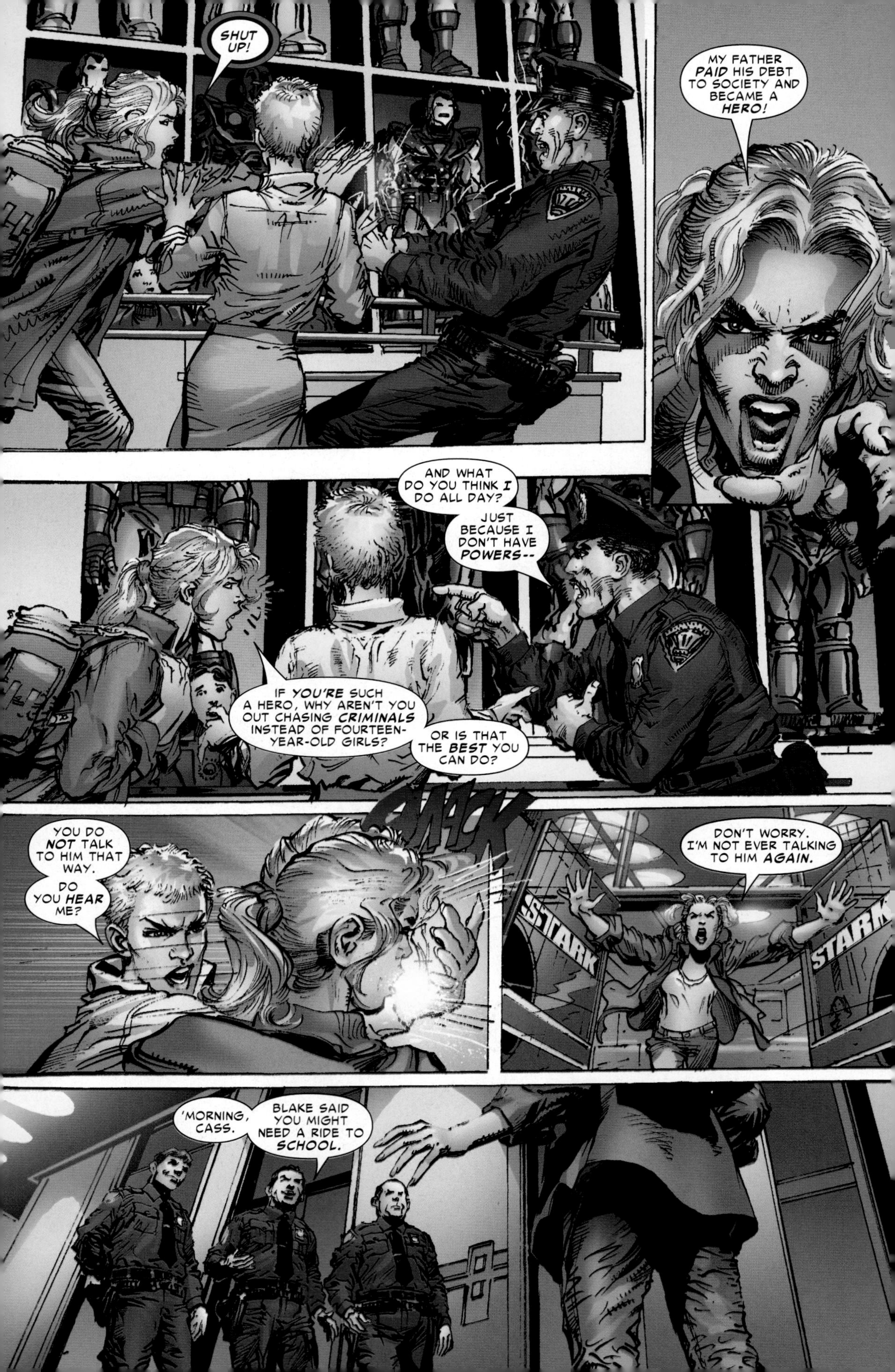
SHUT UP!
MY FATHER PAID HIS DEBT TO SOCIETY AND BECAME A HERO!
AND WHAT DO YOU THINK I DO ALL DAY?
JUST BECAUSE I DON'T HAVE POWERS--
IF YOU'RE SUCH A HERO, WHY AREN'T YOU OUT CHASING CRIMINALS INSTEAD OF FOURTEEN-YEAR-OLD GIRLS?
OR IS THAT THE BEST YOU CAN DO?
CRACK
YOU DO NOT TALK TO HIM THAT WAY.
DO YOU HEAR ME?
DON'T WORRY. I'M NOT EVER TALKING TO HIM AGAIN.
STARK
STARK
'MORNING, CASS.
BLAKE SAID YOU MIGHT NEED A RIDE TO SCHOOL.

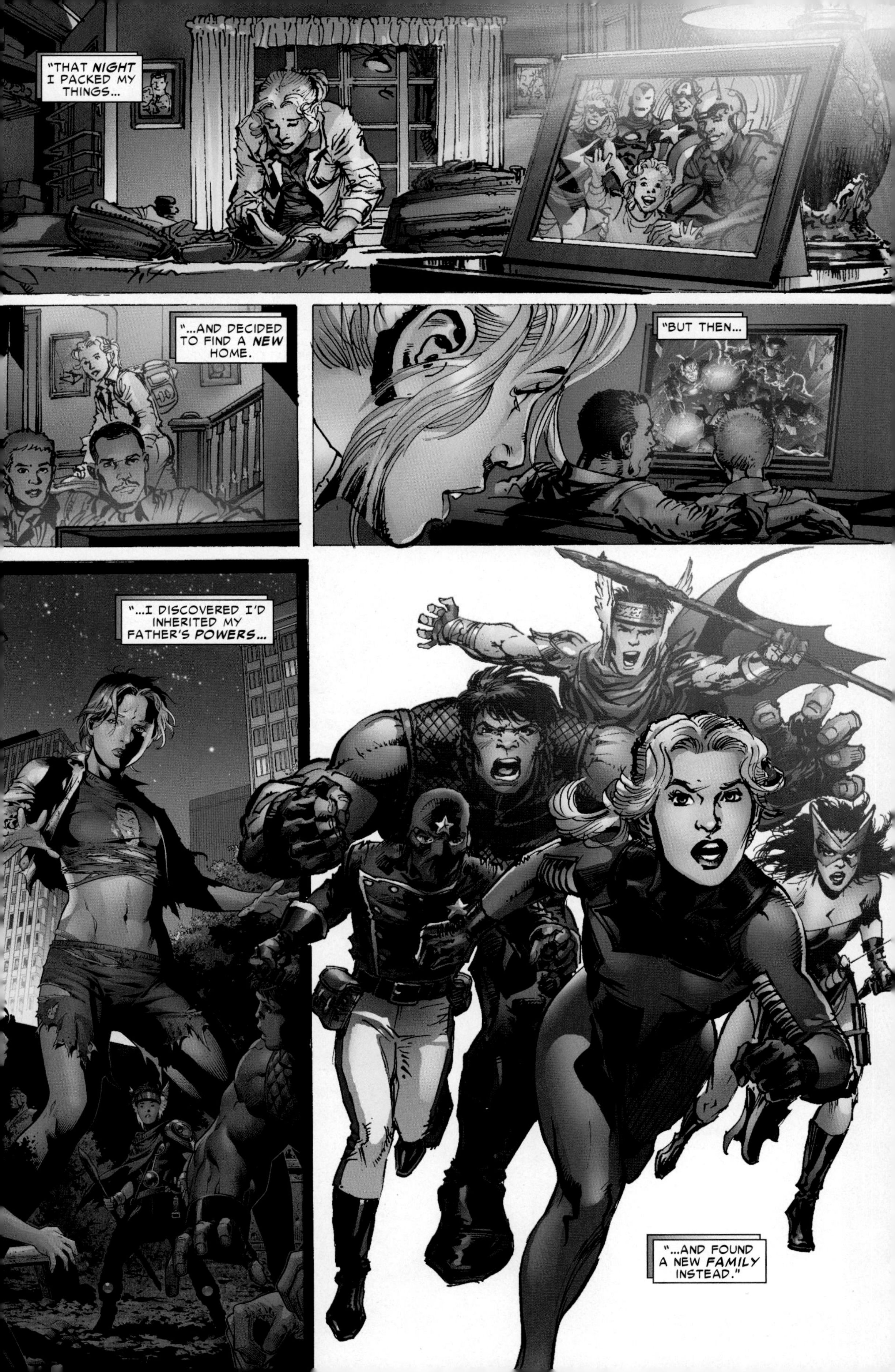
"THAT NIGHT I PACKED MY THINGS...
"...AND DECIDED TO FIND A NEW HOME.
"BUT THEN...
"...I DISCOVERED I'D INHERITED MY FATHER'S POWERS...
"...AND FOUND A NEW FAMILY INSTEAD."

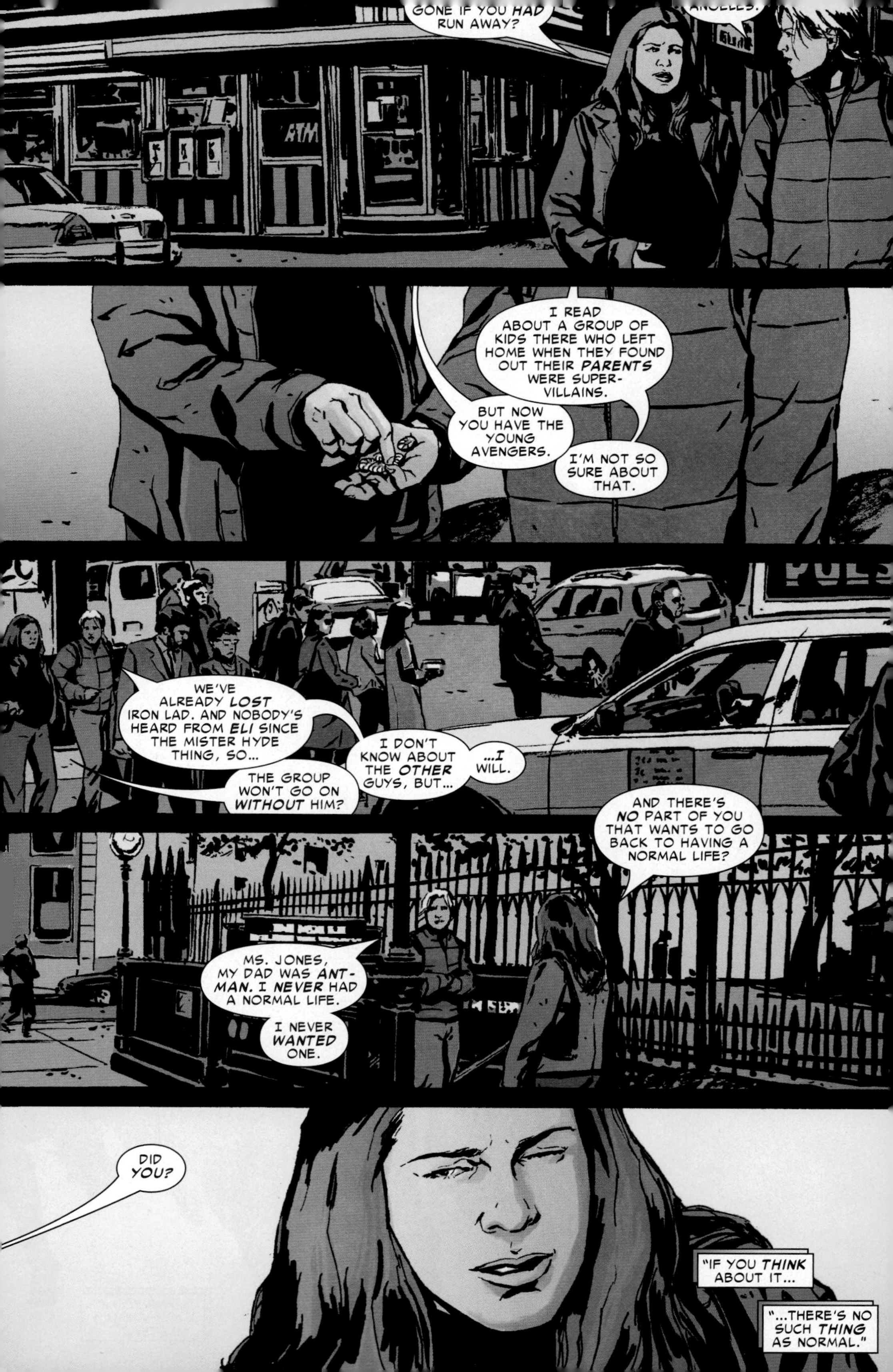
GONE IF YOU HAD RUN AWAY?
I READ ABOUT A GROUP OF KIDS THERE WHO LEFT HOME WHEN THEY FOUND OUT THEIR PARENTS WERE SUPER-VILLAINS.
BUT NOW YOU HAVE THE YOUNG AVENGERS.
I'M NOT SO SURE ABOUT THAT.
WE'VE ALREADY LOST IRON LAD. AND NOBODY'S HEARD FROM ELI SINCE THE MISTER HYDE THING, SO...
THE GROUP WON'T GO ON WITHOUT HIM?
I DON'T KNOW ABOUT THE OTHER GUYS, BUT...
...I WILL.
AND THERE'S NO PART OF YOU THAT WANTS TO GO BACK TO HAVING A NORMAL LIFE?
MS. JONES, MY DAD WAS ANT-MAN. I NEVER HAD A NORMAL LIFE.
I NEVER WANTED ONE.
DID YOU?
"IF YOU THINK ABOUT IT...
"...THERE'S NO SUCH THING AS NORMAL."

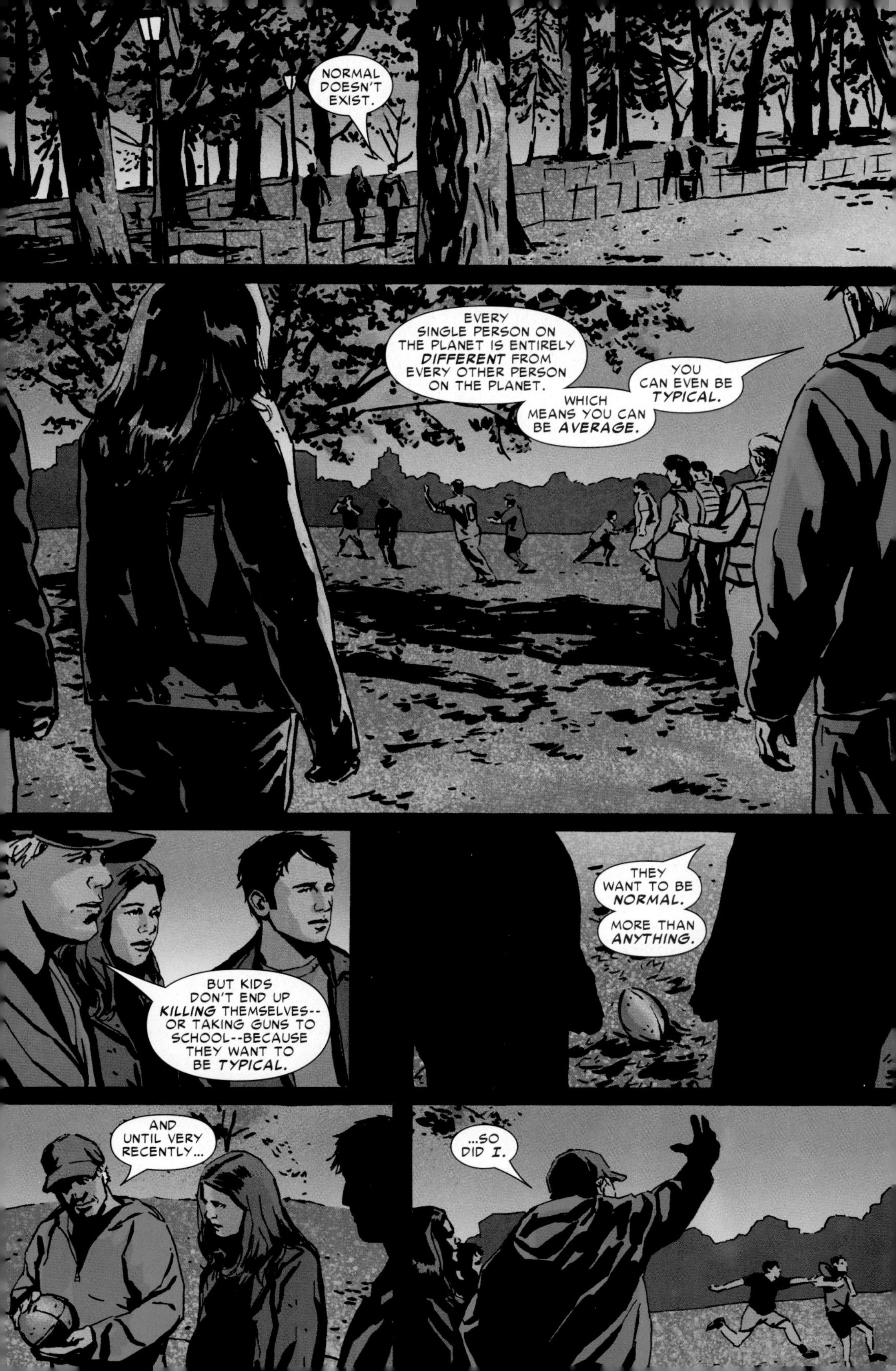
NORMAL DOESN'T EXIST.
EVERY SINGLE PERSON ON THE PLANET IS ENTIRELY *DIFFERENT* FROM EVERY OTHER PERSON ON THE PLANET.
WHICH MEANS YOU CAN BE *AVERAGE*.
YOU CAN EVEN BE *TYPICAL*.
BUT KIDS DON'T END UP *KILLING* THEMSELVES-- OR TAKING GUNS TO SCHOOL--BECAUSE THEY WANT TO BE *TYPICAL*.
THEY WANT TO BE *NORMAL*.
MORE THAN *ANYTHING*.
AND UNTIL VERY RECENTLY...
...SO DID *I*.

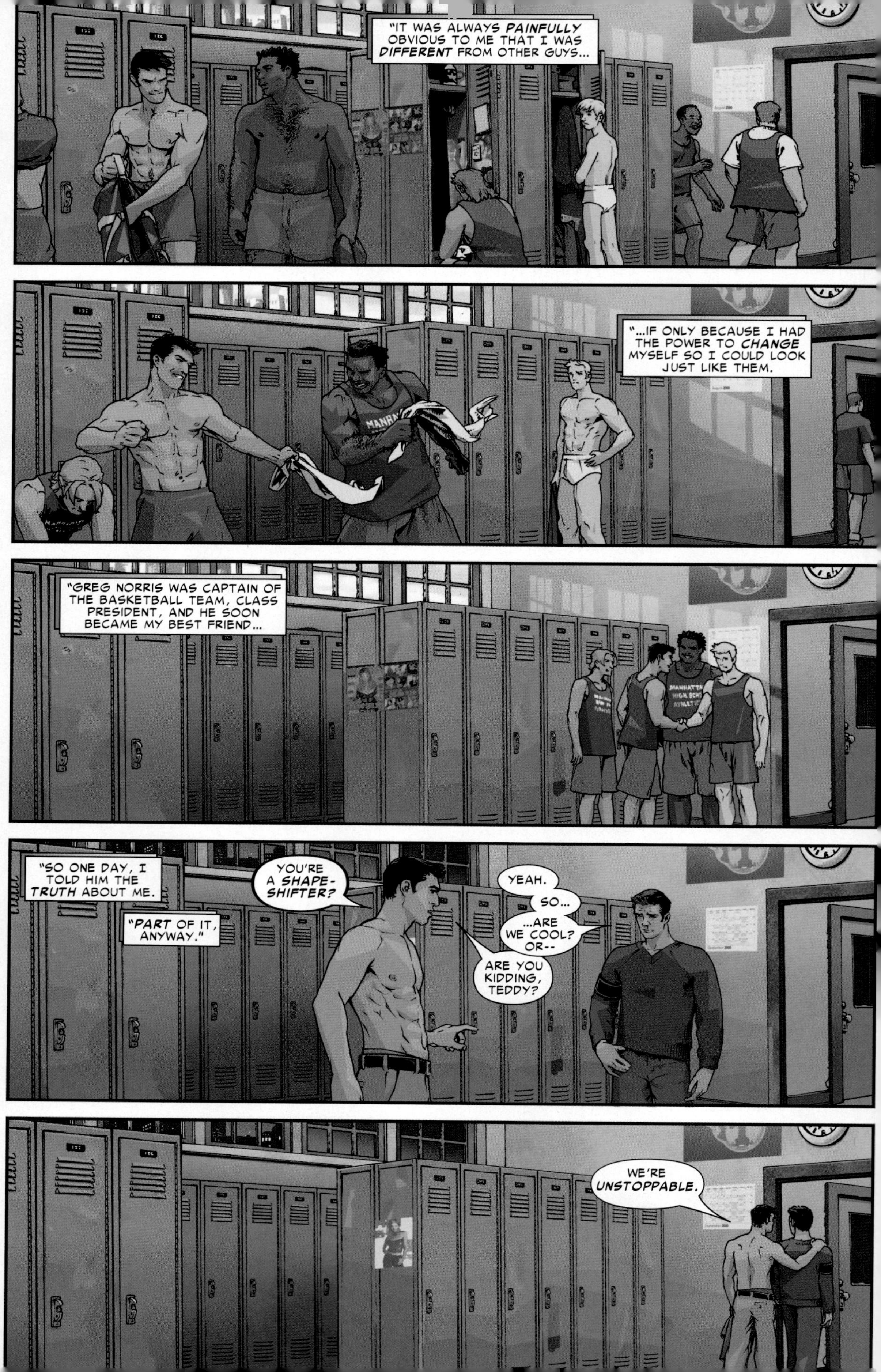
"IT WAS ALWAYS PAINFULLY OBVIOUS TO ME THAT I WAS DIFFERENT FROM OTHER GUYS...
"...IF ONLY BECAUSE I HAD THE POWER TO CHANGE MYSELF SO I COULD LOOK JUST LIKE THEM.
"GREG NORRIS WAS CAPTAIN OF THE BASKETBALL TEAM, CLASS PRESIDENT, AND HE SOON BECAME MY BEST FRIEND...
"SO ONE DAY, I TOLD HIM THE TRUTH ABOUT ME.
"PART OF IT, ANYWAY."
YOU'RE A SHAPE-SHIFTER?
YEAH.
SO...
...ARE WE COOL? OR--
ARE YOU KIDDING, TEDDY?
WE'RE UNSTOPPABLE.

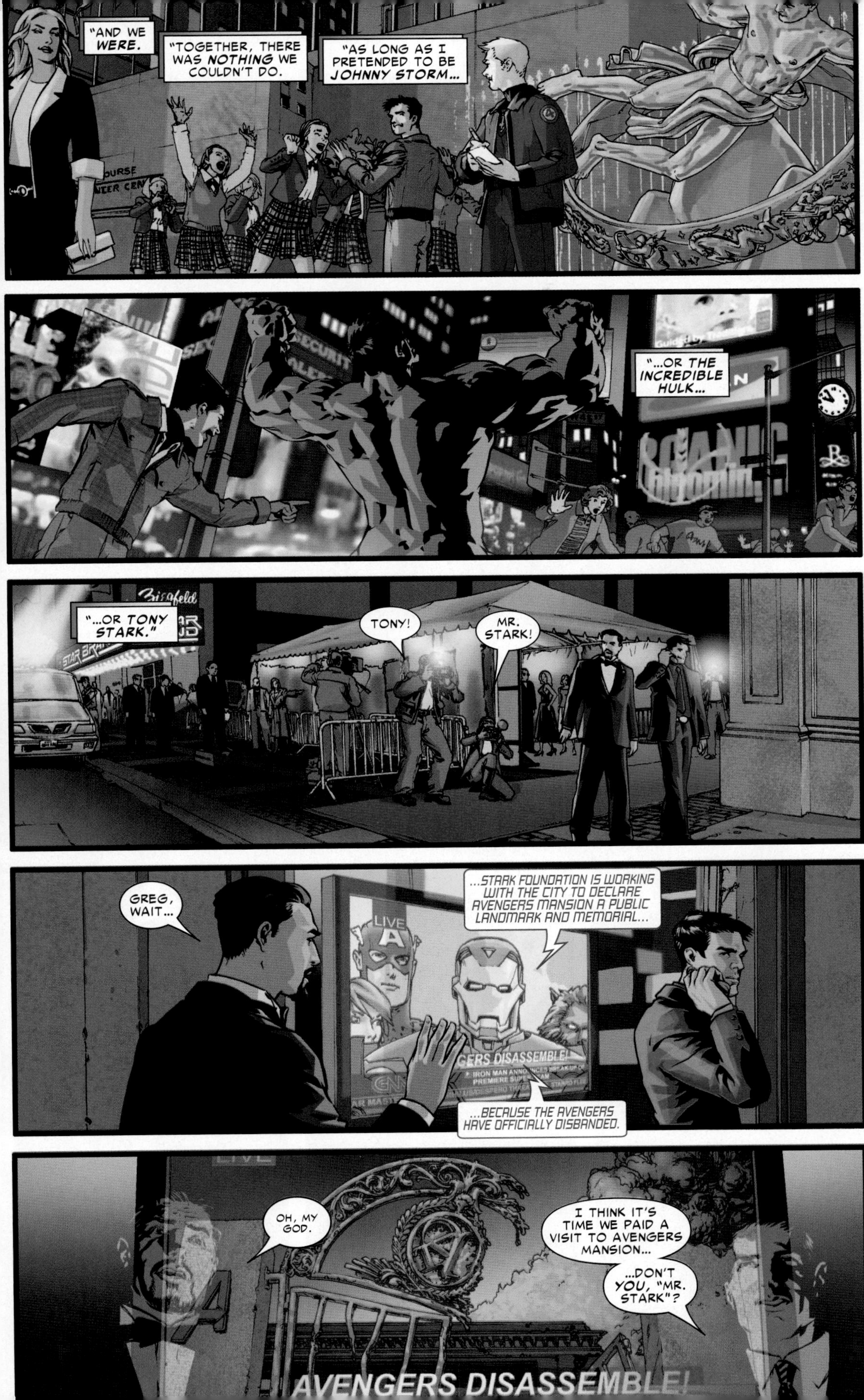
"AND WE WERE.
"TOGETHER, THERE WAS NOTHING WE COULDN'T DO.
"AS LONG AS I PRETENDED TO BE JOHNNY STORM...
"...OR THE INCREDIBLE HULK...
"...OR TONY STARK."
TONY!
MR. STARK!
GREG, WAIT...
...STARK FOUNDATION IS WORKING WITH THE CITY TO DECLARE AVENGERS MANSION A PUBLIC LANDMARK AND MEMORIAL...
...BECAUSE THE AVENGERS HAVE OFFICIALLY DISBANDED.
OH, MY GOD.
I THINK IT'S TIME WE PAID A VISIT TO AVENGERS MANSION...
...DON'T YOU, "MR. STARK"?
AVENGERS DISASSEMBLE!

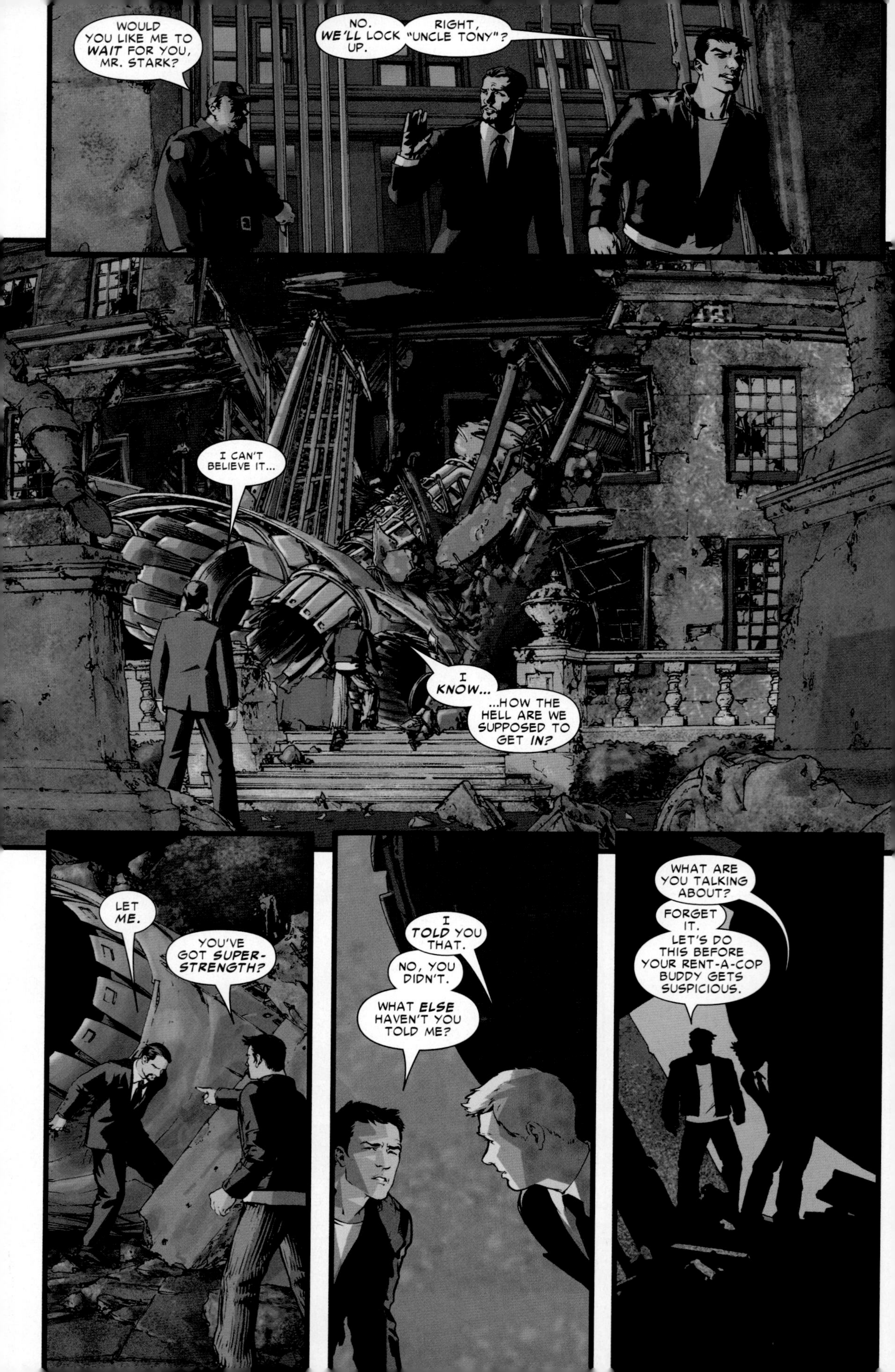
WOULD YOU LIKE ME TO WAIT FOR YOU, MR. STARK?
NO. WE'LL LOCK UP.
RIGHT, "UNCLE TONY"?
I CAN'T BELIEVE IT...
I KNOW...
...HOW THE HELL ARE WE SUPPOSED TO GET IN?
LET ME.
YOU'VE GOT SUPER-STRENGTH?
I TOLD YOU THAT.
NO, YOU DIDN'T.
WHAT ELSE HAVEN'T YOU TOLD ME?
WHAT ARE YOU TALKING ABOUT?
FORGET IT.
LET'S DO THIS BEFORE YOUR RENT-A-COP BUDDY GETS SUSPICIOUS.

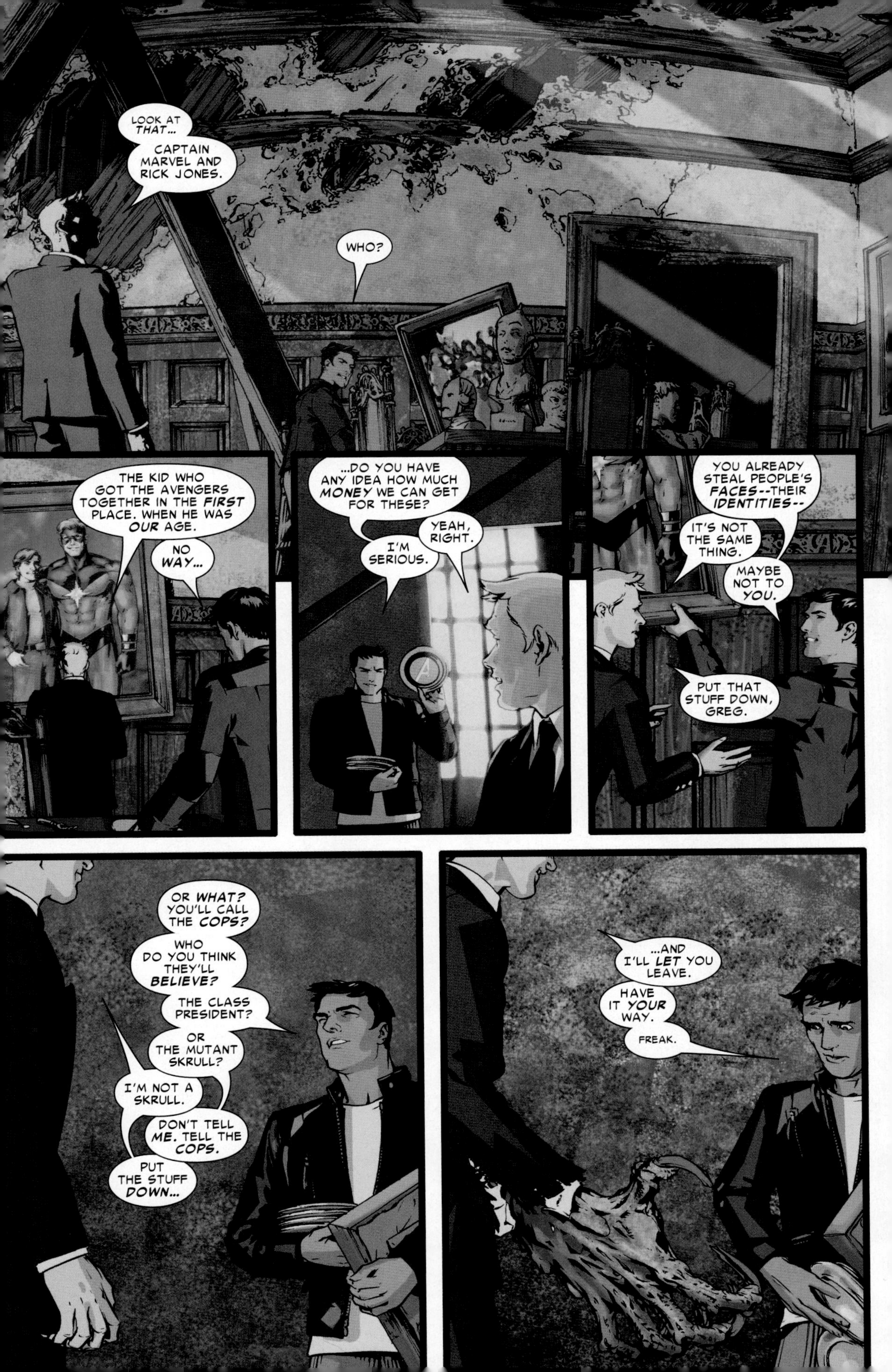
LOOK AT THAT...
CAPTAIN MARVEL AND RICK JONES.
WHO?
THE KID WHO GOT THE AVENGERS TOGETHER IN THE FIRST PLACE. WHEN HE WAS OUR AGE.
NO WAY...
...DO YOU HAVE ANY IDEA HOW MUCH MONEY WE CAN GET FOR THESE?
YEAH, RIGHT.
I'M SERIOUS.
YOU ALREADY STEAL PEOPLE'S FACES--THEIR IDENTITIES--
IT'S NOT THE SAME THING.
MAYBE NOT TO YOU.
PUT THAT STUFF DOWN, GREG.
OR WHAT? YOU'LL CALL THE COPS?
WHO DO YOU THINK THEY'LL BELIEVE?
THE CLASS PRESIDENT?
OR THE MUTANT SKRULL?
I'M NOT A SKRULL.
DON'T TELL ME. TELL THE COPS.
PUT THE STUFF DOWN...
...AND I'LL LET YOU LEAVE.
HAVE IT YOUR WAY.
FREAK.

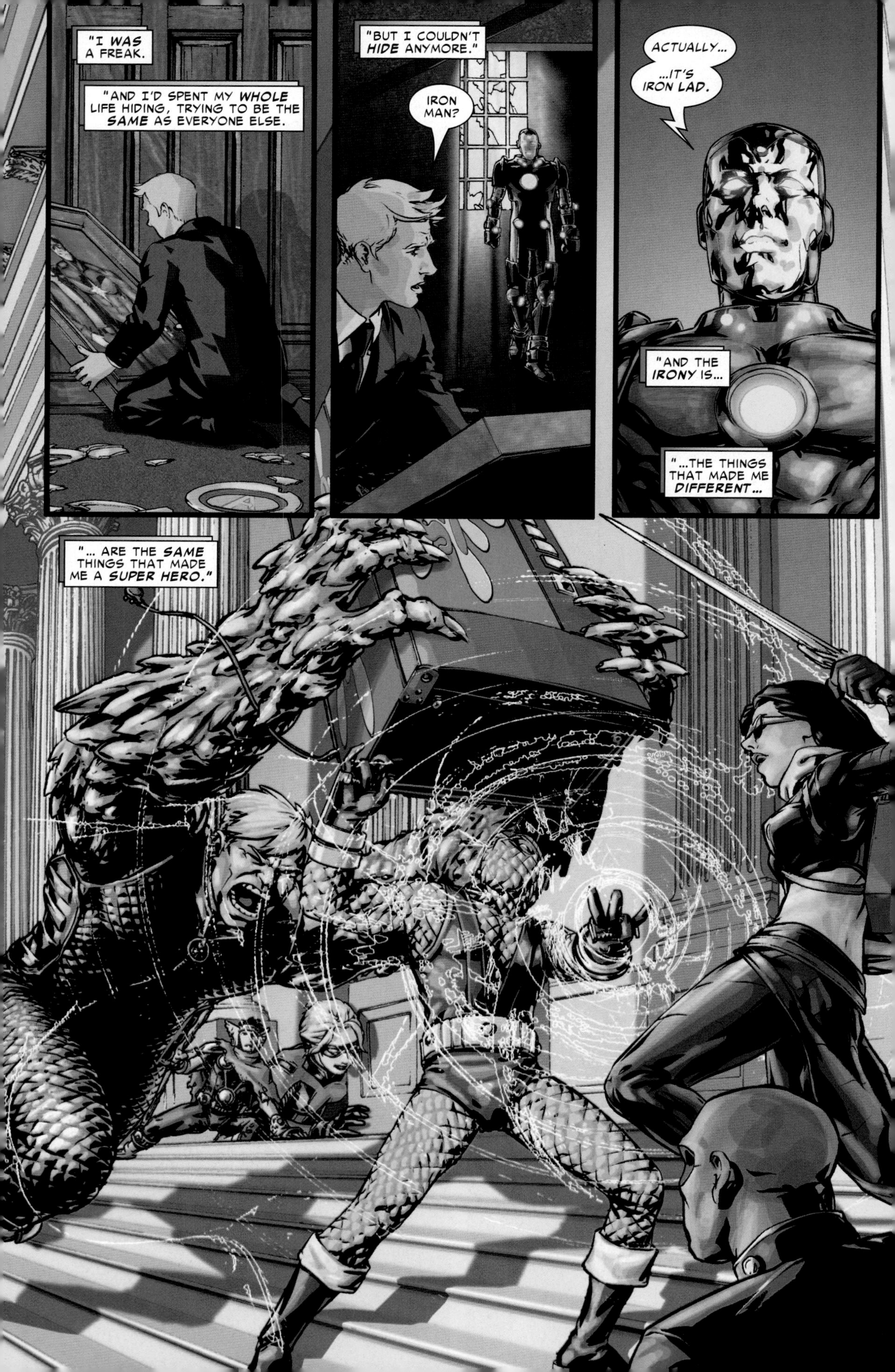
"I WAS A FREAK.
"AND I'D SPENT MY WHOLE LIFE HIDING, TRYING TO BE THE SAME AS EVERYONE ELSE.
"BUT I COULDN'T HIDE ANYMORE."
IRON MAN?
ACTUALLY...
...IT'S IRON LAD.
"AND THE IRONY IS...
"...THE THINGS THAT MADE ME DIFFERENT...
"... ARE THE SAME THINGS THAT MADE ME A SUPER HERO."

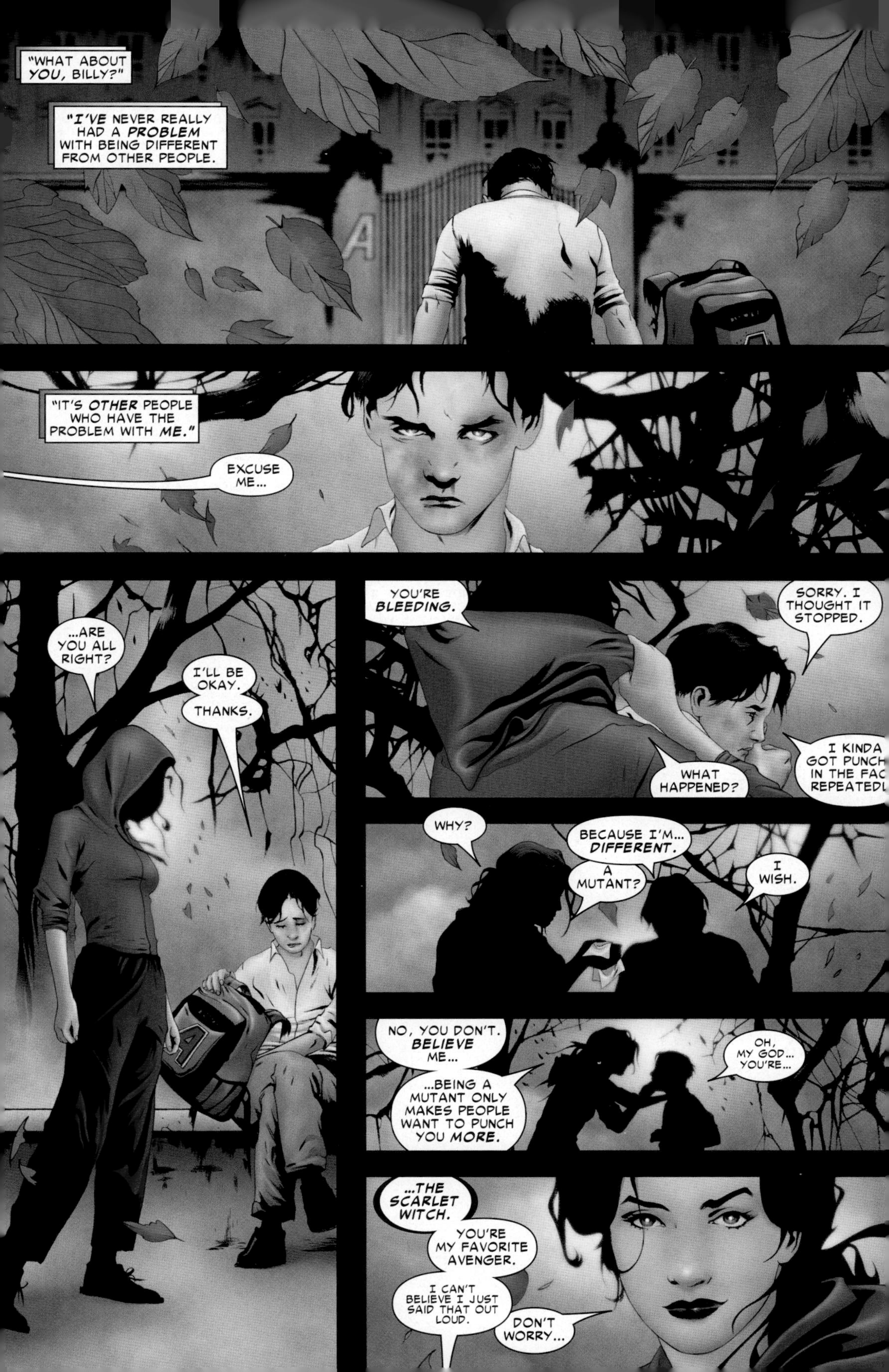
"WHAT ABOUT YOU, BILLY?"
"I'VE NEVER REALLY HAD A PROBLEM WITH BEING DIFFERENT FROM OTHER PEOPLE.
"IT'S OTHER PEOPLE WHO HAVE THE PROBLEM WITH ME."
EXCUSE ME...
...ARE YOU ALL RIGHT?
I'LL BE OKAY.
THANKS.
YOU'RE BLEEDING.
SORRY. I THOUGHT IT STOPPED.
WHAT HAPPENED?
WHY?
BECAUSE I'M... DIFFERENT.
A MUTANT?
I WISH.
NO, YOU DON'T. BELIEVE ME...
...BEING A MUTANT ONLY MAKES PEOPLE WANT TO PUNCH YOU MORE.
OH, MY GOD... YOU'RE...
...THE SCARLET WITCH.
YOU'RE MY FAVORITE AVENGER.
I CAN'T BELIEVE I JUST SAID THAT OUT LOUD.
DON'T WORRY...

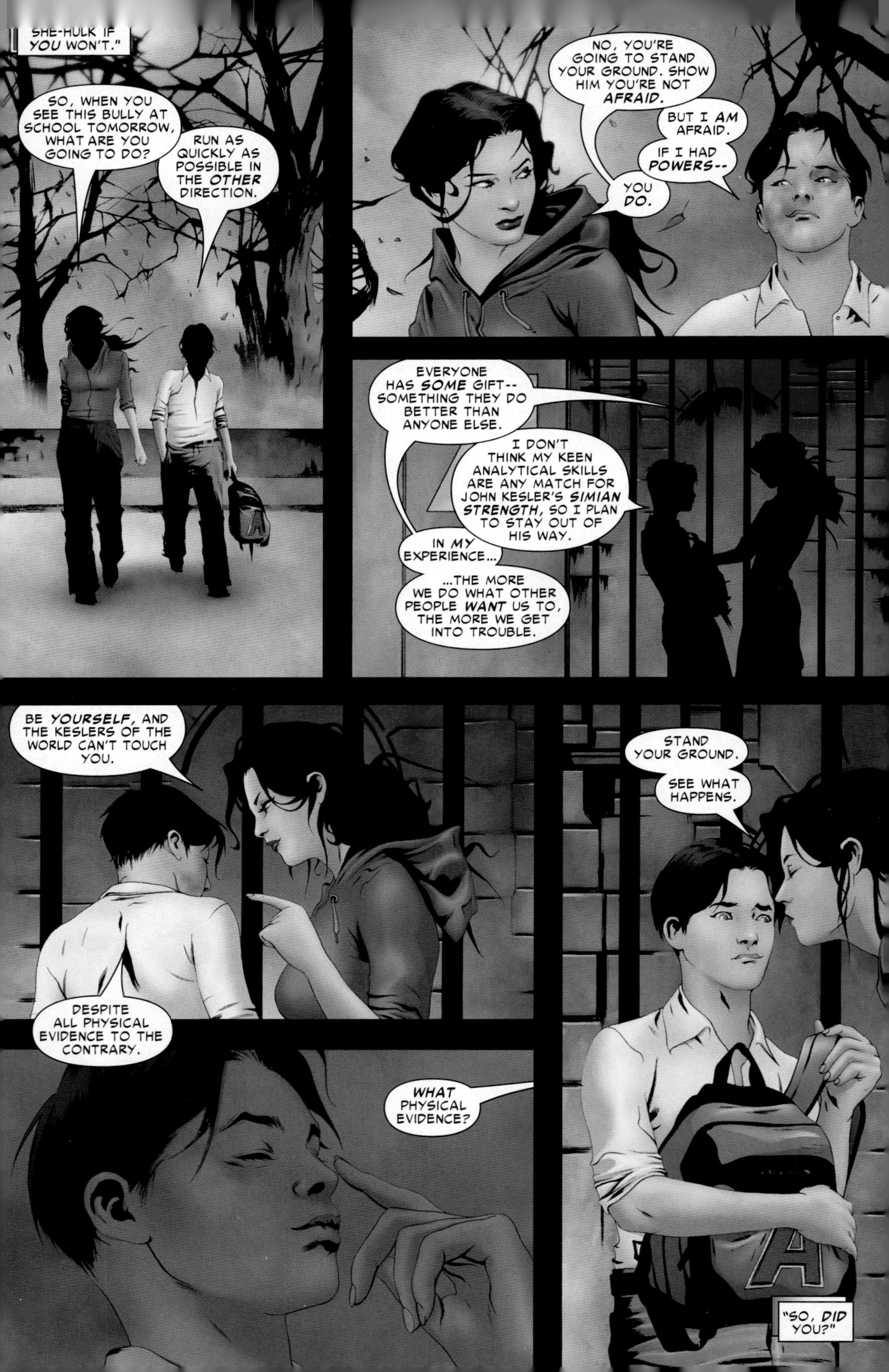
SHE-HULK IF YOU WON'T."
SO, WHEN YOU SEE THIS BULLY AT SCHOOL TOMORROW, WHAT ARE YOU GOING TO DO?
RUN AS QUICKLY AS POSSIBLE IN THE OTHER DIRECTION.
NO, YOU'RE GOING TO STAND YOUR GROUND. SHOW HIM YOU'RE NOT AFRAID.
BUT I AM AFRAID.
IF I HAD POWERS--
YOU DO.
EVERYONE HAS SOME GIFT-- SOMETHING THEY DO BETTER THAN ANYONE ELSE.
I DON'T THINK MY KEEN ANALYTICAL SKILLS ARE ANY MATCH FOR JOHN KESLER'S SIMIAN STRENGTH, SO I PLAN TO STAY OUT OF HIS WAY.
IN MY EXPERIENCE...
...THE MORE WE DO WHAT OTHER PEOPLE WANT US TO, THE MORE WE GET INTO TROUBLE.
BE YOURSELF, AND THE KESLERS OF THE WORLD CAN'T TOUCH YOU.
DESPITE ALL PHYSICAL EVIDENCE TO THE CONTRARY.
WHAT PHYSICAL EVIDENCE?
STAND YOUR GROUND.
SEE WHAT HAPPENS.
"SO, DID YOU?"

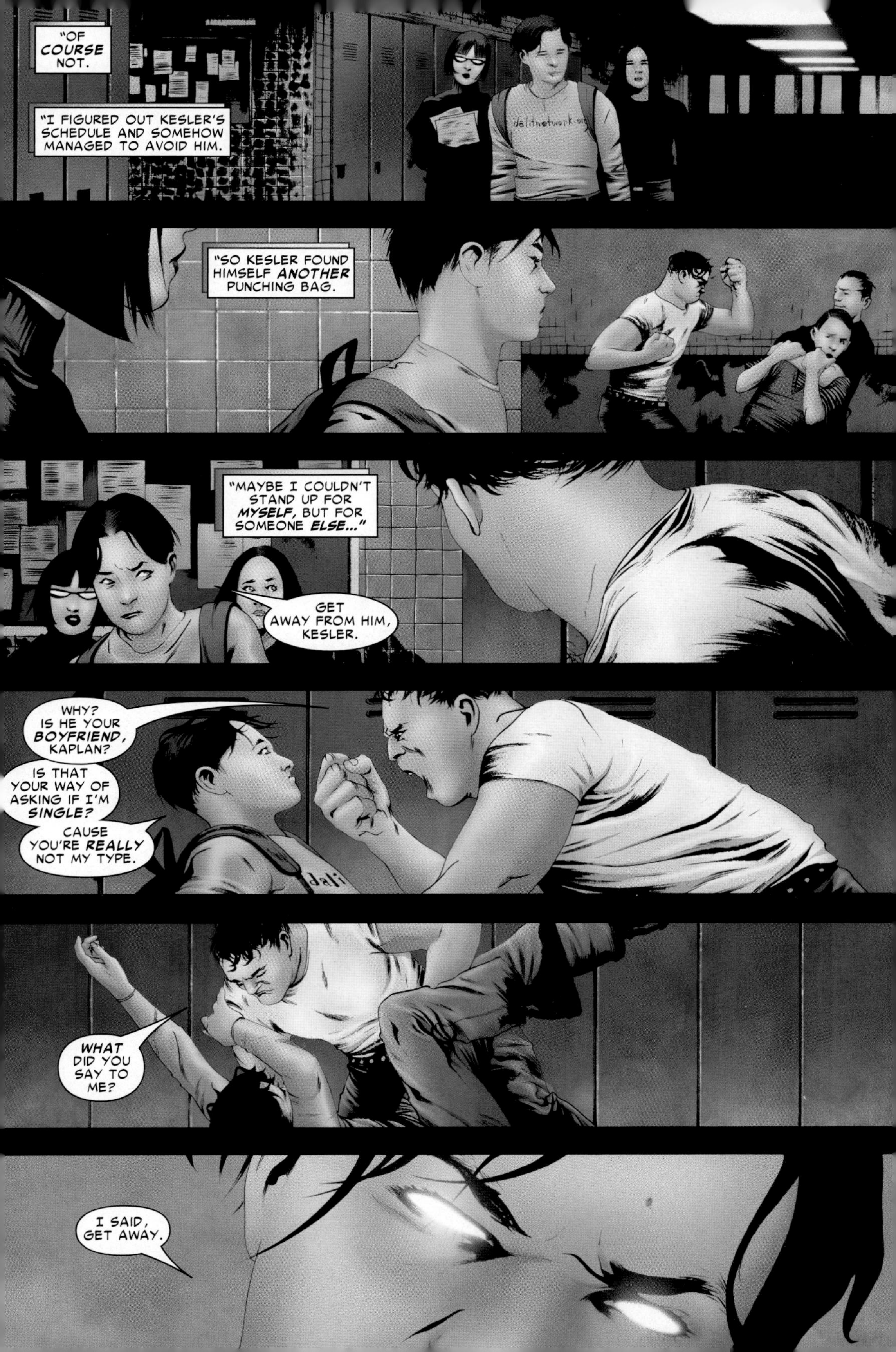
"OF COURSE NOT.
"I FIGURED OUT KESLER'S SCHEDULE AND SOMEHOW MANAGED TO AVOID HIM.
dalitnetwork.org
"SO KESLER FOUND HIMSELF ANOTHER PUNCHING BAG.
"MAYBE I COULDN'T STAND UP FOR MYSELF, BUT FOR SOMEONE ELSE..."
GET AWAY FROM HIM, KESLER.
WHY? IS HE YOUR BOYFRIEND, KAPLAN?
IS THAT YOUR WAY OF ASKING IF I'M SINGLE?
CAUSE YOU'RE REALLY NOT MY TYPE.
dali
WHAT DID YOU SAY TO ME?
I SAID, GET AWAY.

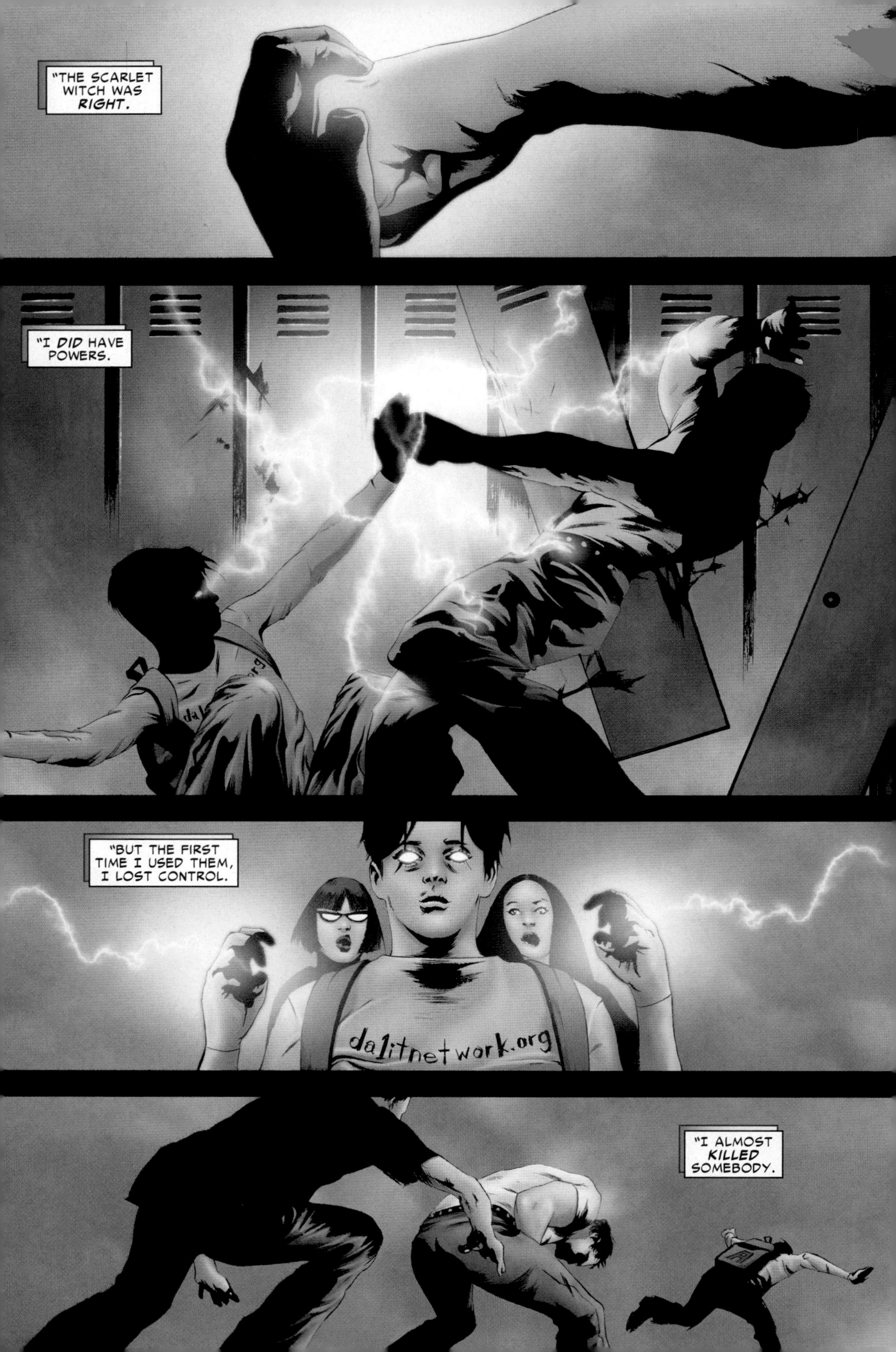
"THE SCARLET WITCH WAS RIGHT.
"I DID HAVE POWERS.
dalitnetwork.org
"BUT THE FIRST TIME I USED THEM, I LOST CONTROL.
dalitnetwork.org
"I ALMOST KILLED SOMEBODY.

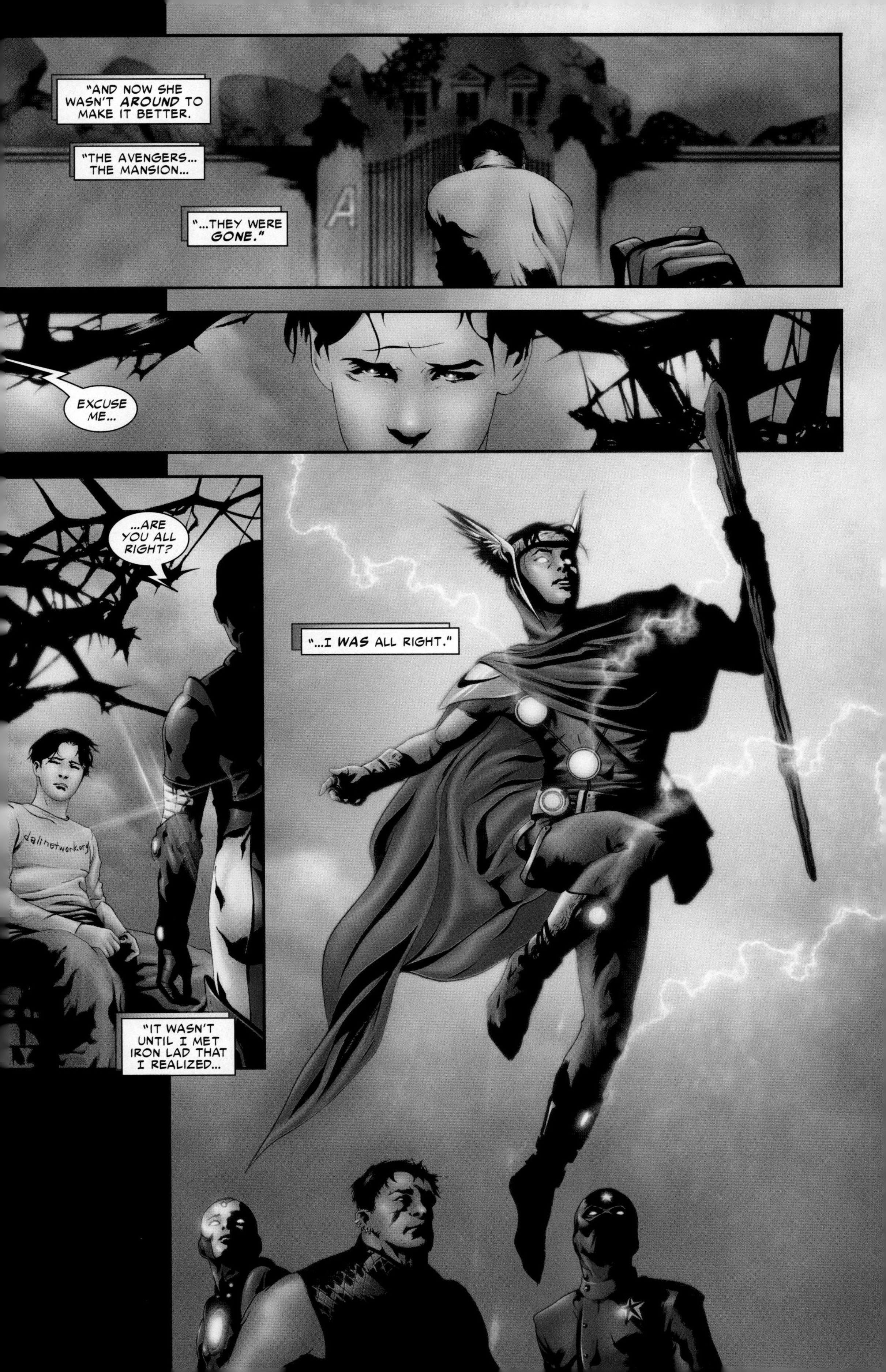
"AND NOW SHE WASN'T AROUND TO MAKE IT BETTER.
"THE AVENGERS... THE MANSION...
"...THEY WERE GONE."
EXCUSE ME...
...ARE YOU ALL RIGHT?
dalinetwork.org
"IT WASN'T UNTIL I MET IRON LAD THAT I REALIZED...
"...I WAS ALL RIGHT."

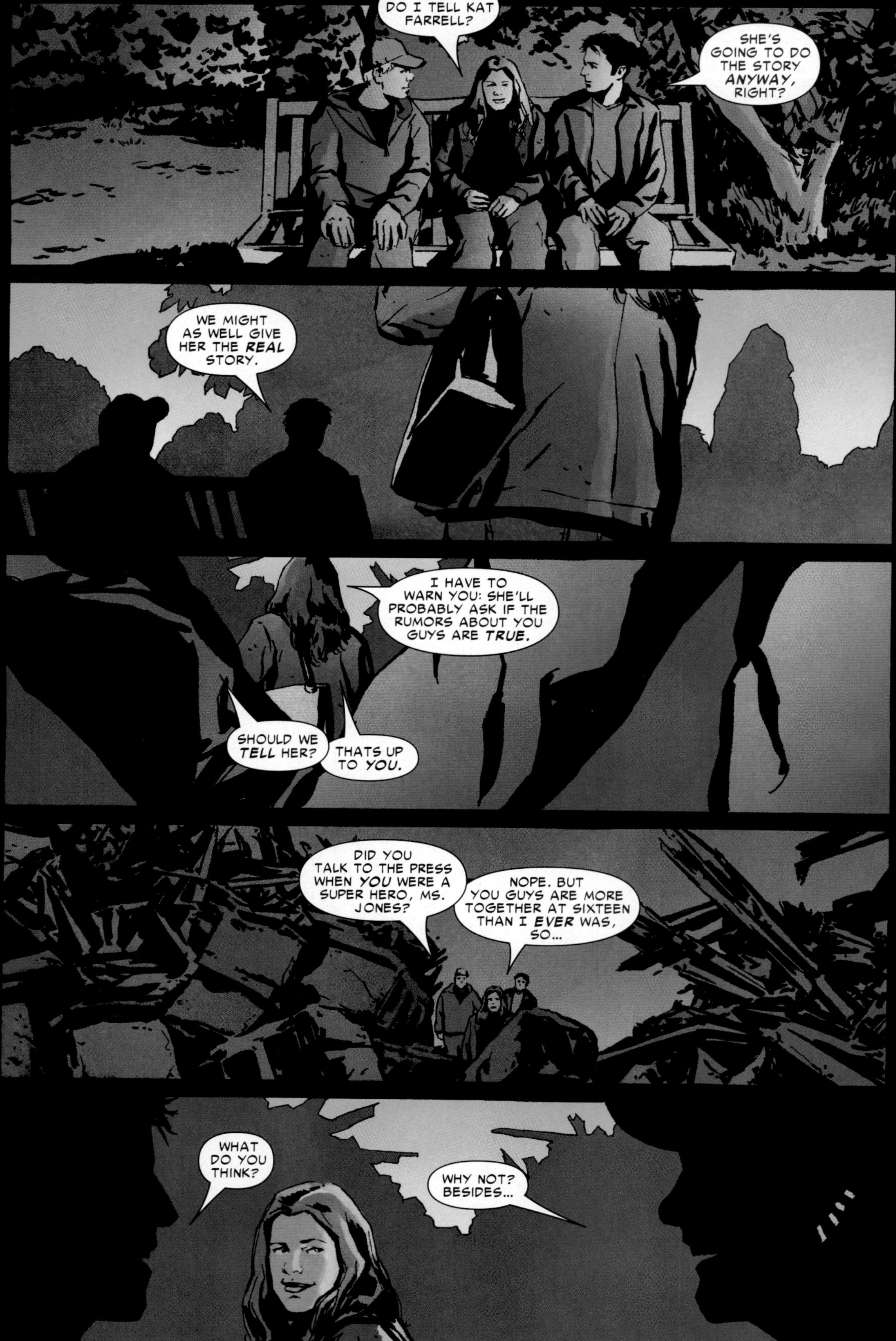
SO, WHAT DO I TELL KAT FARRELL?
SHE'S GOING TO DO THE STORY ANYWAY, RIGHT?
WE MIGHT AS WELL GIVE HER THE REAL STORY.
I HAVE TO WARN YOU: SHE'LL PROBABLY ASK IF THE RUMORS ABOUT YOU GUYS ARE TRUE.
SHOULD WE TELL HER?
THATS UP TO YOU.
DID YOU TALK TO THE PRESS WHEN YOU WERE A SUPER HERO, MS. JONES?
NOPE. BUT YOU GUYS ARE MORE TOGETHER AT SIXTEEN THAN I EVER WAS, SO...
WHAT DO YOU THINK?
WHY NOT? BESIDES...

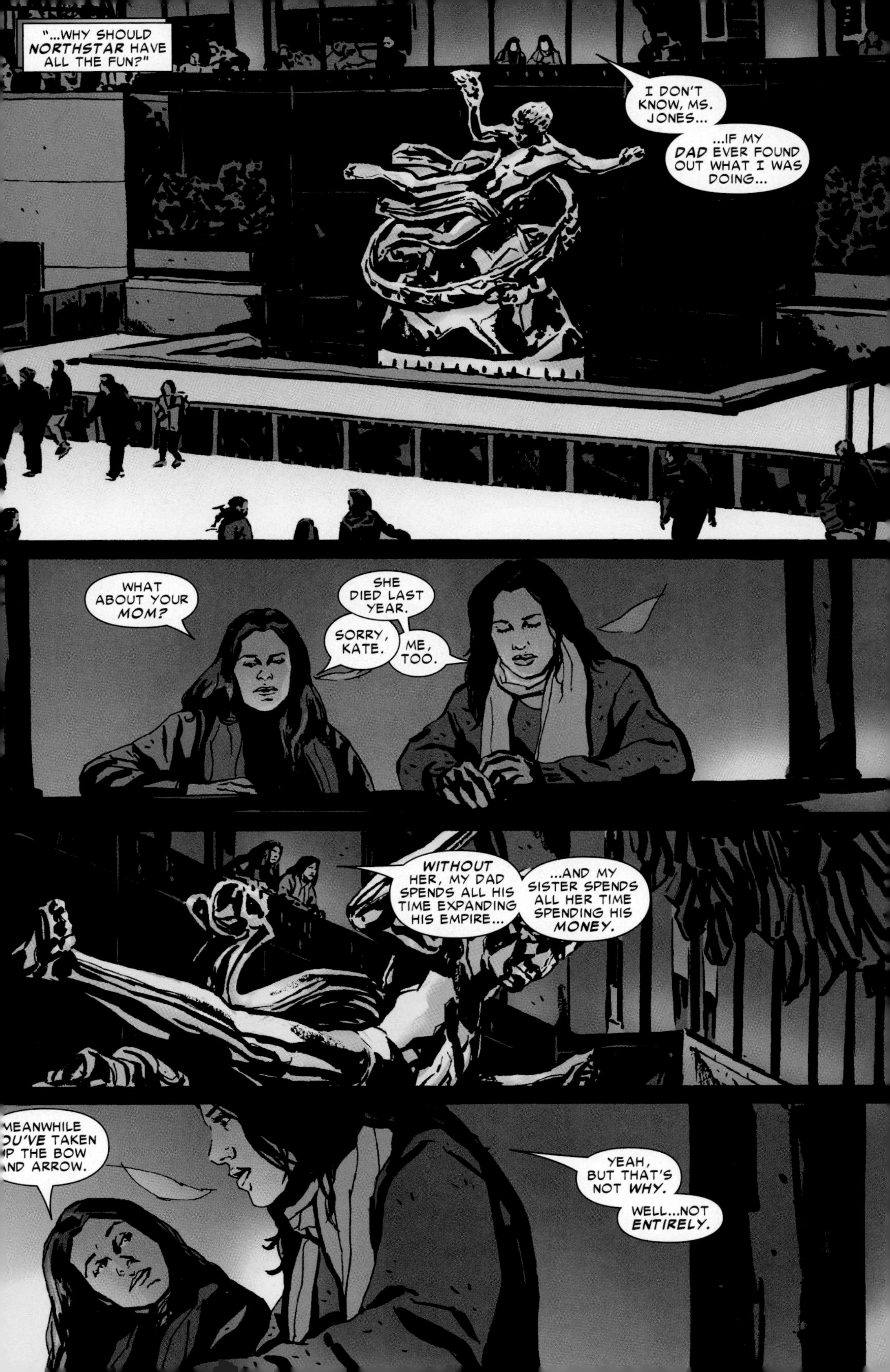
"...WHY SHOULD NORTHSTAR HAVE ALL THE FUN?"
I DON'T KNOW, MS. JONES...
...IF MY DAD EVER FOUND OUT WHAT I WAS DOING...
WHAT ABOUT YOUR MOM?
SHE DIED LAST YEAR.
SORRY, KATE.
ME, TOO.
WITHOUT HER, MY DAD SPENDS ALL HIS TIME EXPANDING HIS EMPIRE...
...AND MY SISTER SPENDS ALL HER TIME SPENDING HIS MONEY.
MEANWHILE OU'VE TAKEN P THE BOW AND ARROW.
YEAH, BUT THAT'S NOT WHY.
WELL...NOT ENTIRELY.

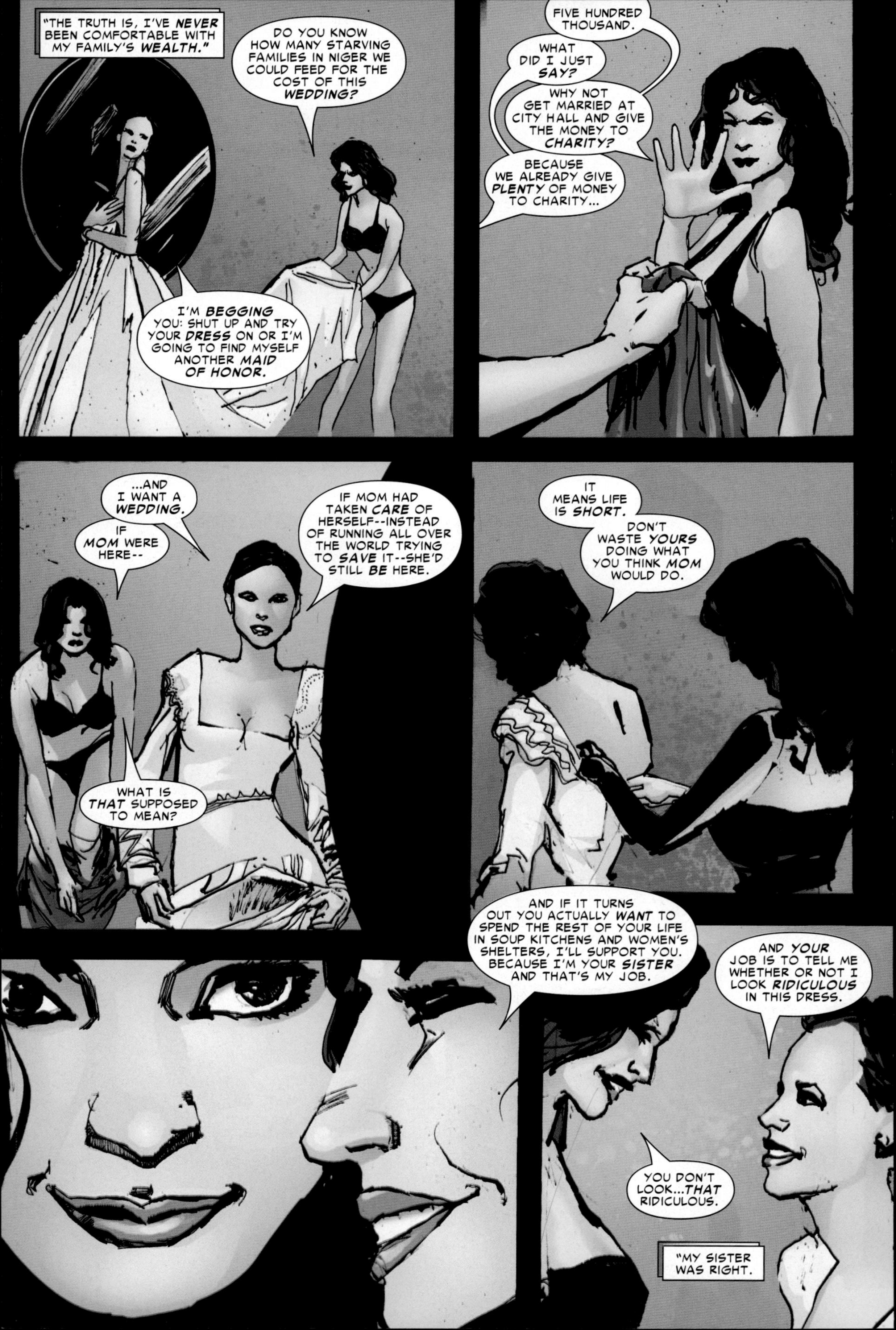
"THE TRUTH IS, I'VE NEVER BEEN COMFORTABLE WITH MY FAMILY'S WEALTH."
DO YOU KNOW HOW MANY STARVING FAMILIES IN NIGER WE COULD FEED FOR THE COST OF THIS WEDDING?
I'M BEGGING YOU: SHUT UP AND TRY YOUR DRESS ON OR I'M GOING TO FIND MYSELF ANOTHER MAID OF HONOR.
FIVE HUNDRED THOUSAND.
WHAT DID I JUST SAY?
WHY NOT GET MARRIED AT CITY HALL AND GIVE THE MONEY TO CHARITY?
BECAUSE WE ALREADY GIVE PLENTY OF MONEY TO CHARITY...
...AND I WANT A WEDDING.
IF MOM WERE HERE--
IF MOM HAD TAKEN CARE OF HERSELF--INSTEAD OF RUNNING ALL OVER THE WORLD TRYING TO SAVE IT--SHE'D STILL BE HERE.
WHAT IS THAT SUPPOSED TO MEAN?
IT MEANS LIFE IS SHORT.
DON'T WASTE YOURS DOING WHAT YOU THINK MOM WOULD DO.
AND IF IT TURNS OUT YOU ACTUALLY WANT TO SPEND THE REST OF YOUR LIFE IN SOUP KITCHENS AND WOMEN'S SHELTERS, I'LL SUPPORT YOU. BECAUSE I'M YOUR SISTER AND THAT'S MY JOB.
AND YOUR JOB IS TO TELL ME WHETHER OR NOT I LOOK RIDICULOUS IN THIS DRESS.
YOU DON'T LOOK...THAT RIDICULOUS.
"MY SISTER WAS RIGHT.

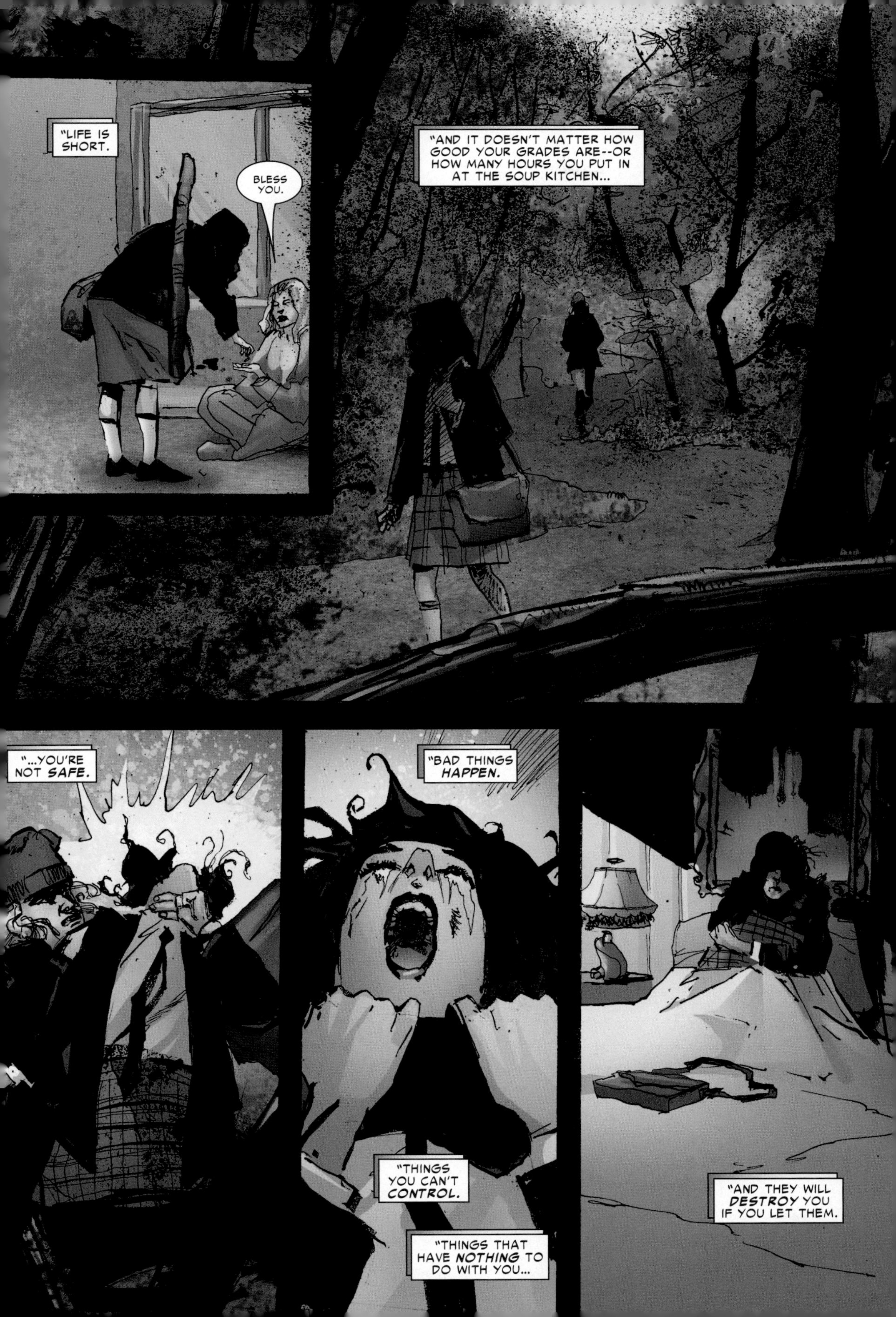
"LIFE IS SHORT.
BLESS YOU.
"AND IT DOESN'T MATTER HOW GOOD YOUR GRADES ARE--OR HOW MANY HOURS YOU PUT IN AT THE SOUP KITCHEN...
"...YOU'RE NOT SAFE.
"BAD THINGS HAPPEN.
"THINGS YOU CAN'T CONTROL.
"THINGS THAT HAVE NOTHING TO DO WITH YOU...
"AND THEY WILL DESTROY YOU IF YOU LET THEM.

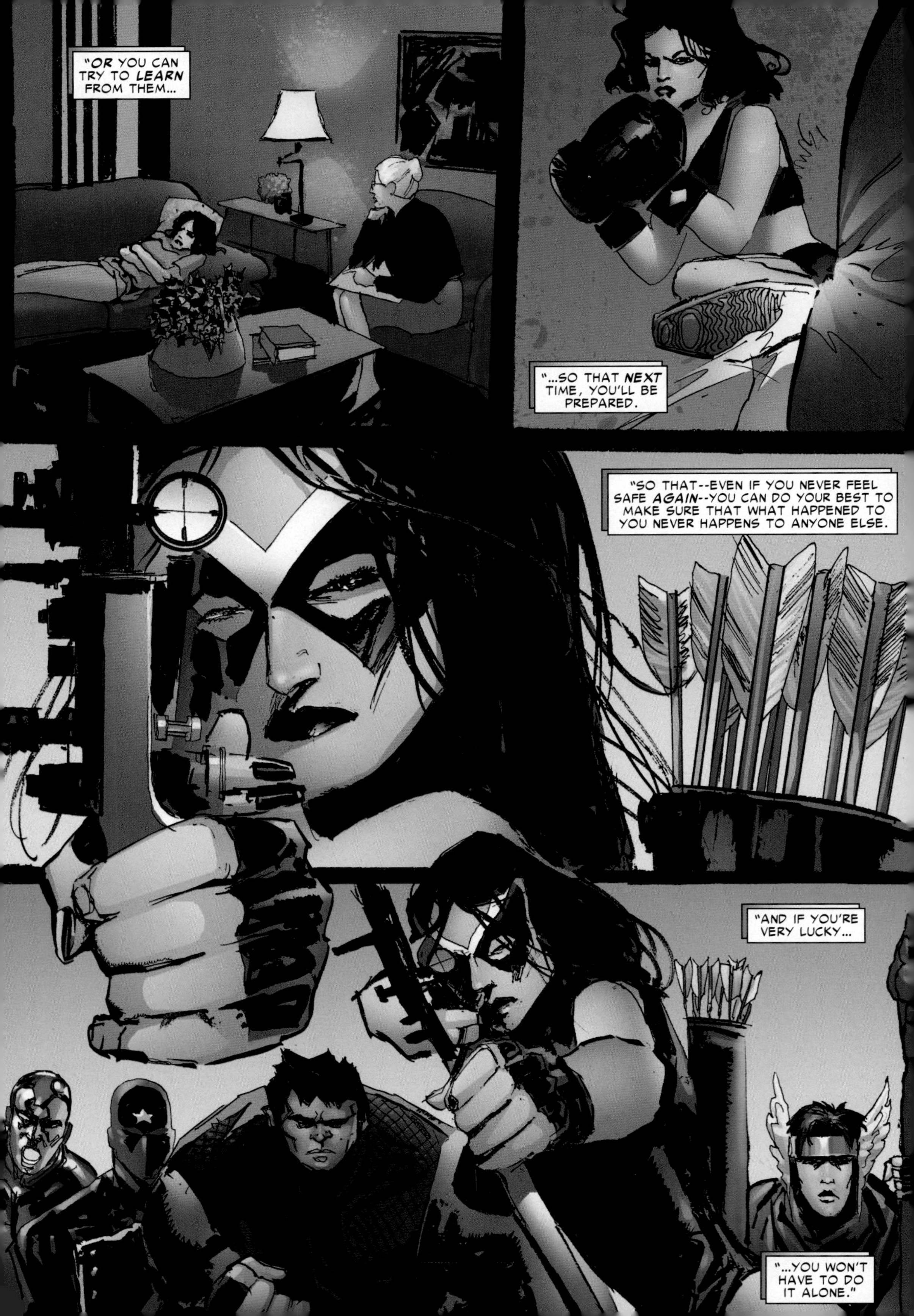
"OR YOU CAN TRY TO LEARN FROM THEM...
"...SO THAT NEXT TIME, YOU'LL BE PREPARED.
"SO THAT--EVEN IF YOU NEVER FEEL SAFE AGAIN--YOU CAN DO YOUR BEST TO MAKE SURE THAT WHAT HAPPENED TO YOU NEVER HAPPENS TO ANYONE ELSE.
"AND IF YOU'RE VERY LUCKY...
"...YOU WON'T HAVE TO DO IT ALONE."

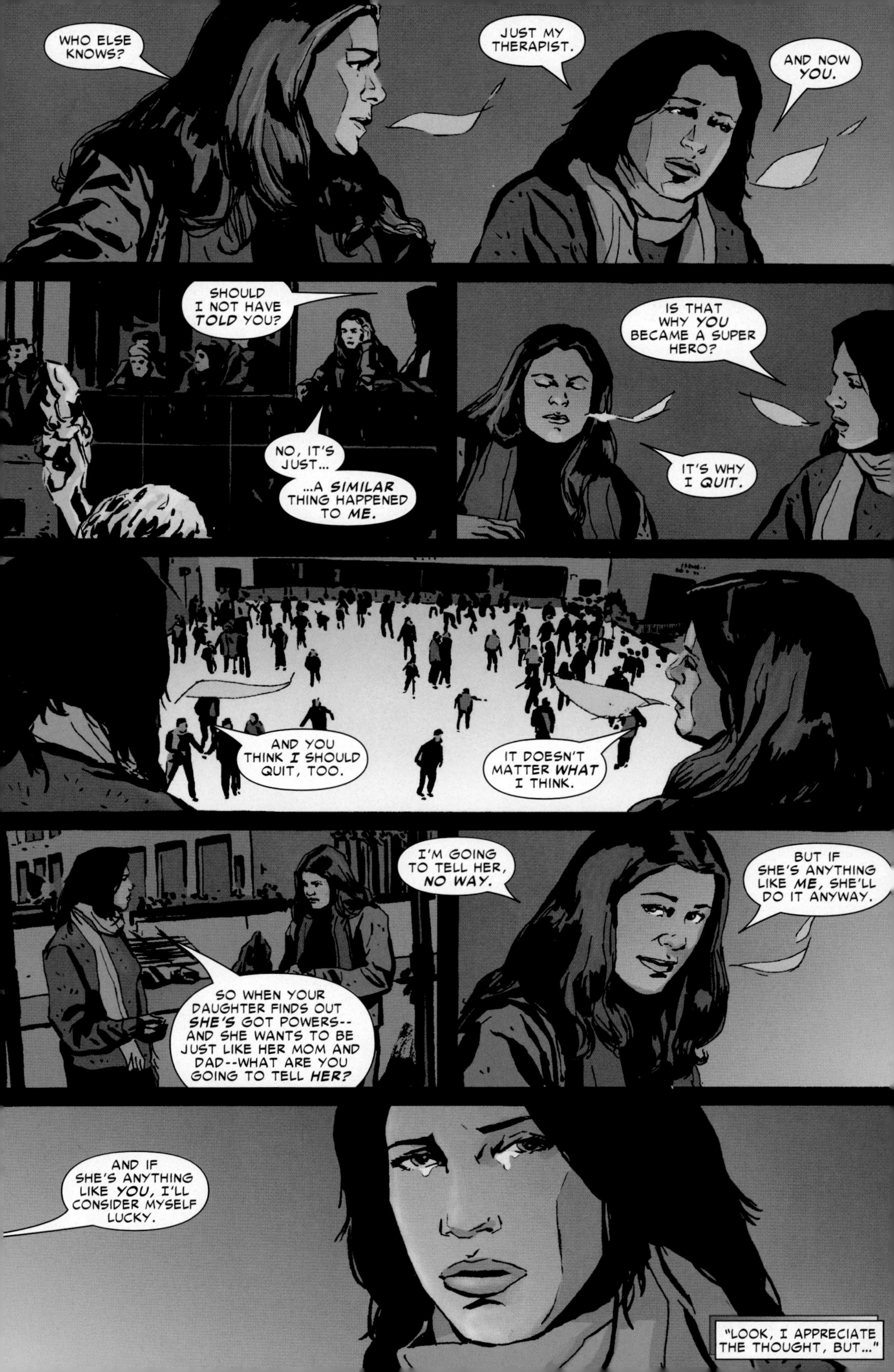
WHO ELSE KNOWS?
JUST MY THERAPIST.
AND NOW YOU.
SHOULD I NOT HAVE TOLD YOU?
NO, IT'S JUST...
...A SIMILAR THING HAPPENED TO ME.
IS THAT WHY YOU BECAME A SUPER HERO?
IT'S WHY I QUIT.
AND YOU THINK I SHOULD QUIT, TOO.
IT DOESN'T MATTER WHAT I THINK.
SO WHEN YOUR DAUGHTER FINDS OUT SHE'S GOT POWERS--AND SHE WANTS TO BE JUST LIKE HER MOM AND DAD--WHAT ARE YOU GOING TO TELL HER?
I'M GOING TO TELL HER, NO WAY.
BUT IF SHE'S ANYTHING LIKE ME, SHE'LL DO IT ANYWAY.
AND IF SHE'S ANYTHING LIKE YOU, I'LL CONSIDER MYSELF LUCKY.
"LOOK, I APPRECIATE THE THOUGHT, BUT..."

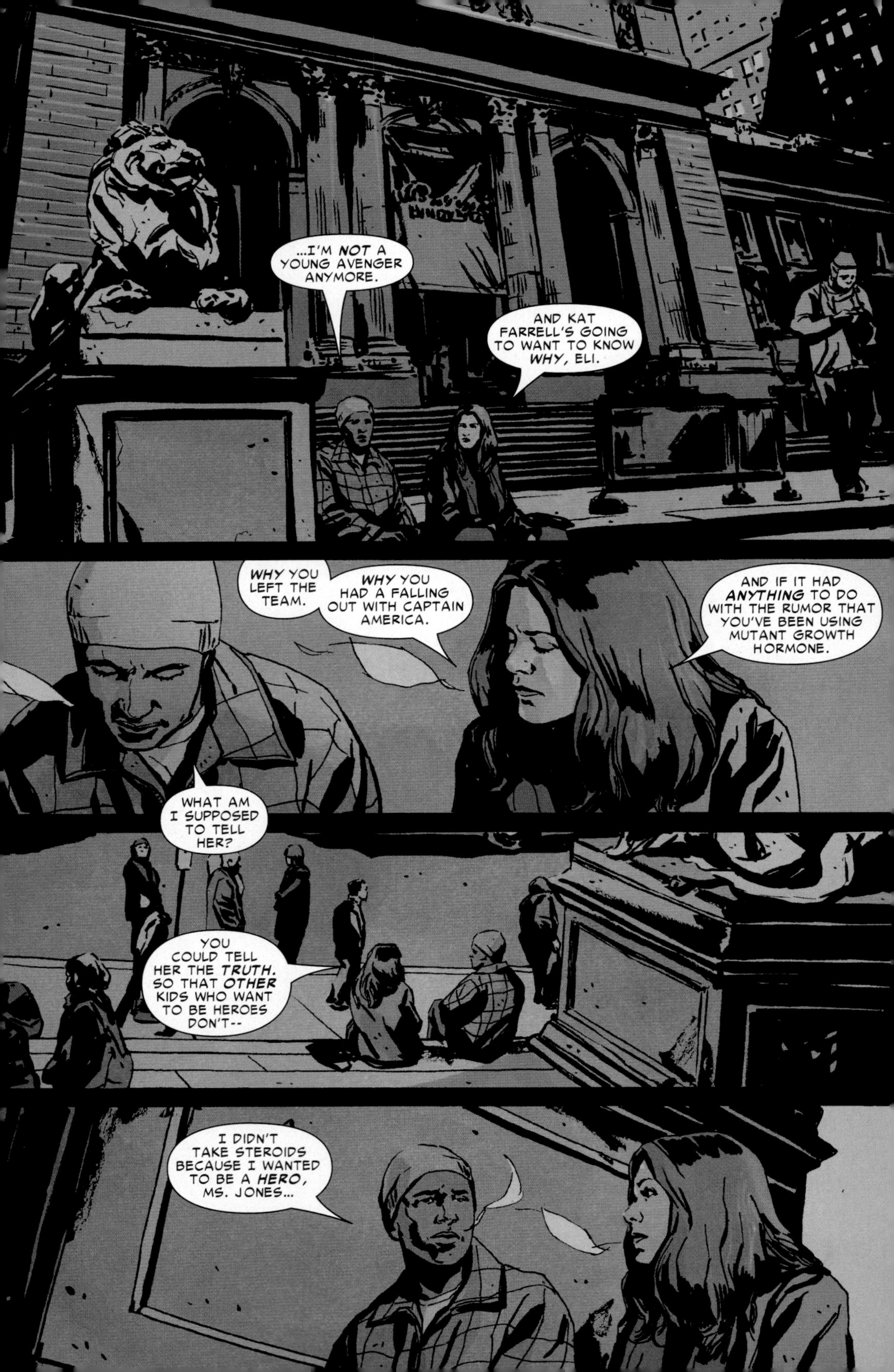

...I'M NOT A YOUNG AVENGER ANYMORE.
AND KAT FARRELL'S GOING TO WANT TO KNOW WHY, ELI.
WHY YOU LEFT THE TEAM.
WHY YOU HAD A FALLING OUT WITH CAPTAIN AMERICA.
AND IF IT HAD ANYTHING TO DO WITH THE RUMOR THAT YOU'VE BEEN USING MUTANT GROWTH HORMONE.
WHAT AM I SUPPOSED TO TELL HER?
YOU COULD TELL HER THE TRUTH. SO THAT OTHER KIDS WHO WANT TO BE HEROES DON'T--
I DIDN'T TAKE STEROIDS BECAUSE I WANTED TO BE A HERO, MS. JONES...

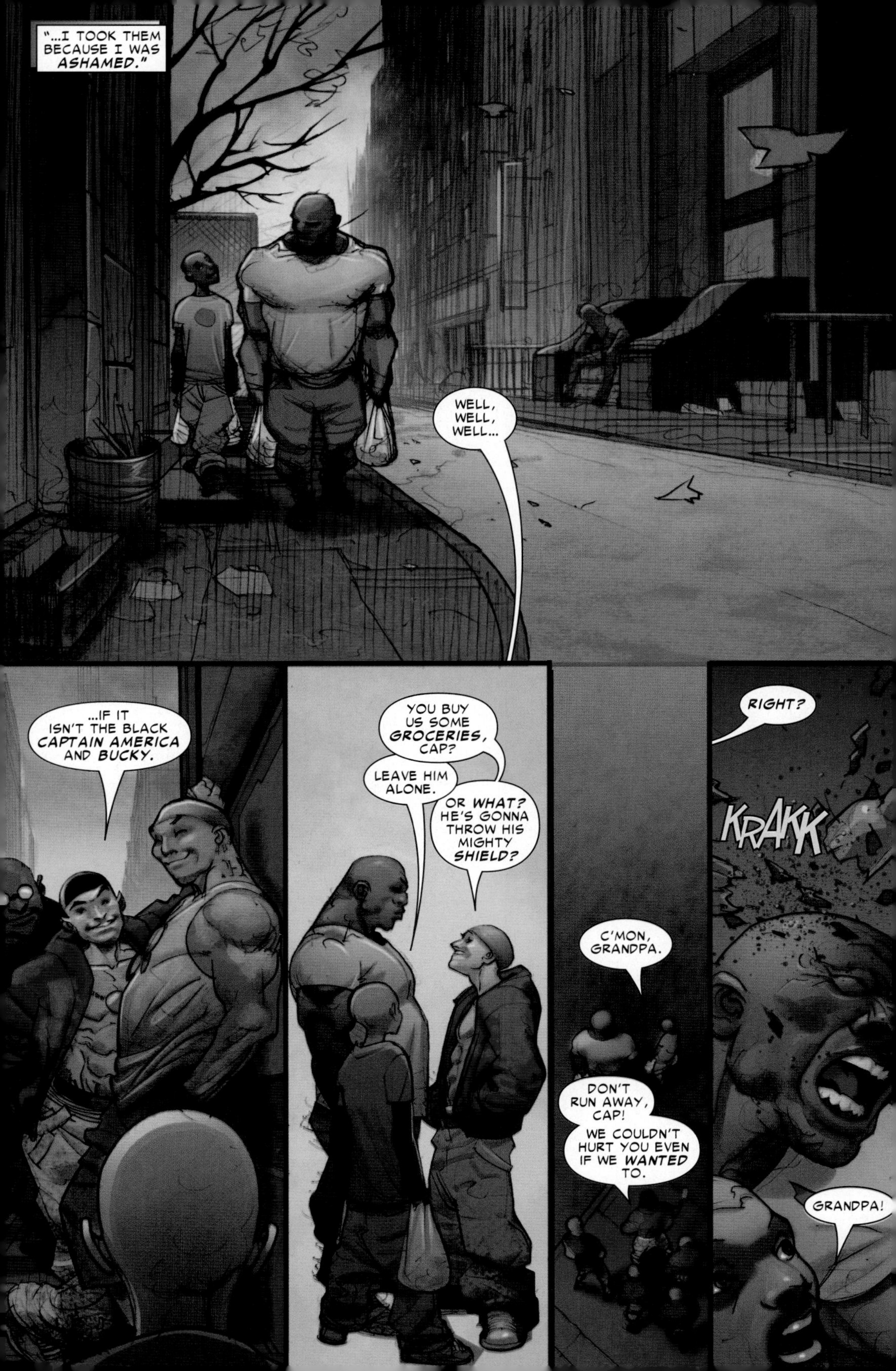
"...I TOOK THEM BECAUSE I WAS ASHAMED."
WELL, WELL, WELL...
...IF IT ISN'T THE BLACK CAPTAIN AMERICA AND BUCKY.
YOU BUY US SOME GROCERIES, CAP?
LEAVE HIM ALONE.
OR WHAT? HE'S GONNA THROW HIS MIGHTY SHIELD?
C'MON, GRANDPA.
DON'T RUN AWAY, CAP!
WE COULDN'T HURT YOU EVEN IF WE WANTED TO.
RIGHT?
KRAKK
GRANDPA!

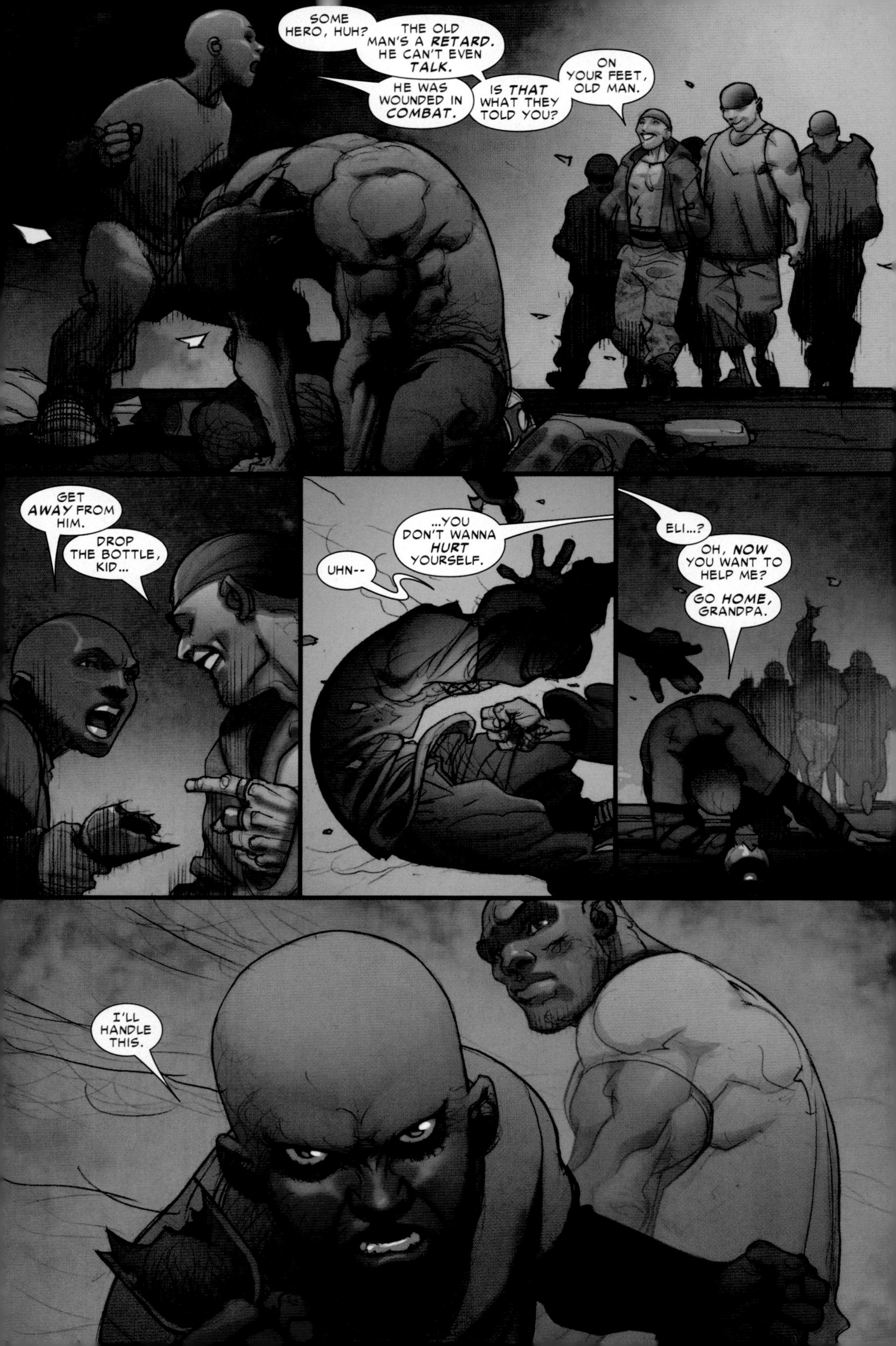
SOME HERO, HUH?
THE OLD MAN'S A RETARD. HE CAN'T EVEN TALK.
HE WAS WOUNDED IN COMBAT.
IS THAT WHAT THEY TOLD YOU?
ON YOUR FEET, OLD MAN.
GET AWAY FROM HIM.
DROP THE BOTTLE, KID...
...YOU DON'T WANNA HURT YOURSELF.
UHN--
ELI...?
OH, NOW YOU WANT TO HELP ME?
GO HOME, GRANDPA.
I'LL HANDLE THIS.

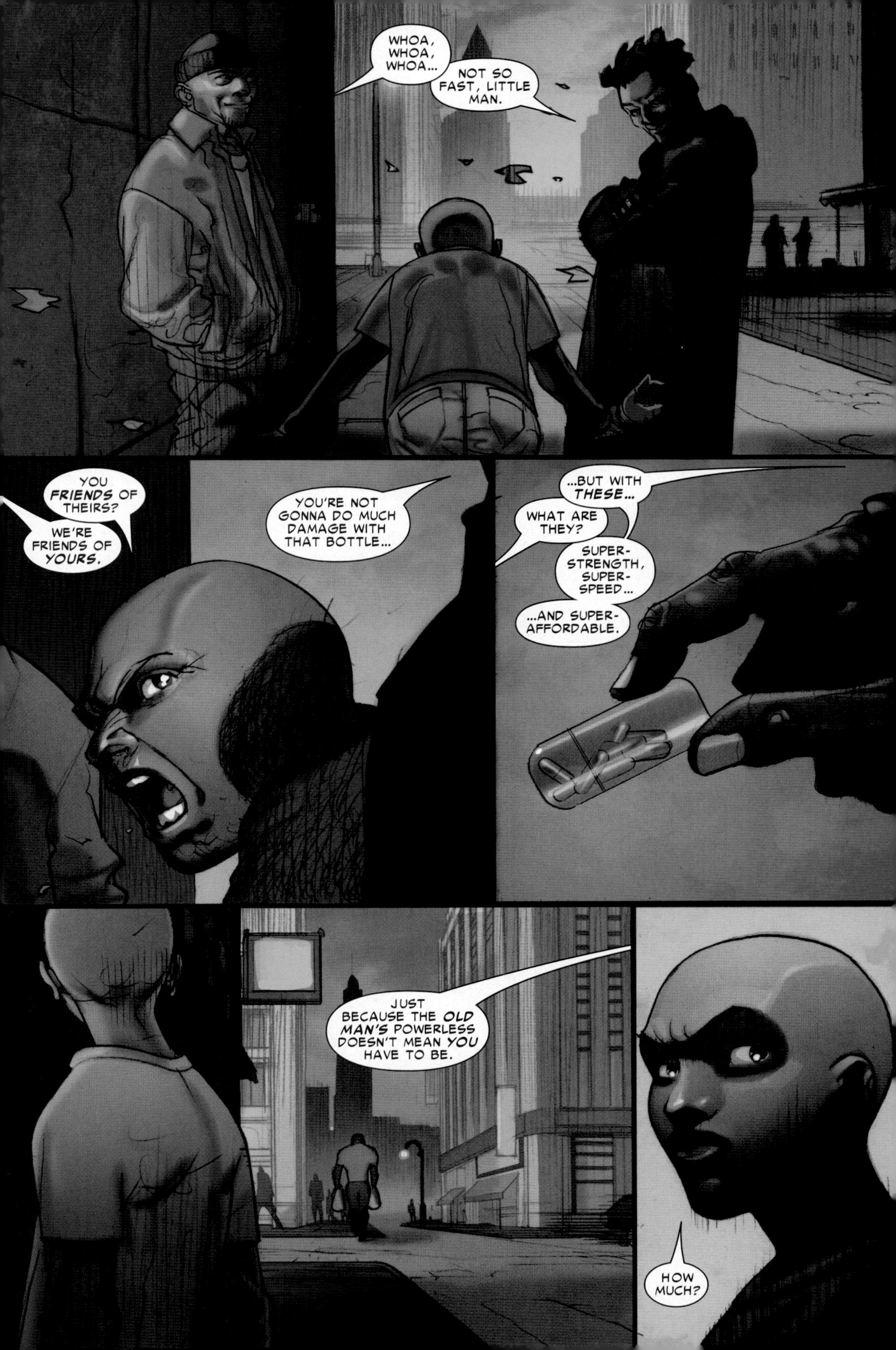
WHOA, WHOA, WHOA...
NOT SO FAST, LITTLE MAN.
YOU FRIENDS OF THEIRS?
WE'RE FRIENDS OF YOURS.
YOU'RE NOT GONNA DO MUCH DAMAGE WITH THAT BOTTLE...
...BUT WITH THESE...
WHAT ARE THEY?
SUPER-STRENGTH, SUPER-SPEED...
...AND SUPER-AFFORDABLE.
JUST BECAUSE THE OLD MAN'S POWERLESS DOESN'T MEAN YOU HAVE TO BE.
HOW MUCH?

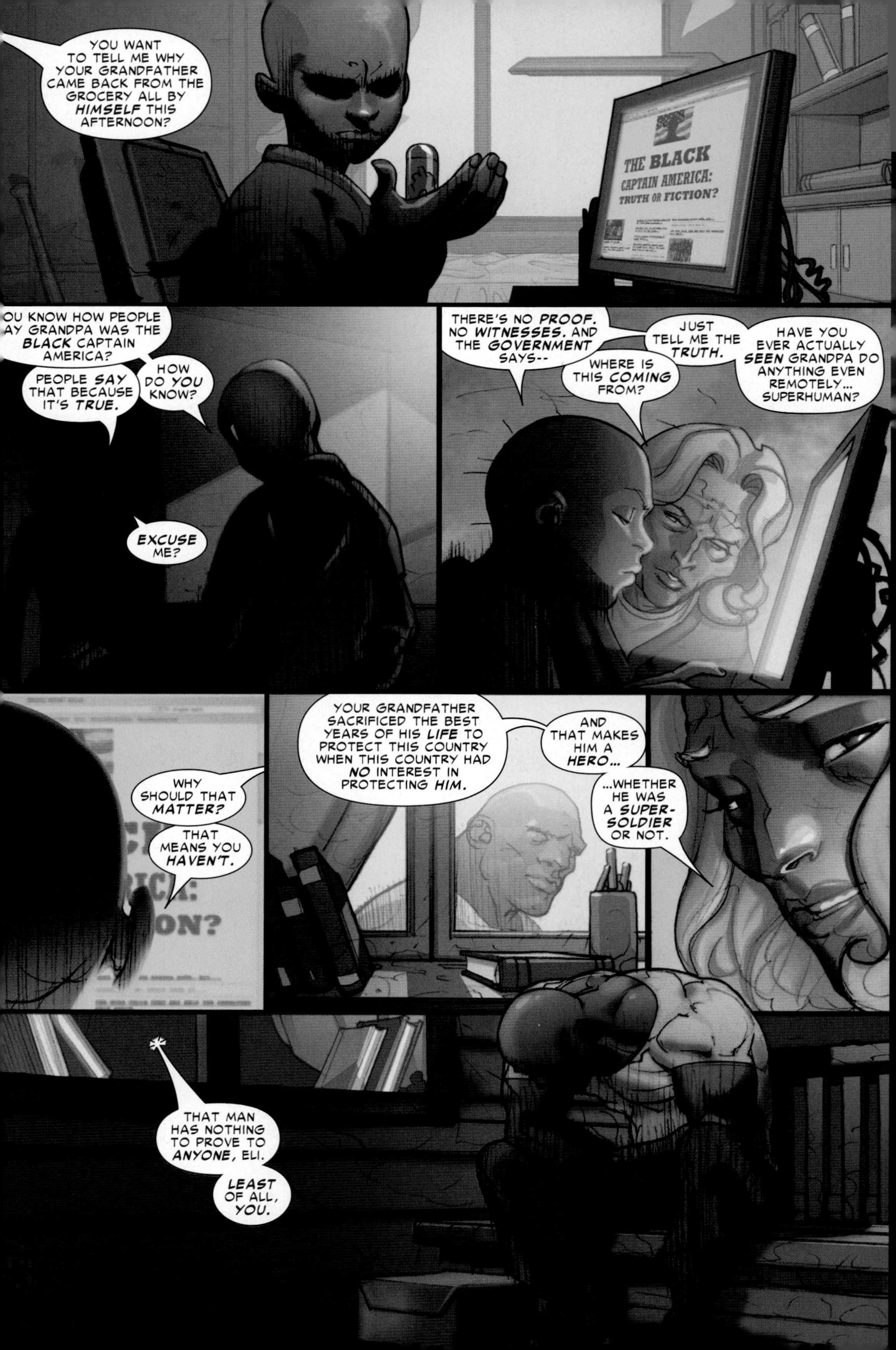

YOU WANT TO TELL ME WHY YOUR GRANDFATHER CAME BACK FROM THE GROCERY ALL BY HIMSELF THIS AFTERNOON?
THE BLACK CAPTAIN AMERICA: TRUTH OR FICTION?
OU KNOW HOW PEOPLE AY GRANDPA WAS THE BLACK CAPTAIN AMERICA?
PEOPLE SAY THAT BECAUSE IT'S TRUE.
HOW DO YOU KNOW?
EXCUSE ME?
THERE'S NO PROOF. NO WITNESSES. AND THE GOVERNMENT SAYS--
JUST TELL ME THE TRUTH.
WHERE IS THIS COMING FROM?
HAVE YOU EVER ACTUALLY SEEN GRANDPA DO ANYTHING EVEN REMOTELY... SUPERHUMAN?
WHY SHOULD THAT MATTER?
THAT MEANS YOU HAVEN'T.
YOUR GRANDFATHER SACRIFICED THE BEST YEARS OF HIS LIFE TO PROTECT THIS COUNTRY WHEN THIS COUNTRY HAD NO INTEREST IN PROTECTING HIM.
AND THAT MAKES HIM A HERO...
...WHETHER HE WAS A SUPER-SOLDIER OR NOT.
THAT MAN HAS NOTHING TO PROVE TO ANYONE, ELI.
LEAST OF ALL, YOU.

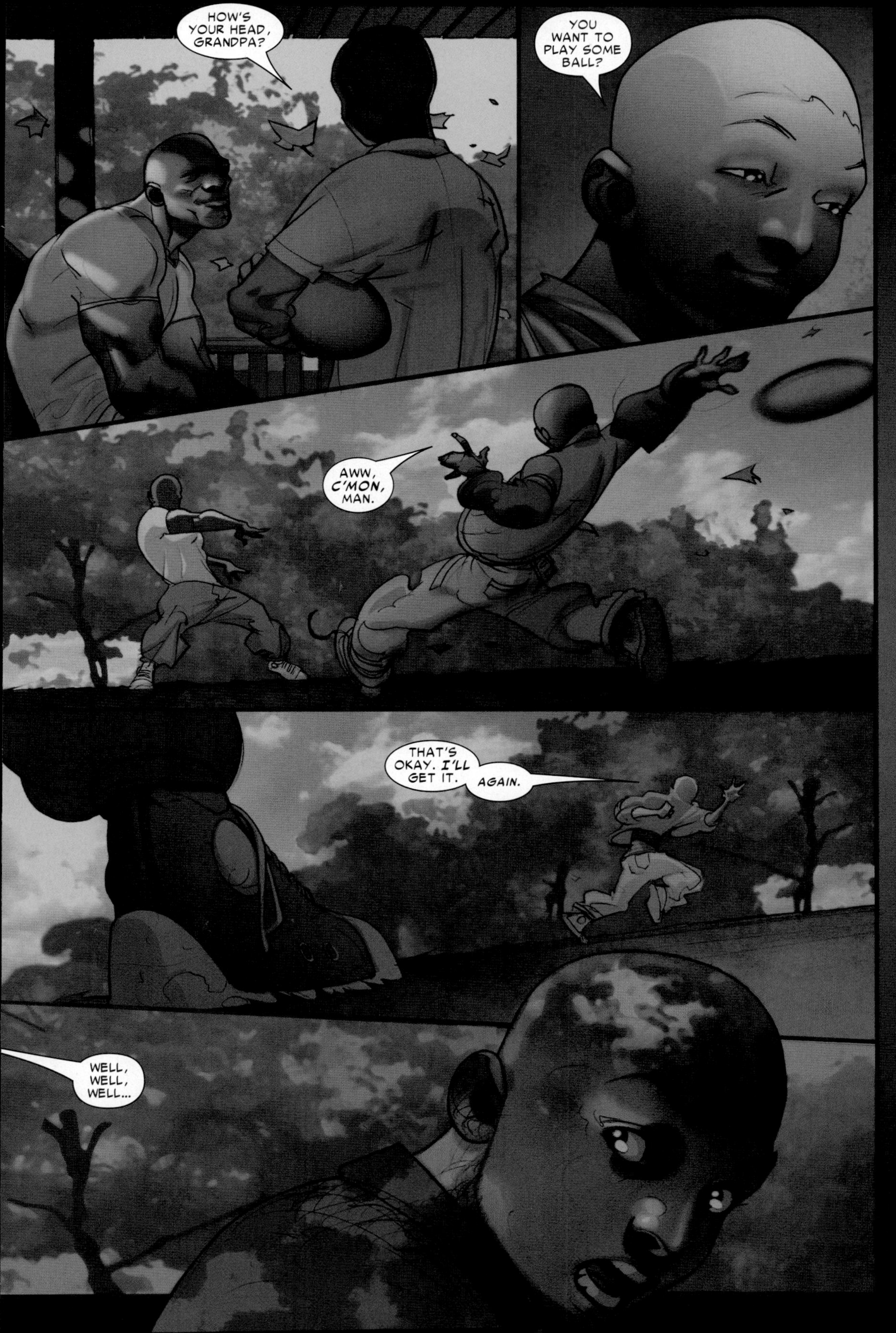
HOW'S YOUR HEAD, GRANDPA?
YOU WANT TO PLAY SOME BALL?
AWW, C'MON, MAN.
THAT'S OKAY. I'LL GET IT.
AGAIN.
WELL, WELL, WELL...

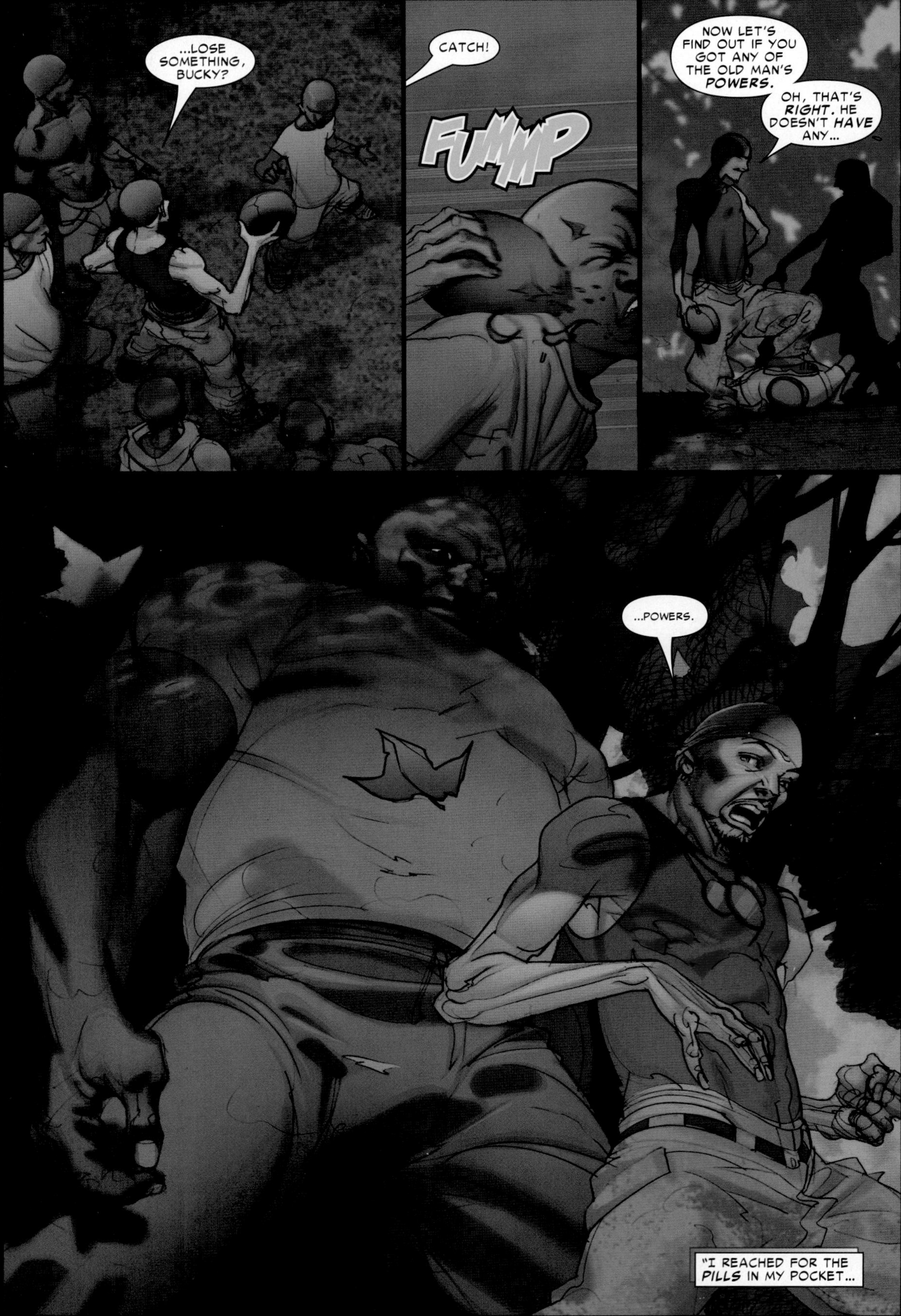
...LOSE SOMETHING, BUCKY?
CATCH!
FUMMP
NOW LET'S FIND OUT IF YOU GOT ANY OF THE OLD MAN'S POWERS.
OH, THAT'S RIGHT. HE DOESN'T HAVE ANY...
...POWERS.
"I REACHED FOR THE PILLS IN MY POCKET...

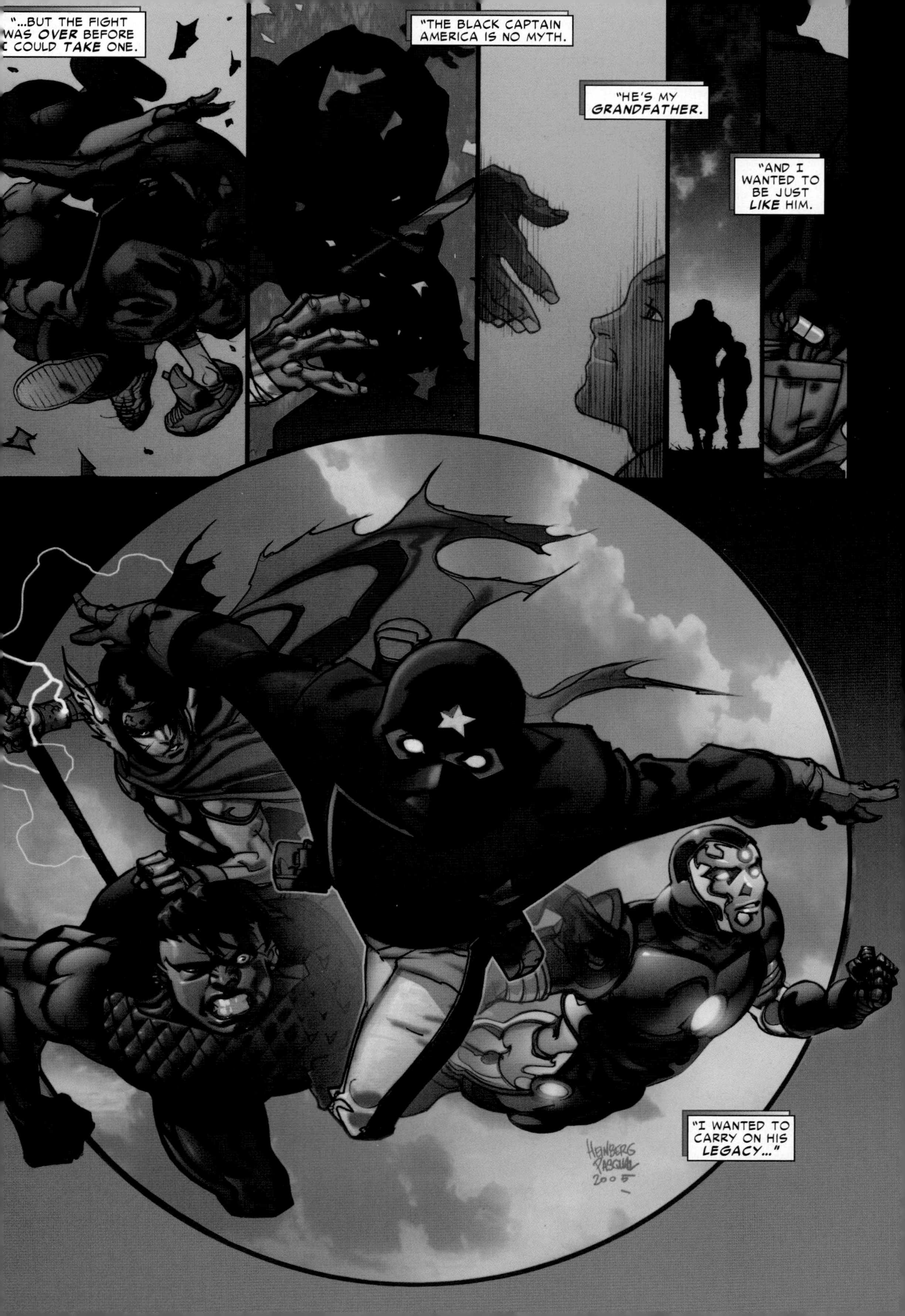
"...BUT THE FIGHT WAS OVER BEFORE I COULD TAKE ONE.
"THE BLACK CAPTAIN AMERICA IS NO MYTH.
"HE'S MY GRANDFATHER.
"AND I WANTED TO BE JUST LIKE HIM.
"I WANTED TO CARRY ON HIS LEGACY..."
HEINBERG PASQUAL 2005

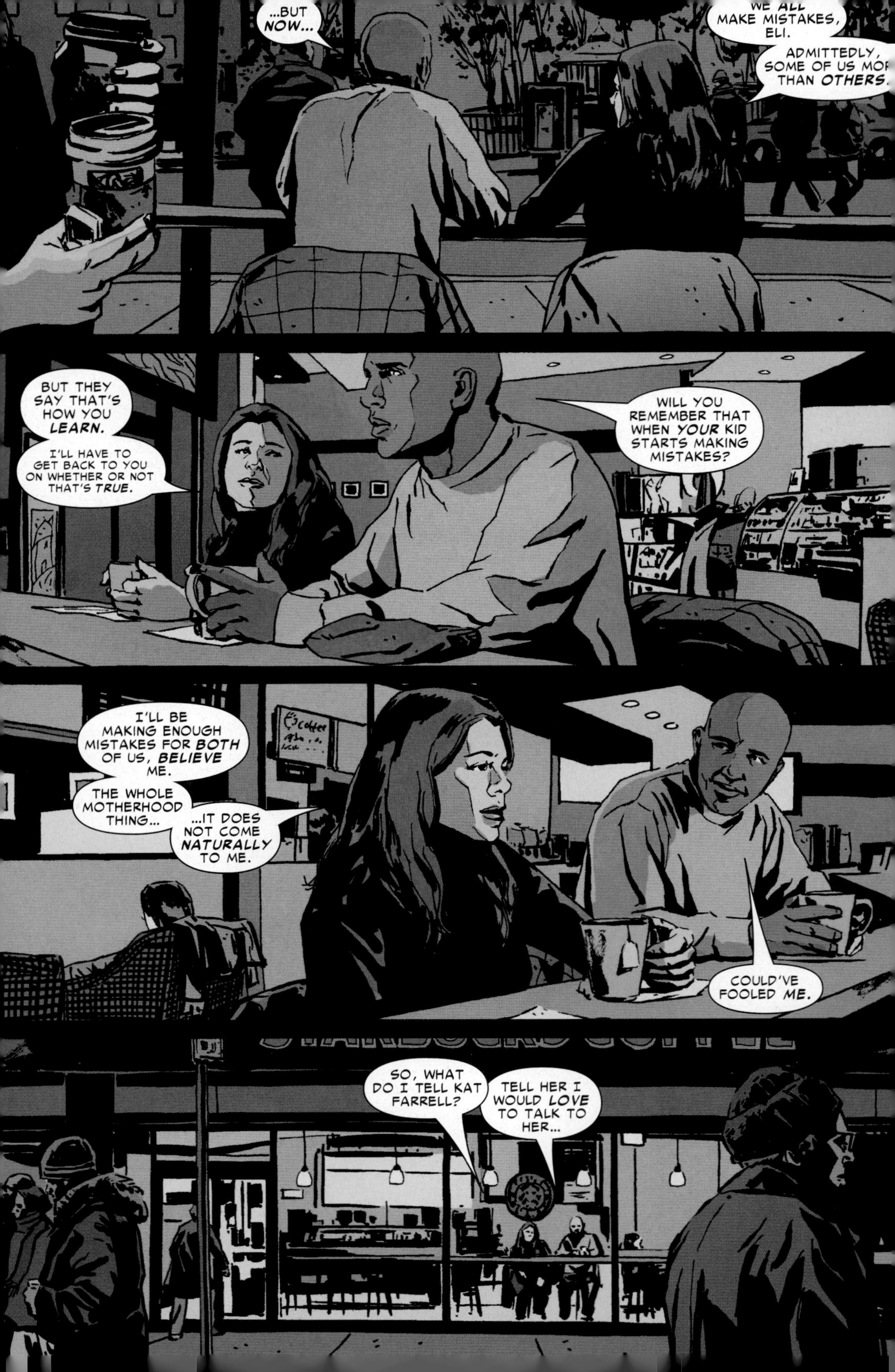
...BUT NOW...
WE ALL MAKE MISTAKES, ELI.
ADMITTEDLY, SOME OF US MOR THAN OTHERS.
BUT THEY SAY THAT'S HOW YOU LEARN.
I'LL HAVE TO GET BACK TO YOU ON WHETHER OR NOT THAT'S TRUE.
WILL YOU REMEMBER THAT WHEN YOUR KID STARTS MAKING MISTAKES?
I'LL BE MAKING ENOUGH MISTAKES FOR BOTH OF US, BELIEVE ME.
THE WHOLE MOTHERHOOD THING...
...IT DOES NOT COME NATURALLY TO ME.
COULD'VE FOOLED ME.
SO, WHAT DO I TELL KAT FARRELL?
TELL HER I WOULD LOVE TO TALK TO HER...

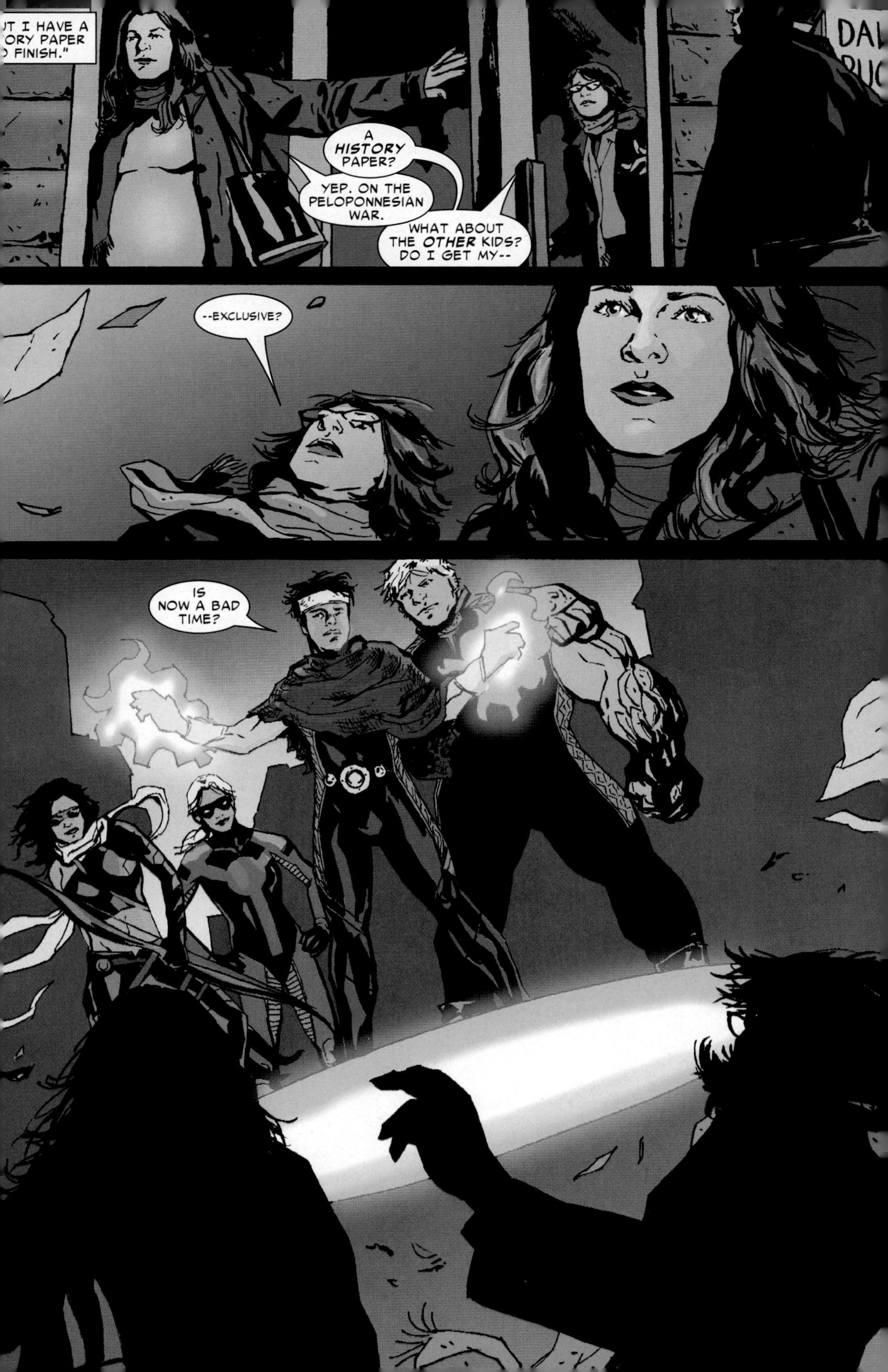

"UT I HAVE A
TORY PAPER
O FINISH."
A HISTORY PAPER?
YEP. ON THE PELOPONNESIAN WAR.
WHAT ABOUT THE OTHER KIDS? DO I GET MY--
--EXCLUSIVE?
IS NOW A BAD TIME?

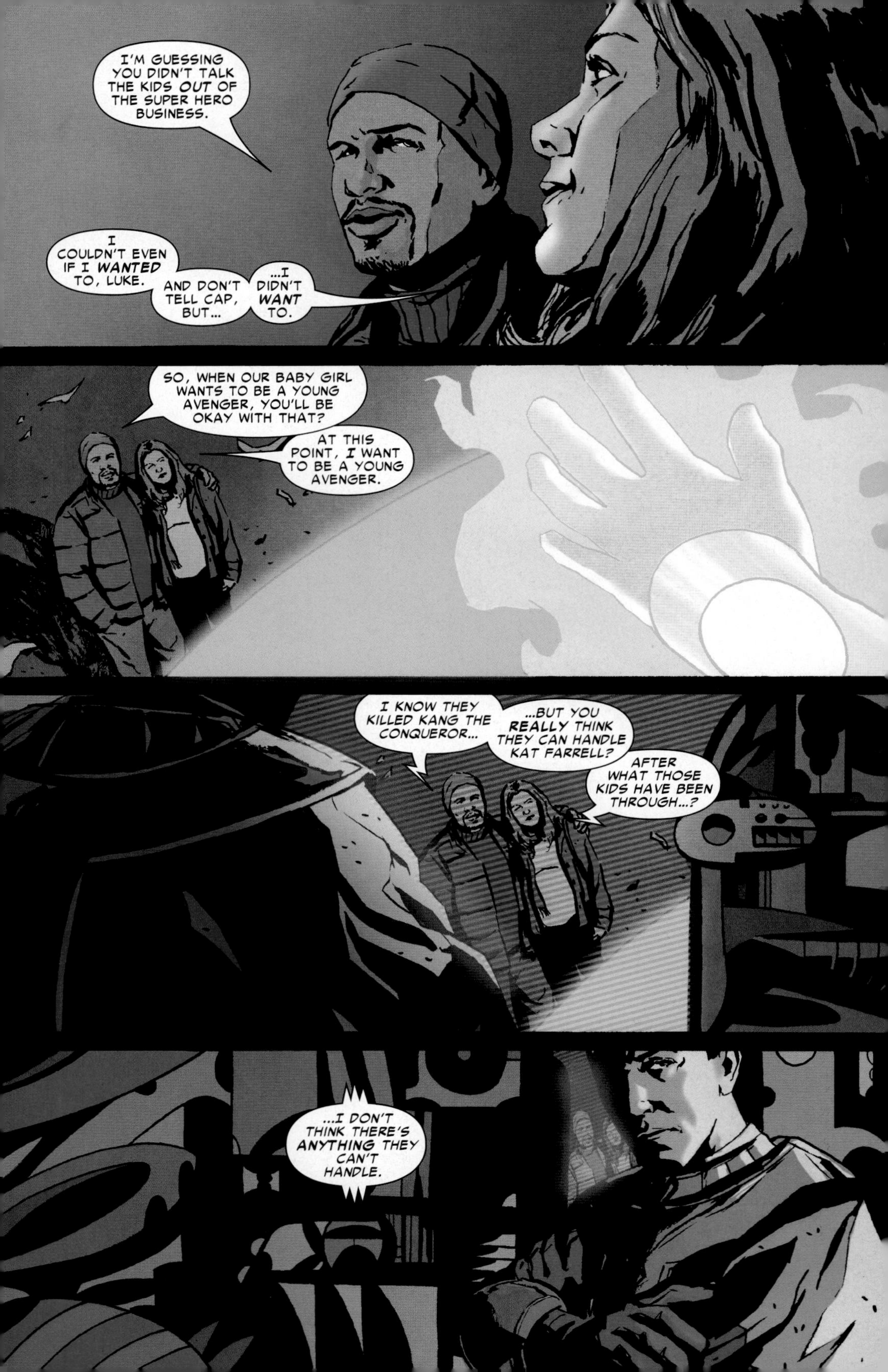
I'M GUESSING YOU DIDN'T TALK THE KIDS OUT OF THE SUPER HERO BUSINESS.
I COULDN'T EVEN IF I WANTED TO, LUKE.
AND DON'T TELL CAP, BUT...
...I DIDN'T WANT TO.
SO, WHEN OUR BABY GIRL WANTS TO BE A YOUNG AVENGER, YOU'LL BE OKAY WITH THAT?
AT THIS POINT, I WANT TO BE A YOUNG AVENGER.
I KNOW THEY KILLED KANG THE CONQUEROR...
...BUT YOU REALLY THINK THEY CAN HANDLE KAT FARRELL?
AFTER WHAT THOSE KIDS HAVE BEEN THROUGH...?
...I DON'T THINK THERE'S ANYTHING THEY CAN'T HANDLE.

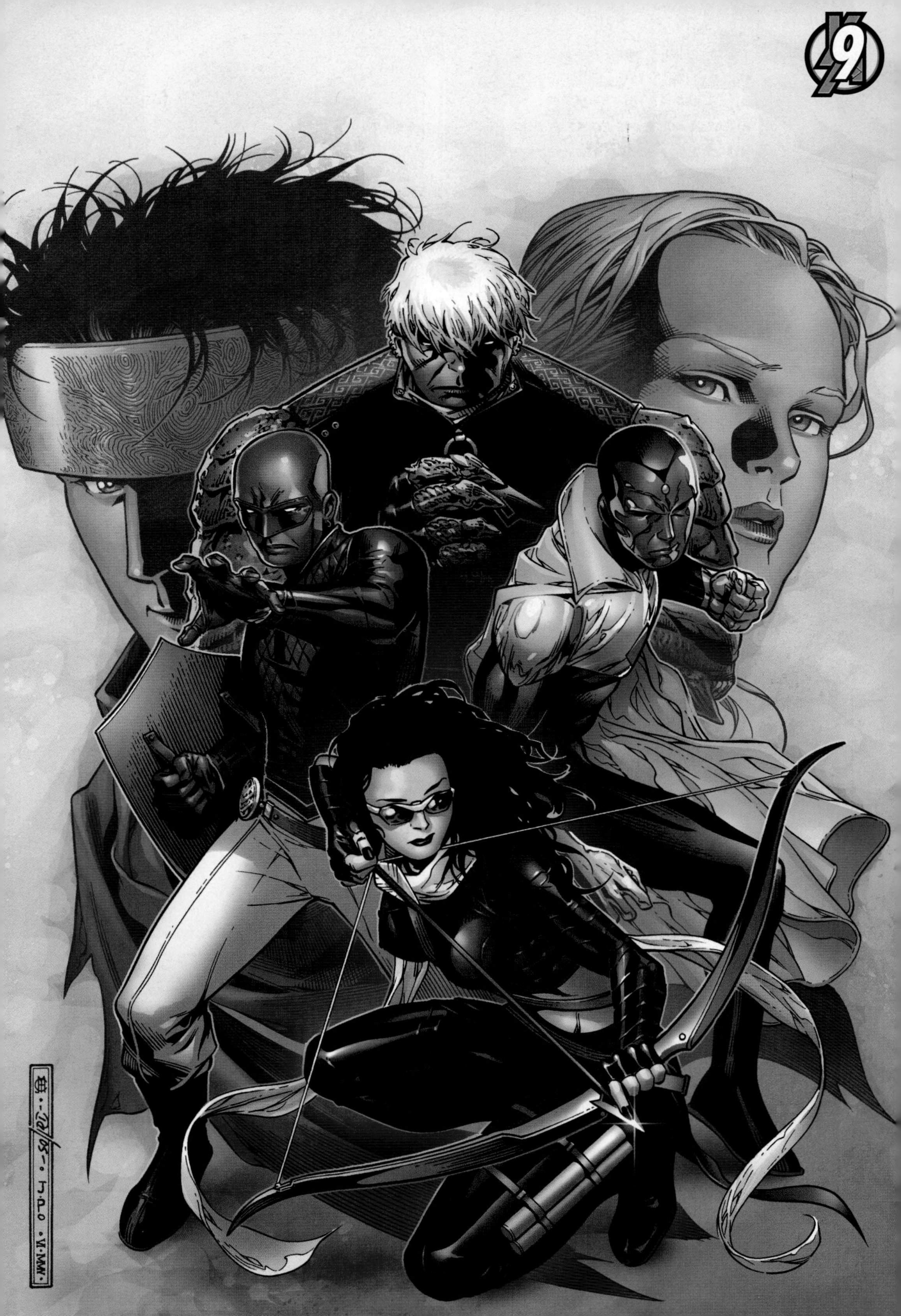

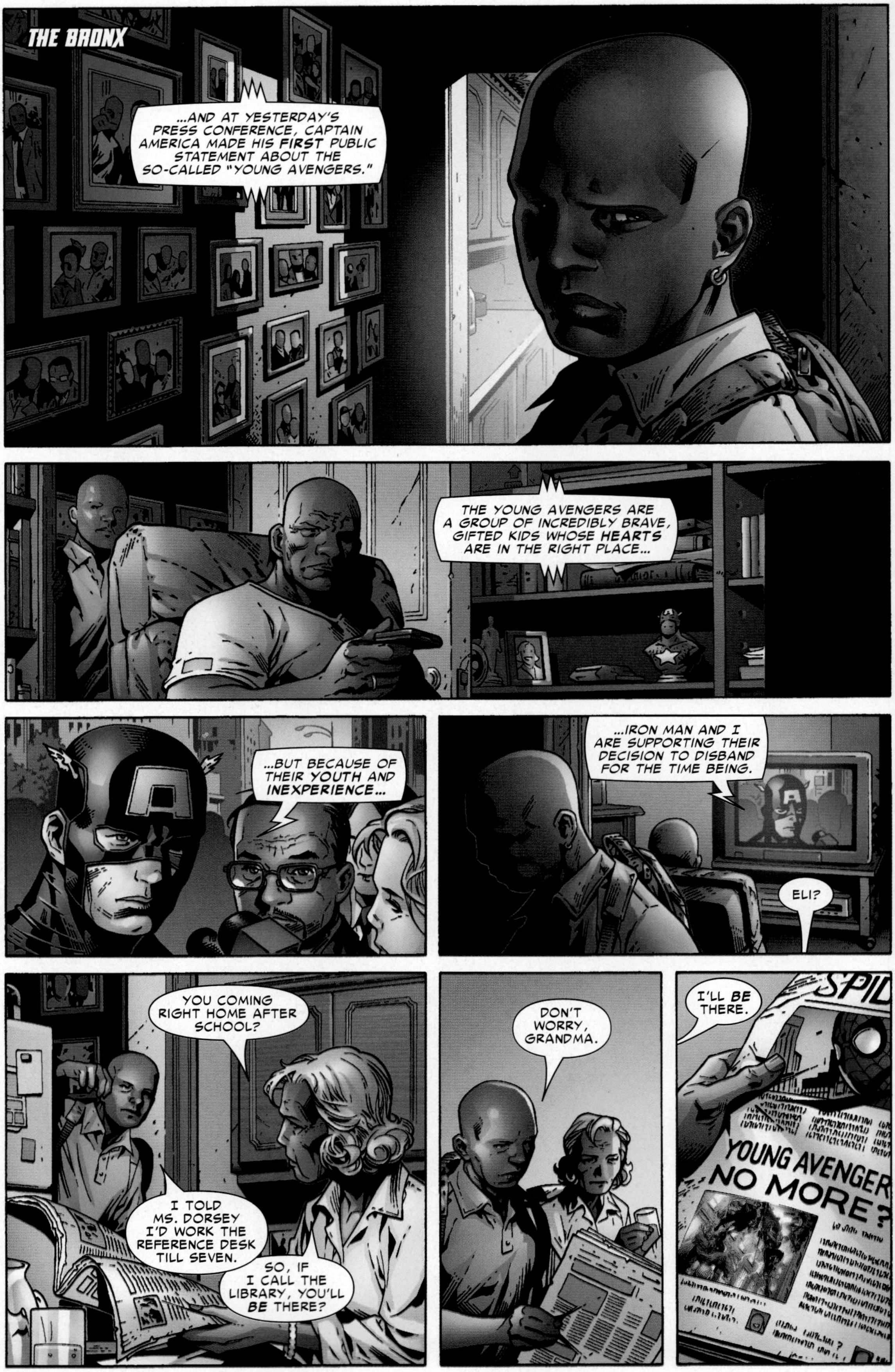
THE BRONX
...AND AT YESTERDAY'S PRESS CONFERENCE, CAPTAIN AMERICA MADE HIS FIRST PUBLIC STATEMENT ABOUT THE SO-CALLED "YOUNG AVENGERS."
THE YOUNG AVENGERS ARE A GROUP OF INCREDIBLY BRAVE, GIFTED KIDS WHOSE HEARTS ARE IN THE RIGHT PLACE...
...BUT BECAUSE OF THEIR YOUTH AND INEXPERIENCE...
...IRON MAN AND I ARE SUPPORTING THEIR DECISION TO DISBAND FOR THE TIME BEING.
ELI?
YOU COMING RIGHT HOME AFTER SCHOOL?
I TOLD MS. DORSEY I'D WORK THE REFERENCE DESK TILL SEVEN.
SO, IF I CALL THE LIBRARY, YOU'LL BE THERE?
DON'T WORRY, GRANDMA.
I'LL BE THERE.
YOUNG AVENGER NO MORE?

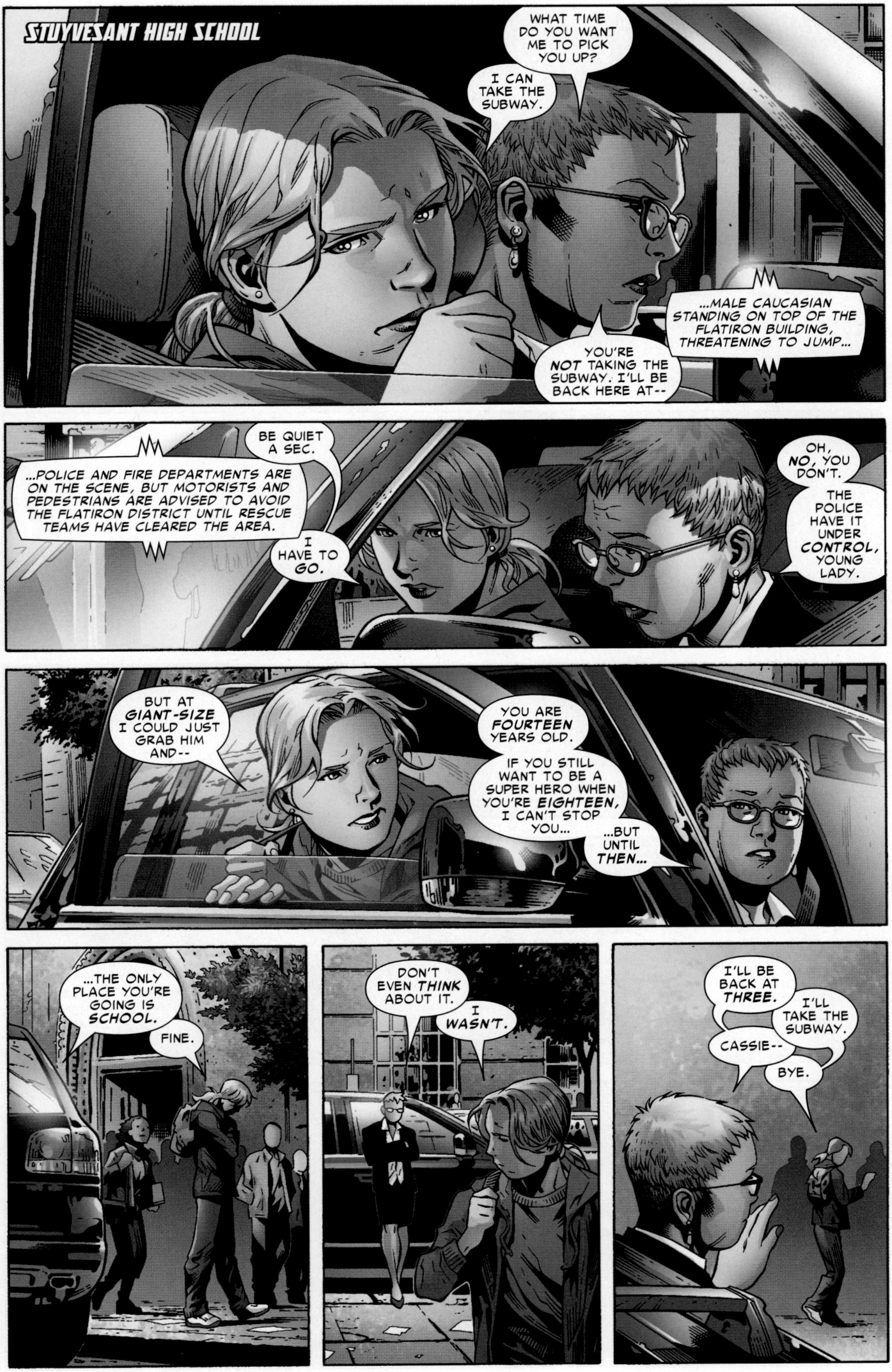
STUYVESANT HIGH SCHOOL
WHAT TIME DO YOU WANT ME TO PICK YOU UP?
I CAN TAKE THE SUBWAY.
...MALE CAUCASIAN STANDING ON TOP OF THE FLATIRON BUILDING, THREATENING TO JUMP...
YOU'RE NOT TAKING THE SUBWAY. I'LL BE BACK HERE AT--
...POLICE AND FIRE DEPARTMENTS ARE ON THE SCENE, BUT MOTORISTS AND PEDESTRIANS ARE ADVISED TO AVOID THE FLATIRON DISTRICT UNTIL RESCUE TEAMS HAVE CLEARED THE AREA.
BE QUIET A SEC.
I HAVE TO GO.
OH, NO, YOU DON'T.
THE POLICE HAVE IT UNDER CONTROL, YOUNG LADY.
BUT AT GIANT-SIZE I COULD JUST GRAB HIM AND--
YOU ARE FOURTEEN YEARS OLD.
IF YOU STILL WANT TO BE A SUPER HERO WHEN YOU'RE EIGHTEEN, I CAN'T STOP YOU...
...BUT UNTIL THEN...
...THE ONLY PLACE YOU'RE GOING IS SCHOOL.
FINE.
DON'T EVEN THINK ABOUT IT.
I WASN'T.
I'LL BE BACK AT THREE.
I'LL TAKE THE SUBWAY.
CASSIE--
BYE.

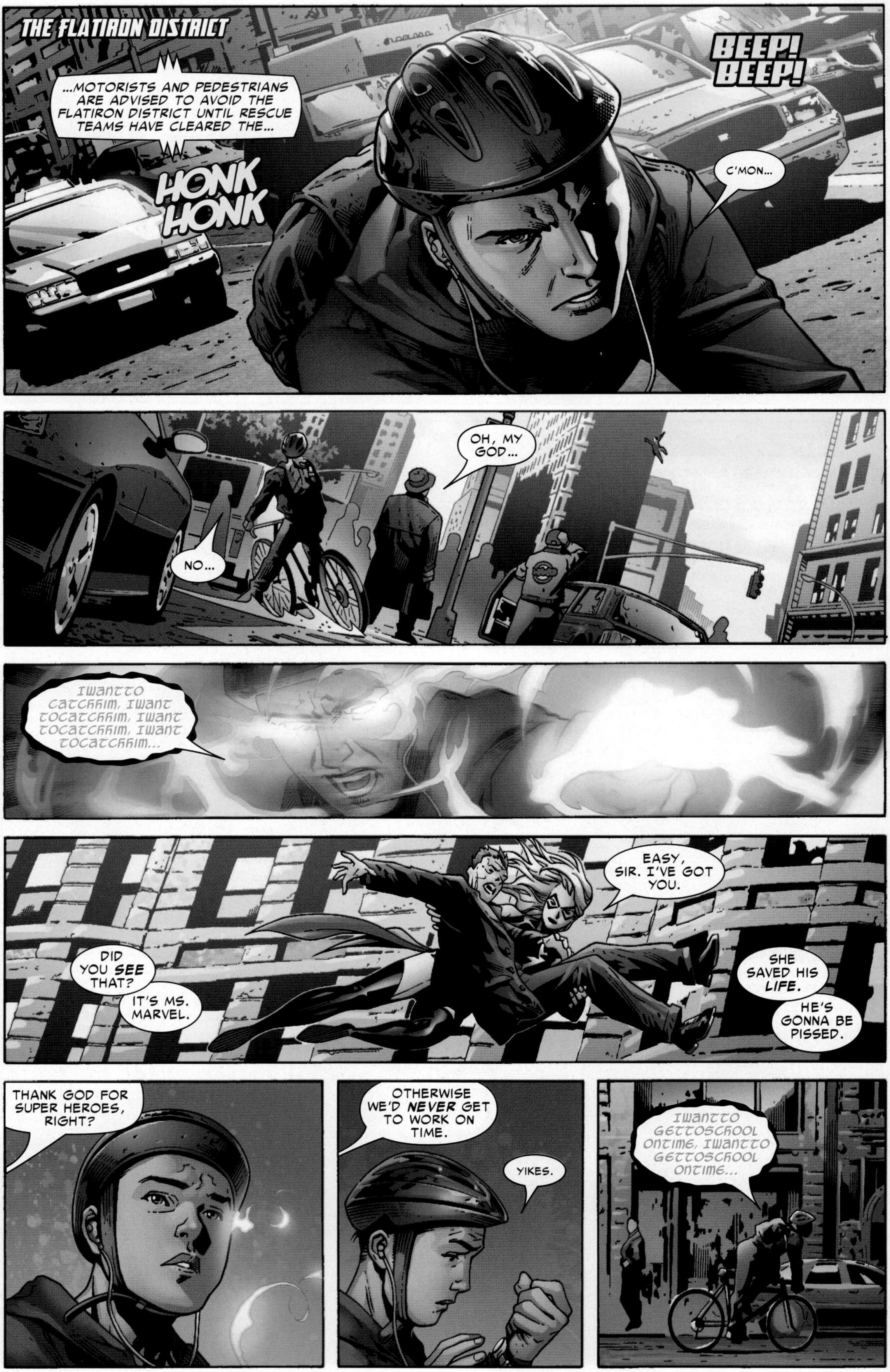
THE FLATIRON DISTRICT
...MOTORISTS AND PEDESTRIANS ARE ADVISED TO AVOID THE FLATIRON DISTRICT UNTIL RESCUE TEAMS HAVE CLEARED THE...
HONK HONK
BEEP! BEEP!
C'MON...
OH, MY GOD...
NO...
IWANTTO CATCHHIM, IWANT TOCATCHHIM, IWANT TOCATCHHIM, IWANT TOCATCHHIM...
EASY, SIR. I'VE GOT YOU.
DID YOU SEE THAT?
IT'S MS. MARVEL.
SHE SAVED HIS LIFE.
HE'S GONNA BE PISSED.
THANK GOD FOR SUPER HEROES, RIGHT?
OTHERWISE WE'D NEVER GET TO WORK ON TIME.
YIKES.
IWANTTO GETTOSCHOOL ONTIME, IWANTTO GETTOSCHOOL ONTIME...

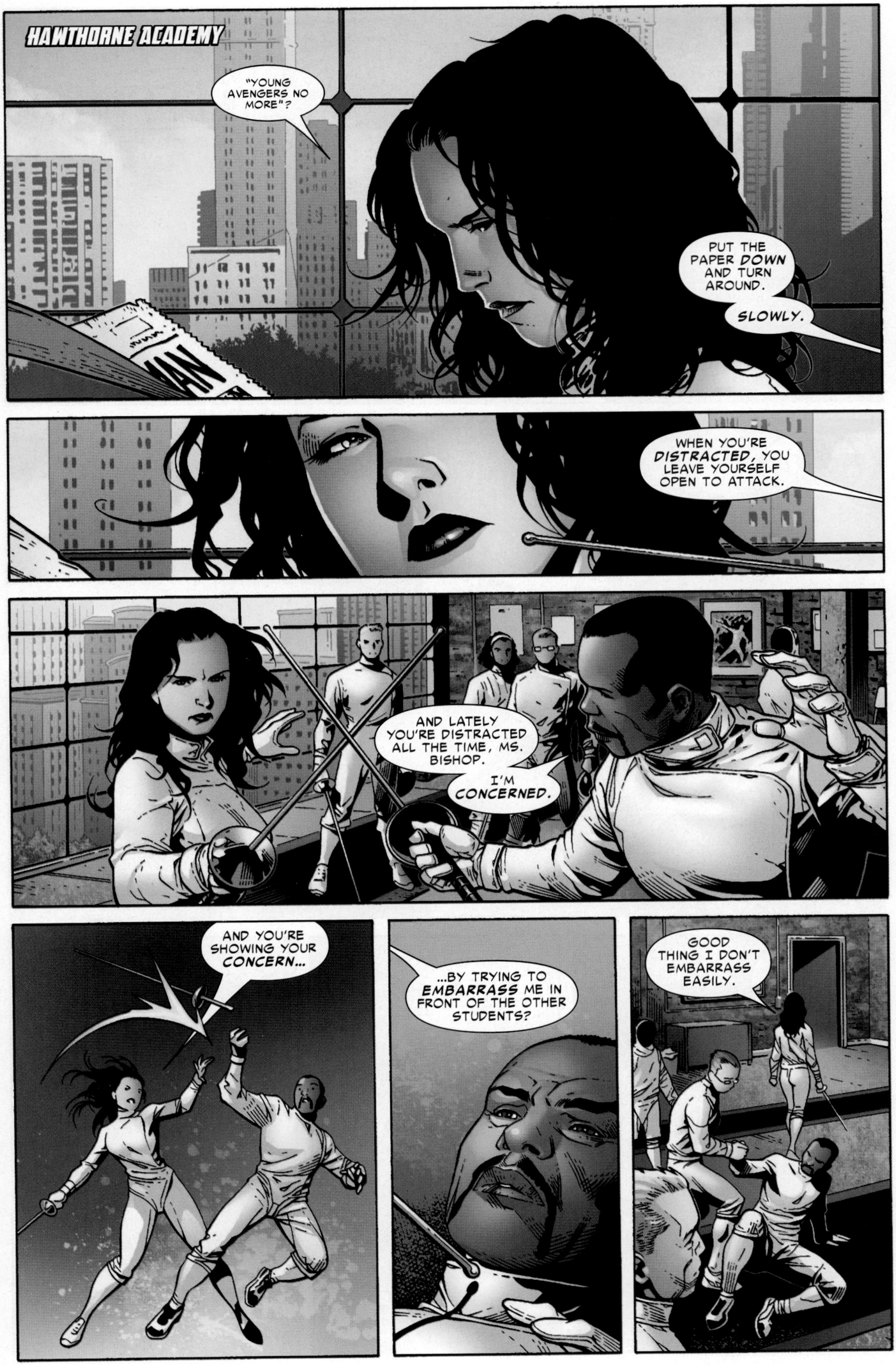
HAWTHORNE ACADEMY
"YOUNG AVENGERS NO MORE"?
PUT THE PAPER DOWN AND TURN AROUND.
SLOWLY.
WHEN YOU'RE DISTRACTED, YOU LEAVE YOURSELF OPEN TO ATTACK.
AND LATELY YOU'RE DISTRACTED ALL THE TIME, MS. BISHOP.
I'M CONCERNED.
AND YOU'RE SHOWING YOUR CONCERN...
...BY TRYING TO EMBARRASS ME IN FRONT OF THE OTHER STUDENTS?
GOOD THING I DON'T EMBARRASS EASILY.

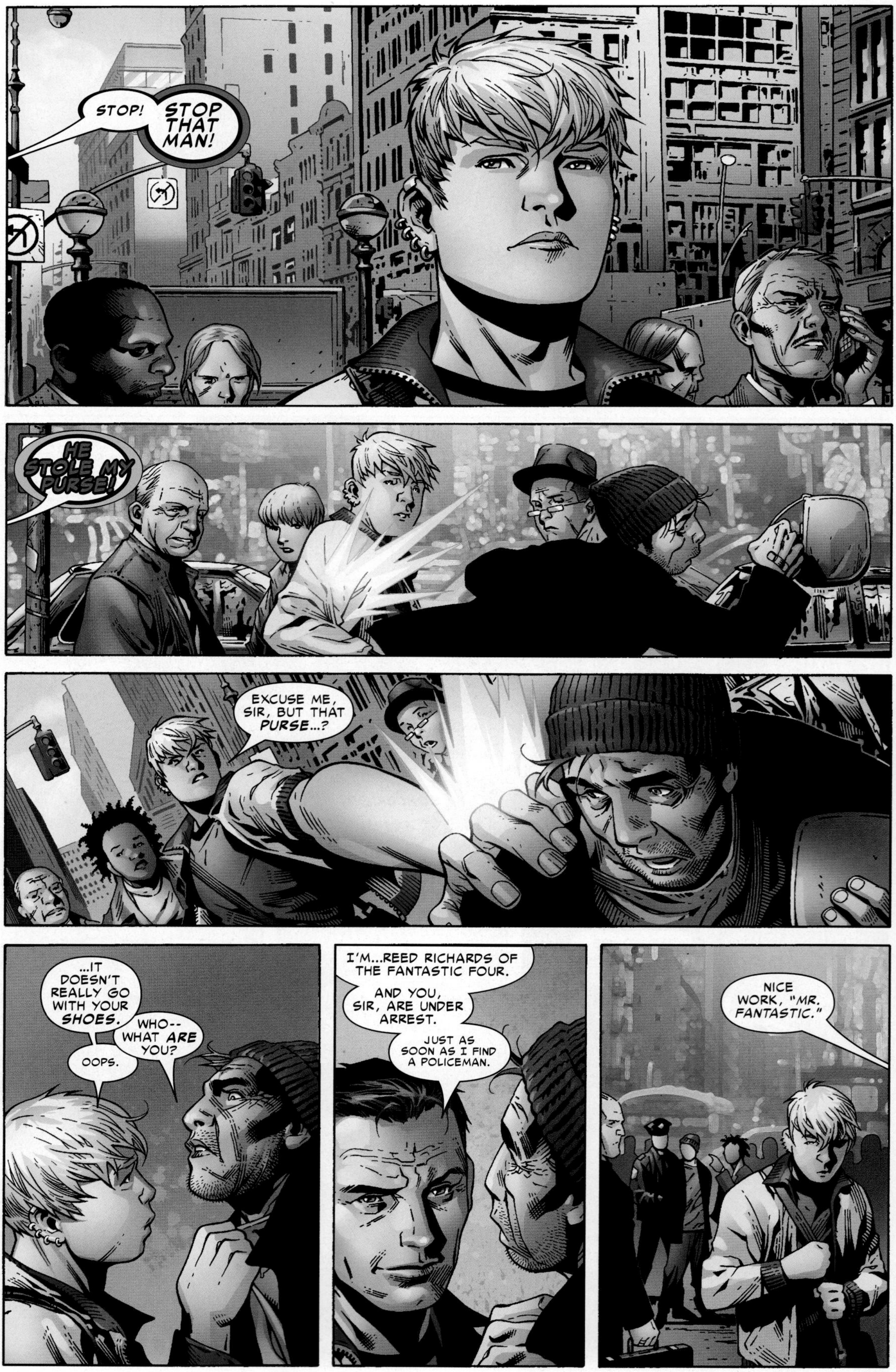

STOP!
STOP THAT MAN!
HE STOLE MY PURSE!
EXCUSE ME, SIR, BUT THAT PURSE...?
...IT DOESN'T REALLY GO WITH YOUR SHOES.
OOPS.
WHO--WHAT ARE YOU?
I'M...REED RICHARDS OF THE FANTASTIC FOUR.
AND YOU, SIR, ARE UNDER ARREST.
JUST AS SOON AS I FIND A POLICEMAN.
NICE WORK, "MR. FANTASTIC."

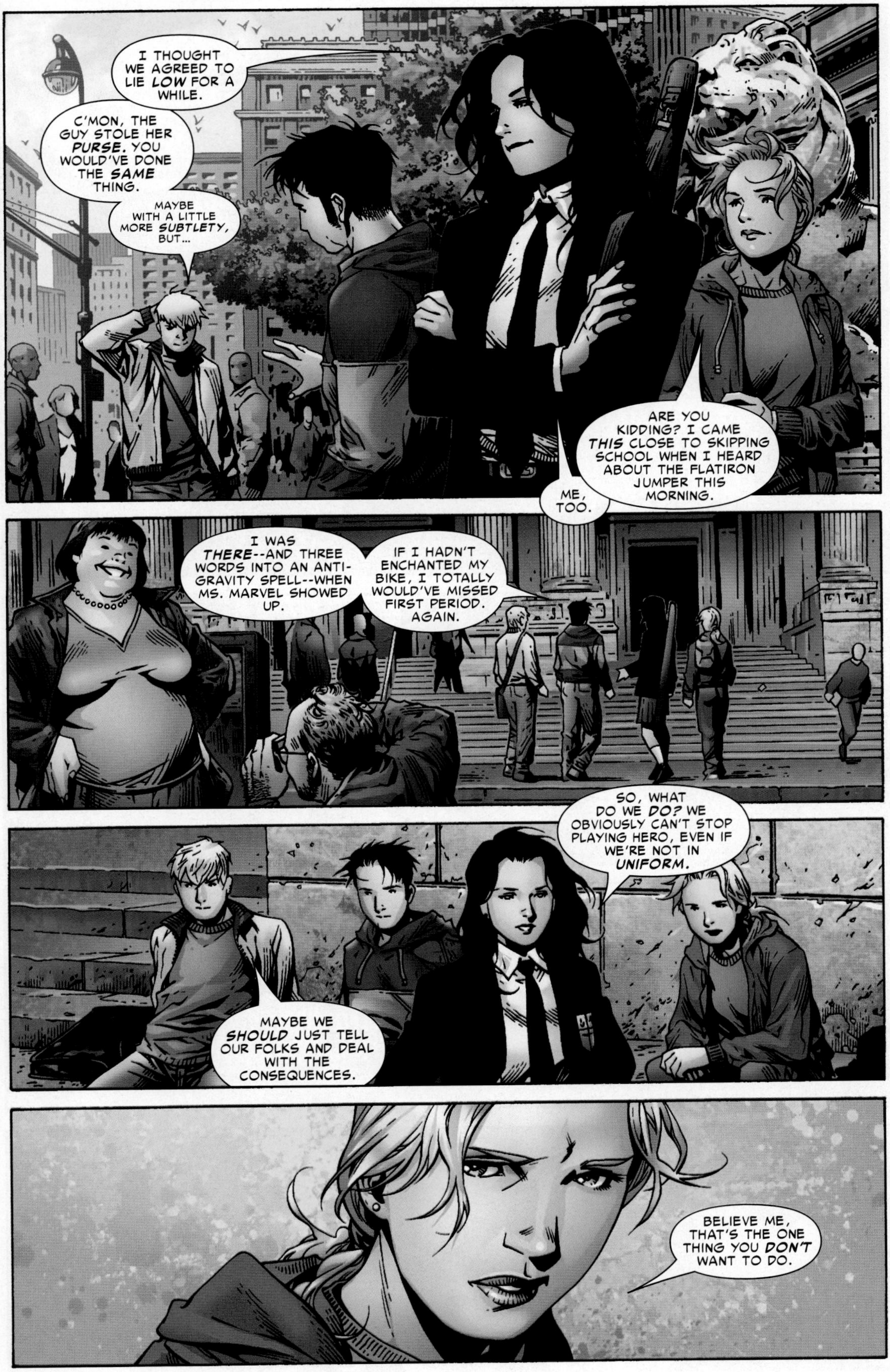
I THOUGHT WE AGREED TO LIE LOW FOR A WHILE.
C'MON, THE GUY STOLE HER PURSE. YOU WOULD'VE DONE THE SAME THING.
MAYBE WITH A LITTLE MORE SUBTLETY, BUT...
ARE YOU KIDDING? I CAME THIS CLOSE TO SKIPPING SCHOOL WHEN I HEARD ABOUT THE FLATIRON JUMPER THIS MORNING.
ME, TOO.
I WAS THERE--AND THREE WORDS INTO AN ANTI-GRAVITY SPELL--WHEN MS. MARVEL SHOWED UP.
IF I HADN'T ENCHANTED MY BIKE, I TOTALLY WOULD'VE MISSED FIRST PERIOD. AGAIN.
SO, WHAT DO WE DO? WE OBVIOUSLY CAN'T STOP PLAYING HERO, EVEN IF WE'RE NOT IN UNIFORM.
MAYBE WE SHOULD JUST TELL OUR FOLKS AND DEAL WITH THE CONSEQUENCES.
BELIEVE ME, THAT'S THE ONE THING YOU DON'T WANT TO DO.

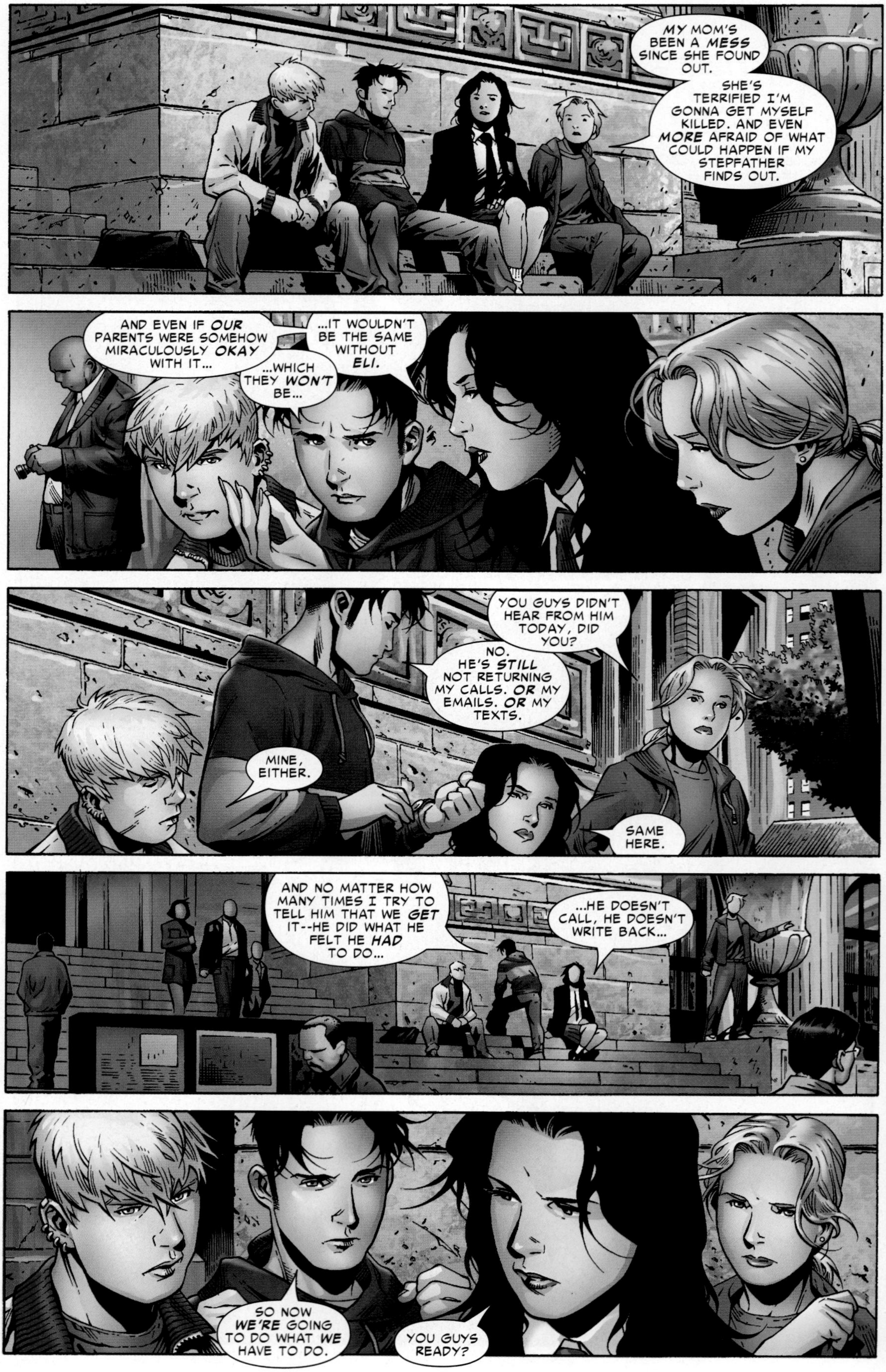
MY MOM'S BEEN A MESS SINCE SHE FOUND OUT.
SHE'S TERRIFIED I'M GONNA GET MYSELF KILLED. AND EVEN MORE AFRAID OF WHAT COULD HAPPEN IF MY STEPFATHER FINDS OUT.
AND EVEN IF OUR PARENTS WERE SOMEHOW MIRACULOUSLY OKAY WITH IT...
...WHICH THEY WON'T BE...
...IT WOULDN'T BE THE SAME WITHOUT ELI.
YOU GUYS DIDN'T HEAR FROM HIM TODAY, DID YOU?
NO. HE'S STILL NOT RETURNING MY CALLS. OR MY EMAILS. OR MY TEXTS.
MINE, EITHER.
SAME HERE.
AND NO MATTER HOW MANY TIMES I TRY TO TELL HIM THAT WE GET IT--HE DID WHAT HE FELT HE HAD TO DO...
...HE DOESN'T CALL, HE DOESN'T WRITE BACK...
SO NOW WE'RE GOING TO DO WHAT WE HAVE TO DO.
YOU GUYS READY?

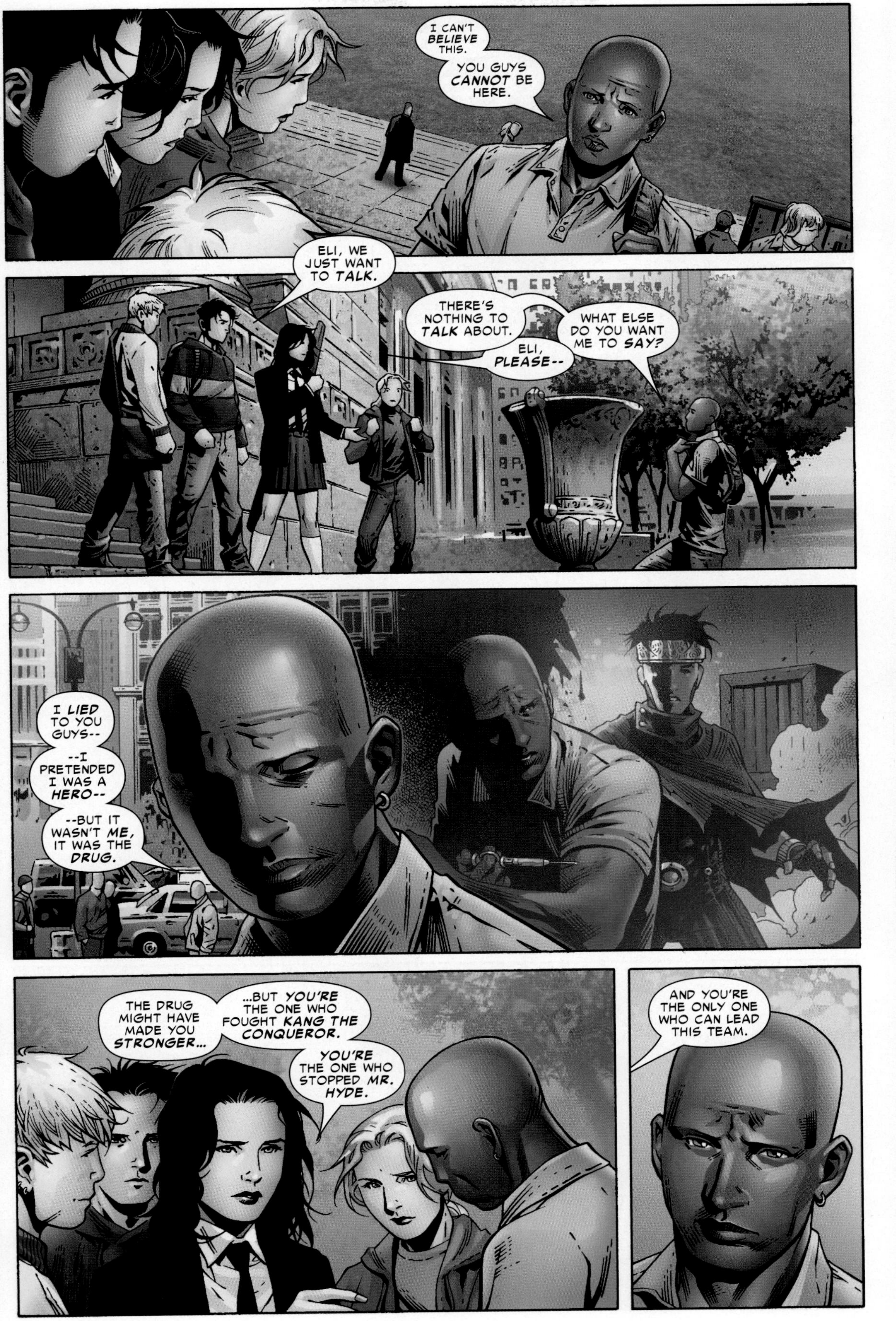
I CAN'T BELIEVE THIS.
YOU GUYS CANNOT BE HERE.
ELI, WE JUST WANT TO TALK.
THERE'S NOTHING TO TALK ABOUT.
ELI, PLEASE--
WHAT ELSE DO YOU WANT ME TO SAY?
I LIED TO YOU GUYS--
--I PRETENDED I WAS A HERO--
--BUT IT WASN'T ME, IT WAS THE DRUG.
THE DRUG MIGHT HAVE MADE YOU STRONGER...
...BUT YOU'RE THE ONE WHO FOUGHT KANG THE CONQUEROR.
YOU'RE THE ONE WHO STOPPED MR. HYDE.
AND YOU'RE THE ONLY ONE WHO CAN LEAD THIS TEAM.

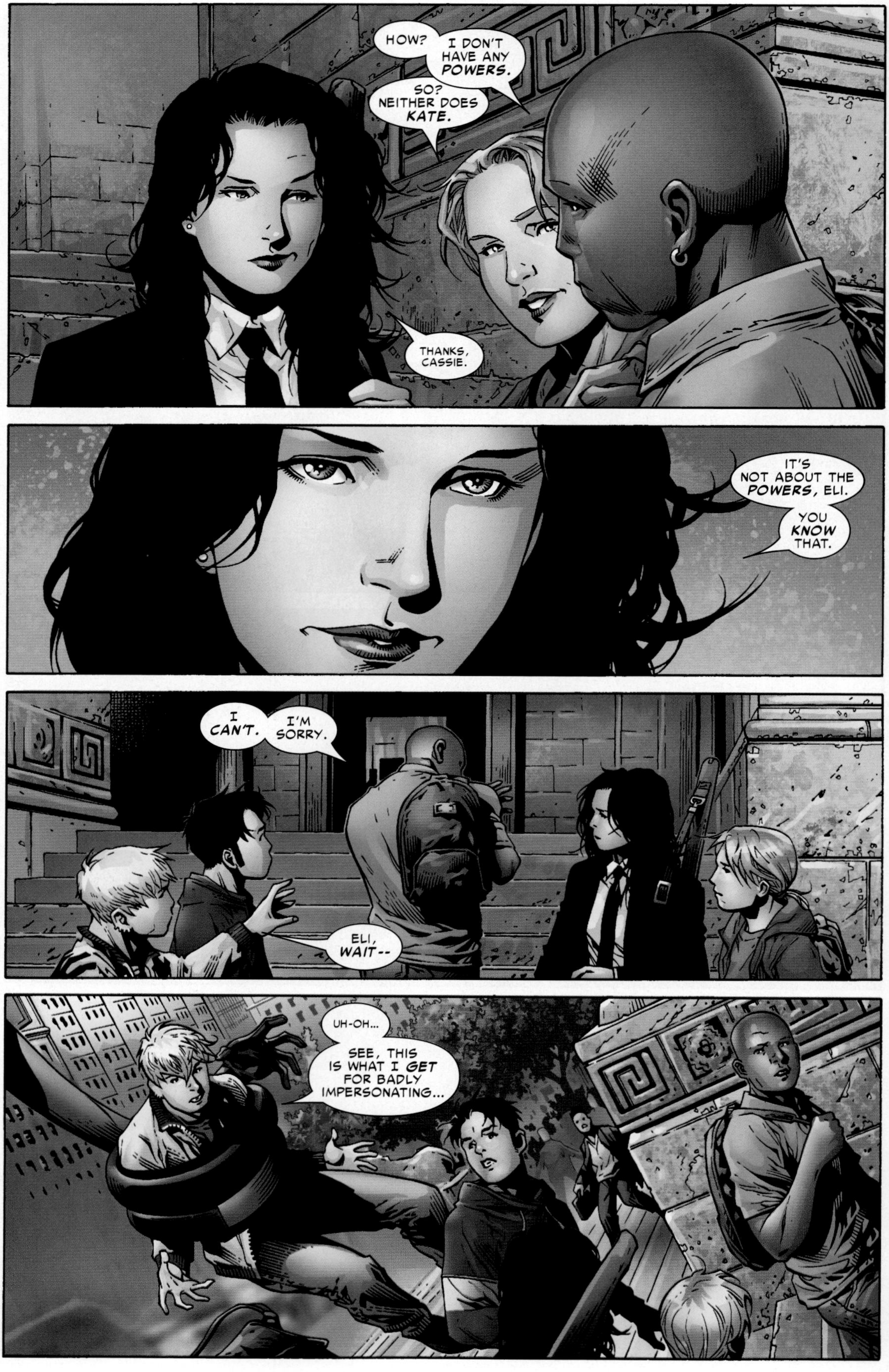
HOW?
I DON'T HAVE ANY POWERS.
SO? NEITHER DOES KATE.
THANKS, CASSIE.
IT'S NOT ABOUT THE POWERS, ELI.
YOU KNOW THAT.
I CAN'T.
I'M SORRY.
ELI, WAIT--
UH-OH...
SEE, THIS IS WHAT I GET FOR BADLY IMPERSONATING...

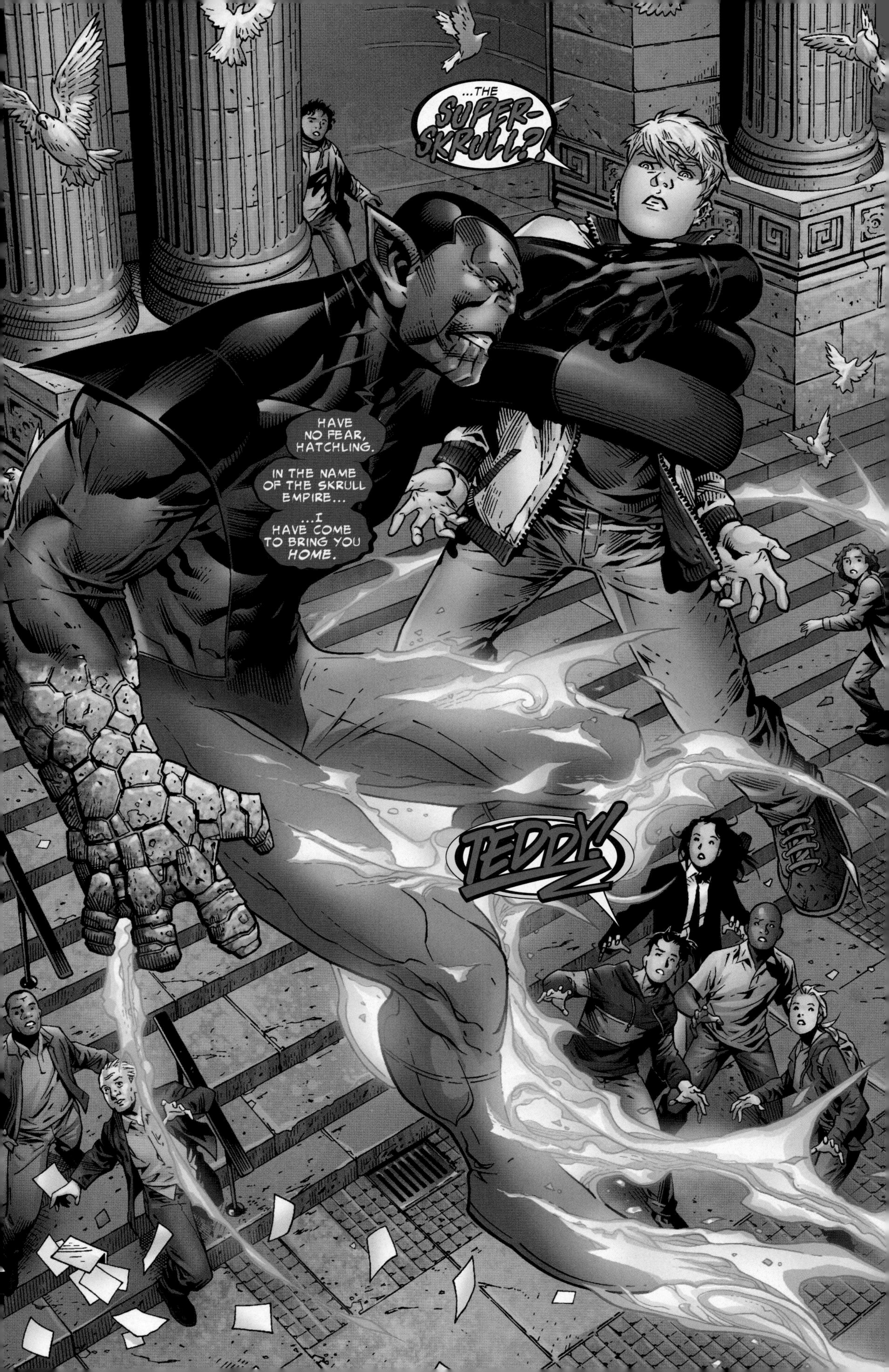
...THE SUPER-SKRULL?!
HAVE NO FEAR, HATCHLING.
IN THE NAME OF THE SKRULL EMPIRE...
...I HAVE COME TO BRING YOU HOME.
TEDDY!

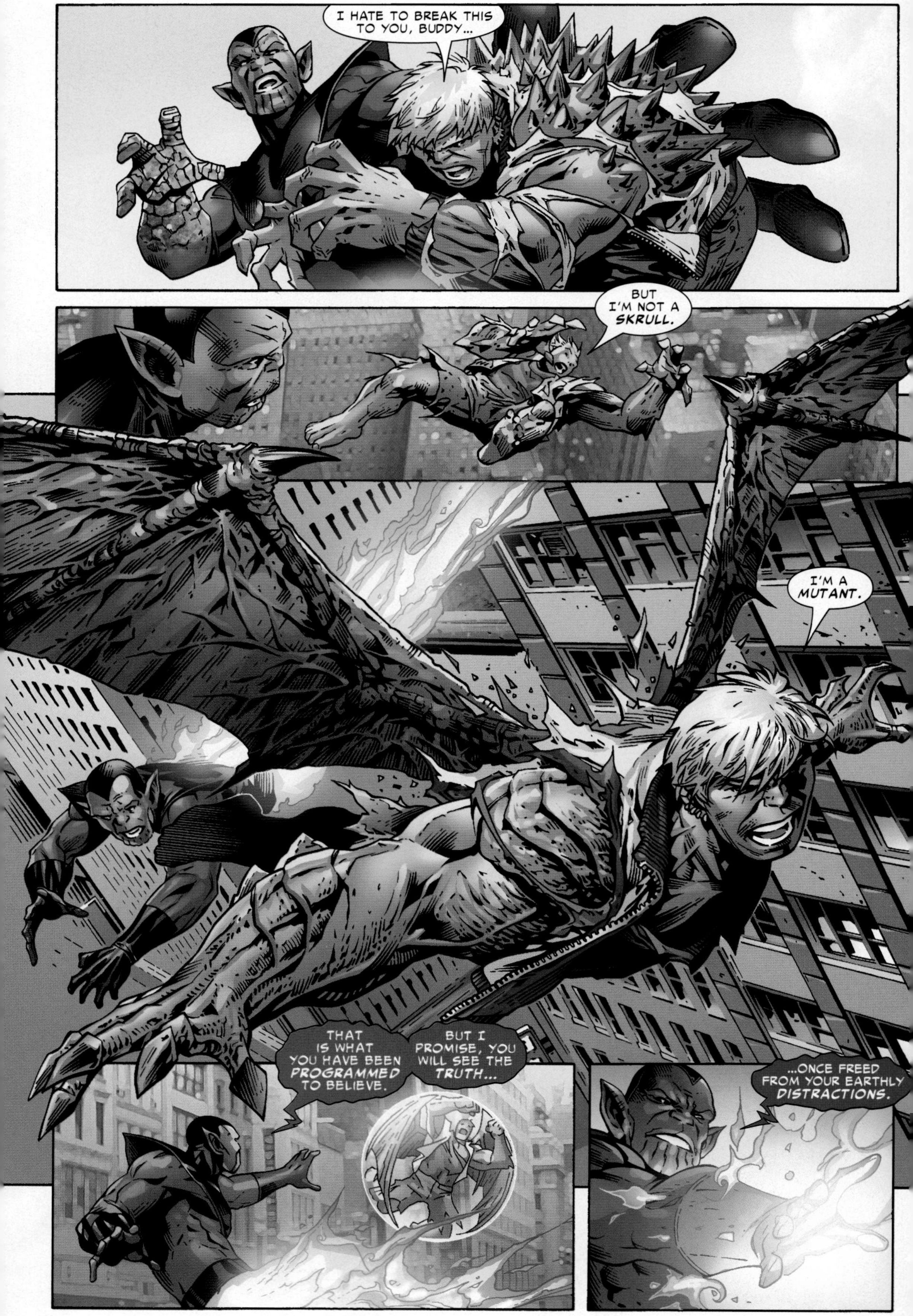
I HATE TO BREAK THIS TO YOU, BUDDY...
BUT I'M NOT A SKRULL.
I'M A MUTANT.
THAT IS WHAT YOU HAVE BEEN PROGRAMMED TO BELIEVE.
BUT I PROMISE, YOU WILL SEE THE TRUTH...
...ONCE FREED FROM YOUR EARTHLY DISTRACTIONS.

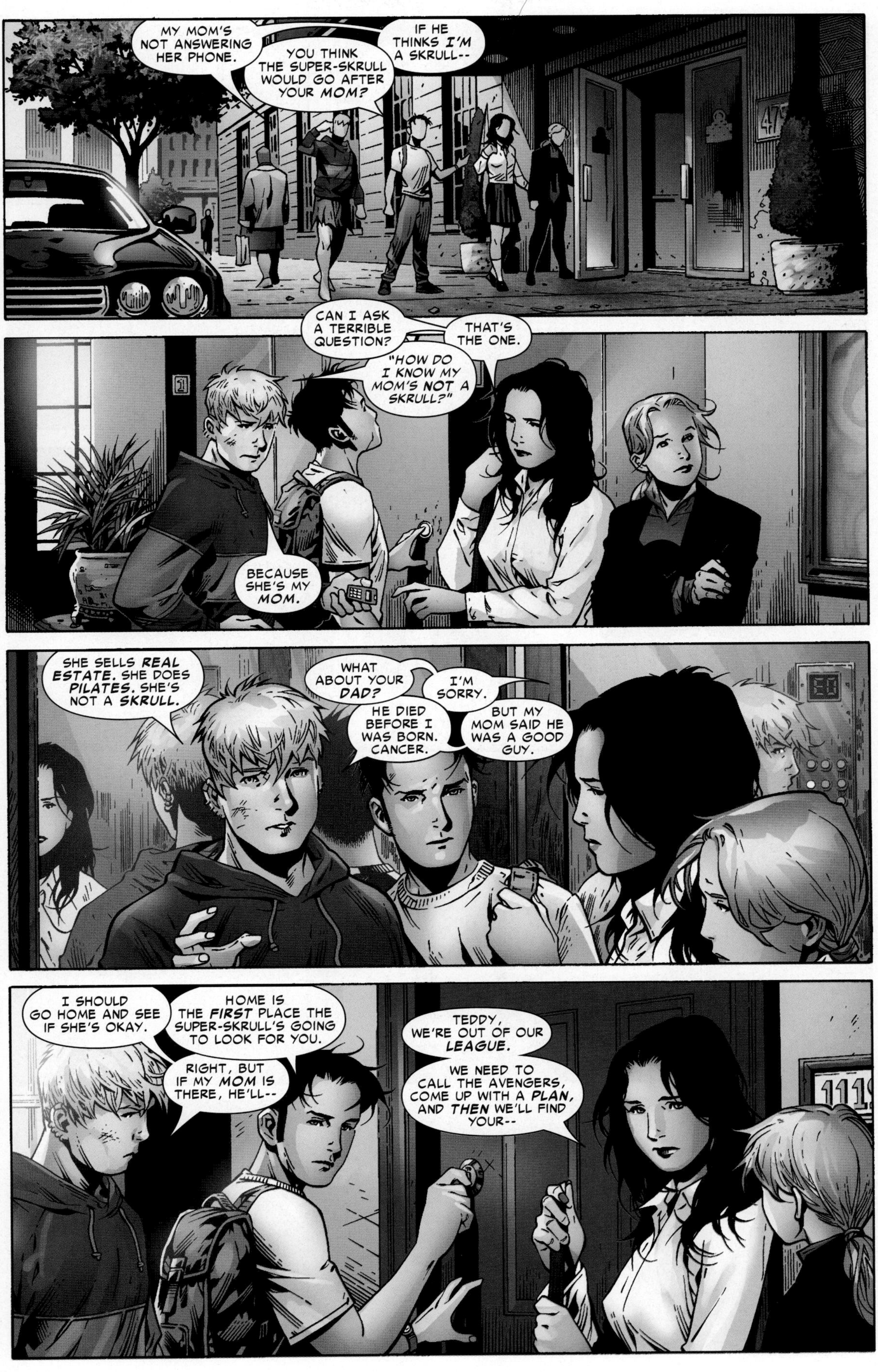
MY MOM'S NOT ANSWERING HER PHONE.
YOU THINK THE SUPER-SKRULL WOULD GO AFTER YOUR MOM?
IF HE THINKS I'M A SKRULL--
CAN I ASK A TERRIBLE QUESTION?
THAT'S THE ONE.
"HOW DO I KNOW MY MOM'S NOT A SKRULL?"
BECAUSE SHE'S MY MOM.
SHE SELLS REAL ESTATE. SHE DOES PILATES. SHE'S NOT A SKRULL.
WHAT ABOUT YOUR DAD?
I'M SORRY.
HE DIED BEFORE I WAS BORN. CANCER.
BUT MY MOM SAID HE WAS A GOOD GUY.
I SHOULD GO HOME AND SEE IF SHE'S OKAY.
HOME IS THE FIRST PLACE THE SUPER-SKRULL'S GOING TO LOOK FOR YOU.
RIGHT, BUT IF MY MOM IS THERE, HE'LL--
TEDDY, WE'RE OUT OF OUR LEAGUE.
WE NEED TO CALL THE AVENGERS, COME UP WITH A PLAN, AND THEN WE'LL FIND YOUR--

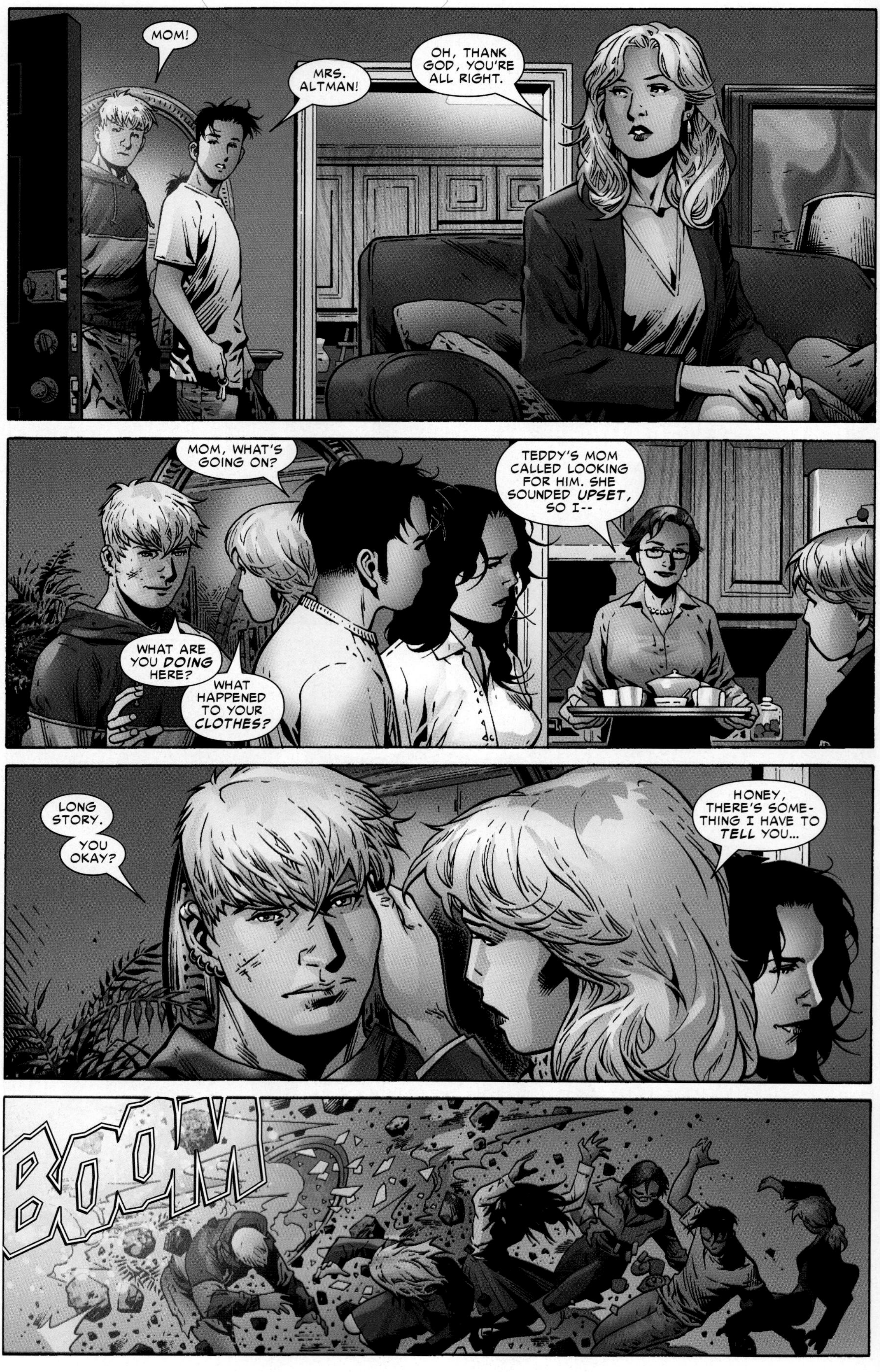
MOM!
MRS. ALTMAN!
OH, THANK GOD, YOU'RE ALL RIGHT.
MOM, WHAT'S GOING ON?
TEDDY'S MOM CALLED LOOKING FOR HIM. SHE SOUNDED UPSET, SO I--
WHAT ARE YOU DOING HERE?
WHAT HAPPENED TO YOUR CLOTHES?
LONG STORY.
YOU OKAY?
HONEY, THERE'S SOME-THING I HAVE TO TELL YOU...
BOOM

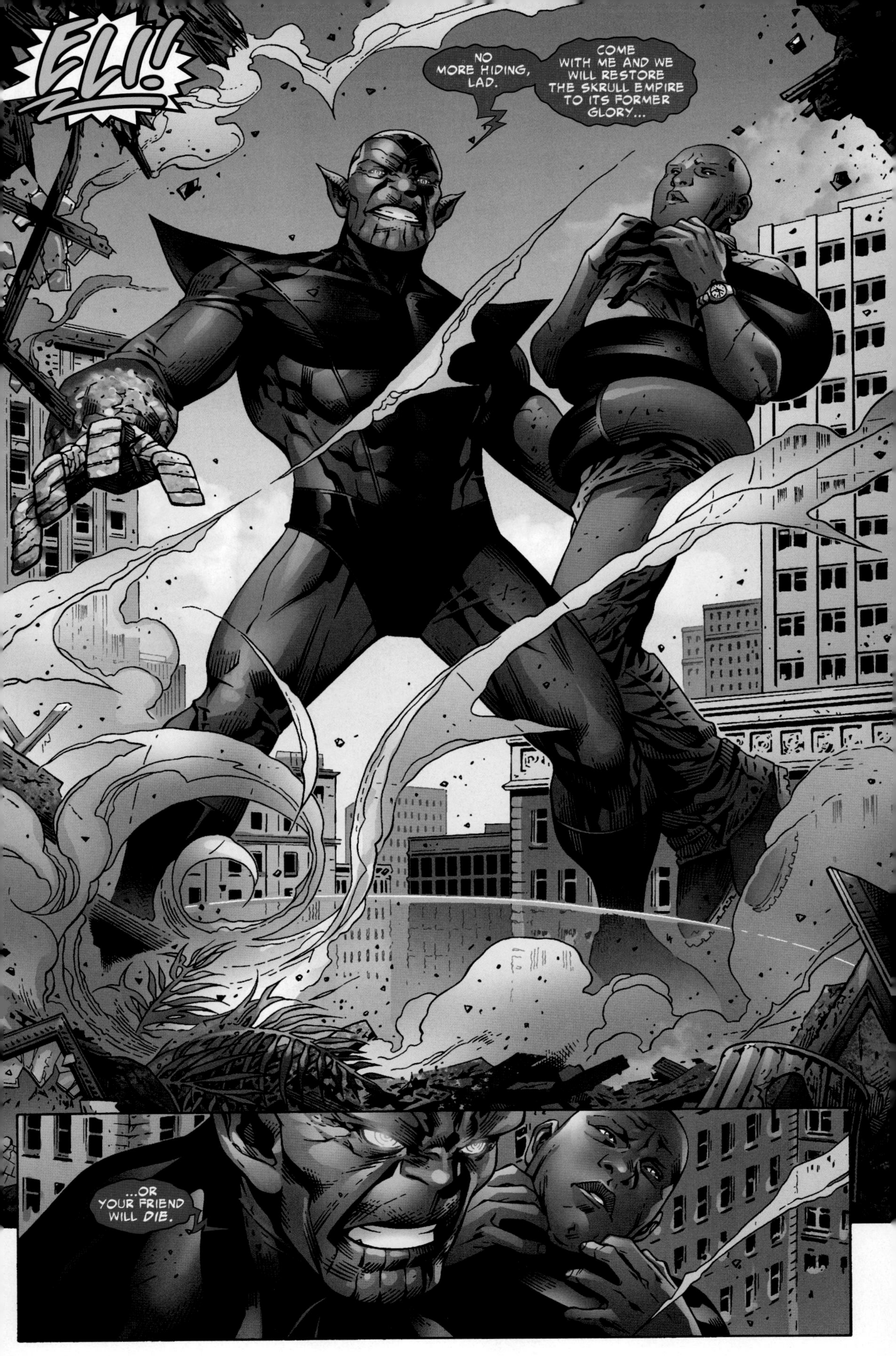
ELI!
NO MORE HIDING, LAD.
COME WITH ME AND WE WILL RESTORE THE SKRULL EMPIRE TO ITS FORMER GLORY...
...OR YOUR FRIEND WILL *DIE*.

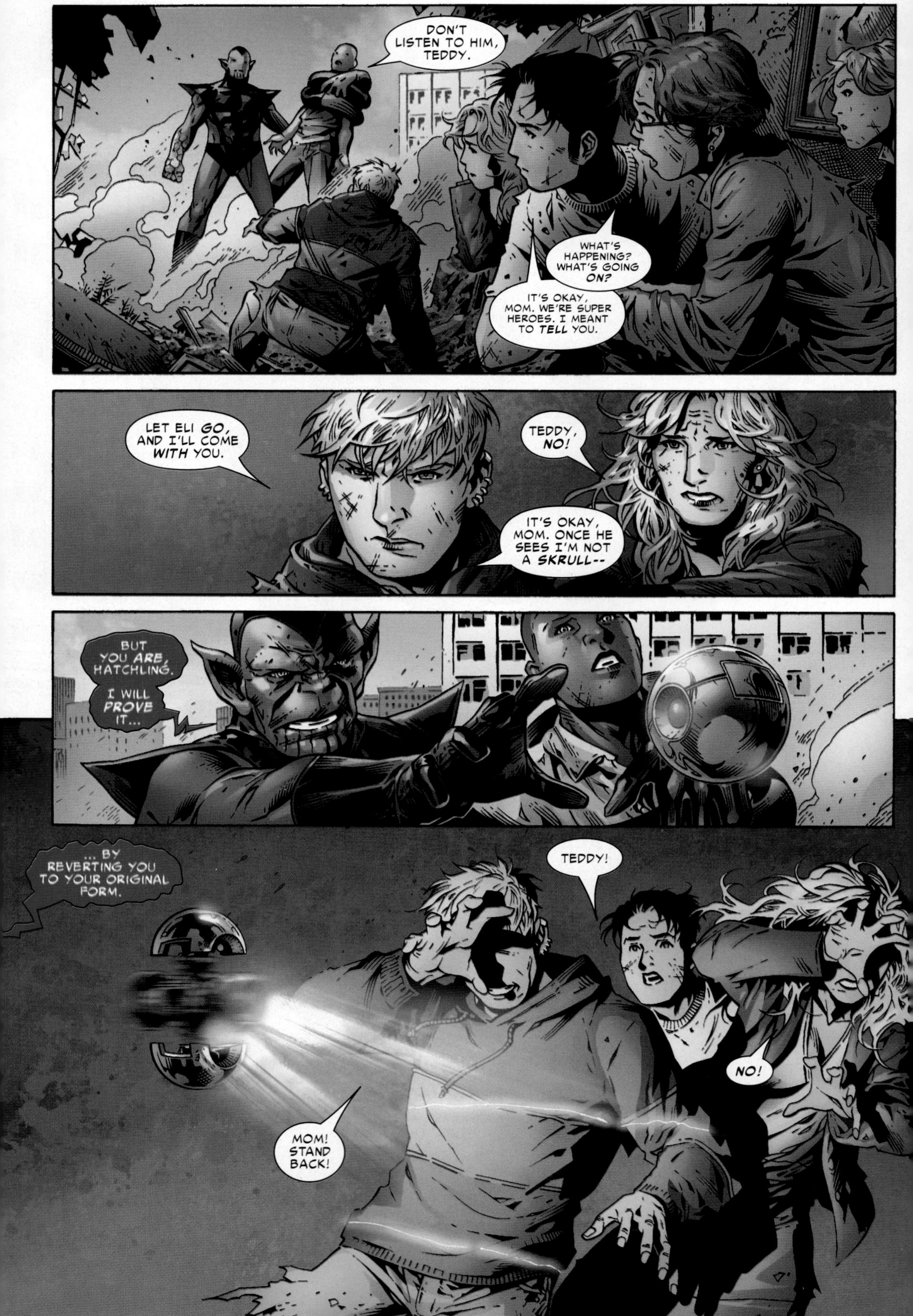
DON'T LISTEN TO HIM, TEDDY.
WHAT'S HAPPENING? WHAT'S GOING ON?
IT'S OKAY, MOM. WE'RE SUPER HEROES. I MEANT TO TELL YOU.
LET ELI GO, AND I'LL COME WITH YOU.
TEDDY, NO!
IT'S OKAY, MOM. ONCE HE SEES I'M NOT A SKRULL--
BUT YOU ARE, HATCHLING.
I WILL PROVE IT...
... BY REVERTING YOU TO YOUR ORIGINAL FORM.
TEDDY!
NO!
MOM! STAND BACK!

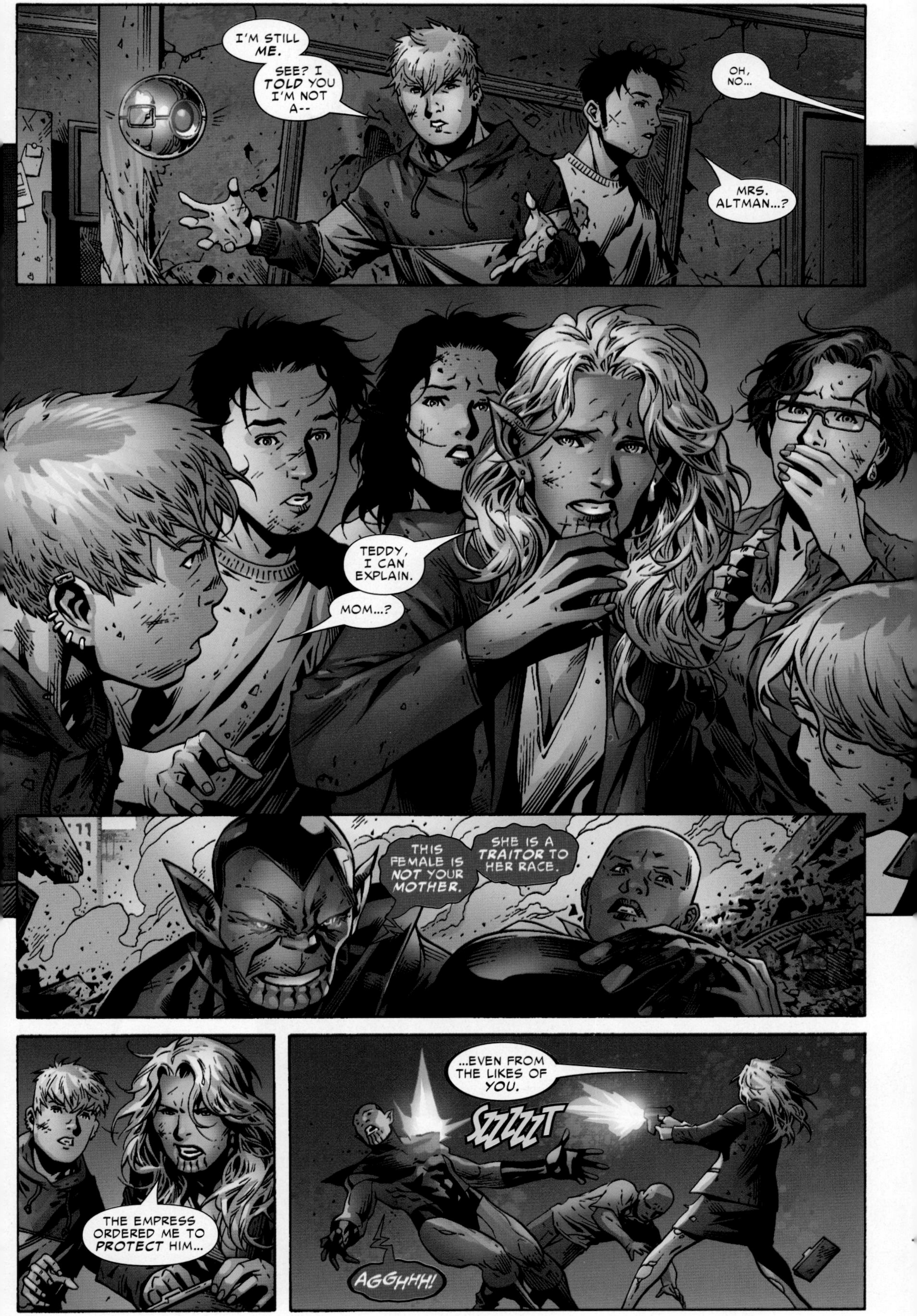
I'M STILL ME.
SEE? I TOLD YOU I'M NOT A--
OH, NO...
MRS. ALTMAN...?
TEDDY, I CAN EXPLAIN.
MOM...?
THIS FEMALE IS NOT YOUR MOTHER.
SHE IS A TRAITOR TO HER RACE.
THE EMPRESS ORDERED ME TO PROTECT HIM...
...EVEN FROM THE LIKES OF YOU.
SZZZZZT
AGGHHH!

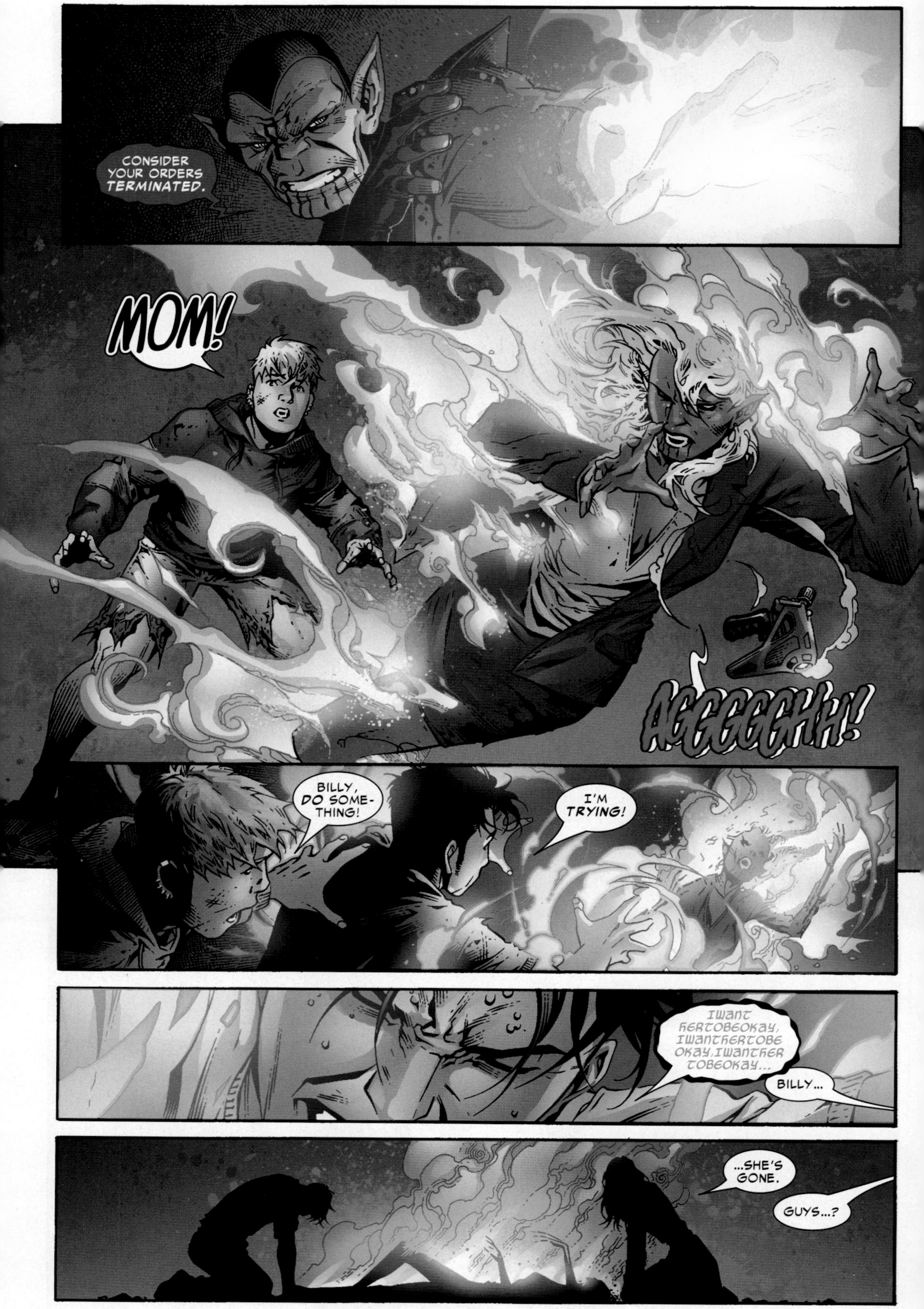
CONSIDER YOUR ORDERS TERMINATED.
MOM!
AGGGGGHH!
BILLY, DO SOME-THING!
I'M TRYING!
IWANT HERTOBEOKAY, IWANTHERTOBE OKAY,IWANTHER TOBEOKAY...
BILLY...
...SHE'S GONE.
GUYS...?

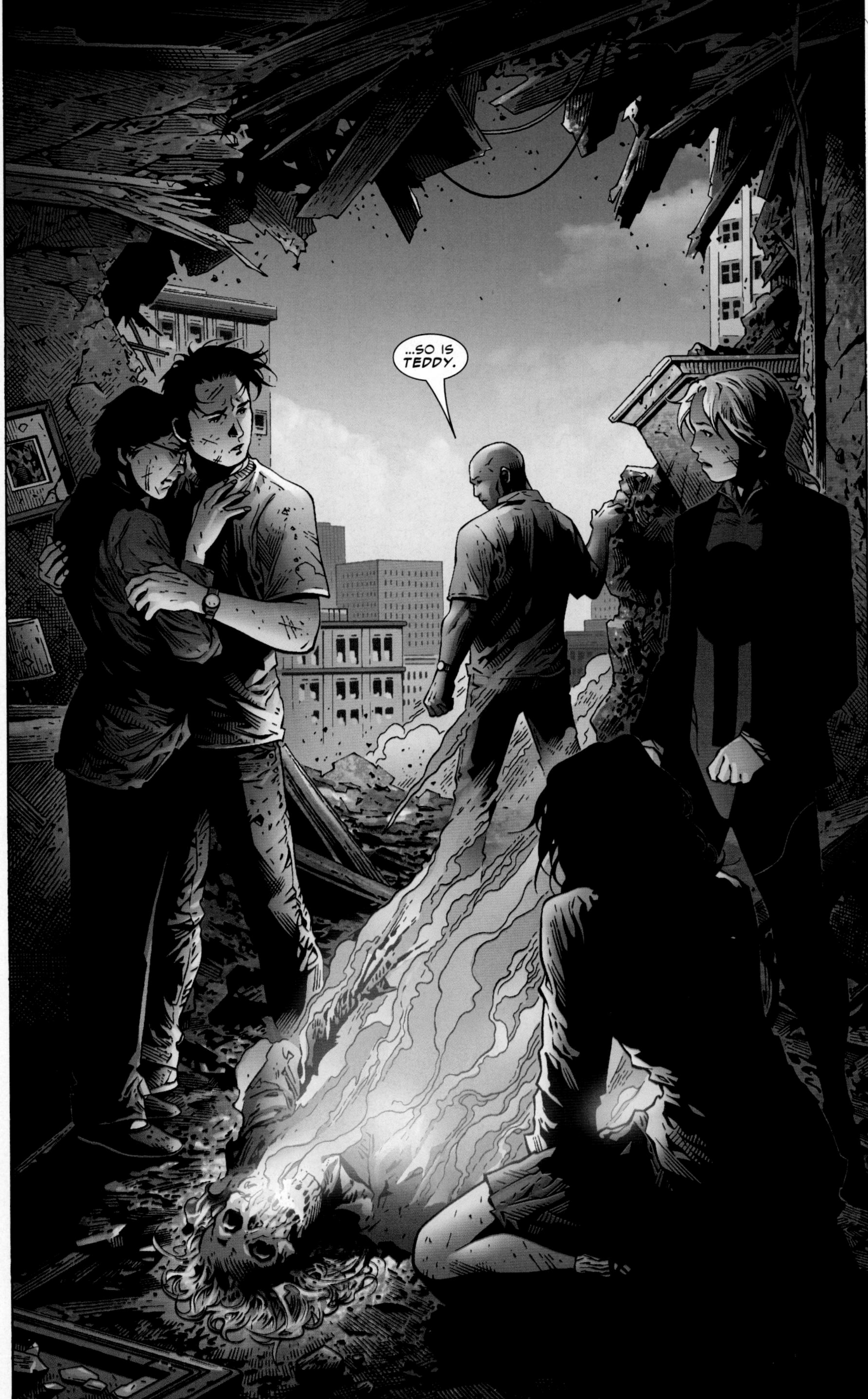
...SO IS TEDDY.

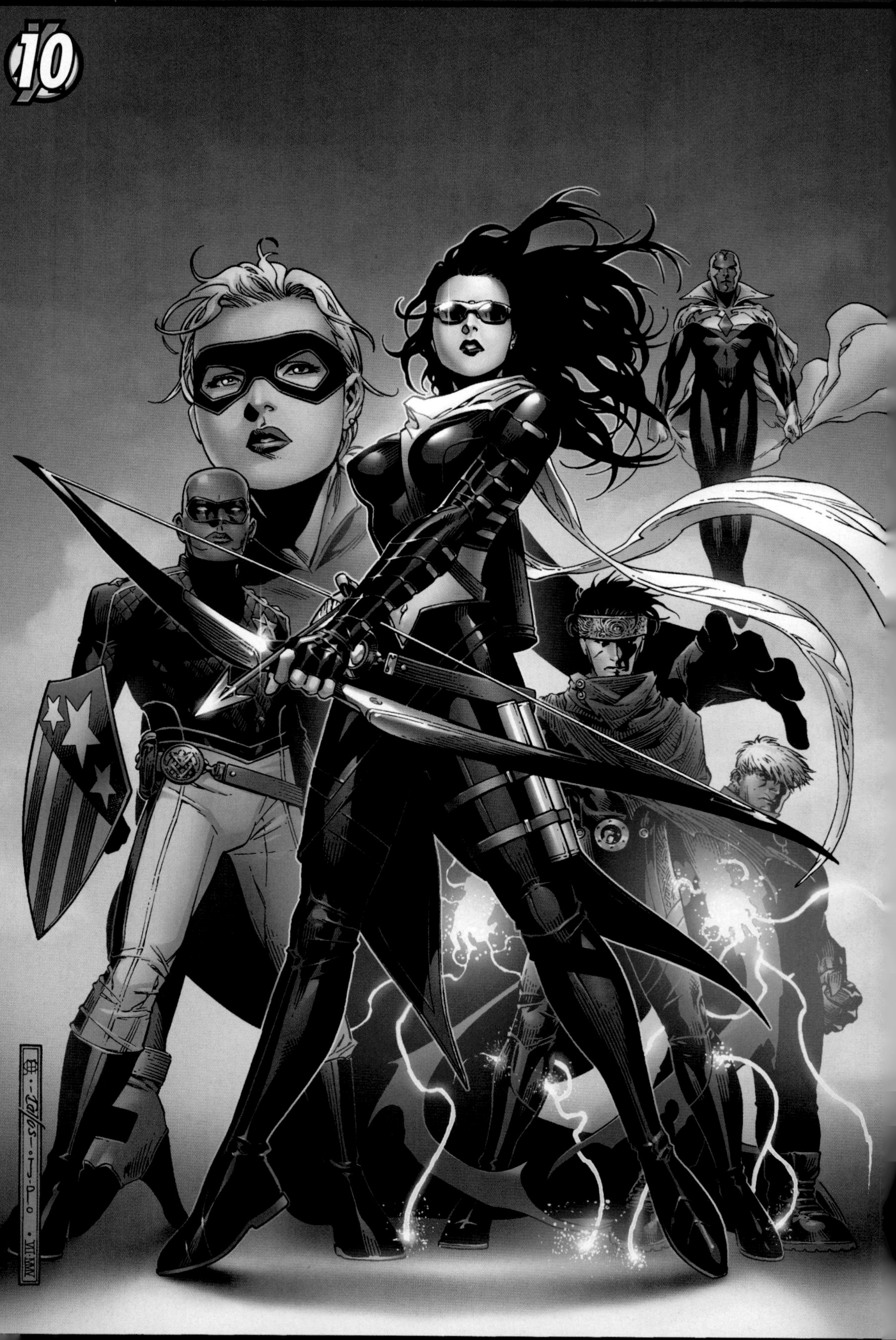
10

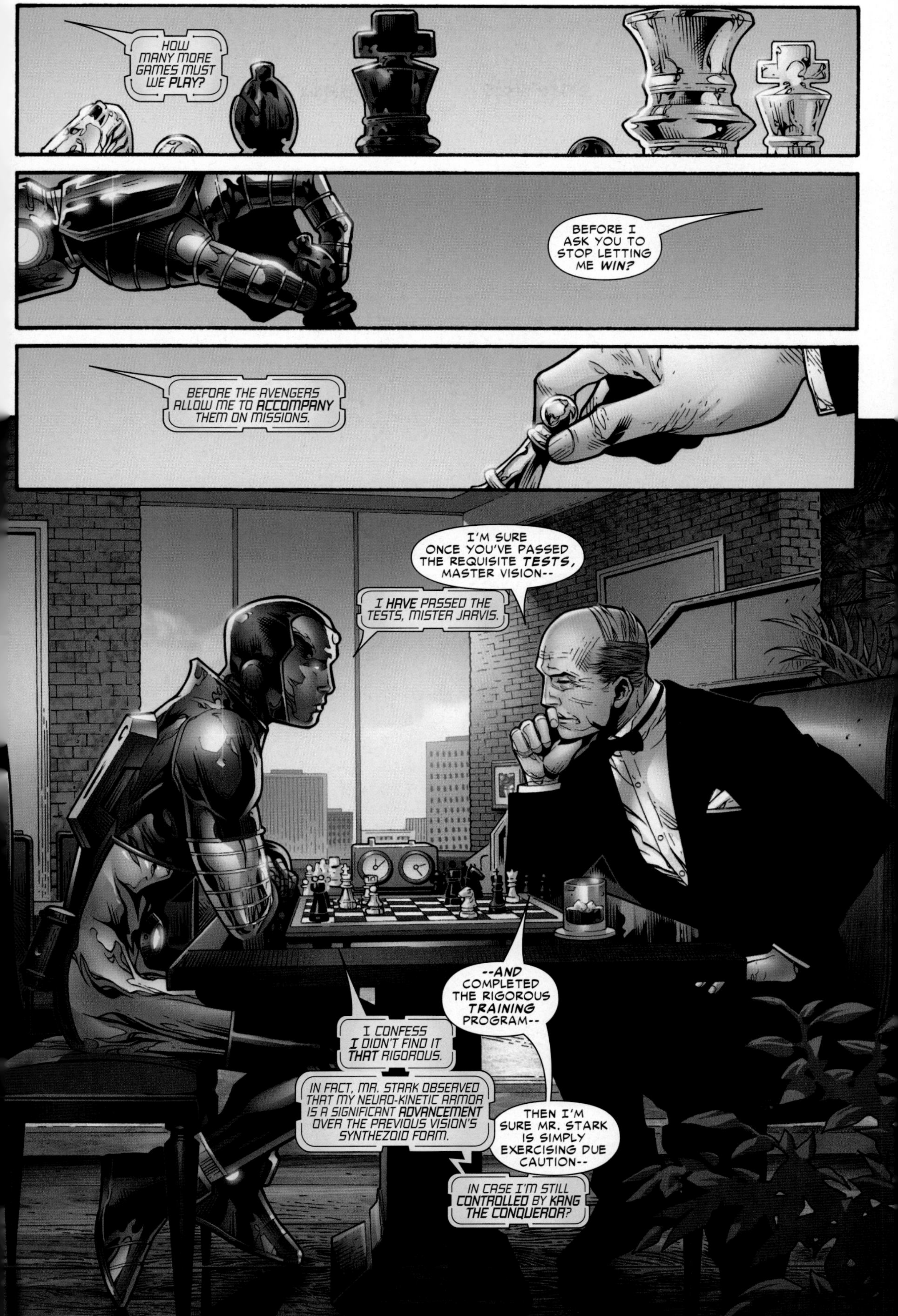

HOW MANY MORE GAMES MUST WE PLAY?
BEFORE I ASK YOU TO STOP LETTING ME WIN?
BEFORE THE AVENGERS ALLOW ME TO ACCOMPANY THEM ON MISSIONS.
I'M SURE ONCE YOU'VE PASSED THE REQUISITE TESTS, MASTER VISION--
I HAVE PASSED THE TESTS, MISTER JARVIS.
--AND COMPLETED THE RIGOROUS TRAINING PROGRAM--
I CONFESS I DIDN'T FIND IT THAT RIGOROUS.
IN FACT, MR. STARK OBSERVED THAT MY NEURO-KINETIC ARMOR IS A SIGNIFICANT ADVANCEMENT OVER THE PREVIOUS VISION'S SYNTHEZOID FORM.
THEN I'M SURE MR. STARK IS SIMPLY EXERCISING DUE CAUTION--
IN CASE I'M STILL CONTROLLED BY KANG THE CONQUEROR?

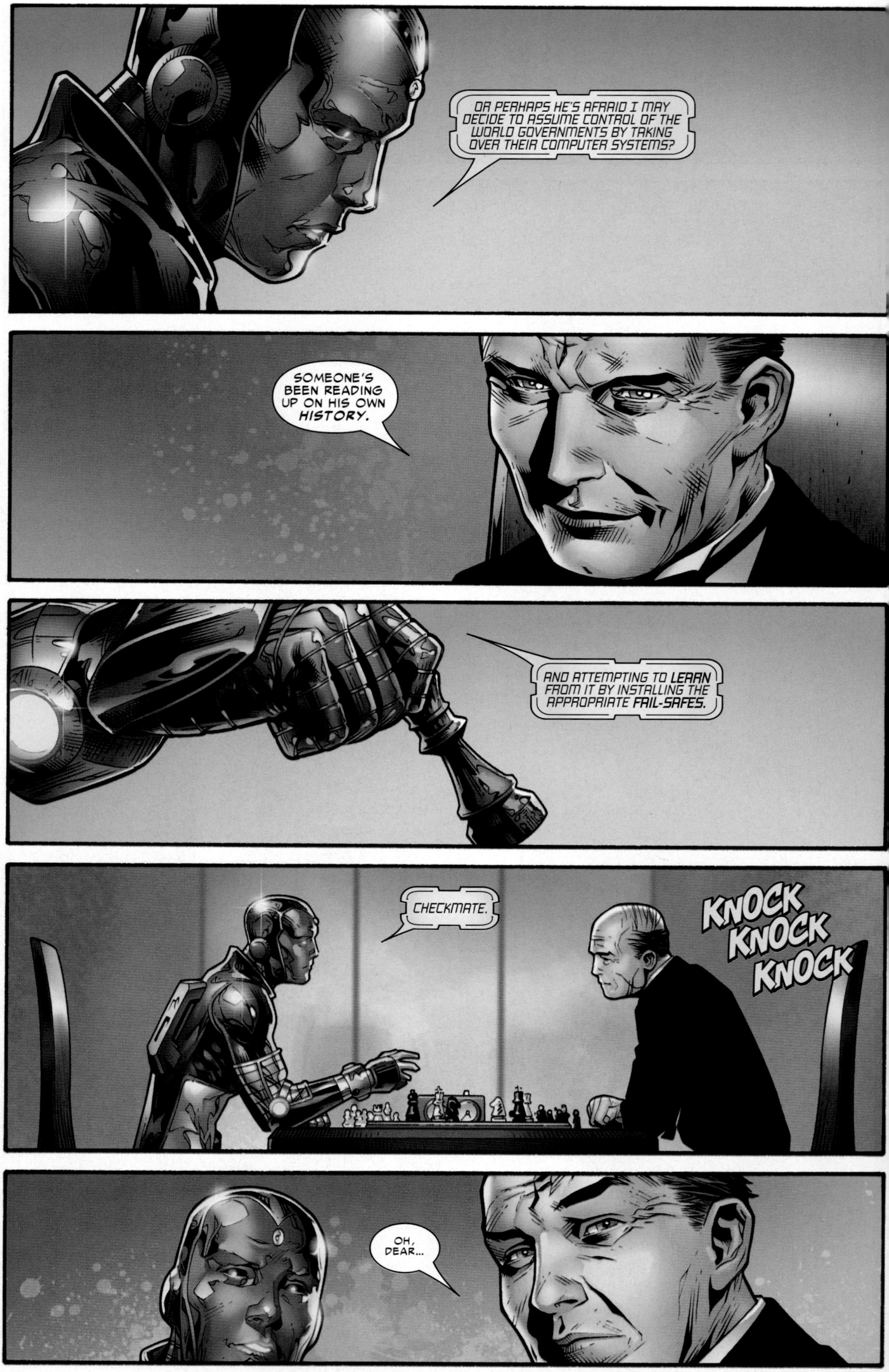
OR PERHAPS HE'S AFRAID I MAY DECIDE TO ASSUME CONTROL OF THE WORLD GOVERNMENTS BY TAKING OVER THEIR COMPUTER SYSTEMS?
SOMEONE'S BEEN READING UP ON HIS OWN HISTORY.
AND ATTEMPTING TO LEARN FROM IT BY INSTALLING THE APPROPRIATE FAIL-SAFES.
CHECKMATE.
KNOCK KNOCK KNOCK
OH, DEAR...

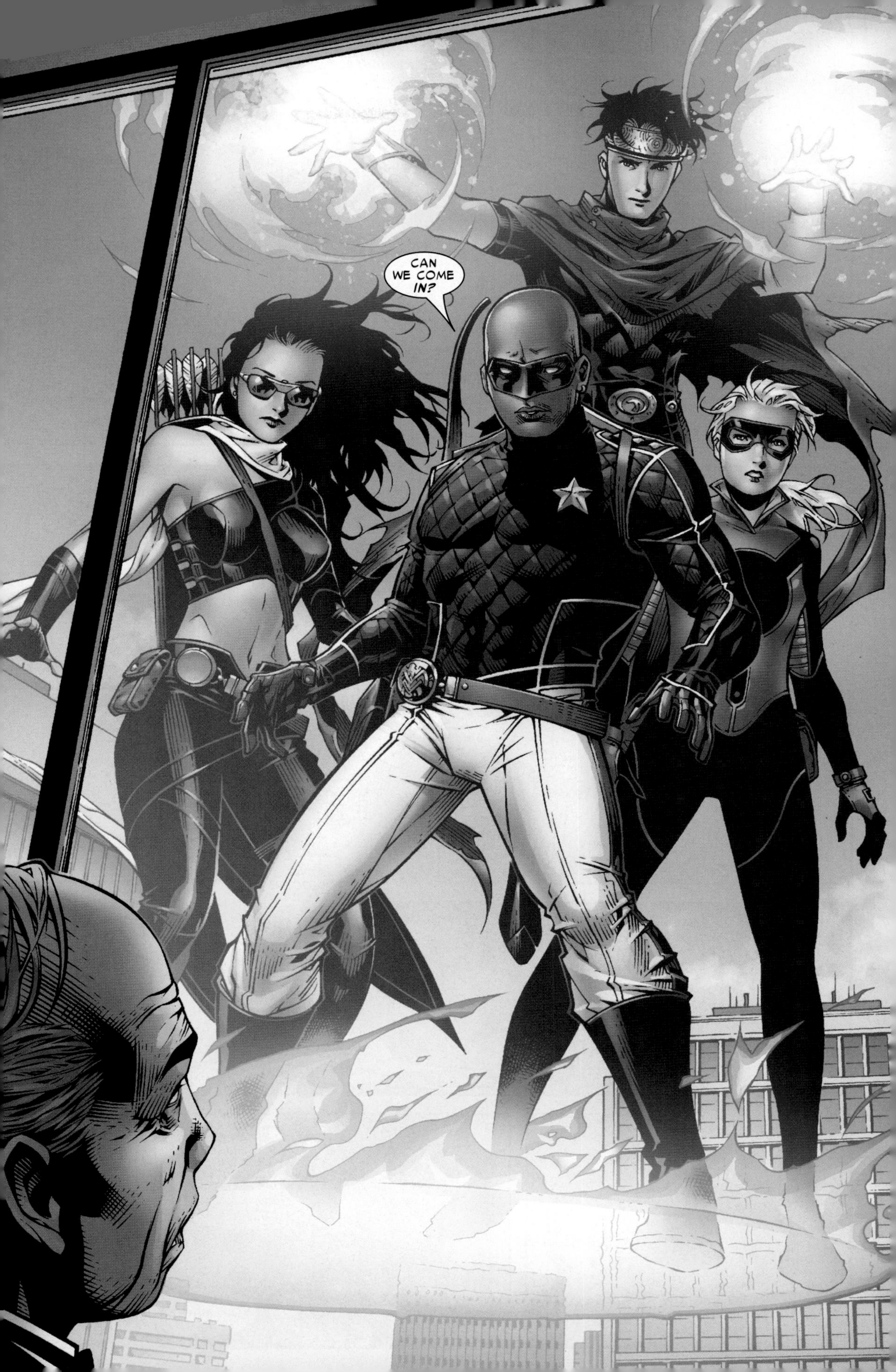
CAN WE COME IN?

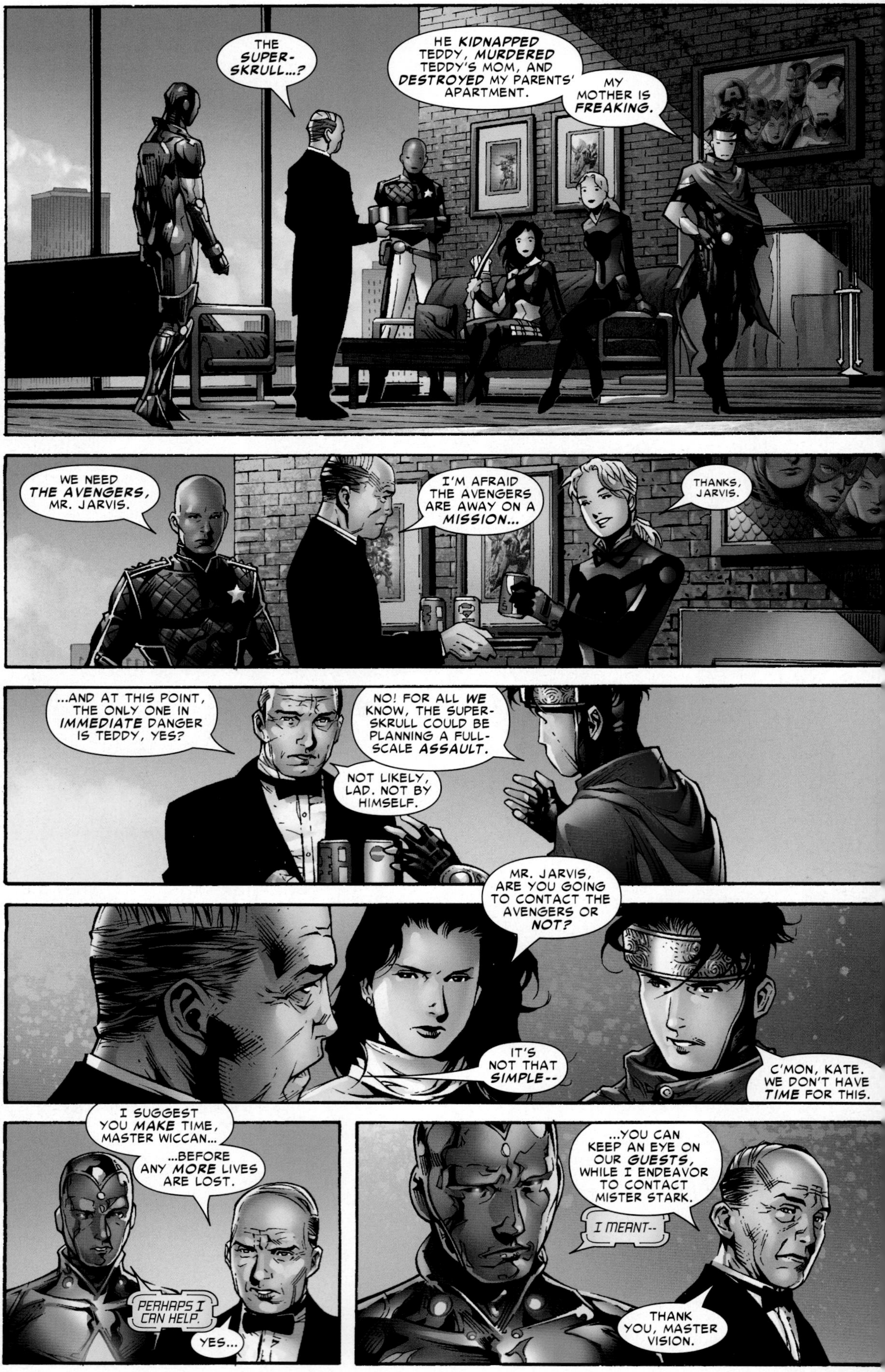
THE SUPER-SKRULL...?
HE KIDNAPPED TEDDY, MURDERED TEDDY'S MOM, AND DESTROYED MY PARENTS' APARTMENT.
MY MOTHER IS FREAKING.
WE NEED THE AVENGERS, MR. JARVIS.
I'M AFRAID THE AVENGERS ARE AWAY ON A MISSION...
THANKS, JARVIS.
...AND AT THIS POINT, THE ONLY ONE IN IMMEDIATE DANGER IS TEDDY, YES?
NO! FOR ALL WE KNOW, THE SUPER-SKRULL COULD BE PLANNING A FULL-SCALE ASSAULT.
NOT LIKELY, LAD. NOT BY HIMSELF.
MR. JARVIS, ARE YOU GOING TO CONTACT THE AVENGERS OR NOT?
IT'S NOT THAT SIMPLE--
C'MON, KATE. WE DON'T HAVE TIME FOR THIS.
I SUGGEST YOU MAKE TIME, MASTER WICCAN...
...BEFORE ANY MORE LIVES ARE LOST.
PERHAPS I CAN HELP.
YES...
...YOU CAN KEEP AN EYE ON OUR GUESTS, WHILE I ENDEAVOR TO CONTACT MISTER STARK.
I MEANT--
THANK YOU, MASTER VISION.

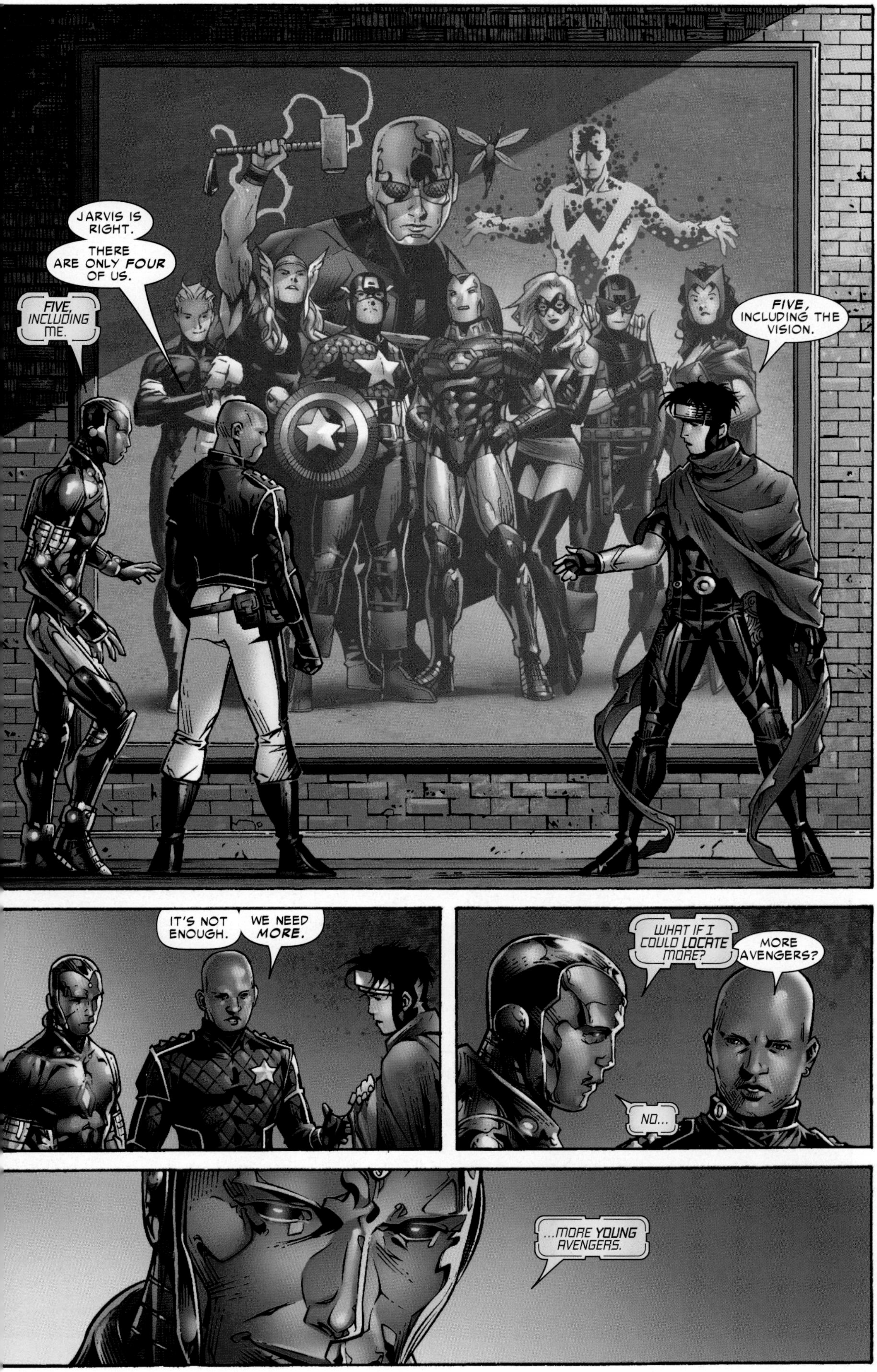
JARVIS IS RIGHT.
THERE ARE ONLY FOUR OF US.
FIVE, INCLUDING ME.
FIVE, INCLUDING THE VISION.
IT'S NOT ENOUGH.
WE NEED MORE.
WHAT IF I COULD LOCATE MORE?
MORE AVENGERS?
NO...
...MORE YOUNG AVENGERS.

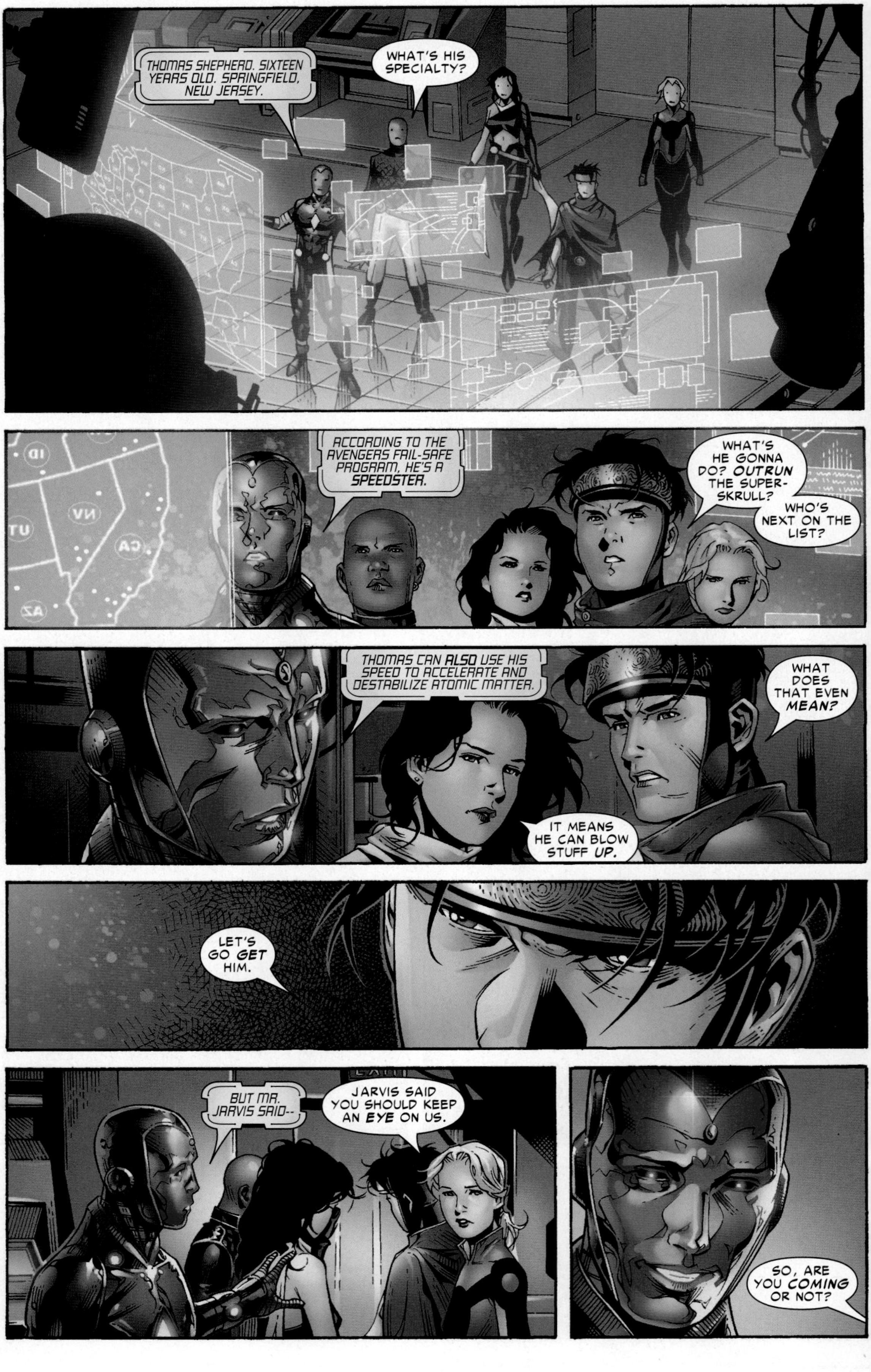
THOMAS SHEPHERD. SIXTEEN YEARS OLD. SPRINGFIELD, NEW JERSEY.
WHAT'S HIS SPECIALTY?
ACCORDING TO THE AVENGERS FAIL-SAFE PROGRAM, HE'S A SPEEDSTER.
WHAT'S HE GONNA DO? OUTRUN THE SUPER-SKRULL?
WHO'S NEXT ON THE LIST?
THOMAS CAN ALSO USE HIS SPEED TO ACCELERATE AND DESTABILIZE ATOMIC MATTER.
WHAT DOES THAT EVEN MEAN?
IT MEANS HE CAN BLOW STUFF UP.
LET'S GO GET HIM.
BUT MR. JARVIS SAID--
JARVIS SAID YOU SHOULD KEEP AN EYE ON US.
SO, ARE YOU COMING OR NOT?

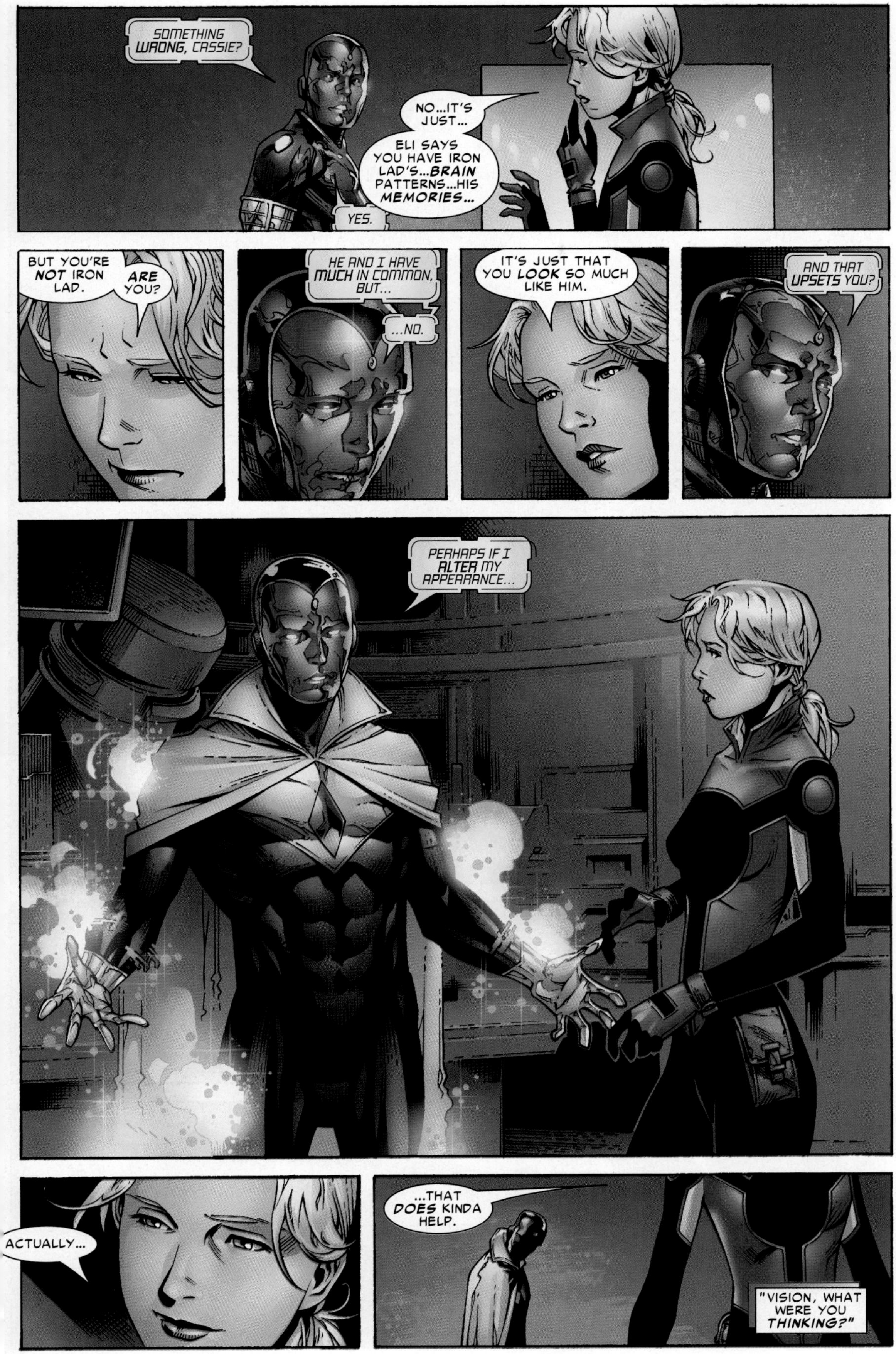
SOMETHING WRONG, CASSIE?
NO...IT'S JUST...
ELI SAYS YOU HAVE IRON LAD'S...BRAIN PATTERNS...HIS MEMORIES...
YES.
BUT YOU'RE NOT IRON LAD.
ARE YOU?
HE AND I HAVE MUCH IN COMMON, BUT...
...NO.
IT'S JUST THAT YOU LOOK SO MUCH LIKE HIM.
AND THAT UPSETS YOU?
PERHAPS IF I ALTER MY APPEARANCE...
ACTUALLY...
...THAT DOES KINDA HELP.
"VISION, WHAT WERE YOU THINKING?"

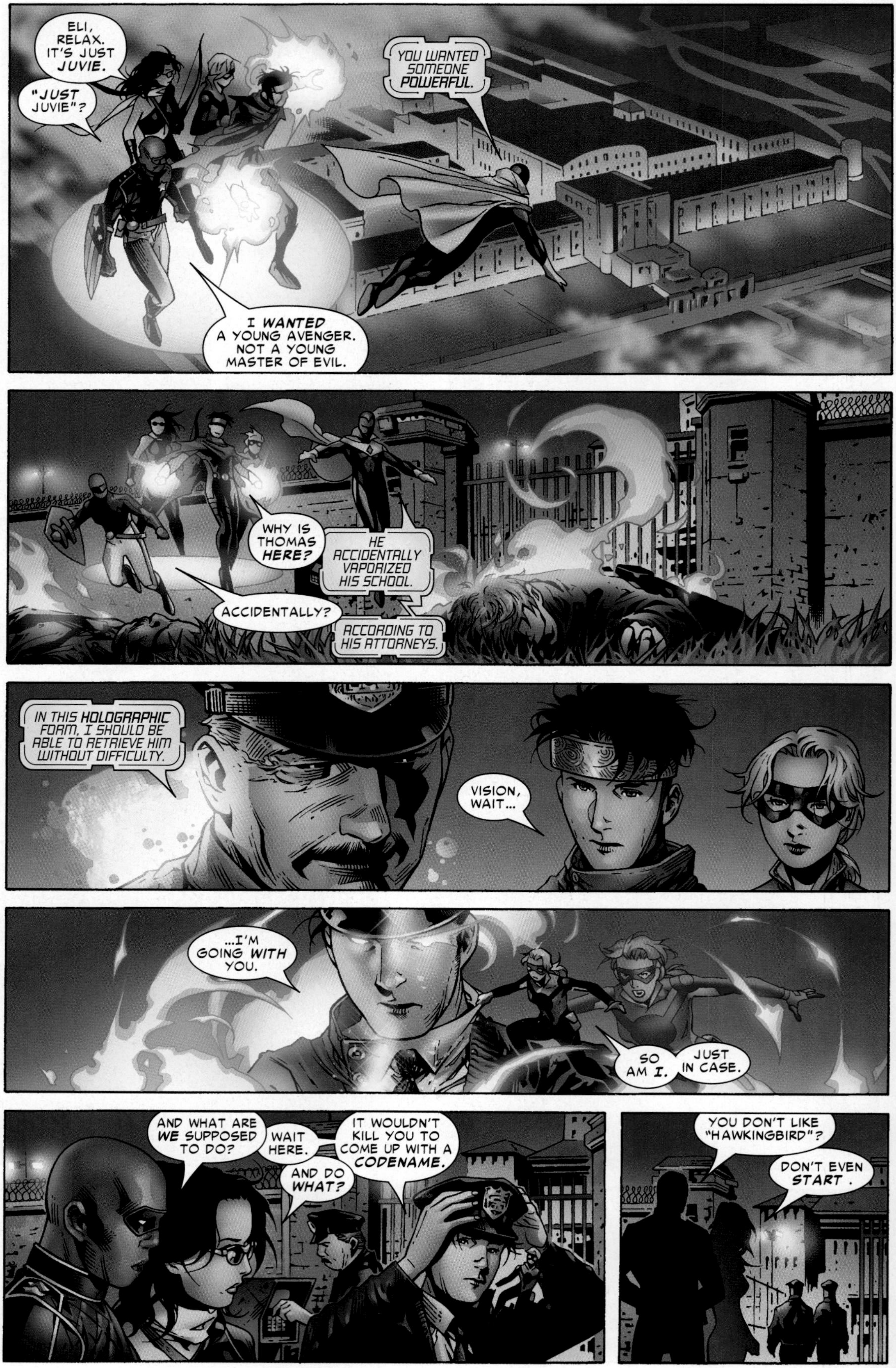
ELI, RELAX. IT'S JUST JUVIE.
"JUST JUVIE"?
YOU WANTED SOMEONE POWERFUL.
I WANTED A YOUNG AVENGER. NOT A YOUNG MASTER OF EVIL.
WHY IS THOMAS HERE?
HE ACCIDENTALLY VAPORIZED HIS SCHOOL.
ACCIDENTALLY?
ACCORDING TO HIS ATTORNEYS.
IN THIS HOLOGRAPHIC FORM, I SHOULD BE ABLE TO RETRIEVE HIM WITHOUT DIFFICULTY.
VISION, WAIT...
...I'M GOING WITH YOU.
SO AM I.
JUST IN CASE.
AND WHAT ARE WE SUPPOSED TO DO?
WAIT HERE.
AND DO WHAT?
IT WOULDN'T KILL YOU TO COME UP WITH A CODENAME.
YOU DON'T LIKE "HAWKINGBIRD"?
DON'T EVEN START.

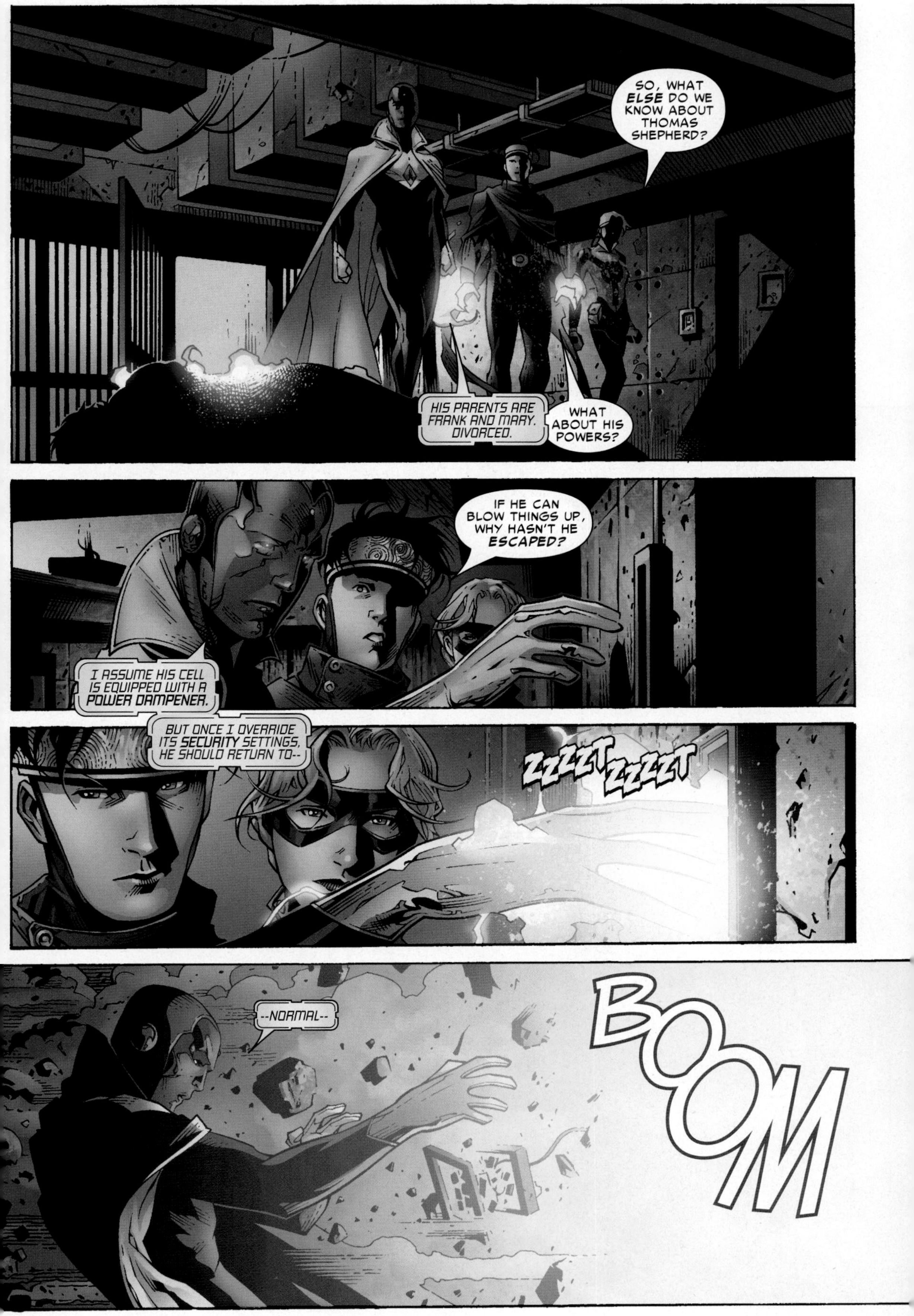
SO, WHAT ELSE DO WE KNOW ABOUT THOMAS SHEPHERD?
HIS PARENTS ARE FRANK AND MARY. DIVORCED.
WHAT ABOUT HIS POWERS?
IF HE CAN BLOW THINGS UP, WHY HASN'T HE ESCAPED?
I ASSUME HIS CELL IS EQUIPPED WITH A POWER DAMPENER.
BUT ONCE I OVERRIDE ITS SECURITY SETTINGS, HE SHOULD RETURN TO--
ZZZZT ZZZZT
--NORMAL--
BOOM

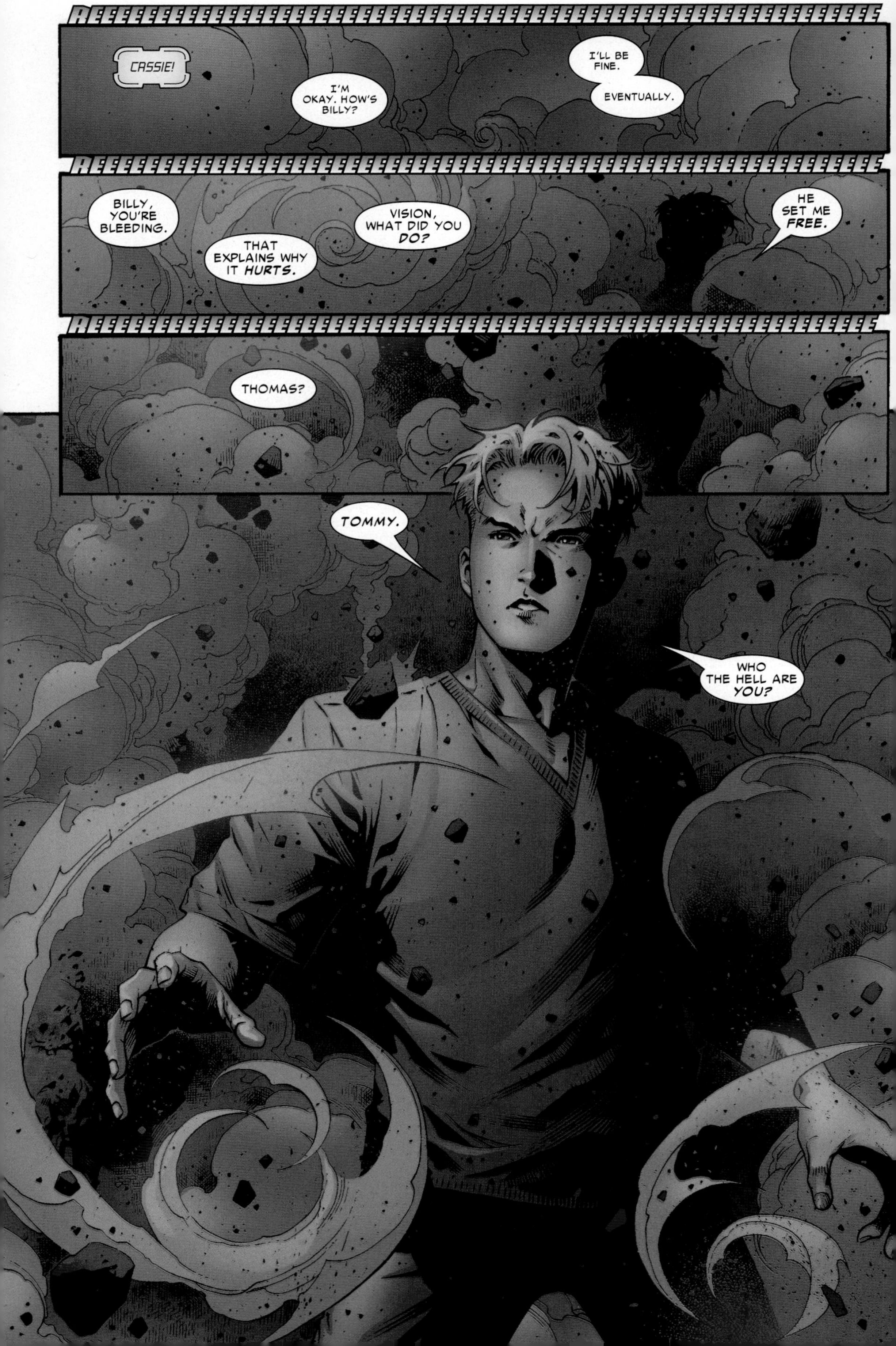

REEEEEEEEEEEEEEEEEEEEEEEEEEEEEEEEEEEEEEEEEEEEEEEEEEEEEEEEEEE
CASSIE!
I'M OKAY. HOW'S BILLY?
I'LL BE FINE.
EVENTUALLY.
REEEEEEEEEEEEEEEEEEEEEEEEEEEEEEEEEEEEEEEEEEEEEEEEEEEEEEEEEEE
BILLY, YOU'RE BLEEDING.
THAT EXPLAINS WHY IT HURTS.
VISION, WHAT DID YOU DO?
HE SET ME FREE.
REEEEEEEEEEEEEEEEEEEEEEEEEEEEEEEEEEEEEEEEEEEEEEEEEEEEEEEEEEE
THOMAS?
TOMMY.
WHO THE HELL ARE YOU?

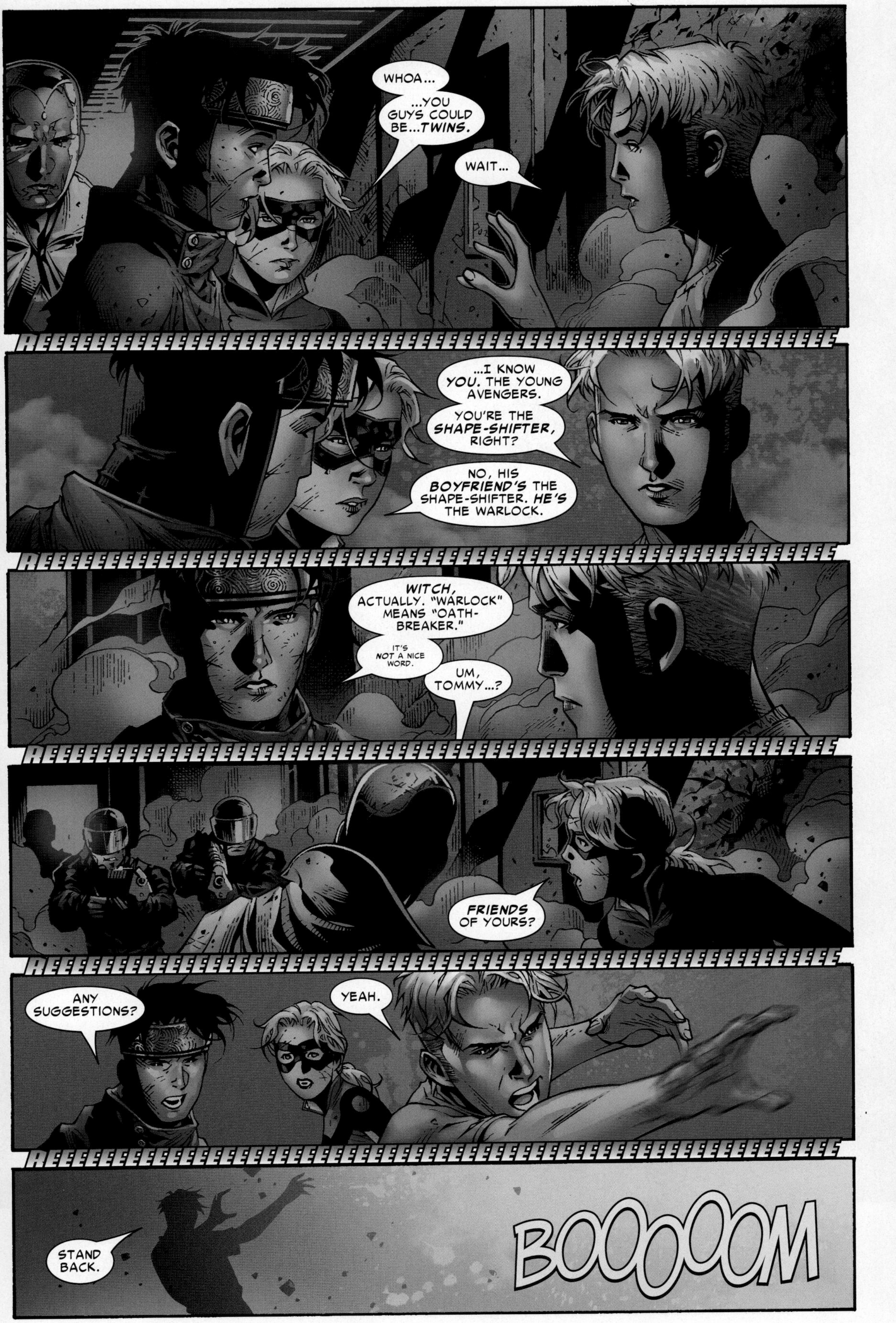
WHOA...
...YOU GUYS COULD BE...TWINS.
WAIT...
...I KNOW YOU. THE YOUNG AVENGERS.
YOU'RE THE SHAPE-SHIFTER, RIGHT?
NO, HIS BOYFRIEND'S THE SHAPE-SHIFTER. HE'S THE WARLOCK.
WITCH, ACTUALLY. "WARLOCK" MEANS "OATH-BREAKER."
IT'S NOT A NICE WORD.
UM, TOMMY...?
FRIENDS OF YOURS?
ANY SUGGESTIONS?
YEAH.
STAND BACK.
BOOOOOM

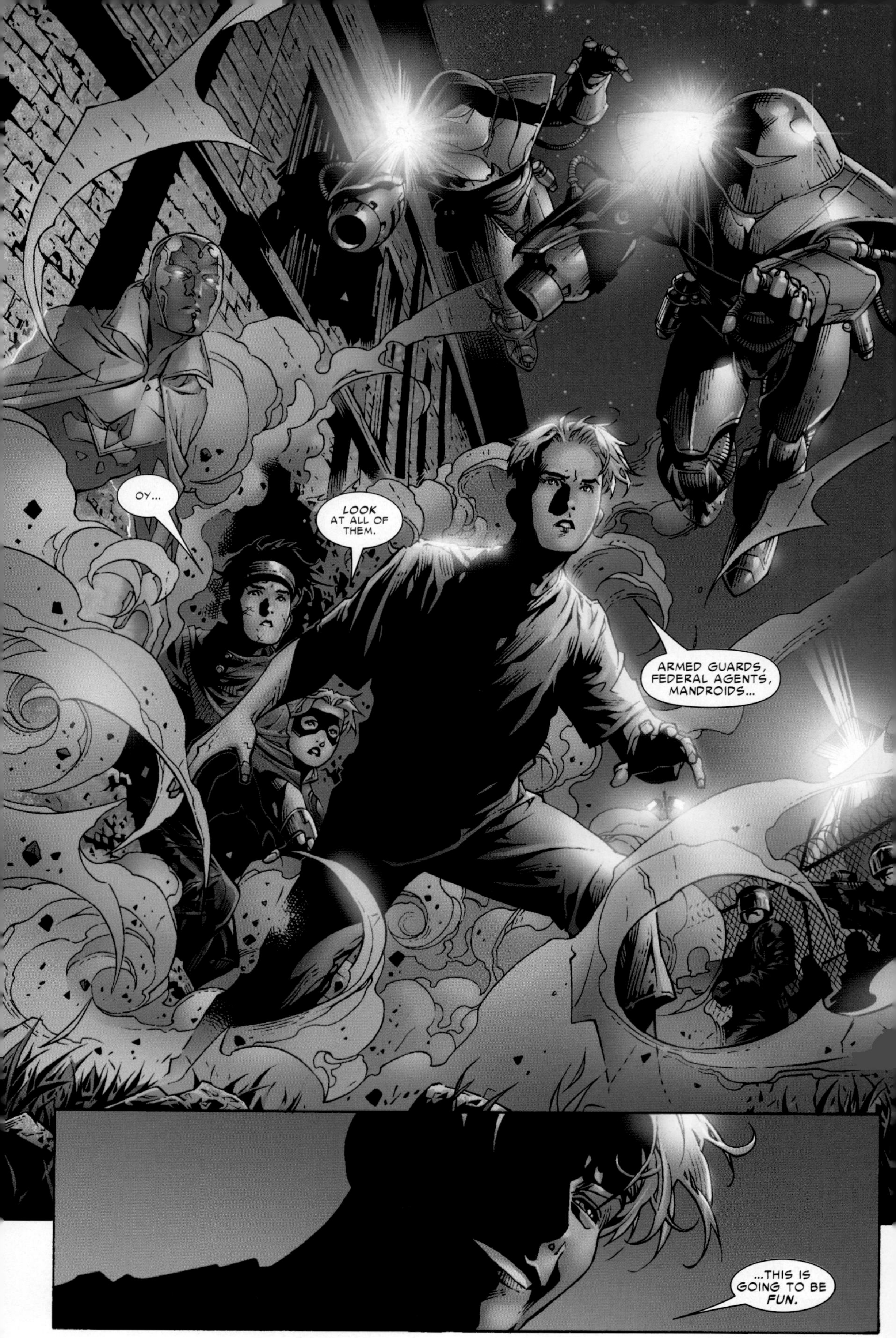
OY...
LOOK AT ALL OF THEM.
ARMED GUARDS, FEDERAL AGENTS, MANDROIDS...
...THIS IS GOING TO BE FUN.

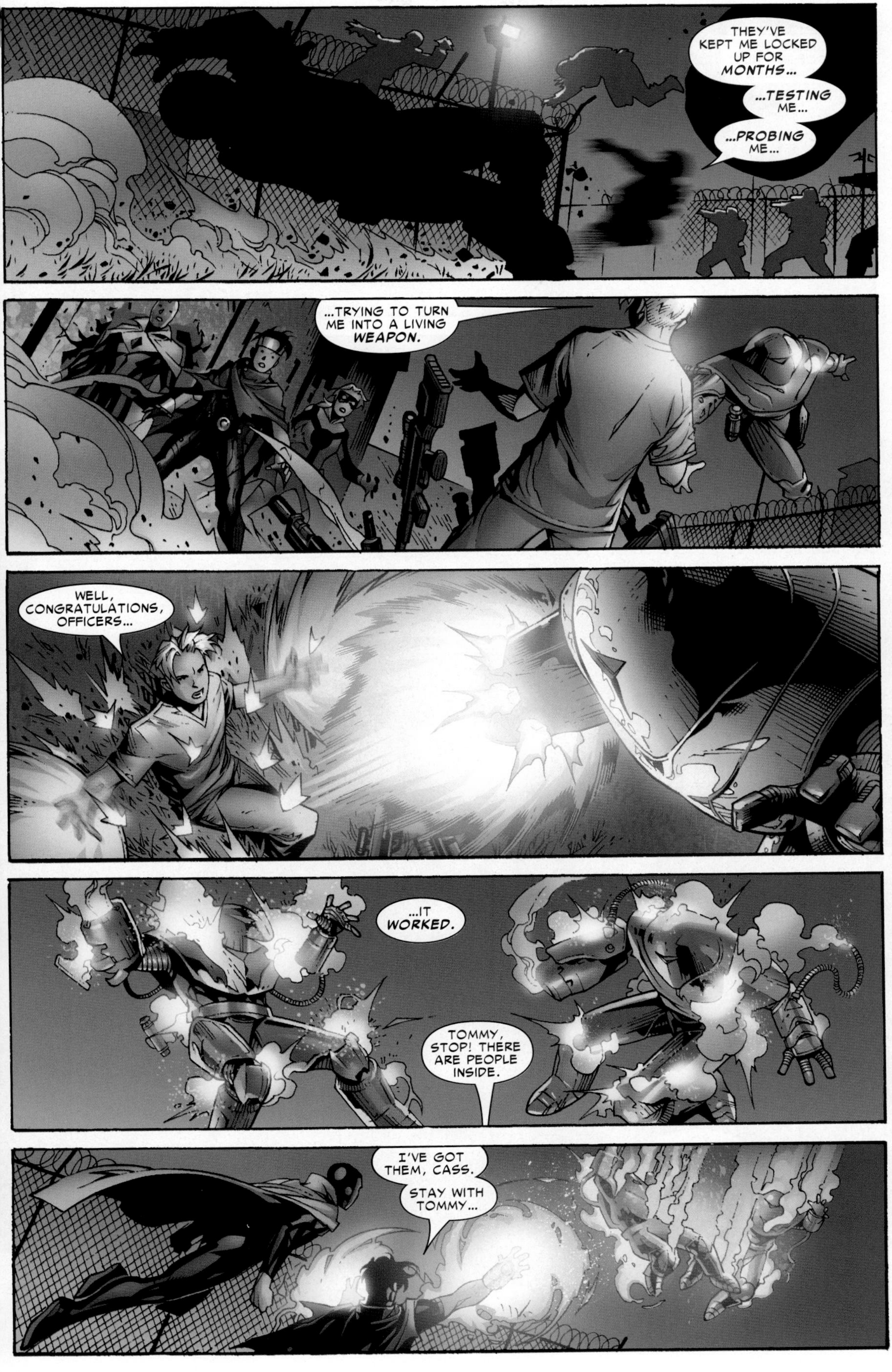
THEY'VE KEPT ME LOCKED UP FOR MONTHS...
...TESTING ME...
...PROBING ME...
...TRYING TO TURN ME INTO A LIVING WEAPON.
WELL, CONGRATULATIONS, OFFICERS...
...IT WORKED.
TOMMY, STOP! THERE ARE PEOPLE INSIDE.
I'VE GOT THEM, CASS.
STAY WITH TOMMY...

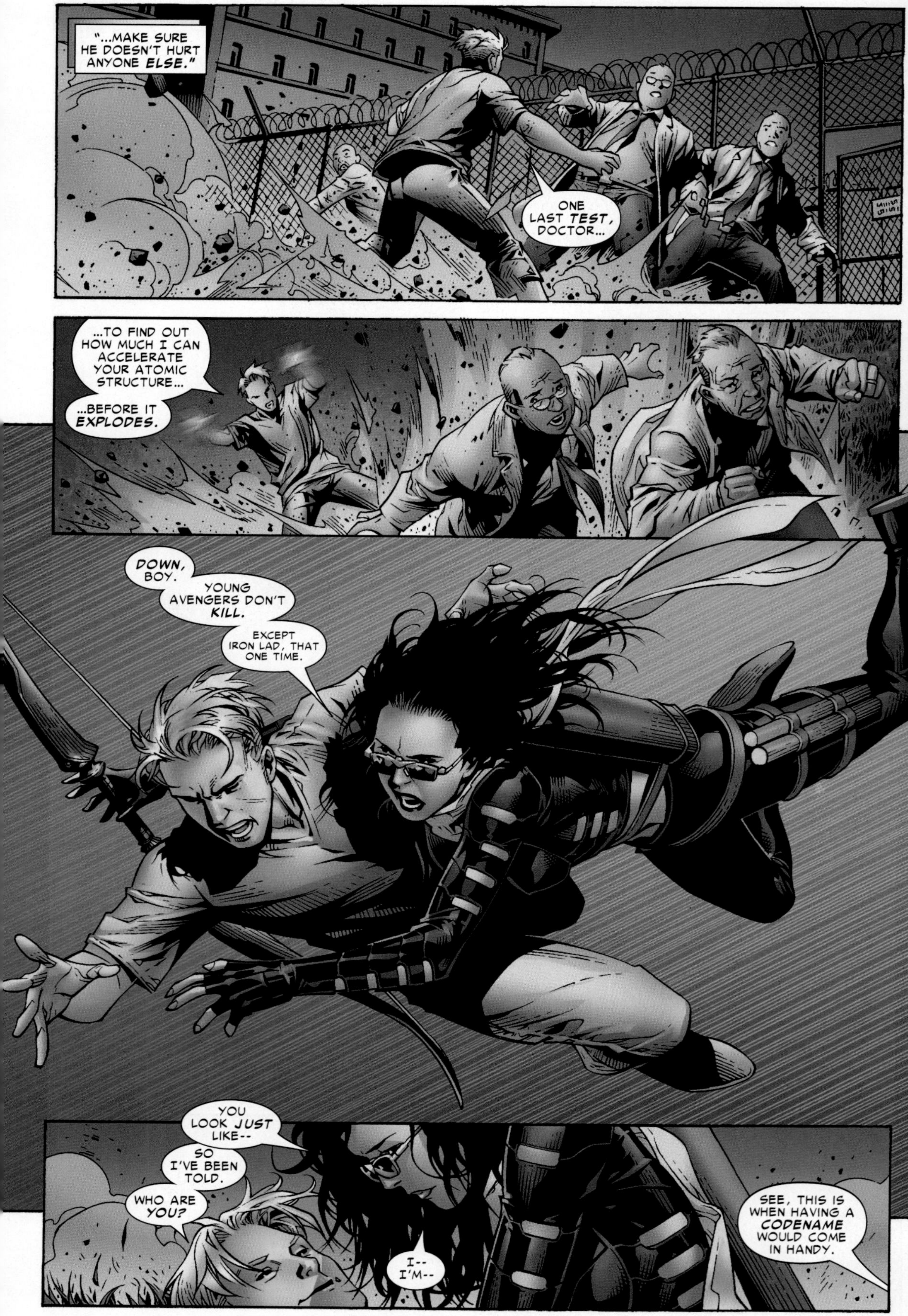
"...MAKE SURE HE DOESN'T HURT ANYONE ELSE."
ONE LAST TEST, DOCTOR...
...TO FIND OUT HOW MUCH I CAN ACCELERATE YOUR ATOMIC STRUCTURE...
...BEFORE IT EXPLODES.
DOWN, BOY.
YOUNG AVENGERS DON'T KILL.
EXCEPT IRON LAD, THAT ONE TIME.
YOU LOOK JUST LIKE--
SO I'VE BEEN TOLD.
WHO ARE YOU?
I-- I'M--
SEE, THIS IS WHEN HAVING A CODENAME WOULD COME IN HANDY.

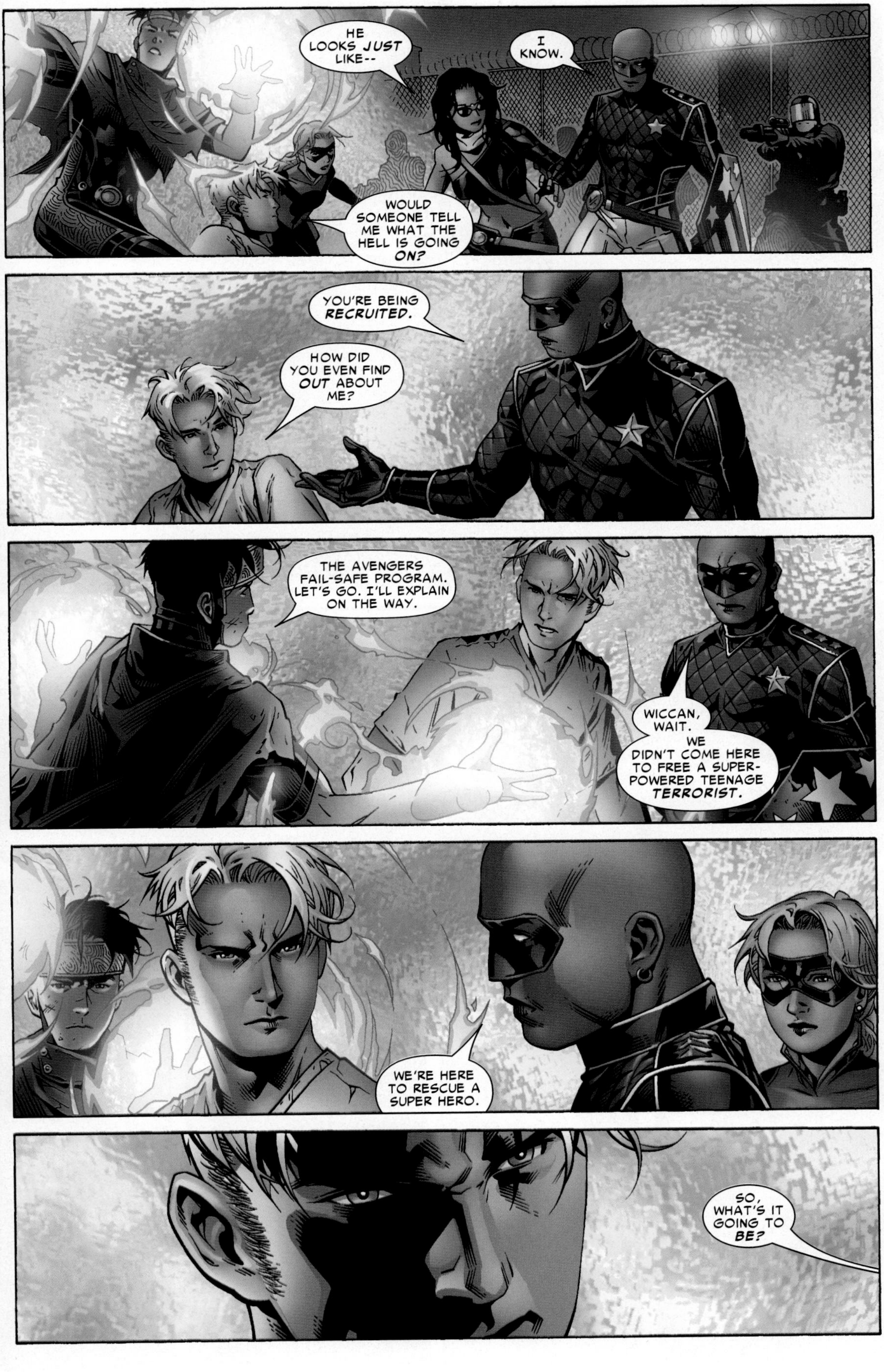
HE LOOKS *JUST* LIKE--
I KNOW.
WOULD SOMEONE TELL ME WHAT THE HELL IS GOING *ON?*
YOU'RE BEING *RECRUITED.*
HOW DID YOU EVEN FIND *OUT* ABOUT ME?
THE AVENGERS FAIL-SAFE PROGRAM. LET'S GO. I'LL EXPLAIN ON THE WAY.
WICCAN, WAIT.
WE DIDN'T COME HERE TO FREE A SUPER-POWERED TEENAGE *TERRORIST.*
WE'RE HERE TO RESCUE A SUPER HERO.
SO, WHAT'S IT GOING TO *BE?*

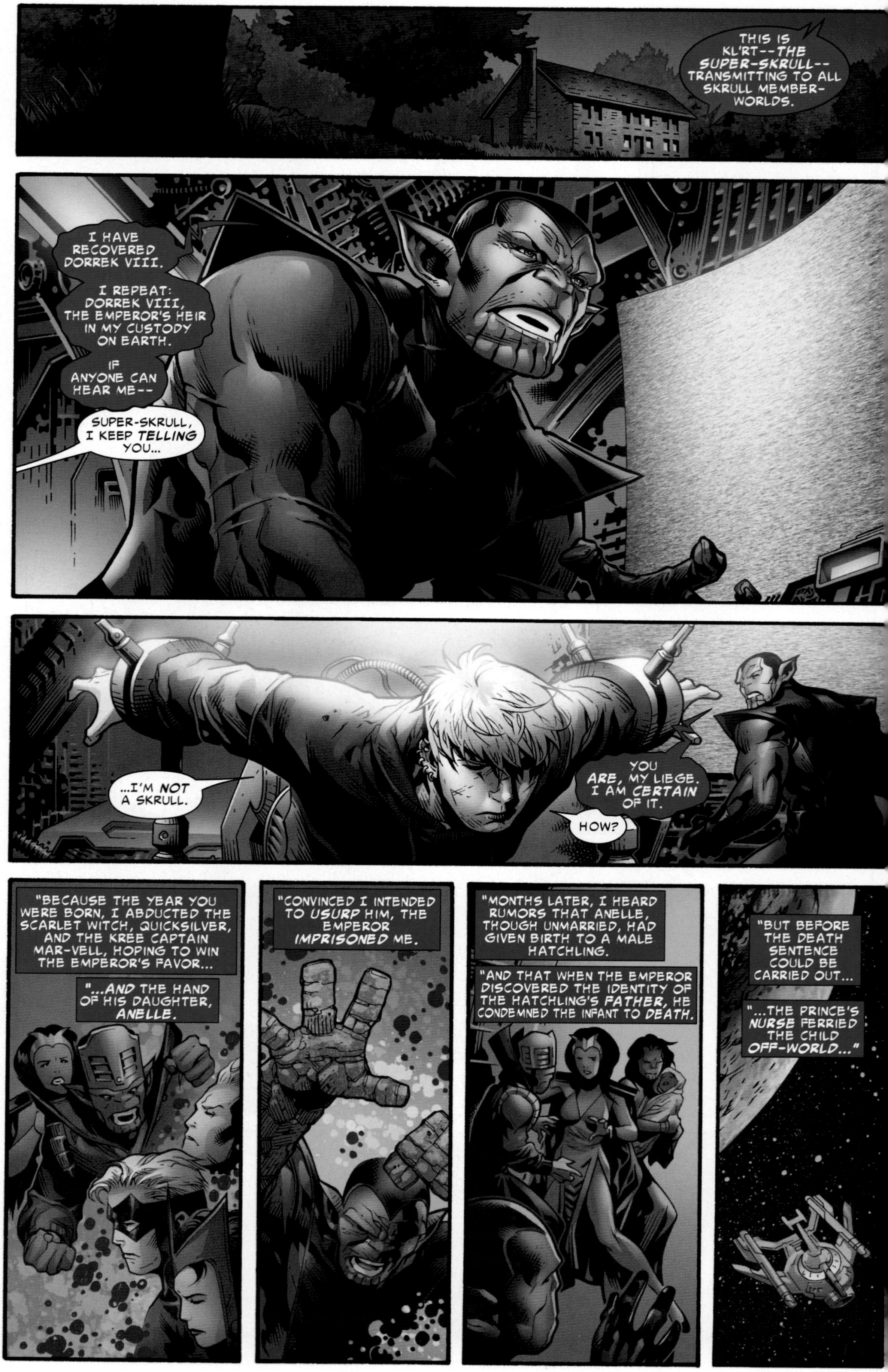
THIS IS KL'RT--THE SUPER-SKRULL--TRANSMITTING TO ALL SKRULL MEMBER-WORLDS.
I HAVE RECOVERED DORREK VIII.
I REPEAT: DORREK VIII, THE EMPEROR'S HEIR IN MY CUSTODY ON EARTH.
IF ANYONE CAN HEAR ME--
SUPER-SKRULL, I KEEP TELLING YOU...
...I'M NOT A SKRULL.
YOU ARE, MY LIEGE. I AM CERTAIN OF IT.
HOW?
"BECAUSE THE YEAR YOU WERE BORN, I ABDUCTED THE SCARLET WITCH, QUICKSILVER, AND THE KREE CAPTAIN MAR-VELL, HOPING TO WIN THE EMPEROR'S FAVOR...
"...AND THE HAND OF HIS DAUGHTER, ANELLE.
"CONVINCED I INTENDED TO USURP HIM, THE EMPEROR IMPRISONED ME.
"MONTHS LATER, I HEARD RUMORS THAT ANELLE, THOUGH UNMARRIED, HAD GIVEN BIRTH TO A MALE HATCHLING.
"AND THAT WHEN THE EMPEROR DISCOVERED THE IDENTITY OF THE HATCHLING'S FATHER, HE CONDEMNED THE INFANT TO DEATH.
"BUT BEFORE THE DEATH SENTENCE COULD BE CARRIED OUT...
"...THE PRINCE'S NURSE FERRIED THE CHILD OFF-WORLD..."

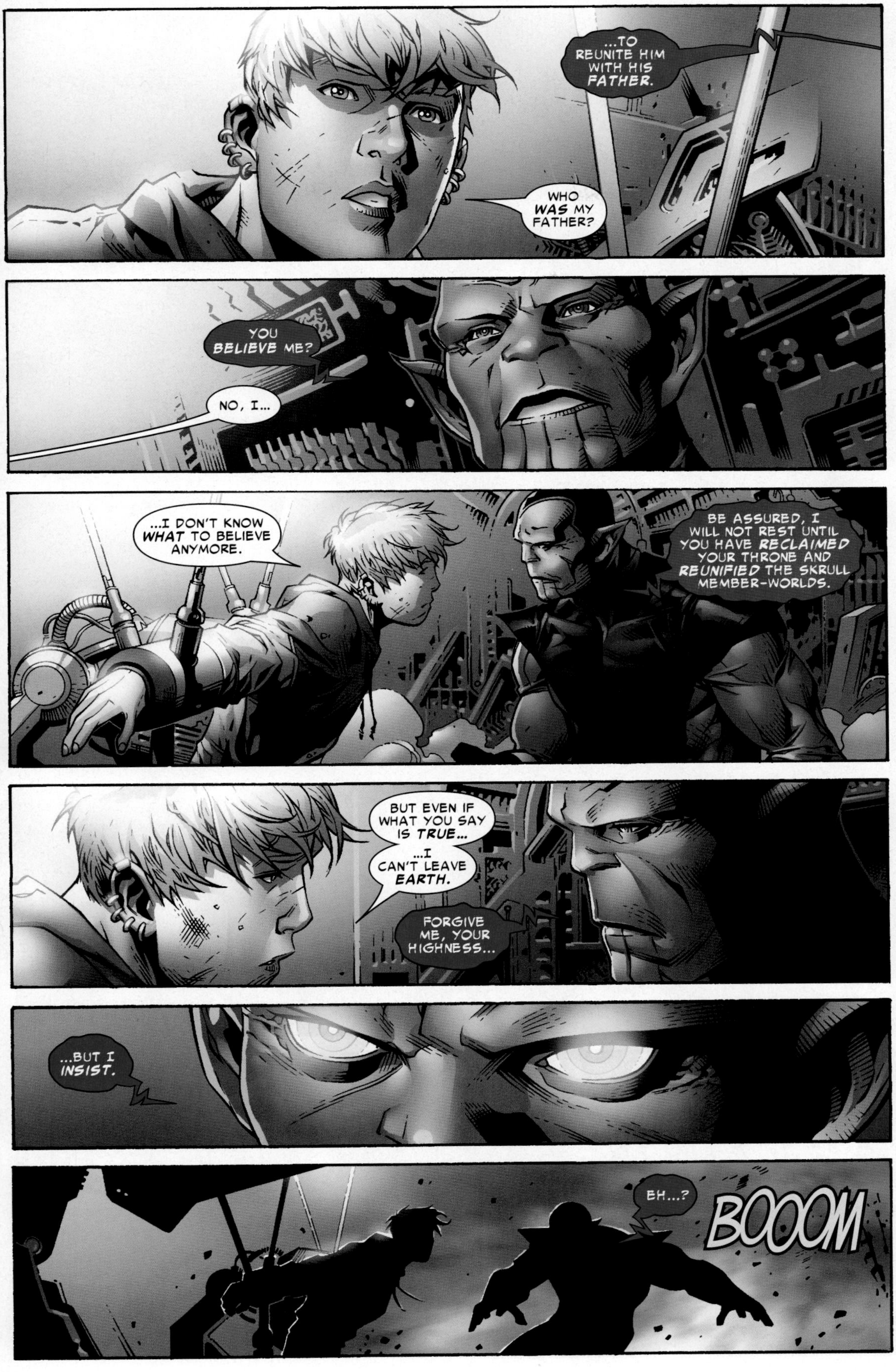
...TO REUNITE HIM WITH HIS FATHER.
WHO WAS MY FATHER?
YOU BELIEVE ME?
NO, I...
...I DON'T KNOW WHAT TO BELIEVE ANYMORE.
BE ASSURED, I WILL NOT REST UNTIL YOU HAVE RECLAIMED YOUR THRONE AND REUNIFIED THE SKRULL MEMBER-WORLDS.
BUT EVEN IF WHAT YOU SAY IS TRUE...
...I CAN'T LEAVE EARTH.
FORGIVE ME, YOUR HIGHNESS...
...BUT I INSIST.
EH...?
BOOOM

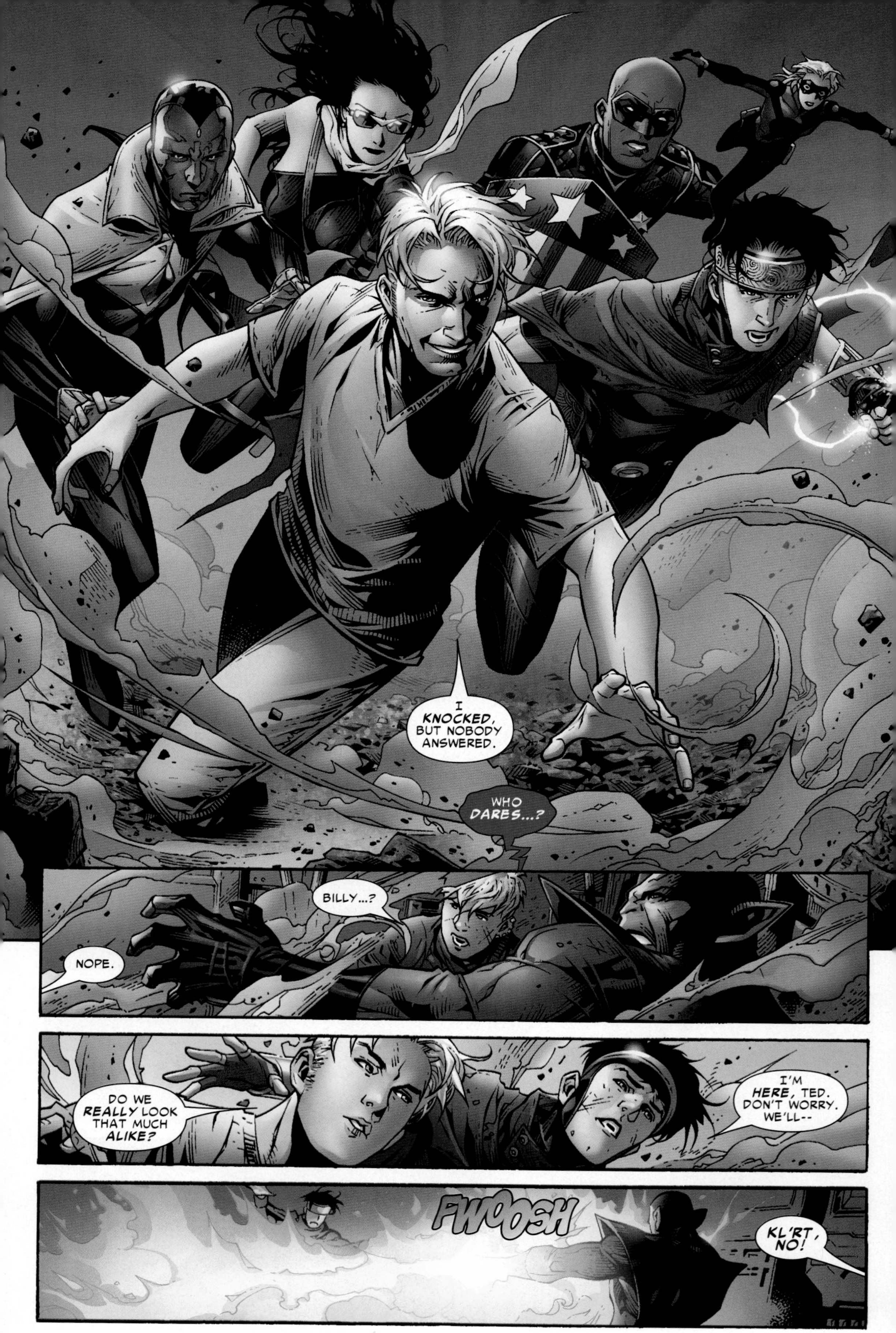
I KNOCKED, BUT NOBODY ANSWERED.
WHO DARES...?
BILLY...?
NOPE.
DO WE REALLY LOOK THAT MUCH ALIKE?
I'M HERE, TED. DON'T WORRY. WE'LL--
FWOOSH
KL'RT, NO!

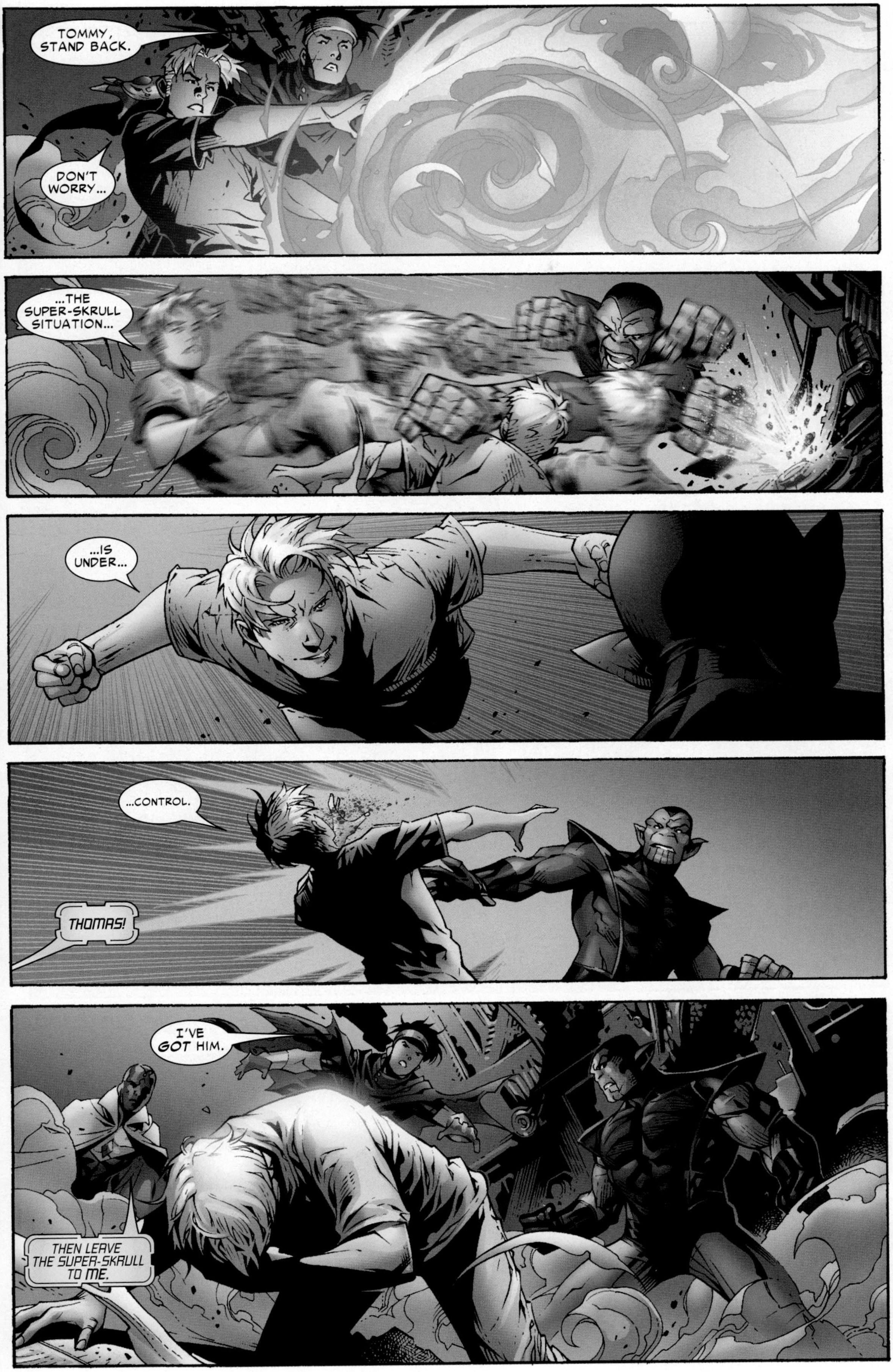
TOMMY, STAND BACK.
DON'T WORRY...
...THE SUPER-SKRULL SITUATION...
...IS UNDER...
...CONTROL.
THOMAS!
I'VE GOT HIM.
THEN LEAVE THE SUPER-SKRULL TO ME.

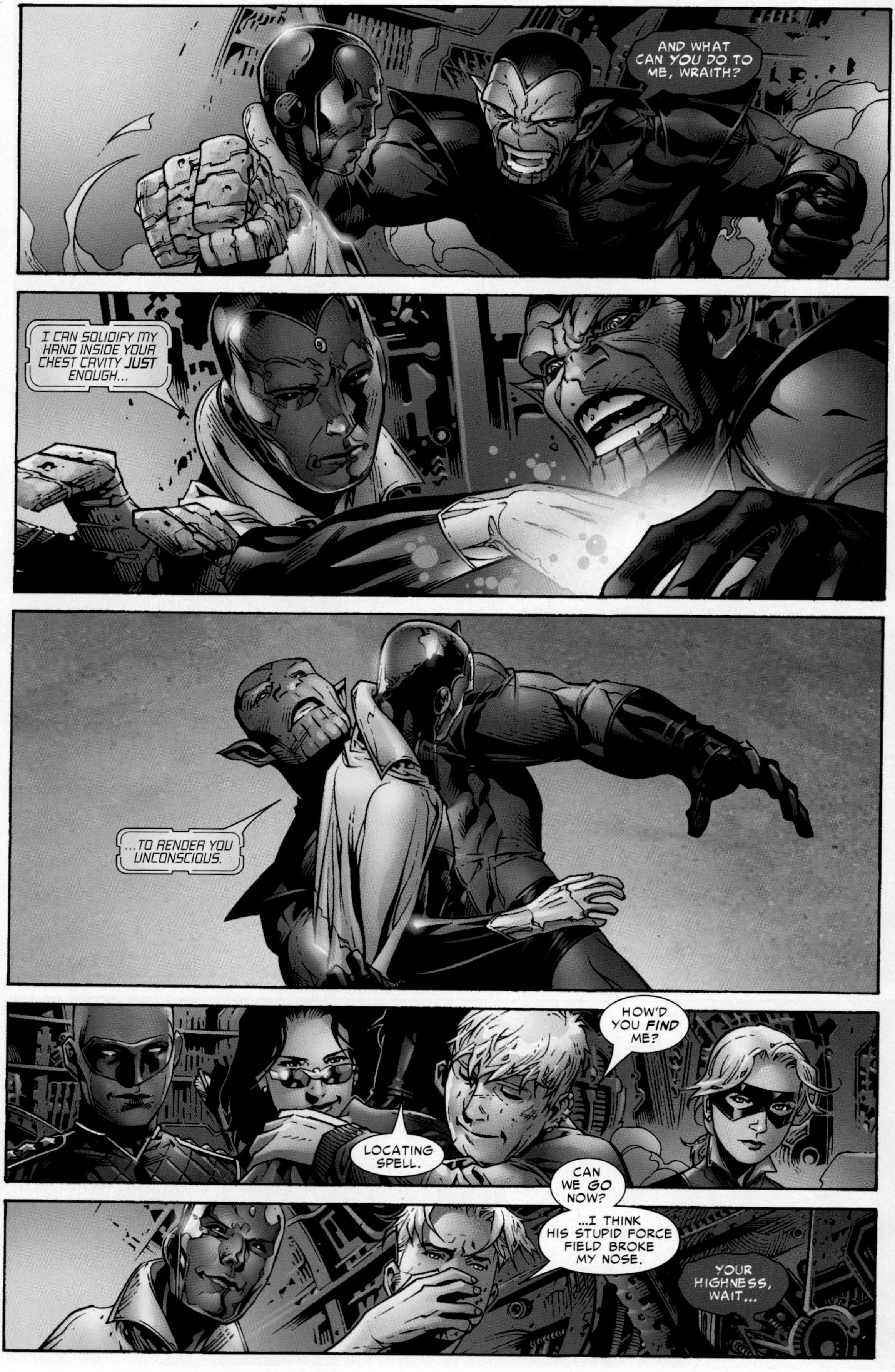
AND WHAT CAN YOU DO TO ME, WRAITH?
I CAN SOLIDIFY MY HAND INSIDE YOUR CHEST CAVITY JUST ENOUGH...
...TO RENDER YOU UNCONSCIOUS.
HOW'D YOU FIND ME?
LOCATING SPELL.
CAN WE GO NOW?
...I THINK HIS STUPID FORCE FIELD BROKE MY NOSE.
YOUR HIGHNESS, WAIT...

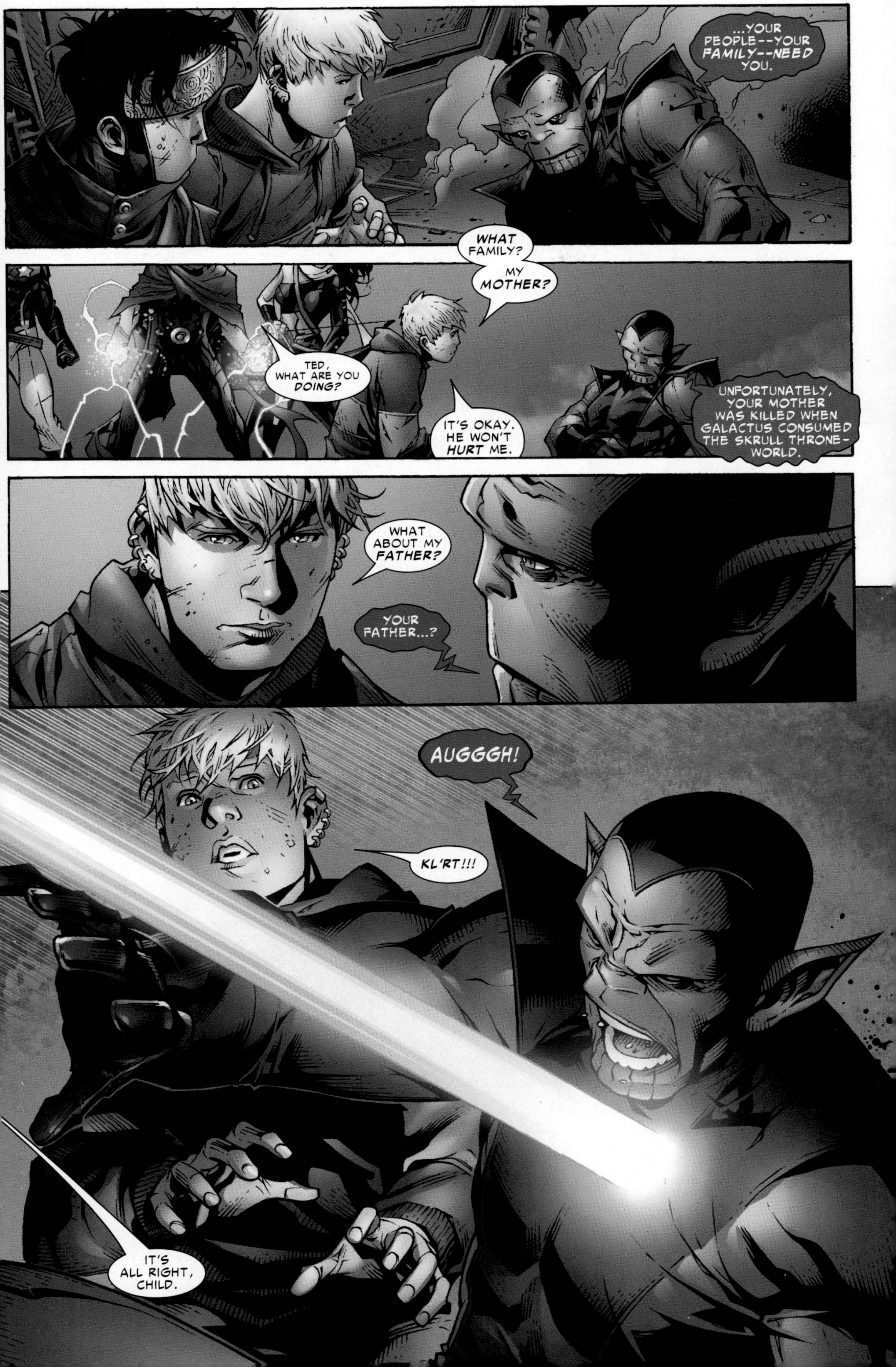
...YOUR PEOPLE--YOUR FAMILY--NEED YOU.
WHAT FAMILY?
MY MOTHER?
TED, WHAT ARE YOU DOING?
IT'S OKAY. HE WON'T HURT ME.
UNFORTUNATELY, YOUR MOTHER WAS KILLED WHEN GALACTUS CONSUMED THE SKRULL THRONE-WORLD.
WHAT ABOUT MY FATHER?
YOUR FATHER...?
AUGGGH!
KL'RT!!!
IT'S ALL RIGHT, CHILD.

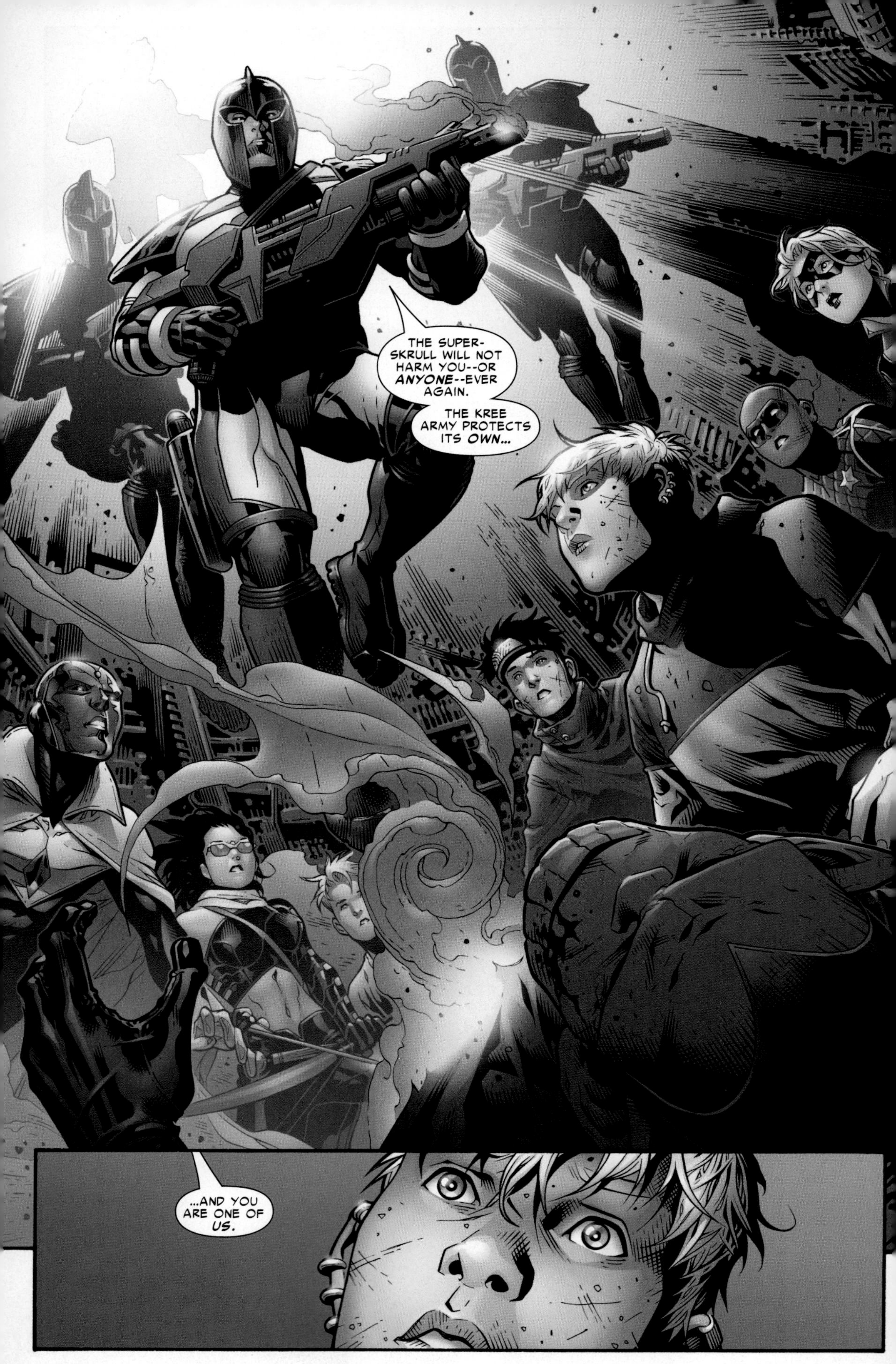

THE SUPER-SKRULL WILL NOT HARM YOU--OR ANYONE--EVER AGAIN.
THE KREE ARMY PROTECTS ITS OWN...
...AND YOU ARE ONE OF US.

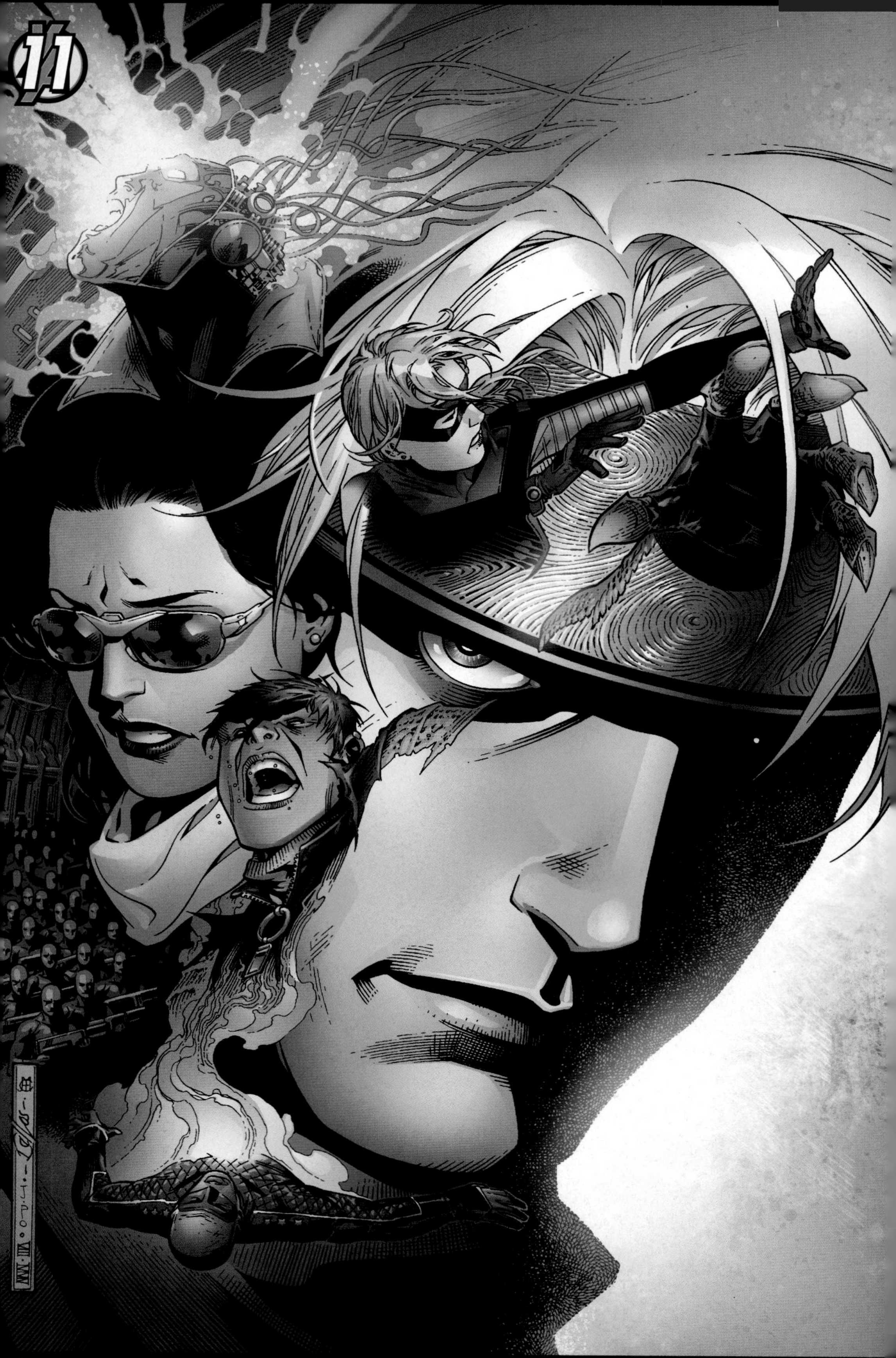

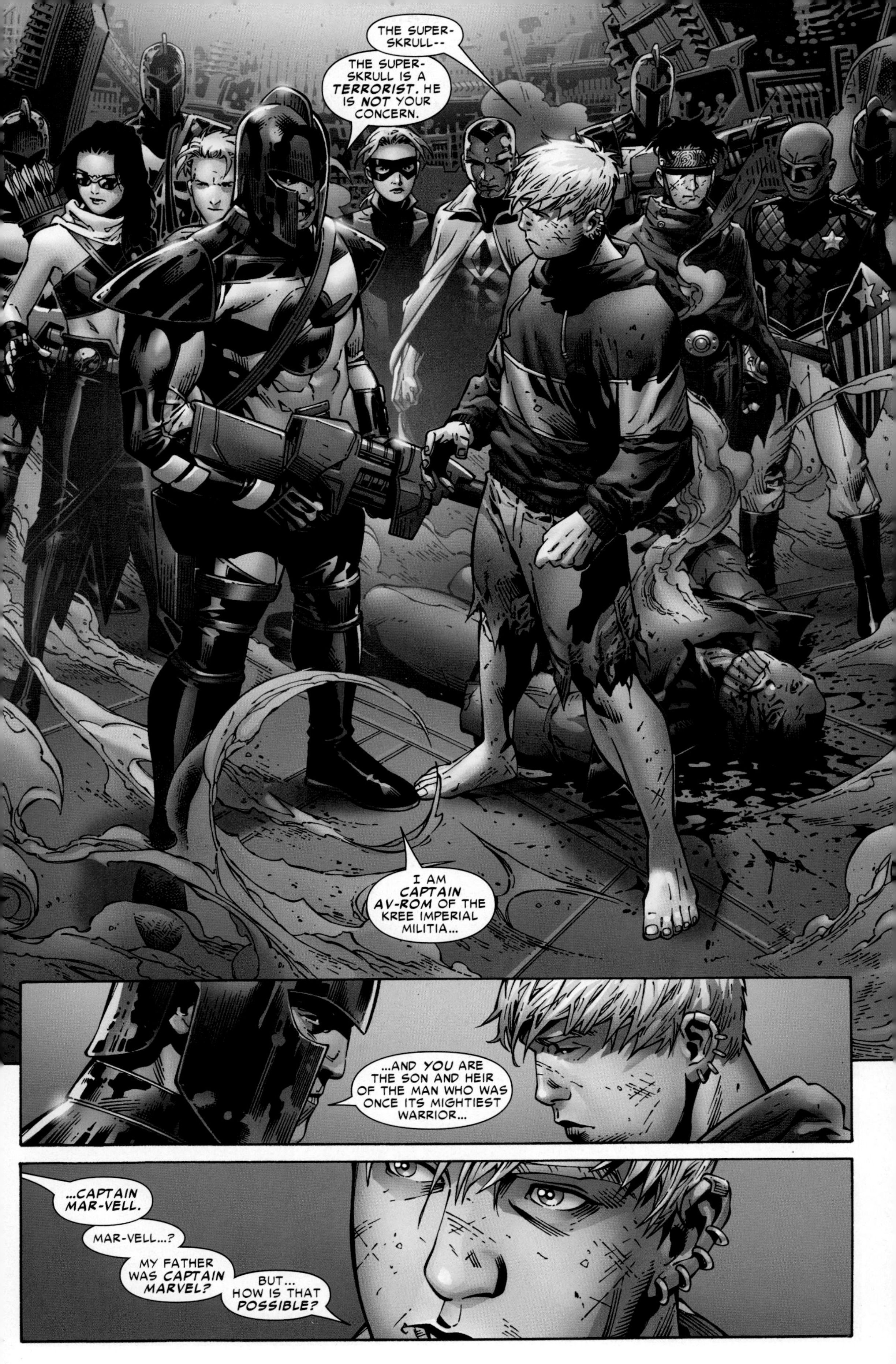
THE SUPER-SKRULL--
THE SUPER-SKRULL IS A TERRORIST. HE IS NOT YOUR CONCERN.
I AM CAPTAIN AV-ROM OF THE KREE IMPERIAL MILITIA...
...AND YOU ARE THE SON AND HEIR OF THE MAN WHO WAS ONCE ITS MIGHTIEST WARRIOR...
...CAPTAIN MAR-VELL.
MAR-VELL...?
MY FATHER WAS CAPTAIN MARVEL?
BUT... HOW IS THAT POSSIBLE?

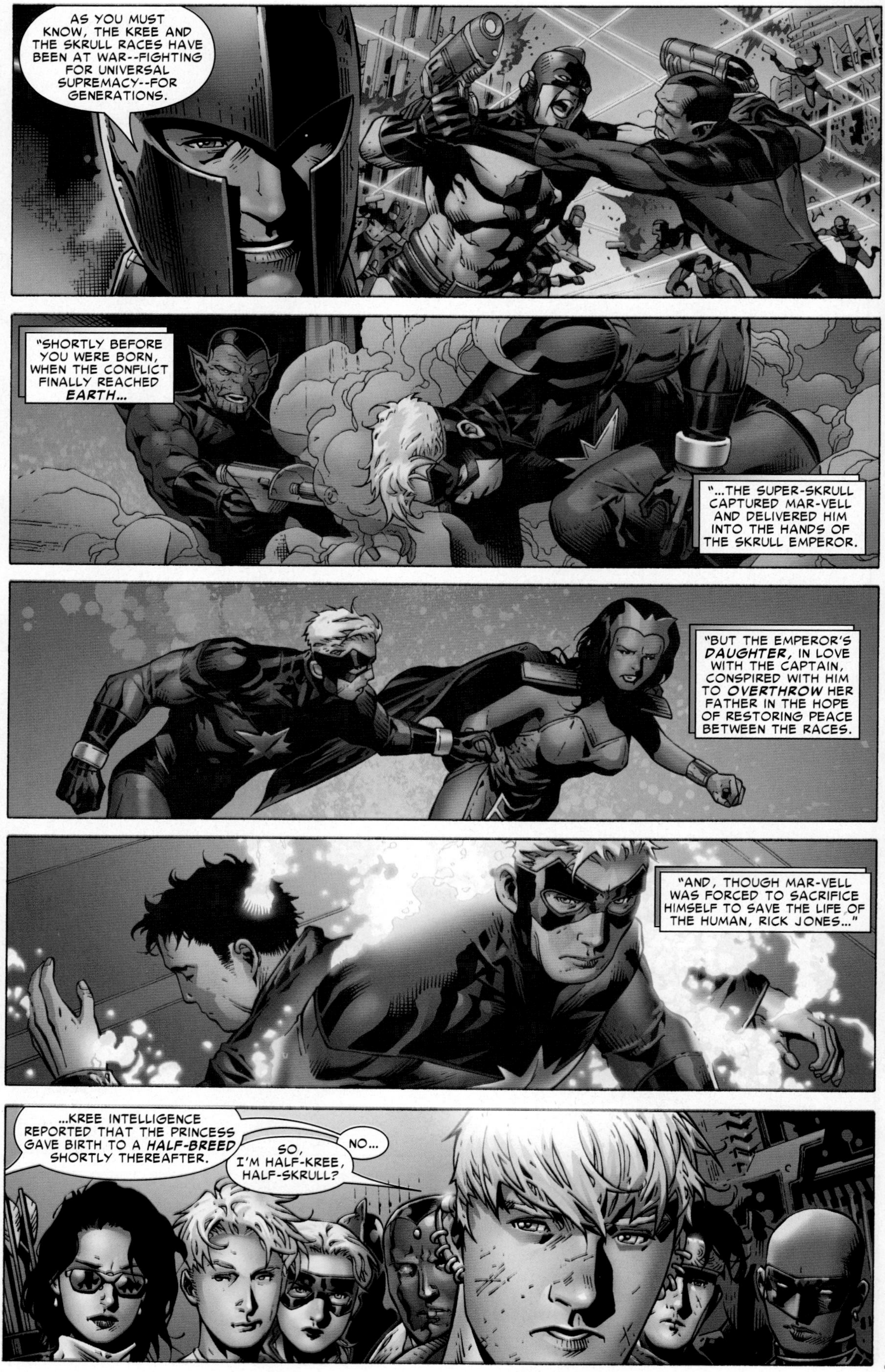
AS YOU MUST KNOW, THE KREE AND THE SKRULL RACES HAVE BEEN AT WAR--FIGHTING FOR UNIVERSAL SUPREMACY--FOR GENERATIONS.
"SHORTLY BEFORE YOU WERE BORN, WHEN THE CONFLICT FINALLY REACHED EARTH...
"...THE SUPER-SKRULL CAPTURED MAR-VELL AND DELIVERED HIM INTO THE HANDS OF THE SKRULL EMPEROR.
"BUT THE EMPEROR'S DAUGHTER, IN LOVE WITH THE CAPTAIN, CONSPIRED WITH HIM TO OVERTHROW HER FATHER IN THE HOPE OF RESTORING PEACE BETWEEN THE RACES.
"AND, THOUGH MAR-VELL WAS FORCED TO SACRIFICE HIMSELF TO SAVE THE LIFE OF THE HUMAN, RICK JONES..."
...KREE INTELLIGENCE REPORTED THAT THE PRINCESS GAVE BIRTH TO A HALF-BREED SHORTLY THEREAFTER.
NO...
SO, I'M HALF-KREE, HALF-SKRULL?

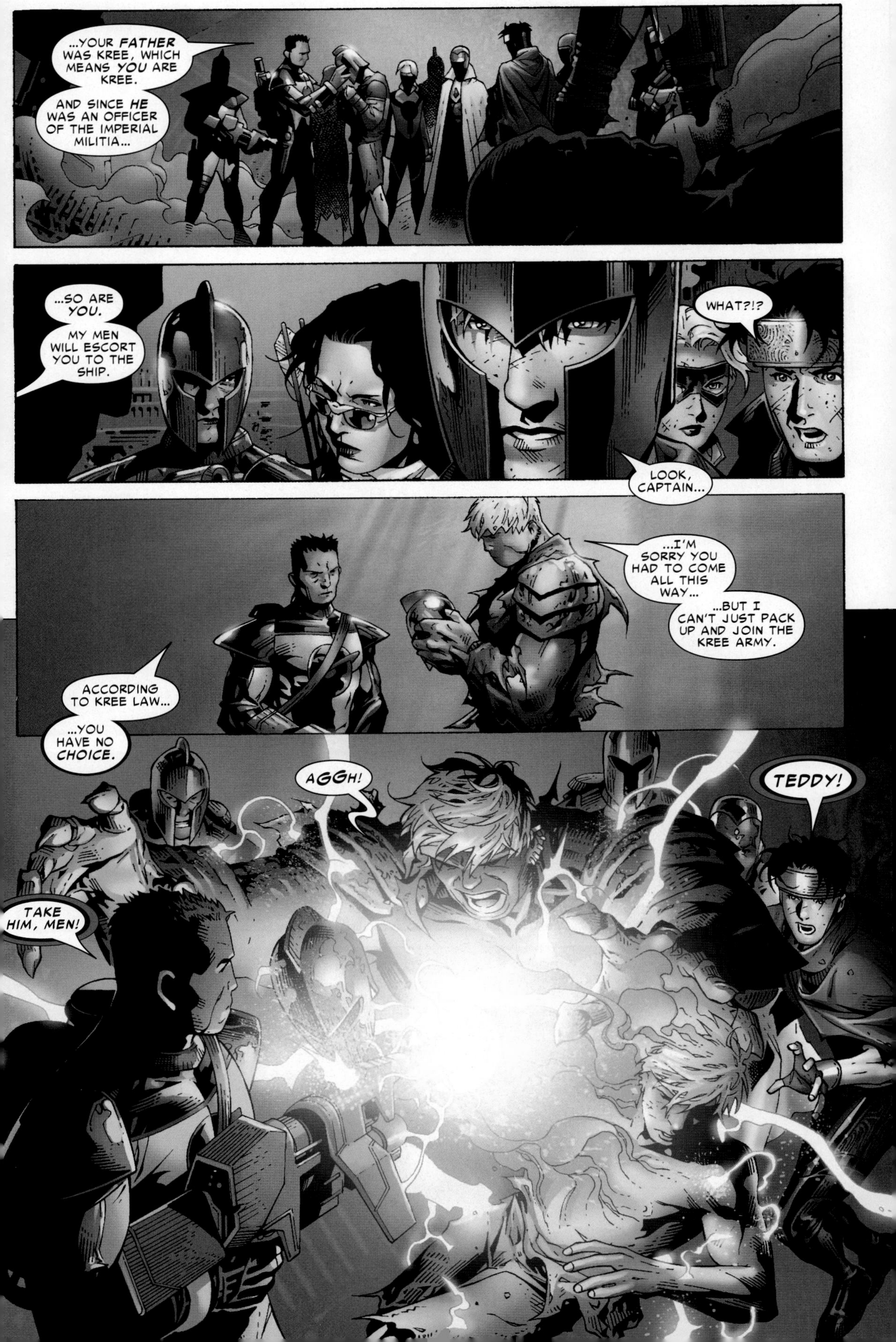
...YOUR FATHER WAS KREE, WHICH MEANS YOU ARE KREE.
AND SINCE HE WAS AN OFFICER OF THE IMPERIAL MILITIA...
...SO ARE YOU.
MY MEN WILL ESCORT YOU TO THE SHIP.
WHAT?!?
LOOK, CAPTAIN...
...I'M SORRY YOU HAD TO COME ALL THIS WAY...
...BUT I CAN'T JUST PACK UP AND JOIN THE KREE ARMY.
ACCORDING TO KREE LAW...
...YOU HAVE NO CHOICE.
AGGH!
TEDDY!
TAKE HIM, MEN!

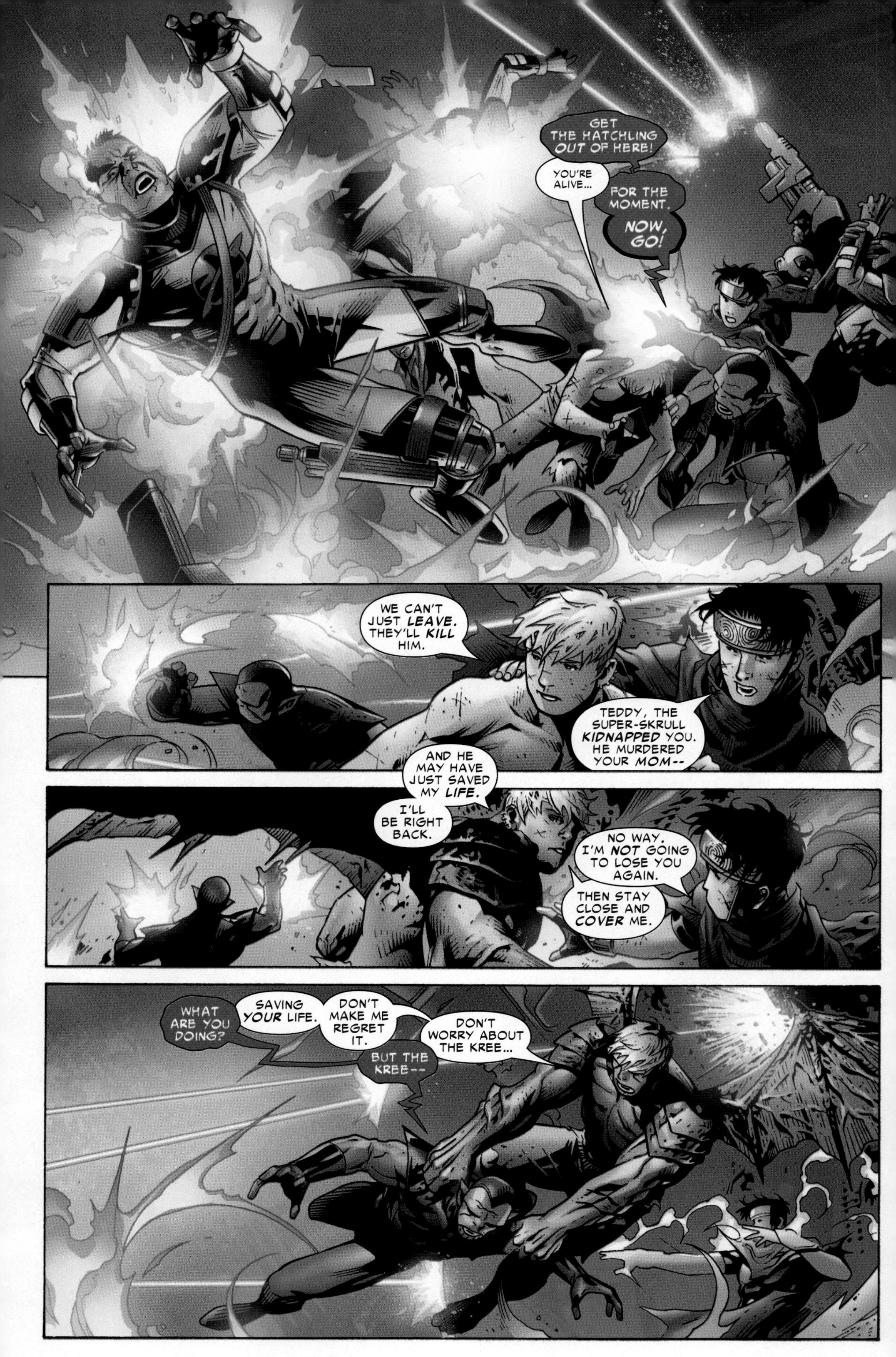
GET THE HATCHLING OUT OF HERE!
YOU'RE ALIVE...
FOR THE MOMENT. NOW, GO!
WE CAN'T JUST LEAVE. THEY'LL KILL HIM.
TEDDY, THE SUPER-SKRULL KIDNAPPED YOU. HE MURDERED YOUR MOM--
AND HE MAY HAVE JUST SAVED MY LIFE.
I'LL BE RIGHT BACK.
NO WAY. I'M NOT GOING TO LOSE YOU AGAIN.
THEN STAY CLOSE AND COVER ME.
WHAT ARE YOU DOING?
SAVING YOUR LIFE.
DON'T MAKE ME REGRET IT.
BUT THE KREE--
DON'T WORRY ABOUT THE KREE...

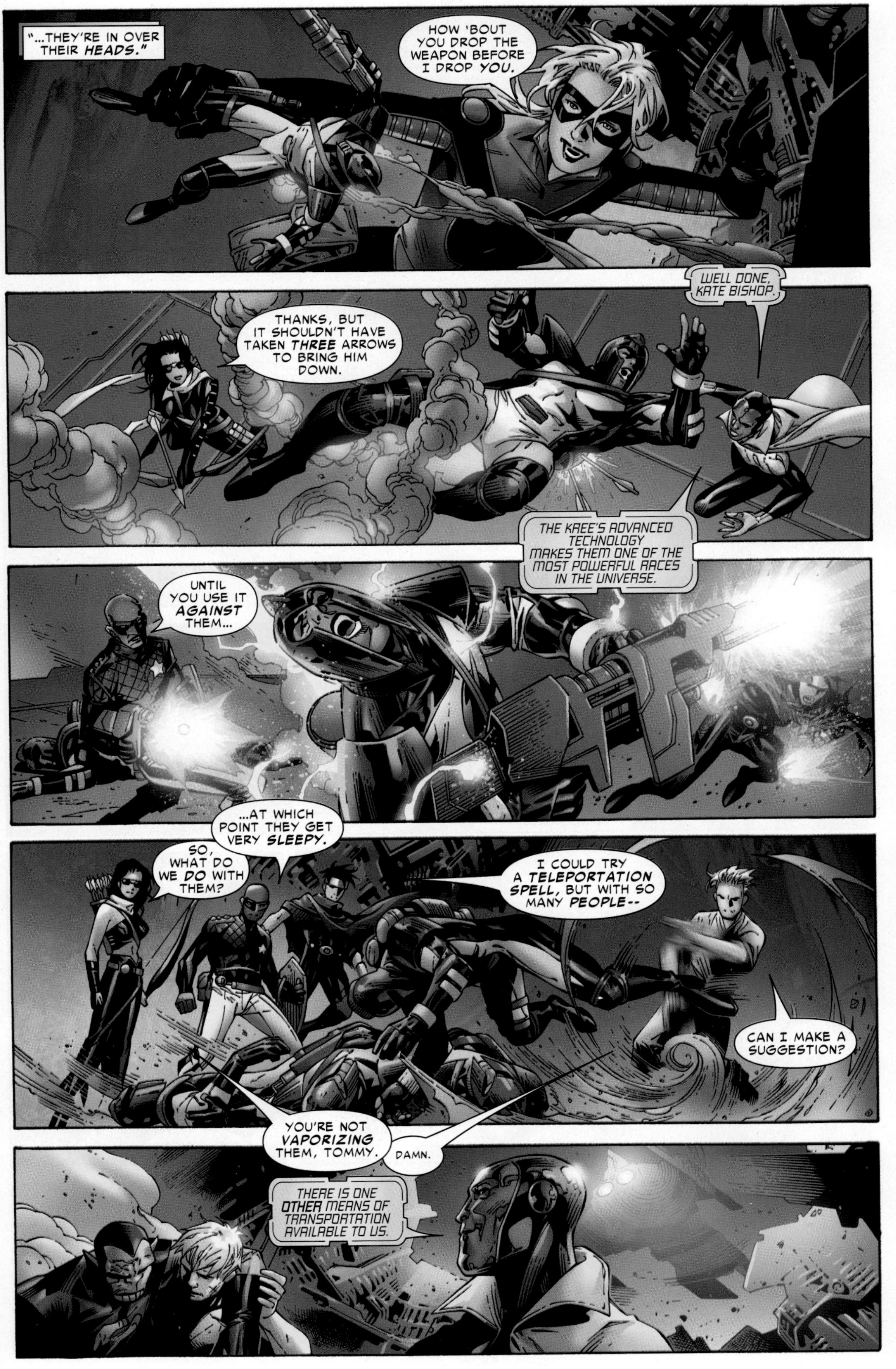
"...THEY'RE IN OVER THEIR HEADS."
HOW 'BOUT YOU DROP THE WEAPON BEFORE I DROP YOU.
WELL DONE, KATE BISHOP.
THANKS, BUT IT SHOULDN'T HAVE TAKEN THREE ARROWS TO BRING HIM DOWN.
THE KREE'S ADVANCED TECHNOLOGY MAKES THEM ONE OF THE MOST POWERFUL RACES IN THE UNIVERSE.
UNTIL YOU USE IT AGAINST THEM...
...AT WHICH POINT THEY GET VERY SLEEPY.
SO, WHAT DO WE DO WITH THEM?
I COULD TRY A TELEPORTATION SPELL, BUT WITH SO MANY PEOPLE--
CAN I MAKE A SUGGESTION?
YOU'RE NOT VAPORIZING THEM, TOMMY.
DAMN.
THERE IS ONE OTHER MEANS OF TRANSPORTATION AVAILABLE TO US.

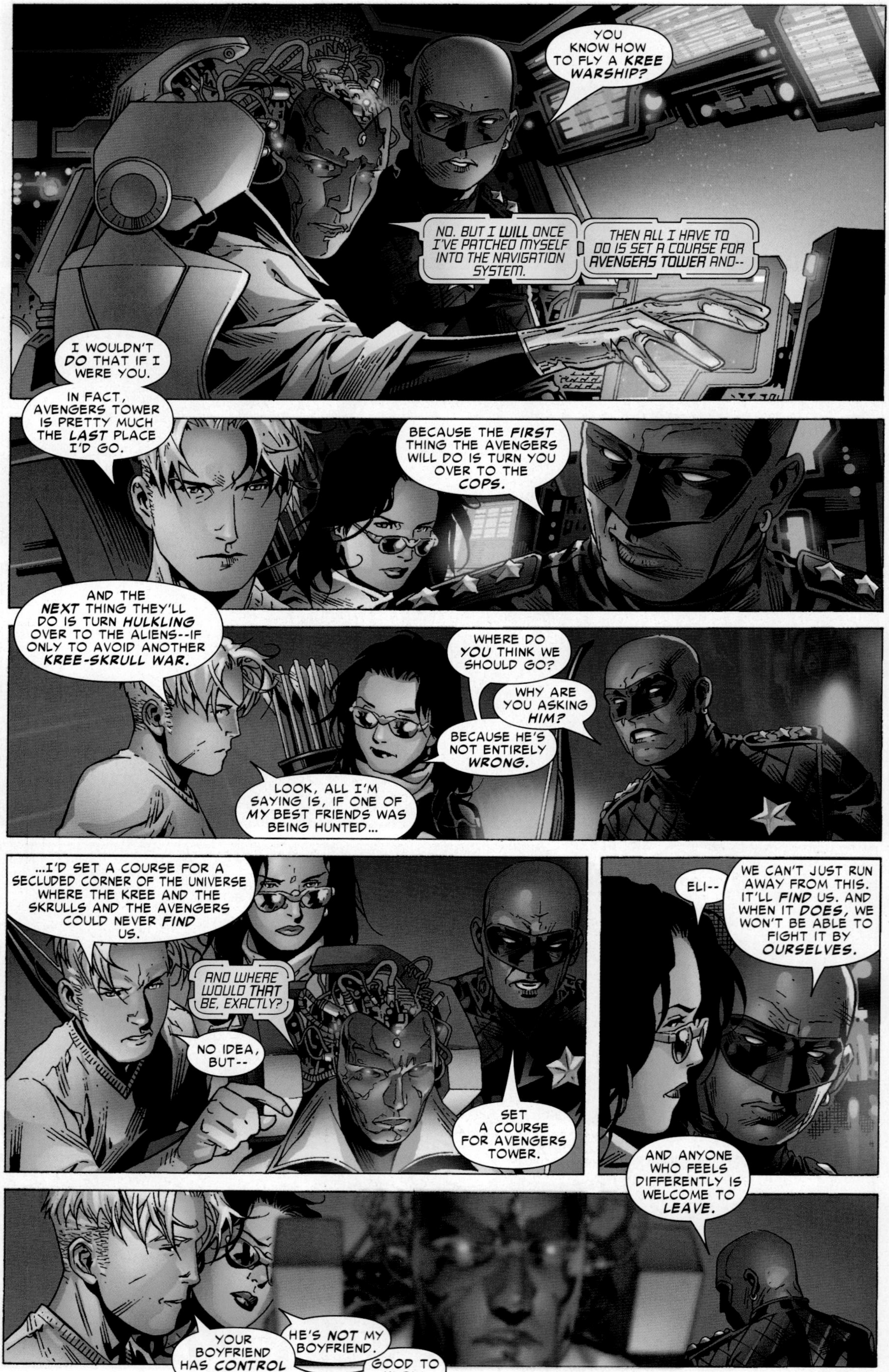
YOU KNOW HOW TO FLY A KREE WARSHIP?
NO. BUT I WILL ONCE I'VE PATCHED MYSELF INTO THE NAVIGATION SYSTEM.
THEN ALL I HAVE TO DO IS SET A COURSE FOR AVENGERS TOWER AND--
I WOULDN'T DO THAT IF I WERE YOU.
IN FACT, AVENGERS TOWER IS PRETTY MUCH THE LAST PLACE I'D GO.
BECAUSE THE FIRST THING THE AVENGERS WILL DO IS TURN YOU OVER TO THE COPS.
AND THE NEXT THING THEY'LL DO IS TURN HULKLING OVER TO THE ALIENS--IF ONLY TO AVOID ANOTHER KREE-SKRULL WAR.
WHERE DO YOU THINK WE SHOULD GO?
WHY ARE YOU ASKING HIM?
BECAUSE HE'S NOT ENTIRELY WRONG.
LOOK, ALL I'M SAYING IS, IF ONE OF MY BEST FRIENDS WAS BEING HUNTED...
...I'D SET A COURSE FOR A SECLUDED CORNER OF THE UNIVERSE WHERE THE KREE AND THE SKRULLS AND THE AVENGERS COULD NEVER FIND US.
AND WHERE WOULD THAT BE, EXACTLY?
NO IDEA, BUT--
SET A COURSE FOR AVENGERS TOWER.
ELI--
WE CAN'T JUST RUN AWAY FROM THIS. IT'LL FIND US. AND WHEN IT DOES, WE WON'T BE ABLE TO FIGHT IT BY OURSELVES.
AND ANYONE WHO FEELS DIFFERENTLY IS WELCOME TO LEAVE.
YOUR BOYFRIEND HAS CONTROL ISSUES.
HE'S NOT MY BOYFRIEND.
GOOD TO KNOW.

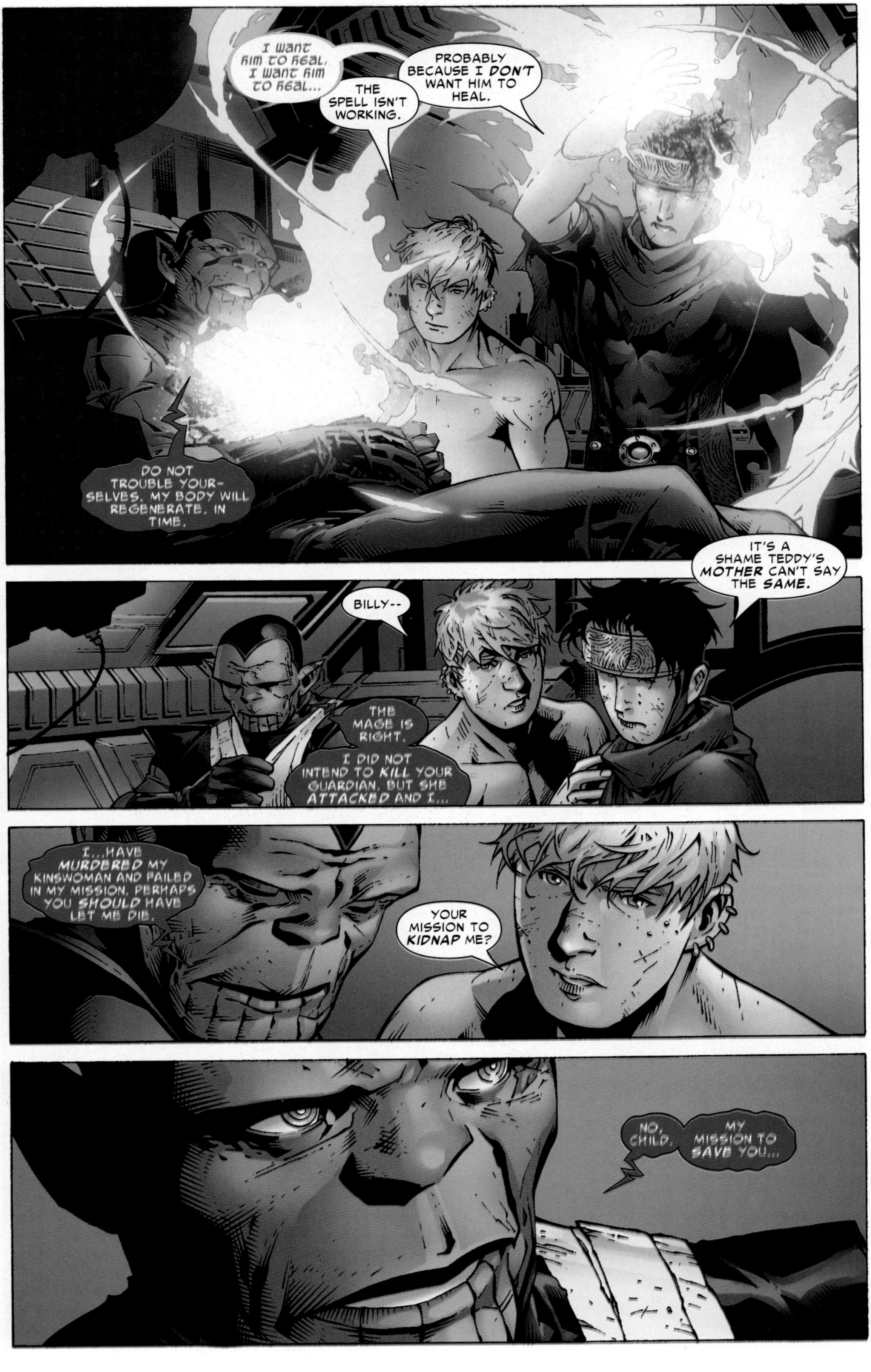
I WANT HIM TO HEAL, I WANT HIM TO HEAL...
THE SPELL ISN'T WORKING.
PROBABLY BECAUSE I DON'T WANT HIM TO HEAL.
DO NOT TROUBLE YOURSELVES. MY BODY WILL REGENERATE, IN TIME.
BILLY--
IT'S A SHAME TEDDY'S MOTHER CAN'T SAY THE SAME.
THE MAGE IS RIGHT.
I DID NOT INTEND TO KILL YOUR GUARDIAN, BUT SHE ATTACKED AND I...
I...HAVE MURDERED MY KINSWOMAN AND FAILED IN MY MISSION. PERHAPS YOU SHOULD HAVE LET ME DIE.
YOUR MISSION TO KIDNAP ME?
NO, CHILD.
MY MISSION TO SAVE YOU...

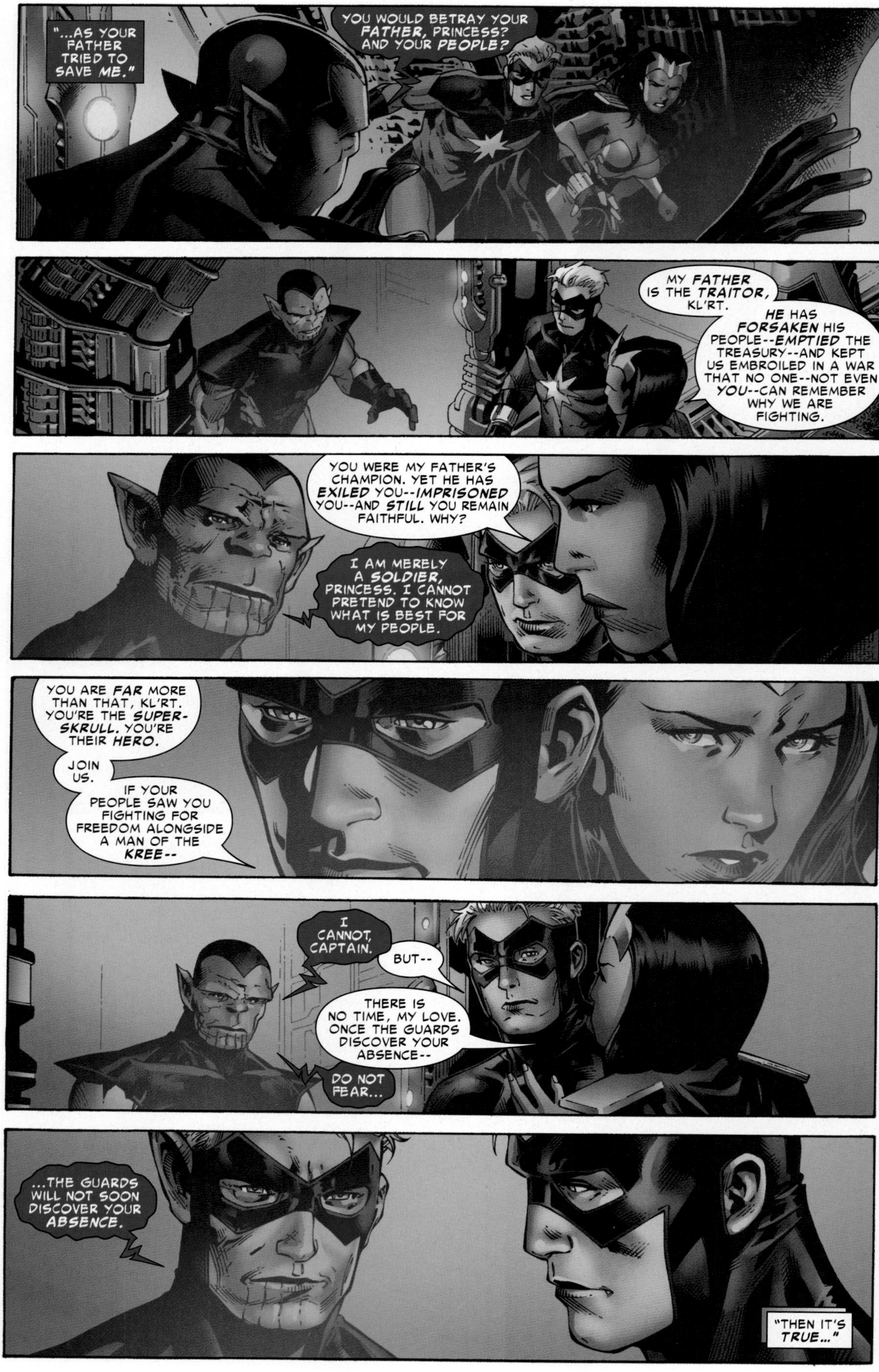
"...AS YOUR FATHER TRIED TO SAVE ME."
YOU WOULD BETRAY YOUR FATHER, PRINCESS? AND YOUR PEOPLE?
MY FATHER IS THE TRAITOR, KL'RT.
HE HAS FORSAKEN HIS PEOPLE--EMPTIED THE TREASURY--AND KEPT US EMBROILED IN A WAR THAT NO ONE--NOT EVEN YOU--CAN REMEMBER WHY WE ARE FIGHTING.
YOU WERE MY FATHER'S CHAMPION. YET HE HAS EXILED YOU--IMPRISONED YOU--AND STILL YOU REMAIN FAITHFUL. WHY?
I AM MERELY A SOLDIER, PRINCESS. I CANNOT PRETEND TO KNOW WHAT IS BEST FOR MY PEOPLE.
YOU ARE FAR MORE THAN THAT, KL'RT. YOU'RE THE SUPER-SKRULL. YOU'RE THEIR HERO.
JOIN US.
IF YOUR PEOPLE SAW YOU FIGHTING FOR FREEDOM ALONGSIDE A MAN OF THE KREE--
I CANNOT, CAPTAIN.
BUT--
THERE IS NO TIME, MY LOVE. ONCE THE GUARDS DISCOVER YOUR ABSENCE--
DO NOT FEAR...
...THE GUARDS WILL NOT SOON DISCOVER YOUR ABSENCE.
"THEN IT'S TRUE..."

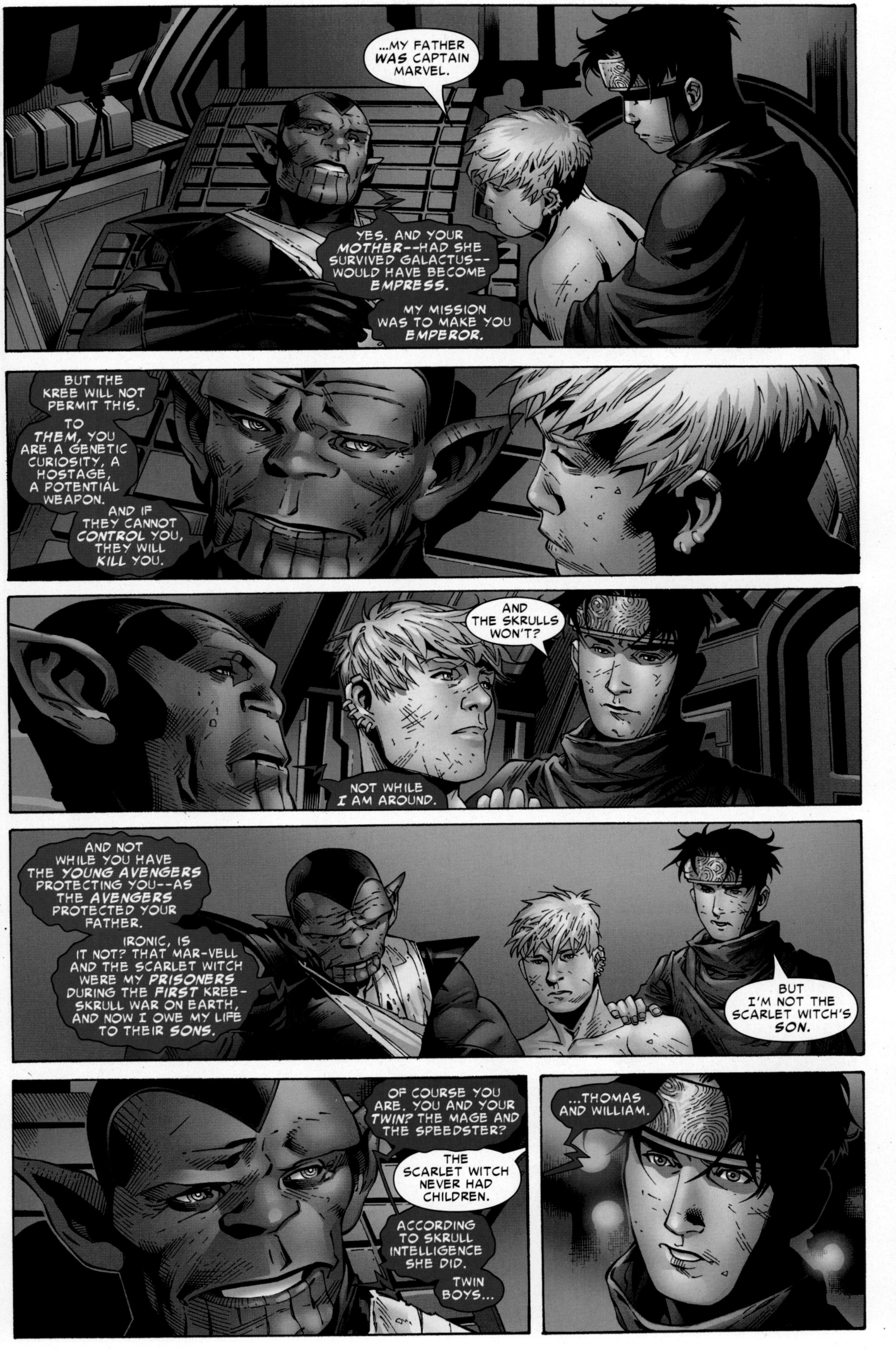
...MY FATHER WAS CAPTAIN MARVEL.
YES. AND YOUR MOTHER--HAD SHE SURVIVED GALACTUS--WOULD HAVE BECOME EMPRESS.
MY MISSION WAS TO MAKE YOU EMPEROR.
BUT THE KREE WILL NOT PERMIT THIS.
TO THEM, YOU ARE A GENETIC CURIOSITY, A HOSTAGE, A POTENTIAL WEAPON.
AND IF THEY CANNOT CONTROL YOU, THEY WILL KILL YOU.
AND THE SKRULLS WON'T?
NOT WHILE I AM AROUND.
AND NOT WHILE YOU HAVE THE YOUNG AVENGERS PROTECTING YOU--AS THE AVENGERS PROTECTED YOUR FATHER.
IRONIC, IS IT NOT? THAT MAR-VELL AND THE SCARLET WITCH WERE MY PRISONERS DURING THE FIRST KREE-SKRULL WAR ON EARTH, AND NOW I OWE MY LIFE TO THEIR SONS.
BUT I'M NOT THE SCARLET WITCH'S SON.
OF COURSE YOU ARE. YOU AND YOUR TWIN? THE MAGE AND THE SPEEDSTER?
THE SCARLET WITCH NEVER HAD CHILDREN.
ACCORDING TO SKRULL INTELLIGENCE SHE DID.
TWIN BOYS...
...THOMAS AND WILLIAM.

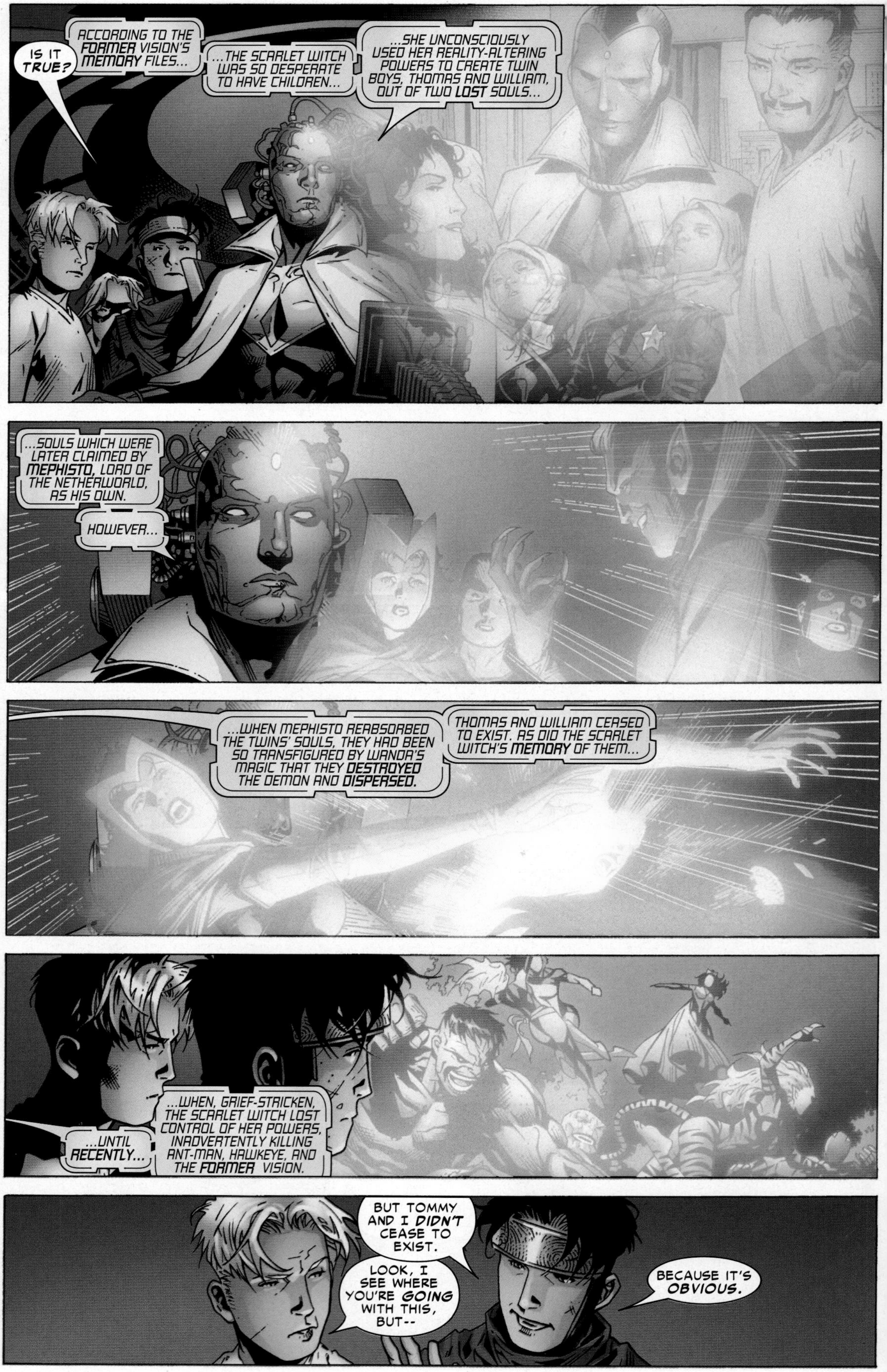

IS IT TRUE?
ACCORDING TO THE FORMER VISION'S MEMORY FILES...
...THE SCARLET WITCH WAS SO DESPERATE TO HAVE CHILDREN...
...SHE UNCONSCIOUSLY USED HER REALITY-ALTERING POWERS TO CREATE TWIN BOYS, THOMAS AND WILLIAM, OUT OF TWO LOST SOULS...
...SOULS WHICH WERE LATER CLAIMED BY MEPHISTO, LORD OF THE NETHERWORLD, AS HIS OWN.
HOWEVER...
...WHEN MEPHISTO REABSORBED THE TWINS' SOULS, THEY HAD BEEN SO TRANSFIGURED BY WANDA'S MAGIC THAT THEY DESTROYED THE DEMON AND DISPERSED.
THOMAS AND WILLIAM CEASED TO EXIST. AS DID THE SCARLET WITCH'S MEMORY OF THEM...
...UNTIL RECENTLY...
...WHEN, GRIEF-STRICKEN, THE SCARLET WITCH LOST CONTROL OF HER POWERS, INADVERTENTLY KILLING ANT-MAN, HAWKEYE, AND THE FORMER VISION.
BUT TOMMY AND I DIDN'T CEASE TO EXIST.
LOOK, I SEE WHERE YOU'RE GOING WITH THIS, BUT--
BECAUSE IT'S OBVIOUS.

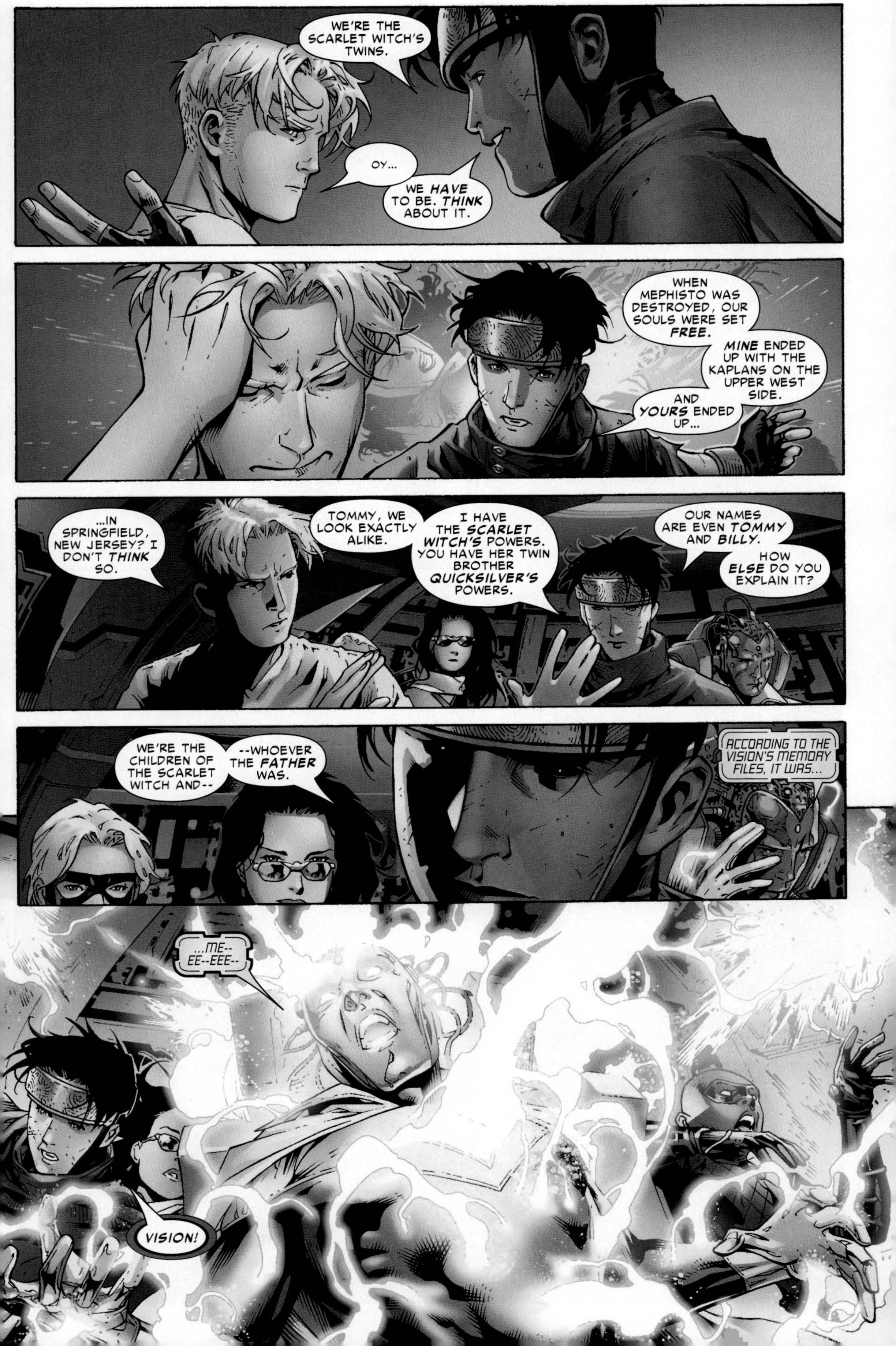

WE'RE THE SCARLET WITCH'S TWINS.
OY...
WE HAVE TO BE. THINK ABOUT IT.
WHEN MEPHISTO WAS DESTROYED, OUR SOULS WERE SET FREE.
MINE ENDED UP WITH THE KAPLANS ON THE UPPER WEST SIDE.
AND YOURS ENDED UP...
...IN SPRINGFIELD, NEW JERSEY? I DON'T THINK SO.
TOMMY, WE LOOK EXACTLY ALIKE.
I HAVE THE SCARLET WITCH'S POWERS. YOU HAVE HER TWIN BROTHER QUICKSILVER'S POWERS.
OUR NAMES ARE EVEN TOMMY AND BILLY.
HOW ELSE DO YOU EXPLAIN IT?
WE'RE THE CHILDREN OF THE SCARLET WITCH AND--
--WHOEVER THE FATHER WAS.
ACCORDING TO THE VISION'S MEMORY FILES, IT WAS...
...ME--EE--EEE--
VISION!

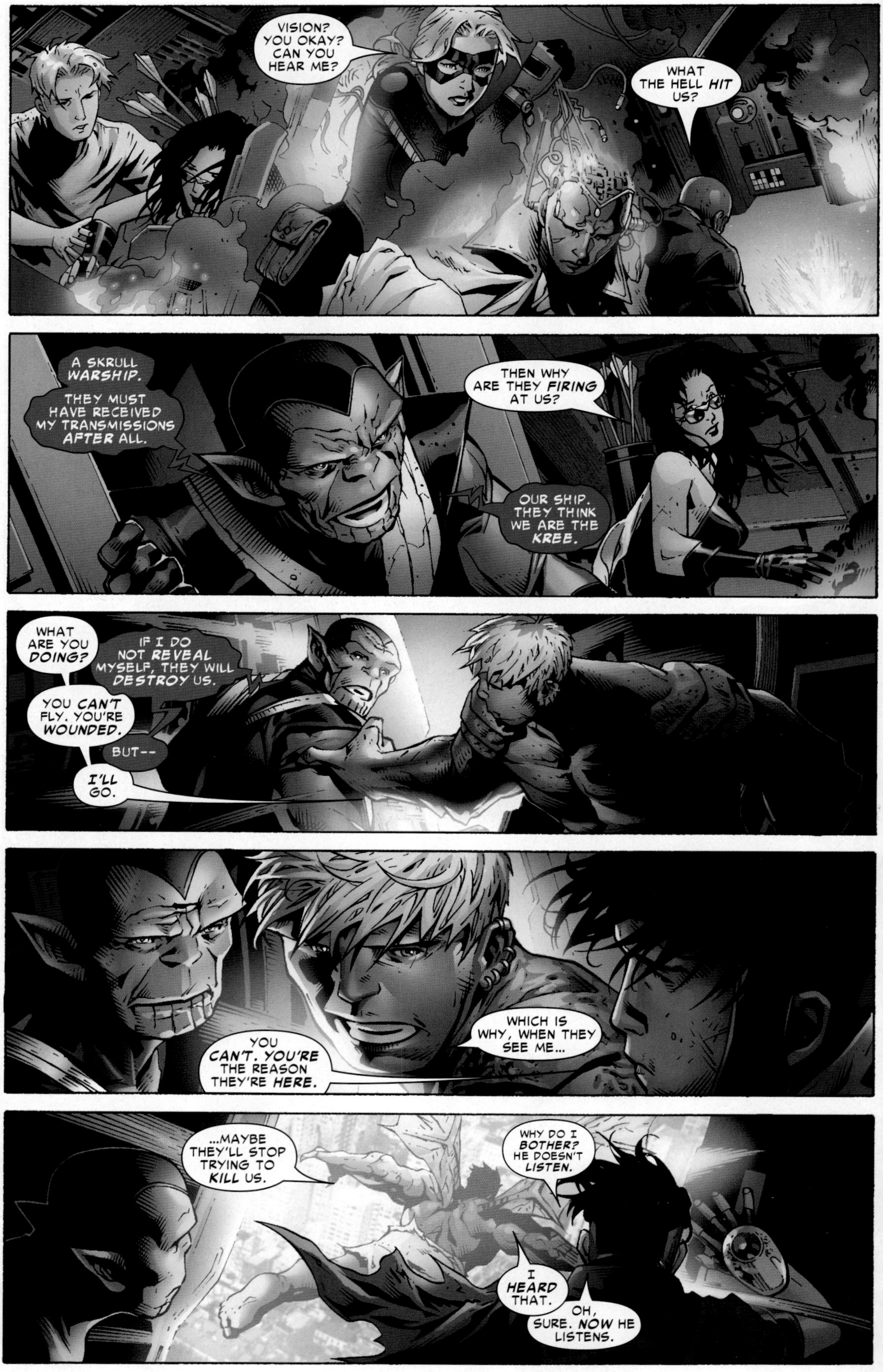

VISION? YOU OKAY? CAN YOU HEAR ME?
WHAT THE HELL *HIT* US?
A SKRULL *WARSHIP*.
THEY MUST HAVE RECEIVED MY TRANSMISSIONS *AFTER* ALL.
THEN WHY ARE THEY *FIRING* AT US?
OUR SHIP. THEY THINK WE ARE THE *KREE*.
WHAT ARE YOU *DOING?*
IF I DO NOT *REVEAL* MYSELF, THEY WILL *DESTROY* US.
YOU *CAN'T* FLY. YOU'RE *WOUNDED*.
BUT--
I'LL GO.
YOU *CAN'T. YOU'RE* THE REASON THEY'RE *HERE*.
WHICH IS WHY, WHEN THEY SEE ME...
...MAYBE THEY'LL STOP TRYING TO *KILL* US.
WHY DO I *BOTHER?* HE DOESN'T *LISTEN*.
I *HEARD* THAT.
OH, SURE. *NOW* HE LISTENS.

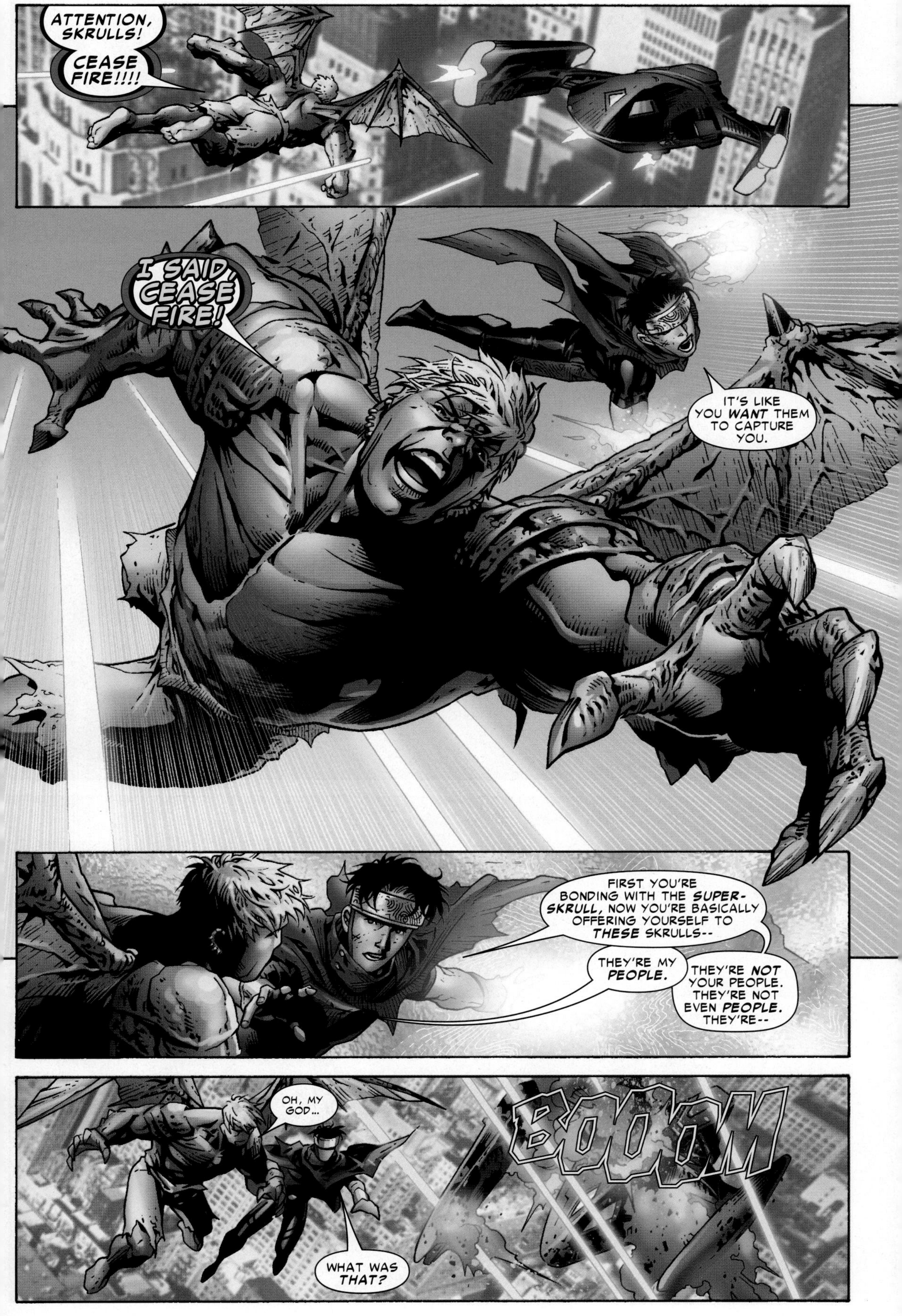

ATTENTION, SKRULLS!
CEASE FIRE!!!!
I SAID, CEASE FIRE!
IT'S LIKE YOU WANT THEM TO CAPTURE YOU.
FIRST YOU'RE BONDING WITH THE SUPER-SKRULL, NOW YOU'RE BASICALLY OFFERING YOURSELF TO THESE SKRULLS--
THEY'RE MY PEOPLE.
THEY'RE NOT YOUR PEOPLE. THEY'RE NOT EVEN PEOPLE. THEY'RE--
OH, MY GOD...
BOOOM
WHAT WAS THAT?

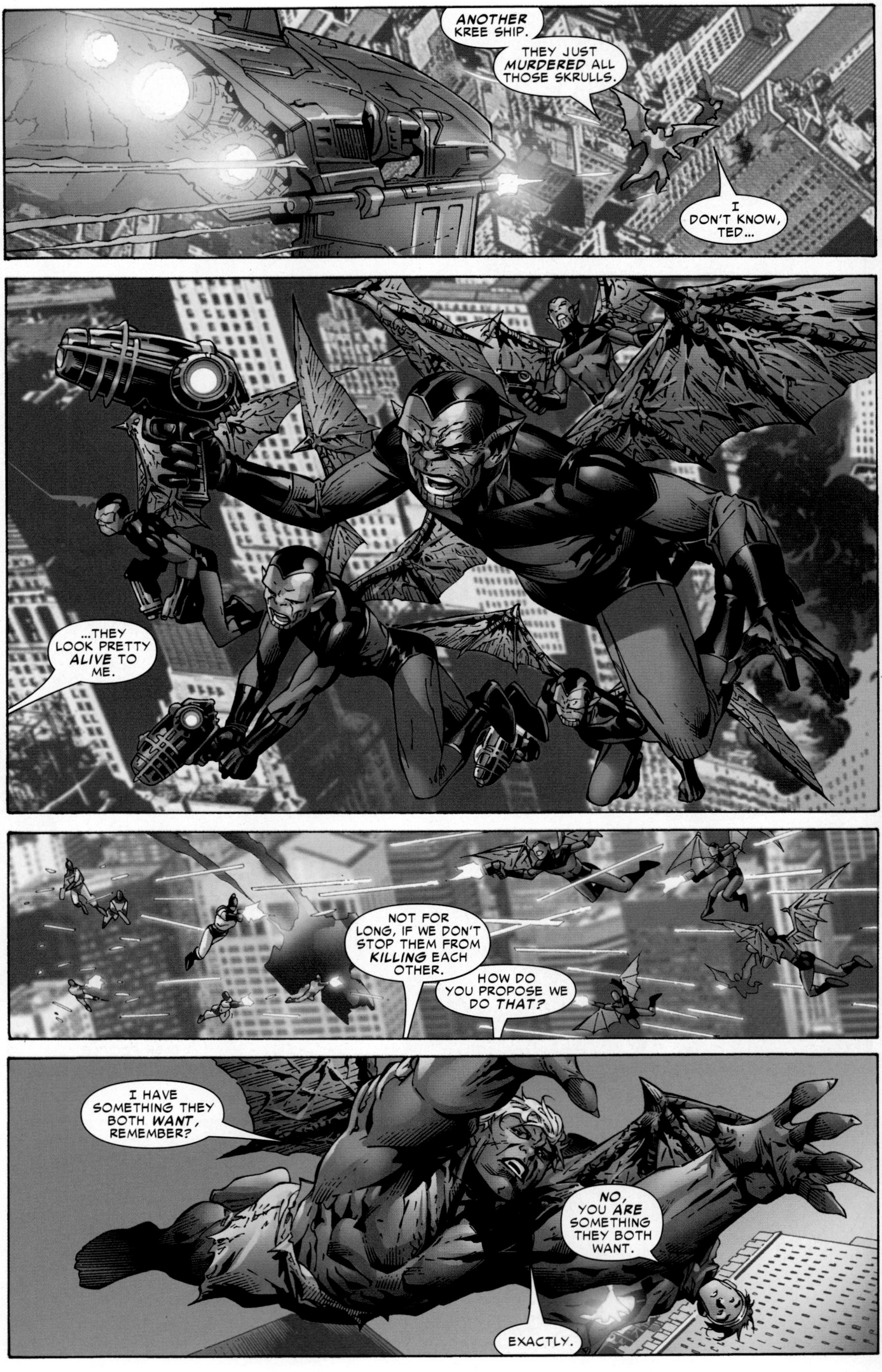
ANOTHER KREE SHIP.
THEY JUST MURDERED ALL THOSE SKRULLS.
I DON'T KNOW, TED...
...THEY LOOK PRETTY ALIVE TO ME.
NOT FOR LONG, IF WE DON'T STOP THEM FROM KILLING EACH OTHER.
HOW DO YOU PROPOSE WE DO THAT?
I HAVE SOMETHING THEY BOTH WANT, REMEMBER?
NO, YOU ARE SOMETHING THEY BOTH WANT.
EXACTLY.

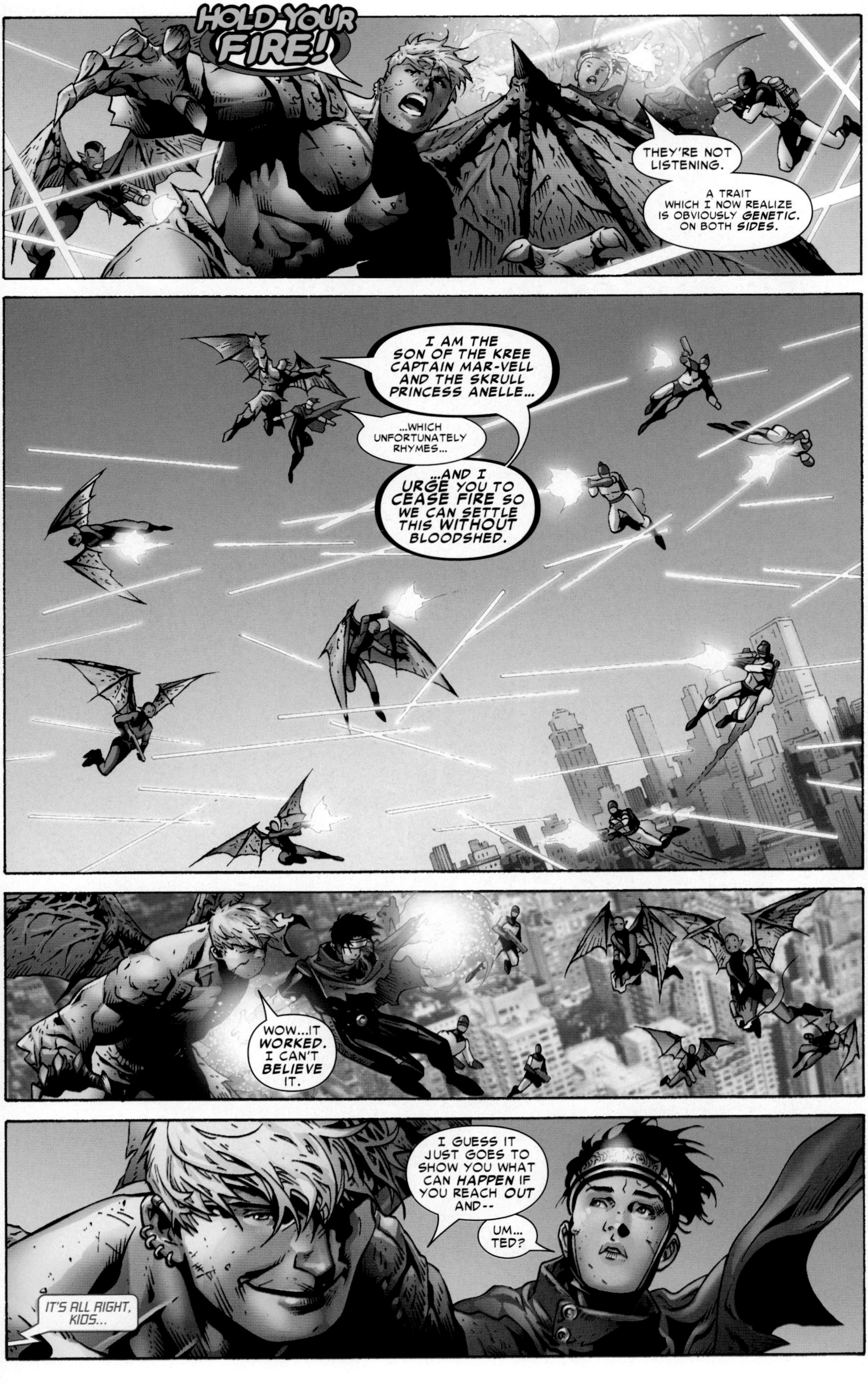
HOLD YOUR FIRE!
THEY'RE NOT LISTENING.
A TRAIT WHICH I NOW REALIZE IS OBVIOUSLY GENETIC. ON BOTH SIDES.
I AM THE SON OF THE KREE CAPTAIN MAR-VELL AND THE SKRULL PRINCESS ANELLE...
...WHICH UNFORTUNATELY RHYMES...
...AND I URGE YOU TO CEASE FIRE SO WE CAN SETTLE THIS WITHOUT BLOODSHED.
WOW...IT WORKED. I CAN'T BELIEVE IT.
I GUESS IT JUST GOES TO SHOW YOU WHAT CAN HAPPEN IF YOU REACH OUT AND--
UM... TED?
IT'S ALL RIGHT, KIDS...

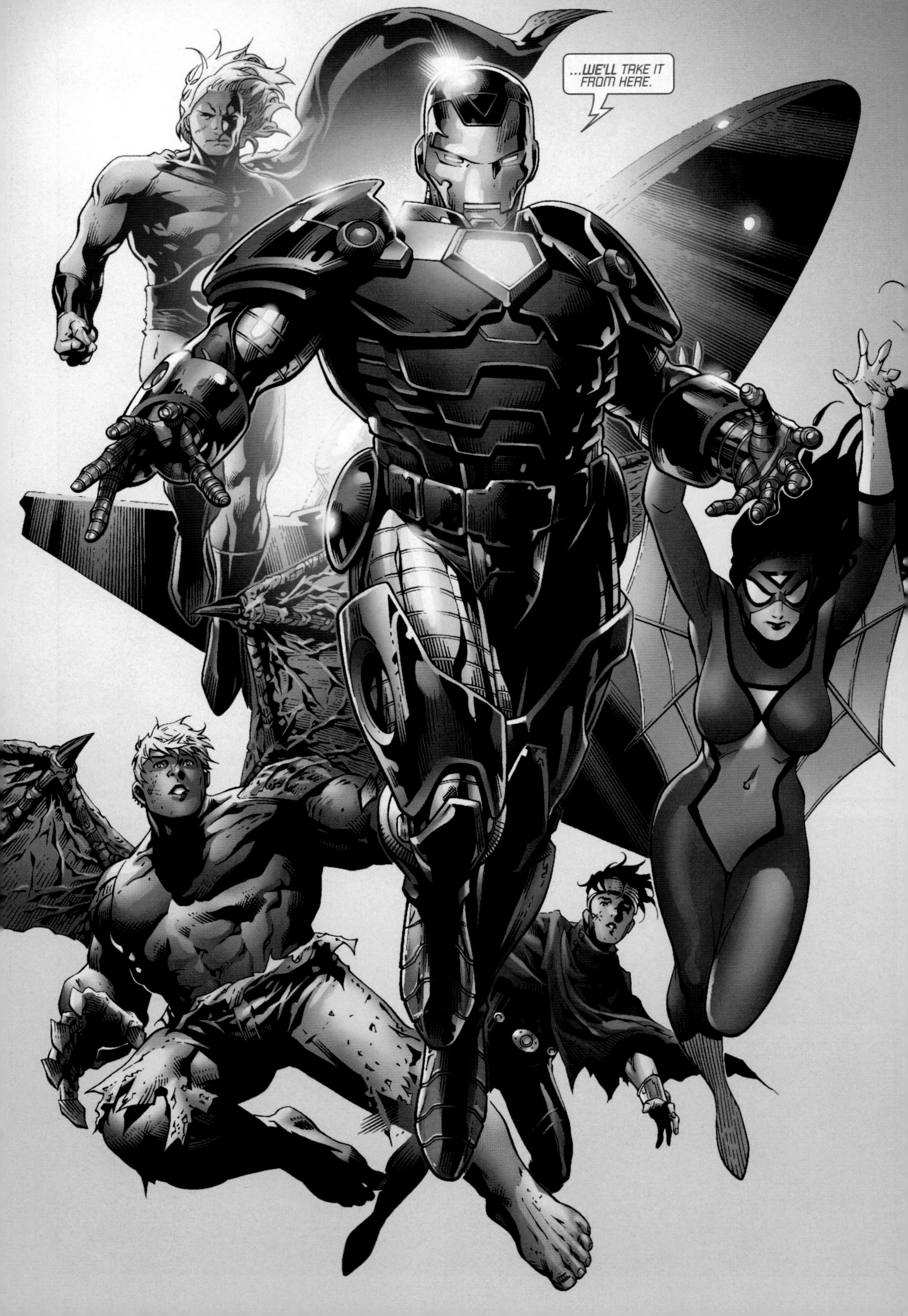
...WE'LL TAKE IT FROM HERE.

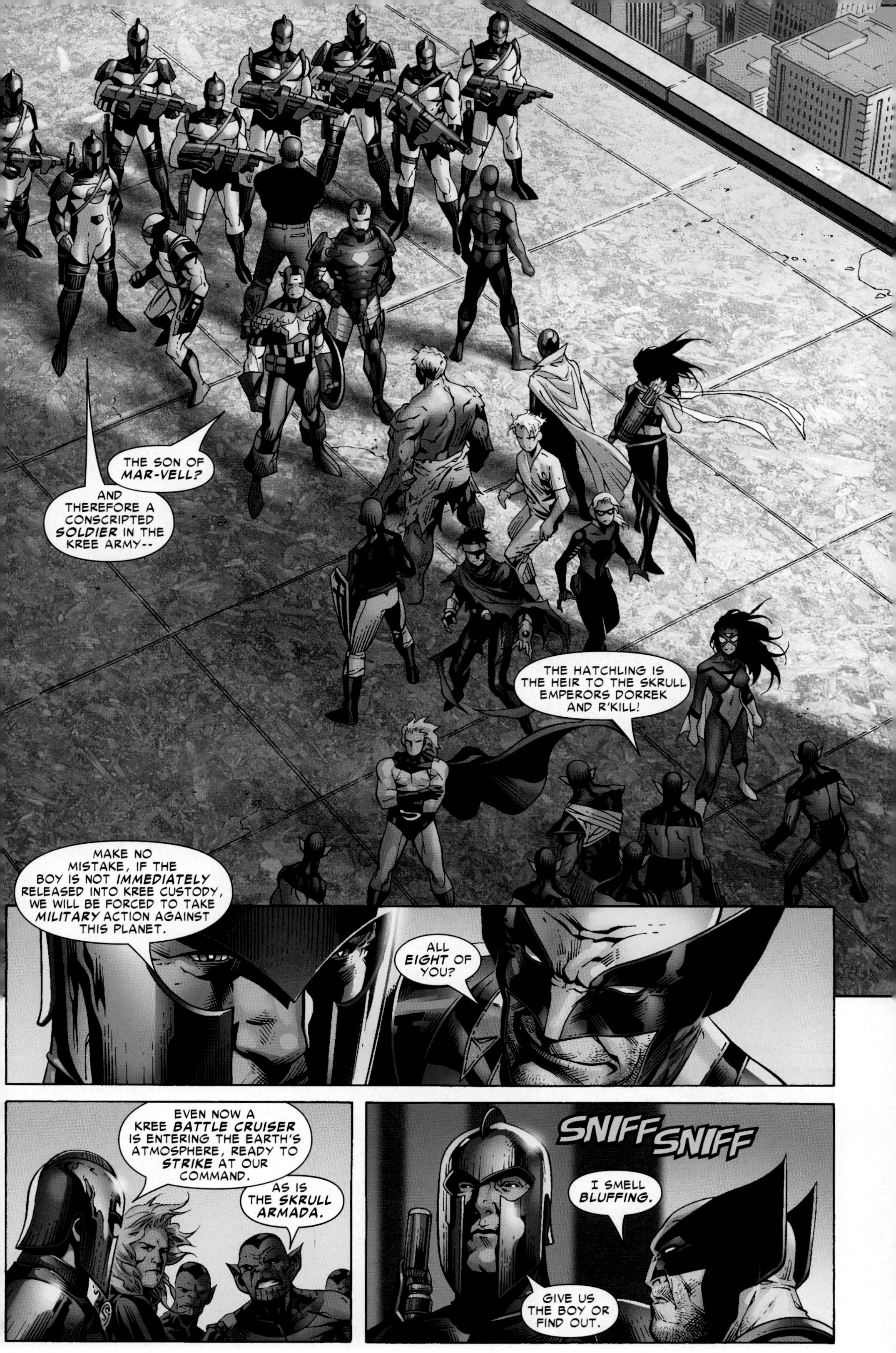
THE SON OF MAR-VELL?
AND THEREFORE A CONSCRIPTED SOLDIER IN THE KREE ARMY--
THE HATCHLING IS THE HEIR TO THE SKRULL EMPERORS DORREK AND R'KILL!
MAKE NO MISTAKE, IF THE BOY IS NOT IMMEDIATELY RELEASED INTO KREE CUSTODY, WE WILL BE FORCED TO TAKE MILITARY ACTION AGAINST THIS PLANET.
ALL EIGHT OF YOU?
EVEN NOW A KREE BATTLE CRUISER IS ENTERING THE EARTH'S ATMOSPHERE, READY TO STRIKE AT OUR COMMAND.
AS IS THE SKRULL ARMADA.
SNIFF SNIFF
I SMELL BLUFFING.
GIVE US THE BOY OR FIND OUT.

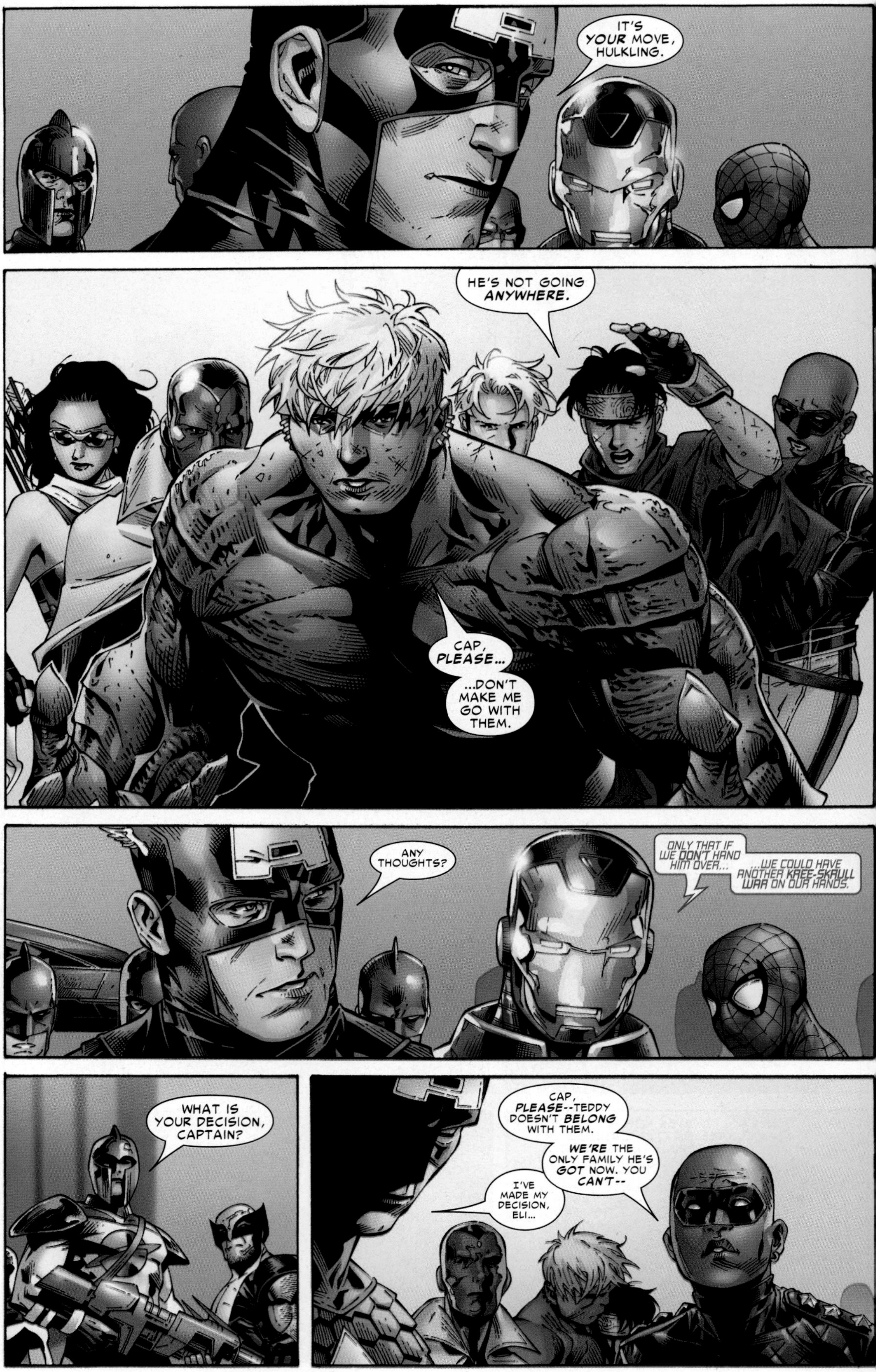
IT'S YOUR MOVE, HULKLING.
HE'S NOT GOING ANYWHERE.
CAP, PLEASE...
...DON'T MAKE ME GO WITH THEM.
ANY THOUGHTS?
ONLY THAT IF WE DON'T HAND HIM OVER...
...WE COULD HAVE ANOTHER KREE-SKRULL WAR ON OUR HANDS.
WHAT IS YOUR DECISION, CAPTAIN?
CAP, PLEASE--TEDDY DOESN'T BELONG WITH THEM.
WE'RE THE ONLY FAMILY HE'S GOT NOW. YOU CAN'T--
I'VE MADE MY DECISION, ELI...

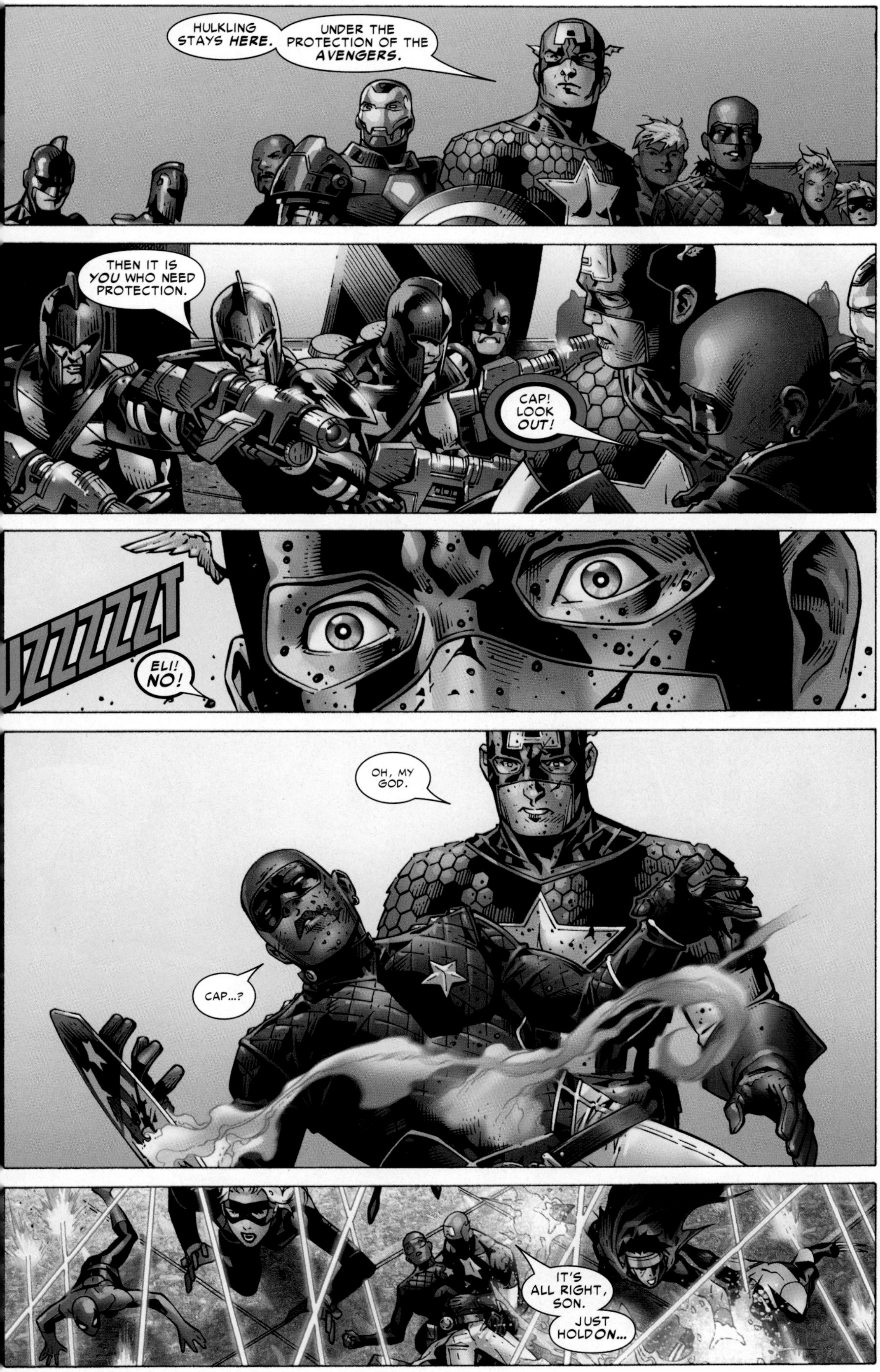
HULKLING STAYS HERE.
UNDER THE PROTECTION OF THE AVENGERS.
THEN IT IS YOU WHO NEED PROTECTION.
CAP! LOOK OUT!
ZZZZZZZT
ELI! NO!
OH, MY GOD.
CAP...?
IT'S ALL RIGHT, SON.
JUST HOLD ON...

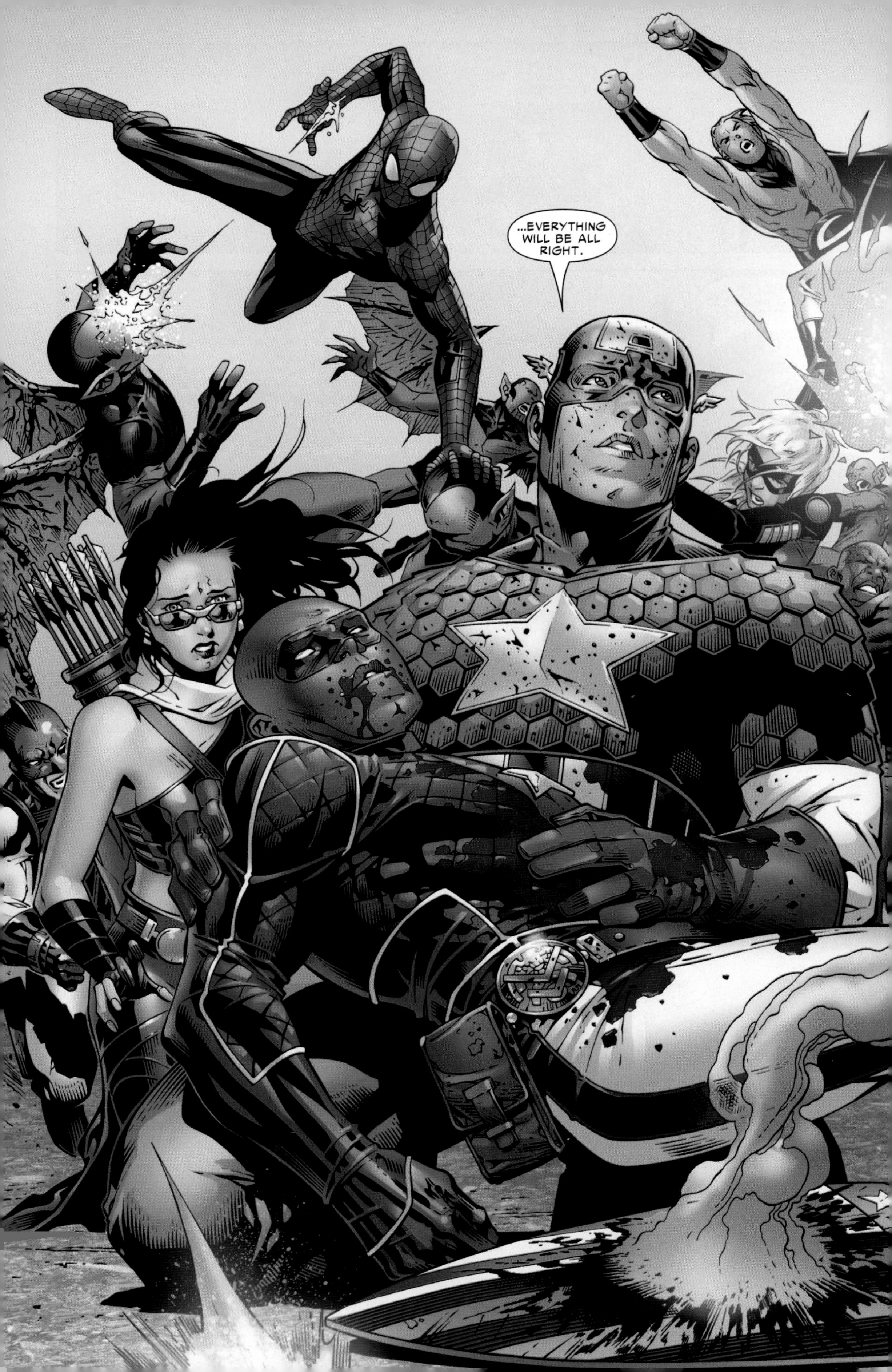
...EVERYTHING WILL BE ALL RIGHT.

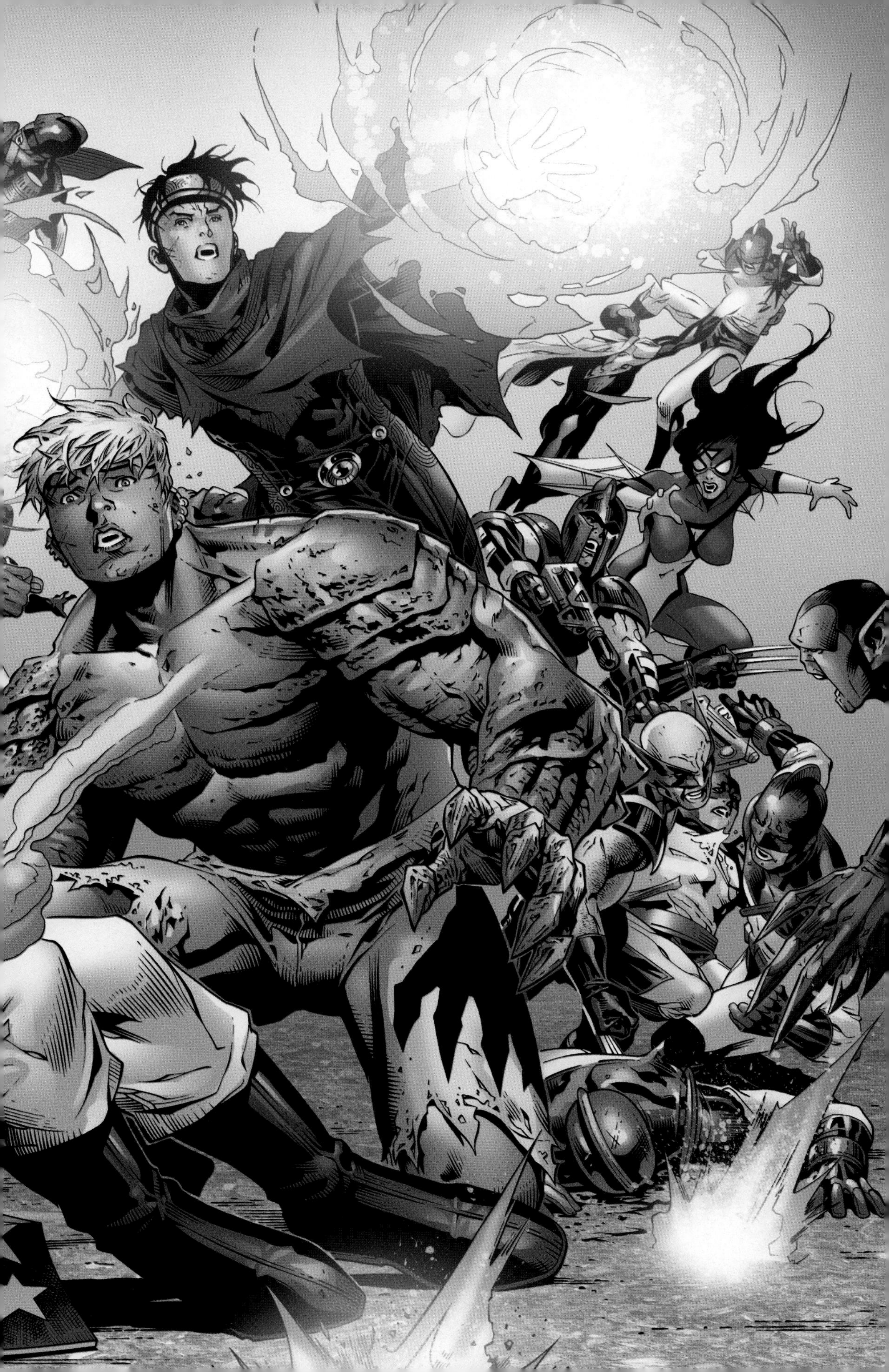

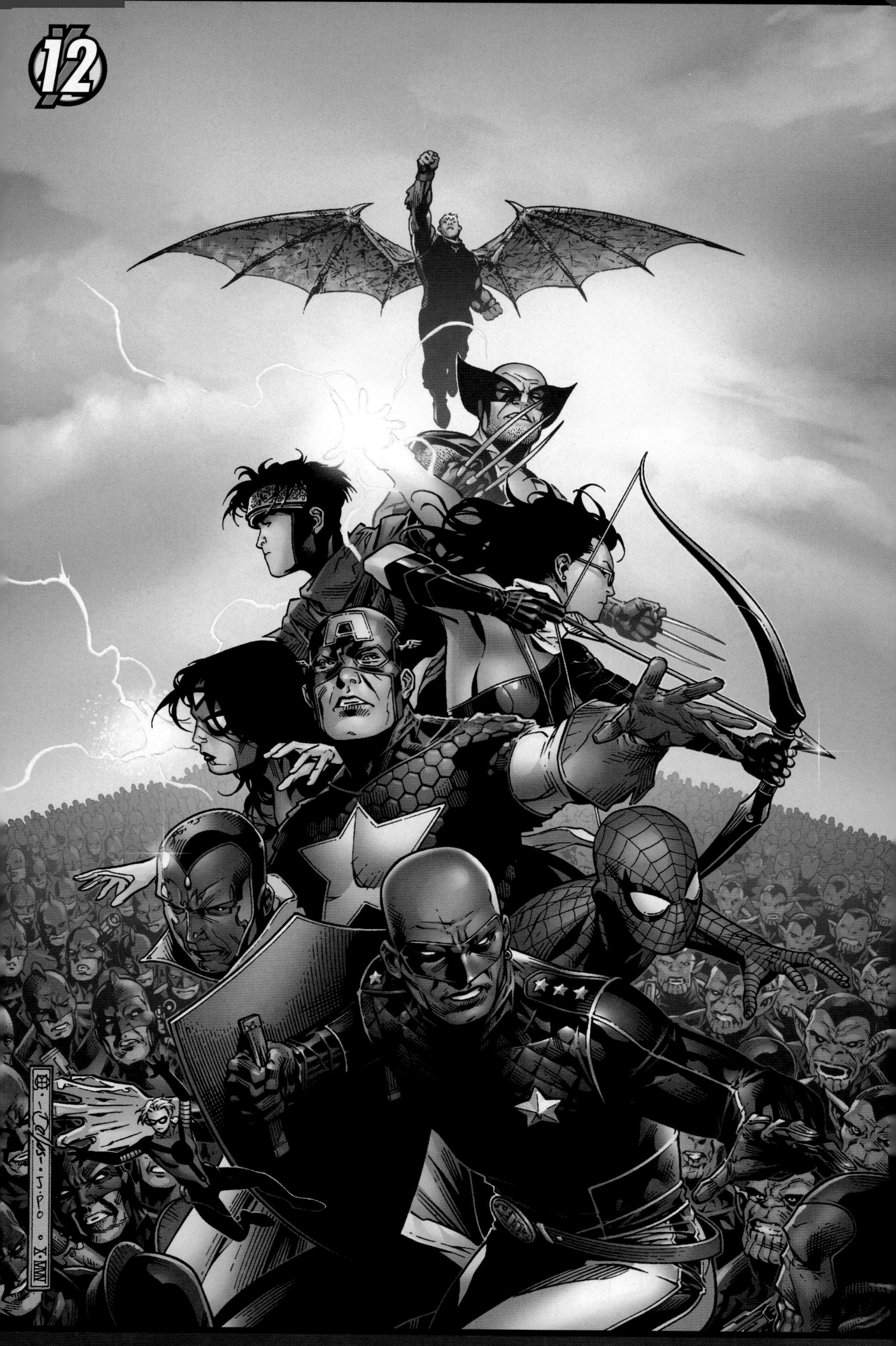

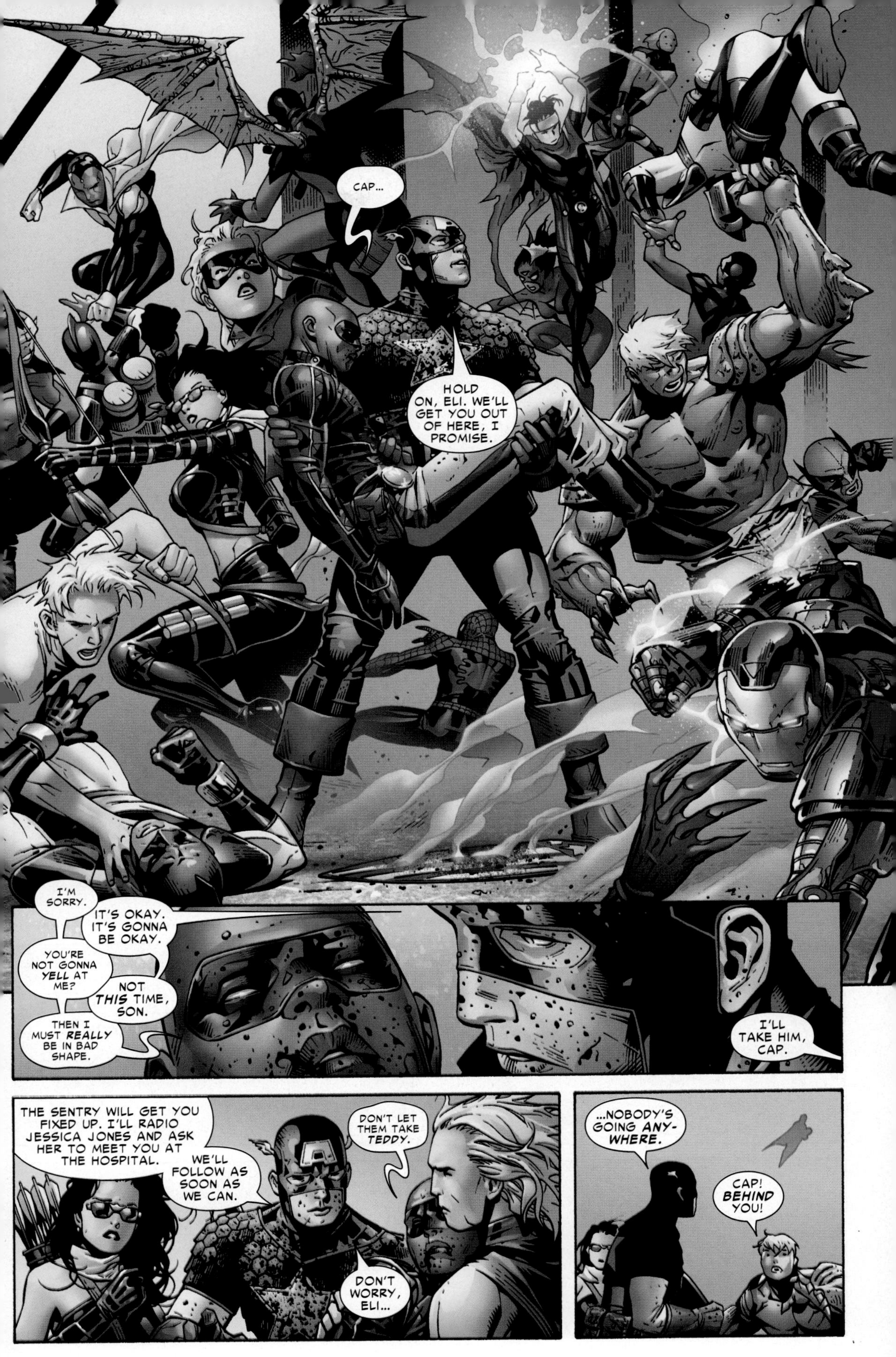
CAP...
HOLD ON, ELI. WE'LL GET YOU OUT OF HERE, I PROMISE.
I'M SORRY.
IT'S OKAY. IT'S GONNA BE OKAY.
YOU'RE NOT GONNA YELL AT ME?
NOT THIS TIME, SON.
THEN I MUST REALLY BE IN BAD SHAPE.
I'LL TAKE HIM, CAP.
THE SENTRY WILL GET YOU FIXED UP. I'LL RADIO JESSICA JONES AND ASK HER TO MEET YOU AT THE HOSPITAL.
WE'LL FOLLOW AS SOON AS WE CAN.
DON'T LET THEM TAKE TEDDY.
DON'T WORRY, ELI...
...NOBODY'S GOING ANY-WHERE.
CAP! BEHIND YOU!

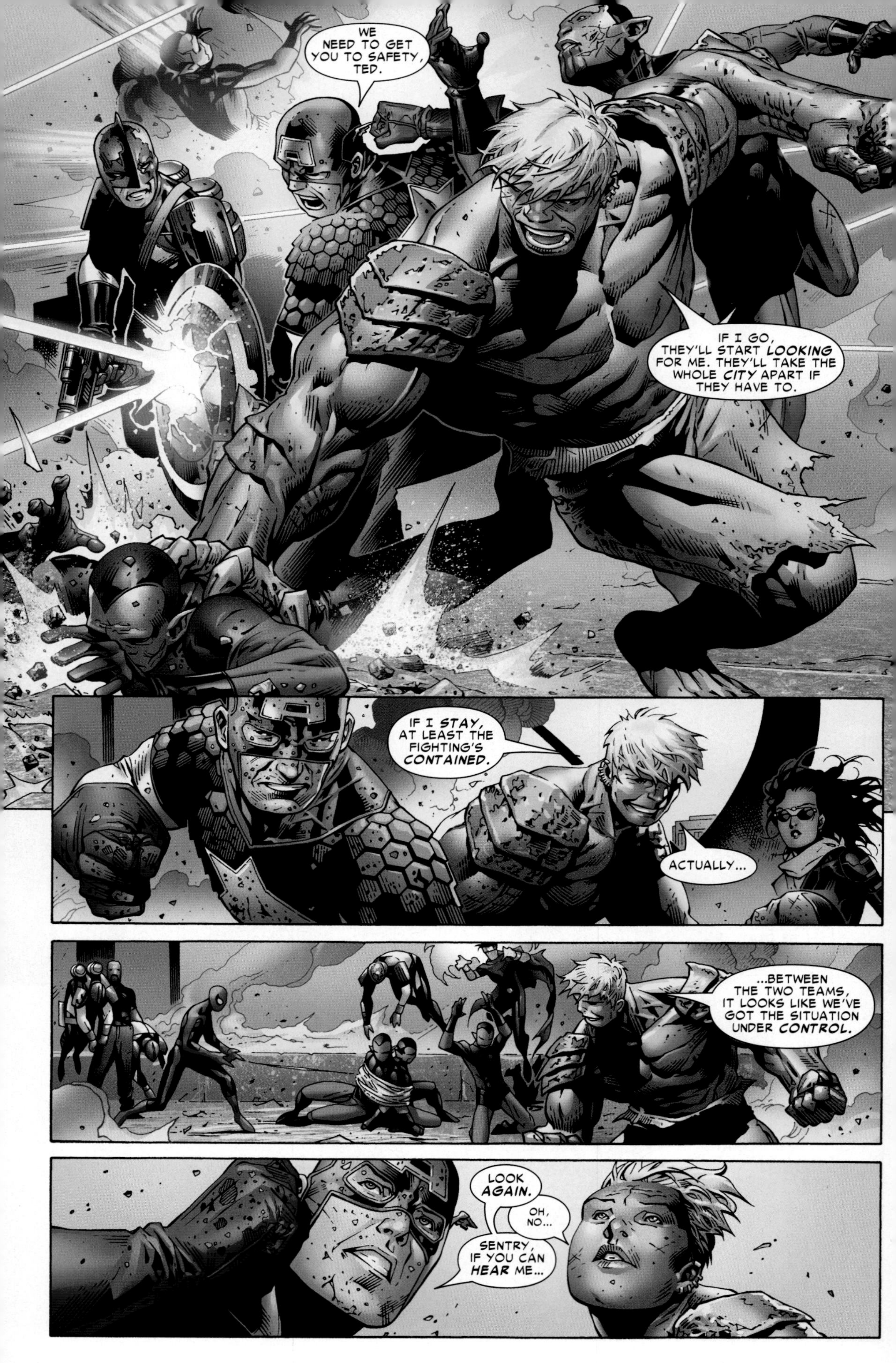
WE NEED TO GET YOU TO SAFETY, TED.
IF I GO, THEY'LL START LOOKING FOR ME. THEY'LL TAKE THE WHOLE CITY APART IF THEY HAVE TO.
IF I STAY, AT LEAST THE FIGHTING'S CONTAINED.
ACTUALLY...
...BETWEEN THE TWO TEAMS, IT LOOKS LIKE WE'VE GOT THE SITUATION UNDER CONTROL.
LOOK AGAIN.
OH, NO...
SENTRY, IF YOU CAN HEAR ME...

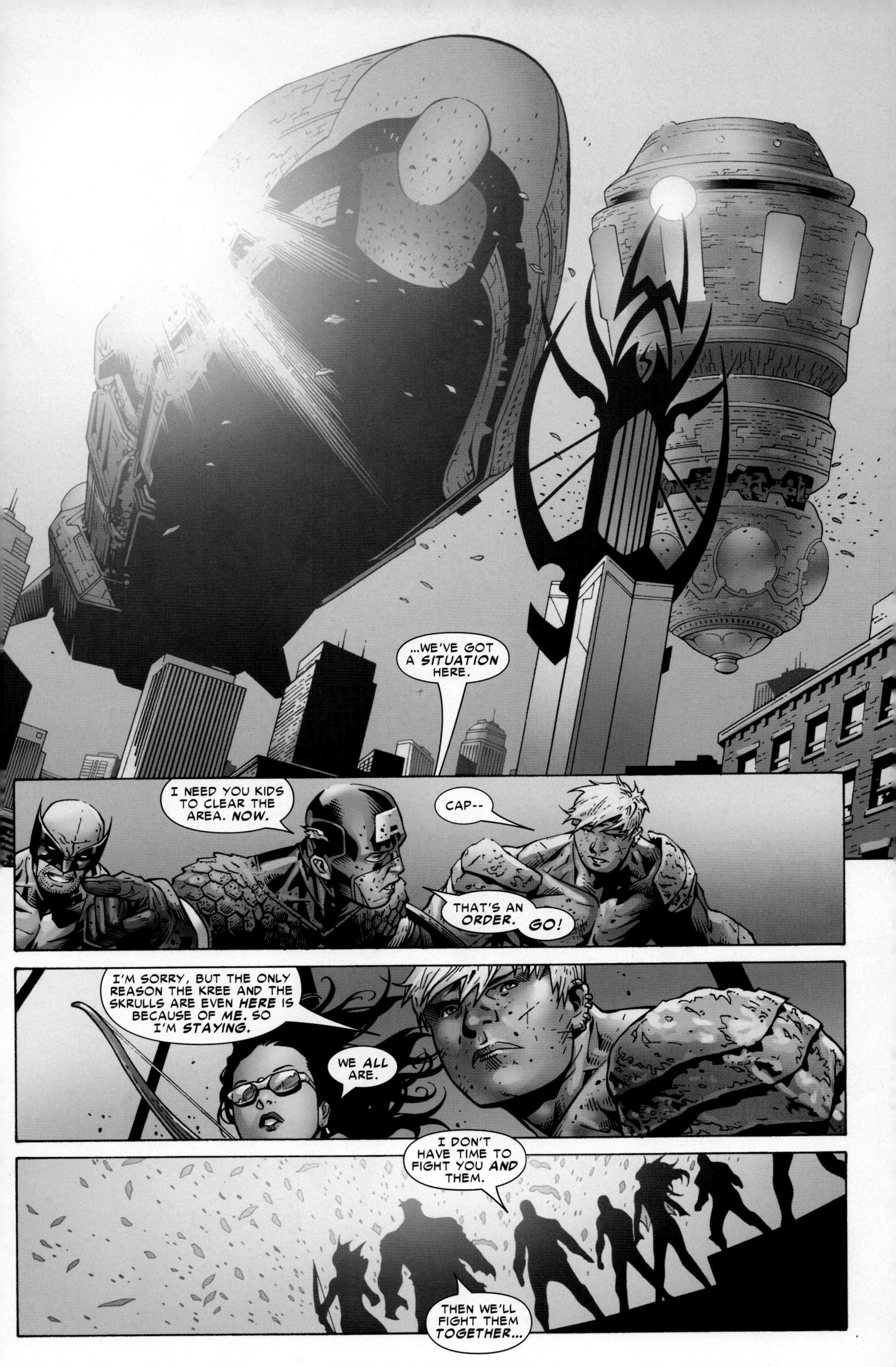
...WE'VE GOT A *SITUATION* HERE.
I NEED YOU KIDS TO CLEAR THE AREA. **NOW.**
CAP--
THAT'S AN *ORDER*. *GO!*
I'M SORRY, BUT THE ONLY REASON THE KREE AND THE SKRULLS ARE EVEN *HERE* IS BECAUSE OF *ME*. SO I'M *STAYING*.
WE *ALL* ARE.
I DON'T HAVE TIME TO FIGHT YOU *AND* THEM.
THEN WE'LL FIGHT THEM *TOGETHER*...

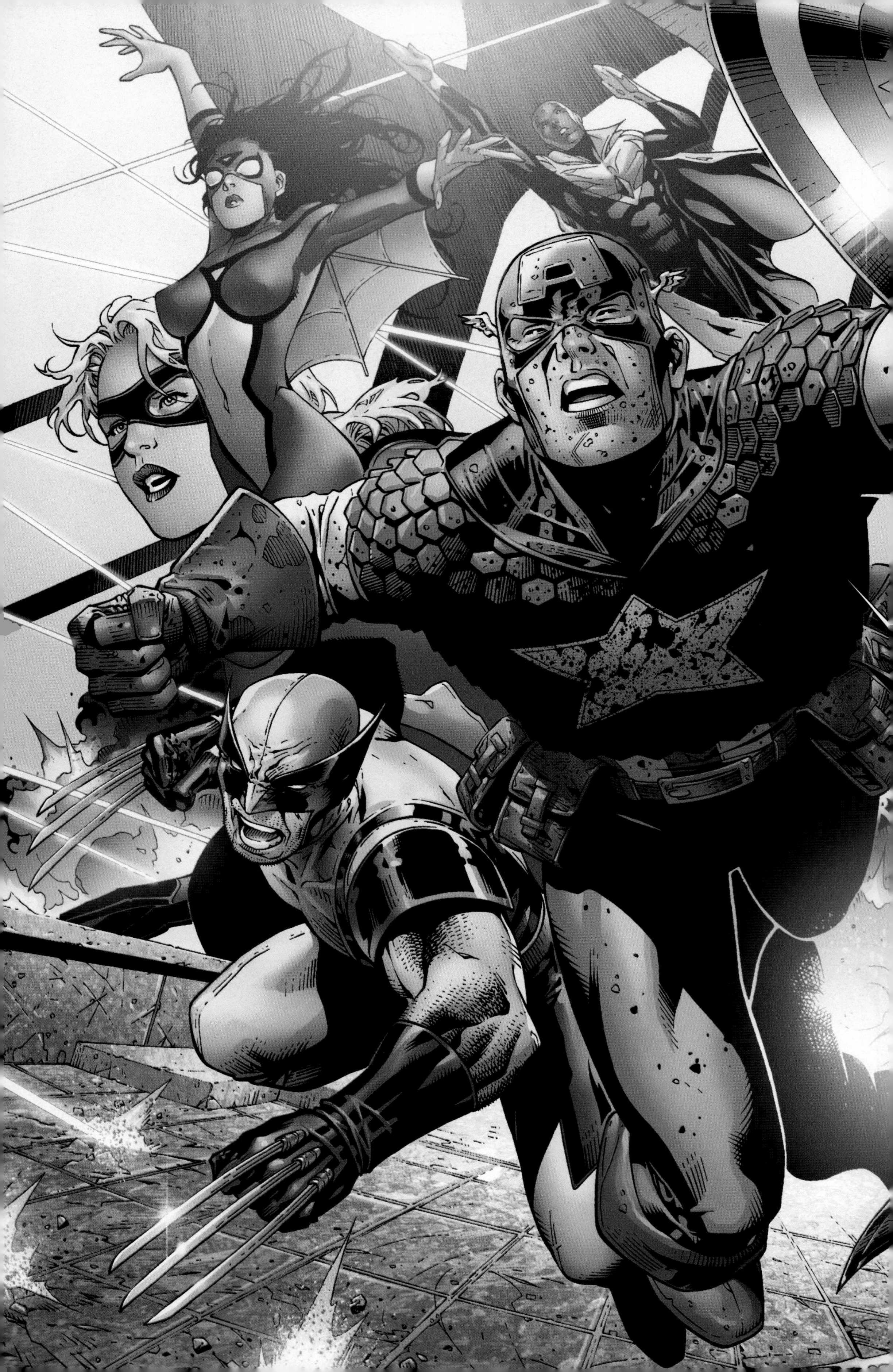

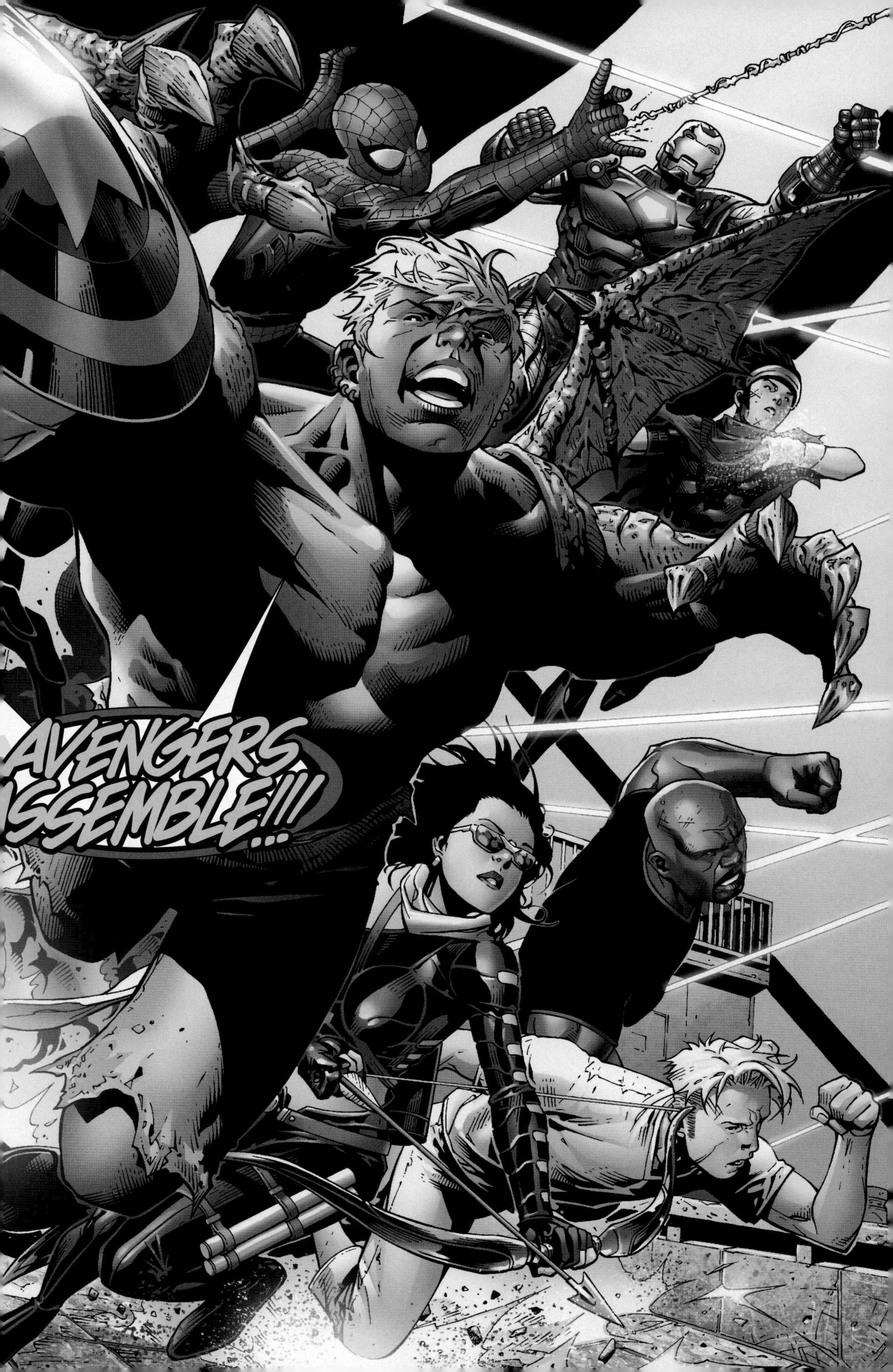
AVENGERS
SSEMBLE!!!

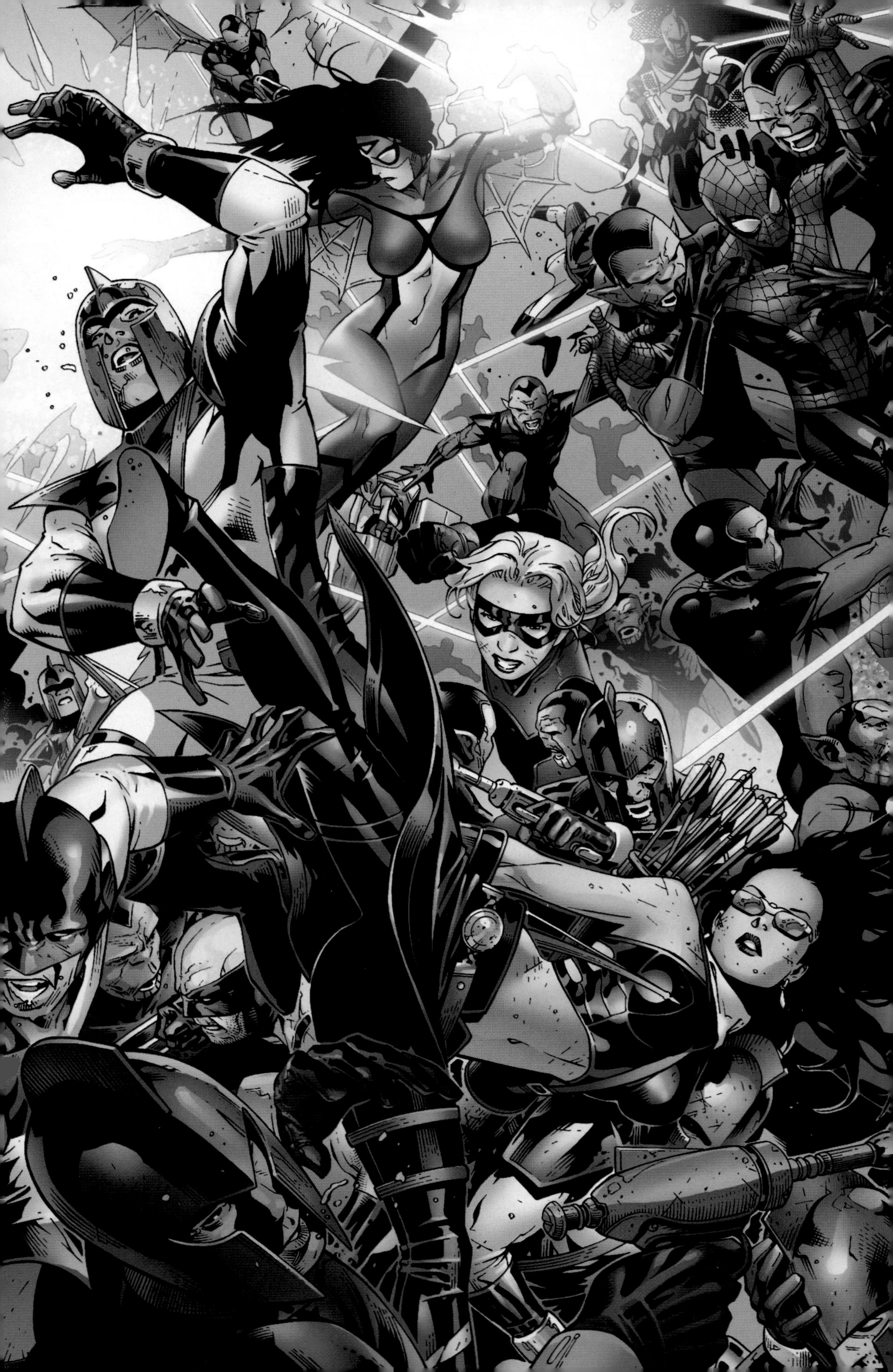

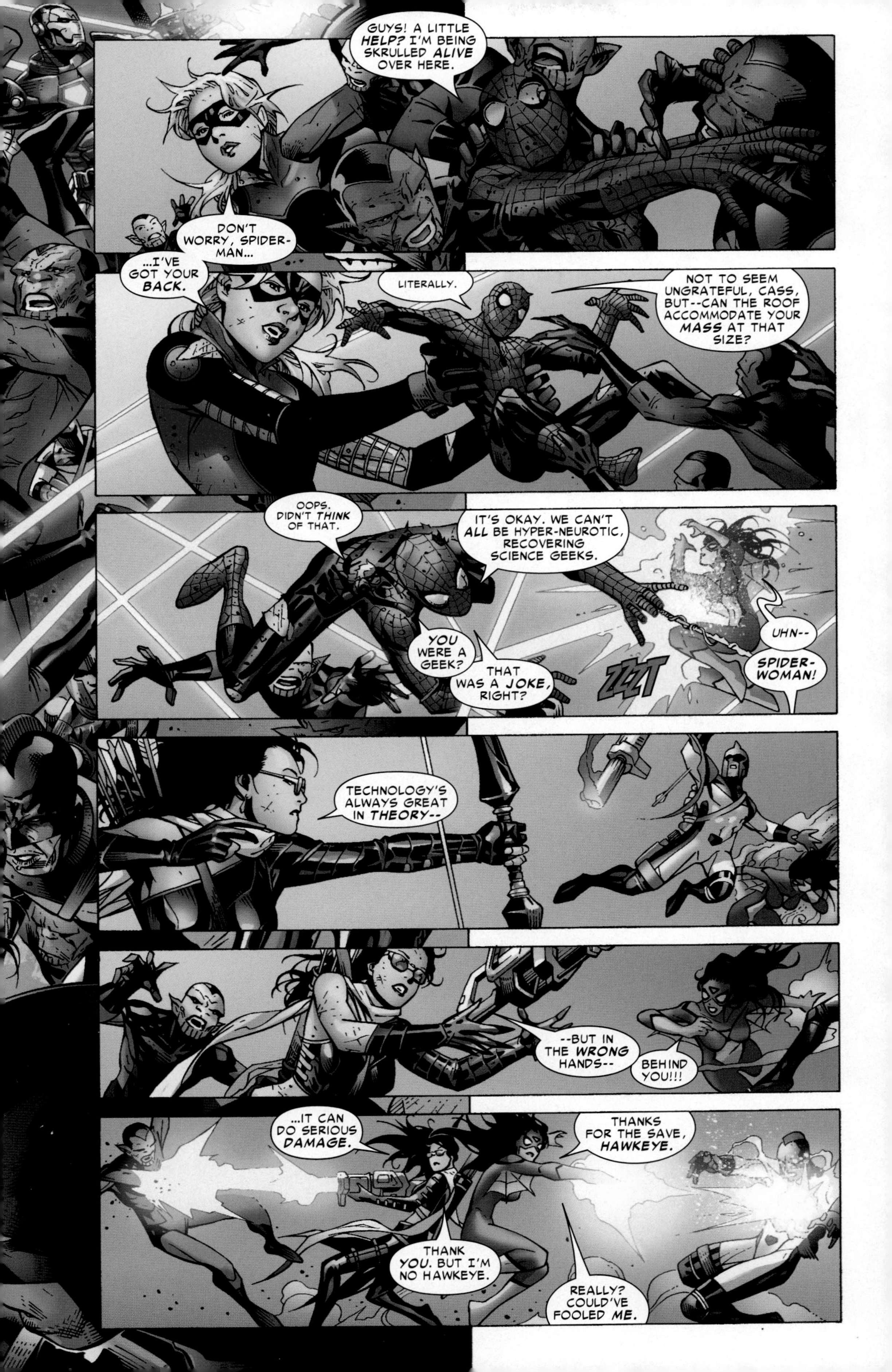
GUYS! A LITTLE HELP? I'M BEING SKRULLED ALIVE OVER HERE.
DON'T WORRY, SPIDER-MAN...
...I'VE GOT YOUR BACK.
LITERALLY.
NOT TO SEEM UNGRATEFUL, CASS, BUT--CAN THE ROOF ACCOMMODATE YOUR MASS AT THAT SIZE?
OOPS. DIDN'T THINK OF THAT.
IT'S OKAY. WE CAN'T ALL BE HYPER-NEUROTIC, RECOVERING SCIENCE GEEKS.
YOU WERE A GEEK?
THAT WAS A JOKE, RIGHT?
ZZZT
UHN--
SPIDER-WOMAN!
TECHNOLOGY'S ALWAYS GREAT IN THEORY--
--BUT IN THE WRONG HANDS--
BEHIND YOU!!!
...IT CAN DO SERIOUS DAMAGE.
THANKS FOR THE SAVE, HAWKEYE.
THANK YOU. BUT I'M NO HAWKEYE.
REALLY? COULD'VE FOOLED ME.

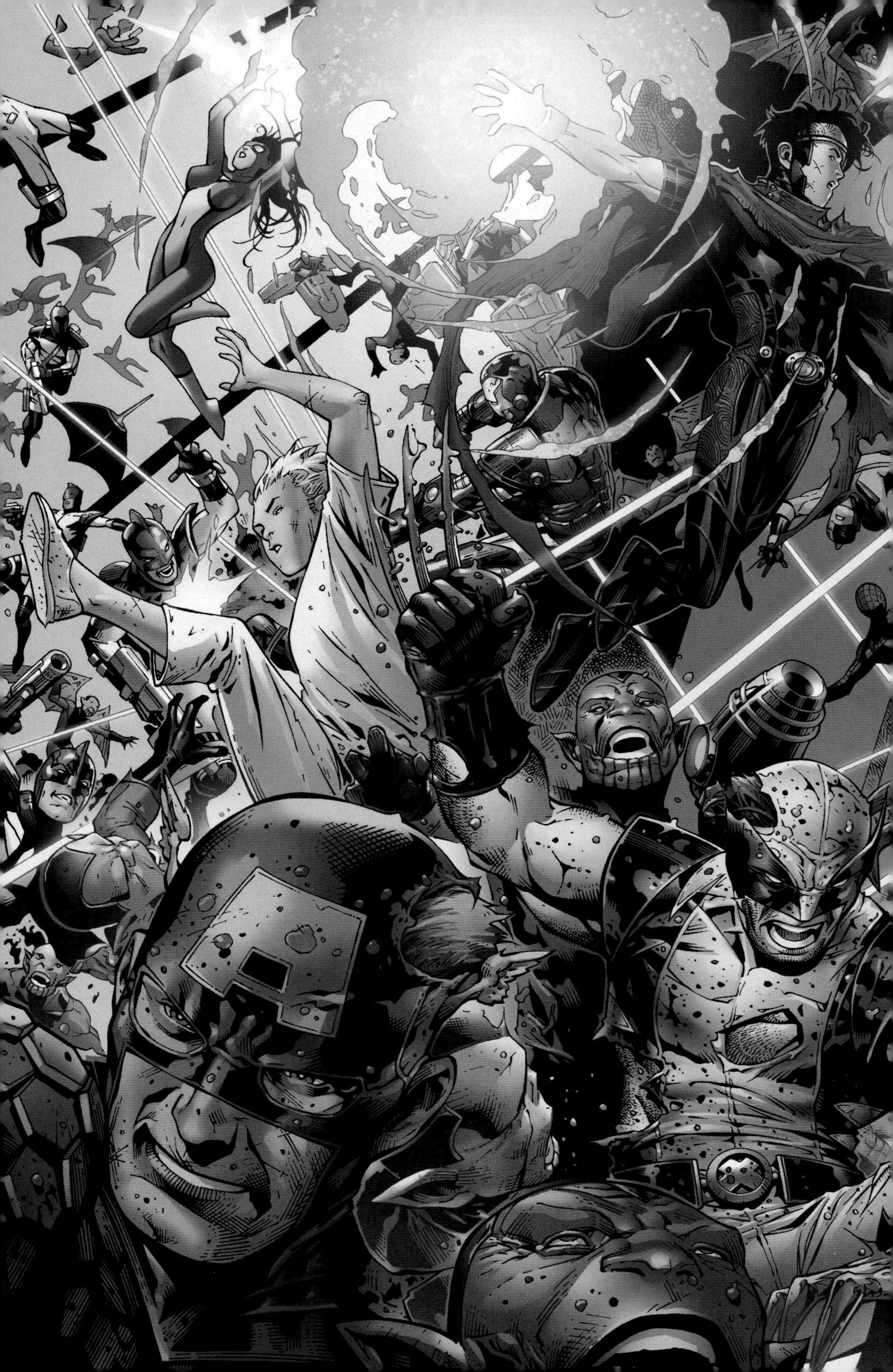

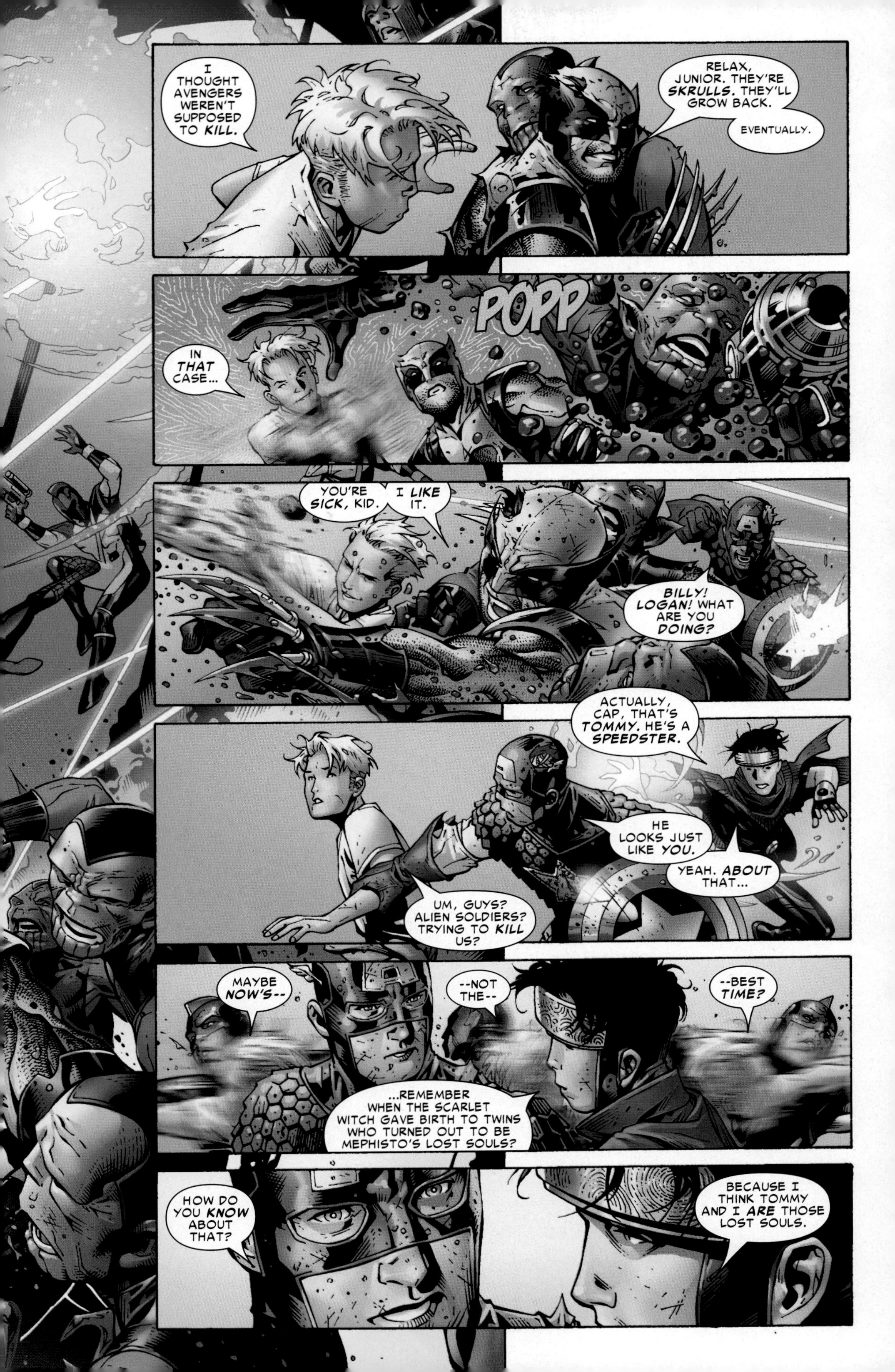
I THOUGHT AVENGERS WEREN'T SUPPOSED TO KILL.
RELAX, JUNIOR. THEY'RE SKRULLS. THEY'LL GROW BACK.
EVENTUALLY.
IN THAT CASE...
POPP
YOU'RE SICK, KID.
I LIKE IT.
BILLY! LOGAN! WHAT ARE YOU DOING?
ACTUALLY, CAP, THAT'S TOMMY. HE'S A SPEEDSTER.
HE LOOKS JUST LIKE YOU.
YEAH. ABOUT THAT...
UM, GUYS? ALIEN SOLDIERS? TRYING TO KILL US?
MAYBE NOW'S--
--NOT THE--
--BEST TIME?
...REMEMBER WHEN THE SCARLET WITCH GAVE BIRTH TO TWINS WHO TURNED OUT TO BE MEPHISTO'S LOST SOULS?
HOW DO YOU KNOW ABOUT THAT?
BECAUSE I THINK TOMMY AND I ARE THOSE LOST SOULS.

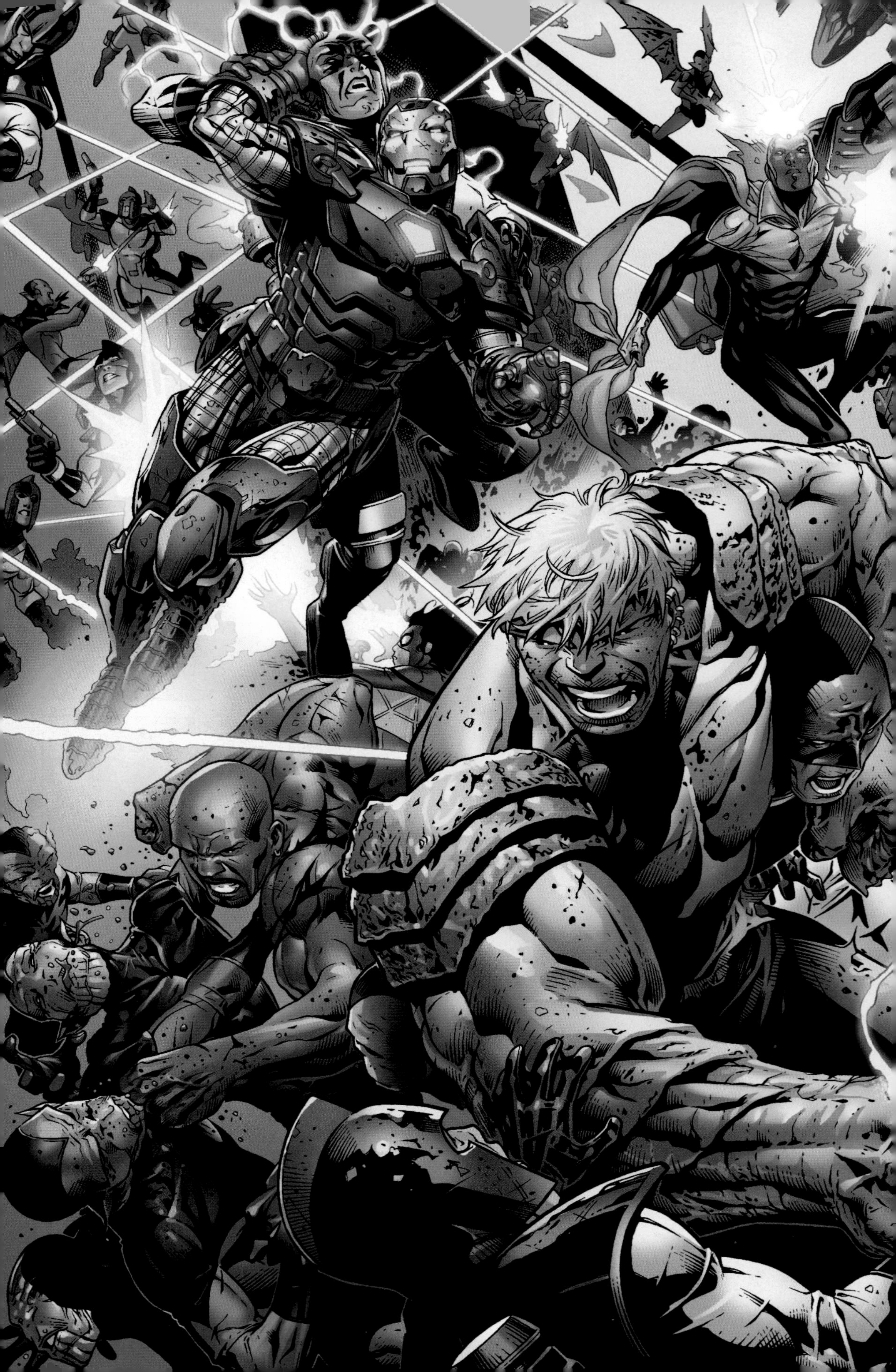

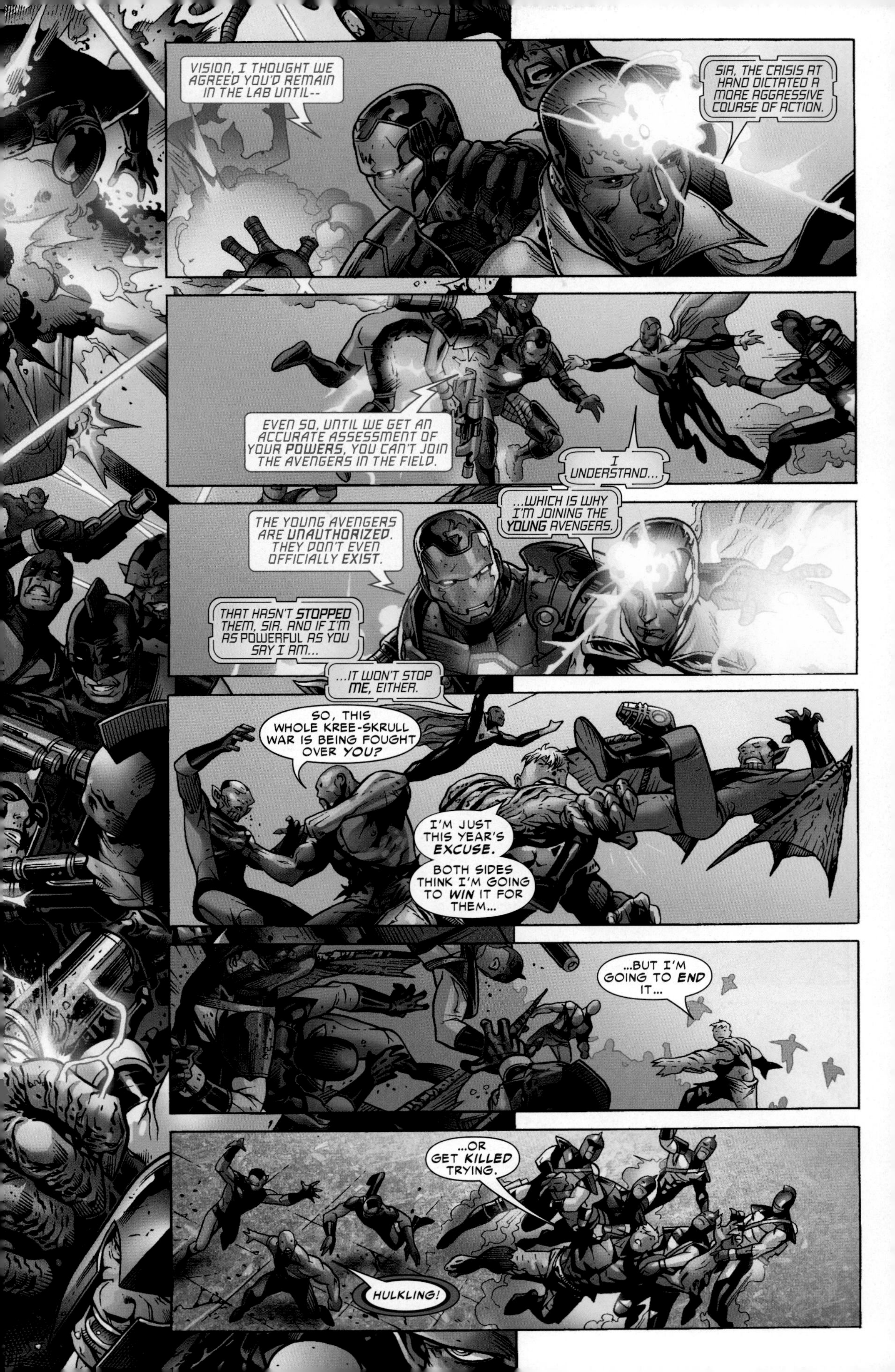
VISION, I THOUGHT WE AGREED YOU'D REMAIN IN THE LAB UNTIL--
SIR, THE CRISIS AT HAND DICTATED A MORE AGGRESSIVE COURSE OF ACTION.
EVEN SO, UNTIL WE GET AN ACCURATE ASSESSMENT OF YOUR POWERS, YOU CAN'T JOIN THE AVENGERS IN THE FIELD.
I UNDERSTAND...
...WHICH IS WHY I'M JOINING THE YOUNG AVENGERS.
THE YOUNG AVENGERS ARE UNAUTHORIZED. THEY DON'T EVEN OFFICIALLY EXIST.
THAT HASN'T STOPPED THEM, SIR. AND IF I'M AS POWERFUL AS YOU SAY I AM...
...IT WON'T STOP ME, EITHER.
SO, THIS WHOLE KREE-SKRULL WAR IS BEING FOUGHT OVER YOU?
I'M JUST THIS YEAR'S EXCUSE.
BOTH SIDES THINK I'M GOING TO WIN IT FOR THEM...
...BUT I'M GOING TO END IT...
...OR GET KILLED TRYING.
HULKLING!

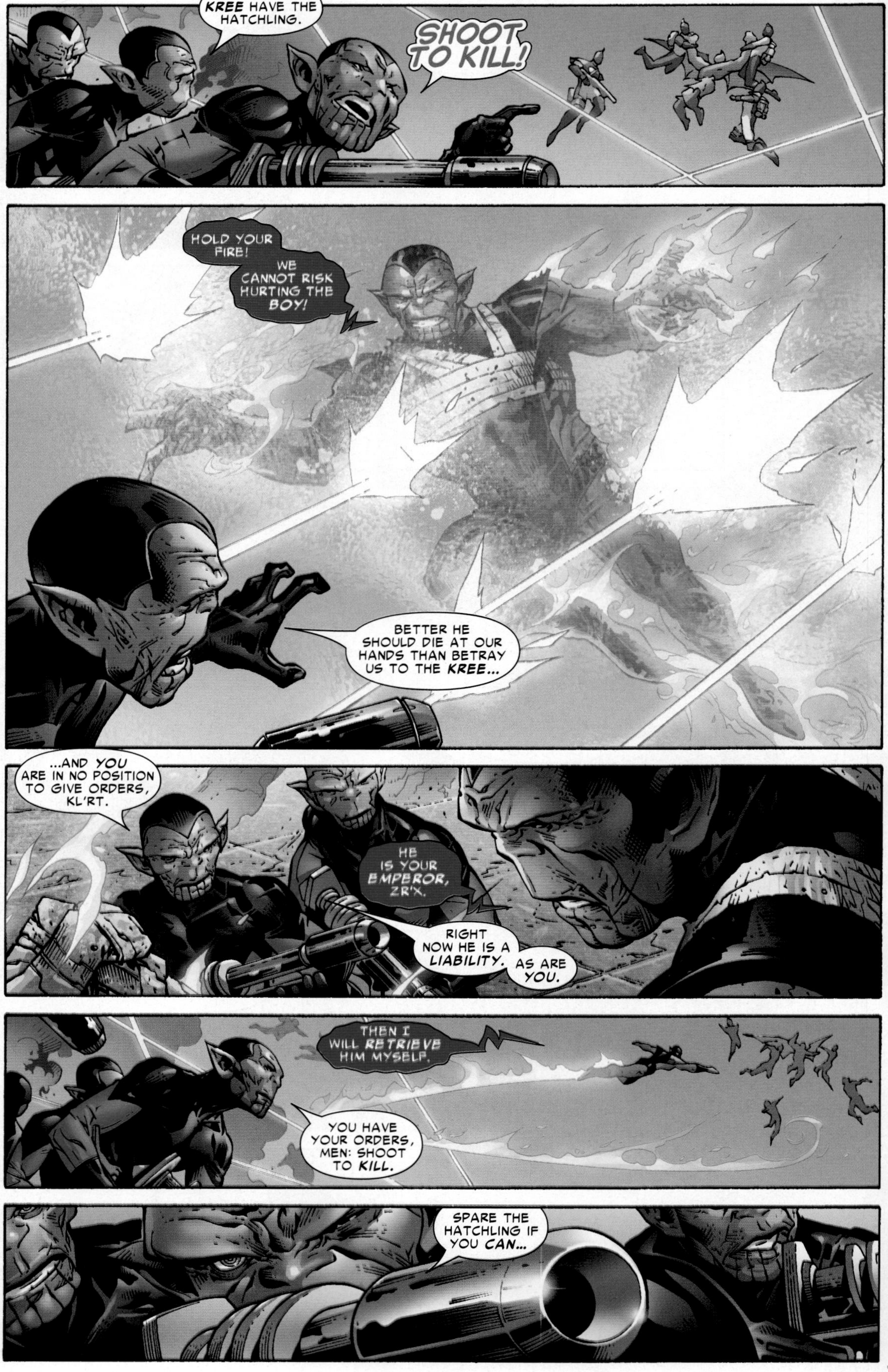
THE KREE HAVE THE HATCHLING.
SHOOT TO KILL!
HOLD YOUR FIRE!
WE CANNOT RISK HURTING THE BOY!
BETTER HE SHOULD DIE AT OUR HANDS THAN BETRAY US TO THE KREE...
...AND YOU ARE IN NO POSITION TO GIVE ORDERS, KL'RT.
HE IS YOUR EMPEROR, ZR'X.
RIGHT NOW HE IS A LIABILITY.
AS ARE YOU.
THEN I WILL RETRIEVE HIM MYSELF.
YOU HAVE YOUR ORDERS, MEN: SHOOT TO KILL.
SPARE THE HATCHLING IF YOU CAN...

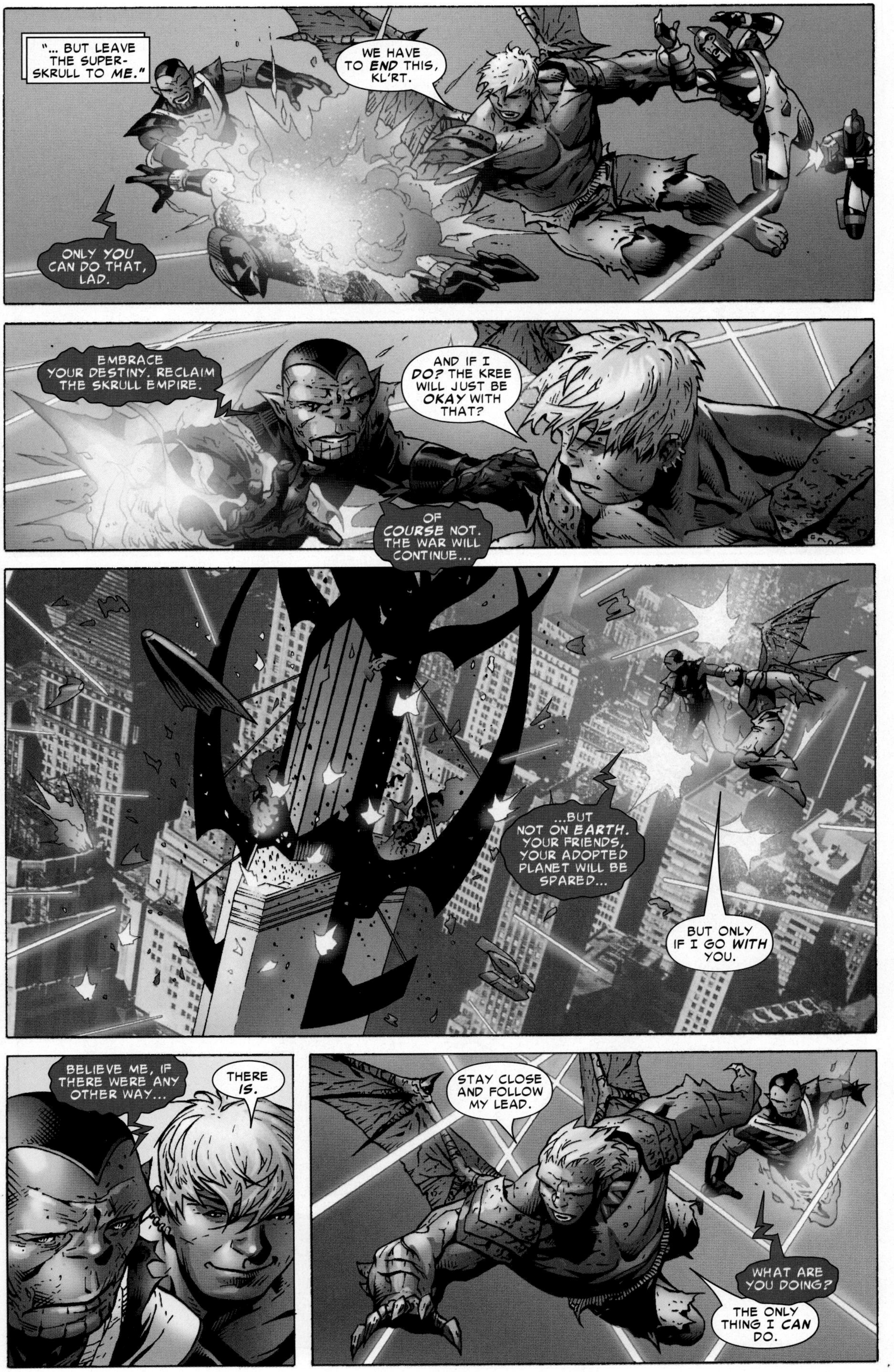

"... BUT LEAVE THE SUPER-SKRULL TO ME."
WE HAVE TO END THIS, KL'RT.
ONLY YOU CAN DO THAT, LAD.
EMBRACE YOUR DESTINY. RECLAIM THE SKRULL EMPIRE.
AND IF I DO? THE KREE WILL JUST BE OKAY WITH THAT?
OF COURSE NOT. THE WAR WILL CONTINUE...
...BUT NOT ON EARTH. YOUR FRIENDS, YOUR ADOPTED PLANET WILL BE SPARED...
BUT ONLY IF I GO WITH YOU.
BELIEVE ME, IF THERE WERE ANY OTHER WAY...
THERE IS.
STAY CLOSE AND FOLLOW MY LEAD.
WHAT ARE YOU DOING?
THE ONLY THING I CAN DO.

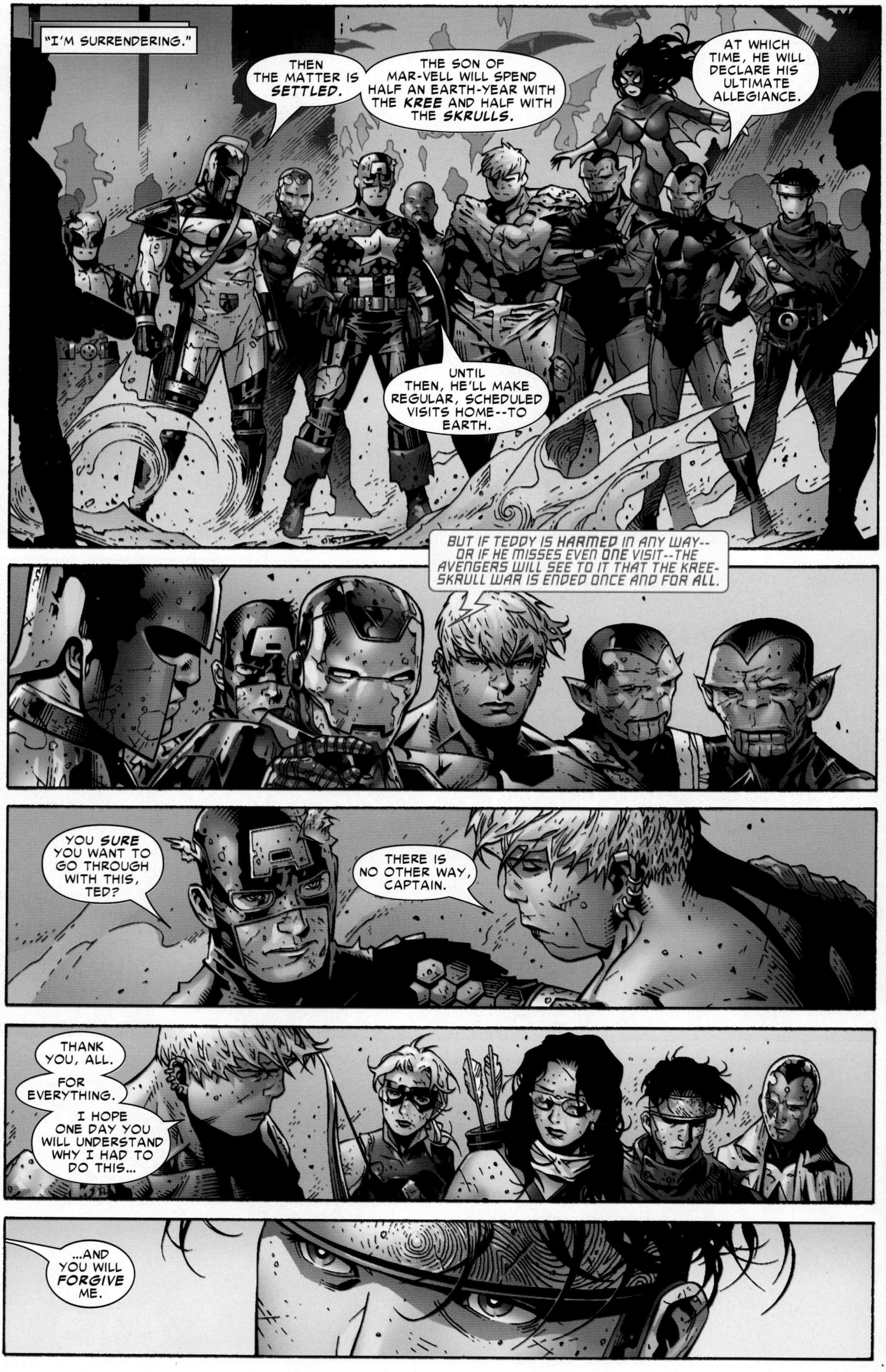

"I'M SURRENDERING."
THEN THE MATTER IS SETTLED.
THE SON OF MAR-VELL WILL SPEND HALF AN EARTH-YEAR WITH THE KREE AND HALF WITH THE SKRULLS.
AT WHICH TIME, HE WILL DECLARE HIS ULTIMATE ALLEGIANCE.
UNTIL THEN, HE'LL MAKE REGULAR, SCHEDULED VISITS HOME--TO EARTH.
BUT IF TEDDY IS HARMED IN ANY WAY--OR IF HE MISSES EVEN ONE VISIT--THE AVENGERS WILL SEE TO IT THAT THE KREE-SKRULL WAR IS ENDED ONCE AND FOR ALL.
YOU SURE YOU WANT TO GO THROUGH WITH THIS, TED?
THERE IS NO OTHER WAY, CAPTAIN.
THANK YOU, ALL.
FOR EVERYTHING.
I HOPE ONE DAY YOU WILL UNDERSTAND WHY I HAD TO DO THIS...
...AND YOU WILL FORGIVE ME.

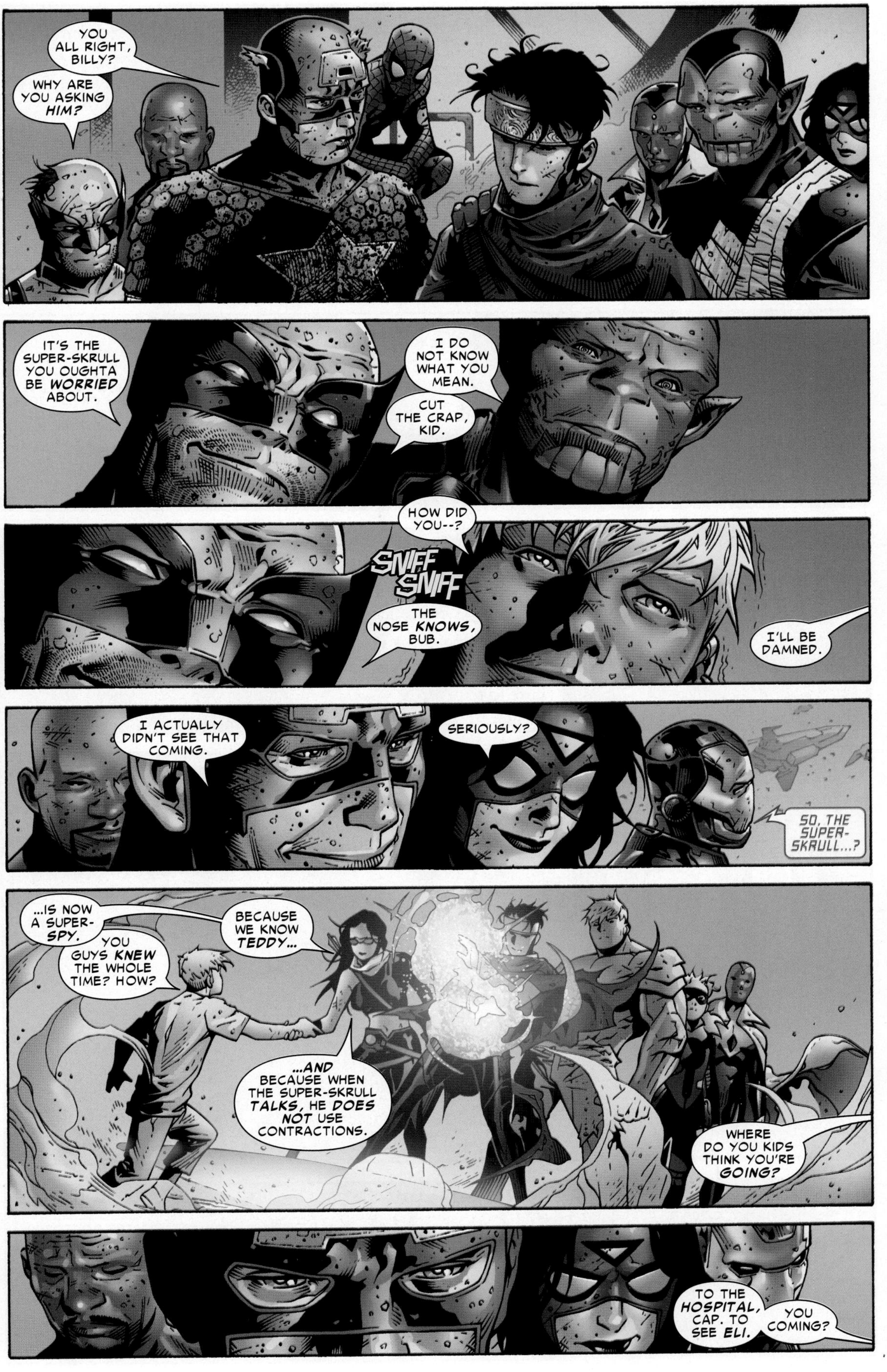
YOU ALL RIGHT, BILLY?
WHY ARE YOU ASKING HIM?
IT'S THE SUPER-SKRULL YOU OUGHTA BE WORRIED ABOUT.
I DO NOT KNOW WHAT YOU MEAN.
CUT THE CRAP, KID.
HOW DID YOU--?
SNIFF SNIFF
THE NOSE KNOWS, BUB.
I'LL BE DAMNED.
I ACTUALLY DIDN'T SEE THAT COMING.
SERIOUSLY?
SO, THE SUPER-SKRULL...?
...IS NOW A SUPER-SPY.
BECAUSE WE KNOW TEDDY...
YOU GUYS KNEW THE WHOLE TIME? HOW?
...AND BECAUSE WHEN THE SUPER-SKRULL TALKS, HE DOES NOT USE CONTRACTIONS.
WHERE DO YOU KIDS THINK YOU'RE GOING?
TO THE HOSPITAL, CAP. TO SEE ELI.
YOU COMING?

LENOX HILL HOSPITAL

HE'S LOST A LOT OF BLOOD, SO THE DOCTORS CAN'T *OPERATE* UNTIL--

UNTIL THEY FIND A *DONOR*, I KNOW.

CAP, YOU DON'T *HAVE* TO.

YOU *KNOW* HOW HARD I'VE BEEN ON ELI, JESS. AND HE *STILL* TOOK THE HIT FOR ME.

GIVING BLOOD IS THE *LEAST* I CAN DO.

AND I'M SURE HE'D *APPRECIATE* IT, BUT...

...THE *OTHER* SUPER-SOLDIER BEAT YOU *TO* IT.

ISAIAH...

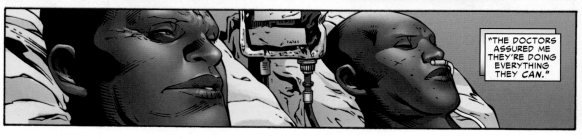

"THE DOCTORS ASSURED ME THEY'RE DOING EVERYTHING THEY *CAN*."

IF THE SURGERY IS SUCCESSFUL, ELI WILL BE ABLE TO LEAD A COMPLETELY NORMAL LIFE.

AND I'M HOPING THAT-- IN LIGHT OF WHAT HAPPENED TO HIM--YOU KIDS WILL, TOO.

SIR, WITH ALL DUE RESPECT...

...THE MINUTE ELI'S BACK ON HIS FEET, HE'LL BE CHASING DOWN BAD GUYS, POWERS OR NO POWERS. THAT'S JUST WHO HE IS.

IT'S WHO WE ALL ARE.

THE SAME AS YOU.

I KNOW YOU AND IRON MAN DON'T APPROVE OF US, BUT I CAN'T HELP THINKING...

...IF YOU GUYS HAD SUPPORTED US--IF YOU HAD TAKEN THE TIME TO TRAIN US--

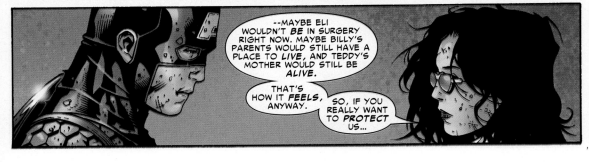

--MAYBE ELI WOULDN'T BE IN SURGERY RIGHT NOW. MAYBE BILLY'S PARENTS WOULD STILL HAVE A PLACE TO LIVE, AND TEDDY'S MOTHER WOULD STILL BE ALIVE.

THAT'S HOW IT FEELS, ANYWAY.

SO, IF YOU REALLY WANT TO PROTECT US...

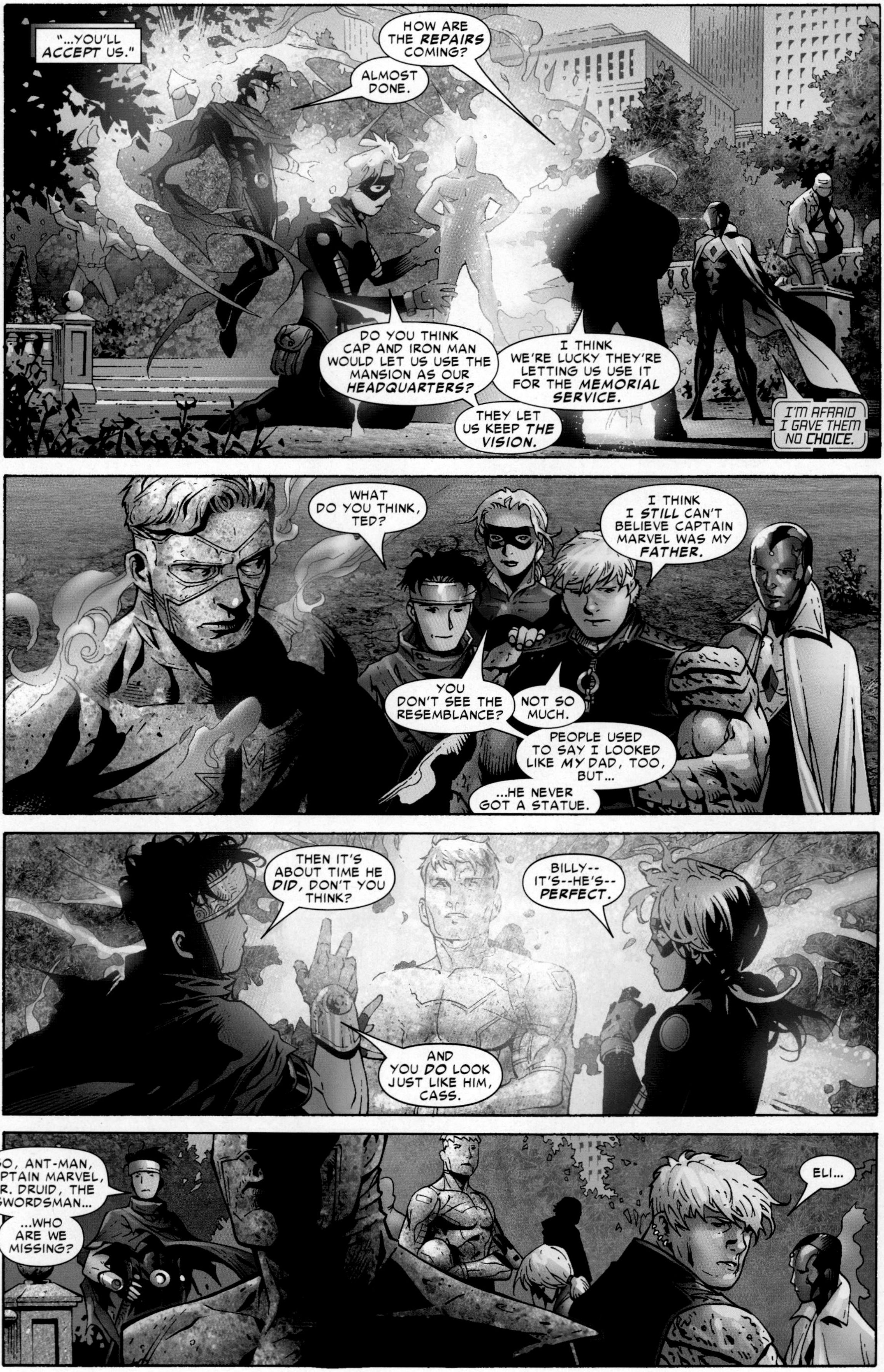
"...YOU'LL ACCEPT US."
HOW ARE THE REPAIRS COMING?
ALMOST DONE.
DO YOU THINK CAP AND IRON MAN WOULD LET US USE THE MANSION AS OUR HEADQUARTERS?
I THINK WE'RE LUCKY THEY'RE LETTING US USE IT FOR THE MEMORIAL SERVICE.
THEY LET US KEEP THE VISION.
I'M AFRAID I GAVE THEM NO CHOICE.
WHAT DO YOU THINK, TED?
I THINK I STILL CAN'T BELIEVE CAPTAIN MARVEL WAS MY FATHER.
YOU DON'T SEE THE RESEMBLANCE?
NOT SO MUCH.
PEOPLE USED TO SAY I LOOKED LIKE MY DAD, TOO, BUT...
...HE NEVER GOT A STATUE.
THEN IT'S ABOUT TIME HE DID, DON'T YOU THINK?
BILLY-- IT'S--HE'S-- PERFECT.
AND YOU DO LOOK JUST LIKE HIM, CASS.
SO, ANT-MAN, CAPTAIN MARVEL, DR. DRUID, THE SWORDSMAN...
...WHO ARE WE MISSING?
ELI...

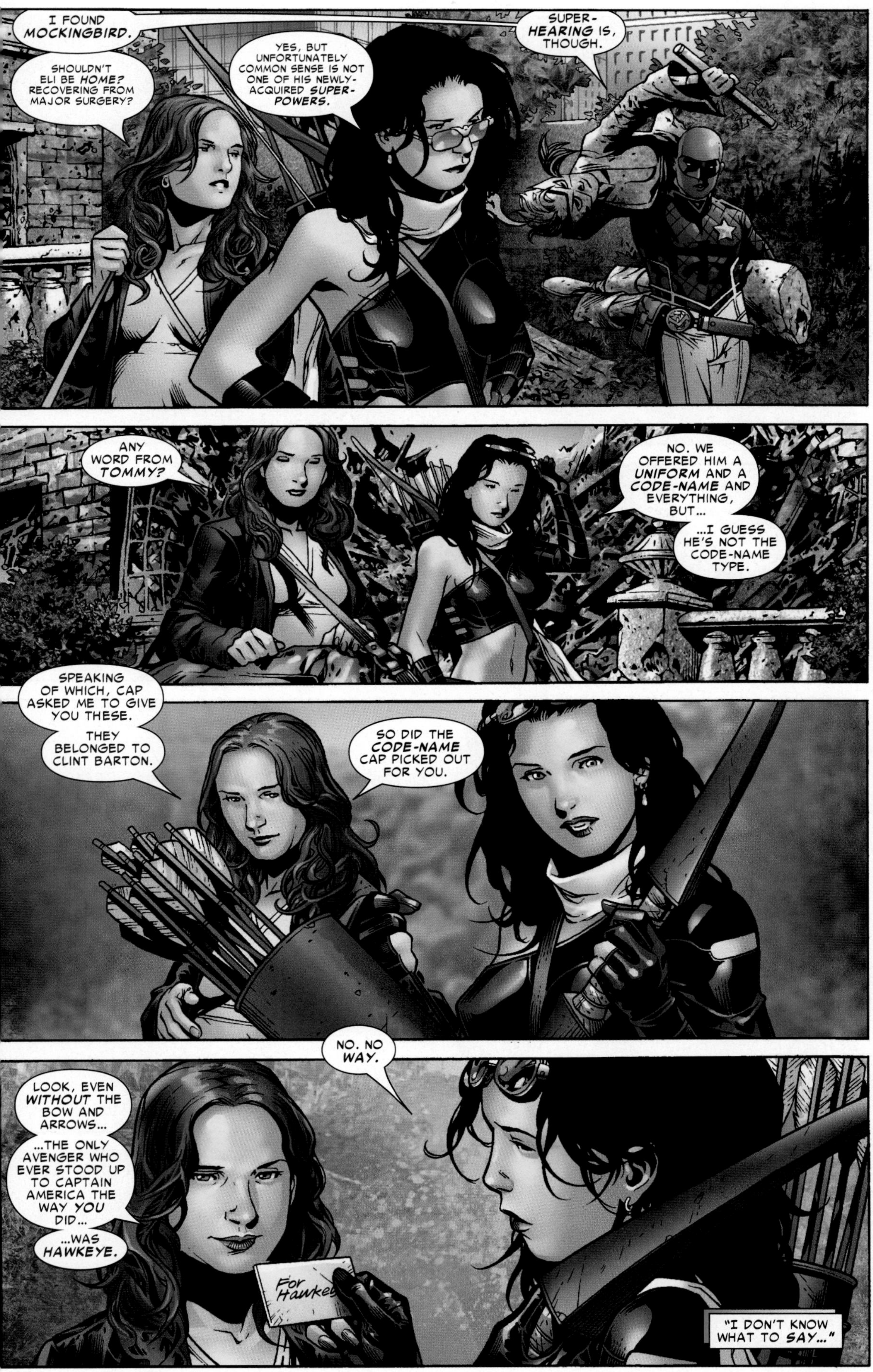
I FOUND MOCKINGBIRD.
SHOULDN'T ELI BE HOME? RECOVERING FROM MAJOR SURGERY?
YES, BUT UNFORTUNATELY COMMON SENSE IS NOT ONE OF HIS NEWLY-ACQUIRED SUPER-POWERS.
SUPER-HEARING IS, THOUGH.
ANY WORD FROM TOMMY?
NO. WE OFFERED HIM A UNIFORM AND A CODE-NAME AND EVERYTHING, BUT...
...I GUESS HE'S NOT THE CODE-NAME TYPE.
SPEAKING OF WHICH, CAP ASKED ME TO GIVE YOU THESE.
THEY BELONGED TO CLINT BARTON.
SO DID THE CODE-NAME CAP PICKED OUT FOR YOU.
NO. NO WAY.
LOOK, EVEN WITHOUT THE BOW AND ARROWS...
...THE ONLY AVENGER WHO EVER STOOD UP TO CAPTAIN AMERICA THE WAY YOU DID...
...WAS HAWKEYE.
For Hawkey
"I DON'T KNOW WHAT TO SAY..."

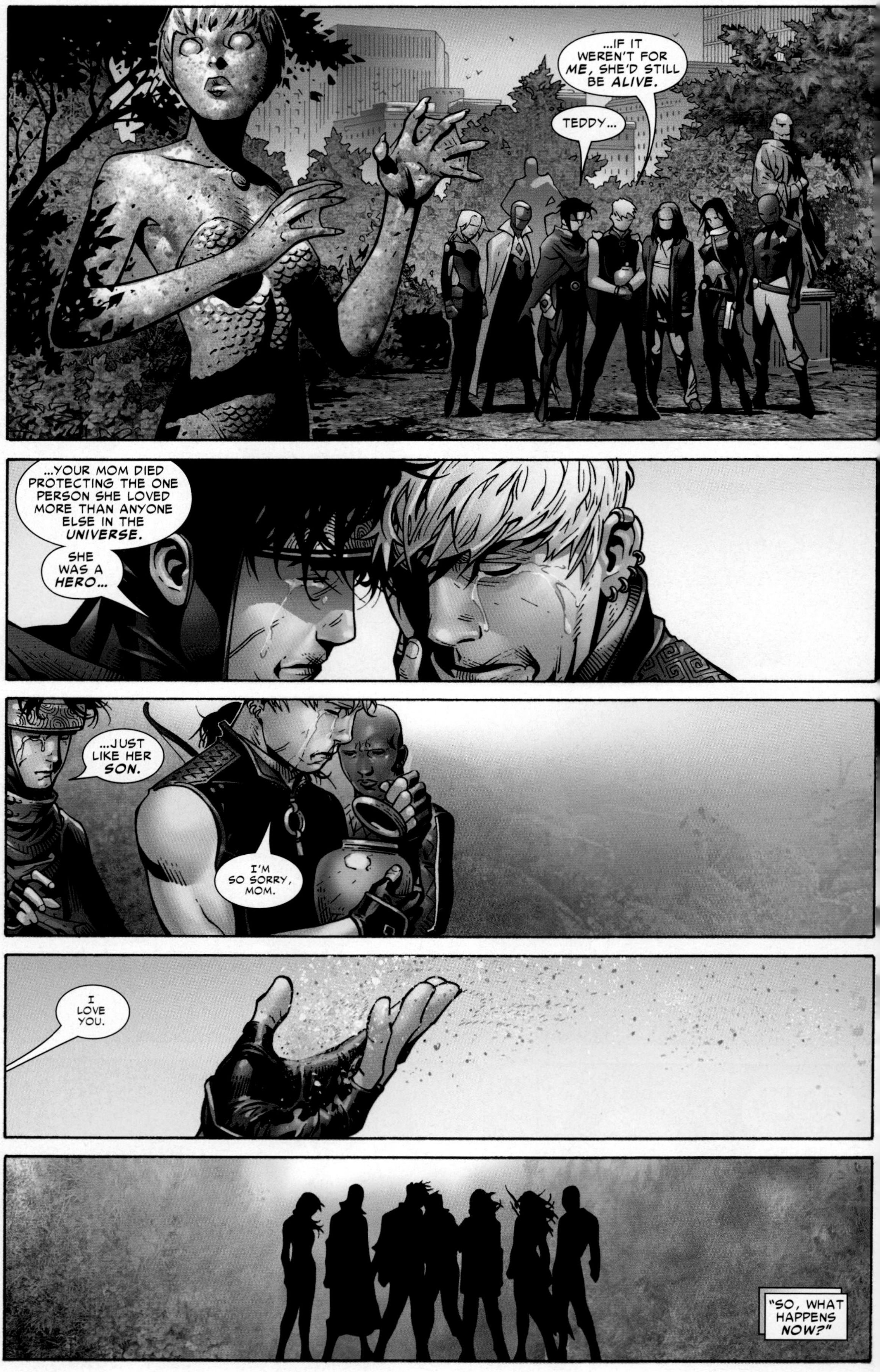

...IF IT WEREN'T FOR ME, SHE'D STILL BE ALIVE.
TEDDY...
...YOUR MOM DIED PROTECTING THE ONE PERSON SHE LOVED MORE THAN ANYONE ELSE IN THE UNIVERSE.
SHE WAS A HERO...
...JUST LIKE HER SON.
I'M SO SORRY, MOM.
I LOVE YOU.
"SO, WHAT HAPPENS NOW?"

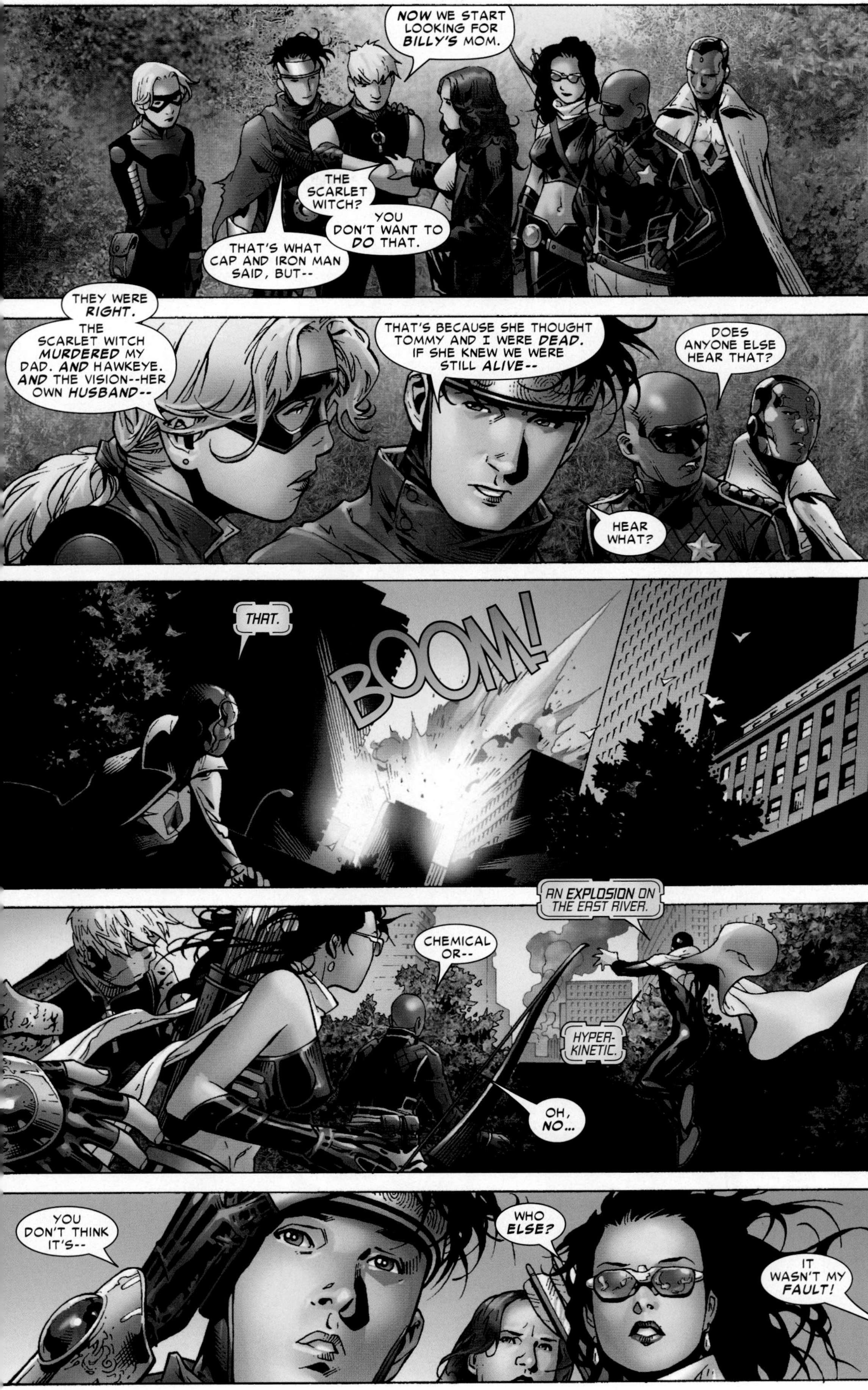
NOW WE START LOOKING FOR BILLY'S MOM.
THE SCARLET WITCH?
YOU DON'T WANT TO DO THAT.
THAT'S WHAT CAP AND IRON MAN SAID, BUT--
THEY WERE RIGHT.
THE SCARLET WITCH MURDERED MY DAD. AND HAWKEYE. AND THE VISION--HER OWN HUSBAND--
THAT'S BECAUSE SHE THOUGHT TOMMY AND I WERE DEAD. IF SHE KNEW WE WERE STILL ALIVE--
DOES ANYONE ELSE HEAR THAT?
HEAR WHAT?
THAT.
BOOM!
AN EXPLOSION ON THE EAST RIVER.
CHEMICAL OR--
HYPER-KINETIC.
OH, NO...
YOU DON'T THINK IT'S--
WHO ELSE?
IT WASN'T MY FAULT!

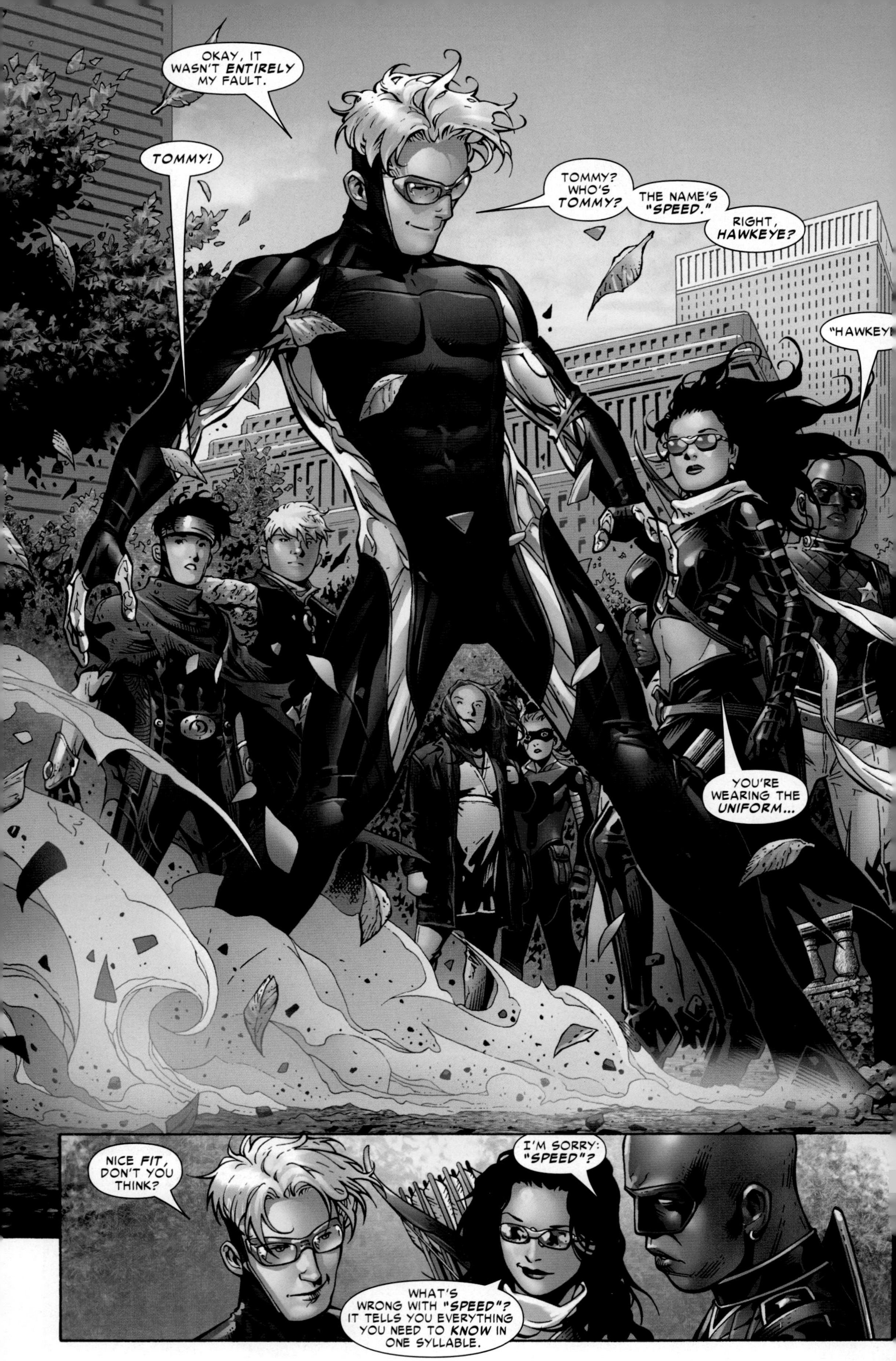
OKAY, IT WASN'T ENTIRELY MY FAULT.
TOMMY!
TOMMY? WHO'S TOMMY?
THE NAME'S "SPEED."
RIGHT, HAWKEYE?
"HAWKEYE
YOU'RE WEARING THE UNIFORM...
NICE FIT, DON'T YOU THINK?
I'M SORRY: "SPEED"?
WHAT'S WRONG WITH "SPEED"? IT TELLS YOU EVERYTHING YOU NEED TO KNOW IN ONE SYLLABLE.

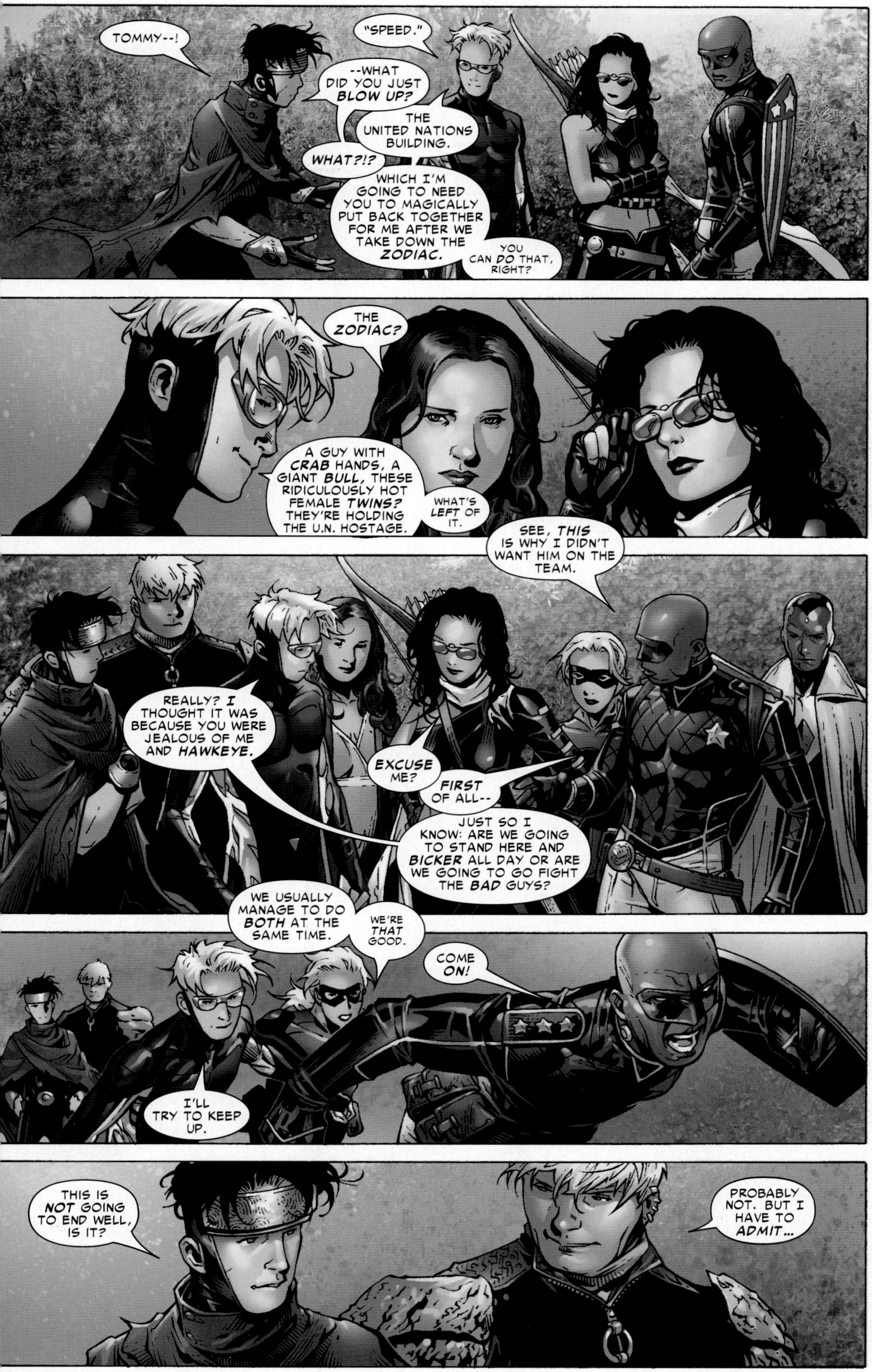
TOMMY--!
"SPEED."
--WHAT DID YOU JUST BLOW UP?
THE UNITED NATIONS BUILDING.
WHAT?!?
WHICH I'M GOING TO NEED YOU TO MAGICALLY PUT BACK TOGETHER FOR ME AFTER WE TAKE DOWN THE ZODIAC.
YOU CAN DO THAT, RIGHT?
THE ZODIAC?
A GUY WITH CRAB HANDS, A GIANT BULL, THESE RIDICULOUSLY HOT FEMALE TWINS? THEY'RE HOLDING THE U.N. HOSTAGE.
WHAT'S LEFT OF IT.
SEE, THIS IS WHY I DIDN'T WANT HIM ON THE TEAM.
REALLY? I THOUGHT IT WAS BECAUSE YOU WERE JEALOUS OF ME AND HAWKEYE.
EXCUSE ME?
FIRST OF ALL--
JUST SO I KNOW: ARE WE GOING TO STAND HERE AND BICKER ALL DAY OR ARE WE GOING TO GO FIGHT THE BAD GUYS?
WE USUALLY MANAGE TO DO BOTH AT THE SAME TIME.
WE'RE THAT GOOD.
COME ON!
I'LL TRY TO KEEP UP.
THIS IS NOT GOING TO END WELL, IS IT?
PROBABLY NOT. BUT I HAVE TO ADMIT...

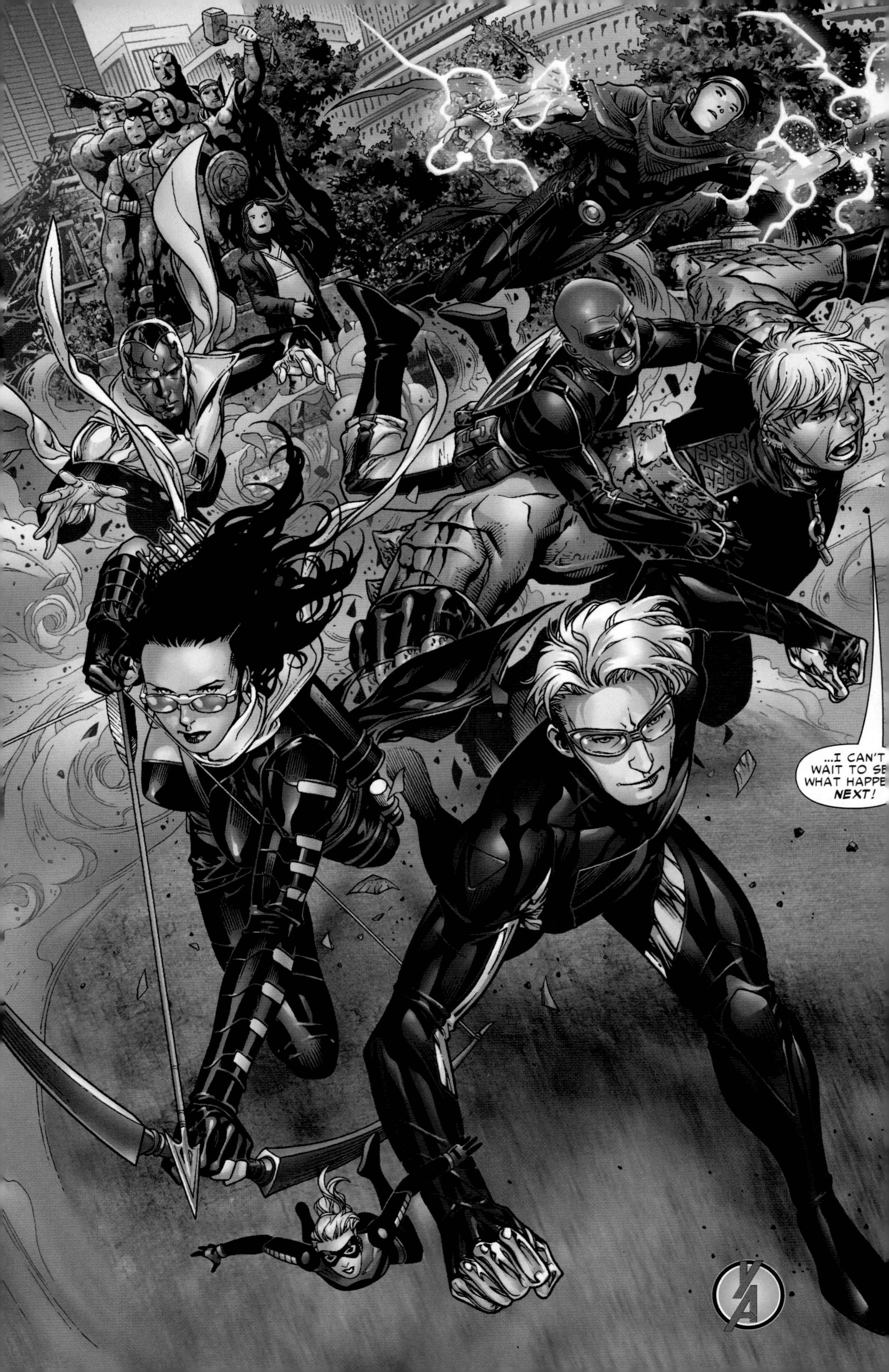
...I CAN'T WAIT TO SE WHAT HAPPE NEXT!

THE YOUNG AVENGERS
Conceptual Notes by Allan Heinberg
Wednesday, June 2, 2004

The Premise

THE YOUNG AVENGERS are a group of four teenaged superheroes-in-training who first appear in the Marvel Universe (and on the cover of YOUNG AVENGERS #1) as the teen sidekicks-who-never-were of the classic Avengers: Captain America, Iron Man, Thor, and the Hulk. They are IRON LAD, THE PATRIOT, THE HULKLING, and THE ASGARDIAN.

Since the Marvel Universe has no real teen sidekicks (apart from Bucky and Toro, historically), the goal is for comics readers to see this group of Marvel's teen titans and ask, "Who the hell are these kids?"

At which point, the reader will hopefully buy the book, turn to page one, and find J. Jonah Jameson asking the same question of Pulse reporter Jessica Jones: "Who the hell are these kids?"

Over the course of the first six issues, the teen heroes will be stripped of their "sidekick" identities and forced to evolve into heroes in their own right, thereby earning the trust of their adult counterparts (the New Avengers) and the right to officially call themselves the Young Avengers.

The Characters

Iron Lad (Young Kang)

[Movie casting: A teen Keanu Reeves in NEO mode.]

When an adult, time-traveling Kang the Conqueror visits his 15-year-old self in the 30th century, he gives the restless, ambitious YOUNG KANG (already a robotics expert) a preview of his future – and future conquests. Horrified, Young Kang steals Kang the Conqueror's armor (and time-travel equipment) and escapes into the present day Marvel Universe to ensure that his prescribed future never comes to pass. Knowing Kang the Conqueror will soon arrive to force him back to the future, Young Kang seeks out the Avengers to defeat Kang. But when Young Kang discovers that the Avengers have recently been disassembled, he gets a hold of the disassembled Vision's CPU and uses its failsafe program to assemble a team of YOUNG AVENGERS to defeat his older self.

To conceal his identity from Kang the Conqueror, Young Kang transforms his 30th century armor into a futuristic approximation of Tony Stark's Iron Man armor. And thus becomes IRON LAD. Iron Lad's armor houses a vast array of futuristic technology, making it one of the most powerful weapons in the Marvel Universe. In Avengers #8 (Kang's first appearance in Avengers continuity), Kang's armor possesses (among other things): an anti-gravity ray, an anti-matter ray, a force field which can both repel and/or disintegrate anything it comes into contact with (except Thor's mystical hammer), and a paralysis beam. The suit's potential seems almost limitless – provided it remains fully powered.

By the end of YOUNG AVENGERS #6 (or thereabouts), Young Kang will be sent back to the 30th century at the Avengers insistence (and against his will, thereby insuring his grudge against the Avengers). At which point, THE VISION will take over Iron Lad's 30th century armor, redesigning it to more closely resemble the Vision's classic synthezoid body and costume.

The Patriot (Elijah "Eli" Bradley)

[MOVIE CASTING: A teen Tom Cruise, if he were African-American.]

ELI BRADLEY (17) is the grandson of Isaiah Bradley (Marvel's African-American Captain America from TRUTH: RED, WHITE & BLACK), and the nephew of Josiah X (from Marvel's THE CREW).

Eli is a tough, smart, athletic high school junior, who's far more interested in superheroes and upholding his grandfather's superheroic legacy than he is in his schoolwork (to the dismay of his single mom, SARAH). When Eli first appears as the Patriot, it's assumed that his Captain America-like strength and speed derive from the same super-serum that empowered his grandfather and Steve Rogers. But in YOUNG AVENGERS 6-12, it will be revealed that Eli is, in fact, addicted to MGH (see Brian Bendis' DAREDEVIL and ALIAS), thereby endangering his place on the team and, eventually, his own life.

Eli will vie for team leadership with Iron Lad (Young Kang). In YOUNG AVENGERS #2, he will also find himself going head-to-head with Kate Bishop (who will ultimately become the new Hawkeye) when she strong-arms her way onto the team. The two of them will subsequently fall in love, despite themselves. (See ROMANTIC ARCS, below.)

Once the Young Avengers prove themselves as heroes in their own right, Eli will set aside his "Young Captain America" garb to become **THE SENTINEL**. (Essentially Nightwing to Cap's Batman.)

The Asgardian (Billy Kaplan)

[MOVIE CASTING: Jake Gyllenhall]

BILLY KAPLAN (16) first appears as though he's a teenage disciple of Thor, wielding what appear to be lightning powers (which seems appropriate as the Thunder God's "sidekick"). But, in fact, Billy is a young sorcerer who will eventually become **THE WICCAN**.

Billy is neurotic, Jewish, cerebral, ironic, charming – and has no idea whatsoever how attractive he is. He is plagued by self-doubt, thinks way too much, and is never in complete control of his formidable magic powers. Despite his quick wit and sharp mind, Billy's not as articulate about his own feelings – the true source of his powers. Billy's also a huge fan of superheroes (since early childhood) and knows Avengers lore inside and out.

In the course of YOUNG AVENGERS #1-6, Billy will fall thoroughly in love with (and be completely intimidated by) his phenomenally attractive, shape-shifting teammate, Teddy Altman (who first appears as the Hulkling). Over time, Teddy's shape-shifting (and gender-shifting) abilities threaten Billy's ideas about his own sexuality. Ultimately, however, his feelings for Teddy force Billy to accept that real love transcends mere physical appearance.

In issues 6-12, Billy discovers that he was, in fact, adopted by his parents, JEFF and REBECCA KAPLAN. He'll then engage in a search for his real parents... who may (if Marvel signs off) turn out to be the Scarlet Witch and the Vision. This revelation will then lead to the discovery of THOMAS, Billy's equally powerful, but morally ambiguous twin brother.

The Hulkling (Teddy Altman)

[Movie casting: Lindsey Lohan.]

TEDDY ALTMAN (17) is the most mysterious member of the group. As the Hulkling, Teddy appears to be a smarter, more articulate – and completely in control – teenage version of the Hulk, possessing super-strength and comparatively massive size. So, it comes as a complete surprise when the Hulkling reveals himself to be an almost supernaturally attractive, teenage GIRL. Teddy is the designated blonde bombshell of the group and appears to be the most self-possessed. But in truth, because so much of her life experience is dictated by her *appearance*, she's actually the most insecure member of the group. Teddy's never quite sure if people like her for who she really is. Which is compounded by the fact that *she* doesn't quite know who she is. An orphan, Teddy's essentially had to raise herself – even posing as her own parents to avoid being sent to an institution. As a result, she's become a very talented con-artist, constantly changing her appearance to get what she needs to survive.

Over time, it will be revealed that Teddy is, in fact, at least part-Skrull, a child of the Kree-Skrull war, thus making her even more of an outsider.

When the Avengers attempt to disband the Young Avengers, Teddy will set aside her identity as the Hulkling and prove herself as the shape-shifting **CHIMERA**.

Cassie Lang (Titan)

[Movie casting: Kirsten Dunst]

CASSIE LANG (15), the daughter of Scott Lang (Ant-Man) has recently suffered through her parents' divorce and brutal custody battle, her subsequent kidnapping (in Avengers #76), and her father's tragic death in Brian Bendis' upcoming Avengers #500.

When our story begins, Cassie's mother, PEG (and Cassie's new step-father, police officer BLAKE) has taken Cassie out of the New York public school system, away from her friends, and enrolled her in an exclusive, Upper East Side, private prep school for Cassie's own protection. And Cassie hates it.

When Cassie's first introduced (in YA #2), the flame-haired teen is still in shock from her father's death and angry at the world. Mostly, though, Cassie's angry at herself. Though she'd never admit it, Cassie blames herself for her father's death. After all, if Cassie hadn't needed an expensive corrective heart operation as a kid, her father would never have become Ant-Man, and he'd still be alive today.

Before her father died, Cassie dreamed of becoming his sidekick and perhaps one day following in Ant-Man's microscopic footsteps. She learned as much as she could about the insect world, and spent as much time as she could at Avengers mansion and in her father's lab, immersing herself in his work.

As a result, Scott's death and the disassembly of the Avengers has left Cassie feeling angry and powerless. She refuses to give her new school a chance, lashing out at her parents, her clique-ish new schoolmates, and the strict prep school faculty. So when Cassie discovers that a group of so-called Young Avengers have emerged to take the place of the adult team, Cassie takes it upon herself to confront them and take her rightful place among them.

When the Young Avengers ignore Cassie, she loses her temper, and goes off on the team. And the more she yells, the more she starts to grow. And grow. Until Cassie, livid, stands several stories above the team. At which point, it becomes clear that Cassie's long-term exposure to her father's Pym particles has endowed her with impressive (if somewhat scary) size-changing powers. But unlike her dad, Cassie's able to both shrink AND grow. When Cassie finally takes her place among the Young Avengers, she does so as the size-changing **TITAN.**

Kate Bishop **(Hawkeye)**

[Movie casting: Kate Beckinsale, perhaps. But more along the lines of Katherine Hepburn in HOLIDAY and THE PHILADELPHIA STORY.]

At first sight, KATE BISHOP (16) appears to be just another child of wealth and privilege among Manhattan's urban, upper-East-side elite. Her father, DEREK is a powerful New York media baron. And her mother, RACHEL, is a bored heiress who dabbles in charity work. Both Derek and Rachel expect Kate to follow her sister SUSAN's example and take her rightful place among the New York debutante set. Which Kate flatly refuses to do.

Kate is a fierce tom-boy and Olympic-caliber athlete. She despises all the privilege her parents' money can buy. Enrolled in the same private prep school as Cassie, the two girls are bound by their hatred of the place, and their desire to escape, to be bad, to have adventures.

When Cassie petitions to join the Young Avengers, Kate asks for a place on the team, as well. But without super powers, per se, Kate is summarily rejected by the group. She's too vulnerable, too much a liability. However, when the Young Avengers are captured and de-commissioned by Captain America and Iron Man, it's Kate who helps them escape and aid the Avengers in their battle against Kang the Conqueror. In the end, Kate's strength, bravery, and mastery of weaponry (notably Clint Barton's bow and arrow) are instrumental in the Young Avengers defeat of Kang, eventually earning Kate a place on the team as the new **HAWKEYE.**

Romantic Arcs

KATE AND ELI will dislike each other intensely – both alphas – and of course fall in love, engaging in a romantic relationship they have to keep secret in both their identities. (Kate's parents would never approve of her dating him. And the socio-economic difference between them proves a challenge, as well.)

BILLY AND TEDDY Billy become involved, as well, but Billy will be forced to question everything when Teddy reveals that she's neither male nor female. H/she's a shape-shifter. Billy will have to examine the true nature of love.

CASSIE AND YOUNG KANG will become involved, as well. And Cassie's going to object strongly to sending him back into the time stream. Leaving her alone again – after her father's death and mother's remarriage.

YOUNG AVENGERS #1 (Synopsis)

As their story begins, **IRON LAD, THE PATRIOT, THE ASGARDIAN,** and **THE HULKLING** will appear on the scene (and on the cover of YOUNG AVENGERS #1) just as the

Avengers themselves have disbanded, but before the existence of the New Avengers has been revealed to the public.

The first issue will establish the mystery of these heretofore unknown teenage sidekicks. Both the New Avengers (Captain America, Iron Man, Spider-Man, Luke Cage) and (with luck) the comic book buying public will be asking the same question: Who the hell are these kids?

At any rate, that's the question J. JONAH JAMESON is asking. In a story meeting with JESSICA JONES, Jameson, BEN URICH, and ROBBIE ROBERTSON fill Jessica in on what little is known about these kids – their sudden appearance, their recent crime-fighting exploits, etc. (See Bendis' THE PULSE.) Jameson suggests Jessica contact her Avengers buddies to find out why, after the tragic events of "Avengers Disassembled," Cap and Tony Stark are now putting kids' lives at risk.

In the new headquarters of the Avengers, Jessica consults with LUKE CAGE, CAPTAIN AMERICA, SPIDER-MAN, and IRON MAN about the kids, but the New Avengers are just as concerned and curious as Jessica is. Jessica wonders if the Young Avengers aren't simply super-powered fanboys who've made it their mission to carry on the Avengers' legacy in the perceived absence of the team. Cap's concerned that, despite the kids' obvious abilities, they are kids and will inevitably hurt themselves. Stark points out that, just as inevitably, if anything happens to those kids, the Avengers will be held responsible. Therefore, the Young Avengers need to be confronted and stopped.

We then join the Young Avengers themselves in action, excavating the ruins of Avengers Mansion. From their dialogue, we learn that the members of this inexperienced and dysfunctional group are almost constantly at odds with each other. In the course of their argument, we learn that Iron Lad is trying to locate something in the rubble that will aid the team in an upcoming battle against Kang the Conqueror. The Patriot, however, believes they're wasting time. Why prepare themselves for a *possible* attack by an old Avengers foe when the team could be out fighting *actual* crime. And, sure enough, when the team hears sirens in the distance, the Patriot (against Iron Lad's wishes) leads the rest of the team off in their direction.

At which point, we see the Young Avengers go into action – a super-heroic New York City rescue mission which shows off the powers of each individual team member as well as their potential for working together if they ever learned to listen to each other. Despite their in-fighting, however, the Young Avengers save the day and narrowly escape the encroaching media. Iron Lad wants to return to Avengers Mansion to resume his search, but the other kids have to get home before their parents discover their absence.

Alone, Iron Lad returns to the wreckage of Avengers mansion. The Asgardian, feeling guilty about abandoning Iron Lad to his task, is about to join him when he witnesses Iron Lad being surrounded by a disapproving Iron Man, Captain America, and Spider-Man. The Asgardian watches (in paralyzed awe) as, at Cap's stern insistence, Iron Lad finally removes his helmet and the sixteen year-old reluctantly tells the Avengers (because he's sure they won't believe him) that his real name is KANG.

YOUNG AVENGERS #2 (Synopsis)

Issue #2 opens on CASSIE LANG, the daughter of Scott Lang (the now deceased Ant-Man). Since Cassie's kidnapping (in Avengers #76) and her father's death (in Avengers #500), Cassie's mother and step-father have enrolled her in a private girls' school (like the Brearley or Chapin Schools) to better ensure her safety.

Grief-stricken and angry after her father's death, Cassie's only friend at school is KATE BISHOP, a beautiful, athletic tomboy who spends most of her time rebelling against her wealthy parents, who want her to be part of the New York debutante scene.

When news of the Young Avengers latest adventure spreads throughout the school, Cassie cuts class to investigate. Kate tries to talk her out of it and, failing, follows Cassie, instead.

Meanwhile, the Patriot, the Hulkling, and the Asgardian try to figure out what to do without Iron Lad to lead them. Dysfunctional as ever, they don't understand why, if Iron Lad's with Captain America and Iron Man, he hasn't returned to them. They argue about their next move. Should the team try to find Iron Lad? Or should they continue their original mission and prepare for the arrival of Kang. As they kids continue to argue...

Iron Lad, unmasked as Young Kang, learns that the new reconstituted Avengers still exist and proceeds to them his story. Young Kang explains that his life as a robotics prodigy in the 30th Century was interrupted by a visit from his time-traveling adult self, KANG THE CONQUEROR, who, using his advanced technology, showed the boy a glimpse of his future. Young Kang, horrified, then stole Kang's armor and time machine and returned to 2004 to enlist the Avengers' help in vanquishing his older self. Young Kang, however, arrived in the twenty-first century just as the Avengers disassembled.

When Young Kang then visited Stark Industries to try to enlist Tony Stark's help, he was unceremoniously thrown out. So, that night, using Kang's advanced tech, Young Kang infiltrated Stark Industries, where he discovered the remains of THE VISION. Young Kang then "borrowed" the Vision's CPU and returned to his "headquarters," a sub-basement beneath the ruins of Avengers Mansion to try to revive the Vision. In doing so, Young Kang tripped a failsafe program in the Vision's CPU to be accessed only if the Avengers themselves were ever vanquished. Using this failsafe program, Young Kang was able to locate several new, super-powered recruits. The team banded together to carry on the Avengers' legacy and to protect the twenty-first century from Kang's inevitable arrival.

While Young Kang tries to convince the New Avengers that he's telling the truth, the team returns to Avengers Mansion where they come face to face with Cassie and Kate – who've stumbled into Young Avengers "Headquarters." Cassie demands to know who they are and wants to know what gives these kids the right to call themselves Avengers. Kate and The Patriot immediately butt heads, at which point the Asgardian (an Avengers fanboy) recognizes Cassie as the daughter of Scott Lang, Ant-Man. As Cassie argues with Patriot, asserting her right to join the team, she loses her temper, going off on the boys. And as she yells at them, she starts to grow. And grow. Until Cassie, livid, finally stands several stories above the team, shocked at what's just happened to her.

As the team marvels at Cassie's latent size-changing abilities, they fail to notice the arrival of KANG THE CONQUEROR, mad as hell, as poised to capture -- if not kill -- them.

TO BE CONTINUED...

ROUGH CUT: YOUNG AVENGERS #1 SCENE ONE

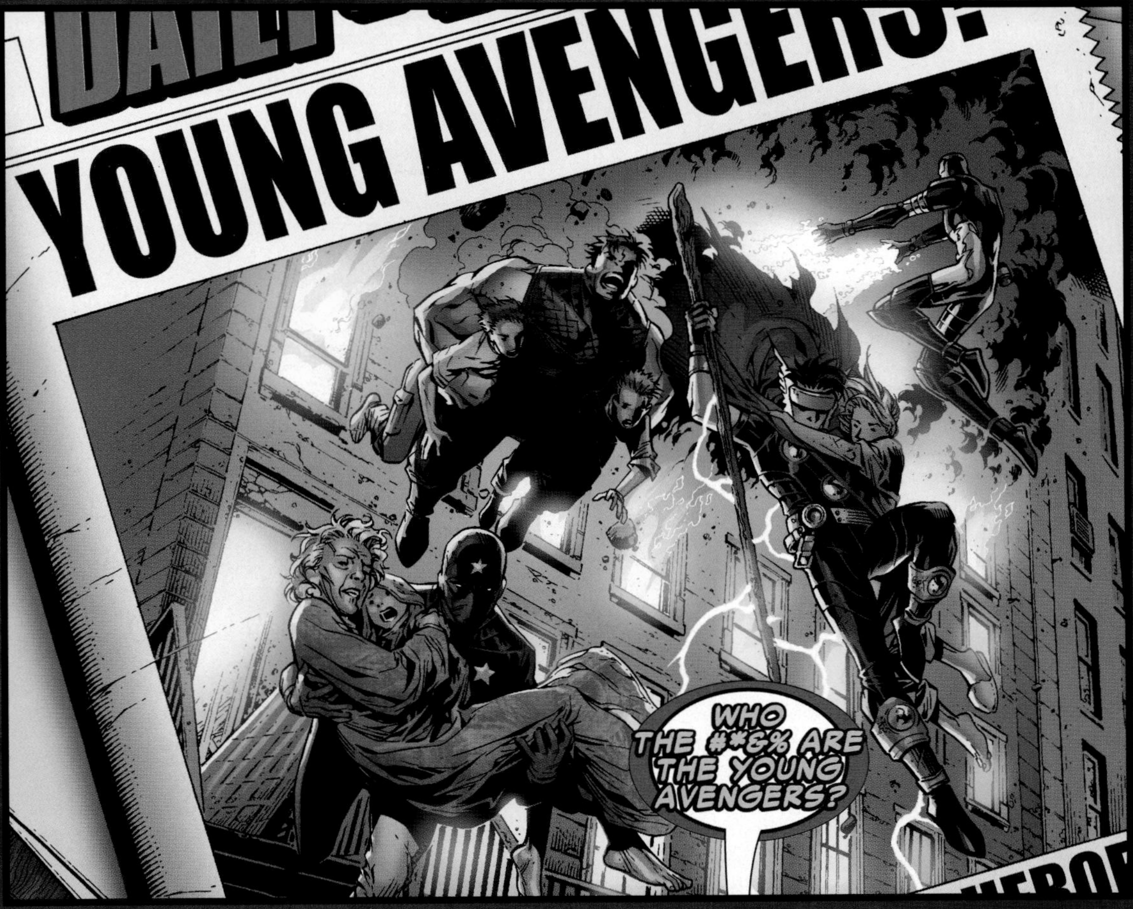
DAILY
YOUNG AVENGERS?
WHO THE #*&% ARE THE YOUNG AVENGERS?

So, here's how the whole thing started:

I had a six-issue story pitch, a detailed outline for *YOUNG AVENGERS #1*, and Marvel's go-ahead to start writing. Only I couldn't start. Every time I'd sit down and type "Page One, Panel One" I'd have no idea what to do next, except to call my editor, Tom Brevoort, and try to quit the book.

Having written teleplays almost exclusively for the past several years, I had no idea how to tell a story panel by panel. So, there I was, a lifelong comic book fan who had no idea how to write a comic book script. I was paralyzed by fear and self-loathing and about to miss my very first Marvel deadline. Fortunately that's when Joe Quesada called and gently suggested I write the first scene of *YOUNG AVENGERS #1* as a teleplay. He then volunteered to personally walk me through the process of dividing that scene into pages and panels and transforming it into a full-fledged comic book script.

So, thanks to Joe, that's what I did. And now, despite my better judgment, the good people at Marvel Comics have convinced me to share what was my first attempt at the first scene of *YOUNG AVENGERS #1* written in teleplay form. It's too long, too talky, and has a few too many characters in it, but it was — at last — a start.

—ALLAN HEINBERG

YOUNG AVENGERS #1

SIDEKICKS, Part One

ALLAN HEINBERG
WEDNESDAY, AUGUST 4, 2004

REFERENCE:

- **THE DAILY BUGLE, J. JONAH JAMESON'S OFFICE: *THE PULSE #1-4* (MARVEL COMICS)**
- **JESSICA JONES: *ALIAS #1-28* (MARVEL COMICS), THE PULSE #1-4**
- **JESSICA JONES AS JEWEL: *ALIAS #25***
- **KAT FARRELL: *THE PULSE, #1-4* (MARVEL COMICS), *DEADLINE #1-4* (MARVEL COMICS)**

PAGE 1

FULL-PAGE IMAGE

EXTREME CLOSE-UP OF THE FRONT PAGE OF THE DAILY BUGLE

The headline reads:

1. YOUNG AVENGERS?

Beneath it is a large (if slightly BLURRED) COLOR PHOTO of IRON LAD, THE PATRIOT, THE ASGARDIAN, and THE

HULKLING in action outside a burning apartment building:

A crowd of refugees and onlookers gathers around the burning building as —

IRON LAD, in mid-air, fires what looks like FIRE EXTINGUISHER FOAM from his palms, dousing the flames;

THE ASGARDIAN, also in flight, rescues a MOTHER and CHILD from the blaze;

THE PATRIOT runs out of the fire cradling an ELDERLY GENTLEMAN in his arms;

and THE HULKING has just leapt from the roof, carrying TWO EMBARRASSED AND FRIGHTENED-LOOKING COLLEGE-AGED GUYS, one guy tucked under each arm.

Then, beneath the photo, in smaller print, another headline:

2. A NEW GENERATION OF HEROES?

Then, in even smaller print:

3. By Bugle reporter Kat Farrell

4. J. JONAH JAMESON (OFF-CAMERA): Who are the Young Avengers?

PAGE 2

INT. DAILY BUGLE – J. JONAH JAMESON'S OFFICE – MORNING (D1)

J. JONAH JAMESON stands behind his desk showing the Young Avengers headline to the small group assembled in his office. His desk is cluttered with PHOTOS, INTERNET PRINTOUTS, rival NEWSPAPERS. He's in full-on story pitching mode – eyes shining – mouth going a mile a minute. Equal parts inspiration and impatience.

PULSE editor ROBBIE ROBERTSON leans against a file cabinet, COFFEE in hand, calmly listening to Jonah's rant. He's used to Jameson's editorial temper tantrums – even enjoys them – and provides an even-tempered counter-balance to Jonah's bluster.

Seasoned PULSE reporter BEN URICH sits in one of the two chairs opposite Jonah's desk. He's leaning forward, re-reading Kat's article. Like Robbie, Ben is used to Jonah's journalistic temper tantrums, and his mind is racing ahead — synthesizing the meager facts provided by Kat's story into his own theory about the Young Avengers.

PULSE super hero consultant JESSICA JONES sits in the chair next to Ben's. Jessica's pregnancy is just beginning to show. She has a copy of the Bugle on her lap, but her eyes are fixed on Jonah. She's listening attentively, still not quite sure what her role is here. Jess is not easily intimidated, but her relationship with Jonah has a vaguely father-daughter dynamic to it. She's knows he's a raving lunatic, but can't help wanting to please him.

PULSE reporter KAT FARRELL sits on a low bookshelf near the office door. Kat is very much like Jonah (in both eagerness and impatience), and they don't quite get along because of it. The Young Avengers are Kat's story, and right now she's anxious to get out of Jonah's office and back on it.

1. JONAH: Last night, four teenagers dressed up to look like the Avengers showed up out of nowhere and saved more than a dozen people from a four-alarm fire in midtown.

Jonah picks up FOUR PHOTOS from his desk, hands two to Ben, two to Jessica.

Jessica looks at the photos as Jonah describes them.

2. JONAH (CONT'D): Teen Thor, a mini-Hulk, a younger-looking Iron Man…

Ben looks at his photos, impressed.

3. … and a kid who seems to want to be Captain America when he grows up.

4. BEN: Who doesn't?

5. JONAH: Me. And it's a little late for you, Urich.

Ben half-smiles at Jess, acknowledging this, as they trade photos.

6. JONAH (CONT'D): After the kids put out the fire, they proceeded to foil an attempted bank robbery in Chelsea…

Jonah passes Ben MORE BLURRED PHOTOS.

7. JONAH (CONT'D): … they busted three drug dealers in Washington Square Park…

8. JONAH (CONT'D): … and they helped Michael Saltzman of Great Neck, Long Island restart his station wagon when it stalled, blocking traffic on the L.I.E.

9. JONAH (CONT'D): And they did all of this before midnight. At which point, they disappeared.

10. JONAH (CONT'D): This morning, all we have are conflicting eyewitness accounts, bad photos, and truly terrible amateur video footage.

11. JONAH (CONT'D): The TV news, the internet, and every other paper in town is ready to embrace these kids as heroes. But the truth is, no one knows anything about them. Who they are, where they come from, or what they're doing here.

12. JONAH (CONT'D) (A SLIGHT SMILE): That, ladies and gentlemen, is where we come in.

PAGE 3

1. JONAH (CONT'D): Tomorrow morning, THE DAILY BUGLE's weekly super hero supplement, THE PULSE, is going to feature an exhaustive profile of the Young Avengers.

2. JONAH (CONT'D): Exclusive interviews. Never-before-seen photos. Ideally taken by photographers who know how to focus a camera.

3. JONAH (CONT'D): We're going to find out who they are and

MS. JONES, YOU'VE READ MS. FARRELL'S ARTICLE?

YEAH, BUT I--

THEN YOU KNOW THAT LAST NIGHT, FOUR KIDS DRESSED UP LIKE JUNIOR AVENGERS SHOWED UP OUT OF NOWHERE AND RESCUED A DOZEN PEOPLE FROM A FOUR-ALARM FIRE IN MIDTOWN.

why they're calling themselves the Young Avengers.

A beat. Kat frowns. Holds up her hand.

4. **KAT:** Um, Jonah?

5. **JONAH:** Kat?

6. **KAT:** They didn't actually call themselves the Young Avengers. I did that.

7. **JONAH (HIS FACE CLOUDING):** You did that?

8. **KAT:** I used a question mark. Young Avengers Question Mark? It's a question.

Off Jonah's stony stare —

9. **KAT (CONT'D) (SHRUGS, DEFENSIVE):** They were kids dressed up as the Avengers.

Jonah's just about to speak his mind when Jessica interrupts:

10. **JESSICA:** Actually they're not.

11. **KAT (CONFUSED):** They're not?

12. **JONAH (WILLING TO HEAR JESS OUT):** They're not?

Jessica holds the Bugle up to Jonah and points to PATRIOT in the PHOTO.

13. **JESSICA:** Look. See? This kid isn't dressed up as Captain America. He's dressed up as Bucky.

14. **ROBBIE (TO JONAH, IMPRESSED):** She's right. The military jacket, the domino mask —

15. **BEN:** The suit's been updated, but that's Bucky all right.

16. **KAT:** Okay, I'm sorry, but —

They all turn to Kat expectantly.

17. **KAT (CONT'D) (EMBARRASSED):** — who's Bucky?

18. **JONAH (APPALLED):** "Who's Bucky?"

19. **BEN:** You don't know Bucky?

20. **ROBBIE:** We've got a file here somewhere.

As Robbie goes to the file cabinet —

21. **KAT:** I've heard of Bucky, but —

22. **JONAH:** As in "Captain America and…"?

Robbie hands Kat the file.

23: **ROBBIE:** Here he is. That's Bucky.

PAGE 4

Kat opens the file to find it's filled with dramatic PHOT[O]
OF CAP AND BUCKY in glorious Golden Age action.

1. **ROBBIE:** Bucky was Cap's sidekick during World War Two

2. **JONAH (TO KAT):** How could you not know Bucky? H[ow]
old are you?

3. **KAT (DEFENSIVE):** It was World War Two. How old are you[?]

4. **JONAH:** I was extremely young back then, thanks [for]
asking. In fact, young enough — and stupid enough —
want to be Bucky at the time. Every kid did.

5. **BEN (SMILES AT JONAH'S ADMISSION):** You wante[d to]
be Bucky? You hate super heroes.

6. **JONAH:** I don't hate anyone, Urich. Except you occasionally

7. **JONAH:** But I don't trust anyone, either.

7. **JONAH (CONT'D):** And during World War Two, Cap[t]
America — who was my hero at the time — le[d]
fourteen-year-old kid into combat…

8. **JONAH (CONT'D):** … and got him killed.

9. **JONAH (CONT'D):** Suddenly I didn't want to be Bu[cky]
anymore. Nobody did.

10. **JONAH (CONT'D):** And from then on, teen sideki[ck]
only showed up in comic books.

12. **JESSICA:** Until now.

...nah looks at Jessica, concerned.

PAGE 5

JONAH: So, that's what you think these kids are? The ...engers' new sidekicks?

JESSICA: No. They're probably just super-powered fanboys.

JONAH: Just what this city needs.

KAT: With no official ties to the Avengers?

JESSICA: No. There is no Avengers. The Avengers disbanded.

JESSICA (CONT'D) (TO JONAH): Besides, Cap would ...ver put another kid in danger.

JESSICA (CONT'D): Ever.

JONAH: How do you know that?

JESSICA: Because I know Cap. And he'd never —

JONAH (EYES GLEAMING): Right. Of course you know ...p. You were a young Avenger.

JESSICA: No, I wasn't.

KAT: Really? I thought you were.

Kat crosses to the file cabinet to retrieve Jessica's file —

JESSICA: No. I was a young idiot with powers who had ... business putting on a stupid costume, let alone calling ...self a super hero.

BEN: Don't say that, Jess. You were great.

...t finds and opens Jessica's file and produces a PHOTO ...her as JEWEL.

KAT: You were hot.

PAGE 6

...produces an extraordinarily sexy photo of Jessica as JEWEL.

--WHO'S BUCKY?

JESSICA: And now I'm mortified.

BEN: Wow. And I mean that in a completely un-sexist way.

KAT (TO JONAH): You wanted to be Bucky when you ...e a kid? I wanted to be Jewel.

JESSICA (STRICKEN): That is maybe the scariest thing ... ever heard.

JONAH (A PLAN FORMING): Are you kidding? This is

exactly why I wanted a super hero on staff in the first place.

6. JONAH (CONT'D): Because if these Young Avenger-types turn out to be mutant fanboys, then they're gonna love you.

7. JESSICA: They're kids. They're not even gonna know who I am.

8. JONAH: So, you'll remind them. You still have the costume, right?

9. JESSICA: Please tell me you didn't just say that.

10. JONAH: We can probably find you a costume, right, Robbie?

11. JESSICA: I'm gonna throw up now. And not just because I'm pregnant.

12. JONAH: So, you can practice your mothering skills on these kids.

13. JESSICA: What mothering skills?

14. JONAH: Skills you never even knew you had.

15. JONAH (CONT'D): You'll find the kids. You'll answer all their little fanboy trivia questions.

16. JONAH (CONT'D): They'll love you. They'll trust you. Then they'll tell you their story.

17. JONAH (CONT'D) (A TRIUMPHANT SMILE): Then you'll tell Ben and Kat. And the BUGLE will have its exclusive.

A beat. Jessica looks at Jonah. Can't resist his smile.

18. JESSICA: How would I even go about finding them?

19. JONAH: I don't know. Put the word out. Call your buddy Captain America.

20. JESSICA: I can't just call Captain America.

21. JONAH: Why not? I thought you said you guys were friends?

22. JESSICA: I said I know him. I didn't say we were —

23. JESSICA (CONT'D): Not that we aren't — it's just —

24. JESSICA (CONT'D): That's not how it works.

25. JONAH: Really. How does it work?

26. JESSICA: That's what I'm asking you.

27. JONAH: Then what am I paying you for?

28. JESSICA: I'm still trying to figure that out.

A stalemate. Jessica and Jonah stare each other down until —

29. JESSICA: I'm not wearing the costume.

After Joe coached me through the process of how to divide the scene into panels and pages, *YOUNG AVENGERS* editor Tom Brevoort sagely suggested I cut Ben Urich and Robbie Robertson from it entirely, allowing the scene to breathe and become more focused. I also tried to trim as much of the dialogue as I could to pace the scene up and to better showcase Jim Cheung and John Dell's extraordinary pencils and inks.

—A. H.

YOUNG AVENGERS #1
SIDEKICKS, Part One

SCRIPT BY ALLAN HEINBERG
PENCILS BY JIM CHEUNG
REVISED WEDNESDAY, DECEMBER 1, 2004

REFERENCE:

GENERAL REFERENCE:

THE DAILY BUGLE, J.JONAH JAMESON'S OFFICE: THE PULSE #1-4

JESSICA JONES: ALIAS #1-28, THE PULSE #1-4; AS JEWEL: ALIAS #25

KAT FARRELL: THE PULSE #1-4, DEADLINE #1-4

PAGE 1

SPLASH PAGE

AN EXTREME CLOSE-UP OF THE FRONT PAGE OF THE DAILY BUGLE. The HEADLINE reads:

YOUNG AVENGERS?

Beneath the headline is a LARGE (if slightly BLURRY) COLOR PHOTO of IRON LAD, PATRIOT, ASGARDIAN, and HULKLING rescuing victims from a BURNING APARTMENT BUILDING:

IRON LAD, in mid-air, faces the building and sprays what looks like FIRE EXTINGUISHER FOAM from his palms, dousing the flames.

ASGARDIAN, also in flight, rescues a TWENTY-SOMETHING GIRL from the blaze.

PATRIOT runs out of the building carrying an ELDERLY WOMAN and CHILD in his arms.

HULKING has just leapt from the roof, carrying TWO TERRIFIED TEEN BOYS — one kid under each arm.

Beneath the photo, in smaller print, is another HEADLINE:

A NEW GENERATION OF HEROES?

And below that, in even smaller print:

By Kat Farrell

1. J. JONAH JAMESON (OFF-PANEL, YELLING): WHO THE #*&% ARE THE YOUNG AVENGERS?

PAGE 2

PANEL 1

An establishing shot of Jonah's office.

J. JONAH JAMESON stands behind a desk cluttered with PHOTOS, INTERNET PRINTOUTS, and the morning BUGLE with its "Young Avengers?" headline.

In the CHAIRS opposite Jonah's desk are: Bugle reporter KAT FARRELL, who sits with a NOTEBOOK COMPUTER on her lap; and JESSICA JONES, the Bugle's new super hero consultant, whose PREGNANCY is just beginning to show.

Kat is not unlike Jonah — aggressive, opinionated, relentless — and perhaps because of this, she and Jonah have a tendency to get on each other's nerves.

Jessica, after a long and twisted history with Jonah (see ALIAS: THE UNDERNEATH for reference), now has a vaguely father-daughter relationship with him. She knows he's a raving lunatic, but can't help wanting to please him despite herself.

Jonah holds up FOUR PHOTOS. Each photo is a somewhat blurred portrait of one of the Young Avengers in action. The photos are badly cropped, amateur-looking stuff with enough blurriness and shadow to create a sense of mystery about the kids.

Kat and Jessica listen attentively, not sure which way Jonah's going with this tirade.

1. JONAH: Ms. Jones, you've read Ms. Farrell's article?

2. JESSICA: Yes, but I —

3. JONAH: Then you know that last night, four kids dressed up like junior Avengers showed up out of nowhere and rescued a dozen people from a four-alarm fire in midtown.

PANEL 2

CLOSE ON a PHOTO of ASGARDIAN waving his STAFF as a LIGHTNING BOLT strikes a FIRE HYDRANT, sending a column of water skyward.

4. JONAH (CONT'D): Witnesses claim THOR JUNIOR had LIGHTNING powers —

PAGE 2

PANEL 4

CLOSE ON a PHOTO of IRON LAD firing FOAM in the direction of the FLAMES.

5. JONAH (CONT'D): — that IRON KID's armor was more advanced than

Iron Man's —

PANEL 3

CLOSE ON a PHOTO of HULKLING handing a PUPPY to a LITTLE GIRL as the GIRL'S MOTHER smiles, astonished.

6. JONAH (CONT'D): — that TEEN-HULK was very polite —

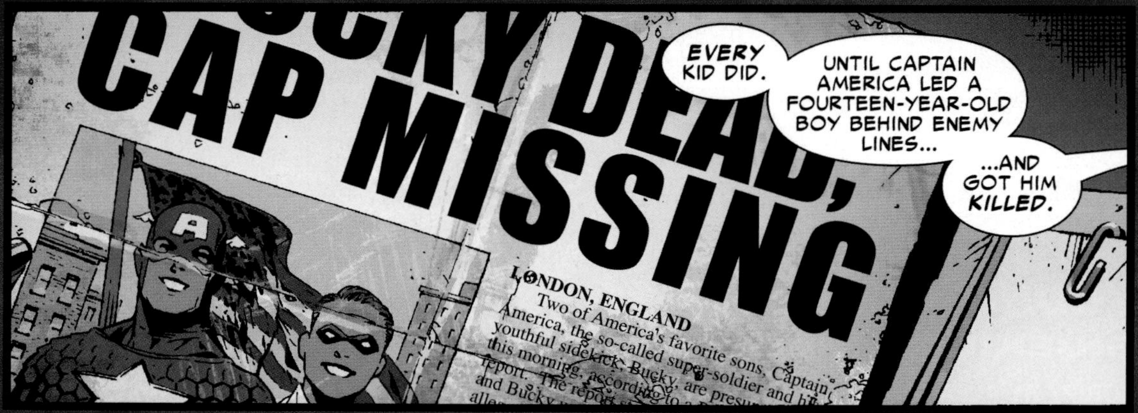
CAP MISSING
EVERY KID DID.
UNTIL CAPTAIN AMERICA LED A FOURTEEN-YEAR-OLD BOY BEHIND ENEMY LINES...
...AND GOT HIM KILLED.
LONDON, ENGLAND
Two of America's favorite sons, Captain America, the so-called super-soldier and his youthful sidekick, Bucky, are presu
this morning, according to a
report.

CLOSE ON a PHOTO of PATRIOT directing the crowd away from the BLAZE.

7. JONAH (CONT'D): — and that LIEUTENANT AMERICA was — according to Farrel here — extremely BOSSY.

PANEL 6

KAT turns to JESS, explaining.

8. KAT: He told me to MOVE, like, TEN times.

9. JESSICA: Where WERE you?

10. KAT: In his face, asking him questions.

11. JESSICA: While he was trying to put out the FIRE?

12. KAT: What's your point?

13. JONAH (OFF-PANEL): The POINT is nobody knows WHO they are, WHERE they came from, or WHY they're here.

PAGE 2

PANEL 7

JONAH turns away from his office window to face JESS and KAT. He almost smiles.

14. JONAH (CONT'D): That's where WE come in.

PAGE 3

PANEL 1

JONAH leans over his desk, holding the BUGLE in one hand and indicating its "Young Avengers?" headline with the other.

1. JONAH (CONT'D): By the time we put tomorrow's Bugle to bed tonight, you ladies will have found out exactly WHO these kids are and what gives them the RIGHT to call themselves "The Young Avengers".

PANEL 2

KAT frowns. Holds up her hand.

2. KAT: Um... Jonah?

3. JONAH (OFF-PANEL): Yes, Kat?

4. KAT: They didn't exactly call THEMSELVES the Young Avengers.

5. KAT (CONT'D): I did that.

PANEL 3

ON JONAH, his face clouding.

6. JONAH: YOU did that?

PANEL 4

KAT shrugs defensively.

7. KAT: I used a question mark. "Young Avengers?" It was a QUESTION.

8. KAT (CONT'D): They're dressed like young AVENGERS.

9. JESSICA (OFF-PANEL): Actually… they're NOT.

PAGE 3

PANEL 5

JESS looks at the PHOTOS as Kat and Jonah look at JESS.

Jess holds up the photo of PATRIOT for Kat to see.

10. JESSICA (CONT'D): Look. SEE?

11. JESSICA (CONT'D): This kid isn't wearing Captain America's uniform…

12. JESSICA (CONT'D): … he's wearing BUCKY'S.

PANEL 6

JONAH takes the PHOTO, examines it.

13. JESSICA (OFF-PANEL) (CONT'D): The suit's been UPDATED, but —

14. JONAH: Let me see that.

15. JONAH (CONT'D): You're right. The military jacket, the domino mask —

16. JONAH (CONT'D): It IS Bucky.

17. KAT (OFF-PANEL): Okay, I'm sorry, but —

PANEL 7

ON KAT, at a loss.

18. KAT (CONT'D): — who's BUCKY?

PAGE 4

PANEL 1

JONAH and JESSICA are astonished by the question. KAT, embarrassed, types.

1. JONAH (INCREDULOUS): "Who's Bucky?"

2. JESSICA: Bucky was Captain America's teen sidekick during World War Two.

PANEL 2

JONAH hands KAT a yellowed FILE FOLDER.

3. JONAH: How could you not know BUCKY? How old are you?

4. KAT: It was World War TWO. How old are YOU?

PANEL 3

KAT opens the file. JONAH and JESS (on either side of her) look over her shoulder at the folder's contents admiringly, smiles on their faces.

5. JONAH: I was extremely YOUNG back then, thank you for asking.

6. JONAH: (CONT'D): Young enough — and naïve enough — to want to BE Bucky.

7. JESSICA (SURPRISED): YOU wanted to be BUCKY?

PAGE 4

PANEL 4

CLOSE ON the folder's contents: a 1945 NEWSPAPER ARTICLE announcing Bucky's death and Captain America's subsequent disappearance at the hand of Baron Zemo.

The HEADLINE reads:

BUCKY DEAD, CAP MISSING

Below it is an iconic PUBLICITY PHOTO OF CAPTAIN AMERICA AND BUCKY.

8. JONAH (OFF-PANEL): EVERY kid did.

9. JONAH (OFF-PANEL) (CONT'D): Until Captain America led a fourteen-year-old boy behind enemy lines...

10. JONAH (OFF-PANEL) (CONT'D): ...and got him KILLED.

PANEL 5

ON JONAH, caught in a rare moment of vulnerability, his head bowed.

11. JONAH (CONT'D): Suddenly I didn't WANT to be Bucky anymore. Nobody did.

12. JONAH (CONT'D): From then on, kid sidekicks only showed up in comic books.

PANEL 6

ON JESSICA, holding up the PHOTO OF PATRIOT —

13. JESSICA: Until NOW.

PAGE 5

PANEL 1

KAT re-examines the YOUNG AVENGERS PHOTOS on her LAPTOP SCREEN. JESSICA looks over her shoulder.

1. KAT: So, these kids are the Avengers' new SIDEKICKS?

2. JESSICA: The Avengers DISBANDED. There ARE no Avengers.

3. JESSICA (CONT'D): These kids are probably just super-powered FANBOYS.

PANEL 2

ON JONAH, mistrustful as always.

4. JONAH: How do you KNOW?

5. JESSICA (OFF-PANEL): Well, I DON'T. It's just —

6. JONAH: How do you know the Avengers aren't still operating in SECRET? That these kids aren't just a DISTRACTION? A publicity stunt?

PANEL 3

CLOSE ON JESS, taking offense at the suggestion, but with calm assurance.

7. JESSICA: Because I know Captain America.

8. JESSICA (CONT'D): And he would NEVER put another kid's life in danger.

PANEL 4

A three-shot: JONAH and KAT both lean into Jess, intrigued. They both smell a way into the story. JESS instantly regrets her choice of words.

9. KAT (OFF-PANEL): You know CAPTAIN AMERICA?

10. JESSICA: It's not like we HANG OUT —

11. KAT: But YOU were a young Avenger once, too, WEREN'T you?

12. JESSICA: No. I was a young IDIOT who had no business putting on that ridiculous costume in the first place.

PAGE 5

PANEL 5

KAT looks at her LAPTOP, clearly enjoying the image on-screen. JONAH looks over her shoulder at the screen.

13. KAT: I LIKED that costume.

14. KAT (CONT'D): It was HOT — in an early-90's, Jem-and-the-Holograms kinda way.

15. KAT (CONT'D): Check it out...

PAGE 6

PANEL 1

CLOSE ON Kat's laptop, which features a very sexy PHOTO of Jessica in the early 90's as the Marvel super heroine JEWEL.

1. KAT (OFF-PANEL): Jessica Jones as JEWEL.

1. JESSICA (OFF-PANEL): Oy... where did you get that?

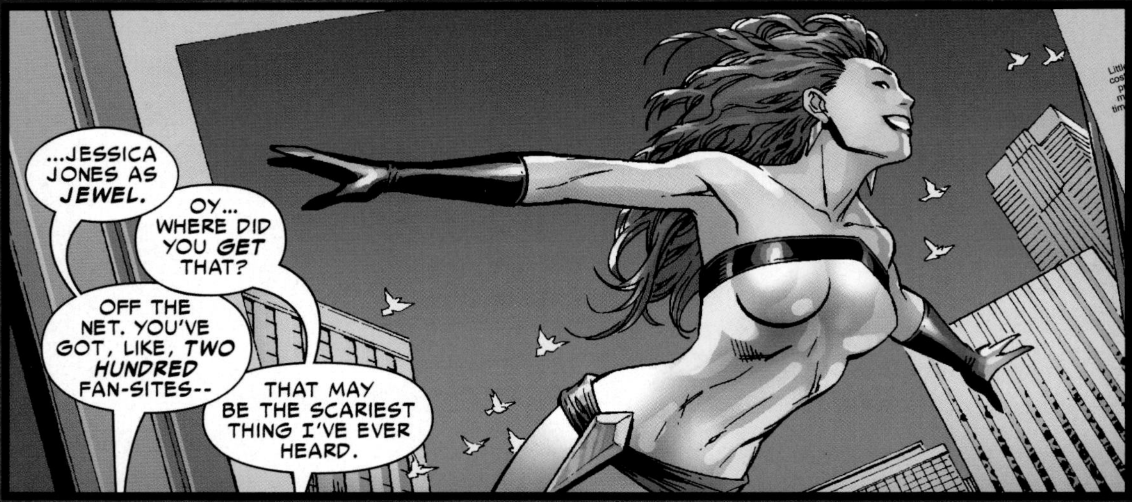
...JESSICA JONES AS JEWEL.
OY... WHERE DID YOU GET THAT?
OFF THE NET. YOU'VE GOT, LIKE, TWO HUNDRED FAN-SITES--
THAT MAY BE THE SCARIEST THING I'VE EVER HEARD.

2. KAT (OFF-PANEL): Off the 'net. You've got, like, two hundred fan-sites —

3. JESSICA (OFF-PANEL): That may be the scariest thing I've ever heard.

PANEL 2

JONAH joins KAT and JESS behind Kat's laptop. He half-smiles, going into his pitch.

4. JONAH: So, who better to track down a gang of super-powered FANBOYS…?

5. JESSICA: Oh, no…

6. KAT: … than super-powered, fan-favorite JEWEL?

7. JESSICA: Guys, they're KIDS. They're not gonna remember ME.

8. JONAH: So, you'll REMIND them. You still have the COSTUME, right?

PANEL 3

ON JESS, appalled.

9. JESSICA: Okay, I'm gonna be sick now.

10. JESSICA (CONT'D): And not just because I'm PREGNANT.

PANEL 4

ON JONAH, an expert salesman, enjoying himself.

11. JONAH: You'll FIND the kids, GET their story, and practice your mothering skills all at the same time.

PAGE 6

PANEL 5

JONAH's back behind his desk already moving on to other business. KAT stands at the door, ready to go, but JESSICA just stands looking at Jonah, incredulous.

12. JESSICA: WHAT mothering skills?

13. JONAH: Exactly.

14. JESSICA: And how am I supposed to FIND these kids?

15. JONAH: How should I know? Ask that super hero boyfriend of yours, Luke Cage. Or call your buddy Captain America.

PANEL 6

ON JONAH, annoyed, over JESS' shoulder.

16. JESSICA: It doesn't work that way.

17. JONAH: So, how does it work?

18. JESSICA: I have NO idea.

19. JONAH: Then what am I PAYING you for?

PANEL 7

CLOSE ON JESS, summoning what's left of her pride.

20. JESSICA: I'm NOT wearing the costume.

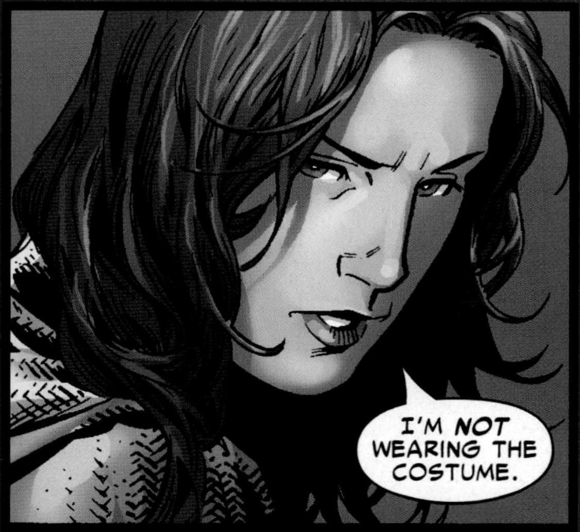
I'M NOT WEARING THE COSTUME.

ALLAN HEINBERG:
THE JOE QUESADA INTERVIEW

Allan Heinberg is one of those rare cats you find in Hollywood from time to time. He's a huge comic's fan, the kind like all of us, who at one point would have given their eye teeth to be in the business of writing comics. What's unusual about Allan is that even with his amazing success in the world of TV, writing such hit shows as The O.C. and Sex and the City among his many credits, he still has this incredible love of comics and he has this pining desire to actually write some! I now own his eye teeth!

Guys like Allan make my job as EIC easy. He comes with the resume, the skills, the work ethic and the incentive to make a difference. But, what's ultimately really fun to see is a guy like him, coming from the big pond called Network Television, geek out over getting a chance to write a Marvel Comic!

JOE QUESADA: Allan, I have to tell this story, because Bendis and I always get a good chuckle at your expense whenever we recount it. I remember when we had you up for your first panel, I think it was San Diego Con, it was an Avengers thing. Anyway, I remember introducing you and leaving you unmercifully in the hands of this hostile Avengers crowd ready to lynch us for what we were doing to their beloved characters. Suddenly we just saw panic flash across your face as I asked you to tell us a bit about Young Avengers.

ALLAN HEINBERG: I think I was in shock for most of it. From what I remember, I had a nice little seat hidden behind Ed Brubaker and then suddenly I'm standing in front of a few hundred anxious Avengers fans who had no idea who I was or why I was potentially compromising the integrity of Earth's Mightiest Heroes with a highly suspect spin-off title. I knew I had to say SOMETHING, if only to try to allay their worst fears about the book. But at the same time, I couldn't really say ANYTHING because the book's premise was a huge secret.

So, I'm standing there at the mike, paralyzed, and I look to Brian Bendis for help. Brian smiles at me and says, "Go ahead."

So, with Bendis' blessing, I opened my mouth and started talking, but to this day, I have no idea what I said or if the words flying out of my mouth made any sense. But I do remember TRYING to let this crowd of dedicated fans know that I, too, shared their fears about a book called YOUNG AVENGERS. And that artist and co-creator Jim Cheung and I were working hard to make it something new, yet thoroughly respectful of Avengers history.

The crowd was unconvinced, to put it mildly. From the looks on their faces, I was clearly making them even more cranky and suspicious. So I KEPT talking, thinking maybe if I told them some specifics about the book, they wouldn't hate me quite so much. That's when I hear Bendis whisper, "And now you've said too much."

Not my finest moment, no.

QUESADA: I have to say, that was one of those endearing moments when the fans could see in that one short moment your humility and love of the medium. You may have all these other credits, but heck, comics are serious business. Serious enough to hyperventilate over!

HEINBERG: It's true, though. I've been a fanboy my whole life, so to have the opportunity to create new characters in the Marvel Universe AND to have those characters interact with Captain America, Iron Man, and Jessica Jones? That was beyond my wildest fanboy fantasies. And a daunting proposition, to say the least. And then to enter a field where heroes of mine -- Alan Moore, Neil Gaiman, Frank Miller, Brian Bendis (the list goes on and on) -- continue to raise the bar and redefine the medium? It's a humbling experience. And after years and years of being an incredibly opinionated fanboy, it was suddenly put-up-or-shut-up time.

QUESADA: Speaking of credits, why don't you give the fans out there a short bio on some of the stuff you've done?

HEINBERG: I was a working actor and playwright and songwriter in New York until 1997 when I moved to Los Angeles to become a writer on the NBC/Tea Leoni sitcom "The Naked Truth." After that, I spent two seasons writing and producing "Party of Five" for FOX, and then two seasons writing and producing "Sex and the City" for HBO (including an episode where Carrie dates "Power Lad," a struggling comic book writer/artist). After "Sex and the City," I worked on "Gilmore Girls" for a season. And for the past two years, I've been writing and producing "the O.C.", a dream job for many reasons -- not least of which is that Seth Cohen's comics obsession allows me to write about and feature several of my favorite creators, titles, and characters on national television. It just doesn't get any better than that.

QUESADA: Let's talk a bit about Young Avengers. I remember your first meeting with us thanks to C.B. Cebulski hunting you down. I was so impressed by your love of the medium and your knowledge of it. You liked Bendis but I didn't want to hold that against you. I know we left that first meeting agreeing to do something but really with nothing in mind. What were your thoughts right afterwards, did you start mulling over ideas or mentally going through the Marvel catalog?

HEINBERG: My first thought was, "There's no way I can write a television series and a monthly comic book at the same time." My second thought was, "I'm going to do it anyway." And then I think I went home and re-read the entire OFFICIAL HANDBOOK OF THE MARVEL UNIVERSE. I think you and I even talked about maybe doing a mini-series about the private lives of several Marvel super heroines. Sort of a super-powered "Sex and the City." (Which still sounds like fun to me, actually...)

QUESADA: I have to be honest, the idea of something called "Young Avengers" would never had crossed my mind if I hadn't have met you. When I blurted out Young Avengers to you during our second meeting, I still had no idea what that actually meant, I think we all just knew exactly what it couldn't mean. But you said you had this affinity for teen characters, so I think that's what kind of got the idea stuck in my head.

HEINBERG: I do love writing teenage characters. Probably because I never got over being a teenager myself. I don't know if anyone does. It's such a tumultuous, deeply felt period in a person's life: you're struggling to define yourself in relation to your family and friends; you're expected to behave like an adult, but you're not permitted to enjoy any of the rights and privileges that most adults take for granted; and you're falling in love for the first time. There's so much about being a teenager that goes unsaid and so many wounds that never heal. It's an incredibly rich experience to be able to write about. And as a teen who grew up reading comics, I always loved teenage characters. The X-Men, the Titans, the Legion -- these were my favorite characters growing up. And I still love those characters.

So when you said the words "Young Avengers" to me, I was initially thrown, since the Avengers didn't have teen sidekicks from which to build a team. But the idea of creating a group of teenage super heroes in the Avengers universe was irresistible to me. The one question I couldn't answer for myself in that initial meeting was "Who ARE the Young Avengers?" Which turned out to be the PERFECT question for a book about teenagers, since being a teenager is all about the beginning of one's search for identity. And that question, "Who are the Young Avengers," haunted me such a degree that it became the soul of my subsequent pitch.

QUESADA: Speaking of that pitch, let's talk a bit about that. I have to admit, it's one of the best and most thought-out pitches anyone has ever presented here at Marvel. I'm not alone in this, many of our editors feel the same way. It's like you have a complete road map of where everything fits and is going. Does this come from your TV background or is it more of a comics-related thing?

HEINBERG: I think with YOUNG AVENGERS it was a combination of both actually.

In television, when you write a pilot for a new series, that first script has to introduce all the new characters and the world of those characters in the context of a story that will hopefully engage viewers from the moment they start watching. And in that first story, you have to lay the groundwork for all the stories that will take you through the rest of the season, which on FOX can be anywhere from 24 to 30 episodes. So, when you pitch a show to a studio or a network, you should ideally be able to talk about the broad strokes of Episode Thirteen even though you haven't written Episode One yet.

And with YOUNG AVENGERS, I did an enormous amount of research and planning before pitching it to you guys. As an Avengers fan, I wanted to be sure that the premise of the book had a deep, organic connection to Avengers history, so I read as many issues of THE AVENGERS, WEST COAST AVENGERS, CAPTAIN AMERICA, THOR, and IRON MAN as I could get my hands on -- as well as several Avengers-related mini-series, and the entire original run of THUNDERBOLTS. I also re-read all of Brian Vaughn's RUNAWAYS and Geoff Johns' TEEN TITANS (both of which I love), because I wanted to be sure that YOUNG AVENGERS offered its readers characters and storytelling that they couldn't get anywhere else. And I also wanted to be sure that I had at least two years worth of solid stories to tell before I made my pitch to Marvel.

QUESADA: I have to tell you, what floored me most about the pitch was that almost every issue has a major revelation that has you saying, "gee, I never saw that coming!"

HEINBERG: That must be my television background coming through. Or years of growing up watching Adam West and Burt Ward in reruns and hearing, "Tune in next week, etc." I have to say, though, that as much as I love building surprises and cliffhangers into the book, they have to reveal something essential about the characters in order to be effective. And, as a reader, there's nothing like that feeling of getting to the end of an issue and wanting to read the next one RIGHT NOW.

QUESADA: So far, what have been the major changes in craft that you've discovered between comics and TV?

HEINBERG: The biggest adjustment for me was having to "direct" every panel of every page. In TV, you write a scene and encouraged to do as little "directing" on the page as possible. You'd never dare to dictate shots or angles since directing is the sole (and union-protected) province of the television director. But in comics, the writer is free (and encouraged) to direct every element of every panel of every page of every scene. And as someone who's worked principally on dialogue-driven shows, I like to think it's helped me become a more visual storyteller.

QUESADA: Allan, thanks so much, I know you're swamped. Any last shout outs?

HEINBERG: Yeah, actually. First of all, I owe a profound debt of thanks to Jim Cheung, co-creator of YOUNG AVENGERS, who is one of the most gifted and generous artists in comics and an ideal collaborator. Thanks, too, to Brian Bendis and Geoff Johns for their continued input, support and -- most of all -- friendship. I'm also grateful to Tom Brevoort, Andy Schmidt, Molly Lazer, and Nicole Wiley for their extraordinary editorial efforts on behalf of YOUNG AVENGERS. And to you, Joe, for saying the words YOUNG AVENGERS in the first place.